REPRESENTATION, INTEGRATION AND POLITICAL PARTIES IN CANADA

This is Volume 14 in a series of studies commissioned as part of the research program of the Royal Commission on Electoral Reform and Party Financing

REPRESENTATION, INTEGRATION AND POLITICAL PARTIES IN CANADA

~

Herman Bakvis
Editor

Volume 14 of the Research Studies

ROYAL COMMISSION ON ELECTORAL REFORM
AND PARTY FINANCING
AND CANADA COMMUNICATION GROUP –
PUBLISHING, SUPPLY AND SERVICES CANADA

DUNDURN PRESS
TORONTO AND OXFORD

Published by Dundurn Press Limited in cooperation with the Royal
Commission on Electoral Reform and Party Financing and Canada
Communication Group – Publishing, Supply and Services Canada.

Canadian Cataloguing in Publication Data

Main entry under title:
Representation, integration and political parties in Canada

(Research studies ; 14)
Issued also in French under title: Les Partis politiques au Canada.
ISBN 1-55002-110-9

1. Political parties – Canada. 2. Representative government and
representation – Canada. I. Bakvis, Herman, 1948– . II. Canada. Royal
Commission on Electoral Reform and Party Financing. III. Series: Research
studies (Canada. Royal Commission on Electoral Reform and Party
Financing) ; 14.

JL195.R47 1991   324.271   C91-090526-6

Dundurn Press Limited
2181 Queen Street East
Suite 301
Toronto, Canada
M4E 1E5

Dundurn Distribution
73 Lime Walk
Headington
Oxford, England
OX3 7AD

CONTENTS

FIGURES

8. NEW POLITICS, THE CHARTER AND POLITICAL PARTICIPATION

9. INCENTIVES CREATED BY THE INSTITUTIONS OF REPRESENTATIVE DEMOCRACY: THEIR EFFECTS ON VOTERS, POLITICAL PARTIES AND PUBLIC POLICY

TABLES

7. THE CONSEQUENCES OF ELECTORAL VOLATILITY: INEXPERIENCED MINISTERS 1949–90

8. NEW POLITICS, THE CHARTER AND POLITICAL PARTICIPATION

9. INCENTIVES CREATED BY THE INSTITUTIONS OF REPRESENTATIVE DEMOCRACY: THEIR EFFECTS ON VOTERS, POLITICAL PARTIES AND PUBLIC POLICY

FOREWORD

THE ROYAL COMMISSION on Electoral Reform and Party Financing was established in November 1989. Our mandate was to inquire into and report on the appropriate principles and process that should govern the election of members of the House of Commons and the financing of political parties and candidates' campaigns. To conduct such a comprehensive examination of Canada's electoral system, we held extensive public consultations and developed a research program designed to ensure that our recommendations would be guided by an independent foundation of empirical inquiry and analysis.

The Commission's in-depth review of the electoral system was the first of its kind in Canada's history of electoral democracy. It was dictated largely by the major constitutional, social and technological changes of the past several decades, which have transformed Canadian society, and their concomitant influence on Canadians' expectations of the political process itself. In particular, the adoption in 1982 of the *Canadian Charter of Rights and Freedoms* has heightened Canadians' awareness of their democratic and political rights and of the way they are served by the electoral system.

The importance of electoral reform cannot be overemphasized. As the Commission's work proceeded, Canadians became increasingly preoccupied with constitutional issues that have the potential to change the nature of Confederation. No matter what their beliefs or political allegiances in this continuing debate, Canadians agree that constitutional change must be achieved in the context of fair and democratic processes. We cannot complacently assume that our current electoral process will always meet this standard or that it leaves no room for improvement. Parliament and the national government must be seen as legitimate; electoral reform can both enhance the stature of national political institutions and reinforce their ability to define the future of our country in ways that command Canadians' respect and confidence and promote the national interest.

In carrying out our mandate, we remained mindful of the importance of protecting our democratic heritage, while at the same time balancing it against the emerging values that are injecting a new dynamic into the electoral system. If our system is to reflect the realities of Canadian political life, then reform requires more than mere tinkering with electoral laws and practices.

Our broad mandate challenged us to explore a full range of options. We commissioned more than 100 research studies, to be published in a 23-volume collection. In the belief that our electoral laws must measure up to the very best contemporary practice, we examined election-related laws and processes in all of our provinces and territories and studied comparable legislation and processes in established democracies around the world. This unprecedented array of empirical study and expert opinion made a vital contribution to our deliberations. We made every effort to ensure that the research was both intellectually rigorous and of practical value. All studies were subjected to peer review, and many of the authors discussed their preliminary findings with members of the political and academic communities at national symposiums on major aspects of the electoral system.

The Commission placed the research program under the able and inspired direction of Dr. Peter Aucoin, Professor of Political Science and Public Administration at Dalhousie University. We are confident that the efforts of Dr. Aucoin, together with those of the research coordinators and scholars whose work appears in this and other volumes, will continue to be of value to historians, political scientists, parliamentarians and policy makers, as well as to thoughtful Canadians and the international community.

Along with the other Commissioners, I extend my sincere gratitude to the entire Commission staff for their dedication and commitment. I also wish to thank the many people who participated in our symposiums for their valuable contributions, as well as the members of the research and practitioners' advisory groups whose counsel significantly aided our undertaking.

Pierre Lortie
Chairman

INTRODUCTION

THE ROYAL COMMISSION'S research program constituted a comprehensive and detailed examination of the Canadian electoral process. The scope of the research, undertaken to assist Commissioners in their deliberations, was dictated by the broad mandate given to the Commission.

The objective of the research program was to provide Commissioners with a full account of the factors that have shaped our electoral democracy. This dictated, first and foremost, a focus on federal electoral law, but our inquiries also extended to the Canadian constitution, including the institutions of parliamentary government, the practices of political parties, the mass media and nonpartisan political organizations, as well as the decision-making role of the courts with respect to the constitutional rights of citizens. Throughout, our research sought to introduce a historical perspective in order to place the contemporary experience within the Canadian political tradition.

We recognized that neither our consideration of the factors shaping Canadian electoral democracy nor our assessment of reform proposals would be as complete as necessary if we failed to examine the experiences of Canadian provinces and territories and of other democracies. Our research program thus emphasized comparative dimensions in relation to the major subjects of inquiry.

Our research program involved, in addition to the work of the Commission's research coordinators, analysts and support staff, over 200 specialists from 28 universities in Canada, from the private sector and, in a number of cases, from abroad. Specialists in political science constituted the majority of our researchers, but specialists in law, economics, management, computer sciences, ethics, sociology and communications, among other disciplines, were also involved.

In addition to the preparation of research studies for the Commission, our research program included a series of research seminars, symposiums and workshops. These meetings brought together the Commissioners, researchers, representatives from the political parties, media personnel and others with practical experience in political parties, electoral politics and public affairs. These meetings provided not only a forum for discussion of the various subjects of the Commission's mandate, but also an opportunity for our research to be assessed by those with an intimate knowledge of the world of political practice.

These public reviews of our research were complemented by internal and external assessments of each research report by persons qualified in the area; such assessments were completed prior to our decision to publish any study in the series of research volumes.

The Research Branch of the Commission was divided into several areas, with the individual research projects in each area assigned to the research coordinators as follows:

F. Leslie Seidle	Political Party and Election Finance
Herman Bakvis	Political Parties
Kathy Megyery	Women, Ethno-cultural Groups and Youth
David Small	Redistribution; Electoral Boundaries; Voter Registration
Janet Hiebert	Party Ethics
Michael Cassidy	Democratic Rights; Election Administration
Robert A. Milen	Aboriginal Electoral Participation and Representation
Frederick J. Fletcher	Mass Media and Broadcasting in Elections
David Mac Donald (Assistant Research Coordinator)	Direct Democracy

These coordinators identified appropriate specialists to undertake research, managed the projects and prepared them for publication. They also organized the seminars, symposiums and workshops in their research areas and were responsible for preparing presentations and briefings to help the Commission in its deliberations and decision making. Finally, they participated in drafting the Final Report of the Commission.

On behalf of the Commission, I welcome the opportunity to thank the following for their generous assistance in producing these research studies – a project that required the talents of many individuals.

In performing their duties, the research coordinators made a notable contribution to the work of the Commission. Despite the pressures of tight deadlines, they worked with unfailing good humour and the utmost congeniality. I thank all of them for their consistent support and cooperation.

In particular, I wish to express my gratitude to Leslie Seidle, senior research coordinator, who supervised our research analysts and support staff in Ottawa. His diligence, commitment and professionalism not only set high standards, but also proved contagious. I am grateful to Kathy Megyery, who performed a similar function in Montreal with equal aplomb and skill. Her enthusiasm and dedication inspired us all.

On behalf of the research coordinators and myself, I wish to thank our research analysts: Daniel Arsenault, Eric Bertram, Cécile Boucher, Peter Constantinou, Yves Denoncourt, David Docherty, Luc Dumont, Jane Dunlop, Scott Evans, Véronique Garneau, Keith Heintzman, Paul Holmes, Hugh Mellon, Cheryl D. Mitchell, Donald Padget, Alain Pelletier, Dominique Tremblay and Lisa Young. The Research Branch was strengthened by their ability to carry out research in a wide variety of areas, their intellectual curiosity and their team spirit.

The work of the research coordinators and analysts was greatly facilitated by the professional skills and invaluable cooperation of Research Branch staff members: Paulette LeBlanc, who, as administrative assistant, managed the flow of research projects; Hélène Leroux, secretary to the research coordinators, who produced briefing material for the Commissioners and who, with Lori Nazar, assumed responsibility for monitoring the progress of research projects in the latter stages of our work; Kathleen McBride and her assistant Natalie Brose, who created and maintained the database of briefs and hearings transcripts; and Richard Herold and his assistant Susan Dancause, who were responsible for our research library. Jacinthe Séguin and Cathy Tucker also deserve thanks – in addition to their duties as receptionists, they assisted in a variety of ways to help us meet deadlines.

We were extremely fortunate to obtain the research services of first-class specialists from the academic and private sectors. Their contributions are found in this and the other 22 published research volumes. We thank them for the quality of their work and for their willingness to contribute and to meet our tight deadlines.

Our research program also benefited from the counsel of Jean-Marc Hamel, Special Adviser to the Chairman of the Commission and former

Chief Electoral Officer of Canada, whose knowledge and experience proved invaluable.

In addition, numerous specialists assessed our research studies. Their assessments not only improved the quality of our published studies, but also provided us with much-needed advice on many issues. In particular, we wish to single out professors Donald Blake, Janine Brodie, Alan Cairns, Kenneth Carty, John Courtney, Peter Desbarats, Jane Jenson, Richard Johnston, Vincent Lemieux, Terry Morley and Joseph Wearing, as well as Ms. Beth Symes.

Producing such a large number of studies in less than a year requires a mastery of the skills and logistics of publishing. We were fortunate to be able to count on the Commission's Director of Communications, Richard Rochefort, and Assistant Director, Hélène Papineau. They were ably supported by the Communications staff: Patricia Burden, Louise Dagenais, Caroline Field, Claudine Labelle, France Langlois, Lorraine Maheux, Ruth McVeigh, Chantal Morissette, Sylvie Patry, Jacques Poitras and Claudette Rouleau-O'Toole.

To bring the project to fruition, the Commission also called on specialized contractors. We are deeply grateful for the services of Ann McCoomb (references and fact checking); Marthe Lemery, Pierre Chagnon and the staff of Communications Com'ça (French quality control); Norman Bloom, Pamela Riseborough and associates of B&B Editorial Consulting (English adaptation and quality control); and Mado Reid (French production). Al Albania and his staff at Acart Graphics designed the studies and produced some 2 400 tables and figures.

The Commission's research reports constitute Canada's largest publishing project of 1991. Successful completion of the project required close cooperation between the public and private sectors. In the public sector, we especially acknowledge the excellent service of the Privy Council unit of the Translation Bureau, Department of the Secretary of State of Canada, under the direction of Michel Parent, and our contacts Ruth Steele and Terry Denovan of the Canada Communication Group, Department of Supply and Services.

The Commission's co-publisher for the research studies was Dundurn Press of Toronto, whose exceptional service is gratefully acknowledged. Wilson & Lafleur of Montreal, working with the Centre de Documentation Juridique du Québec, did equally admirable work in preparing the French version of the studies.

Teams of editors, copy editors and proofreaders worked diligently under stringent deadlines with the Commission and the publishers to prepare some 20 000 pages of manuscript for design, typesetting and printing. The work of these individuals, whose names are listed elsewhere in this volume, was greatly appreciated.

Our acknowledgements extend to the contributions of the Commission's Executive Director, Guy Goulard, and the administration and executive support teams: Maurice Lacasse, Denis Lafrance and Steve Tremblay (finance); Thérèse Lacasse and Mary Guy-Shea (personnel); Cécile Desforges (assistant to the Executive Director); Marie Dionne (administration); Anna Bevilacqua (records); and support staff members Michelle Bélanger, Roch Langlois, Michel Lauzon, Jean Mathieu, David McKay and Pierrette McMurtie, as well as Denise Miquelon and Christiane Séguin of the Montreal office.

A special debt of gratitude is owed to Marlène Girard, assistant to the Chairman. Her ability to supervise the logistics of the Commission's work amid the tight schedules of the Chairman and Commissioners contributed greatly to the completion of our task.

I also wish to express my deep gratitude to my own secretary, Liette Simard. Her superb administrative skills and great patience brought much-appreciated order to my penchant for the chaotic workstyle of academe. She also assumed responsibility for the administrative coordination of revisions to the final drafts of volumes 1 and 2 of the Commission's Final Report. I owe much to her efforts and assistance.

Finally, on behalf of the research coordinators and myself, I wish to thank the Chairman, Pierre Lortie, the members of the Commission, Pierre Fortier, Robert Gabor, William Knight and Lucie Pépin, and former members Elwood Cowley and Senator Donald Oliver. We are honoured to have worked with such an eminent and thoughtful group of Canadians, and we have benefited immensely from their knowledge and experience. In particular, we wish to acknowledge the creativity, intellectual rigour and energy our Chairman brought to our task. His unparalleled capacity to challenge, to bring out the best in us, was indeed inspiring.

Peter Aucoin
Director of Research

PREFACE

~

CANADIANS DISTRUST BOTH politics and politicians at a level of apprehension that has undoubtedly affected the standing of political parties. As demonstrated by survey evidence gathered for the Commission, the ranking of political parties as organizations for which Canadians have a high regard has dropped precipitously over the past decade so that they now rank below other institutions such as banks and trade unions.* In brief, these are not the most propitious of circumstances for political parties.

Yet many of the functions performed by political parties are more important than ever. Parties remain the primary means for recruiting individuals to run for political office at the provincial and federal level; in this sense, they act as the main gatekeepers for those wishing to compete for political office. Parties are the all-important link in the accountability mechanism, allowing citizens to link government performance to past and proposed party policies at election time. Ultimately, notwithstanding the increasing attractiveness of single-issue groups as vehicles for political participation, political parties constitute the only organizations capable of integrating and reconciling a wide range of interests in society, including those diffuse interests that ordinarily may not find means for expression through specialized groups.

These are significant functions and, in the absence of political parties, it is obvious that some entity would have to be invented to fulfil these functions. Furthermore, in seeking to understand the low standing of political parties among the general public, it is important to consider that this may be based not so much on rejection of political parties per se as on assessment of the performance of parties in their role as the primary political organizations for participation and as intermediaries between citizens and the state.

---

* Canada, Royal Commission on Electoral Reform and Party Financing, 1991, *Reforming Electoral Democracy: Final Report* (Ottawa: Minister of Supply and Services Canada), vol. 1, chap. 5.

In light of the changing perceptions and an increasingly difficult environment, what is the appropriate role of political parties? What can citizens reasonably expect from political parties? What short- and long-term forces both in the polity and in society challenge political parties as primary political institutions? To what extent does Canadian political geography affect the representation of interests within the parties and how can the parties best organize themselves in response to these constraints?

The nine research studies in this volume speak to several of these considerations. In addition to supporting the deliberations of the Commission with respect to specific issues of electoral reform, the research program was also designed to examine the broader underpinnings of the Canadian party system and its role in Canadian society. Canadians will be facing some interesting but difficult choices in the next few years, given the arrival of new political parties and the unfolding of new constitutional options. We may also see innovations in, for example, the way political parties organize themselves in the House of Commons or in opportunities available for the direct participation of citizens in the political process. In making choices and in framing demands for reform, it is useful to know something about the properties and dynamics of the present party system, as well as about the forces driving the demand for change.

The research studies of Volume 14 examine questions ranging from the integrative functions of political parties, to the appropriate relationship between the federal and provincial wings of the national parties, to the specific properties of the electoral system, such as the turnover of seats in the House of Commons in response to changes in voter preferences.

In the first two studies, David Elkins and Maureen Covell were asked to examine Canadian political parties as national institutions. Elkins, through an examination of the Canadian, Australian and American party systems and a rigorous critique of the current literature, reaches the conclusion that we expect too much of our political parties. What he refers to as the uniquely Canadian preoccupation with national unity detracts, in his view, from the more fundamental function of parties, namely, to appeal to and represent a specific array of interests in society in a manner that distinguishes any given political party from other parties. He finds it paradoxical that political parties, as organizations designed to stimulate and manage conflict, should also be expected to encourage national unity. He argues that the efforts of Canadians are misplaced if we expect political parties to carry the burden of national unity or to come up with reforms that will somehow increase the capacity of parties to perform the national unity role.

Covell develops a different argument based on the same theme
and uses an alternative comparative reference point, drawing on the
experience of a number of European party systems, including that of
Belgium with its linguistic cleavage. Covell points out that most countries have multi-party systems, and that in these systems accommodation and integration occur *between* rather than *within* parties. In
Canada, however, even under conditions of minority government, the
expectation has been that each of the major parties will attempt separately to bridge the major regional and linguistic cleavages. According
to Covell, insofar as Canadian parties have always played this role,
and this role is seen as legitimate, it would be awkward if they were now
to cease playing this integrative function. This role has fallen to parties in Canada in part due to the lack of a history of regular alternation
of parties in government. Instead, we have "a history of alternating
periods of one-party dominance ... This creates a 'party of government'
mentality, in which the party concerned adopts the function ... of aggregating a broad range of interests."

At the same time she notes we may well be in a transitional period.
The next election could see the successful electoral début of at least two
new parties, the Bloc québécois and the Reform Party. These parties
may attract sufficient support so that no single party enjoys a majority
in the House of Commons. Whether we like it or not, Covell states,
Canadians may be confronted with the need for, and the possibility of,
European-style coalition government. In the concluding section of her
study she sketches, with their pros and cons, five different scenarios
of coalitions between different pairs of political parties. One advantage
of this type of politics, she argues, is that it should lead to more open
bargaining among parties, thereby "giving the population of the country continuing influence on the policy process beyond the registering
of approval or disapproval at election times." There is no guarantee,
however, that more open bargaining among the parties will indeed
occur. At the same time, a more open bargaining process might make
it more difficult to arrive at a consensus and hence a workable coalition.
It would appear, therefore, that a shift to coalition-style party politics
would need to be accompanied by a change in attitudes, both within
and outside the parties, that would see participants place a high value
not only on openness but also on seeking consensus and tolerating
compromise.

Mackenzie King is once purported to have said that, rather than
too much history, as some countries have, Canada has too much geography. In Canada, the regional and federal-provincial dimension has
always loomed large for political parties. Rand Dyck, in his study,

tackles the issue of linkages between federal and provincial parties of the same partisan stripe. It has generally been thought that weak or absent links between the two levels lower the integrative capacity of national parties, limiting their ability to represent significant groups in Canadian society. In Canada, the linkages are certainly weak. Yet, according to Dyck, there is no necessary relationship between the degree of federal-provincial integration of a political party in Canada and its ability to accommodate regional diversity. His study concludes that increased integration of federal and provincial parties and party systems would not necessarily contribute to national unity. Instead, he argues, a strengthening of the relationship between the federal constituency associations and the national parties and disentangling the federal and provincial wings would be a more productive approach. It would enhance the parties' successes at transcending regional cleavages. Further, it would allow the national parties a greater share of attention and commitment from party activists in each of the provinces.

The study by Paul Thomas focuses on the role of party caucuses within the Parliament of Canada as vehicles for the representation of regional concerns and demands in the national policy process. It is often thought that the Canadian parliamentary system operates in such a rigid fashion that there is no room for members of Parliament to represent regional interests. Thomas' study, however, argues that the capacity of national political institutions to accommodate regional diversity is greater than what is usually attributed to them. Drawing on original interviews conducted specially for this study, Thomas notes how regional party caucuses in particular "have become important forums for the expression of regional concerns."

The limitation of these forums, however, resides in the fact that party caucuses meet and deliberate in secret. Therefore, the public sees neither its interests being represented nor the outcome of these deliberations. As Thomas notes, this failing alone, no matter how effective the regional caucuses and individual MPs may be behind the scenes, could be sufficient to lead to the consideration of institutional changes with the aim of generating greater confidence in national decision making. At the same time, he stresses that these institutional reforms are unlikely to be found in the realm of electoral reform per se. To the extent that enhanced regional representation in the Commons from smaller provinces, for example, is deemed desirable, adoption of such a scheme would require significant departure from the principle of representation by population. Changes in the rules of party discipline and the possibility of more free votes in the House of Commons lie in the purview of Parliament and the parliamentary parties. And, in areas such as Senate reform and the distribution of powers between the federal and provincial governments, most such changes can come about only through constitutional change. In summary, Thomas' study points to the fact that Canadian political parties are undervalued for the important roles they do play in reconciling regional divisions. It also points to the difficulty of finding remedies for defects in the system that would not at the same time undermine the present capacity of parties to represent regional interests.

A further criticism of the performance of parties and the party system relates directly to Canada's single-member plurality (SMP) electoral system. It has been argued that, as in the case of all SMP systems, there is less competition and less choice for voters compared to that found under proportional representation. A complaint also made is that the Canadian electoral system is insufficiently responsive in translating changes in voter preferences into changes in seats or in governments. The study by Donald Blake, however, points out that Canada stands unique among SMP systems in that parties such as the New Democratic Party have been sufficiently strong to prevent dominance of electoral outcomes by Liberals and Progressive Conservatives. Using a specially developed index of volatility based on absolute change in the vote from one election to the next, Blake also shows that levels of volatility are much higher in Canada: "They confirm the relative lack of volatility in U.S. House elections and show that Canada has had more extreme changes than Britain as well as more variability over time." Similar findings are found with respect to turnover – seats changing hands at election time. Incumbents in Canada are far more likely to be defeated – or, to put it differently, there are far fewer safe seats in Canada. He does note that, as in so many things in Canadian political life, there are pronounced regional differences. Manitoba and Saskatchewan, for example, have far lower levels of volatility in federal elections than other provinces.

Blake's evidence helps dispel certain misconceptions about the properties of the Canadian electoral system. The system tends to be far more competitive and responsive to changes in electoral choice than many people believe. In his conclusion he discusses the implications of his findings, noting that the high level of competition is not entirely an unmixed blessing. For example, the high turnover rate does represent an opportunity for more women to enter the House of Commons. Unfortunately, it also means that they are more vulnerable – as are all MPs – to defeat in the next election.

"The Personal Vote in Canada" by John Ferejohn and Brian Gaines addresses many of the same themes visited by Blake. Electoral politics in the United States has been characterized for many years by the "personal vote" phenomenon. Voters base their choice not so much on party labels or policies and programs as on personal loyalty to the incumbent. Senators and congressmen in turn do all they can to cultivate a personal following through advertising and extensive constituency service. One of the consequences has been a significant rise in the level of incumbency. In the last two congressional elections, for example, the success rate for incumbents has been between 95 and 98 percent. In Canada, the comparable figure has been less than 60 percent.

One of the tasks Ferejohn and Gaines set for themselves was to investigate the extent to which the personal vote phenomenon is present in Canada. In the United States, the personal staffs and the resources available to senators and congressmen for campaigning and engaging in personal service are much greater than in Canada or Great Britain. In Canada, however, the staffs of MPs are larger than those for MPs in Britain, leading the two researchers to posit initially that Canada might be somewhere in between the United States and Great Britain. Using both aggregate and survey data, Ferejohn and Gaines arrive at the surprising result that the personal vote factor may in fact be weakest in Canada. While survey data suggest that Canadian MPs are well regarded by their constituents, this does not necessarily translate into a strong incumbent advantage. Canadian election data thus do not display the characteristics associated with incumbency and the personal vote. Rather, in Canada the variability in vote swings is low (indicating little variation from constituency to constituency), electoral margins are small and relatively constant and parliamentary turnover is high and unchanging over time. All this indicates that Canadians are much more likely to vote on the basis of party, party leadership and issues.

In the United States, the trend toward greater incumbency, the seeming incapacity of electors to throw incumbents out of office and the minimal policy responsiveness on the part of legislators have led to widespread dissatisfaction with the electoral process. "When elections cannot act as sensitive barometers of public sentiment ... on the conduct of government, democracy would appear to be on shaky ground." On this basis, Ferejohn and Gaines are reassured by finding only limited evidence of the spread of the "American disease" northward; in their eyes Canadians should be pleased that their system still displays high levels of responsiveness.

High levels of competition and legislative turnover are not an undifferentiated benefit, however. One of the consequences of high turnover has been a relatively inexperienced House of Commons. Inexperienced members, it is said, need at least a term to learn the ropes, the techniques of parliamentary debate, the ways of committees and so on. Unfortunately, that one term may be their one and only term, given the strong possibility of defeat in the next election. Thus the quality of debate, the capacity of the opposition to scrutinize government operations effectively and the restricted selection of experienced candidates for ministerial office are all cited as consequences of inexperience.

In her study, Sharon Sutherland tackles one specific consequence of turnover and volatility – the appointment of ministers who have had little or no parliamentary experience. She addresses two questions: what happens to those individuals appointed to ministerial office without appreciable experience in Parliament? Is electoral volatility an important reason for the appointment of inexperienced politicians to Cabinet?

In the case of the first question she finds overall that inexperienced ministers were more likely to run into trouble. That occurred not necessarily because these ministers were incompetent or because they mishandled their portfolios but, rather, given their inexperience, they became easy prey for opposition attacks in the House of Commons and, not infrequently, the cause of some embarrassment to the government. On the second question, she readily concedes that the high turnover in Canada leads to the recruitment of ministers who would likely have benefited from seasoning in the House of Commons before entering Cabinet. The problem becomes particularly acute when there is a change in government and the new prime minister is faced with only a small pool of experienced parliamentarians.

Sutherland's main recommendations would not entail changes in the electoral system or a reduction in the level of competition; but they do run counter to Canadian political norms concerning the sanctity of constituencies and the prerogative of the constituency associations of the parties. First, she suggests expanding the seasoned core of parliamentary parties by encouraging talented career politicians to move to safe seats that are not in their home territories. Second, she urges that everything be done to encourage political parties to develop policy on a continual basis, including measures such as guaranteed minimum inter-election funding for party organizations to be used to develop ideas.

The final two studies deal with the forces affecting the credibility of parties as primary political organizations and with some of the incentives provided by the present electoral system for parties to pursue certain courses of action. Neil Nevitte examines both the "new politics" thesis and the effect of "Charter politics" in relation to political participation. One of the more noteworthy developments over the past decade has been the increased involvement of Canadians in single-issue groups and in protest activity.

Using survey data for different time periods (particularly 1981 and 1990), Nevitte documents the increased willingness of Canadians to participate in political activities of all types, ranging from talking about politics to engaging in protest activity. Nevitte links this development to two interrelated phenomena. First, the proportion of Canadians cleaving to "post-materialist values" as of 1990 was substantially greater than it was in 1981, a trend that Canada shares with most other advanced industrialized nations. "Post-materialists" are those eschewing traditional materialist values and are more concerned with esthetic values, the rights of minorities, the environment and the like. The increase in post-materialists is attributed to population replacement and increased levels of education.

The second factor is unique to Canada: the arrival of the *Canadian Charter of Rights and Freedoms* in 1982. As Nevitte notes, it is those groups representing minorities, the disabled, feminists and the like – the so-called "Charter groups" – that are most likely to use Charter challenges in the courts to press their claims. For some groups, ethno-cultural minorities for example, social location rather than post-materialism propels them toward supporting Charter challenges. For others, particularly women, adherence to post-materialist beliefs has an important bearing on their position on Charter issues. Thus both separately and in combination with post-materialism the existence of the Charter has helped to transform Canadian politics by making the courts an additional and competing arena for groups to pursue their interests.

The presence of both these forces, according to Nevitte, has important implications for political parties. Partisan loyalties among post-materialists are weaker, thereby contributing to greater voter volatility. Post-materialists are also less inclined to participate in political parties, seeing them as part of an outmoded form of political representation. The challenge for political parties, then, is to respond to the agenda of those advocating "new politics," no easy task insofar as issues important to them, such as environmentalism and animal rights, cut across more traditional lines of political conflict. As well, the manner in which parties conduct their internal life has an important bearing on their ability to attract adherents from among post-materialists. Overall, among this sector of the population there is a stress on openness and acceptance of new ideas from below. In brief, the ability of Canadian political parties to survive and prosper as primary political organizations will depend in good part on how they respond both in policy terms and organizationally.

The final study by Réjean Landry examines some important properties of our present electoral system. Any electoral system constitutes a set of rules for the conduct of elections. Under our SMP system, for example, the candidate with the plurality of votes wins the seat. As with any set of rules, the SMP system provides certain kinds of incentives for candidates and political parties to pursue particular strategies. Thus, in Canada, it is well known that smaller parties are better off cultivating support on a regional basis. Limited voter support across the country as a whole is unlikely to yield many seats, while the same amount of support concentrated in a specific region could result in several seats.

Landry examines how our institutional arrangements structure the context in which voters and party leaders make their decisions. In doing so he notes the incentives and disincentives embedded in the SMP system that result in biases in both electoral outcomes and, ultimately, public policies. The system of election financing also helps structure the behaviour of voters and parties. The biases, Landry argues, are ones that tend to favour producers over consumers, particular over general interests and short-term over long-term interests. These biases tend to be found in all electoral systems, but certain biases, such as the focus on short-term interests, tend to be more pronounced under the SMP system. According to Landry, "these biases should be corrected because they cause an inefficient allocation of resources by encouraging parties, as well as voters ..., to invest resources in creating policies that tend to redistribute wealth rather than increase it."

The means for correcting the biases lies primarily in providing voters with more information. And, rather than changing the electoral system itself, Landry recommends that the legislative process be amended so that, among other things, newly enacted statutes would be accompanied by information on indirect and direct costs, on which categories of citizens and producers would benefit and which would bear the costs, and on the budgetary implications of the statute over a 10-year period. He notes that these are essentially marginal changes, but useful nonetheless in partly reducing the effects of the fiscal illusion and the short-term focus of political parties.

Landry's proposals can also be seen as an argument for improving the overall level of political education of voters and the capacity of parties to deliver more useful and meaningful information to voters on policy choices and the long-term consequences of those choices. In this respect, therefore, the arguments presented by Landry fit well with a number of the other themes both in this volume and in others. Nevitte's study in this volume, for example, notes how Canadian voters are not only increasingly less disposed toward material issues but also more critical consumers of government services and programs. And Sutherland, also in this volume, stresses the need for parties to improve their capacity for policy development.

The nine studies in this volume do not exhaust all questions relating to the performance of political parties and the differing properties of the Canadian electoral system. They address some of the more salient ones, however, and the answers they provide highlight some important characteristics of our parties and electoral system of which many Canadians remain unaware. Many Canadians, for example, would probably be surprised to know that, in comparison to Great Britain and the United States, Canadian elections display much higher levels of responsiveness.

To be sure, the nature of Canada's political geography constitutes a major source of frustration. The high turnover rate notwithstanding, many voters in western Canada, for example, feel stymied that no matter which party is in power, the government still tends to be dominated by MPs from central Canada. The parliamentary system also can make parties at least appear unresponsive. As documented by Paul Thomas, the regional caucuses are important vehicles for the advocacy of regional demands. Yet because caucus deliberations are secret, this form of regional representation lacks visibility.

Electoral reform, however, offers only limited means for remedying these deficiencies. The redress of regional imbalance, for instance by providing a disproportionately greater number of seats in the House of Commons from outlying regions, would entail a major departure from the principle of equality of the vote, something many Canadians would find unacceptable. The issue of regional imbalance is probably more appropriately addressed through improvement of our federal-provincial institutions or a reformed and directly elected Senate. In altering some of the features of our parliamentary system, however, we may at the same time lose some of the qualities we presently enjoy, such as the high level of electoral responsiveness.

In brief, there is little doubt that Canadians are genuinely disenchanted with the political process and this disenchantment directly affects the way Canadians perceive the role performed by political parties. Nonetheless, while some limited reform of the electoral system for the House of Commons and of the rules applying to parties within the House is both possible and desirable, more far-reaching changes would require either difficult or unacceptable trade-offs or would be more appropriately made in institutional arenas other than the electoral system and the party system. It is the hope here that the reader will find the discussion of the different qualities, both positive and negative, of Canadian parties and the party system helpful in understanding the implications of reform.

Volume 14 forms part of the Commission's publication program, reflecting the importance that the Royal Commission on Electoral Reform and Party Financing attached to original research activities to support its deliberations and recommendations.

As with any multifaceted research undertaking, the completion of this volume, one of 23, is due in no small measure to the help and cooperation of several individuals. To begin, I would like to thank the authors of the research studies, first, for agreeing to contribute their knowledge and expertise, in many instances on short notice, and second, for their cooperation in meeting the deadlines that the exigencies of the Commission imposed. Their task entailed not simply crafting the research studies but also making presentations to the Commission and at research seminars, and responding to requests for information during the time that the Commission's report was being prepared.

Several other individuals in universities, political parties, government and the non-government sector assisted by acting as peer reviewers and participants at the research seminars, or by simply being available as resource persons when crucial information was needed on specialized topics. Their willingness to give freely of their time is much appreciated. In particular I would like to thank Grant Amyot, Donald Blake, Kenneth Carty, William Chandler, Jane Jenson, Richard Johnston, Hugh Thorburn and Steven Wolinetz, who willingly shared their time and wisdom on several occasions throughout the life of the Commission.

In addition, I gratefully acknowledge the excellent help and support received from the staff at the Commission in Ottawa and Montreal. They include Paulette LeBlanc, Hélène Leroux, Lori Nazar and Liette Simard, who ensured that the flow of research studies between the coordinator, the researchers and the reviewers moved along appropriate channels and in an expeditious fashion; Richard Herold and Susan Dancause, custodians of the Commission's library; Kathleen McBride, the information system specialist; and Eric Bertram, Peter Constantinou, Keith Heintzman, Hugh Mellon and Donald Padget, the research analysts of the Commission, who spent many late hours preparing background material as well as a number of the research studies. The work of one individual in particular, David Mac Donald, assistant research coordinator with the Commission, proved invaluable in numerous ways, but especially during the preparation of presentations based on the research for consideration by the Commission. To each and every one of them, I would like to extend my appreciation for a job well done.

Finally I would like to express my gratitude to the director of research, Peter Aucoin, the Commissioners, Pierre Fortier, Robert Gabor, William Knight and Lucie Pépin, and, above all, the Chairman, Pierre Lortie, for the opportunity of working with them and for sharing with me their erudition and experiences concerning that most fascinating of all worlds – the internal workings and dynamics of political parties.

Herman Bakvis
Research Coordinator

REPRESENTATION, INTEGRATION AND POLITICAL PARTIES IN CANADA

1

PARTIES AS NATIONAL INSTITUTIONS
A Comparative Study

David J. Elkins

CANADIANS HAVE ALWAYS been concerned with "national unity." After all, the lack of unity and cooperation in the United Province of Canada was a significant factor in seeking "a wider union" in the mid-19th century. Likewise, apprehensions about expansionist tendencies in the United States helped to convince many British North Americans that they should submerge their differences or be swallowed by the American giant.

The recurrent focus on national unity is perfectly understandable. What is puzzling is how often Canadian academics and politicians have suggested that political parties might play a useful role in fostering national unity. How could an organization specifically designed to stimulate and manage conflict be expected to encourage national unity? No other democratic country places such a burden on its political parties, although many communist and Third World countries (especially "one-party democracies") see the party as a unifying force.

This study examines the apparent paradox – the uniquely Canadian paradox – that political parties should be national institutions. That such a view of parties is almost never seen as a paradox by Canadians may reveal something about the nature of Canada or Canadian political culture. Yet equally paradoxical may be the fact that some roles played by some political parties in Canadian history have been decisive in creating Canada and keeping a country otherwise divided from breaking up. Thus, by exploring a peculiarly Canadian puzzle, we may learn something about political parties, about national unity and about political culture.

This study is an essay, not a monograph. Although it includes some data and evidence for some assertions, no effort has been made to document each assertion. The focus throughout will be on parties and the roles they might play in different kinds of political situations. To understand the roles and the situations, we will need to branch out to think about federalism (and Canada's peculiar version), responsible government, electoral systems, leadership selection, the Senate and the Constitution.

The aim is to assess, fairly and objectively, the reasons why political parties cannot be asked to solve the problem of national unity and to recount many important ways in which parties have contributed to the operation of politics. To understand this obsession with parties as national institutions, we must understand Canadian political culture. Indeed, to confront almost any apparently paradoxical conclusion and understand why it is not seen as absurd will lead to a greater understanding of the culture or political culture which underlies the paradox (Elkins and Simeon 1979).

DEFINITIONS

Some terms need to be clarified at the beginning. "Party" can be disposed of quickly, since it is less contentious than the set of concepts related to "national unity."

We all know that the Liberal and Conservative parties, under slight variants of these names, have been political parties since Confederation or thereabouts (Laponce 1969). Subsequently, other parties have arisen and some have disappeared: Progressives, United Farmers, Co-operative Commonwealth Federation (CCF) and Social Credit. There is probably no danger that any of these will be confused with other entities such as a faction, a pressure group, a charitable foundation or a consulting firm. Yet some entities going by the name of party might be so confused: Reform Party, Confederation of Regions party, Christian Heritage party and Family Coalition party.

There are several reasons for thinking the latter examples could be confused with other types of organizations. These help us to highlight what parties do and which of their undertakings are less likely to be done by other organizations. Without attempting to be exhaustive, here are some things political parties do:

- nominate candidates in elections;
- formulate policies on a wide range of issues;
- try to get candidates elected so that the party can form the government;

- support or oppose the government in Parliament;
- choose, support and publicize a leader; and
- motivate supporters to vote.

Social Credit, the CCF and several other parties listed above have done all of these things. Several have not, however, and only time will tell if they evolve into functioning parties, wither away or admit that they are only a pressure group, a single-issue group or a lobbying tool.

Two conclusions may be drawn: first, parties are what parties do; rather than relying on whether an organization says it is a party, we shall want to ask what it does. Second, even among the entities that we decide are parties, not all are of equal interest. As candidates for the role of "national institution," some may be ignored. But which ones should be ignored depends on what we mean by the term "national."

The modern nation-state is a recent invention, roughly two centuries old. Political parties (then called factions) predate the nation-state, but modern mass parties in Canada are a 20th-century invention, building on important 19th-century organizational developments. The coincidence that mass parties grew up during the childhood and adolescence of the nation-state can lead one to speculate that they are an essential governing instrument in any such state. Indeed, they probably are, but that does not justify assigning them a status beyond the role they actually play. Parties, it will be seen, are not national institutions but instead are organizations with much more modest functions or purposes: electoral management, candidate recruitment, policy development, representation and so on.

To move the analysis to the next stage, we must distinguish carefully among the meanings of "nation," "nation-state," "state," "country" and some related terms, such as "national." Country is the term with the broadest reference. A nation-state is a subcategory of "country"; it is a juridical concept and involves mutual recognition in the international system.

A nation is a community with shared identity, self-awareness and some common characteristics. It is often referred to as "a people." It may coincide with a nation-state (Japan), or it may be divided among several countries (the Kurds), or there may be more than one nation fully "nested" within a single state or country (Canada?). A state consists of the apparatus for running a nation or nation-state. We often refer to the state as "government," and, as in Canada, the state may be divided among several governments.

One must note that Canada has been characterized as "two nations warring in the bosom of a single state," as Lord Durham put it. It could also be said that French-speaking Canada is a single nation divided up among several parts of the Canadian state (provinces). These two ways of describing our situation have radically different implications: is Quebec the nation with its own incipient state, or does the nation consist of French-speaking people across Canada with a consequent focus on the federal government in Ottawa as the major part of its state? In crude terms, these represent the different visions of René Lévesque and Pierre Trudeau. Note that both ways of thinking about the matter leave open the question of whether Canada is a nation.

Lest "warring" and "divided up" give the wrong impression, multinational states may take many forms and have many origins, some quite peaceful. Canada, it can be argued, is one such example.

This is not the place to debate the peacefulness of Canada's origins. The crucial point is that Canada is a country and a nation-state (i.e., recognized as such by other countries, the United Nations and so on) in which 11 sovereign governments make up "the state" and in which there are arguably two nations I say "arguably" principally because some people refuse to accept that Quebec or French Canadians might be a nation and because even more doubt that English-speaking Canada is a nation, but also because native groups contest the idea that there are only two nations. Indeed, the fact that it is arguable whether Canada consists of one nation, two nations or scores of nations lies at the heart of this study, because in defining "nation" or "national," we take a position on how many nations we are. It is probably not feasible for one definition to prevail, since each carries many theoretical and practical implications. Nevertheless, it is at least desirable to make clear that "nation" will not be used in this study as synonymous with "state," "nation-state" or "country" when referring to Canada.

If the distinctions among nation, nation-state, state and country are clear enough for the basic purposes of this study, then we can move on to another difficult concept, "national" as in "national unity" or "national institution." For clarity, I will stipulate that "national" means "concerning a nation" but not necessarily a country or state. Hence, one can begin to see the first obstacle to asking how parties can be national institutions or how they can help foster national unity. In Japan there is no problem of national unity, and so parties can be national institutions, but in such circumstances no one cares whether parties serve as such. Only where there is no clear congruence between "nation" and "state" or "country" can the issue of parties as national institutions arise as a serious topic. If the country is divided over "national" identity or unity, then all major organizations may be called upon to help, parties among them.

To use words precisely suited to the task, we should probably refer to whether or how parties can serve as *federal* institutions. That way we shall run no danger of confusing the Parti québécois as a national institution (which it may be) with the role of the Conservative party under Sir John A. Macdonald or the Liberals under Sir Wilfrid Laurier. This hardly solves the problem, because "federal" has a double meaning; as used above, it means "countrywide" or some such phrase, but it can also be contrasted with *provincial*, as in "the federal Parliament." Now, it seems clear that in this study we are not interested in the role of parties as federal institutions at the expense of their roles as provincial and countrywide institutions. Indeed, one of the troublesome topics below concerns the almost complete organizational separation between federal and provincial "wings" of the major parties. We shall ask whether that separation makes the parties more or less useful as instruments of the country's purposes.

The use of "federal" is actually even more complex than has just been suggested. If we look at the use of "federal" in Australia, at least two differences are noteworthy. First, what we call the federal government is usually referred to in Australia as the Commonwealth Government, as well as being spoken of as Canberra and other epithets. Second, most uses of the term "federal government" in Australia would carry the meaning of "federal system of government" and thus would include state governments (or in Canada, provinces) as well as the Commonwealth. In fact, one often hears expressions like, "By resisting the Commonwealth Government, Queensland was upholding the federal [system of] government."

To be stipulative once more, I shall use "federal" to mean "related to Ottawa and the general government." It contrasts with "provincial." When we need a word that denotes countrywide, I recommend "confederal." This is an ugly recommendation, since we are now engaged in a discourse on parties as confederal institutions! However, the Canada that is at risk today was created in 1867 by the Fathers of Confederation, so this word may be historically closer to what we want than any other.

An aside: the reluctance we may feel at using "confederal" reflects an important assumption in our political culture. Most people assume that a confederation is a weak and disjointed version of a federation, and of course some political scientists encourage this view on theoretical grounds (but see Stevenson 1979). After all, the United States experimented first with the Articles of Confederation, which had to be replaced in 1789 by a federal system (and even that led to a civil war before the centre was fully legitimate and strong enough to hold). Thus, reluctance to use the word "confederal" probably reflects the fear, which many citizens share, that their country may be falling apart. Real as those fears may be, they need not be decisive for this study's use of the word "confederal."

PLAN OF THIS STUDY

This overly long introduction has clarified what we mean by the role of political parties as national institutions. In short, the focus is defined as the potential aid that parties might offer to building a strong nation-state by endeavouring to become countrywide in their appeal and thus increasing their ability to represent or to speak on behalf of all groups and all parts of the country.

The first step will involve a brief exposition of why there is a "national problem"; why, in other words, the question arises in the first place. As I suggested above, Canada is probably unique in casting parties in this role. It is not an accident that there is a problem or that parties might be asked to help with the solution, and a bit of history will provide the context which seems most convincing to me.

The next section will outline what analysts have thought the parties could offer in this drama. As presented, these will not be limited only to assertions about actual parties, nor only to conclusions that I share. They are my summary of what is a very disparate literature, and they represent hypotheses or interpretive questions to ask of the events and debates throughout Canadian history.

Throughout this section are a series of observations – mine or those of other observers – that have been offered to explain why parties have not or cannot serve as builders or strengtheners of the nation-state. These brief observations are a mixture of fact and interpretation.

Finally, on the basis of the analysis to this point, the remaining sections of the study will attempt to look behind the claims on behalf of parties and the obstacles noted, in an effort to state positive conclusions about Canadian politics and political culture.

THE NATIONAL PROBLEM

In most democracies, political parties share basic views on fundamental cultural issues, reflecting the popular consensus on culture. Typically, leaders and candidates make ritual patriotic statements from time to time and then get on with the main business of disagreeing over policy matters. The national issues, in other words, are not on the agenda or are only rarely on it. The parties deal instead with issues relating to the state, to governance within an agreed framework of a nation. Indeed, one can find instances where a potentially explosive issue of state policy could become a nation-threatening division, and parties will often collude to keep the issue off the agenda – or at least not become a partisan issue – so that its force is contained, limited or diverted to less harmful arenas. In Australia immigration has been such an issue in recent decades. So has capital punishment in Canada.

Canada finds itself in a different situation and perhaps always has. Parties have been asked to deal with issues of nationhood, of nation-state building, of unifying two nations in a single state. Issues of language, religion, ethnicity or (in 19th-century terms) race are not consensual in Canada; they are the basic cleavages. They are why a federal system was created in the mid-19th century: not a "legislative union" because the English and French were too divided, and not separate colonies in isolation because of their weakness compared with the growing American threat next door. Squaring the circle has always been the task laid before parties, politicians and Canadians generally.

As Pierre Trudeau asserted in 1962, the challenge is enormous: "We must separate once and for all the concepts of state and of nation, and make Canada a truly pluralistic and polyethnic society ... The die is cast in Canada: there are two main ethnic and linguistic groups; each is too strong and too deeply rooted in the past, too firmly bound to a mother-culture, to be able to engulf the other" (Trudeau 1968, 177–78).

Scholars and commentators disagree about the motives of the Fathers of Confederation. Some argue that the division of powers (mainly in sections 91 and 92 of the *BNA Act,* and in 1982, the *Constitution Act, 1867)* was intended to give the general and important powers to the federal government, leaving limited and local concerns to the provinces and municipalities. Others aver that the proper conceptualization is quite different. Ottawa was given control only over matters of common concern to all the colonies or provinces (banking and currency, defence, interprovincial and international trade, etc.); the provinces retained the powers that affected the daily lives of citizens, especially including "property and civil rights," which needed a wide interpretation in light of the *Quebec Act* of 1774. The classic expression of the view that "property and civil rights" constitutes, in effect, a residual power to the provinces may be found in the *Report of the Royal Commission of Inquiry on Constitutional Problems,* known as the Tremblay Report (Kwavnick 1973).

Regardless of one's view on motives, the federal and provincial orders of government were given different, distinct and substantial powers. These can never be spelled out precisely, but they are listed in some detail in relevant sections of the *BNA Act.* This should be contrasted with the practice of other federations, such as Australia and the United States. Both have provided detailed lists of powers for the federal order but not for the states. Instead, the states were given residual powers; all those powers not specifically granted to the federal order of government were retained by the people or the states. This was at the time believed to be a significant limitation on the federal government, and intentionally so. As it happened, courts were often unwilling to uphold state jurisdiction in the absence of "black letter" headings. In Canada, by contrast, the long list of headings in sections 91 and 92 closed this avenue of interpretation.

Of course, there were many other reasons why the provinces have been stronger in Canada than their counterparts in Australia or the United States. "Property and civil rights" has been mentioned. The general growth in importance of education, health and social welfare in countries in all parts of the world has, in Canada, favoured the provinces but only because these jurisdictions are clearly spelled out in section 92. At certain key points, Quebec's tenacious defence of its prerogatives has galvanized other provinces into action; no comparable set of circumstances exists in the United States or Australia.

Whatever the intent, jurisdictions can never be entirely clearcut. In part this is because of the imprecision of words, but in good part it derives from the fact that technology and society evolve and new activities arise or change their character. Telecommunications, for example, is not mentioned in the *BNA Act,* so courts allocated that to federal control (by and large) on the analogy of "canals and telegraph lines," which are listed in section 91. The lack of clarity, the protean nature of many categories and the attempts by both orders of government to enhance their own powers have put governments in conflict.

These conflicts are inevitable and inherent in the concept of a true federal system. They derive only in the smallest part from the personal ambitions or self-aggrandisement of politicians or their public servants. Those elected to govern a province or the federal government will find enormous powers at their disposal, and they will find that the other order of government will take actions within its heads of power that conflict with their own actions.

This perspective was well stated by the Rowell-Sirois Report as long ago as 1940:

> It is the duty of a provincial legislature and government to pursue the interests of the province as they conceive them to be, just as it is the duty of Parliament and the Dominion Government to push forward what they believe to be the national interest ... The federal scheme of government was devised precisely because of the lack of complete identity of interest between the whole and the component parts. Where

differences of interest exist they become manifest simply through officials and politicians doing their duty. (Smiley 1963, 209, 212)

If intergovernmental conflict inevitably occurs, how might political parties respond? They can take sides: one party backs the federal
claim of jurisdiction, another backs the provincial claim. Alternatively,
a party can endeavour to mediate the dispute within its own ranks by
ensuring that representatives of the opposing points of view are made
to feel welcome in the party. To some degree this may keep an issue off
the public agenda if the major parties are trying to mediate the conflict
rather than taking sides. If the conflict is between provincial governments
– or regional groupings of provinces – then the same alternatives confront the parties. A third way in which the conflict may arise, perhaps
most often, involves the federal government and some provinces arrayed
against the other provinces. In all cases, "taking sides" and mediation
seem to be the only possibilities in the Canadian case, even though
other logical (but not practical) possibilities exist, such as ignoring the
conflict.

This discussion of mediation is cast in terms of intergovernmental
relations. Partly this simplifies the exposition, but another perspective
should be noted. In the early decades of Confederation, mediation
meant bridging the differences between Protestant and Catholic, English
and French. This occurred within the Conservative party in the federal
government, and it involved cabinet posts, patronage and government
contracts, among other things. Since the provinces were weak and
largely insolvent, there was relatively little of the federal-provincial
conflict that is so visible today. Over the decades, the development of
provincial powers – and not only in Quebec – has made the axis of conflict less exclusively ethnic, linguistic or religious and more intergovernmental. In a later section, I will argue that the new parties which
arose in the West also played a pivotal role in enhancing federal-
provincial conflict. Thus, in present circumstances, mediation involves
governments as often as it does religious or linguistic communities.

Whether they take sides or play the mediator may in some cases
reflect the partisanship of the opposing governments. However, having the "same party" in power at both levels of government has been
no guarantee of harmony in the past. Likewise, two provincial governments controlled by the same party may still experience considerable disagreement and conflict.

A reasonable generalization might be that whichever path a party
follows, it is damned if it does and damned if it doesn't. If a party never
takes sides, it may alienate one or the other governmental order since

there are strong and legitimate views at stake. If a party never tries to mediate, and especially if it consistently takes a particular side, it may find it difficult to manage the issue when it is in power.

Note also that what one party does may constrain what another party can do. If one party "takes sides," can the other party gain an image of statesmanship by mediating the issue? If one party opts for a mediator's role and does so successfully, will that make it more difficult for the other party to mediate the issue, inducing it to take sides? The option of taking sides is probably necessary at least occasionally in light of court decisions or dramatic events. For example, Joe Clark may have had no choice in 1980 but to oppose Trudeau's attempt to patriate the Constitution unilaterally.

If taking sides is an occasional necessity, it can be argued that confederal parties must as a general rule mediate these major rifts. This, however, inevitably leads to tensions within the parties, tensions which will generally coincide with other cleavages, such as region, province or culture. In these circumstances, why should we be surprised that parties have often failed as confederal institutions? After all, they were asked to play the part only because other institutions failed to resolve the problem.

In short, parties that aspire to federal power – or to be confederal institutions – inevitably find themselves divided in many of the same ways as is Canada itself. Part of what it means to succeed in representing all parts of the country is that you must end up incorporating the cleavages that characterize the country. Hence, to suggest that the parties might, could or should unify the country is to redefine the problem as one of party unity. If the problem of national unity did not exist, then the parties could organize differently and behave otherwise than they do now. The reason they cannot do the trick is because the problem is really tough!

Beyond the difficulty of the problem, there is a deeper issue. Parties were created, historically, as organizations designed to manage conflict, but not in the sense of federal-provincial or ethnic conflict. The concept of free elections and the structure of responsible government require that opposition be structured around cleavages that concern and motivate voters or potential voters. Historically, this has usually pitted rich against poor or business against labour; in other words, a social cleavage has provided the emotional base for an organizational opposition.

Note how radically different is the task we set our parties. Instead of defining a cleavage (within a national consensus) and letting the parties take sides, we demand that each party desiring to be a confederal institution take both sides of a fundamental cleavage! Because we do not have a nation in the strict sense, but two nations or none, we expect the parties to paper over the fundamental cleavages.

The stresses placed on party unity in a situation where the party must take both sides of a cleavage account for one of the peculiarities of the Canadian party system. Unlike Australia or most areas of the United States, Liberals and Conservatives in Canada (and the NDP in Quebec) are organized into parallel federal and provincial wings of the party. Thus, for example, the federal wing of the Conservative party in British Columbia has been very successful in recent years while remaining completely distinct from its provincial sibling, which has performed disastrously for two decades. The separation refers not just to different numbers of voters but to the fact that the wings have different organizations, officers, facilities, active members and sources of funding. In some provinces, this degree of separation has not occurred, but it is found to some degree almost everywhere (Black 1972).

The origins of separate federal and provincial wings will be found to be quite different in each case. But the broad reasons remain fundamentally the same: trying to straddle the cleavages discussed earlier. The first example of this separation of party wings, as one might expect, was in Quebec in the mid-1950s (Behiels 1985, 259ff.). Reform of the Liberal party in Quebec to make it a more viable alternative to the Union nationale was hindered in the eyes of many by the actions and policies of the St. Laurent Liberal government in Ottawa. Its efforts to engineer uniform policies across the country in university financing, health and social welfare made it extremely difficult for Liberals in Quebec to appeal to the growing nationalist and neonationalist sentiments which had helped to keep Duplessis and the Union nationale in power. Hence, a totally separate organization was created and proved successful under the leadership of Jean Lesage. Other parties and other provinces slowly learned the same lesson for different specific reasons (Wearing 1981; Whitaker 1977).

It should come as no surprise, therefore, to find that the major parties are internally divided. Burke (1980) has shown that the social coalitions (categories of people voting for a party) are diverse. He found that intraparty variations between provinces were greater than interparty contrasts within any one province. For example, NDP and Social Credit in British Columbia have more similar social bases than the NDP in British Columbia has with the NDP in Ontario; likewise with Liberals in Quebec, Ontario and other provinces.

This peculiar partisan pattern of internalized cleavages should not be seen as a failure of the parties. The reason they diverge so much across the country is because they have done a good job of appealing to the voters in more than one province or region and of reflecting their views. This, of course, raises the fascinating question of whether a party can get away with saying different things in different regions, of "being all things to all people."

One can again usefully quote former Prime Minister Trudeau, even though he might not agree today with what he wrote in the sixties:

> Now it should be obvious to all these groups that no national party can keep its integrity while preaching a gospel which varies as it moves *a mari usque ad mare;* neither can it keep its status as a national party if it seeks support only in narrow regionalism. Yet, on the other hand, if the party preaches the same gospel everywhere, its partisans in some areas will desert it as being too reactionary, whereas in other areas the party will fail to find adherents because it appears too revolutionary.
>
> That dilemma can easily be solved by making full use of our federative form of government. Socialists *can* stand for varying degrees of socialism in the various provinces of Canada by standing in autonomous provincial parties. (Trudeau 1968, 128)

As noted above, this has happened in the Liberal party in most provinces, and it caused Mr. Trudeau some inconvenience when he was prime minister.

If fragmented parties are inevitable, we should also not blame the provincial populations or their governments for the divisions in the country or in the parties. Why should we assume that policies must be homogeneous across the country (i.e., confederal), that the federal government knows best, and that our loyalties to province or region need to be subordinated to Canadian loyalty or identity? Surely, there is a reason for federalism, and it concerns a desire and a need to respect diversity. Loyalties are real, have long historical roots and are not necessarily zero-sum (Elkins and Simeon 1980).

By the same token, policies should reflect reality. They need not all be either national or local. Depending on topic, knowledge or technology, policies should be federal or provincial or local, as enumerated in sections 91 and 92 of the *Constitution Act, 1867.* Of course, one can argue that some headings in section 91 would be better as provincial headings, and vice versa. But one can hardly quarrel with the idea that currency, national defence, etc. should be uniform throughout the country and thus under federal control, while other matters should properly be different in each region or locality, according to local culture, taste or custom, and thus left to provincial jurisdiction. (For an American perspective that reaches the same general conclusion, see Dahl 1967.)

If one grants that some policies should be adapted to local conditions, then it is a political question as to which policies should be uniform and which should not. Different people and different parties disagree over this question, and some strange consequences may arise. For example, unemployment insurance rests with the federal government, but over time regional variations (between and within provinces) in criteria and guidelines have been implemented. It may be humane that shorter periods of work qualify for benefits in areas of high unemployment. Nevertheless, if even federal jurisdictions must recognize that countrywide (confederal) homogeneity is inappropriate, how can one dispute the right of provincial governments in their own jurisdictions to pursue different policies? Of course, the federal government has frequently disputed such policy heterogeneity. Carried to its logical end, such reasoning leads to the conclusion that provincial legislatures are not needed and that provincial governments should be administrative organs of the federal government. Whatever one's views on the wisdom of this perspective, it is clearly illegal and unconstitutional under current and historical Canadian arrangements.

From the foregoing, one can conclude several things relevant to this inquiry. Whether there is a "national problem" depends on who defines the problem. For centralists who favour federal government tutelage of policies, obstreperous provinces and Quebec's nationalist pretensions are the problem. For proponents of federalism as a compromise between central and local control, the problem is a federal government whose resources and ambitions exceed its proper jurisdictions. To bridge, unite or mediate these contrasting perspectives, the parties would have to square a circle, or at least appear to espouse contradictory goals.

We can be more specific about the dilemma we have imposed on our parties. A full understanding must await the discussion of representation, brokerage and governance in later sections, but an overview at this point may be helpful in structuring these later topics.

The character or identity of a country may be identified with the puzzle it cannot solve or which it repeatedly tries to solve. As I see it, the puzzle or conundrum on which Canada is founded derives from the fact that language communities do not quite coincide with political boundaries. Not all French speakers live in Quebec, and not all who live in Quebec are French speakers. (See the interesting conclusions drawn from these facts in Dufour 1990.) If the boundaries and the communities had coincided at key historical moments, there would be no

Canada as we know it; instead, there would be several independent nations or several more American states.

Imagine another scenario. Suppose that the distribution of language, ethnic and religious communities had been more or less the same in each colony in the mid-19th century or that they were so now in each province. No matter how diverse each political unit, territorial borders would not have created cleavages that coincided with regional economies or other differences. This is roughly the case in Australia, where the proportion of Irish or of Catholics or of immigrants is roughly the same in every state. For a party to speak for a social group does not put it in the position of appearing as an advocate for one part of the country at the expense of another. Obversely, each state or provincial government must express concern for the full range of social, demographic and ethnic groups.

Canada lies between these two ideal types. That is why it exists as a country, and that is why it faces many of the political problems it does. One of the consequences of our puzzle is that our parties must endeavour to be confederal institutions, and another consequence is that they will fail.

Because the cleavages almost but do not quite coincide with territorial political boundaries, provincial governments often appear to be advocates of ethnic, linguistic or religious interests. Likewise, parties espousing confederal (countrywide) policies that affect these groups will, as a by-product whether intended or not, appear to favour one province or region over others. This is another reason why I previously discussed mediation as though it involved intergovernmental bargaining.

Now, parties are supposed to be conflictual. But if strengthening them in one region necessarily weakens their support elsewhere, they cannot be confederal institutions. We shall see examples of this dilemma in several subsequent sections, and we shall see how different this is from the situation in Australia.

WHAT PARTIES MIGHT DO

Although one cannot expect parties to solve the "national problem," there are many things they can do. This section will outline some of these roles and will review the reasons that make it difficult for the parties to perform their functions. The five functions, which overlap to a substantial degree, are representation, leadership, brokerage, governance and policy formulation.

Representation

This is one of the most contested terms in political discourse. At root it concerns the impossibility, on practical grounds, of direct democracy in countries, as opposed to direct democracy in Greek city-states or New England towns. (Leave aside for now questions about restrictions on participation even in those earlier democracies, such as the exclusion of women or the presence of slaves.) Hence, one has to delegate authority to representatives who can, for a period of time, speak on behalf of those too numerous to attend the place where decisions are made. The questions that have vexed theoretical and practical discussions include: Who can speak on behalf of others? Which others? On what issues? With what authority? This is not the place to enter this contested area. Instead, I take note that such debates exist and focus instead on current challenges to the ability of Canadian parties to speak on behalf of various groups. As we shall see, there are several significant challenges and Canada's differ from Australia's.

If representation involves authority to speak on behalf of others, one may ask what is represented about those others. More precisely, does a representative represent opinions, preferences, individuals, groups or what? Many answers have been given over the two or three centuries in which the question has been asked in that way, but only a few need be addressed for our purposes.

In early modern times, "interests" or "estates" were what most people thought should be represented. For the most part, this meant propertied interests and legal entities like boroughs and guilds. As the concept of "the people" broadened to include the commercial interest of the middle classes and later the working classes, representation changed as well. Interests were involved, but of a less tangible sort: hours of work, age of child labour, dangerous conditions of work, enforcement of contracts and the like.

Most of the 20th century has witnessed another conception. As mass media spread and as mass parties mobilized millions instead of hundreds or thousands of citizens, representatives were more and more expected to consider the preferences and opinions of constituents as well as their interests and other matters. Since the advent of public opinion polling, one has had the means to measure the degree to which a representative (or group of representatives in a party) speaks adequately on behalf of this or that group. There has been enough public discussion of the value and pitfalls of polls that I need not belabour the point that there are now two means of ascertaining opinions, one by polling and the other in the legislature. If their results do not appear to coincide, more of the public and politicians place their faith in polls than in the representatives.

The latest development in the evolution of the concept of representation involves what Merton (1973) calls "insiders" and "outsiders."

The basic idea is simple: you must be one to know one. In other words, a representative should be a member of the group represented, should share personal and social characteristics with those represented. It is no longer sufficient, so runs the new concept, for a representative to speak on behalf of opinions or preferences; the representatives must share certain privileged life experiences with the constituents. What should be shared depends entirely on the group whose interests are at stake. Women do not think men can represent them, according to this conception, nor can gays and lesbians be adequately represented by people with a different sexual orientation. This line of reasoning has been powerfully enunciated by Alan Cairns in regard to the groups mentioned in the *Canadian Charter of Rights and Freedoms* (Cairns 1988). He refers to it as "constitutional minoritarianism," but the challenge is wider than the "Charter groups" (Cairns 1990).

In addition to an overly dogmatic assumption about the social and personal bases of opinions and preferences, this new conception poses serious challenges to parties, especially those aspiring to the status of confederal institutions. If a party is willing to admit that it speaks on behalf of a limited clientele (e.g., Christian Heritage), then few confusions are likely to arise. If, on the other hand, a party aspires to confederal status and tries to broker the major cleavages, the stress on party unity may become intolerable. Not only must the party speak on behalf of opinions, preferences and goals that appear to be contradictory, but it must also include within its active core (and perhaps in the legislature too) individuals who have had the privileged life experiences which one believes to have led to those opinions and points of view.

The desire for representation by "insiders," by "one's own kind," is not restricted to Canada. Blacks, Hispanics and women in the United States, for example, make the same claims on their political processes. Likewise, Australian Aborigines, women and immigrants prefer "insiders" to represent them. What sets the Canadian process apart from these other countries is the puzzle or conundrum I mentioned earlier. Certain groups who demand "insider" advancement can easily achieve it because they are dominant in certain areas, such as French-speaking Catholics in Quebec or in parts of Ontario or New Brunswick. In other words, a province can be used for advancement because the group is very unevenly distributed across the country. By contrast, women, gays and lesbians, the disabled and many other groups are either quite small or evenly distributed. Thus, they cannot "capture" a government, a major party or even, in most cases, a single constituency.

One consequence of this pattern is that some groups find it much more difficult to achieve "insider" representation. Another consequence is that parties are torn between representing major groups (which are quite different in each province) in order to win provincial power, or representing the full range of groups across the country. The latter strategy necessarily puts in conflict the dominant groups in one area and the minority groups that may be quite large countrywide. If a party can have only one deaf MP, where should this person run for election? Representing a tiny minority everywhere, any one place will say that some other group is more important. "Not in my backyard" applies to some social groups as well as to garbage sites, nuclear power plants and mental institutions.

Please note that I am not espousing or rejecting this conception of representation. Nor do I know how widespread this view is. The point is more basic: a significant number of groups feel that they have been left out because no member of their group is in a decision-making body that purports to speak on their behalf. Since groups or life experiences are not "fixed" in number, the potential claimants under this conception are truly infinite. Classifications are not nested but are cross cutting, so their multiplication is exponential; and as groups or life experiences are incorporated into a party, other "outsiders" become conscious of their exclusion.

It should be clear from this overview of the historical evolution of the concept of representation that different assumptions about what is to be represented, and how, can make a great deal of difference in one's judgement of whether parties are doing an adequate job as representatives. To drive home this fundamental point, I want to turn to examples of Canadian and Australian cultural assumptions about majorities and representation, and how our institutions reflect our assumptions. If these examples mean what I think they mean, then changing the assumptions may be as crucial as changing the institutions. A royal commission charged with changing institutions (parties, electoral systems) should be especially sensitive to the underlying cultural assumptions.

As liberal democracies in the British Commonwealth, Canada and Australia share a host of traditions, values and institutions. A chasm separates them, however, in terms of electoral reform. Australia has for over a century been the greatest innovator of any country in the world in the realm of electoral arrangements. At some point, virtually every form of electoral system has been tried, rejected, embraced or at least considered seriously. Some of these innovations – especially the secret ballot and uniform ballots – are now commonly accepted in many countries, including Canada. By contrast, Canada has, to the best of my knowledge, propagated not a single innovation in the field of electoral reform. Indeed, Canada has steadfastly resisted most reforms championed elsewhere, such as preferential ballots, proportional representation, direct primaries and referenda. Some political units at some times have experimented with them, but all other arrangements have been rejected by now or are viewed with great suspicion.

A contrast that is so striking must mean something. Canada has, after all, been innovative in other aspects of political life, especially federalism. Thus, one cannot easily attribute the difference to Canadian "conservatism" or to clinging to British traditions.

The surprises in this arena do not end with innovation or its absence. Australia is also much more varied and complex in its electoral arrangements, while Canada is quite simple and has been becoming more uniform across regions and levels of government. This trend runs counter to the usual perception that Canada is a country increasingly riven by regional, ethnic and linguistic cleavages. Australia, on the other hand, is frequently viewed as reasonably homogeneous by comparison.

Simple and complex are very imprecise terms. For present purposes, however, they are adequate: Australian electoral arrangements are more complex than those in Canada and always have been. This is true in several senses.

Preferential voting is more complex than single-member plurality voting, especially when one requires a complete set of preferences which in some Australian Senate races may exceed 60 candidates.

Different procedures are used for different offices: single-member electorates with preferential voting for the Australian House of Representatives and multi-member (statewide) electorates using a form of proportional representation (PR) for the Senate. The states also share most of these features, except Tasmania, which uses a form of PR in its Lower House. In Canada, all provincial and federal elections rely on the same method of single-member plurality voting (except for Prince Edward Island and until recently a few constituencies in British Columbia). Three provinces (British Columbia, Alberta and Manitoba) have at various times used other procedures, but no longer (Qualter 1970).

Concrete evidence of how complex the procedures are in Australia has been apparent in every election since the Second World War: the parties feel compelled to distribute "how-to-vote" cards to their supporters. These have two purposes: identifying the party affiliation of the large numbers of alphabetically or randomly listed candidates (especially in Senate races) and the need to control the allocation of second and third preferences.

Complexity over time also varies by country. Canada used to have more varied features in the 1867–1920 period, such as different federal franchises in different provinces, staggered elections, open voting and some experiments with PR or single-transferable vote in some provinces. These have all been abandoned for the nearly uniform system throughout the 11 jurisdictions.

Australia, on the other hand, has seen variety at all historical points, but if anything there has been greater complexity in the last few decades. For example, from 1920 to 1948, Senate elections used the majority-preferential method, as did most elections to the House. In 1948, Senate elections were changed to the present quota-preferential form of PR, while the House of Representatives retained the earlier system.

The majority-preferential method in Australia clearly places a value on achieving a majority. But the majority sought is a special kind, and it is quite different from the form of majority deemed valuable in Canada. Assumptions about the type of majority are related to concepts of representation, and both have implications for the ability of parties to be confederal institutions.

By definition, majority-preferential methods achieve a majority vote for the winning candidate. Implicit in the procedure is the premise that the "majority will" should be imposed on the outcome, and also the premise that this is a majority of individual voters in that constituency. Plurality methods as used in Canada without a second ballot exhibit no such concern. Implicit in the Canadian system is a premise to the effect that the constituency consists of "natural" groups, and the victory goes to the largest group, whether a majority or not. (Notice that this assumption runs counter to the concept of representation implicit in "insiders" and "outsiders.") Simplicity is affirmed, as well, by the Canadian practice to the extent that most observers believe that a plurality system leads to a reduction in the number of parties (perhaps tending toward only two) and thus helps one to create or "manufacture" a majority government (Cairns 1968; Blais 1990). Note how different is the meaning of "majority" at the beginning and end of this paragraph.

Hence, implicit in the electoral procedures are different notions of which type of majority is preferred if one cannot achieve both simultaneously. The Australian system is prepared to sacrifice a majority (party) in Parliament if that is necessary to ensure that a majority of voters in each House electorate supports the winning candidate. The obverse is true in Canada. This "preference" for different types of majorities manifests itself in actual governance: coalitions are common in the Australian legislatures but are rare in Canada, where parties almost always govern alone, even if that entails having a minority government. I will return to this feature in the section on governance.

This analysis can be strengthened by examining the use of the concept of "frustrated" or "disappointed" voters. Such usage is common in Australia, whereas in Canada one more frequently hears complaints that provinces or regions are "underrepresented." The Australian concept refers to voters who supported an unsuccessful candidate. It implies that voters are represented individually, or at least only by the member for their constituency. Some Canadians no doubt share such views, but the more usual complaint concerns provinces. For example, the Progressive Conservatives in Quebec in the 1970s were seen as having a problem because there were too few MPs from Quebec in the caucus (or, in 1979–80, too few in the Cabinet). The problem was most emphatically not that some people in Quebec were unrepresented because the Conservative candidate was defeated in their constituency; such defeats were important collectively, and not because of one constituency. I should note, parenthetically, that Australian political culture, like that of the United States, is very individualistic and egalitarian. Canada exhibits, by contrast, many collective and communitarian features that cannot be expounded here (Elkins 1989). I emphasize the contrast in order to buttress the point above that the institutions we devise and use are intimately related to underlying cultural assumptions, and thus it is difficult to change one element in isolation.

Different notions of majority relate to different understandings of representation. Beyond majoritarian concepts, however, the electoral systems of Canada and Australia reveal additional dimensions of political cultural understandings of representation. Although many aspects could be pursued, I want to focus on one in particular: one person, one vote, one value. It is my hypothesis that both countries share a cultural assumption about the importance of "one person, one vote." They differ to the degree that "one vote, one value" has become a significant controversy in Australia, while hardly mentioned in Canada.

Wright (1980) distinguishes "competition between candidates" and the process of "choosing representatives" as two radically different ways of interpreting electoral outcomes. He asserts that the first-past-the-post system presumes that the only issue is which candidate will win, whereas the proper understanding should be how to translate voters' views into a choice of representatives, which he argues can only be done through proportional representation in multi-member constituencies. I do not want to get sidetracked on whether he is correct about the inexorable link between the particular voting methods and the broader conception of elections. I do agree, however, that his two alternatives – competition between candidates versus choosing representatives – probably reflect quite different cultural conceptions; and Canada is closer to a pure case of the former and Australia to the latter.

Consider double-member constituencies in British Columbia provincial elections or in Prince Edward Island voting for assemblymen and councillors. In those constituencies with two candidates to be chosen, each voter has two votes; in other constituencies, each voter has only one vote. By my commonsense understanding, this violates the "one person, one vote" rule. But no one in either province (except me) has ever put it that baldly. In fact, the usual view is that "one person, one vote" means "one vote per member to be elected." This discrepancy between what is commonly assumed and what the proverbial Martian visitor would say signals that this is a cultural assumption, and perhaps doubly so. For one thing, it makes almost impregnable the belief in "one person, one vote." Besides, it clearly focuses attention on "competition between candidates," since the issue is defined as getting a say in the choice between candidates, rather than whether there will be one or two representatives from the constituency and who voted for them.

In Australia, the use of preferential ballots means that every voter (for House elections, at least) must vote for every candidate, although generally only the first or second preference is counted. Again, there is a commonsense understanding by which one could say that each voter gets more than one vote. This is vehemently denied by most Australians, however, on the grounds that only one candidate is chosen in the end, and *that* is the vote that counts, regardless of what our Martian says. Some voters have their ballots counted a second (or third, etc.) time, while others do not; despite this, no one to my knowledge uses this obvious fact to challenge the belief that "one person, one vote" has been achieved.

Both countries, therefore, have electoral rules which appear to violate (in different ways) the maxim of "one person, one vote." But the almost universal denial of these facts shows the power of the cultural understanding. The two political cultures thus appear to share equally this commitment to "one person, one vote," but the meanings differ in ways captured by Wright's distinction. In Canada, to get to vote for one candidate is sufficient, regardless of whether someone else gets to vote for two. In Australia, the crucial issue is how to create a majority of individual votes for the representative, even if this means that some people's ballots are counted only once and thus these people have only one vote, while other people have their second or third preferences counted and thus have more than one vote. Very different interpretations of the outcome can be generated despite the same deeper assumption about "one person, one vote."

Turning to comparisons between constituencies, one must ask about the adherence to "one vote, one value." Within a constituency, every voter having the same number of votes (one or many) can be seen as equality. If one constituency has many more voters than another, however, a vote in the smaller constituency counts for more (has a higher "value") than a vote in the larger constituency. This is agreed in both countries, but they differ over whether it is a serious problem and what to do about it.

Both countries have legislation which in one way or another asserts that votes should count equally or have equal value. Constituency boundaries, therefore, must be drawn in such a way as to make the number of voters as nearly equal as is feasible. The overt norm, in other words, is "one vote, one value." Both countries (and their states or provinces) allow some deviation around the norm, whether the task is performed by parliamentarians, election commissioners, judges or others. In Canada, at least since the 1960s, the prescribed limits of variation are 25 percent in population size above or below the average in most jurisdictions, with some noteworthy exceptions (Qualter 1970; Carty 1985). In Australia, the limits were 20 percent until 1974, since then 10 percent (Goot 1985; Wright 1980). From this evidence alone, one can conclude that "one vote, one value" has been taken more seriously in Australia (see also Sancton 1990).

Although not such precise evidence, my observation of the debates about apportionment in the two countries leads to the stronger conclusion that until recently "one vote, one value" has hardly been an issue in Canada, whereas it has long been a serious concern in Australia. These observations derive partly from scholarly literature; for example, Carty's (1985) review of electoral boundary legislation concluded that gerrymandering is the overriding concern in Canada, whereas apportionment is the greater concern in Australia and the United States. In part, however, I base my view on reading newspapers and talking to politicians, party workers and journalists. In Australia, the issue of apportionment comes up regularly; but in Canada, hardly at all. I suspect (but cannot prove) that this harks back to Wright's distinction: the focus in Canada is on choosing between candidates within a constituency, so "one vote, one value" loses much of its force. In Australia, on the contrary, a greater concern seems evident about the broad character of representation that results from an election; this requires comparisons between constituencies and in particular requires attention to party shares of seats and votes. This reflects also on the greater value of partisanship as an organizing principle or cleavage in Australian politics, as I will argue in a later section.

At the end of this study I will return to the question of why Australia has been more innovative and complex in its electoral arrangements; but at this point my focus must be restricted to some implications of these cultural contrasts for our understanding of parties as confederal institutions.

Canada rests its electoral system on several implicit assumptions about the value of communities of interest. Australia diverges by assuming that individuals are to be represented. The first-past-the-post single-member constituency favours large, concentrated social groups who can mobilize to elect one of "theirs" to Parliament. This implicitly concedes that other groups, if they are to be represented by an "insider," must look to a representative from another constituency. Preferential voting in Australia, by contrast, forces each voter to vote for each candidate. The emphasis on a majority within each constituency lends authority to the representative, since there is majority support compared with the more usual minority vote in Canada.

It would appear, therefore, that Canadian parties are more vulnerable to the allegations by Charter groups or others that they are not adequately represented. The emphasis in Canada on trying to create majority governments plays down the importance of individual majorities in constituencies. There is a good reason for the Canadian concern with majority government: brokerage politics within a party is hard enough without simultaneously negotiating a deal with an opposition party that in turn has its own brokerage problem. Furthermore, the ultimate objective of brokerage politics is to have significant representation in each region and among each major group in the country; to do so virtually guarantees the party a majority in Parliament. Hence, brokerage and majority are easily blurred into one concept in practical terms.

Recall the references to how major groups (French, English, etc.) do not quite coincide with provincial boundaries. We can now see another reason for the dilemma of parties as confederal institutions. The rules of the Canadian electoral game implicitly give advantages to major groups concentrated in provinces or regions. They disadvantage small groups or those that are very evenly distributed across the country. Parties that do a good job of representing regions may sacrifice their ability to represent other kinds of groups or interests. This may not be a function of inadequate parties but of a particular social distribution overlaid on a peculiar state structure. Indeed, it is not surprising that the "rules" favour large, concentrated social groups. After all, they were also the large, concentrated groups who sent the Fathers of Confederation to Charlottetown and Quebec City in the 1860s. The tension between regional representation and group representation may help to explain why, as noted above, parties have found it expedient to create quite separate federal and provincial wings. This may be a sensible response, but the question is open as to whether it is helpful in building confederal parties.

Leadership

Most of what has been said about representation also applies to the leadership function. The party must choose a leader who can appeal widely and thereby speak on behalf of the diverse interests and perspectives within the party and the country. Needless to say, one leader cannot represent very many groups in the "insider" sense, and thus it becomes especially crucial to have a process of leadership selection that appears to involve all significant groups. The contrast between Canada and Australia, we shall see, is stark and total: timing of selection, range of candidates, opportunities for group participation and other features are entirely contrary in the two countries.

Leaders of Australian parties are chosen by secret ballots in parliamentary caucuses. The same is true of state parties as well. Canadian parties, by contrast, use leadership conventions. Members of Parliament, if they attend the convention, have no greater influence than other delegates; and some are not chosen as delegates.

Organizing a convention to select a leader takes time and money. Thus, there can be no quick or secret changes of leadership in Canada. In Australia, such sudden and private "spills" of a leader are common. Prime Minister Bob Hawke, for example, was elevated to the leader's position and replaced Bill Hayden in the few hours it took the incumbent Prime Minister, Malcolm Fraser, to contact the Governor-General, drive to his office and dissolve Parliament (Kelly 1984).

The nature of the selection process in the two countries constrains the type of people who can plausibly be candidates. In Australia, it is theoretically possible for the caucus to choose any type of person, but in fact only experienced MPs will be considered. In Canada, a wider range of possibilities may be considered, because the convention may find appealing someone with provincial experience or even someone with no legislative experience. The fact that a long campaign across the country to select delegates involves enormous expense and a great deal of time limits the people who can realistically be serious candidates. The 1990 leadership convention that chose Audrey McLaughlin qualifies this generalization only slightly.

A major concomitant of leadership selection methods is the strength of Parliament. Caucus control of leadership selection enhances the

Australian Parliament's role in governance. Canadian conventions may reflect the fact that our Parliament has declined in importance over the past century. Since the questions of parliamentary control of government and of executive dominance through party discipline are the subject of a later section, I will do no more than mention them here and instead turn to some implications of the difference in leadership selection methods in Canada and Australia.

Canadian parties have used leadership conventions as nation-building exercises. This has been partly by intent and partly as a by-product of the publicity that attends such conventions, especially in the era of television. Although the idea of large, open conventions was adopted from the United States, the nature and use of the conventions in the two countries are widely variant. Block voting without secret ballots in Democratic and Republican conventions contrasts sharply, for example, with the secret ballot used in Canada; such private voting means that "bosses" cannot deliver votes here. Furthermore, the concept of leader in Canadian terms is quite different from that of presidential nominee in the United States. A defeated presidential candidate has little power or prestige, whereas the Leader of the Opposition is a significant actor and not simply because of being prime-minister-in-waiting.

As media attention to conventions grew with the advent of televised coverage, party strategists realized the value of this publicity. Thus, the campaign leading to the convention has, on average, lengthened with the hope that the new leader and policies may catch the attention of potential voters. The selection of delegates, by the same token, can be viewed as opportunities for groups, localities, regions and provinces to become more actively involved in a party's internal affairs. If the parliamentary caucus alone made the choice, then areas or groups that had failed to elect an MP would feel excluded, so the reasoning goes; thus, to insist on having delegates from areas of past electoral weakness as well as areas of strength, it is hoped, will make the party more attractive as a confederal institution.

The point must not be pressed too far. Conventions may or may not create confederal parties. The publicity may or may not be entirely beneficial. The divisiveness of campaign rhetoric may receive more attention than the final vote for the winner. My point is not that conventions have fully served the purposes assigned to them, but rather that party activists, leaders and observers have agreed that one of the main reasons for using conventions for leadership selection is the desire to further the role of the party as a confederal institution. It is perhaps the most dramatic illustration of our belief that parties may serve the nation-building enterprise even if other evidence raises questions about the likely result.

Brokerage

The idea that a party should resolve some conflicting interests by aggregating them in organizational and/or policy compromises is common throughout the British-influenced democracies. But some of the specific ways it has worked in the Liberal and Conservative parties have been peculiarly Canadian. I will argue that past success as aggregators or mediators or brokers may have had the unexpected consequence that parties will be less successful in the future. Hence, this dilemma further undermines the chances that the role of broker will allow one or more parties to be confederal institutions.

Brokerage is a concept with several distinct meanings. Sometimes it means no more than mediation or helping to arrange a compromise. Whenever this usage is intended, I have used the word mediation. Often brokerage connotes the use of side payments, especially patronage, to "buy off" persons or groups when their ideological or policy positions cannot be met. In such cases, I have used the terms "patronage" or "patronage machine." More narrowly, brokerage has come to be understood in Canada as a form of group cooptation. This has usually involved mediation and patronage as well, but it can be distinguished by the fact that a party will incorporate leaders of contending groups within the "inner circle" and try to "make a deal" in closed meetings rather than in open debate in election campaigns or in the legislature. These are not rigid distinctions, but they are useful ones for understanding confederal parties and why brokerage in the strict sense defined here is less and less a panacea for our political difficulties.

Historically, the development of Parliament saw its central role as that of representing the taxpayers. Parties (then called factions) were divisions within Parliament, no more than shifting coalitions, partly principled and partly opportunistic. For centuries, no one claimed that parties should do the work of Parliament. Instead, Parliament was the representative body and parties were merely one of the informal means of managing the institution.

The broadening of the franchise in the 19th century contributed to a change in Parliament and in party organization. By then, more diverse interests and points of view were found within Parliament, and parties had taken on ideological contours. Gradually, party discipline became more regular, and government came to depend on the support of a single party. Although this process was ongoing at the period of

Confederation, the outlines were already visible. However, the centuries of British tradition were not directly relevant to guide the governance of the new country, any more than they were for the United Province of Canada, in the area of religious and linguistic conflict. Therefore, Prime Minister Macdonald felt it wise to incorporate French and English, Protestant and Catholic within his Conservative party. His use of patronage thus went beyond smoothing over minor differences of opinion in order to confront the opposition party, whose views were widely different. Instead, Macdonald's strategy was to minimize interparty differences by absorbing both sides of the fundamental cleavages in the young country. By the 1890s, Laurier was successfully following the same strategy. The success of both leaders and their parties blurred the lines between government and party.

By pursuing a brokerage strategy, mainly through use of a "patronage machine," the two major parties usurped some of Parliament's historic functions and contributed to its lessened status. Of course, many other factors contributed to executive dominance of Parliament, and the next section will examine the phenomenon. The crucial point here is that brokerage was originally a parliamentary function but that it became a party function in Canada (at least at the federal level). This is part of the reason why parties as confederal institutions are uniquely Canadian: we have not trusted Parliament to do its job, and we have then asked another institution to remedy the defect.

A comparison with an American perspective may highlight the point. In *The Federalist*, Madison (1949) developed the argument that one virtue of federalism was that it would weaken the power of parties ("factions" was his word). By this he meant that federalism would keep alive the interests of different localities and regions, making it less likely that a single wave of emotion or interest could gain a majority and thus tyrannize the rest of the country.

Madison's advice was, of course, offered in the context of a very different system of government from that which Canada adopted from Britain. Nevertheless, it bears examination because of the similar reason for creating federal systems in the two countries: different social and cultural interests in different colonies. No debate in Canada took place at Confederation comparable to that in response to which *The Federalist* was written. Had a lengthy public debate taken place, one might not have heard any argument like Madison's. We can, however, make the argument ourselves.

If federalism can be defended in both countries on the grounds of incompatible interests in different regions, the defence of those interests by incorporation within a single party would constitute in Madison's eyes a case of tyranny. By tyranny he meant that power was concentrated too much. If one party could reconcile the major contending forces, what was left to oppose it effectively? (See the further implications of this interpretation in the later section on governance, below.)

American parties eventually attempted brokerage politics, and some would say that tyranny resulted. Be that as it may, the contrast between Madisonian logic and Canadian practice emphasizes that the use of patrons and brokers in the Conservative party, and later in the Liberal party, was a strategy tailored to the Canadian context. The fact that the country survived and prospered may or may not be due primarily to brokerage of fundamental cleavages by the parties, but this helped and may have been crucial. The question then may be asked if brokerage can continue to be a successful strategy or function of our parties. Let us examine a few implications of brokerage and some possible variants in the present situation.

Notice that the concept of brokerage entails the "insider" concept of representation discussed above. If the party is to be confederal, it must incorporate the people on different sides of the cleavage. For a long time, this meant Protestant and Catholic, French and English, Quebec and the other regions. As the demography of the country has changed, new groups have sought incorporation. As values change, new groups are created, in the sense of becoming self-conscious or visible to themselves and others; these include groups based on physical characteristics such as skin colour or disability, on psychological traits such as religiosity, or on lifestyle or other combinations of features. Once it has been granted that cleavages that matter to us must be brokered, then as new cleavages are defined and become significant, how does one resist incorporation of these cleavages in the new brokerage efforts?

For decades, incorporation of the brokered groups meant that "insiders" in Merton's sense played a key role. The attitudes, sympathies or commitments of the leader and other allies were less important than the direct involvement of spokespersons from the French or English, Catholic or Protestant communities. Indeed, a combination of personal characteristics was essential, so that it was not sufficient to have either a French speaker *or* a Catholic *or* someone from Quebec; brokerage required that the spokespeople be French *and* Catholic *and* Québécois. Thus, for example, the Joe Clark government in 1979–80 was perceived as unable to broker the cleavages despite the facts that Clark himself was a Catholic, that he was deeply committed to Quebec's interests and that his party received nearly one-sixth of the votes in Quebec.

Without any intention to do so, traditional brokerage politics in Canada thereby laid the foundation for the successful demands of new groups seeking representation. Regional, linguistic, ethnic, religious, aboriginal and lifestyle groups have come to expect direct involvement of one or more of their "insiders" in party, legislature and government. So deeply rooted is this concept that some "outsiders" accept other groups' claims. Many groups that have had privileged status – for example, men, white Anglo-Saxons, central Canadians and upper-middle-class lawyers – now seem to accept that they cannot represent some other groups. People who are not "insiders" in the newly active groups believe that certain of those groups must be represented by their own "insiders." For example, the absence of women on a royal commission would be disastrous today and of concern to most men as well as women, although not 20 years ago. Native groups must be directly involved where their interests are clear, but perhaps not so often as women. Gays and lesbians, on the other hand, will probably wait quite a while before achieving that honoured position.

The need to broker a larger number of groups poses a serious threat to parties as confederal institutions. Let us examine two avenues that have been suggested as ways out of the dilemma that brokerage poses to parties: party reform and proportional representation.

In Canada and Australia, much of the animus behind calls for party reform derives from a desire for greater involvement by the extra-parliamentary membership. This desire complements the fear or belief that the leader (or a small central group) is too powerful. Leadership conventions, of course, are partly intended to increase the sense of involvement. Recent experiments by the Parti québécois and by the Progressive Conservatives in Ontario allow the entire membership to vote without the intermediate step of delegate selection. The consequences may be self-contradictory: the greater the degree of membership involvement, the better; but as the involvement broadens, so much stronger and more legitimate is the leader. Hence, the leader can claim to speak on behalf of the party in a way not open to a leader chosen by a small group or by caucus; and the leader can then exercise more centralized control.

It is worth looking briefly at a structural aspect of party members' involvement in party policy making. In a later section I will return to the process of policy making from a substantive perspective. When parties were factions, there was a perceived need for them because of the large number of members of Parliament. Coordination and management of parliamentary business seemed to require a small core of activists. At that time there was no conception of the party-in-the-electorate or mass parties; the caucus was the party.

In the 19th century, more attention was given to getting out the vote, to constituency service, and the like. This meant that eventually, and especially in this century, "the party" had come to include large numbers of extraparliamentary activists. As mass mobilization followed the granting of almost universal suffrage (after roughly 1920), the number of people who could claim to be in one degree or another involved in the parties was in the millions rather than hundreds or thousands. At the time, this was felt to make the parties much more democratic than the factions of MPs in earlier eras. Of course, millions of party members or voters, like citizens of a country, cannot deal with one another face to face. Thus, parties, like governments, became large-scale organizations, and many developed their own permanent bureaucracies.

Being hierarchical, bureaucracies engender central coordinating positions that wield effective power over many party functions. They become to an important degree "a party within the party." Indeed, in the Australian Labor Party (ALP), there are highly organized (and named) factions very similar to the 18th-century factions in Parliament, except more disciplined. Other parties in Canada or Australia have less structured factions, but one need only think of "Red Tories" or of "wets" and "dries" to realize that large organizations always have a structure. As the structure becomes effective, it comes under attack from people or groups who feel excluded.

The success of mass parties in mobilizing enormous numbers of people – which seems like a democratic development – creates the conditions for charges of hierarchy, élitism and concentration of power. Two lessons may be mentioned: party reform seems to be part of a cyclical process and thus not necessarily a long-term answer to particular current events. The cyclical nature of the process may be related to the brokerage function, since there are always new groups to incorporate. As the new groups become fully incorporated, other groups lose status or newer groups see an opportunity to lay claim to a share of power or spoils. Both lessons suggest to me that party reform is beneficial as a source of renewal of party energies but that it is not a stable solution to our wish to create confederal institutions. This is another way in which the parties mirror the country: both exist in unstable equilibrium and must be re-created or restructured periodically.

A superficial review of the benefits of proportional representation (PR) offers promise for parties as confederal institutions. Deeper analysis reveals some costs that need to be weighed against the benefits. Of course, a judgement on the desirability of PR must take account of more than its value as assistance in creating parties of a confederal nature. But that is the focus here, so I limit my remarks to this aspect of PR. (See also Bakvis 1981.)

The reasoning that links PR and brokerage politics is fairly straight-forward and can be developed in two ways. Most simply, PR aims to achieve a close relationship between the proportion of votes and the proportion of seats won by a party. That is why it is called proportional representation. There can be no doubt whatsoever that PR would make the caucuses of large parties more broadly representative of the regions of Canada and probably therefore more representative of other aspects of our diversity. Instead of the Liberals gaining no seats west of Winnipeg in the 1980 election, their share of the vote would have guaranteed them roughly one-fifth of the seats. Likewise, Joe Clark's government in 1979 would have ended up with quite a few Quebec seats, since it received almost one-sixth of the votes. Of course, more seats in one region might be balanced by fewer in another, since PR evens out in both directions. In the next section, "Governance," we shall return to this point when noting the frequency of minority governments; they would almost certainly be more frequent under PR, especially in the future fragmentation of votes likely to follow the demise of the Meech Lake Accord.

The second type of link between PR and the brokerage role of par-ties concerns the effect of particular types of PR. The use of a list ver-sion of PR in Australian Senate elections may serve as an instructive example. No party expects to win more than half the seats available (six in half-Senate elections, twelve if there is a double dissolution), since no party expects to gain much more than 50 percent of the votes. Thus, with (let us say) six vacancies in the normal case, Labor (ALP) candidates who ranked first and second are guaranteed election, and the third-ranked candidate has a very good chance. Lower-ranked can-didates know that they have zero chance of winning; they hope to move up to one of the safe seats in future elections.

As it happens, the brokering in the ALP involves its factions and not the same groups as in Canada, but the principle is the same. If you really want to show your party's commitment to a region, an ethnic group or a faction, put them first or second. At first glance, this appears to be a way out for Canadian parties, especially if one had longer lists as would be feasible in larger provinces. For example, Quebec has 75 seats and Ontario over 90. If a party could count on even one-quarter or one-half of these seats, it could offer many groups a safe seat.

Notice the down-side of this benefit: not all groups can be placed in safe seats. This is, of course, true in our present system, so one might say they are equivalent. The difference is serious, however: under a list system, the rank order is printed on every ballot and thus is public knowledge, whereas in single-member constituencies we know the winner but not the rank order among the losers in the nomination process. As I noted above, other advantages may outweigh this "cost," but one cannot deny that there is a potential cost.

Could one evade this cost by using a different form of PR? There are many, many versions of PR, but for present purposes the crucial types are list (just discussed) and nonlist. If the party cannot determine the rank order among the candidates, then the voters will. If they are allowed to vote for individual candidates, and the party elects its proportional quota, then no group can claim that the party engineered its loss by an unfair rank order. But recall why PR was examined in the first place: brokerage requires that the party affirm the importance of groups whose support it needs, and the list-PR methods allow it to do this. If another form of PR allows the party to avoid offending some groups, this also makes it difficult to guarantee which groups will succeed.

The dilemma of choosing between list and nonlist forms of PR may be indicative of the broader dilemma that brokerage politics poses to parties as confederal institutions. Parties that successfully straddle fundamental cleavages must endure the internal divisions characteristic of the country. The more successful, the more chance the party will be unable to contain the divisiveness.

Success as brokers may make the parties less able to govern, and success as confederal institutions guarantees divided parties. Parties cannot unite the country if they represent it too well, and they cannot govern it well if they do not represent some major parts of the country. Again, we come to the apparent conclusion that we are asking parties to undertake an impossible task because of the failure of other institutions.

An example of one negative consequence of brokerage confined to parties has been suggested by Dufour's (1990) analysis of the breakdown or stalemate in French-English relations in the "new Quebec." Dufour argues that, as a result of the conquest, English people, institutions and culture are a small but significant part of Quebec; and likewise, the French fact is an integral part of Canada. Because of unresolved tensions growing out of Quebec's special place in Canada, the Government of Quebec feels compelled to pretend that the English fact in Quebec either does not exist or is not an essential component of the Quebec identity. The use of the "notwithstanding" clause to protect Bill 101 in December 1988 serves as an example. Thus, brokerage can occur, if it does, only within the Liberal party (provincial wing) and cannot carry the authoritative weight it otherwise would if it were openly acknowledged government policy. As a consequence, the federal government by default must promote the interests of English speakers in Quebec and of French speakers in other provinces (with some help from the Government of New Brunswick), with a concomitant increase in tensions between the federal and provincial governments.

Governance

Previous sections have included reference to the fact that institutions and political cultural assumptions reinforce each other. To change one feature may have wide ramifications. This perspective underlies much of what I have to say about governance. Two examples or avenues into the topic of governance will reveal a number of interesting contrasts between Canada and Australia: minority governments versus coalition governments, and the contradictions between federalism and responsible government. To deal with these topics, it will be necessary to pay some attention to related institutions of governance, especially the Senate and provincial governments.

I have argued that parties that try to be effective confederal institutions face contradictory demands and find themselves in a double bind. One might ask, however, whether the process of governing serves to exacerbate or complicate any of these dilemmas. Alternatively, one can examine whether related institutions of government may make parties more or less likely to be confederal institutions.

One of the first observations pertinent to these queries is that Canada has experienced minority government at various periods in its history. Several points need to be emphasized about this phenomenon. First, there may be a temporal pattern with minority governments becoming more common in the recent past and perhaps in the future. Second, one should note that Canada is almost unique among democratic regimes in allowing minority governments to occur; most countries in our situation create majority coalition governments. Third, there may be a connection between our reluctance to use coalition governments and our particular type of federalism. Finally, the deficiencies of our Senate and the strength of our provincial governments may underlie our need for parties as confederal institutions while making that goal more difficult for the parties.

Focusing only on the federal government, it is fair to say that minority government is a 20th-century phenomenon, and one that has occurred mostly since the First World War. Is there significance in this pattern? Two interpretations may be suggested, and both might be correct. For one thing, some commentators have alleged that the great nation-building tasks of the late 19th century (railroads, economic integration, immigration, populating the West) simultaneously provided common purposes and were facilitated by a strong federal government facing relatively weak provincial governments. By the end of the First World War, it is argued, these crucial tasks were complete, and provincial governments were utilizing more fully the powers granted them in the *BNA Act.* Hence, regional forces (especially in the newly formed Prairie provinces) grew in significance. Equally important, these dynamic regional thrusts were channelled not through the Senate but through provincial governments.

The second interpretation relates directly to the party system. With the creation of Alberta and Saskatchewan in 1905, a new equilibrium was needed, and it was not possible to achieve that within the two old parties: many new parties were created. Although most did not last very long, they weakened the grip of Liberals and Conservatives and made it less likely that these older parties could validly claim to be confederal institutions. I shall return to the reason for this development after exploring other aspects of the significance of minority governments.

It is probably safe to speculate that minority governments will be quite common in the next decade or two. The most immediate cause of this trend concerns the demise of the Meech Lake Accord. Both the campaign in favour of Meech and the bitter aftermath have loosened the traditional loyalties that voters have felt for the three largest parties in federal politics and have deeply divided each party. If one or another party could pull the pieces together, it would stand a good chance of creating a broad base for a long string of majority governments. However, this seems so implausible that I dismiss it in favour of speculation on erosion of Liberal and Conservative strengths in different areas of the country and the continuing inability of the NDP to gain any significant foothold in Quebec. Hence, I cannot see how any party can put together a stable majority in the next decade or so.

Some of the supporting logic for this conclusion must await later parts of this section and the next. At this point, let us note that minority government is not necessarily bad, despite the common desire for "stable" majority governments. For one thing, some minority governments have passed significant legislation and implemented innovative policies. This is no guarantee of productive minority governments in the future, but it forces one to consider that, at the least, they are not doomed by past experience. Furthermore, almost all minority governments are responsive to the public. Some see this as a defect because these governments may undertake expensive programs, but at least they are likely to be attractive programs because the party in power wants to gain a majority at the next election while undercutting one or more of the other parties.

Leaving aside our judgements of particular minority governments, why do we allow them to occur even though we repeatedly lament their occurrence? To understand this very peculiar situation, we need a comparative perspective. In general, very few countries try to govern themselves with minority governments (Bakvis 1981). Typically, parties negotiate coalitions after any election in which no one party has a majority; and in Australia the non-Labor parties sometimes establish a coalition before the election or even when the Liberals have a majority of seats on their own. Several reasons may be offered for our unusual practice; whether these actually justify the practice is less important than the fact that they enlighten us about assumptions apparently underlying our system of governance.

One must note first that Canada and most countries with coalition governments fall into a particular category of nation-state. Such countries contain more than one nation, or at least are deeply divided over certain fundamental questions that are consensual in some other countries. In such situations, there are two logical avenues in the formation of governments: either each party can be internally homogeneous, endeavouring to represent one major interest such as a region, an ethnic group or an ideology; or the parties can try to bridge or broker several major interests and be, in effect, coalitions in their own right. Obviously, the first alternative results in a majority government only if the major interest encompasses the vast majority of the population, which cannot be true of the divided countries in this category such as Belgium, Holland, Austria and perhaps Germany (West or united). Hence, "pure" parties lead inevitably to coalition governments, since by definition no one group or party can speak on behalf of more than a fraction of the country.

Where, as in Canada, parties try to mediate or broker interests, they are coalitions. The purpose of brokering and thus the purpose of being coalitions involves a belief that this is how one builds a majority government. When that succeeds, one confirms the presumption. Recall, in another section, I argued that "majority" and "brokerage" are closely related concepts in practice, at least in Canada. When more than two major parties compete, minority governments often result. By itself, this reasoning is not satisfying, since it borders on a tautology. If your party is a coalition of interests, you can avoid coalition government because you are a coalition, and so a minority government is a coalition anyway. Thus, the question is: Will we have a formal coalition (government) or an informal coalition (party)? Since we are analysing cultural assumptions, we cannot expect them to be fully coherent when held up to logical scrutiny. Nevertheless, one can learn from the fact that something like a tautology may underlie our pattern of minority governments. There are other strands to the argument to which I now turn.

A second concern expressed about coalition governments is that they blur the lines of responsibility or (more exactly) of accountability. That is, if two or more parties jointly take responsibility for a policy, and voters do not like it, whom do they hold accountable? Again, I emphasize that this is not logical, since this reasoning could just as well apply to a confederal party since it is by definition a coalition of interests. As I have repeatedly argued, however, we learn about political cultures by trying to see why apparently illogical conclusions are not noticed or are not a matter of concern to those who operate within the culture. The missing link in the above logic may be that one can deny that one's party is a coalition in the same sense as a coalition of several parties in government. Perhaps one should, in our political culture, say that brokerage parties are alliances and that only formal coalitions in government will be called coalitions. Either way, the government encompasses several distinct interests, and each party does too.

A third perspective on the preference for minority governments harks back to the earlier discussion of Madison's views on federalism. Recall that brokerage of opposites would constitute tyranny in Madison's analysis. Few people today define tyranny in that way but notice a hidden assumption in our use of brokerage. If all major groups (or "sides") are adequately represented in a party, then any other party can be chastized as illegitimate or unrepresentative. If opponents lack legitimacy or credibility, why form a coalition with them?

If the party forming the minority government has been the government for some time, it understands the value of patronage and the importance of holding office. Thus, besides viewing opposing parties as illegitimate, the governing party prefers the insecurity of a minority situation to sharing patronage and other benefits with its opponents.

The final interpretation of our willingness to countenance minority governments relates back to the previous discussion of representation. Brokerage entails the accommodation of "insiders" who represent key elements of the society, whether regional, ethnic or ideological. Once a party achieves some kind of equilibrium within its ranks, some balance among activists who are "insiders," then the party must "hang together or hang separately." The intense internal tensions built into brokerage parties require strict party discipline. This is also necessary in parliamentary forms of government in order to support or oppose the government. Such discipline is much less easily imposed on a coalition of parties, as experience shows. Hence, a minority government relying on support in Parliament from first one party and then another may be no less stable than most coalition governments. The tight discipline fostered by responsible government and reinforced by brokerage would work quite well except for the vast regional differences in a federal system like Canada's. This contradiction between federalism and responsible government takes us well beyond the issue of minority government, however, and deserves extensive separate treatment.

There are several ways to characterize the contradictions – or, at least, the poor fit – between federalism and responsible government. The simplest is to note that the Canadian state is organized federally because there are widely different interests in different regions (or colonies, depending on the period one examines), and these regions should be organized as legislatures with executive governments. Parties, historically speaking, were devised to organize interests, ideologies, issues or individuals. That is, parties are a form of conflict management or issue management *within* a particular region, whereas a legislature (and its executive) represents the whole territory. These are two fundamentally different organizational types.

Second, unless a party holds all the seats (as the Liberals did in New Brunswick in 1987–91) it does not represent the territory in the same manner that a legislature does, and perhaps not even then. Majoritarian thinking easily leads one to believe that because one's party controls a majority of constituencies through its MPs, one can speak for the whole. Practically, one may get away with it, but that does not justify thinking of a party as equivalent to a legislature.

Third, parties (even brokerage parties) must deal with many issues or interests that are nonterritorial. These interests or issues may (and often do) have differential effects on each section of the country, because economic, social and demographic elements are unevenly distributed. Nevertheless, ideologies, visions of the future, strategies for development and the like – which are the subject of the next section – are abstract, not specifically territorial in nature and differ on average between parties, more in some cases than in others and usually with some overlap. Thus, the regional or territorial impact of policies or ideologies should not blind us to the fact that these impacts are incidental to the effort to organize a coherent program in partisan terms.

Another way to characterize the tension between federalism and responsible government is to look at the contradictory demands on Canadian MPs. Each MP is expected to speak on behalf of the unique interest in the constituency. Some of those interests will be territorially based, such as the fact that wheat, fisheries and automobile plants are concentrated in only a few places. These groups expect the MP to work on their behalf, and MPs will do a lot of that if they wish to be re-elected. At the same time, MPs are part of a party that imposes discipline to ensure MPs vote a particular way even if that is contrary to the interests of the MP's constituents. The mutual influence of regionalism and federalism reinforces the tendency to see almost all issues in Canada as though they were territorial, whether they are or not. This tendency will be clearer after enunciation of the third and final perspective on how federalism and responsible government oppose each other.

The final perspective on federalism and responsible government that I will mention concerns other institutions of governance. The Senate and the provincial legislatures and governments also bear some of the burden of representation of territories and the range of interests in them. They are intended to do so in ways quite distinct from the way we expect parties to operate.

The Senate was intended by the Fathers of Confederation to make certain that regional or local matters were expressed within Parliament. They were at pains to build in this perspective because of the fact that the basis of representation in the Commons was population. Thus, as we know, Ontario has always had vastly more seats than Prince Edward Island. The Senate, on the other hand, has the same number of seats (24) from each region, except the Yukon and the Northwest Territories (two each). Equally significant, Ontario and Quebec have the same number of seats despite different population sizes.

The Senate has not performed very well as the "House of the regions." This should not cause us to doubt that federalism requires that some such perspective be built into the system of governance (Smiley 1980; Cairns 1979). The Fathers of Confederation were doubly wrong in their expectations, because they did not foresee the enormous power and varied roles of the provincial legislatures and governments. Thus, the institution they thought would remind the Parliament of its regional concerns has been totally eclipsed by the "subordinate" and "local" institution of the provinces themselves.

What matters for our analysis is not whether the Senate or the provinces articulate regional perspectives. Whichever does so, it poses large problems for parties as confederal institutions. Why would we want a party to compete with the Senate or with a provincial legislature or government as the voice of a regional interest? Parties were not designed to perform this function, and the other institutions were. Since everyone agrees that the Senate has failed completely to speak for the provinces or regions, the real contest seems to be between parties and provincial governments. Since most commentators believe that provincial governments do too good a job of pushing the interests they represent, why ask parties to duplicate the effort?

The answer, of course, is that one needs a countrywide (confederal) perspective that takes account of all major interests. Since provincial legislatures, governments or premiers are manifestly, indeed almost by definition, unsuited to that confederal task, we ask our parties to perform the function. But if provincial governments cannot do the trick, why not ask the federal government to do it? Why turn to a political party? One reason is obvious: we shall try every avenue, including parties. There is, however, a deeper explanation, and it involves our misunderstanding of the demands on parties in our system. An Australian comparison should prove instructive.

Previously, I mentioned the puzzle or conundrum at the heart of Canada's political organization – that social cleavages do not quite coincide with political (provincial or regional) boundaries. Australia is different. Social cleavages are totally unrelated to political (state) boundaries. There is no state that has an overwhelming proportion of any single group in the way in which Quebec is French-speaking (but not totally so). Roman Catholics, farmers, mining interests, immigrants and natural disasters are roughly evenly spread among the units of the Australian federation. Hence, all state governments find themselves subject to the same range of pressures, although the exact form and degree vary somewhat. (Only Tasmania has significant hydroelectric potential, for example, and only Queensland has the Great Barrier Reef.) Obversely, any confederal party based on fundamental social cleavages (class, religion) will find that it has support in every state, although the exact level of support also varies with local events and personalities.

Notice how party discipline operates in systems like Australia's. Since each party stands for a range of interests that are confederal in scope, party discipline rarely forces MPs to choose between the interests of their constituents and the demands of party unity. Obversely, no matter which party forms the Canberra government, there is essentially no chance of one or another state failing to be represented in the government. This is true of the House of Representatives, but doubly so of the Senate. The use of proportional representation in Senate elections ensures that close to half the senators, but no more, will be from the Australian Labor Party in each state; and most of the rest will be Liberal. Australian Democrats, the National Party and an occasional independent will constitute a small but often decisive minority. Again, no territorial division can dominate, nor can one be left out completely. Incidentally, it is worth emphasizing that senators – being democratically elected – are fully acceptable as cabinet ministers, whereas Canadian senators are less able to compensate for a party's deficiency of representation in a province or region.

Notice an important consequence of this fortuitous set of circumstances. Australian parties do not have to compete with the Senate or with state governments as representatives of purely local or regional interests. Hence, they also do not have to play the role of brokers in the Canadian sense. Thus, they can manage and organize conflict over the cleavages deemed critical without wondering if their actions will tear the nation asunder. Hard feelings are common between Australian parties because of intense ideological concerns (big business versus organized labour, for example), but they rarely lead to charges of treason or lack of patriotism. Party organization and discipline work to manage and constrain the interstate social cleavages, contrary to the Canadian situation where they work at cross purposes.

Putting the argument in another way, recall my earlier assertion that, historically, governments speak on behalf of territories, while parties represent nonterritorial interests and ideologies. In Australia, this is how the division of labour has worked out. In Canada, on the other hand, we have asked parties to do both jobs, to represent (and broker) territorially based interests (religion, language, economic base) while also presenting programs which are ideological and nonterritorial in intent.

For many periods in Canadian history, this peculiar set of demands worked. In part, that was because the provinces were slow in learning how to flex their muscles and occupy their heads of jurisdiction. More important for the present topic, party discipline was less strict in several periods. The first 20 to 30 years after Confederation, for example, found Macdonald and other leaders lamenting the "loose fish" who could not be brought into line under threat of the whip. Likewise, during the Second World War, for very different reasons, party lines were blurred. Over a long period, however, we have seen more and more rigid and strict party discipline with debilitating effects on the ability of any parties to broker the territorially based interests. Of course, as discipline was turning backbenchers into "trained seals," as Trudeau once called them, the provincial legislatures and governments were encouraged to speak more forcefully on behalf of their populations.

There may be another link among several strands of this discussion. By and large, the people who call for parties to serve as confederal institutions are the same people who feel that the federal government lacks sufficient power and that the provincial governments are too strong. Is there a hidden agenda here that aims to weaken the provinces? Or is it not noticed that parties as confederal institutions, a reformed Senate and other devices will compete with provincial legislatures and governments in speaking on behalf of provincial populations and interests? Why should we try to hamper the legitimate pursuit of provincial constitutional responsibilities? These are not questions I need answer here, but a related set of questions about some historical motives may serve to complete this review of the impact of governance on parties as confederal institutions.

I promised to explore some reasons for the proliferation of third parties and why this corresponded to changes in federal-provincial relations. Obviously, the change from essentially a two-party system to a multi-party system heralds a change in governance: one can almost never have a minority government in a two-party system but will often have one in a multi-party system. So much should be obvious, but the reasons for the rise of new parties, where and when they did appear, counts for as much as the actual impact they had on governance.

Had the new provinces of Alberta and Saskatchewan been populated by Québécois or Franco-Ontarians, or equally by French- and English-Canadian settlers or immigrants, the Prairies would have experienced the same types of conflict that led to Confederation half a century earlier. Instead, settlers were from the United States or were non-British and non-French Europeans, especially Germans and East Europeans who had no interest in the old animosities of the United Province of Canada (Dufour 1990).

The Prairie provinces were also unusual in that their economic bases were so homogeneous: wheat, wheat and more wheat. Not only was the regional economy different from central Canada's, but the base was much narrower, a fact still true nearly a century later. Their interests were thus not only distinct but also extremely focused and visible. Not surprising, they proved to be fertile ground for new parties that could speak on behalf of these narrowly focused intense interests. How could political parties that had mastered the brokering of religious and language conflicts expect to slip easily into the role of advocate for people and regions with no real concern about the cleavages that led to creation of the wider union? The question is especially poignant when one recalls the parliamentary debate that led to the creation of the Prairie provinces. The record shows that a conscious decision was made that there should be three Prairie provinces rather than one, as some had urged. The reason was clear: one such province would eventually rival Ontario and Quebec in population, wealth and power (Nicholson 1979).

By the time of the Great Depression, there were additional motives for abandoning Liberals and Conservatives, and turning to other parties. After all, who had been in power when this calamity befell the country? Even more crucial, the severity of the Depression was unspeakably greater in the Prairies, while the caucus and Cabinet of the Liberals and Conservatives came mainly from areas least affected by the economic devastation. Hence, voters turned to Progressives, United Farmers, Social Credit and the Co-operative Commonwealth Federation (CCF).

Mallory has explored some of these developments in his seminal book on Social Credit in Alberta. His conclusion goes beyond that province and is pertinent to this discussion:

> The western provinces were in an exceptionally weak bargaining position. The things that concerned them most – immigration, agricultural policy, and transportation – were either fields exclusively federal under the constitution or concurrent fields in which the Dominion possessed a dominant initiative. Inevitably there emerged a struggle between the federal government and the provinces ... Thus Canadian federalism produced at times an odd modification of parliamentary government in which the main focus and strength of the opposition to the government of the day was not in the parliamentary opposition but in the provincial governments. (Mallory 1954, 59)

It is easy to see the new parties as regional protest voices. And to some degree they were. But the fundamental challenge they posed to the traditional parties lay in a different dimension. The new parties were *ideological*. True, the voters who flocked to them were concentrated in certain regions, so it was natural to assume (at least at first) that they were just more interests that needed brokering.

Notice the specific ideological bases of these parties, however, and the total lack of concern with language, religion, ethnicity or race. Instead, the issues revolved around the relative importance of types of industries (manufacturing, farming, etc.) and who was protected by tariffs and for whose benefit. Other issues included the morality of banking and finance, monopoly versus competition in the transportation and marketing of wheat, and the significance of governments as economic actors. These were not issues of patronage or matters to be dealt with in traditional brokerage politics.

Their ideologies also meant that many western protest parties had a vision of society and of the country that went beyond economic interests. Some of them conceived of a transformation of the very basis of society and the creation of a new type of human being. In this, there were millenarian overtones that have since been lost or muted. For all such parties, there were hopes that old feuds, divisions and habits might be left behind! Such hopes would not augur well for their integration into a system that assumed the relevance of linguistic and religious rivalries dating from 1759 or the 1860s.

What the West forced upon the country was a new rhythm, a new basis for parties and party systems. The new parties were much closer to what parties have been historically in most Western democracies. By capturing provincial governments in the West, their party discipline did not work at cross purposes to territorial interest, as had happened with the federal Liberals and Conservatives. Of course, as Social Credit and the CCF tried to build confederal parties later, they found the situation as contradictory as their predecessors had done. Being in no danger of forming the government in Ottawa, the new parties could act out their ideological roots more consistently; this in turn ensured that they would not be confederal parties; and so on. Thus, the one-dimensional party system based on territory almost coinciding with social cleavages was replaced by a two-dimensional party system based separately on territory and ideology. If we could ever count on brokerage to underpin confederal parties, that logic broke down with the advent of a more complex party system, and no amount of electoral reform can change the logic back to its original simplicity.

Decades of patronage and brokerage under the former system were followed by stopgap measures to hold the new system in equilibrium. As new groups in the West, in the cities and in central Canada itself sought accommodation in the large, confederal parties, the old style of governance survived by other means. These included the extreme centralization of the war years, the prosperity of the immediate postwar years, and finally the use of federal taxing and spending powers to "buy off" groups and regions. The cost of these latter measures accounts in large part for the debilitating deficits and accumulated debt of recent federal governments.

To sum up, note some themes running through this section. Parties are coalitions rather than homogeneous bodies, or at least this characterizes the major parties. They thus perform some of the representative and brokerage functions of Parliament. Party discipline that serves a parliamentary function works contrary to Parliament's need to speak on behalf of regional interests, thus leaving a vacuum for the provincial governments to fill. The parties that most clearly embody the ideological function that parties perform elsewhere are regionally based and thus virtually certain to work through (and strengthen) provincial governments, rather than becoming confederal institutions. They thereby challenge the legitimacy of the Senate and the House of Commons to speak on behalf of many interests, further weakening those bodies and making them even more appendages of the traditional parties.

It may be argued, therefore, that the motives that lead us to build parties that are confederal may reflect and exacerbate the weakness of Parliament. In Australia, by contrast, the role of parties strengthens Parliament. In the United States, there is no party discipline because there is no responsible government; and thus there is no persistent dilemma for the representative or senator between serving the party and serving the constituents back home. Is the dilemma we impose on our parties a false one, and should we focus instead on why executive dominance prevails and why Parliament no longer (or only rarely) serves its function of limiting and constraining government? As noted, nationwide leadership conventions reinforce these tendencies. Fortunately, I have not been asked to solve the problem that Parliament is a "paper tiger." I emphasize once again, however, that it is very difficult to change an isolated part of the system – whether parties or Parliament – without an understanding of how that one part derives its nature from linkages with the other elements. That does not make diagnosis impossible or change undesirable; but it makes both more unpredictable.

Reform may follow several tracks. Whether we pursue party reform, Senate reform, electoral reform or changes to responsible government, the end product should be kept in mind. We do not pursue these changes for their own sake. What matters is not the number or type of parties but the government that is formed. We have examined some aspects of governance, but ultimately the central concern is what policies are formulated and how they are implemented.

Policy Formulation

Most Canadians probably assume that parties generate policies that will get the party elected and that the purpose of getting elected is to be able to implement the policies. Of course, there is no compelling reason why policy should be developed only by parties, nor any guarantee that the policies developed by a party will be implemented once it is elected. Nevertheless, parties and policies are closely linked in many people's minds.

Many observers go further and suggest that the policies put forward by a party follow logically from the particular set of people active in the party. For example, if Quebec (or the West) is underrepresented (or overrepresented) in a party, then of course the party will propound certain policies rather than others. This assumption or expectation derives in part from experience, but it is reinforced in many cases by assumptions like the "insider" view of representation. If you observe some degree of correlation between certain influential people in a party and the party's policies, then you do not settle for trying to pressure those people; you insist on getting some of "your people" into key positions. To the extent that you succeed, you will stimulate other groups to emulate your efforts.

This line of reasoning runs directly counter to the most widely cited theory of party election strategy and voting, that of Anthony Downs (1957). In this theory, parties exist in order to get elected; for this purpose they develop policies that will appeal to voters (specifically the median or average voter). Unlike the other theory, there is no assumption that, once elected, the party will implement the policies it used to get elected. Instead, it will be developing policies to get itself re-elected. The policies are emphatically not just expressions of the personal or collective preferences of those members active in policy formulation. This theory, like the "insider" approach, is an abstraction and rests on certain simplifications. One of these – a unidimensional "space" along which voters' ideological positions are arrayed – is likely false, since we have just seen that the party system, at least since the 1930s, has been two-dimensional. Nevertheless, the clarity of these two theories and their almost diametrically opposed views of where policies come from suggest that together they may shed some light on parties as policy formulators.

Since I have already discussed at length the "insider" view of representation, there is little more that needs elaboration at this point. Downs's view, on the other hand, will lead us down some interesting avenues and back to the "insider" view again. Before this journey, however, I want to mention what appears to be a radically different approach but probably is not.

The third approach to policy formulation is an idealistic view, although not without merit for that reason. This approach suggests that a party (or a person or group within it) might develop a policy because it is good for the country. Of course, that's what they all say! Even if we grant that the motive behind a policy is really altruistic, that is not helpful, nor does it differ from the other two theories just outlined. The problem is conceptual: How do you decide what is "good for the country" before the policy is implemented and before it either succeeds or fails? The "insider" theory answers that you trust the right people ("your people") to know what the country needs. This begs the question, but then this is the problem with the theory as it applies to representation too. Nevertheless, it is a coherent answer that has profoundly affected many people in several parties, regardless of the intellectual merits of the theory. Downs's theory gives a similar answer: that the policy which the median voter thinks is best for the country is the best policy for the country. Again, the test turns out to be whom you trust. Thus, I propose to leave aside this idealistic notion and focus on the other theories.

Downs's theory rests on an appeal to the median voter. It is fairly clear what that might mean in regard to certain kinds of cleavages and policies. Social class, rich and poor, and income redistribution have reasonably clear interpretations in Downsian terms. People with high status or high income have opinions that differ in degree from those of people just below them, and they in turn differ in degree from those of the people even lower. For example, the differences may fall along an ideological gradation from pro-business–anti-labour to anti-business–pro-labour, with ambivalence about one or both targets in between. Another example concerns taxes such as succession duties, or how progressive income tax should be. Such examples are useful, and Downs's theory handles them easily, because they involve a continuum of opinions or ideologies that can be calibrated into finely or coarsely marked points. It is meaningful to speak of a median voter because one can imagine that zero percent succession duties and 100 percent duties define a range, and some point (say, 20 percent) divides the population in half; that is, half want higher duties and half want lower duties.

Even more complex issue spaces may be amenable to analysis in Downsian terms. For example, an earlier section examined conflicting views of centralization and decentralization: whether the federal government should intervene in policy areas under provincial jurisdiction in order to achieve countrywide uniformity. Again, one can imagine a median voter; it might be one who felt that such intervention was acceptable in areas *A* and *B* but not in others. Half the people want more intervention and half want less. A party can, if it wishes, appeal to the electorate by targeting a policy on that hypothetical voter.

Imagine a more realistic situation. People espousing views on centralization and decentralization will differ in three ways at least: they will disagree on the number of areas of acceptable federal intervention, as in the example given; they will differ on which particular areas should be subject to intervention and their opinions will have varying intensity. Where is the median voter with so many ways in which the voters can be classified? Logically and theoretically, it is possible to locate median positions, although in a multidimensional space there may be several medians and thus the policy may be unstable. Given the sophistication of modern public opinion polling, it should therefore be feasible (even if costly) to ascertain opinions (and intensity) on a range of options and to devise a policy appropriate to the hypothetical median position.

While granting that something like this actually occurs in some parties, there are limits to its use as a general procedure. There are two major obstacles and both are common; but either one can make it virtually meaningless to say that policy formulation is just a matter of finding out what "the people" want and giving them that policy.

The first and most obvious problem is that one must have priorities. If we ask people (or ourselves, for that matter) a series of questions about preferred policies, we will get answers from most people; but preferences are not policies, since one must give up some preferences in order to achieve others, and that is what the policy means. For example, I want subsidized public child care available to everyone (with a means test of some sort), but I also want to reduce government spending and protect personal privacy. Thus, I cannot have subsidized child care unless I am prepared to cut elsewhere; and I cannot have a means test without access to information about individual incomes and expenses (e.g., tax returns).

In principle, even this sort of complication can be met by sufficient polling. Sufficient, in this case, may mean several years and millions of dollars. (Of course, it is a policy question whether the cost exceeds the benefit from the polling!) Over that period of time, opinions may change; perhaps they will reflect changes in the economy or family structure or whatever. Nevertheless, with effort, the problem can probably be overcome. The next obstacle cuts deeper.

There is nothing in Downs's theory which guarantees that the policy aimed at the median voter will be found on the first try, or several tries. Given the complications just mentioned, it seems realistic to assume that the process will be protracted; and this is, of course, what we find. A poll is taken, a policy formulated and another poll tests out the policy. As a result, it is modified, and tested again in a poll or in an election campaign; and so on. In fact, the collection of ideas and the testing of possible policies will often occur in a multiplicity of arenas: polls, campaigns, leaks, in-depth interviews, editorial and other commentary, academic research, the experience of other jurisdictions, royal commissions, parliamentary debate and reaction to other parties' policies, to name only a few.

In this protracted process of seeking opinions, debating them publicly and privately and seeking revised opinions, public preferences are changed. Some people will be made aware of options they had never imagined; others will realize that their favourite position is impractical, too costly or violates other cherished values. As the public's opinions evolve, so do the public pronouncements of their representatives who are "testing the waters." The public pronouncements may help to clarify opinions, but they may also lead to an impression of vacillation or insincerity. To avoid this, manipulation is required: newspaper leaks, trial balloons, unnamed sources, deep background briefings and many others; that is, the party activists and elected officials find ways of putting forward views that are not attributed to them, in order to carry forward the process of opinion evolution.

The exact details of the evolution are interesting but not crucial here. We will take for granted that something like what I have just described actually occurs. The damning question does not depend on the details. What meaning do we give to representation when the elected representatives lead, form, mould, shape and change the opinions we expect them to represent? Can one really be said to represent people's opinions when one has (to an unknown degree) helped to create those opinions? Given what I have outlined as theoretically required and realistically practised, can one ever represent opinions that have not yet been influenced by the representatives?

I suggested earlier that Downs's theory would eventually lead us back to the "insider" theory, despite the differences between the two. There are several linkages. First of all, much of the exploration of trade-offs, intensities and reactions to incipient policies occurs within the party, in conventions, in nomination races, in study groups and elsewhere. Hence, "insiders" are insiders in a double sense, having privileged life experiences and privileged access to the policy process. Second and equally critical, the success of the process depends on an open party, one in which every group wanting access has some chance. The self-interest of the party requires that a sufficient range of groups is incorporated in this process so that all major points of view are taken into account.

Both points are important aspects of any attempt to answer the questions above. How open the party is, and how many forums there are for moulding opinion other than the parties, is critical in making our system of government representative rather than just manipulative. This is not the place to pursue the answers to these troubling questions, but the process of policy formulation and opinion evolution has some implications for our goal of confederal parties.

A third connection between the two theories concerns the answer that "insiders" might give to the questions above. They would say that the questions are irrelevant for their type of representation because "insiders" faithfully represent each other, since their privileged life experiences explain why they share opinions, preferences and points of view.

If one accepts the "insider" theory, one is led to such a conclusion; and that is one reason the Downsian theory is so different. Both are, however, theories and are thus subject to scrutiny.

One type of scrutiny has just been described – how the policy formulation process actually works in many parties. Since the description fits all the major parties in Canada as far as I can tell, this might put the "insider" theory on the defensive. Another type of scrutiny concerns implications of the theories for brokerage politics and for building confederal parties. I shall explore two implications to conclude this section. The two theories stand on opposite sides of both implications, and each seems to have the advantage in one.

One implication of the "insider" theory and of brokerage politics generally is that policies are not the only (or perhaps even the most important) way for parties to attract votes. This directly contradicts the fundamental assumption of Downs's theory. If "insiders" are representative almost by definition, that is not their only advantage. Presumably, voters who notice that one of "theirs" has a prominent place in the party or in Parliament will draw the conclusion that the party respects them, their group and its importance. This inference may be completely devoid of policy or opinion representation, or even contrary to them, although I doubt if the two elements are frequently that separate. Nevertheless, the 19th-century origins of party as broker were more concerned with this notion of respect and recognition, to say nothing of patronage, than with pure policy or ideology (Simpson 1988). Since these are powerful motives, a theory like Downs's that can take only policies into account should be graded down, despite its other merits.

The other implication requires that we recall why brokerage puts such terrible strains on parties. Instead of picking sides, a brokerage party endeavours to incorporate representatives of both sides of cleavages. It is able to satisfy both sides – or at least the representatives – by means other than policy alone; these include patronage, respect, log rolling and perhaps espousing different policy in different parts of the country. Whatever the means, the tension remains.

Downsian analysis could not be more different. Instead of compromise, patronage and so on, a party operating on the Downsian principle must balance pressures that are entirely policy based or ideological. In particular, each party must try to appeal to the median voter by espousing that voter's policy stance while at the same time remaining distinct from opposing parties. Hence, parties tend to cluster very close to the hypothetical median voter.

Policies that attempt to bridge opposite sides of fundamental cleavages are unthinkable in a Downsian system. In fact, they are also rare in practice. Instead, brokerage parties have to take a stand and try to hold their support through the other means already discussed. Hence, Downs's theory seems to offer a more solid explanation for the policy positions actually observed. The insider theory, on the other hand, accurately points to other ways in which parties may attract and hold their support.

CODA: A COMPARISON WITH AUSTRALIA

This study could end at this point. It has explored why we search for ways to create and use confederal parties and why that goal is increasingly illusory. Parties do serve many essential purposes, but building a united nation of Canada cannot be one of them. The debate about whether Canada exists as a nation, as two nations or as many nations explains why we have a problem and why mere political parties cannot solve that problem.

Instead of concluding on this note, I propose to examine some broader questions about our status as a country and our political culture by means of an extended comparison with Australia. As noted, the contrast could not be greater in terms of the extensiveness of electoral reform. The reasons for the differences in electoral systems, in electoral innovations and in the kinds of arguments used in debates about electoral reform serve to highlight Canada's "national problem."

Is Australia More Democratic than Canada?

At a glance, one can build an impressive case for greater democracy in Australian electoral arrangements. A second glance, however, raises doubts.

It is clear that early innovations in Australia were more democratic than Canadian election procedures. One need only contrast the secret ballot and standardized ballots with open voting and staggered elections. In addition, the universal franchise was gained much earlier in Australia than in Canada, or almost anywhere else, for that matter. Likewise, it should be clear that later innovations have often appeared more democratic than Canadian procedures. Note, for example, compulsory voting on the basis of careful enumeration, compared to (until recently) less complete voters' lists in Canada and continuing lower turnout. One can also point to preferential voting with its concern for creating a majority, and to the use of constitutional referenda, a form of "direct" democracy. More frequent elections in Australia (three-year maximum term) suggest more democracy, because they involve "going to the people" more often than in Canada (five-year terms). One need hardly mention an elected rather than an appointed Senate as evidence of democratic intent.

Some of these apparently democratic aspects have another inter-pretation. Compulsory voting has been challenged by some Australians as coercion, and compulsory preferences as forcing voters to express views they may wish to withhold. Referenda have been criticized as useless and thus not fulfilling their democratic potential on two grounds: they almost never pass, and they are nearly always fought on purely partisan grounds. The Senate, while undeniably more democratic than Canada's, fails to measure up in some eyes for at least two reasons: it can frustrate the will of the people expressed through the Lower House, which in the British tradition is the proper source of "confidence" in a government; in addition, like its American model, the motive for elect-ing only half of the senators in each election (and thus for longer terms) was to remove it some distance from "tides of opinion."

There are thus good arguments for describing Australian electoral arrangements as more democratic than Canadian ones and some good counter-arguments. This is not, however, the end of the matter. The next two sections try to put this question in a broader context. They imply that the two countries conceive of democracy, or "democratic-ness," in different ways – one about procedural matters and the other about substantive statecraft.

The Argument from Simplicity

In a previous section, I dismissed the view that Canada's lack of inno-vation and complexity could be attributed to conservatism in general or to factors like "the Tory touch." It is now time to ask what might account for the difference and what this tells us about Canadian poli-tics and political culture. One of the most persuasive indicators of the unstated assumptions of any political culture is what kinds of argu-ments have "the burden of proof." In other words, which arguments or grounds are accepted without proof, taken for granted or taken as given, and which encounter resistance and need elaborate justifications? Canada and Australia exhibit markedly different patterns of argument in support of reform in general and of particular reforms.

In Canada, one can adequately defend many electoral arrange-ments by pointing out that they are simple and easily understood by most voters. This has been, I believe, the hidden and unnoticed premise behind resistance to proportional representation (PR), and especially to "mixed systems" (on the German model) proposed by Irvine (1979) and others. Its opponents allege that PR is complex; and a combination of plurality, single-member constituencies with a "topping up" of addi-tional members of the legislature chosen by some form of PR is even more complex.

Buttressing the argument from simplicity is the Canadian conception of representation previously discussed. If one is concerned with choosing between candidates so that the largest group or community is represented, one thereby gives less heed to concerns about the representativeness of MPs collectively or to concerns about minority views or "disappointed voters."

Arguments about electoral reform in Australia take a very different form. Not only are the elements of the electoral system more complex and more mixed than in Canada, but, more important, other values override the argument from simplicity. In particular, the starting point or premise in Australian reforms focuses on achieving equality or fairness. Of course, one may allege that the Australian system does not successfully attain fairness or equality, but these values serve as potent arguments against simplicity. Equality and fairness put on the defensive those people in Australia who point to the value of simple procedures.

The values of equality and fairness are congruent also with Australian conceptions of representation and majority. Note that "one vote, one value" carries weight if one assumes that individuals, rather than groups or communities, are to be represented. Likewise, a majority within a constituency requires equality among individual voters, even if that results in less chance of a majority government.

A word is in order about the content of these other values, whether we label them equality or fairness or evenhandedness or standardization. It is worth a long paper to explore whether equality in a Benthamite sense (Collins 1985) is the fundamental Australian political value, and whether that reflects a presumption for fairness. One can also argue whether equality might deteriorate in practice into mere standardization. Instead of pursuing these details, I assert that other values are often given greater priority than simplicity in arguments about electoral reform. For present purposes, I shall lump together these values under the label "fairness" without putting too much emphasis on that one word at the expense of equality or other ways of characterizing fundamental values.

If one assumes that electoral arrangements have value as means to an end, then one will be less concerned with the degree to which they have independent value. If one believes, on the other hand, that they are important political goals in their own right, then one will take seriously questions about whether they achieve equality or fairness.

The unstated premise of arguments from simplicity in Canada is that it is very difficult to construct a government. Hence, electoral arrangements should be judged by their effectiveness in giving Canadians stable and strong governments. This is also why we are concerned with confederal parties. The government so constituted has substantive concerns, including fairness and equality. One fights for values through government, not through electoral arrangements in the abstract.

In Australia, by contrast, simplicity carries little weight because the electoral arrangements, it is implicitly assumed, should further certain goals. These include a fair reflection or translation of popular opinion into partisan representation. Fair in this context subsumes individual equality. Most Australians do not want strong government, since most are deeply suspicious of government. This leads them to want to build fairness of representation into the process of selecting a government, so that the government has less scope for unusual deviations.

Games, Rules and Outcomes

To play the game, you must know the rules. In politics as in sports, there are people who never question the rules because of a desire to get on with the game. What matters to them is the play itself or the outcome. Other people are dissatisfied with the game or the outcome and feel it appropriate to give more thought to setting the rules.

My reading and observations about these two countries lead me to characterize them as diverging over whether setting the rules or the outcomes are the real game. The fundamental premise of Australian political culture as revealed in its electoral arrangements is that one should value equally or more so the means, the setting of the rules, than the ends or the outcome of the game. In Canada, one may not ignore the rules or the means, but they seem less important because the ends or goals or possible outcomes involve high stakes. This sharp dichotomy does a disservice to both countries, but I believe it highlights a very significant difference in their political cultures.

It is easy to miss the significance of the contrast by failing to keep in mind the full historical picture. Canadian politics in recent years has dealt so fully with constitutional change that one can forget that this mania has not always been at the top of the agenda. In any event, electoral reform has never been high on the political agenda. Equally important or more important than constitutional change in most eras has been how to counter American influence, culture, or expansion, how to diversify an economy too heavily dependent on the export of raw materials and how to integrate a small and extremely scattered population in the second-largest land mass in the world. Although conflict between federal and provincial governments often is expressed in the rhetoric of rules or constitutional change, most of the first century since Confederation consisted of federal and provincial governments gradually learning to use the jurisdictional realms they had. Seldom has there been any attention to redefining federal and provincial jurisdictions.

It is also easy to believe that Australians have dealt with nothing but the rules of the game. As a country, Australia has had many of the same concerns about nation building as Canada, because it too has few people and much geography. Until recently, however, the people were much more homogeneous in origin; and such variety as there was (Irish Roman Catholic versus British Protestant) characterized each colony in roughly the same way. There was never an Australian equivalent of Quebec, nor is that a possibility in the future. Australia shares no border with any other country, and it is not in the shadow of a neighbourly giant.

Thus, Australia in its antipodean isolation could devote more time and effort to the rules of the game. The nature of this focus on rules, I allege, has changed in character over the decades. At first, it was motivated by ideas and values on a grand scale; more recently, tinkering is probably an appropriate epithet.

The apparently awesome amount of electoral innovation has been of two very different types, and they are largely confined to particular periods. The creative innovations for which Australia is justly renowned – secret ballots, universal suffrage and the like – were complete and accepted by 1902. Since then, there have been many other innovations, such as compulsory preferences, compulsory voting and quota-preferential proportional representation for the Senate. Thus, one can form an impression that innovation is an ongoing process, that Australia is constantly pushing ahead of other countries in electoral arrangements. This is, I believe, incorrect and misleading.

My hypothesis is this: from the mid-19th century until about 1902, Australia was innovative in a positive respect; the measure of this is other countries' acceptance of Australia's lead. This is why I referred earlier to "creative innovation," which would otherwise be a redundant phrase. More recently, however, the innovations consist of efforts to extricate the country from the box it put itself in by means of the earlier innovations when coupled with institutions and practices of a non-electoral sort: strong extraparliamentary wings of parties (because of the labour and class origins), unstable leadership (because of caucus democracy), organized factions within parties (especially the Australian Labor Party) and the deadlocks between House and Senate precisely because they are both electorally legitimate. Too much democracy can be a hindrance, or at least it can lead to further innovations to try to get the system out of deadlock.

Consciously or unconsciously, Australians have sought means of breaking out of their pattern of intense, bitter and quite evenly balanced partisan forces (Graham 1962). Each group of opponents has experimented with ways of ensuring, through apparently ever more democratic procedures, a decisive advantage. For example, if it is believed that low turnout favours an opposing group, interest or party, then try compulsory voting: it may help the innovator while being justifiable on democratic grounds. Or consider optional preferential voting versus compulsory preferential voting: for those potential allies in a coalition, make Labor voters cast a second and third choice vote for a non-Labor party. It may help and it looks democratic. Or if your party has been defeated too often by a Senate controlled by another party, try a procedure (quota-preferential proportional representation) that is overtly democratic and that will gain you more seats even if you cannot increase your vote share.

I do not wish to allege that all political tinkering in Australia, even since 1920, has been motivated solely by such concerns. Especially I do not think the innovators have always consciously intended the consequences that we know in hindsight to have occurred. But there are too many coincidences to overlook. And to the extent that current tinkering reflects earlier motives, we can substantiate some matters more easily. The enlargement of the Senate after 1984, from 10 to 12 senators per state, was, by all off-the-record accounts, motivated by two Labor party goals: eliminate (if possible) the minor parties, or at least make them more sensitive to Labor; and if that works, half-elections (six per state) will result in 50 percent of the senators being Labor. Hence, Labor can block non-Labor, but non-Labor can only rarely block Labor's wishes when it controls the House (Sharman 1986).

If my hypothesis is plausible, it leads to further speculations, which have implications far beyond the electoral arena. One concerns the relationship of regions and parties to the central cleavages. The other concerns the incidence of nation-threatening political issues.

Where fundamental cleavages are thwarted by party discipline, they must seek expression in other arenas. In Canada's case, Catholic versus Protestant was the original cleavage; although still significant, it was later redefined as French versus English. More recently, it has been translated into Quebec versus the rest of Canada and more generally as regionalism, province building or related phrases. Whatever the terminology, these are cleavages that cannot be captured fully by parties, in good measure because of the regional nature of the cleavages and in part because the parties have tried to bridge or broker the cleavages. As argued in a previous section, party discipline in the 11 legislatures exacerbates the problem, leading to the search for more elaborate forms of federal-provincial relations. This, in turn, reduces the need for, or potential effectiveness of, electoral reform, because this is seen as weakening provinces as actors on the national stage.

The obverse situation characterizes Australia's political system. Originally, class (which corresponded closely to religion) was the fundamental cleavage, accurately (more or less) reflected in partisan divisions that were roughly the same in all states, ignoring some cyclical fluctuations. Whether Kemp (1978) and others are correct that party itself has become the fundamental cleavage as class relations have become more complex and blurred, there can be no doubt that party is a more useful analytic tool in Australia. Electoral tinkering to ensure that voters' preferences are accurately reflected in partisan distributions of seats means that party discipline does not work at cross purposes to basic cleavages.

Australia can afford to tinker with its electoral system because nothing rides on the outcome except a better electoral system or better parties. Canada, on the other hand, has faced at least two nation-threatening issues that could be decided differently depending on the type of electoral reform: American dominance and Quebec nationalism. Electoral reform in Canada could destroy one of the major parties, or could weaken a party's claim to be a confederal party or could raise the status of the NDP or other smaller parties enough to foreclose all hope of any majority government; so goes the usual argument. If it is correct, electoral reforms cannot be judged on their merits but must be weighed on the scales of their effect on Canada's continued existence.

By this logic, electoral reform is at best a sideshow in Canada. It distracts one from intergovernmental conflicts, whether they involve the provinces and the federal government or the federal government and the United States government. For Australians, however, the problem is electoral, and thus the solution can apparently be sought through electoral reform. It is in this sense, more than any of the details above, that electoral reform and the arguments that support it reveal Australian political culture and its difference from that of Canada.

POLITICS AND COMMUNITY

I have emphasized repeatedly the contradictions, tensions and cleavages found throughout Canadian history. These explain why Canada had to become a federal system and why it continues to experience conflict, animosities and misunderstanding. These make Canada a very political place, because politics is about managing conflict, especially fundamental disagreements. Where rules may be used to settle disputes, we set up bureaucracies and courts. Where rules conflict, where values collide and where visions of nationhood contend, politics is the necessary handmaiden. Politics must enter any public situation in which we seek to resolve the priorities among equally valued goals or in which we must choose the lesser of two evils.

"Two nations warring in the bosom of a single state" is a recipe for interesting politics. The incorporation of new immigrant groups and the efforts to find a dignified status for native groups lead in the same direction. The "insider" view of representation and policy formulation only complicates what was already a profoundly political situation.

The premise on which Canada was founded involved communities: how to protect French and English, Catholic and Protestant since assimilation was not feasible. As I noted, the dilemma is compounded by group boundaries that almost but not quite coincide with political boundaries. Canada is truly founded on contradictions and on efforts to balance what are, in principle, irreconcilable concepts of collective rights and community.

The never-ending effort to balance contrary needs and different types of communities that do not quite coincide goes to the heart of politics. The repeated renewal of balance among conflicting groups is how we create a political community, "a wider union" that can function but does not corrode those natural communities that we also value. Each generation of Canadians has had to fashion a political compromise that leaves no group fully satisfied and has then been challenged and reworked and challenged again. Sometimes we try to enlist our political parties in this effort.

If we ask our parties to construct a compromise, that is an entirely appropriate task. That is part of leadership, governance and policy formulation. If we hope or believe, however, that any party can make such a compromise last forever, or if we assume that any party can unite the country without a painful compromise, then we search in vain for confederal parties. We also thereby fail to understand the nature of our political community.

REFERENCES

Bakvis, Herman. 1981. *Federalism and the Organization of Political Life: Canada in Comparative Perspective*. Kingston: Queen's University, Institute of Intergovernmental Relations.

Behiels, Michael D. 1985. *Prelude to Québec's Quiet Revolution: Liberalism versus Nationalism, 1945–1960*. Montreal and Kingston: McGill–Queen's University Press.

Black, Edwin R. 1972. "Federal Strains within a Canadian Party." In *Party Politics in Canada*, ed. Hugh Thorburn. Scarborough: Prentice-Hall of Canada.

Blais, André. 1990. "The Debate Over Electoral Systems." In *Papers in Political Economy*. London: University of Western Ontario, Political Economy Research Group.

Burke, Mike. 1980. "Dimensions of Variation in Electoral Coalitions, 1965–1974." In *Small Worlds*, ed. David J. Elkins and Richard Simeon. Toronto: Methuen.

Cairns, Alan C. 1968. "The Electoral System and the Party System in Canada, 1921–1965." *Canadian Journal of Political Science* 1:55–80.

———. 1979. *From Interstate to Intrastate Federalism in Canada.* Kingston: Queen's University, Institute of Intergovernmental Relations.

———. 1988. "Citizens (Outsiders) and Government (Insiders) in Constitution-Making: The Case of Meech Lake." *Canadian Public Policy* 14 (supplement): 121–45.

———. 1990. "Constitutional Minoritarianism in Canada." The J.A. Corry Lecture delivered 6 March at Queen's University, Kingston.

Carty, R. Kenneth. 1985. "The Electoral Boundary Revolution in Canada." *American Review of Canadian Studies* 15:273–87.

Collins, Hugh. 1985. "Political Ideology in Australia: The Distinctiveness of a Benthamite Society." In *Australia: The Daedalus Symposium*, ed. Stephen R. Graybard. Sydney: Angus and Robertson.

Dahl, Robert A. 1967. "The City in the Future of Democracy." *American Political Science Review* 61:953–70.

Downs, Anthony. 1957. *An Economic Theory of Democracy.* New York: Harper.

Dufour, Christian. 1990. *The Canadian Challenge/Le défi québécois.* Lantzville, BC: Oolichan Books and Halifax, NS: Institute for Research on Public Policy.

Elkins, David J. 1989. "Facing Our Destiny: Rights and Canadian Distinctiveness." *Canadian Journal of Political Science* 22:699–716.

Elkins, David J., and Richard Simeon. 1979. "A Cause in Search of Its Effect, or What Does Political Culture Explain?" *Comparative Politics* 11:127–45.

———. 1980. *Small Worlds: Provinces and Parties in Canadian Political Life.* Toronto: Methuen.

Goot, Murray. 1985. "Electoral Systems." In *Surveys of Australian Political Science*, ed. Don Aitkin. Sydney: Allen and Unwin.

Graham, B.D. 1962. "The Choice of Voting Methods in Federal Politics, 1902–1918." *Australian Journal of Politics and History* 8:161–81.

Irvine, William P. 1979. *Does Canada Need a New Electoral System?* Kingston: Queen's University, Institute of Intergovernmental Relations.

Kelly, Paul. 1984. *The Hawke Ascendency.* Sydney: Angus and Robertson.

Kemp, David. 1978. *Society and Electoral Behaviour in Australia.* St. Lucia: University of Queensland Press.

Kwavnick, David, ed. 1973. *The Tremblay Report: Report of the Royal Commission of Inquiry on Constitutional Problems.* Toronto: McClelland and Stewart.

Laponce, Jean A. 1969. "Canadian Party Labels: An Essay in Semantics and Anthropology." *Canadian Journal of Political Science* 2:141–57.

Madison, James. 1949. "Federalist no. 10." In *Selections from "The Federalist,"* ed. Henry Steele Commager. New York: Appleton-Century-Crofts.

Mallory, J.R. 1954. *Social Credit and the Federal Power in Canada.* Toronto: University of Toronto Press.

Merton, Robert. 1973. *The Sociology of Science: Theoretical and Empirical Investigations.* Chicago: University of Chicago Press.

Nicholson, Norman. 1979. *The Boundaries of the Canadian Confederation.* Toronto: Macmillan of Canada.

Qualter, Terence H. 1970. *The Election Process in Canada.* Toronto: McGraw-Hill.

Rusk, Jerrold G. 1970. "The Effect of the Australian Ballot Reform on Split-Ticket Voting: 1876–1908." *American Political Science Review* 64:1220–38.

Sancton, Andrew. 1990. "Eroding Representation-by-Population in the Canadian House of Commons: The *Representation Act, 1985*." *Canadian Journal of Political Science* 23:441–57.

Sharman, Campbell. 1986. "The Senate, Small Parties, and the Balance of Power." *Politics* 21:29–38.

Simpson, Jeffrey. 1988. *Spoils of Power: The Politics of Patronage.* Toronto: Collins.

Smiley, Donald V., ed. 1963. *The Rowell-Sirois Report: An Abridgement of Book I of the Royal Commission Report on Dominion-Provincial Relations.* Toronto: McClelland and Stewart.

Smiley, Donald V. 1980. *Canada in Question: Federalism in the Eighties.* Toronto: McGraw-Hill Ryerson.

Stevenson, Garth. 1979. *Unfulfilled Union: Canadian Federalism and National Unity.* Toronto: Macmillan of Canada.

Trudeau, Pierre Elliott. 1968. *Federalism and the French Canadians.* Toronto: Macmillan of Canada.

Ward, Norman. 1950. *The Canadian House of Commons: Representation.* Toronto: University of Toronto Press.

Wearing, Joseph. 1981. *The L-Shaped Party: The Liberal Party of Canada 1958–1980.* Toronto: McGraw-Hill Ryerson.

Whitaker, Reginald. 1977. *The Government Party: Organizing and Financing the Liberal Party of Canada, 1930–58.* Toronto: University of Toronto Press.

Wright, J.F.H. 1980. *Mirror of the Nation's Mind: Australia's Electoral Experiments.* Sydney: Hale and Iremonger.

2

PARTIES AS INSTITUTIONS OF NATIONAL GOVERNANCE

Maureen Covell

INTRODUCTION

POLITICAL PARTIES ARE generally considered to be among the central institutions of modern political systems, performing essential linkage and organizational functions. Even systems that do not claim to be liberal democracies use the single party for a whole series of functions, including the recruitment, socialization and screening of aspirants to government office, the mobilization of the general population, and the supervision of the government bureaucracy. Pluralist party systems offering competing candidates at free elections are so identified with the political practices of liberal democracy that they constitute part of the definition of the term, and a demand for freedom to form political parties has been part of movements for liberalization in all countries, including the countries of southern Europe in the 1970s and the countries of Eastern Europe in the more recent past.

However, if parties are among the essential institutions of governance in liberal democracies, their performance has not escaped questioning and criticism. Critics argue that the major functions of parties – their ability to present citizens with choices among candidates and policies, their ability to represent and reconcile interests, and their ability to organize both the personnel and policies of government – have been taken over by other institutions including the bureaucracy, the media, the court system and movements like interest groups. It was a recognition of the importance of parties and of the challenges to their ability to perform the functions we expect of them that led to the formation of the Royal Commission for which this study was written.

This study will examine the performance of parties as institutions of national governance in Canada in a comparative context and will look at some of the factors affecting the quality of that performance. It begins with a discussion of the functions usually attributed to parties in liberal democracies, focusing in particular on those functions that link citizen and political system: organizing electoral choice between candidates and parties, channelling non-electoral political participation, and representing economic and non-economic interests. It then considers the claim that parties are no longer able to perform these functions and that they either have been taken over by other institutions or, more seriously, are not being performed.

This description of party functions and the challenges to their performance is followed by a section on the historical development of parties in Europe and in Canada. Differences in the circumstances of origin and development have led to differences in party structure and in the range of functions parties perform in Europe and in Canada, but parties on both sides of the Atlantic have been exposed to the same challenges in the postwar period. It can be argued that the two types of party system are undergoing a degree of convergence, with European parties acquiring the looser organization and links with voters that have characterized Canadian parties. Meanwhile, Canadian parties, as many of the recommendations to the Commission show, are aspiring to the greater degree of organization and more continuous contact with the population that is characteristic of many European parties.

What happens when parties fail to perform the functions expected of them? There are two possibilities: the decay of the party system, or the creation of new parties. This study examines the reasons for choosing means other than parties, such as the court system or the bureaucracy for the pursuit of political goals, and the conditions for the creation of new parties. One possible consequence for Canada of encouraging the creation and activities of new parties could be the development of a multi-party system with, as a possible result, the need to form coalition governments. The formation and management of coalitions is a type of political activity with which Canadians have little experience. The study concludes, therefore, with a consideration of the principles of types of government other than the single-party majority government that we assume to be the norm. It also includes a consideration of coalition scenarios for a five-party parliament, applying the principles of the last section to a hypothetical Canadian case.

The Choice of Comparisons
The systems used as the basis of comparisons with the Canadian party system are mainly drawn from Western Europe. Many of these coun-

tries have multi-party systems in which the basis of party formation and organization is different from that of Canadian parties and in which the dynamics of interparty relationships are different from those of the Westminster model. However, there are also significant similarities between Western European party systems and the Canadian system. Like Canadian parties, European parties operate in a parliamentary system (or, in France, a mixed parliamentary/presidential system) in which the provision of a legislative base for a coherent government is one of the functions attributed to parties. This distinguishes both types from, for example, the American system. In addition, both European and Canadian systems have been subject to the same changes that are said to have affected the parties' ability to perform their functions. These include the rise of government bureaucracies, the development of the mass media, and the recent development of interest groups with new, often non-economic, agendas.

Framing Some Answers

Before discussing the functions of parties and challenges to the ability of parties to perform those functions, some clarification of the terms party and party system is needed. The term party is used in diverse ways, and parties have many aspects. At its largest, a party includes its voters. In this usage, the size of a party will vary from election to election. A smaller and more stable group is comprised of those who identify with the party, followed by smaller circles of members, activists and office holders. Parties differ in the relationship of the size of these circles to each other. A mass membership party like many of the European parties examined will have a circle of members that is larger in relation to the circle of voters, but smaller in relation to the circle of activists than the typical Canadian party.

Parties in liberal democracies do not exist in isolation, but interact with each other in a party system. The characteristics of this system will also affect the ways in which parties perform their functions as institutions of national governance. These characteristics include the number of parties and the nature of their relationship with each other, including the degree of conflict among them and the basis of the conflict, whether ideology, regionalism, economic interests or the division of government office (Sartori 1976). For example, parties in a political system could be regionally based, but if their relationship with each other is one of peaceful bargaining, then we can say that the party system facilitates the resolution of regional conflict even if individual parties do not.

Most of the party systems discussed in this study are multi-party systems. Generally, a party system is considered to be a two-party system if there are only two parties that stand a realistic chance of participating in a government. Under this rule of counting, Britain is considered to be a two-party system in spite of the existence of third parties that have gained as much as 25 percent of the vote, and Canada is also considered to be a two-party system, in spite of the existence of the New Democratic Party. On the other hand, Germany is considered to be a multi-party system although its third party, the Free Democrats, rarely receives as high a percentage of the popular vote as the New Democrats do in Canada, because this party has a realistic chance of participating in government (and frequently does). Of course, many European systems have more than three parties. In Belgium, for example, there are 10 parties in the lower house of the current legislature.

PARTIES IN LIBERAL DEMOCRACIES

Parties have the potential to perform a wide range of functions in liberal democracies. Perhaps their main function is to offer and organize electoral choice among competing candidates and ideas. Parties recruit candidates and distribute information about their candidates. The party label aids voters in the choice among candidates, and party platforms offer at least the potential of a choice among policies.

Parties organize the most important act of participation of the general population, that of voting; they also organize the participation of those who wish to play a more active role in political life and, most crucially, are the main vehicle for the recruitment and promotion of aspirants to governmental office. It is through activities in parties and through securing party nominations that most elected officials begin their political careers, and it is through acceptability to their party that they acquire leadership positions. Party is the basis of the "team" that governs in parliamentary systems, and party organizes the opposing teams who would replace them. Parties also organize the flow of information between political leadership and the population. Information about leaders is conveyed to the population through the party, and the party organization conveys information about popular attitudes and reactions to policies to the leadership.

Parties also represent and aggregate interests. Through party competition in elections and in the legislature, the diverse interests of the national population are presented, reconciled where possible, and, where this is not possible, a decision is made about which interests shall prevail. This process of public representation and competition among interests plays a role in national integration since the process implies, and often explicitly states, that the losing interests have at least had a chance to present their case and to attempt to persuade others of its value.

Because of their importance in the political system, parties are able to set the limits of political discourse and to identify issues as worthy of serious attention. In the absence of discussion by parties, issues may not be given public consideration at all. Parties can also have an educational function. Mass membership parties, to be discussed below, had as one of their major functions the inculcation of political ideas in nonpoliticized groups. Some parties, such as the Greens in many European countries and the Canadian CCF (Co-operative Commonwealth Federation) in its early days, give primacy to this educational function over the electoral function.[1]

Like parties in other liberal democracies, Canadian parties are expected to perform a wide range of functions. It is generally agreed that they emphasize the function of recruiting candidates to office and organizing election campaigns. Canadian parties are also considered to have a particular responsibility for the function of national integration. While in other systems national integration usually refers to the integration of economic groups, in Canada this function includes both socio-economic integration and the articulation and reconciliation of regional and language interests. Most studies of the Canadian party system argue that the country's diversity is such that the maintenance of national integration must be accomplished through a variety of institutions, with parties, given their importance in the political system, playing a major role in this area (Aucoin 1985; Thorburn 1985; for a contrary view, see Elkins 1991).

Challenge to Parties

Although political parties have been celebrated for many years as key institutions in liberal democracies, they have also been challenged, as inappropriate and ineffective institutions. From the time of the appearance of parties, the wisdom of organizing so many aspects of political life through their structures and activities has been questioned from what Daalder calls the "statist" and the "democratist" points of view (Daalder and Mair 1983, Introduction).

The statist point of view argues that parties, particularly a large number of parties, introduce artificial divisions in the population and lead to government decisions based on "political" criteria rather than a consideration of what would be the best decision. The modern version of the statist view of parties can be seen in the argument that most of the problems of running a modern society are so complex that solutions are better discovered by the studies of professional experts than through the debates of professional politicians. (See the 1982 Report of the Canadian Bar Association Committee on the Reform of Parliament, cited in Smith (1985, 22), which criticizes Parliament for being "too partisan." This misconception of the role of Parliament is especially striking given the number of lawyers in that body.) This view assumes that there is one correct solution to any problem, visible only to the trained eye, and that policy formation is a series of choices among more or less technically correct answers, rather than a series of political choices among necessarily imperfect alternatives.

On the other hand, the "democratist" point of view argues that parties actually constitute a barrier to effective participation, screening out issues that do not fit their ideologies and promoting the welfare of office holders rather than that of the population. This attitude was prominent in the American Reform movement of the late 19th and early 20th centuries and gave rise to extensive regulation of party activity and organization, as well as provisions like the use of the primary election as a means of candidate selection, recall of incumbents and the use of the referendum rather than party decision making as a means of settling important issues. These measures were explicitly designed to weaken parties and diminish their role in the political system. Similar attitudes appeared in Canada in the Progressive Party in the 1920s and have characterized many "new-politics" groups who often reject the use of the party system as a way of furthering their causes.

Another strand of criticism, and the one that this study will address most directly, accepts the legitimacy of the role parties play in the political system, but argues that changes in modern society have reduced the ability of parties to link the population and the leaders, as well as to organize political life at both the mass and élite level. These functions, the argument runs, are now being performed by other institutions – both public and private – or are not being performed at all.

The changes in question include several that, like the increased mobility of the population, the rise of modern education and the development of the mass media, have all loosened the ties between parties and their electorate, so that parties are no longer able to mobilize support for political personnel or policies. Other changes are said to have reduced the role of parties in political recruitment and the reliance of political leaders on party support. These include the increased personalization of politics and the use of the mass media and modern polling techniques to create a flow of information between leaders and the population unmediated by a party organization.[2]

At the level of governing, there have been challenges to the ability of parties to set a distinct course in policy making. In part, these challenges arise from the increasing complexity and bureaucratization of government activity. Do parties have the resources to match the knowledge of bureaucrats in policy making, or does the combination of expertise and permanent links between bureaucracies and interest groups lead to the development of standing policy orientations not susceptible to change by the party or parties nominally in charge of the government? Have national societies become so fragmented with the rise of single-interest groups, the exacerbation of ethnic and regional antagonisms, and the re-emergence of challenges to the postwar democratic consensus that parties are no longer able to perform their function of aggregating interests and mediating conflict? (See Castles 1982; Galipeau 1989; King 1969; Lewis-Beck 1988; Rose 1984.)

The ability of Canadian parties to perform the desired range of functions has also been questioned. While it is agreed that Canadian parties concentrate on electoral organization and political recruitment, many argue that they do not perform even these functions well. Critics of the Canadian party system often trace its ills to the "brokerage" style that dominates Canadian politics (Brodie and Jenson 1988; Meisel 1985; Smith 1985). This style of politics rests on the accommodation of material demands, usually either local in nature or coming from distinct groups in the population, and on electoral appeals based on uncorrelated promises to various groups. Brokerage politics does not tie voters to parties in any stable way, but encourages them to shop around for the party that offers the best accommodation of their short-term interests. Politics necessarily focuses on party leaders rather than policies, because differences in leadership style are the main distinguishing marks of the competing parties.

Several negative consequences follow from brokerage politics. Because many votes are the result of calculations of short-term interest rather than of a commitment to a party and its policies, governments cannot count on a stable basis of support for their policies once in office (Clarke et al. 1984). The brokerage style of politics does not encourage the formation of coherent government policies or the presentation of clear policy alternatives in elections. This deprives the political system of an essential source of policy innovation and leaves the role to be filled, if it is at all, by the minor parties of the system (Brodie and Jenson 1988). The overall conservatism of the system can also be seen in political recruitment which underrepresents new groups and those who do not enjoy the advantage of social prestige. The function of education is not performed during or between elections, while the function of encouraging participation occurs only during the electoral campaign.

Under these circumstances, the changes in modern society that have undermined parties in other political systems have been particularly hard on Canadian parties which are already weak as organizations, leader dominated, and inadequately tied to the population. The influence of the mass media has reinforced the dominance of party leaders, and television and professional pollsters have cut into the communications role of party activists. Participation, even in elections, is further reduced as politics becomes a spectator sport. The brokerage style of politics, uninhibited by the constraints of ideological stance or even policy direction, leaves the parties defenceless before the demands of intense single-interest groups. Finally, the failure of the parties to establish firm ties with the electorate leaves the party system vulnerable to incursions by new, sectionally based parties (Gagnon 1989).

Not all commentators on Canadian parties paint such a bleak picture, and it should be pointed out that the Canadian party system has at least demonstrated a capacity to survive. The two major parties have dominated national politics since Confederation, absorbing both new territories and new citizens. One or the other, and sometimes both, is a major player in the political system of every province except British Columbia. This longevity cannot be attributed solely to the difficulties our political system puts in the way of new parties. While the replacement of a major party by a challenger is rare in liberal democracies, it has happened. In Britain, which operates under the same single-member plurality system used in Canada, the Labour Party replaced the Liberals as the alternate party of government to the Conservatives. Nor are there signs, in the form of a decline of electoral participation, that voters are becoming alienated from the party system as a whole, as appears to be happening in the United States (Bakvis 1988; Wolinetz 1988). The innovative capacity of the system is more difficult to evaluate, but comparison suggests that it has been able to avoid both a fixation on old ideological quarrels and the stunning inertia of the American system (Thorburn 1985).

Have Canadian parties been more vulnerable to the disintegrative effects of social and economic change than European parties with their more coherent base of support and stronger organizations? In order to answer this question, it is necessary, first, to examine the development of each type of party system to see whether the contrast drawn between Canadian parties and European parties is accurate or exaggerated, and, then, to examine the ways in which each party system has been affected by the changes described above.

The Development of Parties

The prehistory of Canadian parties and of many European parties has certain similarities. Proto-parties often began as groups of notables and their followers, organized as much by personal ties as by policy, and devoted to the capture of government office and its associated spoils. However, Canadian parties, operating in a more diffuse but arguably less diverse environment, kept an organization closer to that of the early parties, while European parties became increasingly attached to the deeper divisions of their societies.

Canadian parties began as coalitions of local interests under local leaders who delivered the support of their followers to form a government around a central leader in Ottawa. Escott Reid has written a lively description of Canadian politics in the elections of 1867, 1872 and 1874 in which the combination of open voting and staggered elections encouraged the existence of "ministerialists," or uncommitted candidates who shifted their support as the election results indicated the likely winner. An intelligent government began the election in ridings it was sure to win and gradually extended the election to less safe seats. Although a modicum of party organization was already necessary for the electorate and the candidates to decide which way to jump, as Reid puts it, "The ideal election of these political realists was an uncontested one in which the member was not definitely committed to any party and could therefore make good terms for his constituency in return for giving his support to the strongest party in the House" (Reid 1932, in Thorburn 1985, 12).

Although the introduction of the secret ballot and simultaneous elections in 1878 led to a tightening of the party system and the elimination of the independents, this description aptly conveys the basis of early party development in Canada: the acquisition of government office and the distribution of patronage on a personal and local basis. Although the Conservative and Liberal parties might differ on policy issues like free trade with the United States, these policy differences were not clearly connected to ideological bases (Brodie and Jenson 1988).

The party system was able to assimilate the immigration of the late 19th and early 20th centuries to a certain degree, but the strains of the First World War and economic crisis led to a weakening of the two-party system. The Prairie provinces were the site of much of the recent immigration, and the disenfranchisement of large numbers of new immigrants from Germanic countries in the 1917 election did not strengthen their allegiance to the two existing parties, both of whose English-speaking members agreed to this step (Brodie and Jenson 1988; Gibbins 1980). The same election saw a regionalization of the two parties after the Conservative government formed a coalition with English-speaking Liberals and passed a conscription bill. The Unionist coalition gained only three seats in Quebec, while the Liberals gained over two-thirds of their vote in that province and only eight seats in Ontario.

In 1921, in the first election after the war, the Conservatives were eliminated in Quebec, and the Liberals gained over one-half of their seats in that province. As significantly, a new party made its appearance at the federal level for the first time since Confederation. The Progressive Party gained 64 seats in Parliament, more than the Conservatives. Forty of its seats came from the western provinces, where it surpassed both Liberals and Conservatives. These results at the national level were accompanied by the emergence of nontraditional parties at the provincial level. The United Farmers of Ontario formed a short-lived minority government in 1919, and the United Farmers of Alberta formed a government in 1921 that lasted until they were replaced by Social Credit in 1935.

Although the Progressives had disappeared as an effective political force by the 1926 election, the pattern of the Canadian party system established in 1921 has persisted. The system is characterized by two major parties, each with a national focus, but usually with a regional centre of gravity, and by at least one "third" party that often combines regional and socio-economic protest with a critique of the practices of "politics as usual."

The major parties continued to be cadre parties largely oriented around elections, shrinking and almost disappearing as organizations between elections. (See Duverger 1959, for the distinction.) The attempts of the CCF/NDP to create a mass membership, policy-oriented party have not been successful enough to change the basic characteristics of the system. Voters tend not to identify strongly with a given party, and party systems can be quite different at the provincial and federal levels, further reinforcing the flexibility of party identification. While there are some social distinctions between habitual voters for any given party, the parties do not represent coherent social blocs as is so often the case in Europe.

Party Development in Europe

Although the parties that existed at an early stage in European political systems followed the Canadian pattern of being factions in the legislature, the development of their modern form is closely connected with long-standing religious cleavages and with the extension of the suffrage to the growing industrial working class, two conditions that were not as strong in Canada as they were in Europe (Lipset and Rokkan 1967; Sartori 1976).

Early extensions of the suffrage to the non-aristocratic upper and middle classes led to the creation of parties that reflected the divisions of those classes. These divisions were usually based on religion, giving rise, for example, to Catholic and Protestant parties in countries like the Netherlands. A related division was that over the role of religion in political life. This division between supporters of a large role for religion, particularly in education, and the supporters of a laic state, gave rise in countries like Belgium and France to confrontation between Catholic parties and nonreligious parties, usually called Liberal, Radical, or even Radical Liberal. The British party system that developed in the 19th century combined religious and regional cleavages, with the Conservative party largely based on the Church of England and the central and southern regions, while the Liberal party drew disproportionately from the "nonconformist" Protestant religions and the Celtic fringe (Wolinetz 1988; Mair and Smith 1989; Mair 1990; Budge et al. 1976; Inglehart 1977).

With the industrialization of most European countries and the granting of universal manhood suffrage, divisions based on class were added to European party systems. One result was the appearance of a socialist or labour party in almost all systems, often enlisting members through unions and cooperative societies even before those members were eligible to vote. In many countries the conservative religious party attempted to develop a cross-class base, and these parties, like the Conservative party in Britain and the Catholic party of Belgium, were leaders in mobilizing the working class vote via membership in the party and the associated organizations.

In most countries, the socialist party eventually displaced the secular or non-established religious party as the second largest party in the system. In the British two-party-oriented system, the Liberal party lapsed into governmental irrelevance; but in systems organized around proportional representation and coalition government parties like the Belgian Liberals and, after the Second World War, the German Free Democratic Party survived and continued to participate in governments. The final major change in many European systems was the addition of Communist parties after the Russian revolution of 1917.

Party Development and Party Functions

Many of the European parties that developed with the extension of the suffrage were mass membership parties: that is, they aspired to enrol as members a large proportion of their voters and to involve them in the life of the party in ways beyond the act of voting. This type of party organization was related to the need to mobilize and stabilize the votes of an often illiterate and frequently newly urbanized working class in the absence of modern media of communication. Both conservative religious and socialist parties fell into this category, while the secular conservative liberals, who did not aim at a working class base of support, usually had relatively small memberships and organizational networks that were only shadows of those of the other parties.

Mass membership parties aspired to perform other functions for their members beyond organizing the act of voting, often to the point of providing them with a total environment. The parties had youth wings, associated trade unions, social assistance organizations, and at the extreme, bands, libraries, football teams and burial societies. Voting patterns associated with this type of party organization were extremely stable since the vote was an expression both of political choice and of membership in a "political family."

The mass membership parties of the early 20th century in Europe are credited with integrating the working class into the political system and providing its members with the tools of political efficacy (Lipset and Rokkan 1967; Rokkan 1970). However, the mass membership party system had a darker side, manifested in the emergence of "segmented societies" where the typical citizen's first loyalty was to a partisan "family" rather than to the society as a whole and where, in the absence of overarching loyalties to the larger society, political disputes were often bitter and paralysing. Examples of segmented societies include the Netherlands with its Protestant, Catholic, Socialist and Liberal segments and Belgium, with its division into religious and secular families manifested in the Catholic and Belgian Workers' (later Socialist) party. Political conflict in segmented societies could come close to civil war as did the conflict between the Communist and Nazi parties in Germany and the Christian Social and Social Democratic parties in Austria in the 1930s. (For studies of segmented polities, see Daalder 1966; Lijphart 1977.)

The development of European parties led to important differences in organization and function from those of Canadian parties. The major European parties usually have an extraparliamentary organization that rivals in importance the party in parliament and that has its own ties with party members. The existence of this organization facilitates the educational function of the party and the discussion of policy issues between elections. In contrast, in Canadian parties, the parliamentary wing is clearly dominant, and the function of the extraparliamentary organization is seen as that of supporting the parliamentary and electoral activities of incumbent and aspiring office holders.

The contrast can be exaggerated, however. When parliamentary and extraparliamentary wings of European parties quarrel, it is usually the parliamentary wing that wins, in part because of the greater legitimacy and visibility its official status gives it. Furthermore, as will be seen below, the organization of European political parties as "families" has been weakening. Studies of mass membership parties since the Second World War argue that their relationship with their members has become more clientelistic – the provision of services for loyalty – and that the adherence of the members is therefore more conditional and open to change (Huysen 1988). Certainly the rise of new parties in Europe suggests a weakening of the tie between member/voter and party.

From Persistence to Change in Party Systems

Both Canadian and European party systems went through a period of instability in the 1960s marked by increased voter volatility, by the rise of new parties, and by periods of governmental instability and/or minority governments. Although this period was followed by a period of relative stability in the 1980s, it left its mark on the political system. Moreover, the rise of new parties in both Canada and Europe in recent years suggests the arrival of another period of effervescence, if not change, in the party systems of many countries. These series of changes in party systems have been one of the bases of arguments that the links between parties and the electorate have been weakening.

In the 1960s in Canada, the re-emergence of the Social Credit party and the emergence of the Créditistes pushed the third-party vote from its historical low of 9.5 percent in 1958 to a historical high of 25.2 percent in 1962 and led to a series of minority governments (Gagnon 1989). At the provincial level, the most striking change in this period was the emergence of the Parti québécois as the alternative to the Liberal party in Quebec. However, the last Créditiste disappeared from Parliament in 1980, and the NDP by itself was never able to reach 20 percent of the vote. The 1980s were in general a period of stability as far as the operation of the two-party system was concerned.

There are signs that the Canadian party system may be entering a new period of fragmentation in the 1990s. In the most recent federal election, the number of parties presenting over 50 candidates increased to 13 from 11, and the share of the vote going to parties other than the Liberals or Conservatives rose from 21 to 25 percent (Frizzell et al. 1989). Since that election, party standings in the polls have been subject to wide fluctuations, the Bloc québécois has been formed and declared its intention to present candidates at the next federal election, and the Reform Party has elected a member of Parliament and a senator and has begun an attempt to move out of its western base into Ontario.

European party systems also underwent significant change beginning in the late 1960s, returned to stability, although often with an altered party landscape, in the early 1980s, and have now entered a new period of party creation. So far the changes that occurred in the earlier period have been more significant. In that period, new parties, organized on a variety of issues, emerged and caused the established parties of the system to suffer significant electoral losses. Old parties shrank, disappeared, split and merged with other parties. Party membership declined, and electors switched their vote from party to party with greater ease (Budge et al. 1976; Inglehart 1977; Dalton et al. 1984; Lawson and Merkl 1988; Mair 1989; Smith 1989).

Signs of these changes occurred, for example, in Great Britain, long considered the model of stable two-party democracy, where the Conservative and Labour parties had monopolized the votes of an overwhelming majority of the electorate, their alternation in power undisturbed by the existence of the remains of the Liberal party. (See table 2.1.) In the 1970s, their hold on the voters was challenged both by a decline in electoral participation and by the emergence of two "ethnonational" parties, the Scottish National Party and the Welsh Plaid Cymru (Breckenridge 1988). In the February 1974 election, these parties and the Liberal party gained enough seats in Parliament to force the Labour Party into a minority government. The Labour Party was then forced into using the votes of the Liberal members of Parliament to maintain themselves in power. In 1981 a new, nonregional party, the Social Democrats, was formed by dissatisfied leaders of the Labour Party, and

Table 2.1
British elections, 1970–87

Year	Conservatives		Labour		Liberals		Nationalists	
	%	N	%	N	%	N	%	N
1970	46.4	330	43.1	288	7.5	6	1.7	1
1974F	37.9	297	37.2	301	19.3	14	2.6	9
1974O	35.8	277	39.2	319	18.3	13	3.5	14
1979	43.9	339	37.0	269	13.8	11	2.0	4
1983	42.4	397	27.6	209	25.4	23*	1.5	4
1987	42.3	375	30.8	229	22.6	22*	1.7	6

Source: Breckenridge (1988, 210).

Notes: Major party share of vote, 1970, 89.5%; 1987, 73.1%. Percentages do not add to 100.0 because of rounding.

N = MPs.

*Liberal–Social Democratic Alliance, 1983, 1987.

in 1983, in alliance with the Liberals, succeeded in coming to within two percentage points of the Labour vote (Norton 1984).

Similar changes occurred in almost all other European systems. In Denmark, in 1973, the "earthquake election" saw a stable party system of the classic type disrupted by the emergence of new parties on both the right and the left. (See table 2.2.) In Belgium, the "traditional parties" split into Dutch-speaking and French-speaking organizations, and their total share of the vote declined from 95.4 percent in 1958 to 75.4 percent in 1974 (Covell 1988; Dewachter 1987). In the Netherlands, religious parties merged, parties on the left split, and new parties appeared, further increasing the fragmentation of an already complex system (Wolinetz 1988).

This instability in the strength of the established parties weakened their ability to participate in governments and led to considerable uncertainty about the nature of the governing coalition that might emerge from any given election. By the mid-1980s, most European party systems had returned to a period of stability. Most of the ethnonationalist parties lost votes and even disappeared, and the British Social Democrats

Table 2.2
Party share of vote in Denmark, 1971, 1973
(percentages)

	Share of vote	
Party	1971	1973
Communist	1.4	3.6
Left Socialist	1.6	1.5
Socialist People's Party	9.1	6.0
Social Democrats	37.3	25.6
Radical Liberals	14.4	11.2
Justice Party	1.7	2.9
Agrarian Liberals	15.6	12.3
Centre Democrats	—	7.8
Christian People's Party	2.0	4.0
Conservatives	16.7	9.2
Progress Party	—	15.9

Source: Pedersen (1987, 18).

Note: Percentages do not add to 100.0 because of rounding.

no longer threatened to displace the Labour Party. Other new parties became established parties and were accepted as regular coalition partners. However, in the last several years, new parties have emerged on the left and right of the political spectrum. These include the various Green parties of Europe and anti-immigrant parties like the French National Front.

Parties and Voters

It is this instability in the party systems of Canada and Western Europe that has provided much of the evidence for the argument that links between parties and voters have been weakening and that the traditional parties are no longer able to dominate the political system as they once did. However, the importance of the changes is not easy to estimate. There are at least three possible interpretations of the available evidence from Europe. The first is that the instability of the 1970s and early 1980s was simply a hiccup in the system, and that the established European parties and party systems will return to their habitual form. There is some evidence for this argument since many of the new parties that disrupted the system have proved to be short-lived, and the established parties have, in many cases, recovered much of their old position. Another possibility is that we are seeing a realignment of the electorate, in which new issues and parties replace the old ones that have been around since the beginning of the century. A final possibility, and the most serious for the parties' performance of their functions, is that we are in a situation of dealignment, of abandonment of parties as institutions by significant numbers of citizens.

A New Politics?

The case for realignment argues that the abandonment of established parties represents the development of a new set of political interests as a result of the conditions of advanced industrialization and the emergence of a new political generation. The conditions of advanced industrialization include relative affluence for a larger segment of the population than in the past, and for the rest, a welfare net that alleviates immediate concerns for economic survival (Inglehart 1977). They also include the decline of the industrial working class, the development of service-based economies, and the emergence of a new middle class whose status is based on education and the professions rather than business activities. These voters bring a new set of values and demands to the political system. Earlier studies called these values "post-materialist" in contrast to the "materialist" values of economic security and economic growth that interested earlier generations, although, in view of the reputation acquired by this generation in the most recent decade, this is perhaps not the most accurate term. "Post-industrial" and "lifestyle" issues have also been used to describe the type of policy in which these voters are interested (Inglehart 1977).

Issues espoused by this new orientation include protection of the environment, even at the cost of economic growth; the promotion of social and economic equality for groups neglected by earlier, class-based redistributionist demands, most notably women, but also other, often diverse, minority groups; the defence of the culture of groups threatened by the homogenizing tendencies of industrial society, notably ethnic and regional groups; and an end to hierarchical "politics as usual" (Nevitte 1991).

These issues, it is argued, constitute a "new-politics" agenda that the traditional parties have not been able to adopt. Neither labour-based nor conservative parties have been able to abandon the idea of economic growth as the chief goal of government policy and the chief solution for political problems while many of the "new-politics" demands are contrary to the economic interests and conservative social values of their existing base of support. As a result, voters interested in these new issues either vote for new parties, whether "green" or "nationalist," move from established party to established party in search of one that corresponds to their interests, or simply do not vote at all.

The existence and attitudes of the post-materialist citizen have been extensively studied, and there is evidence that new issues and attitudes have emerged to a certain degree in advanced industrial societies both in Europe and elsewhere. However, there are several reasons to reject the conclusion that their existence is a harbinger either of a new set of dominant political issues or of a drastic permanent change in party systems, at least in the near future.

First, the proportion of the electorate identified as having these attitudes is still relatively small. In multi-party systems with proportional representation, the shifts of a small number of voters can have large, even if temporary, effects on the balance between the established parties of the system. However, their numbers do not yet appear to be large enough to support a major new party in these systems, or to lead to changes in party systems using the less flexible single-member plurality electoral system. Second, even for these voters, it is not always clear that post-materialist considerations will win out when they conflict with material considerations as they might, for example, in times of economic scarcity. Finally, the concerns listed do not explain the decade-long support for conservative parties and policies in systems like Britain and the United States, since most of these concerns would usually be placed on the "left" side of the political spectrum. (The alternative term, "lifestyle" politics, however, might well explain support for the redistributive policies of the Thatcher and Reagan governments and for parties like the French National Front and the Canadian Reform Party.)

A Rejection of Parties?

A more serious threat to the functions of political parties lies in the possibility that the increased electoral volatility might reflect dealignment, or a disengagement from parties as institutions. Realignment has serious consequences for the parties that disappear, the office holders who lose office, and the interests shut out of the "new political discourse"; but if the old parties are simply replaced by new parties performing essentially the same linking function, the consequences for the political system as a whole are less severe. Dealignment, on the other hand, might well lead to the failure of the parties to perform their functions of linkage and organization. As Ian Budge puts it: "The more electors are attached by enduring psychological links to political parties, the more the polity is ensured against flash parties and sudden demagogic incursions. Conversely, the greater the legitimacy, authority and power of established party elites, the greater the time available for the vital bargaining and compromise that allow democracies to solve problems in an orderly and peaceful fashion with the largest possible degree of peaceful consent" (Budge et al. 1976, 3).

There are several reasons why a disaffection from parties might be occurring. One characteristic of the new politics is a willingness to use political tactics that do not involve links with parties. These include demonstrations, direct mobilization of groups, helped by modern techniques of communication, including the fax revolution, media campaigns, and access to the courts as well as direct links with the bureaucracy. (In fact, the last two methods of pursuing policy goals are also used by established interest groups with no new-politics orientation at all.) The development of the mass media, particularly television, introduces another powerful institution with a claim of its own to the function of defining and commenting on political issues, while a more educated and socially and geographically mobile electorate contains a larger number of "free-range voters" (Mair 1989, 182), less attentive to voting as an expression of permanent group membership and more attentive to candidates and issues.

In European party systems, other social changes have also undercut the base of permanent party support and support expressed as party membership. These include secularization, which has undercut the base of the religious parties, and deindustrialization, which has undercut the labour-based parties. The development of the welfare state has undercut the clientelistic functions of parties. Polls have made party organization less necessary as a source of feedback for politicians, and public financing of parties has further reduced the need for a stable body of party adherents. In other words, both voters and political leaders might now find parties less necessary as institutions than they did in the past.

It is also possible that the performance of parties themselves has led to a distancing of the electorate from the parties. Parties in government have been constrained since the oil crisis of the 1970s and the deficit and debt crises of the 1980s in their ability to deliver policies and services to their populations. Since parties are identified with the act of governing, they inherit some of the blame for this situation. Party splits and/or the takeover of a party by an extremist faction can also disorient and discourage voters. For example, the splits in the British Labour Party and the activities of its left wing in the late 1970s and early 1980s must bear some of the responsibility for its losses to the new Social Democratic Party (Breckenridge 1988).

Stability and Change

However, the degree to which we are witnessing a high degree of dealignment and rejection of parties as institutions can be questioned. Several studies of party identification in Europe suggest that while ties to party are loosening, parties still remain the key institution through which voters exercise their political options (Mair 1989; Tate 1980). The system in which dealignment, with a concomitant fall in electoral participation, seems to have gone the furthest is the American system; but this system has several features, including the primary system of candidate selections and government institutions organized around the division of powers with fixed elections for both executive and legislature that by themselves undercut the role of parties as organizers of political life (Wolinetz 1988). (A contrast to the effect of the American system lies in the French system, where the president can dissolve the legislature in an attempt to achieve one with a majority of his party. This tends to reinforce the importance of party as an organizer of political life.)

Parties themselves have shown some adaptability. The British Conservatives were able to capitalize on voter discontent with the performance of both major British parties in the 1970s by rejecting the centrist policies of the Heath government; the Labour Party has undergone a major reorganization; and on the Continent, parties like the Socialist party in France and the Social Democrats in Germany have attempted to integrate elements of the new politics into their platforms with some success. Although Green parties, the most obvious proponents of new-politics issues, have gained some votes and have been able to elect some candidates, they are far from establishing themselves as major contenders in European party systems (Ladrech 1989; Levy 1988; Rothacher 1984).

CANADIAN PARTIES AND VOTERS

In a sense, Canadian parties have long operated under the circumstances of low and loose party identification that seem to be developing in Europe. The characteristics of an immigrant society, with a fragmented social and economic organization lacking large clearly delineated groups on which distinctive parties might base themselves, coupled with the refusal of parties at the national level to develop distinct policies, to say nothing of ideologies, have removed most of the bases for the formation of clear and fixed party identification. Historically, region and family have been the major determinants of party identification, and further internal migrations coupled with the loosening of family structures suggest that even these supports for the development of party identification may be declining.

While studies of the Canadian electorate emphasize the degree to which "durable partisans" constitute a minority of the electorate, they do not support the thesis of a major decline in "flexible" identification or in the total proportion of party identifiers in the electorate. The 1984 Clarke et al. survey of voters found that while Canadians were quite willing to change their vote from election to election, the proportion of the electorate that reported some degree of identification with a party did not decline over the period they studied, nor was there a tendency for younger voters to be less attached to parties than older voters (Clarke et al. 1984; see table 2.3).

The participation rate in Canadian elections fits comfortably in the range of liberal democracies that do not have compulsory voting (table 2.4). It has been stable, or even increasing slightly. The data, therefore, do not suggest a major case of dealignment or rejection of the party system as a vehicle for electoral choice. Recent polls do suggest that voters are becoming even more flexible in the range of party alternatives they are willing to consider. The gains in support for the NDP and for two new parties, the Bloc québécois and the Reform Party, are indicative of this increased flexibility, while the recent election of an NDP government in Ontario suggests that voters may also be willing to translate this hypothetical support into actual votes.

While voters are willing to consider a wider range of party alternatives, it is not at all clear that the new-politics agenda has been influ-

Table 2.3
Partisan identification in Canada

Party	% respondents reporting partisan identification	
	1974	1980
Liberal	50	45
Conservative	23	28
NDP	12	15
Social Credit	3	1
No party	12	10

Source: Clarke et al. (1984, 60).

Note: Percentages do not add to 100.0 because of rounding.

ential in this change of attitude. Neither the Reform Party nor the Bloc québécois could be considered to be a proponent of new-politics issues, while the electoral fate of the Canadian Green party does not support the idea that there is a large share of the electorate willing to change its vote on the basis of this issue alone. In the 1988 federal election, the Green party was outpolled by the Rhinoceros party 52 173 votes to 47 228. Support for new-politics issues in the abstract may be on the increase, but this support has not yet been translated into votes for a successful challenger party based on a new-politics agenda.

One thing that is striking about the Canadian electorate is the degree to which those who switch parties do so as a result of events and coverage during the election campaign itself (Clarke et al. 1984). This suggests that parties are not very successful in getting messages to the general population between elections. This failure to carry on a dialogue with the electorate between elections can, it has been argued, breed cynicism on the part of governments, who hope that past misadventures will be forgotten by the time of an election campaign.

There are several reasons for the failure of Canadian parties in this area. In the first place, Canadian parties do not attempt to maintain an ongoing dialogue with the population, but prefer to concentrate their resources on the high stakes presented by electoral contests. In fact, the parties lack the resources necessary for policy discussion and communication beyond support for their parliamentary groups. They do not have central offices of a size that could undertake this task, nor do they have a stable base of communicators at the grassroots level.

It seems possible that there would be an audience for this type of communication if the parties were to have the resources and the will to

Table 2.4
Turnout in recent elections

		Turnout (%)
Sweden	1985	89.9
Denmark	1988	85.8
Germany	1987	84.4
Norway	1989	82.3
France	1988 (presidential, first ballot)	82.0
Netherlands	1989	80.1
Germany	1990	77.8
Ireland	1987	76.2
Britain	1987	75.4
Canada	1988	75.0
France	1988 (National Assembly, first ballot)	66.2
Switzerland	1987	46.5

Source: "The Week in Germany," Various Election Reports, *West European Politics* (7 Dec. 1990).

undertake it. A large and stable base of party members is not a prerequisite. Most European parties continue to undertake discussion and communication of political issues between elections, even though the party member who dutifully attended seminars every Friday evening is a thing of the past. In Canada, political participation in nonparty groups seems to be increasing, and parties themselves could take advantage of this increase in political interest. Moreover, most surveys indicate that voters are dissatisfied with having their influence on policy limited to electing the policy makers and then leaving them to do all the work themselves. Most changes to the Canadian political system that have been suggested to meet this demand, including provisions for recall and impeachment, would weaken both the party system and the parliamentary system. An increase in party-public communications between elections might satisfy the demand without making major changes to other parts of the political system. In the absence of any improvement in parties' performance in this area, it continues to be important to regulate the conduct of the electoral campaign itself, including access to advertising, to free time on the media, and to the intervention of nonparty groups.

Parties and Interests

The articulation of competing interests and their reconciliation with each other and with some notion of a general interest is another function attributed to parties in liberal democracies. The preferred model of interest articulation and reconciliation as described in the literature on parties is that of parties assembling interests into policy packages on the basis of an ideological predisposition and offering the electorate a choice among these packages at elections.

There are several systems that do not fit this model. For its realization, the model depends on the existence of at least a significant minority of voters willing to change party choice on the basis of the policy choices offered. It also depends on the existence of parties that on the one hand are not tied to a restricted range of interest groups and, on the other hand, are willing to commit themselves to explicit policy packages. Therefore, it does not fit the segmented systems discussed earlier in which voters are tied to parties by membership in a social/political community or family and where the vote is an affirmation of this membership. In these systems, parties articulate the interests of their segment, and aggregation takes place elsewhere: among parties in a coalition government, in the bureaucracy, or in "corporatist" institutions of interest intermediation.

The other type of system that does not fit the model is one in which parties fail to present clear policy alternatives, but rather try to attract as broad a spectrum of voters as possible by avoiding a distinct and therefore limiting ideological or policy image. In the Canadian system, this strategy is referred to as brokerage politics, while in the European context, parties attempting this type of appeal are known as catch-all parties (Kirchheimer 1966; Wolinetz 1979). In this type of system, the focus of party activity shifts from the articulation of interests to aggregation, but usually by accommodating interests on an individual basis rather than by assembling party responses to demands into a coherent whole.

There are several reasons for the emergence of such a system. The dominance of local interests in the early days of Canadian politics set a pattern that has not changed; attempts of parties like the Progressives and the CCF/NDP to introduce a more policy-oriented style of politics have not been successful in the long run. In Canada, these more policy-oriented parties are under continual pressure to choose between an educational style of politics, with the electoral risks which that entails, and conformity to the prevailing diffuse brokerage style (Brodie and Jenson 1989). If their educational efforts succeed and their policies begin to attract large-scale electoral support, they are notoriously vulnerable to having those policies stolen in piecemeal fashion by the major parties of the system.

Other aspects of the Canadian party system and its history have reinforced the original tendency to accommodation of a wide range of interests rather than identification with specific policies and the interests associated with them. First, Canadian political history is not a history of regular alternation of parties in government, but rather a history of alternating periods of one-party dominance, mitigated by occasional minority governments or temporary eruptions of the nondominant party. This creates a "party of government" mentality, in which the party concerned adopts the function, usually reserved to the governmental level, of aggregating a broad range of interests. The situation also creates pressures on this party not to exclude any interests on a permanent or an a priori basis (Whitaker 1977).

There are analyses that trace the lack of ideology in Canada's parties at the national level to the nature of Canadian federalism, in which a party at the national level will have to reach agreements in many areas of social and economic policy that lie at least partly in the provincial domain with governments led by other parties. However, it should be noted that politics within many provinces has a considerably higher ideological content than politics at the national level, and provincial parties cannot be said to be inhibited by the need to reach agreement with a national government of a different stripe. It is also true that the two main German parties, the Christian Democrats and the Social Democrats, are considerably more distinct than the two major Canadian parties, although Germany is also a federation.

In Europe, there were several motivations for the transformation of existing parties into catch-all parties practising brokerage politics of the type considered typical of the Canadian system. One motivation was a desire to break with the conflict-laden segmented politics of the past. Thus, when parties were formed in Germany after the Second World War, Konrad Adenauer chose to create a broad-based conservative party in the form of the Christian Democratic Union (CDU) rather than to recreate the Catholic party of the Weimar Republic (Chandler 1988; Merkl 1980). The other motivation, of course, was a desire for electoral success. With the growing secularization and de-industrialization of the postwar period, both Christian and Socialist parties faced a numerical decline in the social groups on which they were based.

However, it is an exaggeration to say that European catch-all parties have become indistinguishable. In general, the Christian parties have attempted to transform themselves into a conservative alliance, while the Socialist parties have aimed at attracting progressive-minded white collar workers. Parties that became too indistinct often found themselves faced with internal struggles and attempts to return them to their ideological basis, as the history of the British Labour and Conservative parties shows (Breckenridge 1988; Wolinetz 1979).

European parties show a greater variety of relationships with interests or interest groups than do Canadian parties. In some cases, the party is an emanation of, or at least closely linked to, a specific interest or group. The British trade union movement was the major force behind the creation of the British Labour Party, and its continuing position is reflected in the party's internal electoral system, its finance, and the long-term location of party headquarters in Transport House. In Denmark, the Agrarian Liberals, as the name suggests, were created to further the interests of rural areas. On the other hand, parties may colonize interests, dividing similar groups along party lines. The division of French trade unions into three competing federations of unions reflects that country's party divisions, while the Belgian party system, in which parties have associated unions, insurance societies and charitable organizations, is almost a caricature of the colonization model.

It is also possible for European parties to avoid explicit links with interest groups. This is often the case for parties of the right, like the British Conservative Party. However, the more common pattern is the existence of tighter links between parties and interests than occur in Canada. This has several effects on the style of interest aggregation in these systems. In two-party systems, the result can be a considerable degree of conflict, such as the near civil war that occurred in Austria in the 1930s and the period of industrial unrest in Britain under the Heath government. In multi-party systems with coalition governments, a more common pattern is the movement of interest reconciliation from an intraparty level to an interparty level in the negotiations that accompany the formation of coalition governments and the ongoing process of negotiation that is characteristic of such governments.

In Canada, interests and interest groups may be "party friendly," but they rarely develop formal links with parties. The major current exception is the NDP, which maintains links with the Canadian Labour Congress; historical exceptions include the United Farmers parties and the Progressive Party of the inter-war period. In general, however, Canadian interest groups, like Canadian voters, are free range, rather than tied to a specific party. This style of party-interest relationship both reflects and is reinforced by the brokerage style of politics characteristic of the system. Parties cannot count on a stable collection of interest groups for support, but on the other hand, no group can be considered permanently lost to any party.

New Interest Groups

The development of new groups espousing causes like the protection of the environment and women's rights has posed a challenge to both European and Canadian systems, and both systems have only imperfectly adjusted to the emergence of these groups. There are several reasons for this. It is not that the groups are, as another name for them suggests, "single-interest groups." Espousing a single interest rather than an aggregated set of interests is also characteristic of the economically based groups that preceded the new groups (Galipeau 1989). Rather, the groups differ from other interest groups, first, in the non-economic nature of their demands. For parties and a political system that are used to dealing with demands that can be met by spending money or through redistribution based on economic growth, demands for changes in social practices or demands whose satisfaction may result in a decline in economic growth require responses that are outside the normal range of political discourse.

The demands of these groups are thus often outside the range of "consensus politics," and the electoral impact of meeting or not meeting them is often not clear to parties. The groups themselves are often divided on the utility of contacts with parties as a way of furthering their purposes. In many cases, the groups recruit their leadership from people previously active in political parties, and see parties, because of their domination of the political system, as a necessary channel of influence. For example, a study of the Dutch peace movement shows the centrality of party activists in the movement, and Ladrech quotes a French feminist leader as saying "political parties exist, and we won't be able to change that for some time ... parties are still the place for political intervention" (Ladrech 1989, 273; Kriesi 1989; Machin 1989). However, these movements, as the quotation suggests, are often also hostile to political parties in general and to the traditional political parties of their system in particular.

In Canada the new interest groups have tended to work through the media and the court system as much as through the electoral process. The importance of party in electoral choice protects individual candidates from being targeted by the groups as they often are in the United States, while the focus of Canadian parties on elections reduces the inclination of parties to undertake a dialogue with groups whose electoral impact is not yet proven. Our plurality electoral system means that the formation of separate political parties to promote the interests espoused by these groups, at least in the short run, would not have results commensurate to the effort and expense involved.

A Difficult Balance

In their role as articulators and aggregators of interests, parties must achieve a difficult balance. They must be responsive to the demands of interests, particularly new ones whose emergence serves as an indicator of changing social and economic conditions. At the same time, they must be sufficiently autonomous from groups and their demands to reconcile competing interests and to express some concept of a general interest. This means that changes proposed to the relationship between parties and interest groups also have to strike a balance between ensuring responsiveness and protecting autonomy.

Measures that emphasize the role of the individual candidate and short-term sensitivity to interests, like the primary election method of candidate selection and the recall provisions that exist most notably in many American states, probably go too far in the direction of ensuring responsiveness. Combined with the lack of party discipline in the American Congress, they have had the paradoxical effect of turning that body into a "mutual protection society for incumbents" (Burnham 1982). In the Canadian system, which some argue errs in the other direction, it still seems desirable to strengthen party responsiveness to interests rather than focusing on the individual member of Parliament.

It is also important, as I have argued above, to improve the capacity of parties and their representatives in Parliament to carry on party dialogue on policy between elections. While the ideal model of the role of parties in policy formation that exists in much of the literature stresses the presentation of policy choices to the population at the time of elections, it is quite possible that elections are not the best time for policy choice. Voters in a parliamentary system must already use one vote to select a local representative and a government. To use the election as a plebiscite to pronounce on a single-policy issue, and even more a policy package, is asking the one vote electors have to carry too heavy a load.

It is also true that the role of parties as such in policy formation should not be exaggerated. Parties are among a range of institutions that articulate and aggregate interests in modern liberal democracies. The fact that other institutions such as the bureaucracy and the court system also play a role in this process does not represent a failure of parties, but rather reflects the complexity of modern society. Changes are needed to improve both the process of communication with interest groups and the process of reflection that turns a mix of interests into policy.

Parties and Ethnic-Regional Interests

Ethnic-regional interests are among the most difficult interests for a party system to accommodate. (Nonregional ethnic interests can be accommodated through machine-style politics and "ethnic arithmetic," although it should be noted that it was precisely this style of accommodation in the United States that gave rise to the Reform Movement, many of whose proposals, once adopted, had the effect of drastically weakening the American party system.) Regional and ethnic interests are often those of minority groups within the population, and the dynamic of majoritarian democracy makes the effective representation of such interests difficult. In addition, the major parties of a system are usually committed to the preservation of a status quo that may be challenged by ethnic and regional demands.

The Canadian party system has usually attempted to resolve these problems within its major parties, and the resolution of territorial and language diversity is often seen as one of the roots of the brokerage style of politics. Among the devices used by parties to resolve these interests are the use of regional "lieutenants," and regional ministers with responsibility for representation of the region in the party and of the party in the region (Bakvis 1988). Articulation of regional interests through the party caucus has also been important, as has the judicious distribution of patronage (Thomas 1991; Whitaker 1977).

Several features of the Canadian party system have impeded the accommodation of regional and language interests. First, the party discipline and government-versus-opposition style of politics that are characteristic of the Westminster model of parliamentary government undercut the ability of members to promote regional interests, particularly when those interests are minority interests. Other features of the Canadian party system that make regional representation difficult are the weakness of links between parties at the national and provincial levels, and the tendency of the major parties, even when in government, to have a distinct regional centre of gravity (Dyck 1989; Cairns 1968).

Attempts to articulate a pan-Canadian ideology in the face of these regional imbalances have often been conflict creating rather than conflict resolving, since the ideology has been perceived as a cloak for the interests of central Canada (Smith 1985). As I have remarked above, ethnic-regional interests are often minority interests, and questioning the actual distribution of power in the country involves raising the question whether the interests of the majority of Canadians are the same thing as the interests of Canada. The whole dynamic of majoritarian democracy says that they are.

The existence of the federal system of government has taken some of the burden of resolving these issues from the party system. However, if regional and language interests become more explicitly represented in Parliament, for example, through the election of significant numbers of members from the Reform Party and the Bloc québécois, more overt discussion of these issues in the legislature is likely to result. In these circumstances, behind the scenes resolution within the caucuses of the nonregional parties might not be sufficient to give the appearance of representation of regional-ethnic interests. Demands on members from the West and Quebec to do something could well lead to strains on the unity of these parties.

In spite of the strains imposed on parties, it still seems preferable to give them some role in mediating Canada's language and regional disputes. Canada has always emphasized the value of accommodating ethnic and regional interests within political parties. Even parties that fail to gain votes in a given region (in other words, all three major political parties for a large part of their existence) present themselves as national parties and run candidates in all regions. Given the divided nature of many other aspects of the Canadian polity, the existence of national parties is an important symbol of national integration. To argue, as David Elkins does in this volume (Elkins 1991), that the disputes put too much strain on parties and so should be avoided is a counsel of despair. As long as our parties group members from different regions, regional issues will be debated within the parties. Moreover, if regional disputes are not at least partially resolved in the party system, the strain will simply be passed on to other parts of the system.

An example of the consequences of the failure of parties to play some role in mediating regional disputes comes from the recent history of Belgium, where the Social Christian, Socialist and Liberal parties all split along language lines between 1968 and 1978, leaving the system without any party that grouped Belgians from all regions of the country. In these circumstances, regional interests cannot be reconciled within any given party, but must be dealt with by bargaining among the parties of the governing coalition. The strains of accommodating different regional interests and political styles at the governmental level without prior mediation through parties have been so great that Belgium has moved gradually and, since 1988, decisively to a quasi-federal form of regime. As a unitary state, Belgium could undergo a large amount of decentralization without disintegration. It is not clear that Canada has such a large margin of manoeuvrability.

NEW PARTIES

Almost by definition, the rise of new parties is a sign that the established parties of a system are not accommodating important shades of political opinion in that system. The emergence of Communist and

Fascist parties in Europe in the interwar period was both a sign and a cause of the failure of the postwar political systems, while the emergence of new parties on the left and right in recent years has also been taken as a sign that the parties and party systems established in the period after the Second World War have not adapted to the emergence of new political issues.

In Canada, the period immediately after the First World War and the crisis of the Depression saw the formation of several new parties. The period after the Second World War was calmer, with only the breakthrough of the Social Credit/Créditiste party in 1962 disturbing the two and one-half party balance of power in Parliament. However, recent years have seen the emergence of several new parties, most notably the Reform Party and the Bloc québécois at the national level, and this, too, has been seen as a sign and possibly a future cause of a crisis in the Canadian political system.

If new parties are not uncommon, the displacement of a major established party by a new party is rare. Examples of this type of realignment include the displacement of the Whig party by the Republicans in the United States and the more gradual replacement of the Liberals by the Labour Party in Britain and of the various liberal parties of Continental Europe by Socialist or Social Democratic parties. In Canada, Liberal and Conservative parties have been displaced at the provincial level, but have remained the major parties at the national level since 1867.

The displacement of an established party by a new party requires both the attraction of new generations of voters and a large-scale switch of party allegiance on the part of current voters. (See the discussion of the development of the Labour Party vote in Butler and Stokes 1974.) When this displacement is not associated with a large entry of new voters, as occurred in Europe with the extension of the franchise at the turn of the century and in Canada with large-scale immigration at the same period, it is connected with cataclysmic events: a countdown to civil war in the case of the American Republican Party, and the combined effects of war and depression in the case of the British Labour Party.

However, the displacement of major parties is not the only way in which new parties can affect the political system. Evaluations of new parties differ in the emphasis they give to these other effects. Some see new parties as a destabilizing influence in the political system, disrupting the balance between the established parties and making the achievement or construction of governmental majorities more difficult. New parties may express extreme ideas which are not part of the consensus that unites a political system and may, indeed, be anti-system and even antidemocratic. Their leaders may be new to politics and unused or hostile to the rules of the game that make the system function.

On the other hand, more favourable evaluations of new parties see them as a source of new ideas, important precisely because they have been excluded by the orthodox consensus, and as a source of new people who challenge the self-serving politics-as-usual orientation of the older parties. Recommendations about the degree to which the creation and activities of new parties should be encouraged depend in part on the degree to which they are seen as a destabilizing influence or, on the other hand, a necessary means by which a political system renews itself and ensures long-term stability through change.

The next section of the study will examine new parties in Europe and Canada. Under what circumstances do new parties arise? What are the conditions of their success or failure in perpetuating themselves, in influencing government policy, and in moving into government office? Finally, have the effects of the activities of new parties on the balance of the parties in the system contributed to the ability of political systems to adopt necessary changes or have they caused such fragmentation that their systems lost flexibility?

New Parties in Europe

The new parties of postwar Europe fall into two main categories of origin: ideological parties of the left or right (or, in the case of the British Social Democrats, the centre) and parties of ethnic or regional representation, some of which are revivals or continuations of previously existing movements. Examples of ideologically based parties include the Green parties that have arisen in several systems, the Progress Party of Denmark, the National Front party of France, and the Republican Party of Germany. Examples of regional or ethnic parties include the Scottish National Party and Plaid Cymru of Britain, and the Volksunie, Rassemblement Wallon and Front démocratique francophone of Belgium (Fisher 1980).

The issues involved in the creation of the ideological parties vary according to the left or right orientation of the party. Several of the parties on the left are the result of the debates over internal party democracy and ideological purity and/or renewal that occurred in Labour, Social Democratic or Socialist parties in the late 1960s and 1970s. Challenges to the established practices of these parties were often the work of a younger generation of activists. In Scandinavian systems and in the Netherlands, these groups eventually formed new parties, splintering the left vote, but rarely displacing the original Socialist or Social Democratic Party; while in Britain they were able to gain a temporary ascendancy, leading their opponents to break away to form the British Social Democratic Party. In Germany, these people provided many of the activists for the Green movement (Bille 1989; Breckenridge 1988; Chandler 1988; Daalder 1987; Rothacher 1984; Wolinetz 1988).

The Green parties have been the most spectacular manifestation of ideological new parties, electing members to local and national governments and to the European Parliament. Although many writers on post-materialist values see environmental ideology as cutting across the traditional left-right division of European politics, most Green parties, like the German Greens, draw the bulk of their personnel and many of their votes from the parties of the left. They also tend to be connected with movements advocating neutrality in foreign affairs, usually a left position in those countries that are members of NATO. Green parties often also have an emphasis on intraparty democracy and an anti-establishment suspicion of the institutions and practices of established politics in their systems (Kriesi 1989; Ladrech 1989).

While the ideological parties of the right rarely share the commitment to intraparty democracy of the Green parties, they do adopt the argument that the practices of politics-as-usual have blinded the established parties to the real problems facing their country and a commitment to a change in the status quo. In Scandinavian countries in the 1970s, tax revolt parties, of which the Danish Progress Party is an example, were created to challenge the prevailing consensus on the welfare state and the tax burden it imposed (Bille 1989; Daalder 1987). The French National Front and the German Republican Party have focused on what they see as the dangers to the national culture and way of life posed by non-European immigrants to their countries (Guyomarch and Machin 1988).

The other type of new party common in Europe is the ethno-regional party. Some of these parties, such as the Scottish National Party (SNP) and the Volksunie of Belgium, have histories that go back to the period between the two world wars. In the 1970s these parties grew, and new ones came into existence. In Britain, the SNP was joined by the Welsh Plaid Cymru. At the high point of their success in the October 1974 election, the two parties gained 3.5 percent of the vote and, because of their regional concentration, secured 14 seats in Parliament. In conjunction with the Liberals, who had gained 13 seats (with 18.3 percent of the vote!), they were able to hold the Labour Party to a majority of 3 seats (Norton 1984; Breckenridge 1988). In Belgium, the Volksunie was joined by the Rassemblement Wallon and the Front démocratique francophone from Brussels. In the 1971 election, the three parties gained 22.3 percent of the vote (Rudolph 1977).

The rise of these new parties has been attributed to an increase in the number of voters willing to switch parties and to dissatisfaction with state performance in economic and other areas. However, the new parties have rarely been successful, even in terms of perpetuating their existence. The German Green party, considered to be the most successful of the environmental parties, fell below the 5 percent cutoff point for representation in the Bundestag in the 1990 German election, and the Scottish National Party, Plaid Cymru and Rassemblement Wallon are no longer represented in their national legislatures, while the British Social Democrats and the French National Front have seen their representation drastically reduced.

There are several reasons for the rise of new parties. First, the parties do articulate issues that the established parties are not voicing. These include issues that the established parties have ruled out of discussion. The anti-tax parties of Scandinavia, the anti-immigrant National Front and Republican party, and the parties proposing the federalization of unitary states all put forth issues that the traditional parties of their system considered beyond the pale of acceptable political discourse. Other parties took stands on issues that the old parties avoided because they were divisive. The British Social Democrats took a strong pro-European Community stand when neither the Conservatives nor the Labour Party was able to achieve a united attitude either for or against the Community. New parties are also based on new issues that the established parties have not yet been able to assimilate, with the various Green parties being the clearest example of this phenomenon.

New parties draw their votes from a variety of sources. The most obvious source is voters who are pleased to see "their" issue finally espoused by a political party. However, there are other reasons for voting for a new party besides its stand on issues. Voting for a non-established party is one way of expressing disapproval of the failures of established parties in general, and this motivation is strengthened by the anti-establishment orientation of new parties as diverse as the National Front and the Greens. In addition, new parties, like other non-major parties, offer voters the possibility of expressing disapproval of their usual party without voting for the major "enemy" party (Covell 1981). For example, the Social Democratic Party in Britain gave Labour voters an opportunity to express their disapproval of the leftward trend in the party without voting for the Conservatives.

Reasons for Lack of Success
The reasons for the lack of staying power of many of the new parties are partially related to the reasons for their original successes. Most

new parties appeal to the electorate on the basis of a single issue or a restricted range of issues. This appeal may attract a core of voters who are intensely interested in the issue, but leaves the party vulnerable to a decline in the salience of the issue or to a re-evaluation by the electorate of its importance relative to other issues. The ethnonationalist parties of Europe all lost votes during the economic crisis of the late 1970s and early 1980s, and the Greens were abandoned in the most recent German election by many of their voters who feared a large decline in the vote for the Social Democratic Party, their usual other party of choice.

In general, new parties have difficulty establishing and expanding a stable electorate. Some, like the older ethnonational parties, do have a small electorate with more than one generation's history of voting, but most, because they are new, must, by definition, rely on attracting either those voters most willing to switch parties – marginal voters who vote in some elections but not in others – or voters who are temporarily dissatisfied with their usual party. All of these categories are particularly susceptible to changing their vote again (Mair 1989, 1990).

In addition, many new parties are the electoral manifestations of movements for whom running candidates in elections is only one of several possible strategies. New parties such as the British Social Democrats, whose major purpose is to run and elect candidates, are rare. The parties are therefore vulnerable to both electoral success and electoral failure. Electoral failure leads to debates about the validity of this strategy and the balance between doctrinal purity and vote-catching as it did, for example, in the case of the Scottish National Party and the Belgian Volksunie. The failure to win seats commensurate with its share of the vote undercut the very purpose of the creation of the British Social Democrats and their alliance with the Liberal party, and led to the disintegration of both (Levy 1988). On the other hand, electoral success leads to disputes between elected members of the party and those more identified with its movement aspect, as happened to the German Greens after their successes of 1987. (See table 2.5.)

New parties are also put at a disadvantage by most electoral systems, whether through the operation of the system itself or through rules added to the system with the express purpose of limiting the success of new or extreme parties. The restrictive effect of electoral systems is most obvious in the case of ideologically based parties trying to gain a foothold in single-member plurality systems, as the example of the British Social Democrats shows. In 1983 the party received 25.4 percent of the vote but only 3.5 percent of the seats in Parliament, continuing the sad experience of the British Liberals (Norton 1984).

Table 2.5
Votes for Green parties in various European countries

		Total vote for Green parties (%)
France	1988 (parliamentary, first ballot)	0.4
Denmark	1988	1.4
Italy	1987	2.5
Germany	1990	3.9
Finland	1987	4.0
Austria	1986	4.8
Sweden	1987	5.5
Belgium	1987	7.1
Switzerland	1987	8.3
Germany	1987	8.3
Luxembourg	1989	8.4

Source: "The Week in Germany," Various Election Reports, *West European Politics* (7 Dec. 1990).

(The single-member plurality system can give an advantage to a region-ally based party, as the example of the Scottish National Party in 1974 shows, but this very regional base limits such a party's chances of fur-ther success and influence at the national level.)

The French two-ballot majority system disadvantages parties who cannot make electoral alliances for the second ballot – often the case for new parties. Successive French governments have raised the thresh-old for individual parties appearing on the second ballot, most recently, in 1986, to 12.5 percent. As a result, the National Front, which had won 35 seats in the National Assembly under the proportional system introduced by the Socialist party for the 1986 elections, was reduced to 1 seat in 1988 under the restored two-ballot single-member district system (Guyomarch and Machin 1988). Proportional representation systems are considered to be the most permissive type of electoral system as far as the emergence of new parties is concerned, but most countries that use a proportional electoral system have a threshold which a party must achieve before qualifying for seats in the legislature, 2 percent in the case of Denmark, 5 percent in the case of Germany.

Finally, established parties and the established party system defend themselves in more overt ways. If the issues espoused by the new parties prove their electoral appeal, they may well be stolen by the older parties. In Belgium, the Social Christians of Flanders and the Socialists of Wallonia have successfully taken on the role of defender of regional interests, while the Social Democrats of Germany have added environmental appeals to their program, and the right in France is divided over the wisdom of adopting some of the appeals of the National Front.

In systems characterized by coalition governments, the established parties usually refuse to consider the new parties as potential coalition partners, often explicitly because to do so would give them a respectability that the established parties prefer to refuse them. It is not uncommon for established parties to support a minority government rather than include a new party or give it "blackmailing potential" in the legislature, the most striking example of this being the 22 seat minority government of the Danish Agrarian Liberals in 1973 (Daalder 1987).

Effects of New Parties
Does the appearance of new parties have a destabilizing effect on a party system? The effect or lack of effect depends in part on the electoral system and in part on the balance among the parties in the party system. The SNP and Plaid Cymru were able to cause a period of minority and close to minority government in Britain, even under a single-member plurality system, because they were able to translate their share of the vote into a corresponding share of seats, and because Labour and the Conservative parties were closely balanced at the time. On the other hand, the Social Democratic Party did not have this effect, partly because they were not able to achieve a share of seats in Parliament corresponding to their share of the vote, and partly because they drew votes mainly from the Labour Party. Their existence reinforced the majorities of the Thatcher governments. If the Progress Party in Denmark was able to contribute to a crisis in the party system and the formation of governments, it was both because the proportional representation system allowed it to translate its vote into seats, and because the left and right were closely balanced in Parliament. Where, as in the Netherlands in the 1960s and 1970s, the emergence of new parties is part of a general crisis of the party system, their effect is indeed destabilizing, but their appearance is a symptom of a deeper crisis (Daalder and Mair 1983; Wolinetz 1988).

New Parties in Canada
The appearance of new parties in Canada is connected with periods of crisis and with regional discontent to a greater degree than is true for the emergence of new parties in Europe (Brodie and Jenson 1988; Gagnon 1989). The first new party to elect members to Parliament, the

Progressives, reflected both the political and economic crisis of the First World War and its aftermath and the discontent of agricultural interests, mainly in the West. The Depression of the 1930s saw the appearance at the federal level of two new parties, again from the West: Social Credit and the CCF. Social changes in Quebec saw the emergence of the Créditistes in the 1962 election, and the current double crisis of regional discontent and political alienation has given rise to several new parties, of which the most potentially important are the Reform Party and the Bloc québécois. In each case, part of the appeal of the new parties rested on the perceived failures of the established parties, not just to accommodate regional interests, but also to provide sound government. For example, the divisive tactics of Borden's Union government and the failure of the Conservative party under Diefenbaker to provide an acceptable alternative to the Liberals played a role in the success of the new challengers.

The reasons for the emergence of new parties in Canada suggest that in spite of the weakness of partisan identification in the Canadian electorate, it takes a major crisis for a new party to emerge and attract votes. (The main exception to this is the Social Credit party of British Columbia, whose emergence and success rest more on electoral calculation than crisis.) Advocates of new issues that are not being adopted by any of the established parties but that are not geographically concentrated and not connected with a sense of crisis rarely find that forming a new party at the national level is the most effective way of promoting their concerns.

Unlike the new parties of Europe, Canadian new parties tend to combine ideological stands with regional protest. The Progressive Party attacked the political practices of the established parties, the neglect of agricultural interests, and, by extension, the neglect of the West. The CCF, born in the Depression, attacked the capitalist system, but it also located the headquarters of that system in central Canada. The Créditistes of Quebec were both the party of the Quebec petite bourgeoisie being squeezed by the social and economic changes of the Quiet Revolution and a Quebec party (Lipset 1950; Morton 1950; Young 1969; Pinard 1971; Stein 1973).

New parties that have attempted to expand beyond a regional basis have failed in the task. Although the Progressives elected 24 of their 65 members of Parliament from Ontario in 1921, when the party began to split, it was the Ontario wing that went first (Morton 1950). In the same way, although the Créditistes represented the Quebec wing of a movement that had started in Alberta, their relationships with the western branches of the party were never easy, and the party split in 1963 (Stein 1973).

Although the NDP, and before it, the CCF, saw themselves as national and even anti-regionalist parties, they have never been able to gain large numbers of seats outside western Canada. The Reform Party has rejected suggestions that it attempt to expand to Quebec, and the Bloc québécois is by definition a regional party.

There are several reasons for this regional basis and its persistence. First, given the diversity of the Canadian economy, regional interests often are economic interests, and given the differences in the relative prosperity of the regions and the locations of economic power, it is not hard to interpret these interests in ideological terms. This identification of regional and ideological appeal makes it doubly difficult for a new party to incorporate regions beyond its region of origin. It is also true, as Cairns and others have frequently pointed out, that the Canadian electoral system exaggerates the regional base of all Canadian political parties (Cairns 1968; Irvine 1979).

Party and Movement

Another characteristic that Canadian new parties share is that they were all born out of movements, although this might be debated in the case of the Bloc québécois, whose intraparliamentary origin is unique among Canadian new parties. Often, there is considerable debate within the movement about the wisdom of pursuing its goals through the formation of a political party. The farmers' groups that formed the Progressive Party had links with the Non-Partisan League, and were suspicious both of the utility of substituting action through a party for interest group activities and of party politics in general (Morton 1950). In the same way, the groups that founded the CCF had a long history of interest group activity and only came together to form a political party under the radicalizing conditions of the Depression (Lipset 1950). Both the Progressive Party and the CCF were founded in the hope that they would be unlike the established parties in both doctrine and practice. The Reform Party bases part of its appeal on promises to be unlike the established parties and politicians, and the Bloc québécois avoids taking stands on policy aside from its goal of a new status for Quebec and promises to disband once this goal is achieved.

This rejection of politics-as-usual is an important characteristic of Canadian new parties and is probably one they could not easily shed without losing their appeal to party activists and to voters. However, it has also complicated their considerations of political strategy. The Progressives' rejection both of a coalition government with the Liberals and of the role of Official Opposition led to divisions between those committed to the movement aspect of the party and those who favoured government participation. The CCF and the New Democrats have consistently been divided between those who emphasized the party's education role as the proponent of a consistent left ideology and those who advocated downplaying the role and content of the ideology in the interests of securing government office. Whether the Reform Party and the Bloc québécois will be able to withstand the strains imposed by this type of strategic debate remains to be seen.

Successes and Failures of New Parties

Canadian new parties have often been successful in electing significant numbers of members of Parliament, often enough to force the established parties into minority governments as the Progressives did in 1921 and the Créditistes did in 1962. However, with the exception of the CCF, now the NDP, these parties have not persisted at the federal level. The regional basis of the new parties and the operation of the Canadian electoral system made expansion at the national level difficult, and the existence of a provincial level of government offered an alternative power base that was smaller and easier to capture, and that corresponded to the regional nature of the new parties, many of whose goals were in the provincial sphere of power. Finally, the consistent preference shown by established parties for minority governments rather than coalitions deprived these parties of the leverage they might have enjoyed in many European systems.

Evaluation of the new parties' success in influencing policy must be mixed. In some cases their policy proposals, once their electoral attractiveness was proven, have been adopted by the major parties. The Progressives, for example, had both policies and personnel taken over by the Liberal party, while the construction of the Canadian welfare state in the 1950s borrowed extensively from the platforms of the CCF. But this very success in influencing policy is generally considered to have cost the new parties votes, as the electorate saw that it could gain the same goals by voting for an established party with a chance of forming a government.

Canadian new parties have been significantly more successful at the provincial level, where they have frequently formed governments. The United Farmers of Ontario, Alberta, and Manitoba led the way in 1919, 1921 and 1922 respectively, and although the Ontario government was short-lived, the United Farmers of Alberta stayed in power until 1935, when they were replaced by another new party, Social Credit. The Union nationale came to power in Quebec in 1936, and the CCF formed a government in Saskatchewan in 1944. As the NDP, the party subsequently formed governments in British Columbia, Manitoba and

Ontario. The Parti québécois is the most recent of the new parties to have formed a government. It is only in the Maritime provinces that new parties have not been able to form provincial governments. However, the new parties have not yet been able to translate success at the provincial level into electoral success at the national level.

It is possible that we are entering another period of party effervescence. The Reform Party and the Bloc québécois have been formed to run candidates in the next federal election, and parties such as the Christian Heritage Party have entered politics at both the provincial and federal levels, and in a small number of cases have gained enough votes to affect the result, usually by causing the defeat of the candidate closest to them in ideological terms. So far, parties based on "new-politics issues" have not had a great deal of success. Obviously, the characteristics of our system that work against new parties in general work against new-politics parties in particular. It is more likely that the members, for example, of ecological and feminist movements, have found other means of pursuing their goals, such as court action, which, however unsatisfactory, still offers more satisfactory results than the formation of a political party.

Regulation of New Parties

Most political systems regulate the entry of new parties into the political system and attempt to minimize their electoral impact. However, new parties serve other purposes beyond their ability to elect members to the legislature. Even the emergence of an antidemocratic party like the National Front in France serves as a warning signal to the political system. As this study, and other studies for the Commission have suggested, new parties expand the range of political discourse, and, given the interest of established parties in limiting the range of discourse to issues they are familiar with, new parties provide a useful corrective. The ability of a political system to at least give voice to a wide range of alternative points of view is not only useful in that it builds loyalty to the system and its processes, but also in that it is part of the process of liberal democracy.

It is possible to argue that Canada does not have enough new or minor parties. In particular, the absence of parties other than the regional/ideological parties that have dominated the minor party landscape can be considered to have deprived the system of variety in its political discourse. Some of the reasons for the lack of parties espousing a variety of nongeographical concerns are positive: the existence of a sympathetic legal system reinforced by the *Canadian Charter of Rights and Freedoms* and by media access. Some of the reasons, such as the single-member plurality electoral system, are beyond the scope of this Royal Commission. However, changes in the rules of party financing and a further opening of access to the media might well make it easier for these parties to establish themselves and put forth their points of view.

FORMS OF GOVERNMENT

Single-Party Majority
Single-party majority government is probably the least common form of government in liberal democracies. Parliamentary systems with two parties or with two and one-half parties such as Britain and Canada, enjoy it from time to time, as do multi-party systems with a dominant party, such as the Scandinavian party systems. In the American system, although one party will have a numerical majority in Congress, most legislation is passed by ad hoc majorities drawing on both parties.

The advantages of single-party majority government have attracted much praise. It is generally considered to be more stable than minority or coalition governments and to allow for a clearer attribution of political responsibility. However, there are examples of systems that have chosen to avoid single-party majorities or movement toward such a system. The French Socialists could have ruled alone in 1981 as the Gaullists could have in 1968, but the Socialists chose to form a coalition with the French Communist party, while the Gaullists chose to continue their coalition with the moderate conservatives. Several times in Germany, when it appeared that the Free Democratic Party would fall below the 5 percent threshold for representation in the Bundestag, the Christian Democratic leaders urged their voters to use their list vote to keep it above this level (Blondel and Müller-Rommel 1988; Bogdanor 1983; Herman and Pope 1973; Machin 1989).

There are several reasons why the leaders of a system might refuse the possibility of single-party majority rule. One is that in these systems a single-party majority election result is an exception, more in the nature of an accident than of something that can be expected to repeat itself. Therefore, it is wise not to alienate a past and probable future coalition partner. Also, unlike single-party government, coalition government does share the responsibility, and this might be found to be desirable in times of economic crisis or when a party intends to undertake controversial measures as, for example, the French Socialists did in 1981.

In systems that are used to coalitions, one-party government can appear unnatural and dictatorial. In divided systems, parties might prefer to preserve a centre party whose existence prevents the emergence of a single-party majority but moderates changes in regime, as does the Free Democratic Party in Germany. (A historical example is the introduction of proportional representation by the governing Catholic party in Belgium in 1899. The introduction of manhood suffrage combined with the plurality system threatened to obliterate the Liberal party, and the Catholics preferred a three-cornered system to one in which they directly confronted the Socialists, even though they could expect to win a majority most of the time.)

Minority Governments

Minority governments occur in both two-party and multi-party systems, and in both single-party and coalition forms. Minority government often occurs in two-party systems when third parties gain enough votes to prevent either of the two major parties from forming a majority government. In systems of the British type, minority governments are usually considered preferable to coalitions. Minority governments are not uncommon in multi-party systems, but in a sense require more explaining, since a realistic option of a majority coalition government exists in these systems.

The example of the 1973 Agrarian Liberal government in Denmark, which had 22 of 179 seats in the legislature, is an extreme example of minority governments in multi-party systems, but it illustrates some of the reasons why a minority government might be preferred to a majority coalition. First, the parties of the potential majority government may prefer not to accept that responsibility. In 1973 in Denmark, parties to both the left and right of the Liberals had suffered such electoral losses that they were prey to lack of confidence and internal disputes, and they did not want to subject themselves to the strain of governing. Second, while there might be a mathematically possible majority alternative, this alternative might not be politically possible, especially if some parties are excluded on principle from consideration as potential coalition partners. This was the case in Denmark in 1973, where the anti-tax Progress Party was not recognized by the other parties on the right as an acceptable coalition partner, a refusal that reduced the right's share of parliamentary seats by nearly 16 percent of the total (Pedersen 1987).

Minority governments function under the sufferance of the other parties and under a peculiar set of circumstances that dilutes some of the rules of political responsibility. More consultation, and therefore a diminution of single-party responsibility, usually occurs. This consultation may be general and informal, or it may be the result of a formal agreement, for example, the pact between the Labour government and the Liberal party in Britain in 1974 or the agreement between the Liberals and the

NDP in Ontario after the 1985 election. The junior partner in these agreements hopes to achieve some of its policy goals, and it may hope that this sign of effectiveness will attract votes in a subsequent election. The strategy usually has its critics in such a party, who argue that the responsibility it accepts is not commensurate with the influence it achieves. A minority government will usually accept defeat on some issues without feeling obliged to resign. Both the Liberal government and subsequent conservative minority governments in Denmark have accepted defeat on foreign policy issues by an alternative left majority that manifests itself on those issues.

Majority Coalitions

The majority coalition is probably the most common form of government in liberal democracies. There are several types of such a coalition. The first is the grand coalition, that is, a coalition, usually of the two or more largest parties, that is far larger than the simple majority needed for government. Examples of the grand coalition include that between the Social Democrats and Christian Democratic Party in Germany between 1966 and 1969, and that between the People's Party and the Socialist Party in Austria (Chandler 1988; Engelmann 1988). Switzerland also has a type of grand coalition in that the four largest parties divide the seats on the Federal Council among themselves. Unlike the grand coalitions in Germany and Austria, which have alternated with more normal coalitions, the grand coalition in Switzerland has become a permanent part of national political life (Kerr 1987).

Grand coalitions have been formed during national emergencies such as war, even in two-party systems like Britain and Canada. Other reasons for a grand coalition may lie, ironically, in a history of bitter partisan dispute between the two potential partners, as was the case in Austria. They may also signal the acceptance of one of the partners as a respectable government party, as did the grand coalition in Germany. A desire to minimize the risks of elections, with their all or nothing results for government participation, can be another motivation. The grand coalition partners of Austria were accused of being motivated by a desire to monopolize government patronage, while the grand coalition of Germany was accused of monopolizing the policy formation process and, in the absence of effective opposition within Parliament, gave rise to an often violent extraparliamentary opposition.

This elimination of formal opposition is one of the disadvantages of the grand coalition. If we accent the importance of parties in forming the basis for a stable and effective government, we should not forget their role in articulating the inevitable opposition to the policies of that government and of representing the very principle of the possibility of opposition and alternation. Also, grand coalitions devalue the electoral process and decrease citizen interest, possibly increasing citizen disaffection. The low participation rate of the Swiss electorate in federal elections, 46.5 percent in the last election, is partly explained by the greater importance of the cantonal level of government and the existence of the referendum process; but it is also the result of the fact that the parties to the coalition that will emerge from the election are known in advance, as is the number of seats on the federal council that each party will receive (Papadopoulos 1988).

There are two patterns of normal majority coalition. One is that found in systems with a centre party that allies now to the right and now to the left to form governments. This essential partner may be relatively small, as is the Free Democratic Party in Germany, or it may be a large, dominant party such as the Christian Democrats in Italy or the Social Christians in Belgium. Usually this centre party does very well out of its almost permanent government status and its ability to determine the makeup of the governing coalition (Chandler 1988; Amyot 1988). The other pattern is that of the alternating coalition, usually made up of parties close to each other in the ideological scale of left to right. This pattern can be found in countries like France and in the Scandinavian countries.

In systems where coalition governments are the rule, elections are simply the first step in the process of choosing a government. They register the balance of forces both in terms of total number of seats and gains and losses of seats among the potential members of the future government. The actual formation of the government is the result of negotiations among the parties. This in itself can lead to some voter dissatisfaction, and there is pressure on parties in many systems to declare in advance their coalition preferences.

Coalition formation follows a certain set of rules, with some variation from country to country. Formal studies of coalition formation emphasize two principles that may work in conjunction with each other. The first is the principle of the minimum winning coalition. This principle argues that the most likely coalition is that which groups the minimum number of parties needed to form a majority in the legislature, on the argument that this maximizes the returns to each party. An alternate principle is that of ideological propinquity, which argues that coalitions will group parties that are next to each other on an ideological scale, even if this means that the total coalition will exceed the minimum number of seats necessary to form a majority in the legislature.

While these principles may be a beginning to understanding the process of coalition formation, they are not constraining, and the rules of coalition formation in a given system will include other considerations. Very often there are parties that are excluded a priori from consideration as coalition partners. These include the Communist Party of France for most of the Fourth Republic and the Communist Party of Italy to this day. Neofascist parties in Italy and the National Front in France have also been excluded from coalition consideration. In addition, there are often parties that will refuse to serve together in a coalition, either because of ideological disputes or because of personal enmities among party leaders. In the 1988 government formation process in Belgium, the Socialists refused to join any government that included the Liberal parties.

Other considerations that influence the coalition formation process include the relative size of the available parties. Usually size is an advantage to a party, since this gives the coalition an anchor. Gains and losses in the past election are a contributing factor, since a party that has scored impressive gains has a claim to be included in consideration; but a party that has suffered losses loses a certain amount of its claim to govern, and if it has been in government may prefer to take a *cure d'opposition* (like most cures, intended to be a temporary measure rather than a permanent change of diet). However, dominant centre parties will usually wind up in government whatever their electoral trend. Both Italian and Belgian Christian Democratic parties have been losing votes steadily since the late 1960s, but have remained in government, usually furnishing the prime minister, throughout the period.

The government formation process usually gives an important role to the head of state, whether monarch or president. (Exceptions are Germany, where historical precedent has led to a diminution of the role of president, and Sweden, where the constitution gives the role of presiding over the negotiations to the Speaker of the House rather than to the monarch.) It is normally the head of state who chooses the person to negotiate the formation of the new government, usually a leader of the largest or the winning party in the recent elections. This choice is normally made after consultation with a range of party and nonparty élites. If the first negotiator reports failure, the head of state, again after consultation, decides whether to urge the person to try again or to accept the report and choose another negotiator, from the same party or from another party. After a coalition formula is found, the parties must then negotiate a program and agree on the division of ministerial posts. Often the coalition and program must be approved by extra-parliamentary bodies of the parties involved.

This process – the exploration of alternative formulas, the negotiation of a program, the disposition of ministerial posts, and the approval by extraparliamentary party – is the common European pattern. It is a process that can take a long time, occasionally over 100 days. In most countries, therefore, the outgoing coalition remains in office to handle routine business until it can be replaced by a new government.

The stability of coalition governments depends on two characteristics of the party system. The first is the internal unity of the parties concerned, since revolts within a coalition partner can lead to the collapse of the coalition, as is frequently the case in Italy (Amyot 1988). The second characteristic that affects the stability of coalition governments is the degree of fragmentation of the system, both in the sense of the number of parties that must be included to secure a workable coalition, and the ideological distance between them. In systems like the Italian system, where fragmentation is great in both senses, coalition governments tend to be unstable. However, in systems like those of Germany and France, where coalitions usually involve only two parties of similar ideological leanings, coalitions tend to be quite stable (Sartori 1976).

The life of a coalition government is a continual bargaining process. Most coalitions begin with a basic agreement about the policies they will implement while in office, but these agreements cannot foresee all the policy decisions that will have to be made during the life of the coalition. The degree to which this bargaining process works to the benefit of the democratic resolution of problems depends on other characteristics of the system than the mere existence of the coalition form of government. In highly fragmented systems like Italy and the Fourth French Republic, the bargaining can turn into a game characterized by secret deals and lead to alienation of the population. However, in less fragmented systems, the bargaining leads to an open debate on policy issues that is generally considered to be healthy. New agreements are often submitted to the party organization for approval, thus involving it in policy decisions rather than relegating it to the role of electoral machine.

Canada and Coalitions

Canadians have historically been suspicious of coalitions, preferring minority governments when there is no single-party majority in Parliament. In part, this reflects a prejudice inherited from the Westminster style of parliamentary government which regards coalitions as a Continental practice to be viewed with the same suspicion as Continental cuisine: unnecessarily complicated and possibly even pernicious. The British version of parliamentary government emphasizes a clear distinction between government and opposition and the possibility of a clear attribution of responsibility for the actions of the government. These characteristics are not always easy to maintain under the conditions of coalition government. The examples of noncrisis coalition governments that have existed in the Westminster-type systems of Australia and Ireland are not widely known in Canada and certainly have not served as an inspiration to Canadian political parties.

Canadian suspicion of coalitions also reflects historical experience. There have been few coalition governments in Canadian history, and they have usually occurred under conditions of crisis for the political system and for the major parties. Often the crisis has been blamed on the coalition rather than the other way around.

After the mixed governments of the pre- and post-Confederation period, the first major Canadian experience with coalition government was the wartime coalition between the Conservatives and the Liberals formed in 1917. The formation of the coalition split the Liberal party when the Quebec Liberals under Laurier refused to support the conscription policy it was formed to implement, and the party had to undergo an arduous process of rebuilding. The same conscription policy also cost the Conservatives their base in Quebec, and it was nearly 70 years before the party was to enjoy anything but outsider status in that province.

The period of party instability in the West that followed the First World War also saw the formation of several coalition governments in western provinces: in Manitoba, a Liberal–Progressive coalition was formed in 1932 that lasted until 1936, and an all-party government formed in 1940 survived as a Liberal–Conservative coalition until 1950. In Saskatchewan, the Conservative party joined with the Progressives and some independent members to oust the Liberal party in 1929, only to encounter the Depression and electoral annihilation in 1934 (Gibbins 1980).

The most recent coalition at the provincial level was the 1941–52 coalition between the Liberals and the Conservatives in British Columbia. Originally formed when a wartime election revealed a nearly perfect three-way split of the electorate among the Liberals, Conservatives and the CCF, the coalition persisted after the war as a line of defence against that party. The coalition had been tolerated during the war by the national Conservatives and Liberals, but after the war pressures on the provincial parties to end the coalition increased. The coalition was also vulnerable to the argument that the best way to maintain the line against the CCF was to form a single antisocialist party.

With the 1952 election approaching, and faced with the split of the coalition, the two parties introduced the single transferable vote, hoping that each party would be the second choice of the other's voters. At the same time, however, a Conservative backbencher and unsuccessful candidate for the Conservative leadership, W.A.C. Bennett, took over the small British Columbia branch of the Social Credit party. Under Bennett, Social Credit won enough seats to form a minority government in 1952 and a majority government in 1953, abolishing the single transferable vote shortly thereafter. The Liberals and Conservatives never recovered (Cairns and Wong 1985).

At the provincial level, then, coalitions are associated with crisis situations either in the form of war, and/or in the form of political fragmentation. They have often resulted in electoral disaster for at least one of their participants, although the degree to which this disaster can be attributed to the coalition rather than to the crisis that gave rise to it is debatable.

There are also the "coalitions that never were." In 1921 the Progressives rejected the idea of participating in a coalition, only to be picked off one by one by the Liberals. In part, this reflected their antiparty orientation, since they also rejected the role of official Opposition to which they were entitled by the fact that they were the second-largest party in the House (Morton 1950). The CCF, also with the same suspicion of the processes of party politics, rejected the idea of coalitions during the 1930s, although it allowed its Saskatchewan wing to pursue the idea of an anti-Liberal coalition with the Conservative and Social Credit parties of the province (Gibbins 1980). There are indications that after the 1980 Liberal loss of representation in the West, the Liberal party offered the NDP a coalition arrangement that was refused.

In general, then, Canadian parties have preferred minority governments to coalition arrangements, even when faced with multi-party legislatures. However, it is possible that the next federal election may return a highly fragmented legislature, and I have decided to close this study with some scenarios for a five-party parliament as a speculative and "academic" exercise. Lessons from systems in which coalitions are a normal part of political life and in which single-party majority government is considered unnatural may well be useful to Canada in the future.

SCENARIOS FOR A FIVE-PARTY PARLIAMENT

The considerations involved in the process of forming a government coalition do not appear, at first, to be very familiar to Canadians. Politicians negotiating the formation of a coalition must consider the impact of the combination chosen on the policy output of the prospective government, on party fortunes, on the power of factions within parties, and on individual careers. However, as this list of considerations suggests, although the vocabulary of the coalition process is unfamiliar in Canadian politics, the considerations that lie at its base are not totally unlike those that guide cabinet formation in our system.

Before I begin this exercise, some caveats should be entered. First, speculation about the possibility of a five-party Parliament is based on current public opinion polls which, in some form or other, give the NDP an unprecedentedly high level of support, the Conservatives an unprecedentedly low level, and suggest that two new parties, the Reform Party and the Bloc québécois will gain significant numbers of seats in the West and in Quebec. Polls held at a large distance from an election are not always the best guide to the actual vote in a real election. The NDP, which has often seen impressive gains in polls dwindle to its usual +/− 18 percent of the vote in an actual election, can attest to this. However, it is possible that, between recession and national unity debates, by the next election we may be in the type of crisis situation that leads Canadians to vote for new parties.

It is also necessary to point out that it is almost impossible to predict the number of seats a party will gain in Parliament from the percentage of support it gains in a poll or in an election. Assuming that the five-party Parliament will include the Liberals, the Conservatives, the NDP, the Reform Party and the Bloc québécois, Canada will have at least two four-party regions. In a four-party region, a party that gets 26 percent of the vote could get all of the seats in the region or none of them, depending on how the remaining votes distribute themselves among the other parties.

For the purposes of this exercise, I have assumed that no party will have a majority in the hypothetical five-party Parliament or a minority large enough to form a plausible minority government. I have assumed that the Liberal party and the NDP have roughly the same number of seats, with NDP strength concentrated in the West and Ontario and Liberal strength concentrated in Ontario and points east. In this scenario, the Conservative party has considerably fewer seats than either the Liberals or the NDP, while the Bloc québécois and the Reform Party have varying numbers of seats according to the specific combinations discussed. I have also assumed that neither Ontario nor the Maritimes has developed a regionally specific party with a large number of seats in Parliament.

Finally, I have not discussed all the theoretically possible coalitions. In particular, I have neglected the five-party grand coalition and the four-party combinations. Although every coalition has its problems of cohesion, these combinations would have problems on such a scale that they would probably not be seriously contemplated.

Principles of Coalition Government

The literature on coalition formation identifies two major principles that guide the process. The first is the principle of the minimum winning coalition, which argues that a coalition will contain no more parties than is necessary to attain a simple majority in the legislature. The second is the principle of ideological propinquity, which argues that coalitions will be formed by parties that are close to each other in ideological terms, and that size is a less important consideration (Bogdanor 1983; Browne 1973). Neither of these principles is totally constraining. Coalitions larger than the minimum are quite common, and in a system dominated by nonideological parties, as the Canadian system is, ideological propinquity is a less compelling consideration than it is in systems dominated by ideologically based parties.

There are other considerations that guide parties' behaviour as they consider the possibility of participating in a coalition and the choice of potential partners. The decision to enter a coalition and the choice of partners also affect the internal power balance of a party. For example, the Christian Democratic parties of Europe usually have a right wing that prefers alliances with parties to the right, and a left wing that prefers alliances with Socialist or Social Democratic parties. The choice of partners will depend on the balance of power between these wings, but it will also affect it, since a coalition with, for example, a Socialist party, is likely to undertake policies that strengthen the groups supporting the left wing of the party. Coalition governments often fall, not because of quarrels among their members, but because of quarrels among different factions within one of their members.

Another consideration that parties weigh when considering the composition of a coalition is the distribution of government posts. The post of prime minister, of course, is always an issue, unless one party is clearly dominant, and even here, if this party has monopolized the post it can be subject to claims from the other parties on those grounds. Normally parties want a mixture of prestige posts and posts that allow them to cater to the groups that support them. The German Free Democrats, for example, usually insist on both the Foreign Ministry and the Ministry of Agriculture.

Current policies and posts are important, but so is the next election. A party entering a coalition knows that it will gain some of its policy objectives but will have to compromise on others, a process that can be alienating to party activists and voters. This consideration argues in favour of ideological or policy propinquity, but it also argues in favour of entering a coalition in which the party enjoys a favourable power position, whether through size or centrality. Parties in a coalition are both partners and enemies. Votes may be lost to the parties that form the opposition to the coalition, but, especially if the members of the coalition are close ideologically, they may also be lost to other coalition members. This means that a party looking at possible coalition partners must weigh the costs of compromise against the advantages of having at least some partners who are not attractive to its electorate.

Finally, the choice of a particular coalition also reflects the circumstances at the time of its creation. Periods of crisis favour larger than normal coalitions, periods where economic policy is most important often favour conservative coalitions, while periods where social policy questions dominate favour more left-leaning coalitions. In the case of the five-party Parliament on which I have based my speculations, the period is likely to be perceived as a crisis period, but one that combines, in classic Canadian fashion, economic and regional issues.

Traditional-Party Coalitions

Grand Coalition of the Three Major Parties

Reasons for: The victories of the Reform Party and Bloc québécois are seen as a crisis of the Canadian political system. The three traditional parties agree that this is not the time for partisan quarrels and form a grand coalition to meet the crisis. The NDP has enough seats in the West, and the Liberals and Conservatives have enough seats in Quebec to give the coalition regional plausibility. Each party gains something from the coalition. The Liberals return to power and have a claim to the Prime Ministership based on relative size and previous experience of governing. The NDP achieves national office for the first time, and has, if not a claim to the prime ministership, at least a claim to important ministries. The Conservatives gain a chance to rebuild from a base of some control of government policy and patronage rather than attempting to rebuild from the Opposition.

Reasons against: The coalition might be perceived as an attempt to deprive the two outside parties of the influence on policy that they have earned from their election victories, particularly if these are large (for example, if either party is the first party in its region). Suspicion of the NDP on the part of the two other traditional parties might also prevent the formation of this coalition. It is part of the dynamics of the Westminster system to return to a two-party equilibrium, which means that should the NDP be the largest or second-largest party in Parliament, it would threaten to displace either the Liberals or the Conservatives. At the provincial level, where the NDP has displaced one of the two major parties, it has not consistently been the Liberals who have disappeared; so the Conservatives, especially if they had suffered very heavy losses, might also fear this fate.

Another problem would be the development of policy. It would not be sufficient for the coalition simply to block the two outside parties. Ordinary policy would be difficult enough to achieve because the coalition, containing both the NDP and a Conservative party that is more to the right than Canadian Conservative parties usually are, would be ideologically lumpy. The coalition would also have to formulate policy on the issues of western and Quebec alienation that had produced the election results in the first place. These issues are internally stressful for all three parties now, and would be more so with the two parties outside the coalition standing ready to accuse their regional colleagues in the coalition of a sell-out. Attempts at resolution might split the coalition or the individual parties in the coalition.

A grand coalition might be short-lived and might well be formed only to hold the ring until a new election could be called.

Liberal-Conservative Coalition

Reasons for: The Liberals and Conservatives might decide that they do not want to give the NDP its first participation in government, particularly if they are concerned about recovering their losses to that party as well as to the Reform Party and the Bloc québécois. A Liberal-Conservative combination would be less ideologically lumpy than the grand coalition, and compromises might be easier since neither party would have to deliver results from a first time in office. If the two parties maintained adequate representation from the West and Quebec, the coalition could plausibly claim to be able to tackle the problems of those regions.

Reasons against: Depending on the number of seats each party gained, this combination might have a slim majority. The question of which party would furnish the prime minister and the distribution of major portfolios would be difficult decisions, given the number of people with previous ministerial experience in both parties. The coalition would be attacked by the NDP and the two other excluded parties as a "stand-pat" combination and as one that contradicts the results of the election. Finding accommodation on regional conflict, particularly the status of Quebec, would be internally stressful for both parties, and particularly stressful for this particular coalition since each party would presumably be attempting to re-establish a Quebec base. Personal relationships between Brian Mulroney and Jean Chrétien, assuming that each is still leader of his party, are not likely to be smooth.

NDP-Liberal Coalition

Reasons for: Like the previous combination, this coalition would be less ideologically diverse than a grand coalition. For the two parties involved, it would have the same advantages: a return to power for the Liberals and a first participation in government for the NDP. If the Conservatives had been badly defeated and were wracked by leadership struggles, a Liberal-NDP coalition would have the potential to be more stable than a Liberal-Conservative government. Like the previous coalition, however, it would have to be regionally plausible; that is, the NDP would have to have gained large numbers of seats in the West and the Liberals in Quebec.

Reasons against: The question of the identity of the senior partner in the coalition would be a continuing source of tension. The Liberals would claim the prime ministership and major portfolios on the grounds of their greater experience in office. The NDP's acquiescence in this would depend, in part, on the relative size of the two parties, but they could be expected to demand some high-profile ministries as well as ministries related to their important policy goals. The degree to which the Liberals would allow the NDP to be the policy motor of the coalition is open to question. Dealing with the problems of the West might also divide the coalition, while dealing with the question of greater autonomy for Quebec might be internally divisive for both parties.

NDP-Conservative Coalition

Reasons for: If the Liberals-versus-others dividing line is seen as more important than ideology, this coalition might not be totally implausible, especially if the Liberals fail to gain large numbers of seats in Quebec and the Conservatives hold on to a base there. Since the Conservatives and the NDP are not direct competitors in Quebec in the way that the Liberals and Conservatives are, this coalition might have a higher level of trust than the Liberal-Conservative coalition. If the Conservatives also hold on to Western seats, the coalition might have a firmer base in that region than the NDP-Liberal combination.

Reasons against: This coalition is more contrary to the rule of ideological propinquity than the other combinations. If the Conservatives lose seats in the Maritime region and the New Democrats do not make gains there, that region would be underrepresented in the coalition; while, if the Conservatives' main base is Quebec, having lost their western seats to the Reform Party, the Quebec issue would be an extremely divisive one for this combination. The Conservatives' desire to prevent losses to the Bloc québécois by moving in the direction of greater autonomy for Quebec would clash with the New Democrats' more pan-Canadian focus. As in the previous combination, the issue of junior/senior partner would arise unless the NDP contingent was significantly smaller than the Conservative contingent, since the Conservatives, even if they were the smaller partner, might still claim the prime ministership and important ministries on the grounds of experience.

Coalitions with the Challenger Parties

All of the coalitions described above have the disadvantage that they are more a line of defence against the two challenger parties than a direct answer to the questions that would be raised by their electoral success. Although the three established parties can be expected to argue that they are capable of representing the points of view of those who voted for the Reform Party and the Bloc québécois, it could also be argued that the emergence of those parties would best be dealt with by including them in a governing coalition. This would give direct representation to their positions and would place them under the discipline of government responsibility.

Reform Party Coalitions

Conservative-Reform Party Coalition

Reasons for: This coalition would satisfy the ideological propinquity rule. If the Conservatives hold on to a relatively large number of seats and the Reform Party gains a relatively small number, this combination might appear to the Conservative party as a way of continuing to hold power without having to move away from a free-market stance, as it would have to do in combination with the Liberals or NDP, and also as a way of continuing to govern without excessive sharing of power. If the Conservatives also held on to a Quebec base, the combination would be regionally representative.

Reasons against: Although technically the Reform Party and the Conservative party are next to each other on a right-left scale, this also means that they attempt to attract the same voters, and the Reform Party has been a severe critic of the Conservative party. Suspicions of double-dealing would be high in this coalition. In addition, if the Conservatives held on to a Quebec base, regional tensions in the coalition and within the Conservative party would be high, since many of the policies advocated by the Reform Party are not acceptable to Quebec. Western Conservatives could be expected to argue that it was precisely the attractiveness of Reform policies in the West that caused their party to lose seats there and that failure to adopt them would put their own seats in danger. If the Conservatives did not hold on to a Quebec base, the coalition would not be regionally representative.

Liberal-Reform Party Coalition

Reasons for: The Liberals return to power and might see the promotion of the Reform Party as a way of finishing off a Conservative party badly damaged by the election results. As in the previous coalition, the Reform Party gets the benefits of direct influence on government policy and the use of government patronage to further its party-building effort. If it is the Liberals who do well in Quebec, this combination would also be regionally representative.

Reasons against: This combination would run into ideological problems, and the comments on regional tensions in a Conservative-Reform combination also apply to this coalition. In addition, if the Liberals under Chrétien return to a pan-Canadian policy with an emphasis on issues like nationwide bilingualism, the coalition would come under strain. It is also questionable whether the Liberals would welcome the replacement of the Conservatives by the Reform Party as the major conservative party in the system. A coalition that reflected the ideological agenda of the Reform Party might well lead to defections from the Liberals to the NDP, and debates over policy toward Quebec might either strengthen the Bloc québécois or lead to a revival of the Conservatives in Quebec.

NDP-Reform Party Coalition

Reasons for: Desperation on the part of each party to gain the advantages of government participation.

Reasons against: This coalition suffers from an extreme lack of ideological propinquity on economic and social issues. Since it is numerically possible only if one of the two parties expands beyond its western base, it could not be based on "the revenge of the West." The coalition is also unlikely to have significant strength in Quebec. Tension over the distribution of government posts would be high because neither party can claim governing experience at the national level, and because the parties would probably be close in terms of the number of seats in Parliament.

Combinations with the Bloc Québécois

While it might seem unlikely that a party whose avowed goal is greater autonomy for its region – if not outright independence – would support or participate in the central government of the nation it wants autonomy from, there are precedents. The Irish Home Rule party supported the social legislation of the British Liberal government elected in 1910 in return for the promise of a Home Rule bill. (Such a bill was to be presented in Parliament in the fall of 1914.) All three Belgian regional parties have participated in governments formed to increase regional autonomy. Paradoxically, the Bloc québécois might in some respects be a more comfortable coalition partner than the Reform Party because it would be composed of more experienced politicians, and because it does not have a distinct ideological agenda. Indeed, since it would presumably be participating in the government in return for the gain of a large degree of autonomy for Quebec, the ideological path to be followed by the rest of Canada might well be a matter of indifference to it. The main obstacle to combinations with the Bloc québécois would be the reluctance of other parties to begin the process of granting greater autonomy to Quebec that the Bloc would demand as the price of its support.

Conservative-Bloc Québécois Coalition

Reasons for: Since many members of the Bloc québécois are former Conservatives, ideological propinquity is satisfied. The Conservatives retain power and hope to negotiate a settlement for Quebec that is a midpoint between Meech Lake and the demands of the Bloc québécois. (They also hope that this settlement will diminish the appeal of the Bloc in a subsequent election.) The Bloc québécois hopes to gain a large measure of autonomy for Quebec (and expects that the next national election in the province will be irrelevant).

Reasons against: The level of distrust in this coalition is likely to be high. Like the Reform Party, the Bloc québécois is a direct competitor of the Conservatives in its region. The credibility of this combination would depend on the Conservatives' ability to hold on to seats outside Quebec, particularly in the West. This in itself would make it difficult for the coalition to grant Quebec a larger measure of autonomy. Moreover, the Conservative party might suffer in subsequent elections because it would be accused by the other three parties of selling Canada out to stay in power.

Liberal-Bloc Québécois Coalition

Reasons for: The Liberal party gains government office while the Bloc québécois gains action on its agenda for Quebec.

Reasons against: This combination suffers from a severe lack of ideological propinquity on the Quebec issue and would be troubled by the same lack of trust as the Conservative-Bloc québécois coalition. Unless the Liberal party had been able to gain large numbers of seats in the West, the combination would be regionally unrepresentative.

NDP-Bloc Québécois Coalition

Reasons for: Both parties gain government office. The Bloc québécois would supply the representation from Quebec that the NDP would probably still lack, and it would support NDP social policy in return for more autonomy for Quebec. This is the closest parallel to the Irish Home Rule-Liberal alliance of 1910.

Reasons against: This combination depends on real NDP gains in Ontario for numerical plausibility. Moreover, it is unlikely that the NDP would want its first participation in government, and probably its first prime minister, to be responsible for actions that the other parties would be sure to attack as the destruction of Canada. The NDP itself has always been a pan-Canadian party. The Meech Lake agreement was already looked on with suspicion by many in the party, and any agreement with the Bloc québécois that went further than that in return for an accession to power would be internally divisive, particularly since the NDP has important factions that reject the policy of government participation at the cost of a dilution of party principles.

Reform Party-Bloc Québécois Coalition: An Unholy Alliance

Reasons for: As in the NDP combination, the Bloc québécois supports the social and economic policy agenda of the Reform Party in return for more autonomy for Quebec. At an ideological level, this might be a more plausible combination than the NDP alliance since the agenda of the Reform Party is probably more acceptable to the Bloc québécois than that of the NDP. The Reform Party might welcome a fundamental revision of the organization of the country that diminished the weight of central Canada.

Reasons against: This combination is numerically difficult to achieve. The Bloc québécois would have to win almost all the seats in Quebec, and the Reform Party would have to combine domination of the West with significant gains in Ontario for the coalition to be mathematically possible (see table 2.6). The coalition would probably be marked by a high degree of distrust and would be particularly likely to break down over the discussion of the economic and financial aspects of separation, that is, if it were not blocked at the beginning by disagreement over the prime ministership, since it is unlikely that either Lucien Bouchard or Preston Manning would cede amicably to the claims of the other.

Table 2.6
Election results by province, 1988

Province	PC	Liberal	NDP	Total seats in province
Newfoundland	2	5	0	7
Prince Edward Island	0	4	0	4
Nova Scotia	5	6	0	11
New Brunswick	5	5	0	10
Quebec	63	12	0	75
Ontario	46	43	10	99
Manitoba	7	5	2	14
Saskatchewan	4	0	10	14
Alberta	25	0	1	26
British Columbia	12	1	19	32
Yukon	0	0	1	1
Northwest Territories	0	2	0	2

Source: Frizzell et al. (1989).

Note: Total seats, 295; needed for majority, 148.

CONCLUSIONS

While a move to the practice of coalition government, particularly under the crisis conditions assumed in this exercise, would complicate the process of government in Canada, it would also have advantages. It could even be argued that under a severe crisis of regionalism, giving governmental representation to a broader range of interests than is normally the case with a single-party majority government would be a desirable beginning to coping with the crisis. Open disagreement may give the appearance of greater conflict than disagreement in party caucus, but it also leads to a fuller discussion of the issues and a clearer picture of the situation than disagreements smothered by the fiction of party unity. While Canadians have little experience of formal coalition government, Canadian parties are themselves coalitions, so the practices of coalition bargaining are not totally outside our experience.

Finally, the open bargaining that can characterize coalition government gives an opening to resolve a problem that I have mentioned throughout this study: that of giving the population of the country continuing influence on the policy process beyond the registering of approval or disapproval at election times. People could know that there were differences of opinion, what they were, and who in the government was espousing the opinion they agreed with. The possession of this type of information is essential to the exercise of influence. It is difficult (but not impossible) to legislate coalition government. Fortunately or unfortunately, our future may provide us with the opportunity to practise it.

NOTES

1. The literature on parties in liberal democracies is voluminous and, to a certain degree, repetitive. For some general overviews, see von Beyme (1985); Daalder and Mair (1983); Dalton (1988); Mair (1990).

2. For studies of changes in the role of parties, see Berger (1979); Dalton et al. (1984); Deschouwer (1989); King (1969); Lawson and Merkl (1988); Mair (1989); Maisel (1976); van Mierlo (1986).

BIBLIOGRAPHY

Amyot, G. 1988. "Italy: The Long Twilight of the DC Regime." In *Parties and Party Systems in Liberal Democracies*, ed. S.B. Wolinetz. London: Routledge.

Aucoin, P., ed. 1985. *Party Government and Regional Representation in Canada.* Vol. 36 of the research studies of the Royal Commission on the Economic Union and Development Prospects for Canada. Toronto: University of Toronto Press.

Bakvis, H. 1988. "The Canadian Paradox: Party System Stability in the Face of a Weakly Aligned Electorate." In *Parties and Party Systems in Liberal Democracies*, ed. S.B. Wolinetz. London: Routledge.

Bartolini, S. 1984. "Institutional Constraints and Party Competition in the French Party System." *West European Politics* 7 (4): 103–27.

Berger, S. 1979. "Politics and Anti-Politics in Western Europe in the Seventies." *Daedalus* 108:27–50.

Bille, L. 1989. "Denmark: The Oscillating Party System." *West European Politics* 12 (4): 42–58.

Blais, A. 1973. "Third Parties in Canadian Provincial Politics." *Canadian Journal of Political Science* 6:422–38.

Blondel, J., and F. Müller-Rommel, eds. 1988. *Cabinets in Western Europe.* London: Macmillan.

Bogdanor, V. 1983. *Coalition Government in Western Europe.* London: Heinemann.

Breckenridge, G. 1988. "Continuity and Change in Britain." In *Parties and Party Systems in Liberal Democracies,* ed. S.B. Wolinetz. London: Routledge.

Brodie, J., and J. Jenson. 1988. *Crisis, Challenge and Change: Party and Class Revisited.* Ottawa: Carleton University Press.

———. 1989. "Piercing the Smokescreen: Brokerage Parties and Class Politics." In *Canadian Parties in Transition: Discourse, Organization, and Representation,* ed. A.G. Gagnon and A.B. Tanguay. Scarborough: Nelson Canada.

Browne, E.C. 1973. *Coalition Theories: A Logical and Empirical Critique.* Beverly Hills: Sage Publications.

Budge, I., I. Crewe and D. Fairlie, eds. 1976. *Party Identification and Beyond: Representations of Voting and Party Competition.* New York: John Wiley.

Burnham, W. 1982. *The Current Crisis in American Politics.* Oxford: Oxford University Press.

Butler, D., and D. Stokes. 1974. *Political Change in Britain.* 2d ed. New York: St. Martin's.

Cairns, A. 1968. "The Electoral System and the Party System in Canada, 1921–65." *Canadian Journal of Political Science* 1:55–80.

Cairns, A., and D. Wong. 1985. "Socialism, Federalism, and the B.C. Party Systems, 1933–1983." In *Party Politics in Canada.* 5th ed., ed. H.G. Thorburn. Scarborough: Prentice-Hall.

Castles, F.G., ed. 1982. *The Impact of Parties: Politics and Policies in Democratic Capitalist States.* Beverly Hills: Sage Publications.

Chandler, W.M. 1988. "Party System Transformations in the Federal Republic of Germany." In *Parties and Party Systems in Liberal Democracies,* ed. S.B. Wolinetz. London: Routledge.

Clarke, H.J., J. Jenson, L. Leduc and J. Pammett. 1984. *Absent Mandate: The Politics of Discontent in Canada.* Toronto: Gage.

Covell, M. 1981. "Ethnic Conflict and Elite Bargaining: The Case of Belgium." *West European Politics* 4 (3): 197–218.

———. 1988. "Stability and Change in the Belgian Party System." In *Parties and Party Systems in Liberal Democracies,* ed. S.B. Wolinetz. London: Routledge.

Daalder, H. 1966. "The Netherlands: Opposition in a Segmented Society." In *Political Oppositions in Western Democracies,* ed. R. Dahl. New Haven: Yale University Press.

———, ed. 1987. *Party Systems in Denmark, Austria, Switzerland, the Netherlands, and Belgium.* London: Frances Pinter.

Daalder, H., and P. Mair, eds. 1983. *Western European Party Systems: Continuity and Change.* Beverly Hills: Sage Publications.

Dahl, R. 1966. *Political Oppositions in Western Democracies.* New Haven: Yale University Press.

Dalton, R. 1988. *Citizen Politics in Western Democracies: Public Opinion and Political Parties in the United States, Great Britain, West Germany, and France.* Chatham: Chatham House.

Dalton, R., S. Flanagan and J. Beck. 1984. *Electoral Change in Advanced Industrial Democracies.* Princeton: Princeton University Press.

Deschouwer, K. 1989. "Patterns of Participation and Competition in Belgium." *West European Politics* 12 (4): 28–41.

Dewachter, W. 1987. "Changes in a Particratie: The Belgian Party System from 1944 to 1986." In *Party Systems in Denmark, Austria, Switzerland, the Netherlands, and Belgium,* ed. H. Daalder. London: Frances Pinter.

Duverger, M. 1959. *Political Parties: Their Organization and Activity in the Modern State.* New York: Wiley.

Dyck, R. 1989. "Relations between Federal and Provincial Parties." In *Canadian Parties in Transition: Discourse, Organization, and Representation,* ed. A.G. Gagnon and A.B. Tanguay. Scarborough: Nelson Canada.

Elkins, D. 1991. "Parties as National Institutions: A Comparative Study." In *Representation, Integration and Political Parties in Canada,* ed. Herman Bakvis. Vol. 14 of the research studies of the Royal Commission on Electoral Reform and Party Financing. Ottawa and Toronto: RCERPF/Dundurn.

Engelmann, F.C. 1988. "The Austrian Party System: Continuity and Change." In *Parties and Party Systems in Liberal Democracies,* ed. S.B. Wolinetz. London: Routledge.

Fisher, S.L. 1980. "The 'Decline of Parties' Thesis and the Role of Minor Parties." In *Western European Party Systems*, ed. P. Merkl. New York: Free Press.

Frizzell, A., Jon Pammett and Anthony Westell. 1989. *The Canadian General Election of 1988*. Ottawa: Carleton University Press.

Gaffney, J. 1988. "French Socialism and the Fifth Republic." *West European Politics* 11 (3): 42–56.

Gagnon, A.G. 1989. "Minor Parties of Protest in Canada: Origins, Impact, and Prospects." In *Canadian Parties in Transition: Discourse, Organization and Representation*, ed. A.G. Gagnon and A.B. Tanguay. Scarborough: Nelson Canada.

Gagnon, A.G., and A.B. Tanguay. 1989. *Canadian Parties in Transition: Discourse, Organization, and Representation*. Scarborough: Nelson Canada.

Galipeau, C. 1989. "Political Parties, Interest Groups, and New Social Movements: Toward a New Representation?" In *Canadian Parties in Transition: Discourse, Organization and Representation*, ed. A.G. Gagnon and A.B. Tanguay. Scarborough: Nelson Canada.

Gibbins, R. 1980. *Prairie Politics and Society: Regionalism in Decline*. Toronto: Butterworths.

Guyomarch, A., and H. Machin. 1988. "François Mitterrand and the French Presidential and Parliamentary Elections of 1988: Mr. Norris Changes Trains?" *West European Politics* 11 (4): 196–210.

Herman, V., and J. Pope. 1973. "Minority Governments in Western Democracies." *British Journal of Political Science* 3:191–212.

Huysen, L. 1988. "Pillarisation Reconsidered." *Acta Politica* 19:145–58.

Inglehart, R. 1977. *The Silent Revolution: Changing Values and Political Styles Among Western Publics*. Princeton: Princeton University Press.

Irvine, W.P. 1979. *Does Canada Need a New Electoral System?* Kingston: Queen's University, Institute of Intergovernmental Relations.

Kerr, H.H. 1987. "The Swiss Party System: Steadfast and Changing." In *Party Systems in Denmark, Austria, Switzerland, the Netherlands, and Belgium*, ed. H. Daalder. London: Frances Pinter.

King, A. 1969. "Political Parties in Western Democracies: Some Sceptical Reflections." *Polity* 2:111–41.

Kirchheimer, O. 1966. "The Transformation of European Party Systems." In *Political Parties and Political Development*, ed. J. Lapalombara and M. Weiner. Princeton: Princeton University Press.

Kriesi, H. 1989. "The Political Opportunity Structure of the Dutch Peace Movement." *West European Politics* 12 (3): 295–312.

Ladrech, R. 1989. "Social Movements and Party Systems: The French Socialist Party and New Social Movements." *West European Politics* 12 (3): 262–79.

Lapalombara, J., and M. Weiner, eds. 1966. *Political Parties and Political Development*. Princeton: Princeton University Press.

Lawson, K., and P. Merkl, eds. 1988. *When Parties Fail: Emerging Alternative Organizations*. Princeton: Princeton University Press.

Levy, R. 1988. "Third Party Decline in the United Kingdom: The SNP and SDP in Comparative Perspective." *West European Politics* 11 (3): 57–74.

Lewis-Beck, M.S. 1988. *Economics and Elections: The Major Western Democracies*. Ann Arbor: University of Michigan Press.

Lijphart, A. 1977. *Democracy in Plural Societies: A Comparative Exploration*. New Haven: Yale University Press.

Lipset, S.M. 1950. *Agrarian Socialism: The Cooperative Commonwealth Federation in Saskatchewan*. Berkeley: University of California Press.

Lipset, S.M., and S. Rokkan, eds. 1967. *Party Systems and Voter Alignments*. New York: Free Press.

Luebbert, G.M. 1986. *Comparative Democracy: Policymaking and Governing Coalitions in Europe and Israel*. New York: Columbia University Press.

Luther, K.R. 1989. "Dimensions of Party System Change: The Case of Austria." *West European Politics* 12 (4): 3–27.

Machin, H. 1989. "Stages and Dynamics in the Evolution of the French Party System." *West European Politics* 12 (4): 59–81.

Mair, P. 1988. "The SPD after Brandt: Problems of Integration in a Changing Urban Society." *West European Politics* 11 (1): 40–53.

———. 1989. "Continuity, Change and the Vulnerability of Party." *West European Politics* 12 (4): 168–87.

———, ed. 1990. *The West European Party System*. Oxford: Oxford University Press.

Mair, P., and G. Smith, eds. 1989. "Understanding Party System Change in Western Europe." *West European Politics* (Special issue) 12 (4).

Maisel, L., ed. 1976. *Changing Campaign Techniques: Elections and Values in Contemporary Democracies*. Beverly Hills: Sage Publications.

Mayer, L.C. 1980. "Party Systems and Cabinet Stability." In *Western European Party Systems*, ed. P. Merkl. New York: Free Press.

Meisel, J. 1985. "The Decline of Party in Canada." In *Party Politics in Canada*. 5th ed., ed. H.G. Thorburn. Scarborough: Prentice-Hall.

Merkl, P., ed. 1980. *Western European Party Systems*. New York: Free Press.

Morton, W.L. 1950. *The Progressive Party in Canada.* Toronto: University of Toronto Press.

Nevitte, Neil. 1991. "New Politics, the Charter and Political Participation." In *Representation, Integration and Political Parties in Canada,* ed. Herman Bakvis. Vol. 14 of the research studies of the Royal Commission on Electoral Reform and Party Financing. Ottawa and Toronto: RCERPF/ Dundurn.

Norton, P. 1984. "Britain: Still a Two-Party System?" *West European Politics* 7 (4): 27–45.

Papadopoulos, I. 1988. "The Swiss Election of 1987: A 'Silent Revolution' Behind Stability?" *West European Politics* 11 (4): 146–49.

Pappi, F.U. 1984. "The West German Party System." *West European Politics* 7 (4): 7–26.

Pedersen, M.N. 1987. "The Danish 'Working Multiparty System': Breakdown or Adaptation?" In *Party Systems in Denmark, Austria, Switzerland, the Netherlands, and Belgium,* ed. H. Daalder. London: Frances Pinter.

Pinard, M. 1971. *The Rise of a Third Party.* Montreal: McGill-Queen's University Press.

Pomper, G.M. 1980. *Party Renewal in America: Theory and Practice.* New York: Praeger.

Reid, E. 1932. "The Rise of National Parties in Canada." Reprinted in *Party Politics in Canada.* 5th ed., ed. H.G. Thorburn. Scarborough: Prentice-Hall Canada.

Rokkan, S. 1970. *Citizens, Elections, Parties: Approaches to the Comparative Study of the Process of Development.* New York: D. McKay.

Rose, R. 1984. *Do Parties Make a Difference?* 2d ed. Chatham: Chatham House.

Rothacher, A. 1984. "The Green Party in German Politics." *West European Politics* 7 (3): 109–16.

Rudolph, J.R. 1977. "Ethnonational Parties and Electoral Change: The Belgian and British Experience." *Polity* 9:401–26.

Sartori, G. 1976. *Parties and Party Systems: A Framework for Analysis.* Cambridge: Cambridge University Press.

Smith, D.E. 1985. "Canadian Political Parties and National Integration." In *Party Government and Regional Representation in Canada,* ed. P. Aucoin. Vol. 36 of the research studies of the Royal Commission on the Economic Union and Development Prospects for Canada. Toronto: University of Toronto Press.

Smith, G. 1989. "Core Persistence: Change and the 'People's Party'." *West European Politics* 12 (4): 157–68.

Smith, G., and P. Mair. 1989. "Introduction: How Are West European Party Systems Changing?" *West European Politics* 12 (4): 1–2.

Stein, M. 1973. *The Dynamics of Right-Wing Protest: A Political Analysis of Social Credit in Quebec.* Toronto: University of Toronto Press.

Tate, C.N. 1980. "The Centrality of Party in Voting Choice." In *Western European Party Systems,* ed. P. Merkl. New York: Free Press.

Thomas, P. 1991. "Parties and Regional Representation." In *Representation, Integration and Political Parties in Canada,* ed. Herman Bakvis. Vol. 14 of the research studies of the Royal Commission on Electoral Reform and Party Financing. Ottawa and Toronto: RCERPF/Dundurn.

Thorburn, H.G. 1985. *Party Politics in Canada.* 5th ed. Scarborough: Prentice-Hall.

van Mierlo, H.J.G.A. 1986. "Depillarisation and the Decline of Consociationalism in the Netherlands." *West European Politics* 9 (1): 97–119.

von Beyme, K. 1985. *Political Parties in Western Democracies.* Aldershot, U.K.: Gower.

Whitaker, R. 1977. *The Government Party: Organizing and Financing the Liberal Party of Canada, 1930–58.* Toronto: University of Toronto Press.

Wilson, F.L. 1980. "The Sources of Party Transformation: The Case of France." In *Western European Party Systems,* ed. P. Merkl. New York: Free Press.

———. 1988. "The French Party System in the 1980s." In *Parties and Party Systems in Liberal Democracies,* ed. S.B. Wolinetz. London: Routledge.

Winn, C., and J. McMenemy. 1976. *Political Parties in Canada.* Toronto: McGraw-Hill Ryerson.

Wolinetz, S.B. 1979. "The Transformation of European Party Systems Revisited." *West European Politics* 2 (1): 4–28.

———. 1988. *Parties and Party Systems in Liberal Democracies.* London: Routledge.

Young, W.D. 1969. *The Anatomy of a Party: The National CCF 1932–1961.* Toronto: University of Toronto Press.

3

LINKS BETWEEN FEDERAL AND PROVINCIAL PARTIES AND PARTY SYSTEMS

Rand Dyck

POLITICAL PARTIES SEEK power at two levels in Canada, and our understanding of the subject cannot be complete without an examination of the links between federal and provincial parties and party systems. Indeed, the lack of symmetry and congruence between federal and provincial party systems and the absence of strong direct links between federal and provincial parties is a notable feature of the Canadian party system. This study seeks to clarify the links that do exist, to assess how the lack of integrated parties bears on their capacity to represent significant groupings in Canadian society, to compare Canada to other federations in this respect, and to suggest how the situation might be changed.

With 10 provinces (and two territories) and three large national parties, an amazing array of federal-provincial relationships exists within the Canadian party system. In all this variety and complexity, however, three theoretical models can be used for purposes of categorization and clarification. If a political party functions more or less successfully at both levels of government and if the relations between the two levels are generally close, it can be called an integrated party. If the intraparty relations are not so intimate, it has been termed a confederal party. In some cases, the party may be completely absent at one level or the other, in what might be labelled a truncated state.[1] In reality, there is continuum from integrated to confederal to truncated, and actual federal-provincial party relationships are scattered along this line from one pole to the other. To some extent, the differences are between parties; to some degree, they are regional variations; sometimes there is a difference between being in or out of power; and there are also changes over time. Occasionally a party will even be more friendly to another party at the other level of government than it is to its own counterpart.

The degree of integration between a federal party and its provincial affiliates can be gauged in many ways. Table 3.1 lists the factors by which such a relationship can be measured, at least in the Canadian context. In terms of organization, an integrated national party regards itself as a federation of provincial units: it has joint federal-provincial party memberships and constituency associations, combined federal-provincial executives and conventions at the provincial level, and a single headquarters and staff in each province that looks after both

Table 3.1
Factors measuring degree of integration of federal and provincial parties

1. Organization
    • degree to which the national party regards itself as a federation of provincial units
    • integrated or separate party memberships, constituency associations, provincial executives and conventions
    • integrated or separate party headquarters and staff
    • extent of federal-provincial interaction
    • extent of interprovincial cooperation

2. Finance
    • integrated or separate party revenues
    • integrated or separate party expenditures

3. Elections
    • integrated or separate election campaign team
    • degree of cross-level assistance provided in election campaigns
    • extent of federal leaders' participation in provincial election campaigns and vice versa

4. Leadership
    • personal relationship between federal and provincial party leaders
    • personal relationship between provincial leader and designated federal regional lieutenant, if any
    • degree of cross-level involvement of party establishment in selection of party leaders

5. Policy and Ideology
    • similarity or distinctiveness of federal and provincial ideologies
    • frequency and intensity of policy disputes

6. Personnel
    • overlapping or distinct party activists
    • degree of common voter allegiance
    • integrated or separate party careers
    • extent of contact between federal and provincial elected members
    • degree of cooperation in distribution of patronage

7. Relations with a party of another name at the other level of government

federal and provincial party matters. In such a case, the interaction of federal and provincial party staff is close, as is cooperation among party units in different provinces, especially at election time. Such a party also has integrated finances. In federal elections, the provincial party campaign team functions as the federal campaign committee in each province; at provincial election time, the federal party assists each provincial unit; and federal and provincial party leaders help each other out in their respective electoral efforts. Such leaders continue to maintain close relations between elections, as do provincial leaders with any regional lieutenants or political ministers appointed by the federal party leader. The federal party establishment may also become involved in the selection of provincial party leaders, and vice versa.

When it comes to policy and ideology, an integrated party demonstrates a basic ideological similarity and few policy disputes. In terms of personnel, party activists participate at both federal and provincial levels, the federal and provincial branches of the party share the allegiance of a common set of voters, and elected legislative members and party staff move between federal and provincial levels. Federal and provincial legislators also maintain close contact, and when government patronage is available, it is distributed through the combined party organization. Finally, an integrated federal party does not develop relationships with provincial parties of another name, especially at the expense of its own provincial counterpart, nor do provincial units become intimate with any other federal party.

In a confederal party, on the other hand, the national level has direct links to grassroots federal constituency associations and essentially bypasses the provincial level. It has separate federal and provincial party memberships and constituency associations, and may or may not have federal party executives and conventions in each province. A branch office and staff of the national party exist in each province, but they are not expected to cooperate much with provincial branches of the party, and even less interaction takes place among the provincial units. Federal-provincial finances are totally separate. Each level of the party runs its own election campaigns, extending from the level of leaders through strategists to party staff. In a confederal case, there is little connection between federal and provincial party leaders or between provincial leaders and federally appointed regional lieutenants. The party establishment at one level is not involved in the selection of the party leader at the other. A confederal party is not concerned about the similarity of federal and provincial ideology, and policy disputes may be common. This is related to the fact that each level of the party has its own distinct set of activists as well as voters.

Party careers exist at two separate levels; elected members at the two levels may not interact; and each branch of the party has its own network to distribute patronage. Finally, a provincial branch of the party may develop links to the national party of a different name, or vice versa, even to the detriment of its own counterpart.

The relations between the two levels of the Liberal and Progressive Conservative (PC) parties were closely integrated in almost all respects from the time of Confederation until the conscription and coalition controversies of 1917 (Stevenson 1989; Smith 1975). Those events created rifts within both parties and paved the way for the introduction of new parties, especially in western Canada. Subsequent farmer, coalition and Social Credit governments in the four western provinces complicated relations between the federal and provincial wings of both the Liberal and Conservative parties. In the mid-1930s, the creation of the Union nationale, which operated only at the provincial level in Quebec, and the rupture of the Ontario Liberal party into hostile camps left only the Atlantic provinces with a well-integrated party system. Garth Stevenson (1989) argues that the survival of the traditional two-party system in the Atlantic provinces is related to this closer integration because it is the only region in the country where affiliation with the federal government remained advantageous.

The current links between federal and provincial parties and party systems in Canada can best be discussed in terms of the seven factors in table 3.1. It will be seen that the criteria of an integrated party apply almost perfectly to the New Democratic Party (NDP), that the characteristics of a confederal party are generally applicable to the PC party and that the Liberal party finds itself somewhere between the two theoretical models outlined.[2]

ORGANIZATION

In their basic organization, the three parties currently fall into different categories. The PC party is clearly confederal, except for the truncated cases of Quebec and British Columbia; the NDP is obviously integrated, except for the confederal case of Quebec; and the Liberal party follows two models, one semi-confederal and the other semi-integrated.

Progressive Conservative Party

The national PC party and the provincial PC parties are essentially independent organizations. As one leading student of the party puts it: "Associated with the establishment of strong independent-minded provincial [Conservative] governments was the development of strong independent-minded provincial parties" (Perlin 1980). Two potential links of a formal nature are of little consequence. First, although each province is represented by a vice-president on the national executive committee, such members are not necessarily links with the provincial party. Second, although provincial party leaders (along with the president, women's president, youth president and vice-presidents of all provincial associations) sit on the national executive, this body rarely meets.

The federal-provincial PC relationship varies from one part of the country to another. It is closest in the four Atlantic provinces, variable in Ontario and more distant in the Prairies. The federal party was particularly dependent on the Ontario organization in the Stanfield era and under Mulroney between 1984 and 1988, when the Big Blue Machine moved on to Ottawa. Under Joe Clark, however, federal party relations with Ontario were more strained. Some provincial PC party constitutions commit the provincial wing to supporting the objectives of the federal party and also to backing its candidates at election time. Although this clause is mainly symbolic, the Alberta Conservatives contemplated dropping it in 1990. The provincial wing in British Columbia is extremely weak, and total truncation occurs in Quebec, where no provincial Conservative party has existed at all since 1935–36. The federal party continues to operate in British Columbia and Quebec, of course, but the absence of a provincial party has had different effects. Partly because of the lack of a provincial counterpart since 1935, the federal party was historically weak in Quebec, but after 1984 this gap did not affect federal party fortunes in that province. Nor has the weakness of the provincial party reduced federal party success in British Columbia. In both cases, however, the federal party has acquired some strange provincial bedfellows.

The federal-provincial relationship also depends on which branch of the party is in power. Before 1984, for example, the federal party was somewhat dependent on its provincial wings; but after the PC party formed the national government, it quickly showed that it could take care of itself, both financially and organizationally. Then, as the Mulroney government became increasingly unpopular, the provincial wings tried to distance themselves from the federal party.

As indicated in figure 3.1, a complete set of federal riding associations and executives coexists with PC provincial party organizations at the grassroots level. In many cases, however, federal riding association constitutions provide for executive representation from overlapping provincial constituency associations; in the Atlantic provinces in particular, some of the same people sit on both federal and provincial executives at the local level; and there are still eight or ten joint associations in Ontario. In general, federal and provincial party memberships

Figure 3.1
Progressive Conservative party structures

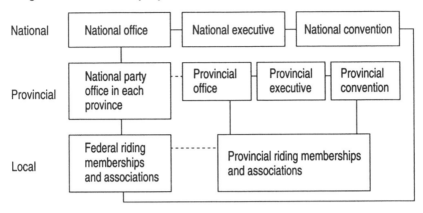

are separate, the main exceptions being the joint associations in Ontario. Separate memberships exist in Manitoba, but one can apply for both on the same form. In some cases, provincial party executives contain federal party representatives, but neither these nor provincial party conventions give much attention to federal matters, except as they overlap with party-organizing activity in the province; and the federal leader rarely speaks at provincial general meetings.

The federal party usually has a field officer in every province and a larger staff headed by a director of operations in Ontario and Quebec. (In Prince Edward Island the same person functions as federal field officer and provincial party executive director.) In the four Atlantic provinces, the federal party's representative works out of the provincial party office and shares support staff and equipment, all of which is one mark of greater proximity between the two wings of the party in that region. These combined offices have encountered few problems, and federal and provincial staff have little hesitation in lending a hand to each other, especially at election time. In the other six provinces, the federal party maintains a separate office, two in the case of Quebec. The federal regional office in Toronto formerly used space belonging to the Ontario party and adjacent to it, but since 1980 its staff has grown and it has moved to its own premises. An earlier trade-off had the eastern Ontario organizer of the provincial party working out of the national office in Ottawa.

The national director of the federal party is in almost daily contact with federal field officers, but contact with provincial party executive directors is fairly infrequent because they are engaged in few joint projects. Relations are cordial, however, and when Malcolm Wickson and

Jerry Lampert were national directors, contacts with the Ontario party staff were particularly close because they had come from that organization. The national director attends as many provincial general meetings and conventions as possible, as well as the annual meeting of provincial party executive directors and presidents.

Most provincial offices report that a close working relationship exists at the staff level of the two wings of the party in the provincial capitals. They have to contend with messages intended for each other, for example, and they attend each other's functions on a regular basis. Partly because the national headquarters is located in Ontario, federal party staff helped out in the 1990 Ontario leadership selection process.

Interprovincial Conservative party cooperation is not extensive. Primarily, it takes the form of the annual meeting of provincial party executive directors and presidents, and the exchange of personnel in the pre-election or election period. For example, because Ontario's Big Blue Machine was once the recognized leader in innovative electoral techniques, it was often asked for assistance by sister provincial parties, and after taking its own immediate needs into consideration it did its best to respond. As mentioned, several former Ontario staffers have gone on to work full time for the party at the federal level or in other provinces, as well as for Social Credit in British Columbia.

New Democratic Party

The NDP has by far the most integrated organization of the three main Canadian political parties. Its national predecessor, the Co-operative Commonwealth Federation, was literally a federation of provincial parties after 1938 (Young 1969), and the NDP maintains this structure in many ways. Its constitution does not use the term "federation," but it does provide for a fully autonomous provincial party in each province.[3] Although there is no provincial party representation on the federal executive, the federal council contains the leader, president, secretary and treasurer of each provincial party, along with three additional representatives from each provincial section. Thus, these key officials formally interact with each other and with their federal counterparts at least twice a year.

Like the other two parties, the NDP is not uniformly strong across the country. Its obvious strengths are Saskatchewan, Manitoba, British Columbia and Ontario, but in the five most easterly provinces it is still a fledgling party. There is a more uniform organizational link between the federal and provincial wings than in the other parties, although there are now separate federal and provincial New Democratic parties in Quebec.

One joins the NDP at the provincial level, but this entails an automatic membership in the national party as well, almost as if the federal party is an afterthought. The relative vitality of federal and provincial constituency associations varies across the country and, at least in the western half, the provincial ridings have traditionally been the party centres of gravity. However, in the three western provinces where it has held power – Manitoba, Saskatchewan and British Columbia – there are now separate federal and provincial riding associations of about equal strength and activity. In Alberta and Ontario, the federal associations are not as active but are becoming stronger. Until the late 1970s, for example, Ontario had only temporary election committees for federal purposes, but it now has full-fledged federal riding executives and annual association meetings. In general, federal associations are strongest in constituencies held by the party and in other priority ridings. The party also employs the concept of "buddy ridings," which links an MP to a second constituency for which he or she maintains some organizational responsibility. In the eastern half of the country, on the other hand, the federal constituency associations are generally more active than the provincial, and the former have been used as a basis of organizing the latter. There were often so few activists available that it made little sense to divide them into tiny provincial constituency executives. Party structures are depicted in figure 3.2.

Provincial executives, councils, and conventions are integrated in the NDP, and they divide their work between the two branches of the party. At a provincial convention, for example, a federal item is always on the agenda – a report from the federal leader, president, secretary and caucus. Moreover, the provincial party often cannot resist the temptation to debate an aspect of international affairs, even though it acknowledges this to be within the federal party's jurisdiction. The provincial

Figure 3.2
New Democratic Party structures

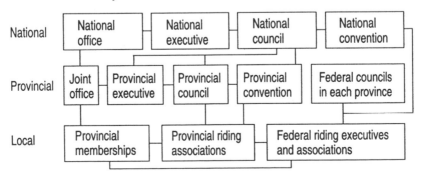

office of the party also serves both levels, a situation that does not ordinarily present a problem because efforts at one level reinforce those at the other. The general orientation of this office is provincial, probably doing on average about 75 percent of its work for provincial purposes. Immediately before federal party conventions and about 12 months before anticipated federal elections, the focus quite consciously shifts, and the organization gears up for such federal efforts. This practice is compromised only if a simultaneous provincial election or leadership convention must be run, as happened in British Columbia in 1983.

Frequent contact is maintained between the federal secretary of the party and the provincial secretaries, and individual contacts are supplemented by encounters at executive, committee and council meetings on which they may sit. With these officials all drawn from the same small pool, often former colleagues, the relationship is usually close and congenial. The federal secretary also attends most provincial conventions.

Despite the generally harmonious and mutually supportive federal-provincial party relationship, federal party officials in recent years have been concerned about the strongly provincial orientation of the party, raising the question of a direct federal membership. The Task Force on Party Structures set up in 1987 sent a questionnaire on this subject to activists, but results indicated that such members did not favour any change. Instead, a Council of Federal Ridings has recently been established in most provinces to combat the dormancy of the federal party at the provincial and constituency levels between federal elections. Such councils meet once a year and contain MPs, nominated federal candidates and a representative of each federal riding association. In Ontario, five regional councils and one ethnocultural council were established. The significance of these councils has yet to be determined.

The federal party has often been embarrassed by what it regarded as radical rhetoric from the provincial NDP in Quebec and has frequently sought to distance itself from that wing. At the same time, especially after 1976, the national party hoped to capture the federal support of provincial Parti québécois members. In consequence, the same 1987 task force proposed constitutional amendments that were passed in 1989 recognizing the NDP of Canada (Quebec) as a separate entity from the Nouveau parti démocratique–Québec. Such a separation involves two NDP memberships and two party offices in Quebec, one federal and the other provincial. In a significant breach of party tradition, it is now possible for a resident of Quebec to belong to a provincial party other than the NDP (most likely the PQ) and still belong to the federal party. The provincial wing is supposed to conduct itself in general consistency with the principles of the federal party, but when it refused to support the federal candidate in an August 1990 Quebec by-election, the federal party effectively severed all links with the provincial wing.

Otherwise, the NDP's integrated nature is clearly revealed by the extent to which the party in one province assists that in another. In the past, this typically involved lending election organizers to one another in their respective campaigns, but it now operates more broadly with respect to creative graphics, polling and other professional services and skills. There is also an Atlantic Apprenticeship Program through which key staff people from that region are temporarily moved to the more established provinces for special training. In fact, this whole operation has been institutionalized in the form of "twinning" smaller provincial and territorial sections of the party with larger ones for such purposes: New Brunswick with British Columbia, Nova Scotia with Saskatchewan, Newfoundland with Ontario, Quebec with Manitoba and Yukon with Alberta.

Liberal Party

The Liberal Party of Canada has replaced the National Liberal Federation as the official name of the Liberal party, but in some aspects it is still a federation of ten provincial and two territorial units (Wearing 1981). The 12 regional presidents, for example, sit on the national executive along with many others, and the provincial and territorial leaders are entitled to attend such meetings as non-voting members, though they rarely do so. The situation is immensely complicated, however, by the extremely weakened, almost truncated, state of the party in certain western provinces since 1957 and by the separation of the provincial parties from the federal wing in Quebec, Ontario and Alberta. This leaves nine provinces and territories where the structure is integrated – called "unitary" or "joint" – and where the provincial organization functions as a branch of the federal party. In the three "split" cases, the Liberal Party of Canada (Quebec) coexists with the Parti libéral du Québec; the Liberal Party of Canada (Ontario) exists alongside the Ontario Liberal party; and the Liberal Party of Canada (Alberta) maintains a separate identity from the Alberta Liberal party.

The provincial Liberal party in Quebec decided to establish itself as a separate entity in 1964 at the height of disputes between the provincial Liberal government of Jean Lesage and the federal Liberal government of Lester Pearson. Fighting over shares of tax revenue and the degree of autonomy that the province wanted in a variety of shared fields of jurisdiction, the two governments simply found it too difficult to rely on a single party organization in the province. In fact, the Liberal party in Quebec always had a quasi-separate status from the national party, and the national headquarters traditionally functioned as the party office for English-speaking Canada (Whitaker 1977). Even after the creation of a distinct federal Liberal organization within Quebec, it remains less closely linked to the national office than any of the other provincial branches. Whatever the relationship between other provincial wings of the Liberal party and the national party, the Quebec party will always insist on a more elaborate infrastructure.

In Ontario the split was less dramatic and coincided with the election of Stuart Smith as provincial leader in 1976. There the provincial party felt short-changed by the federal orientation of the common party organization after the demise of Mitchell Hepburn. It wanted additional money and resources, had certain policy disagreements with the federal Liberal government, and saw the federal leader, Pierre Trudeau, as more of a liability than an asset. The other catalyst of disintegration in Ontario was the 1975 provincial *Election Finances Reform Act*, which separated federal and provincial accounts. Alberta election finance legislation was modeled on that of Ontario and had much to do with the Alberta Liberal party's decision to set itself up as an independent entity in 1977. Such a split was also influenced by the Trudeau government's almost exclusive concern with central Canadian issues, to the detriment of the West.

In these three provinces, Quebec, Ontario and Alberta, there are separate federal and provincial Liberal party memberships, separate federal and provincial executives and conventions, and separate federal and provincial offices and staff. Federal and provincial riding associations are almost all separate, with a handful of Ontario and Quebec exceptions where federal and provincial constituency boundaries still coincide (and where a single joint membership will suffice). From the provincial point of view, the advantages of separation are that the provincial party can take distinctive policy stands, is less burdened by an unpopular national leader, can raise and spend its own money, can employ staff for provincial purposes, can attract better candidates and can generally establish its own image or identity. On the other hand, total costs are increased; the number of creative, talented people available is usually limited; and in spite of attempts to forge a separate identity for the provincial party, the electorate may not make the distinction.

Before 1990 the provincial and territorial parties were essentially the "members" of the national Liberal party, but constitutional amendments passed at the Calgary convention facilitated individual federal party memberships, something previously available only in the split provinces. Now, besides joining a federal constituency association directly, a person can become a member of the federal Liberal party by joining a unitary provincial party or a youth, women's or Aboriginal club, for even though these are provincially oriented, their members are automatically assigned to a federal constituency association.

Even in the integrated provinces, few joint federal-provincial constituency associations remain, largely because of different boundary configurations. But one or other may be basically a "shell," such as the federal Liberal riding associations in Nova Scotia and New Brunswick, in which the provincial constituency organizations are the real engines of activity. Figure 3.3 demonstrates the basic differences between the unitary and split Liberal organizations.

When the federal Liberal party is out of power, the basic orientation of the integrated parties is provincial, especially if the party forms the provincial government, as in Newfoundland, New Brunswick and Prince Edward Island in 1990. In the special case of Newfoundland between 1949 and 1972, Joey Smallwood controlled almost all aspects of the Liberal party at both levels. In Nova Scotia the situation is usually

Figure 3.3
Liberal party structures

Unitary parties

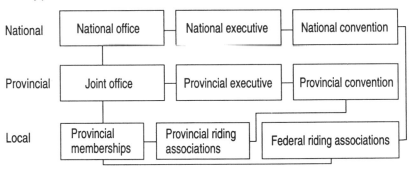

Split parties

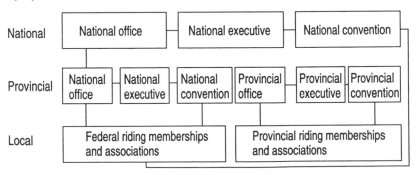

balanced, and for more than 30 years the federal godfather, Allan MacEachen, shared authority with the provincial leader. The Liberal party in that province continues to demonstrate such balance by having an executive committee that includes the presidents of both federal and provincial constituency associations. In the three integrated cases in the West – Manitoba, Saskatchewan and British Columbia – the party has been so weak in recent years that the question of its basic orientation is almost irrelevant, but some federal-provincial conflict has been apparent in Manitoba between Lloyd Axworthy and Sharon Carstairs.

The nature of this orientation is related to the proportion of time or work that is devoted to the respective levels by the integrated party office. This is difficult to quantify, but, as in the NDP, the focus is primarily provincial. Since winning elections is the raison d'être of the party organization, the imminence of an election at one level or the other will be the determining factor. When the integrated Ontario office of the early 1970s had to cope with federal elections in 1972 and 1974 and provincial ones in 1971 and 1975, for example, the staff put 100 percent of their energies into the federal effort at some times and 100 percent into the provincial campaign at others.

The federal party usually suffers from the provincial orientation of its joint members and offices, and national officials would prefer to have a distinct set of federally minded activists and staff. National headquarters even lacks a list of members of the federal Liberal party. On the other hand, the federal party in Ontario closed its Toronto office in 1990 because of financial constraints. Although the office was of some benefit to federal headquarters, it spent too much time and money organizing federal party meetings within the province with little concrete result. Federal party officials would like to have their own staff and office within each province but do not feel that it is necessary to have the elaborate structure of executives and provincewide meetings that the Ontario operation entailed. They prefer the Conservative model of federal field officers and direct links between federal constituency associations and national headquarters.

There is regular contact between national headquarters and the various provincial party offices, since in the unitary cases these provincial offices deliver federal party programs. Less contact exists between the federal head office and the three split provincial parties, although there is some with Ontario, primarily because of proximity. The extent of interprovincial cooperation among provincial Liberal parties is limited. This is probably because they do not see their fates to be intimately interconnected and also because few provincial branches have resources to spare.

FINANCE

Progressive Conservative Party

The second most important measure of the degree of integration between federal and provincial parties involves their financial relationship. Prior to the mid-1970s, both the Liberals and Conservatives raised most of their funds from corporations in Montreal and Toronto and then transferred portions to other parts of the country for both federal and provincial purposes. At that time the provincial PCs in the West became fully self-sufficient in this respect, and today the two wings of the party are totally separate in their finances. This is not to say that requests for funds are not frequently submitted to Ottawa, especially from the Atlantic region, but cash, as such, is rarely transferred. On the other hand, the federal party often helps provincial parties at election time, primarily through the provision of personnel, expertise and services. In 1990, for example, it provided computer assistance in the Manitoba provincial election, and national headquarters staff volunteered for party work after hours in the Ontario campaign.

The federal party may also lend staff to the provincial party for the organization of general meetings or leadership conventions. Provincial parties do not contribute to the federal party's budget, and there are virtually no joint fund-raising events in any province. Ontario officials say, for example, that it is too complicated to agree on the split of the take, as well as to receipt the proceeds properly under different federal and provincial legislation. Instead, federal and provincial parties alternate their fund-raising dinners.

New Democratic Party

The NDP is uniquely integrated in its finances. To a large extent, the federal party is financed by its provincial wings, and the latter are obliged to send the former 15 percent of all provincial moneys received, plus 60 percent of union affiliation fees. How the 15 percent is raised varies from one provincial party to another. In some cases the membership fee is split among federal, provincial and constituency parties, but legislation in such provinces as Ontario, New Brunswick and Alberta prohibits the direct cross-level flow of funds. To comply with these legal requirements, the Ontario party sets up a federal account in its guise as a branch of the federal party. Certain provincial wings quite frequently fall into arrears with the federal party, especially in the wake of a provincial election, and provincial parties use the federal party as a bank from which they borrow money without paying interest. To make up for any shortfall in provincial contributions, the federal party relies on direct mail campaigns.

Although the flow of funds in the NDP is primarily from the provincial to the federal level, the national NDP in turn assists provincial parties, especially in Atlantic Canada and the North. These parties get subventions, which usually take the form of debt forgiveness or cash. The federal party also contributes money or staff to encourage federal activities in these regions, but such efforts are expected to spill over to the provincial parties' advantage. Joint fund-raising events are rare, but the provincial wings may use some or all of the proceeds from their own events to meet their 15 percent federal commitment.

Liberal Party

In the Liberal party, the financial relations between the federal party and its provincial counterparts have always been a nightmare, even when the federal party collected large amounts from national corporations in Ontario and Quebec and redistributed funds across the country for provincial as well as federal purposes. Although this practice put the federal party in a dominant position, it resulted in many heated disputes and left the national organization in the unenviable position of being regarded as a banker of last resort. Since the new federal election finance legislation of 1974, the Liberals as well as the Conservatives have depended more heavily on individual contributions and less on corporate donations. One result has been a heightened competition for funds among federal, provincial and constituency levels of the party. Another effect has been an even closer cross-level link in those places – especially Newfoundland and Saskatchewan – where, in the absence of a provincial equivalent, the federal tax credit was used for provincial party contributions. A third change occurred after the debacle of 1984 when the federal Liberal party simply had no money to spare and vainly hoped that its provincial branches would reverse the flow and help it to reduce its own deficit. Even in these straitened circumstances, however, the indebted Saskatchewan Liberal party managed to pry some $50 000 from the national party and then went back for more. On the other hand, most provinces now also provide tax credits and public subsidy of election expenses, so in these cases there is less need to depend on the national party.

In January 1987 the federal party established a new financial management committee that included provincial party representatives and adopted a new financial plan. This initiative involved retrenchment at both federal and provincial levels and, at least until the federal party's debt was eliminated, a closer federal-provincial financial relationship. In this operation, the national Liberal party has different arrangements with each provincial wing of the party with respect to revenue-sharing and expenses. Every year the federal chief financial officer sits down with each provincial party counterpart to work out an arrangement for the coming 12 months. In most of the unitary cases, the federal party provides provincial wings with 50 percent of their annual budget. Incentives exist for provincial parties to maximize their own fund-raising efforts, although if they raise more than 50 percent of their revenue requirements in the first six months of the year, the federal party reduces its commitment. Such federal funds are supposed to cover the federal political efforts of the joint organization, but the federal party does not usually see much result from the money and would prefer to have it attached to specific federal party activities or personnel.

In contrast to the NDP, then, the flow of funds in the Liberal party is from the federal level to the provinces. In addition, if a provincial party sends federal headquarters its membership list, any money raised in a direct mail campaign is shared 50–50. Somewhat similarly, the proceeds of major joint federal-provincial fund-raising dinners are shared, even in Ontario, Quebec and Alberta. Where provincial electoral law does not provide for a tax credit for contributions, provincial parties use the federal legislation, but the federal party feels that this is unethical, as well as a nuisance, and hopes that the present Royal Commission will recommend that the federal Act cannot be used to fund provincial party activity.

ELECTIONS

Progressive Conservative Party

When it comes to elections (a third aspect of the federal-provincial relationship), each level of the PC party selects its own separate campaign team, although some individuals usually overlap. The guru of the Ontario Big Blue Machine, Norman Atkins, was seconded by Brian Mulroney to run the 1984 federal campaign and was then appointed to the Senate to serve in this capacity again in 1988 (Frizzell et al. 1989). His departure from the Ontario scene was undoubtedly a factor in the party's ill-fated 1985 provincial effort. Below these strategists, at the staff level, the provincial and federal wings usually come to each other's assistance, either during or after working hours, maximizing the value of their time and expertise. In addition, national headquarters helped the Manitoba PCs in 1990 with a sophisticated computerized mail approach that gave voters the impression they were receiving a personal letter from Premier Filmon. Federal officials hoped that knowledge gained from this experiment would also benefit the federal party in the future.

It is expected that the provincial Conservative leader will help the national party in federal election campaigns, an expectation that is normally fulfilled, and often with quite positive results. The commitment of the provincial leader varies, however, and this usually affects the contribution of provincial legislative members, party staff and activists. In Ontario, for example, the tremendous effort of Bill Davis in 1972 and 1984 contrasted with his lack of enthusiasm in 1979 and 1980, and his predecessors also varied in such contributions (Hoy 1985; McDougall 1986; Graham 1990). Such provincial help is not indispensable, however, and in Quebec and British Columbia there is little or no provincial leadership to rely on.

It is probably not as common for the federal leader to participate in provincial elections, for federal leaders have rarely had much prestige to lend to the provincial cause and have not usually been invited. John Diefenbaker was only briefly an unquestionable asset; Robert Stanfield was probably of little advantage outside the Atlantic region; both he and Joe Clark were almost continually under attack from within their own party; and Brian Mulroney's lustre soon diminished after 1984. Mulroney appeared personally via satellite in the 1985 Ontario campaign, but, although asked, he declined to appear in Manitoba and Prince Edward Island in 1986. Nevertheless, Mulroney has been much more active than previous prime ministers, and he has involved the federal government in almost all provincial elections since coming to power. Federal announcements with respect to the Hyundai automobile plant in Quebec in 1985, the Litton plant in Prince Edward Island in 1986 and the $1 billion wheat program during the 1986 Saskatchewan election (while delaying the announcement that the CF-18 maintenance contract would go to Quebec) were all seen as prime ministerial attempts to influence the provincial results.

New Democratic Party
In contrast to the Progressive Conservatives, the national NDP relies heavily on the provincial party's campaign team, usually headed by the provincial secretary, to carry out the directives of the federal Strategy and Election Planning Committee (Frizzell et al. 1989). In fact, the whole integrated staff is normally turned over to the federal election effort. In provincial elections, each provincial party has its own Election Planning Committee, but some provincial units borrow specialized services (such as leader-tour organizers) from the federal party, and the federal party generally turns over all of its polling data and makes available other professional services.

It is normal for the national leader to appear in provincial campaigns, and vice versa, and the popular Ed Broadbent participated in these with relish. Relatively speaking, the national leader is of greater value in the weaker provinces, where he or she does not provide so much media competition for an established provincial party leader. Despite Broadbent's high national standing, he had little effect when he made forays into the 1987 Ontario campaign, and it is not likely that the greater party success in Ontario and Manitoba in 1990 was due to Audrey McLaughlin's appearances in both campaigns.

The federal party pays the airfares of out-of-province organizers in provincial elections, whether these come from the federal party, from vacationing parliamentary party staff or from other provinces. This expense amounted to about $25 000 in each of the 1990 Manitoba and Ontario elections.

Liberal Party

In planning and executing a federal election campaign, the composition of the Liberal team has for many years been the prerogative of the party leader. In most cases, the Liberal party ran parallel campaigns in English-speaking Canada and Quebec, and this entailed considerable variation in advertising and approach, with francophone and anglophone campaign co-chairmen. Keith Davey masterminded the production in English-speaking Canada, and he selected his team without much reliance on the various provincial parties, although there was occasionally some overlap (Davey 1986; McCall-Newman 1982). In the Atlantic provinces in 1988, the federal organization dominated in Newfoundland and Nova Scotia, although in New Brunswick and Prince Edward Island, with the party in power, federal Liberals were overwhelmed by the forces of Premiers McKenna and Ghiz (Frizzell et al. 1989). Certainly, in the case of the three split parties, provincial party strategists are not actively involved in the national campaign. On the other hand, even in a split situation such as that of Ontario, the provincial party headquarters sets aside provincial business as much as possible and turns its staff over for federal electoral purposes. In 1988, many Ontario Liberals were seconded to bolster the staff of the federal party organization, but they could not overcome its inadequacies. Conversely, in the 1986 Alberta provincial election, two Ottawa organizers were contributed, and another two of John Turner's key staff people were integral to the 1985 Ontario campaign. The federal party lent staff to Manitoba in 1988 and to Ontario in 1990; in addition, the national office staff usually help out in the Ottawa area in Ontario provincial elections.

As for cross-level participation of party leaders in election campaigns, the unique case of Joey Smallwood has already been noted. Normally, other provincial Liberal leaders also participate actively in federal elections, especially in the integrated cases, although this was one of many aspects of discord between the Thatcher and Pearson Liberals in Saskatchewan in the 1960s (Smith 1975). In spite of policy differences over Meech Lake and free trade, New Brunswick's Frank McKenna enthusiastically supported the federal Liberal campaign in 1988.

When it comes to the federal leader's participation in provincial elections, there was a striking contrast between Pierre Trudeau and John Turner. The former almost never entered the fray on behalf of his provincial wing, whereas the latter campaigned in almost every provincial contest. Several factors account for this difference in behaviour. First, Trudeau was almost always prime minister, while Turner was usually leader of the Opposition. Some Trudeau advisers considered it inappropriate for the prime minister to engage in such campaigns, and others felt that he lacked the time.

Second, Turner's attitude toward the provinces as well as toward the provincial wings of the Liberal party was quite different from that of his predecessor, who had little use for either. Turner believed that the route to federal power was through capturing provincial governments; he sought to "rebuild the federal party on the basis of strong provincial party foundations" and invested "what resources he could muster to support his Liberal counterparts in their provincial election campaigns" (Frizzell et al. 1989, 30).

Third, Turner was a long-time party man who apparently enjoyed campaigning, but Trudeau was steeped neither in the party nor in politics. His handlers had trouble getting him to help the federal wing of the Liberal party, let alone the provinces.[4] Rather than rely on provincial party organizations (or even federal MPs) as sources of intelligence on local concerns, for example, he set up the regional-desk system in the Prime Minister's Office, although it was dismantled after the near defeat of 1972. Of course, even when Trudeau did not personally participate, the provincial party expected some show of support, possibly in the form of favourable or accelerated federal policy or spending announcements.

Fourth, at least after 1974, Trudeau was rarely asked to participate, while Turner's presence was requested to a greater extent. In the 1985 Ontario election, provincial strategists were undecided about the advisability of making use of the federal leader, who had recently taken the national party to its greatest-ever defeat. Turner ended their indecision by volunteering, and he appeared in a number of constituencies doing no apparent harm. Jean Chrétien participated in several provincial election campaigns even before being chosen federal leader and then immediately helped out in the Ontario and Manitoba campaigns of 1990, although without any apparent effect.

LEADERSHIP

Progressive Conservative Party

Turning from the subject of elections to that of leadership as such, another measure of the degree of intimacy between the federal and provincial parties is the personal relationship between the federal and provincial party leaders. In the past, this relationship in the PC party has frequently been strained. Classic cases include George Drew and Deane Finlayson in British Columbia, as well as the Ontario examples of John Diefenbaker and John Robarts, and Joe Clark and Bill Davis. The Drew-Finlayson feud erupted in a violent public quarrel in 1954 when the provincial party executive approved a motion of nonconfidence in the federal leader. It was partly a personality clash, partly a struggle for control over the party organization, and partly a simple response to disparate organizational needs (Black 1979). Brian Mulroney undoubtedly started out on a closer basis with his provincial counterparts, and some provincial parties still report that the relationship between them is good. Others, however, have become dissatisfied, finding that the prime minister surrounded himself with personal loyalists who kept him from having contact with provincial PC leaders and parties.

The Progressive Conservative party did not officially move in the direction of regional lieutenants or provincial political ministers until mid-1986. Even before that, it was clear who the regional minister was in certain provinces, and he or she often developed a close relationship with the provincial party. Since 1986, certain regional ministers have become even more influential than comparable figures under the Liberals (Bakvis 1989, 1991) and such official designation may have overcome some of the concerns about Mulroney's own ties to the provincial organizations. In addition, the Conservative caucus has chosen an MP in each province to function as a liaison agent between it and the provincial party. The absence of a Quebec leader during the long opposition years was often seen as a fatal flaw in the Conservative party, but when Stanfield tried to recognize Marcel Faribault and then Claude Wagner in this role, the results were not impressive. Conservative fortunes in Quebec in the 1980s were actually better before Mulroney recognized any separate lieutenant there.

As divisive as the national leadership issue has frequently been, there is not much evidence of one level of the party taking sides in leadership conventions against the other. The federal party did try to influence the provincial leadership selection in British Columbia in the coalition period and immediately afterwards, but more typically, Diefenbaker kept the federal party strictly neutral in the 1961 Ontario leadership race, just as Robarts tried to stay out of the federal leadership battles later in that decade (McDougall 1986). Exceptions were the 1956 federal contest when Leslie Frost and the Ontario party worked for Diefenbaker (Graham 1990) and 1967 when some provincial organizations supported native sons: Nova Scotia, Stanfield; Manitoba, Duff Roblin; and British Columbia, Davie Fulton. The most the Ontario party did in connection with the 1983 Tory convention, however, was to poll Bill Davis' chances, and when he declined to run, it did not line up behind a single other candidate.

New Democratic Party

In theory, the NDP puts less emphasis on leadership than the other two parties, and a common ideological commitment generally guarantees a close personal relationship between the federal leader and his or her provincial counterparts. This was true of Broadbent between 1975 and 1989, except perhaps for a period around 1980–82 at the height of the controversy over the federal Constitution (Gruending 1990). The concept of regional lieutenant is foreign to the NDP, although the federal caucus has provincial caucus chairs and sometimes sets up committees or designates spokespersons for provinces in which it lacks representation, such as for Atlantic Canada. Little evidence exists of the party establishment at one level taking sides in a leadership convention against the other.

Liberal Party

In the Liberal case, relations between the federal and provincial leaders have often been serious impediments to party harmony. The most acrimonious was the relationship between Mackenzie King and Mitchell Hepburn of Ontario, but King got along only slightly better with T.D. Pattullo of British Columbia (Whitaker 1977). Lester Pearson had a friendlier personal relationship with provincial Liberal leaders, with the notable exception of Saskatchewan's Ross Thatcher and, increasingly, Jean Lesage (Pearson 1975). Personalities, policies, party finance, and organization were all involved in the Pearson–Thatcher discord. Pierre Trudeau did not have a warm regard for many provincial Liberal leaders during his long tenure, and he demonstrated considerable contempt for Robert Bourassa and disagreement with Bourassa's successor, Claude Ryan. John Turner, being in opposition, had less reason to differ from his provincial counterparts and probably attached more importance to this relationship. His contacts varied with circumstances, issues and personalities – closer with old friend David Peterson than with Bourassa, for example, with whom he eventually had a major falling out. The mutual dislike of Bourassa and Chrétien, stemming in part from issues such as Meech Lake and free trade, and the mutual admiration and support of Bourassa and Mulroney make it exceedingly difficult for the federal Liberal party to maintain close relations with the Liberal party of Quebec. With the corporate sector in Quebec supporting Bourassa and Mulroney (or perhaps even supporting the PQ and the Bloc québécois), the federal Liberals also find it hard to raise money in Quebec.

Especially in the era of Mackenzie King, the role of the federal leader was sometimes of less significance than that of a designated federal regional-lieutenant (Smiley 1987). Because of the special status of the Quebec party even before 1964, the Quebec leader or French lieutenant was even more important (McCall-Newman 1982; English 1986). Classic cases of regional strongmen in the federal party and the Cabinet include Ernest Lapointe and Louis St. Laurent in Quebec, C.D. Howe in Ontario and Jimmy Gardiner in Saskatchewan. Even if the significance of this role has decreased or at least changed (Bakvis 1991), it is possible to identify several regional heavyweights in the period since then, including Allan MacEachen in Nova Scotia, J.W. Pickersgill and Don Jamieson in Newfoundland, Marc Lalonde in Quebec, Otto Lang in Saskatchewan, Romeo LeBlanc in New Brunswick and Lloyd Axworthy in Manitoba. Such lieutenants have often taken a great interest in provincial politics as well as in the federal scene, sometimes being a considerable asset to the provincial party. At other times they became a liability, especially when they did not get along with the provincial leader. The relationship between Otto Lang and Ross Thatcher was particularly bitter (Smith 1975). Except for Raymond Garneau in Quebec, John Turner did not officially designate any such regional chieftains, although some emerged unofficially, such as Lloyd Axworthy in Manitoba and Brian Tobin in Newfoundland. With the possible exception of Axworthy, it would seem that relations with their respective provincial leaders were reasonably congenial.

There have been several instances in which the federal Liberal party establishment has intervened in the matter of provincial leadership. One case occurred in the early 1960s when the federal party wanted Earl Urquhart replaced as provincial leader in Nova Scotia (Wearing 1981). Repeatedly at provincial leadership conventions in Ontario, one candidate was the designated choice of the federal party establishment, especially Walter Harris in 1958. Indeed, the large number of ex officio federal delegates at Ontario leadership conventions was a secondary motive for the 1976 separation. Similarly, federal interference in the selection of provincial leaders occurred in Quebec in 1950, British Columbia in 1957, and Saskatchewan in 1940 and 1954 (Whitaker 1977). The 1986 choice of Vince MacLean in Nova Scotia presumably pleased the federal party establishment, since he came from Cape Breton, just as they did. As far as the influence of provincial party élites in the choice of federal leaders is concerned, the Liberal party has never sought its leadership from the provincial level, and a provincial party has rarely given unanimous support to a single candidate.

POLICY AND IDEOLOGY

Progressive Conservative Party

The federal PC party has often been characterized by internal policy conflicts, but left-right ideological differences have not usually assumed a federal-provincial dimension (Smiley 1987). There have, however, been some serious policy disputes of a nonideological nature between the two levels of the party. Relations between the federal and Newfoundland parties in the Diefenbaker period were severely strained over the federal decision to send RCMP reinforcements into the 1959 loggers' strike and to limit federal grants to the province. The provincial organization temporarily cut its ties with the national body and called itself the United Newfoundland Party. Bill Davis and Richard Hatfield supported Trudeau's 1980–81 constitutional initiative, even to the point of agreeing with his move to patriate unilaterally, at the same time that Joe Clark at the federal level and Tory premiers in several other provinces were fighting the proposal with every weapon at their disposal. This became a very divisive issue for the Ontario party membership in particular, and it prompted many federally oriented Tories to criticize Davis for "being in bed" with Trudeau. It was also a factor that limited Davis' appeal when he contemplated entering the federal leadership race in 1983. During Clark's brief term as prime minister, he had some trouble with Alberta on energy policy.

When Mulroney became the new national leader, to a large extent on the basis of his prospective appeal in Quebec, he immediately faced a provincial wing in Manitoba that was strongly opposed to the extension of bilingualism in that province. Putting the national interest first, Mulroney went to Manitoba to tell his provincial colleagues where he and the federal party stood on the issue. When he took office in 1984, long-standing energy policy disputes with Alberta and Newfoundland were quickly resolved, and Mulroney even persuaded Tory premiers to agree to Quebec's constitutional demands in the Meech Lake Accord. Generally friendly federal-provincial relations followed, apart from minor intergovernmental financial disputes, Don Getty's complaints about federal agriculture and energy policies, and Brian Peckford's concerns about various fishing issues. By 1990, the conflicts were more serious, involving such matters as dam construction in Saskatchewan, federal cutbacks to the Canada Assistance Plan, and the Goods and Services Tax.

New Democratic Party

Perhaps because of the fact that the NDP has the most definitive ideological orientation of the three main parties, it often engages in intense internal ideological disputes. These rarely assume a federal-provincial dimension, but there have been several cross-level disputes within the party over specific policies. The federal party was upset when the NDP government of Manitoba gave a measure of support to Trudeau's wage-and-price control program of 1975, a proposal that had been condemned by David Lewis in the election campaign a year earlier and was fiercely opposed by the Canadian Labour Congress. Energy policy is always difficult for the NDP, but it stakes out its ground carefully and the federal party works closely with its Alberta wing to adopt compatible approaches.

The most serious public policy division was over the Constitution in the early 1980s, when Broadbent and the federal party generally supported the Trudeau initiative (after bargaining for the new section 92A, which they thought was what the provinces wanted), but the Saskatchewan and Alberta parties in particular were very much opposed (Chandler 1986; Gruending 1990). On this point, some of the Saskatchewan MPs sided with their provincial colleagues. The federal and provincial wings also disagreed to a certain extent on the 1987 Meech Lake Accord.

Liberal Party

The Liberal party's ideology is normally sufficiently moderate and flexible that there are no problems between federal and provincial wings.[5] About the only serious left-right divergence of recent years was that between the conservative Thatcher Liberals in Saskatchewan and the welfare-oriented Pearson forces in the 1960s – a discord reminiscent of the split between Mitchell Hepburn's right-wing tangent in the 1937–42 period in Ontario and Mackenzie King's cautious promotion of a federal welfare state. Otherwise, both levels of the Liberal party have occupied a fairly centrist ideological position.

Specific policy disputes, however, have been more common. These are most intense when the party is in power at both levels of government – something rather rare – but they also surface when the party forms the government at one level or the other. Hepburn and King were at odds over such nonideological issues as hydro exports, the Rowell-Sirois Report and especially the war effort. Pattullo in British Columbia also fought with King over Rowell-Sirois recommendations and other matters. In the Pearson period, opposition Liberals in Ottawa could barely stomach Smallwood's anti-union activities in Newfoundland in

1959; and after the Liberals formed the federal government, Ross Thatcher was willing to take them on over almost any issue, including bilingualism, the Constitution and social policy. Meanwhile, Jean Lesage was moved to split the Quebec provincial Liberals off into a separate party. Under Trudeau, the national perspective adopted by the federal caucus often brought it into conflict with the provincial wings of the party, and provincial Liberals found it politically advantageous to maintain some policy distance between themselves and their colleagues at the federal level (Thomas 1985).

As mentioned earlier, it was partly differences in policy that prompted the Ontario Liberals to set up a separate organization in the mid-1970s. Relations between the Trudeau Liberals and the Quebec party under Bourassa and Ryan were not much better than in the Pearson period, with Trudeau pursuing contrary approaches to bilingualism and federalism and being opposed to the provincial government on the FLQ crisis, the Victoria Charter and Bill 22, among other matters (McCall-Newman 1982; Gwyn 1980). As Clarkson writes, "Despite their defeat of separatism, the federal and provincial Liberal parties in Quebec had emerged from the Trudeau era deeply alienated from one another" (Frizzell et al. 1989, 29). Differences over energy policy had a large part to play in the separation of the Alberta Liberals from the national party.

During the 1984–90 period, when the federal Liberals went into opposition under Turner and then came back to power in Ontario, Quebec, Prince Edward Island, New Brunswick and Newfoundland, the two leading national controversies were Meech Lake and free trade. Premiers Bourassa and McKenna both supported free trade, opposition to which was the crusade of federal Liberal leader John Turner's life. Turner's restrained support of Meech Lake was generally consistent with McKenna's position, and although David Peterson and Joe Ghiz supported it more strongly, Clyde Wells in Newfoundland was opposed, as were certain other provincial Liberal leaders such as Sharon Carstairs. Generally speaking, such federal-provincial Liberal policy disputes in the Turner period echoed and exacerbated conflicts that already existed within the federal Liberal party and caucus. In 1990, Jean Chrétien inherited this profound intraparty division on constitutional and linguistic issues. It would thus seem that at least in recent times ideological splits in the Liberal party are no more province-based than in the other two parties.

PERSONNEL

Progressive Conservative Party

The federal-provincial aspects of party personnel can be seen in terms of activists, voters, officials, legislators, leaders and patronage. The question of personnel in the PC party immediately raises the problem of the nonexistent provincial wing in Quebec and the almost extinct branch in British Columbia. These gaps make it almost impossible to assess the percentage of party activists who are involved at both levels of the party, but most estimates put it at about 60–80 percent where a provincial PC party exists. Voters in the two truncated provinces have the same problem as activists: in the virtual absence of a provincial party, they could hardly vote consistently no matter how much they wanted to. Even where such alternatives exist, the phenomenon of split federal-provincial party identifiers is a striking fact of Canadian political life and is not restricted to the Conservative party.[6] Indeed, historically, and with the exceptions of British Columbia and Quebec, Conservative voters have been more consistent than those who voted Liberal (Johnston 1980). Table 3.2 shows the percentage of popular vote gained by the Conservatives in each province in the 1980, 1984 and 1988 federal elections, and in the provincial elections that immediately preceded, intervened and immediately followed these federal elections.

In general, the 1984 federal election was the zenith of party support over the past decade at either level, and the 1980 federal election was its nadir. Most provincial results have fallen between these two extremes.

Table 3.2
Progressive Conservative party, percentage of popular vote, federal and provincial elections, 1977–90

	Provincial	Federal 1980	Provincial	Federal 1984	Provincial	Provincial	Federal 1988	Provincial
Nfld.	50	36	61	38	49	b	42	48
P.E.I.	53	46	52	52	45		41	36
N.S.	46	39	47	51	52	43	41	
N.B.	44	32	47	54	28		40	
Que.	N/Aa	12	N/Aa	50	1		53	N/Aa
Ont.	40	35	44	48	37	25	38	24
Man.	49	38	44	43	40	38	37	42
Sask.	38	39	54	42	45		36	
Alta.	57	65	63	69	51		52	44
B.C.	5	41	1	47	1		35	

Source: Compiled by author from reports of federal and provincial chief electoral officers.

[a] N/A = not applicable (no provincial Conservatives).

[b] Blank spaces indicate no provincial elections.

Traditionally, in Ontario there was a significant disparity, with provincial support being higher than the federal vote, but since 1984 this pattern has been reversed. Newfoundland and New Brunswick have been the other provinces with the greatest federal-provincial variations in the 1977–90 period.

As for political careers, although much provincial-federal migration took place in the early years, there is a general trend in Canada among all parties toward legislators' remaining in the political arena in which they began (Smiley 1987; Whitaker 1977; Barrie and Gibbins 1989). Thus, most PC legislators now remain at either the federal or provincial level. Davie Fulton's mid-1960s foray into the provincial fray in British Columbia between stints at the federal level is one recent exception, and another is Frank Moores' provincial leadership in Newfoundland after serving in the House of Commons.

On the other hand, the federal party has repeatedly recruited provincial premiers when it needed a new leader. This happened in the case of both John Bracken and George Drew in the 1940s, and then again in 1967 in the contest between Robert Stanfield and Duff Roblin. Later still, serious speculation surfaced that John Robarts, Bill Davis and Peter Lougheed might seek the top federal post (Perlin 1980). However, only 8 of the 169 Tory MPs elected in 1988 had served previously in provincial or territorial legislatures – most notably John Crosbie, Marcel Masse, Gerald Merrithew and Kim Campbell[7] – but many senators have previous provincial experience, including ex-premiers Richard Hatfield and John Buchanan who were appointed to the Senate in 1990.

Of the provincial legislators in 1990, it appears that only three had previously been elected as Conservative MPs: John Reynolds, a British Columbia Socred, and two members of the Alberta legislature, Peter Elzinga and Stan Schumacher. Among Tory staffers and strategists there is greater federal-provincial and interprovincial movement. Notable examples include Norman Atkins, Dalton Camp, Jerry Lampert, John Laschinger, Paul Weed and Bill McAleer. Similarly, apart from some of the earlier Liberal–PC arrangements in Ontario and the continuing compacts between the PC and Social Credit parties in British Columbia, federal Tory MPs seem to interact best with fellow Conservative provincial caucus members.

When it comes to patronage, the two levels of the party are relatively independent. An opportunity to reward the faithful at the federal level has rarely existed, but now that it does, some provincial parties report that they are asked to suggest names for various appointments to the Appointments Secretariat; some say they are not asked; and others claim that they submit names anyway. Of course, there is a good deal of overlap among the key players who might be eligible, but the Mulroney government has acted in a fairly unilateral fashion in this regard. Roy McMurtry, for example, went to his reward as Canadian High Commissioner to Britain after a career in Ontario politics, but as a personal friend of the prime minister. Not much evidence exists that provincial Conservative governments behave any differently in their patronage decisions.

New Democratic Party

In the area of personnel, the NDP has the largest proportion of activists involved at both levels, probably at least 80 percent in most provinces, given that most feel they belong to one integrated organization. Although the NDP vote was more uniform between federal and provincial levels than the vote in the other two parties over the 1977–90 period, it was not as high as might have been expected, considering the party's ideological orientation. Table 3.3 shows the percentage of popular vote gained by the party in each province in the 1980, 1984 and 1988 federal elections, as well as in the preceding, intervening and following provincial elections.

Table 3.3
New Democratic Party, percentage of popular vote, federal and provincial elections, 1977–90

	Provincial	Federal 1980	Provincial	Federal 1984	Provincial	Provincial	Federal 1988	Provincial
Nfld.	8	17	4	6	14	a	12	4
P.E.I.	N/A	7	N/A	6	4		7	3
N.S.	15	21	18	15	16	16	11	
N.B.	7	16	10	14	10		9	
Que.	N/A	9	N/A	9	1		14	
Ont.	28	22	21	21	24	26	20	38
Man.	39	33	44	27	41	24	21	29
Sask.	48	36	38	38	45		44	
Alta.	16	10	19	14	29		17	26
B.C.	46	35	45	35	43		37	

Source: Compiled by author from reports of federal and provincial chief electoral officers.

N/A = not applicable (no provincial NDP).

[a] Blank spaces indicate no provincial elections.

The table indicates that the federal party vote is usually about 10 percent lower than provincial support in the four western provinces. In Ontario it is more uniform, with the provincial vote usually slightly higher, and much higher in 1990. In the eastern half of the country, on the other hand, and with the exception of Nova Scotia, the federal vote almost always exceeds that received by the provincial party, but the two levels are not that far apart.

Several prominent migrations between federal and provincial levels have taken place within the NDP – Tommy Douglas, Ed Schreyer, Ian Deans and Michael Cassidy, for example – but the incidence of such integrated careers does not seem to be any greater than in the other two parties. Five of the 43 MPs elected in 1988 had served previously in provincial legislatures, although in 1990 only Bob Rae in Ontario and one NDP member in each of the British Columbia and Saskatchewan legislatures had been MPs. At the staff level, however, such movement is common, not only between federal and provincial levels (Robin Sears, Bill Knight, Dennis Young and Richard Proctor) but even more frequently between provinces. Provincial secretaries are so often selected from the cadre of professional staffers in another province that the party has considered establishing a pension plan for such careerists. The NDP often elects federal and provincial legislative members from the same areas, and they generally work very closely together.

On the question of order-in-council appointments in provinces in which the party assumes power, several prominent personalities have worked for a succession of NDP governments (for example, Marc Eliesen, David Cass-Beggs and Michael Mendelsson) and sometimes for the federal party as well (Cliff Scotten). As one provincial NDP government was defeated and another was elected, a wholesale migration of ministerial advisers sometimes took place. However, when the Saskatchewan party fell in 1982 and the new Tory government fired more than 200 such officials, very few were picked up by the NDP government of Manitoba, which was quite parochial in its appointments. Consultation with the federal party on such matters is even rarer, and the latter has never had the opportunity to make such appointments itself.

Liberal Party

In the unitary cases of the Liberal party, it is estimated that some 80 percent of party activists are involved at both levels of the party. Even when there was federal-provincial hostility at the leadership level in Saskatchewan in the 1960s, the party was united lower down

(Smith 1975). In Quebec, Alberta and British Columbia, the figure on overlapping activists may drop below 50 percent.

The consistency among voters is not as high as for activists. Table 3.4 shows the percentage of popular vote gained by the Liberal party in each province in the 1980, 1984 and 1988 federal elections, and in the provincial elections preceding, intervening and following.

The table indicates that Liberal support in the four western provinces has been low at both levels and that it has also been consistently lower (from 10 to 20 percent) in provincial than in federal elections. Except for British Columbia, this gap has narrowed since 1985 and was actually reversed in Alberta. Even in Quebec, where the party has been strong at both levels, the disparity can rise to 20 percent in either direction. Greater consistency over the 1977–90 period has been evident in Ontario and the Atlantic provinces, where the federal-provincial variance is almost always less than 10 percent, and the advantage can be in either direction.

As in the other parties, most Liberal politicians and party staffers now pursue separate federal and provincial careers. Nevertheless, it is interesting to note recent exceptions to the rule. Jean Lesage was a federal MP and minister before returning to Quebec as provincial leader, as was Don Jamieson in Newfoundland; and Ross Thatcher was a CCF

Table 3.4
Liberal party, percentage of popular vote, federal and provincial elections, 1977–90

	Provincial	Federal 1980	Provincial	Federal 1984	Provincial	Provincial	Federal 1988	Provincial
Nfld.	41	47	35	36	37	a	45	47
P.E.I.	45	47	45	41	49		50	61
N.S.	38	40	31	34	31	40	47	
N.B.	44	50	41	32	60		45	
Que.	34	67	46	35	56		30	50
Ont.	32	42	34	30	38	47	39	32
Man.	12	8	7	22	14	35	37	28
Sask.	14	24	5	18	10		18	
Alta.	6	22	2	13	12		14	29
B.C.	N/A	22	3	16	7		20	

Source: Compiled by author from reports of federal and provincial chief electoral officers.

N/A = not applicable (no provincial Liberals).

a Blank spaces indicate no provincial elections.

MP before his conversion to Liberalism and his move to the Saskatchewan provincial scene. Gerald Regan was first a federal MP, then led the provincial party to victory in Nova Scotia, and finally became a federal minister after losing the 1978 provincial election. Bennett Campbell moved on to Ottawa after his 1979 defeat in Prince Edward Island, Lloyd Axworthy is a former Manitoba MLA, and Raymond Garneau emerged at the federal level several years after a career in the first Bourassa cabinet (and after losing the Quebec leadership to Claude Ryan).

Somewhat ironically, three of the most prominent Ontario Liberal MPPs resigned to run in the 1984 federal election (two of them successfully), just as the federal party went down to defeat and their former colleagues at Queen's Park were forming a government. Only five of the 40-member federal Liberal caucus after 1984 had served previously in a provincial legislature (and 9 of 83 in 1988), but not a single provincial Liberal legislator in 1990 had served in the House of Commons. The number of senators with previous provincial legislative experience is greater, and as with the PCs, many former provincial leaders have been rewarded with a Senate seat.

At the staff level, there is also some integration of careers, but not as much as in the other two parties. Exceptions include David Collenette (former secretary-general of the federal party, who was once executive director of the then-integrated Ontario party) and many of the staffers in the split party offices in Toronto, who are former colleagues. It is probably safe to say that relations between Liberal MPs and provincial elected members are generally close and friendly, with certain exceptions that are noted below.

With respect to the distribution of patronage, there is little federal-provincial interaction. When the federal party was in office, its patronage powers helped keep it dominant over the provincial sections, from whom it rarely requested the names of possible political appointees, except perhaps in the Atlantic provinces. Instead, it relied on the federal organization, the regional lieutenant in the Cabinet or the Prime Minister's Office. For a brief period, Trudeau experimented with a troika system, in which he consulted on such matters with a representative of the provincial party, along with a federal minister and caucus member from the province concerned, but this was abandoned after 1974 (Wearing 1981). Now that the party is out of office federally but in power in four provinces (in 1991), there is a sufficient number of provincial party workhorses waiting in line to obviate the need to seek additional federal party suggestions.

CROSS-PARTY, CROSS-LEVEL RELATIONSHIPS

Progressive Conservative Party

A final point of consideration is whether the national party ever cooperated with a provincial party of another name to the detriment of its own provincial counterpart, or vice versa. In fact, considerable evidence exists to confirm this phenomenon. For the Conservatives, the classic case is the relationship between the federal Tories and Social Credit in British Columbia. Black reports that as early as 1954 the federal party was accused by its provincial wing of having "made a 'saw-off' deal with Social Credit to the effect that Drew's group would keep out of Social Credit's way in British Columbia in return for Social Credit agreement not to oppose federal Conservative candidates" (1979). As provincial leader in the mid-1960s, Davie Fulton managed to reconcile the federal and provincial camps in British Columbia; but after repeated provincial party failure, the federal party came to realize that it would be simpler to develop an informal working arrangement with the British Columbia Social Credit party than to support its own.

To a large extent, those who vote Social Credit provincially support the federal Tories, and vice versa (Blake 1985). The relationship was strengthened after Bill Bennett put together an anti-NDP coalition of Socreds, Liberals and Conservatives in 1975. Since then, it has become virtually impossible to elect a provincial Tory member in the province, and the fledgling British Columbia Conservative party has gone through a succession of unsuccessful leaders. One of them, Brian Westwood, was so upset at the lack of federal support under Joe Clark that he resigned and joined the separatist Western Canada Concept.

This link between the federal PC party and provincial Social Credit also has an Ontario dimension, as can be seen in several instances. Pat Kinsella and Jerry Lampert migrated from the Big Blue Machine and national party to become principal secretaries to Bill Bennett and Bill Vander Zalm; Kinsella and John Laschinger ran the campaigns of Social Credit leadership candidates in 1986; and several of the candidates in that race had federal Tory connections, including the aforementioned John Reynolds. There was even a suggestion that if Brian Smith had won, he might have tried to convert the Social Credit party into an orthodox provincial branch of the national Progressive Conservative party. Instead, he received a federal PC patronage appointment. Most startling, perhaps, is the fact that the federal Conservatives provided staff to assist in the organization of the 1986 Social Credit leadership convention, primarily as a personal favour to Jerry Lampert, a former colleague. In the other direction, Rosemary Dolman, acting national director of the federal PC party, is the former executive director of the British Columbia Social Credit party.

The other strange link is the one between the federal Tories and various provincial parties in Quebec (Perlin 1980). The Union nationale (UN) was created in 1935–36 in large part from the remains of the provincial Conservative party, but the subsequent federal-provincial relationship was not particularly close because the two parties were diametrically opposed on many issues. Indeed, a closer tie often existed between the UN and the federal Liberals. By the mid-1950s, however, the UN leader, Maurice Duplessis, had had enough of this relationship and rendered considerable organizational assistance to the federal Conservatives, especially in 1958. Many of the 50 Tories elected in Quebec in the 1958 federal election were provincial UN members. Shortly afterwards, the party began to decline, but Diefenbaker had a close relationship with Paul Sauvé, and Daniel Johnson frequently sent Diefenbaker encouraging notes (Diefenbaker 1976, 1977; Perlin 1980).

Marcel Masse and Roch LaSalle were the only two UN–PC links in the Stanfield, Clark and Mulroney periods, before the Union nationale disappeared entirely. In the 1984 federal campaign, the Tories capitalized on the Quebec origin and bilingualism of their leader, Brian Mulroney, to attract unprecedented Quebec support from whatever source they could. Much of it, in fact, came from the Parti québécois (PQ), which shared with the PCs an animosity to the Liberals, if little else. Mulroney also tried to maintain friendly ties with the provincial Liberals in 1984 and especially in the 1985 provincial election, when he was accused by both sides of favouring the other. Before that event, he had repulsed the efforts of André Asselin to organize a provincial Conservative party in Quebec, which, lacking Mulroney's encouragement, gained a mere 1 percent of the vote. Mulroney hinted that at some later point he might be interested in developing a provincial wing, but for the time being he preferred to depend on an alliance of those opposed to the federal Liberal party, including provincial Liberals.

As far as provincial PC disloyalty to the federal party is concerned, there were sweetheart deals in Ontario, especially in the north, between Liberal MPs and Conservative MPPs and their respective constituency associations. The Liberals would not contest provincial elections too strongly in certain constituencies, and sometimes not at all, if the Conservatives would run a weak federal campaign in the same area. The frequent indifference of a provincial Conservative government to the fate of the party in a federal election has been referred to earlier. The coalition governments in Manitoba and British Columbia in the

1940s and early 1950s prevented the provincial wings in those locations from providing the federal party with much support.

New Democratic Party
There is no evidence of NDP cross-level, cross-party cooperation at the expense of its own counterpart. However, the Ontario party's 1985–87 deal with the Peterson Liberals aroused displeasure in some quarters, as did Ed Schreyer in Manitoba and Ed Broadbent at the federal level at various times when they were thought by others in the party to be too close to Trudeau.

Liberal Party
In the Liberal case, MPs in Quebec formed nonaggression pacts with provincial Union nationale members in the Duplessis years, leading to a rather frosty federal-provincial Liberal relationship. The sweetheart deals in Ontario between federal Liberals and provincial Conservatives have already been mentioned. During the heyday of Social Credit before 1971, the Alberta Liberal party was frequently upset at the friendly relationship that the federal party had with the provincial government, and an unholy alliance also existed with Social Credit in British Columbia. In Stevenson's frank assessment, the federal party "ruthlessly undermined its faltering provincial affiliates so as to improve relations with the non-Liberal governments of Quebec, Ontario, Alberta, and British Columbia" (Stevenson 1989, 218).

On the other hand, the provincial wing sometimes appeared to be disloyal to the federal party. In the Hepburn era, considerable contact existed between the Ontario Liberals and the federal Conservatives, and Hepburn also attempted to make anti-federal Liberal alliances with the Union nationale and Social Credit (Whitaker 1977). In provincial coalition governments in Manitoba and British Columbia, inevitable tension arose because the provincial Liberal party hesitated to help the federal party for fear of alienating its coalition partner. In recent times, some provincial Liberals in Quebec have taken a cue from Premier Bourassa to vote Conservative in federal elections, while many federal Liberals in British Columbia vote Social Credit provincially. Indeed, the federal Liberal party constitution only prohibits simultaneous membership in any other *federal* party, although in the interests of British Columbians, federal Liberals are permitted to belong to a different provincial party.

ANALYSIS
The foregoing discussion reveals that the federal and provincial wings of Canadian parties are generally quite fragmented and have become

less dependent upon each other over time. Four main reasons have been suggested for this decline in the degree of integration (Dyck 1989). The first is in the realm of party finance. To impose effective limits on party contributions and expenditures, recent election expense legislation at both levels of government has required the maintenance of separate accounts and in some cases has prohibited cross-level funding. Such legislation was a major factor in promoting the separation of the two wings of the Liberal party in Quebec, Ontario and Alberta. In the Conservative case, the autonomy of the provincial parties was also enhanced by increased contributions emanating from the new-found corporate wealth of western Canada.

Second, the level of voter identification with any party is low and appears to be declining. If this is the case at each level of government, it is even less likely that voters will identify with the same party at both federal and provincial levels. Naturally enough, such split identification has been and continues to be most marked in those provinces with distinctive provincial parties: Quebec, British Columbia and the Prairie provinces. To take the British Columbia example, in 1979, 65 percent voted for different parties in federal and provincial elections that were held only 12 days apart (Blake 1985). The phenomenon is also increasingly common in Ontario and the Atlantic provinces, where the same alternatives exist at both levels. More and more voters in any election seem to be motivated by the immediate stimuli of the campaign leaders, issues, candidates and party images, rather than by a consistent federal-provincial party loyalty. Instead of automatically supporting the same party at both levels of government, today's voters are likely to take out their impatience with a government's performance at one level or another by voting against its federal or provincial counterpart.

Third, government decisions made in the forum of federal-provincial conferences tend to leave legislatures and parties out of the picture. This also reduces the mutual dependence of the federal and provincial branches of each party, because governments of different labels may be forced to come to terms with one another in the bargaining process. These accommodations often cause great strain on the federal-provincial party relationship, because they are made at the expense of policies espoused or criticisms expressed by the party at the other level of government.

Fourth, with an ever-increasing reliance on the new technologies of political marketing, such as opinion polling, electronic media, direct mail campaigns and televised leaders debates, neither federal nor provincial parties need the same kind of labour-intensive organization as in the past. Even less do they need the assistance of a party organization at the other level of government, although isolated examples of cross-level assistance in the field of new technologies have been mentioned.

Officials of the Progressive Conservative, New Democratic and Liberal parties demonstrate varied degrees of satisfaction with the existing state of federal-provincial party relationships. The national Progressive Conservative party is quite happy with its confederal relationship with eight provincial PC parties, a sentiment shared by most of these provincial counterparts. Each goes its own way in terms of organization, membership, constituency associations, offices and finance. On the other hand, there is much crossover in terms of personnel, some mutual assistance in elections and an ongoing relationship among senior staff, executives and caucus members. Moreover, cross-level voting is at least as consistent among Conservatives as Liberals. Success at the provincial level has bred further success, whether in developing strong, innovative party organizations, skilled party personnel and attractive leaders, independent sources of funds or electoral victories.

The federal-provincial relationship has been closest in the small, dependent, traditional, Atlantic provinces. Since the PC party has usually been out of power in Ottawa, the federal party could not provide much incentive to provincial wings to develop an intimate connection, and often found it preferable to maintain a certain distance. Even when the federal party did gain power, it quickly declined in popularity and its policies sometimes strained federal-provincial party relations. The principal exception was the occasional dependence of the federal party on the provincial wings to furnish federal leadership candidates, but this can be explained by the party's relatively greater success at the provincial level rather than by the federal-provincial relationship.

The 1984 federal election proved that the PC party could win a majority of seats in every province with or without a provincial wing, and in 1988 the party did better in Quebec, where it lacks a provincial wing, than anywhere else. Federal party officials therefore see no particular advantage in having a provincial Conservative party in Quebec or a stronger provincial wing in British Columbia, and PC organizers unashamedly establish links with other parties in those provinces. The only Conservatives dissatisfied with this situation are the small number in British Columbia who would prefer to strengthen the provincial PC party instead of supporting Social Credit, and the even smaller number in Quebec who are unhappy in choosing between provincial Liberals and the Parti québécois. What it lacks in federal-provincial intimacy, the national PC party makes up for in its close ties to federal constituency associations.

It is quite another story in the case of the Liberals and NDP, who are both concerned about the weakness of their federal organizations. While the federal and provincial branches of the NDP are closely linked by ideology and the feeling of belonging to an undifferentiated movement, federal NDP officials, like the federal Liberals, feel that they must somehow strengthen the federal party presence. Both also spend too much time negotiating over federal-provincial party finances. The Liberals are now developing separate or at least more conscious federal party memberships and would be happy to be relieved of the financial burden of provincial wings. The NDP may yet move to a separate federal membership (having already done so in the case of Quebec), but its initial move to give the federal party more attention between elections was the recent establishment of federal councils of the party in each province. Both parties are characterized by regional strengths and weaknesses: federally and provincially the Liberals are generally strong where the NDP is weak, and vice versa. But, except for Quebec, the NDP is more likely than the Liberals to see the fate of its two levels related, and membership, finances and offices are still all integrated. The NDP counters provincial variations in strength by carrying over its redistributive ethic to internal party affairs, as federal and stronger provincial units help the fledgling provincial parties in the eastern half of the country.

Largely for policy and accounting reasons, the Quebec, Ontario and Alberta wings of the Liberal party severed links with the federal organization. This left the party with two distinct types of federal-provincial relationships. Federal officials see the advantage of having separate federal party offices at the provincial level (as well as separate federal members) but do not feel that the Ontario model of full-fledged federal party meetings and executives within the province should be used. They would be content with Tory-style federal field offices and closer links between federal constituency associations and national headquarters.

What emerges from this discussion of current federal-provincial party links in Canada is that there is no necessary relationship between the degree of integration of a party and its total strength. The Conservative party, though the least integrated, is currently the strongest of the three at both levels (except in Quebec and British Columbia, and these do not materially affect the situation); the greater degree of federal-provincial integration in the Liberals and NDP is, at least to some extent, a detriment to their national parties. Thus, a closer integration with their provincial wings is not necessarily the means to the end of strengthening national parties in Canada.

Turning from the benefits to the parties themselves to what is in the interest of the overall political system, how does this lack of consolidation in parties bear on their capacity to represent significant groupings in Canadian society? This question relates to the function of political parties to aggregate interests in their pursuit of power and their ability, in the process, to act as agents of integration in the country. Some political scientists endorse the broker theory, believing that political parties should do little else than act as brokers among all significant groups. Others condemn this theory but prescribe an alternative means of pursuing the same twin objectives of power and national integration, i.e., by presenting pan-Canadian ideological appeals. The Liberals and Conservatives are usually seen as following the former strategy, while the NDP would prefer to adopt the latter. However, at the time of writing, when an election could well produce five parties of approximately equal strength in the House of Commons, including regional Bloc québécois and Reform parties, neither approach appears to be working.

There are many significant cleavages in Canadian society, including class, religion, gender and age, but the two divisions most capable of leading to the disintegration of the country are region and ethnicity. If a majority federal government with strong support in all regions, and among both French-speaking and English-speaking groups, is taken as the best means of keeping the country together, then the most successful examples in modern times are the Mackenzie King government of the 1940s, the Louis St. Laurent government of the 1950s, the John Diefenbaker government of 1958–62 and the Brian Mulroney government of 1984–88.

In the King and St. Laurent periods, the Liberal party had strong wings in most provinces, including the western provinces, and such strength at both federal and provincial levels was probably mutually advantageous as a general rule. Personality and policy conflicts with the Ontario wing were rampant, however, and the provincial Liberal party in Quebec was overwhelmed by the Union nationale during most of this period. To some extent, the federal Liberal party collaborated with its rival provincial party, but, in any case, the strength of the federal party in Quebec was not dependent upon the provincial wing. Strong regional federal cabinet ministers contributed to the success of the party in all provinces, whether or not they had links to provincial wings of the party.

The Diefenbaker sweep of 1958 was a nationwide phenomenon that did not depend on provincial party strengths, except perhaps in Ontario; indeed, strong provincial PC parties followed in the wake of the national Conservative victory. Furthermore, in 1958, when the party won a majority of seats in Quebec for the first time since 1891, it had no provincial wing in that province and not even much of a federal organization. Such a landslide was partly the result of Quebec's jumping on the bandwagon that was evident in the rest of the country, and partly because of the support of the provincial Union nationale. When Brian Mulroney won an overwhelming national mandate in 1984, this may have been aided by strong provincial parties in several cases, but it was not harmed by the absence of a provincial PC party in Quebec. It was not even hampered by the traditional weakness of the federal Conservative party in Quebec, because links had quickly been forged with provincial Liberal and PQ organizations.

Except for King and St. Laurent, these national mandates quickly eroded. Diefenbaker lost Quebec after only four years in office and Mulroney appears to have lost both Quebec and the West after only six. It could be claimed that the temporary nature of such national mandates is proof that the national parties lacked deep regional or linguistic roots and that strong, integrated wings in *every* province might have prevented such a quick demise. Closer ties with grassroots opinion in Quebec might have helped the Diefenbaker government, although it fell apart on other issues, but Mulroney may yet again prove able to appeal simultaneously to Quebec and the West. Certainly, his policies have attempted to do so, and if the Meech Lake Accord had been adopted instead of being so narrowly rejected, the federal Conservatives would probably stand at an all-time high in popularity in Quebec.

The conclusion that emerges from this analysis is that there is no necessary connection between the federal-provincial integration of a political party in Canada and its ability to accommodate all major regional and ethnic groupings in society. If the objective is to strengthen national parties in Canada so that they can transcend various regional, ethnic and other societal cleavages, it would probably be more fruitful to pursue means of doing so other than by increasing the degree of their federal-provincial integration.

The Situation in Other Federations

Various other research studies for the Royal Commission focus in detail on foreign examples such as Western Europe and the United States (e.g., Chandler and Siaroff 1991; Covell 1991; Elkins 1991). Here it is our purpose to look only briefly at other federations to examine their patterns of federal-provincial party relations and their parties' capacity to accommodate regional and ethnic demands. What can we learn in this respect from Germany and the United States?

Germany is different from Canada in many ways, not only in its federal structure but especially in not having to contend with such deep regional and ethnic cleavages. Federalism in Germany has been termed "administrative" rather than "legislative" because regional units are basically engaged in implementing and administering policies adopted at the central level.[8] The radical re-zoning of Germany by the Allies in 1945 created many new and largely artificial Länder and served to reduce many long-standing regional conflicts and traditional regional loyalties and prejudices. Bavaria was the one distinct region that remained intact. That the Upper House, the Bundesrat, is made up of representatives of state governments is a vital factor in maintaining a close working relationship between federal and state parties (Smiley and Watts 1985).

The three main parties in Germany are the Christian Democrats (CDU), Social Democrats (SPD) and Free Democrats (FDP). The CDU has been a Catholic-conservative broker party that appealed to various regional interests. Its overwhelming early success did not encourage it to build a strong internal organization, although corporate and public funding allowed it to thrive without a strong membership base. The party functioned largely as a U.S.-style campaign committee and even allowed its provincial branches to draw up national candidate lists. After the passing of Adenauer, however, the CDU went to great lengths to build up its own party organization. The Christian Social Union (CSU) has represented the special interests of Bavaria inside the CDU with varying degrees of tension over the years (Chandler 1987). The SPD is closer to the Canadian NDP, with a stronger Protestant and working-class ideological orientation with which to cut across regional differences, and with a more centralized party organization. The FDP (called the Liberals) is somewhere between the other two in combining brokerage and ideological appeals, and like the smaller Green party it is more decentralized than the others.

Over the years, an increasing symmetry between federal and Länder party systems has occurred, and regional variations have diminished (Roberts 1989). This homogenization primarily reflects a federal influence on Länder party systems, the main exception being the introduction of the new Green party at the Länder level. As in Canada, federal and Länder elections do not coincide; but, to a greater extent than in this country, voters prefer the same party at both levels. Indeed, Germany demonstrates "an extremely strong pattern of electoral 'punishment' of Bonn governing parties in Länder elections" (ibid., 111).[9] Roberts also found other evidence pointing to "federal influence on increasingly-subservient Länder party organisations and federal politics spilling over more and more into Länder election campaigns."

The German case also differs from Canada in respects other than the basic cleavages of its society and the federal structure of government. One well-known difference is its electoral system, which provides each voter with two votes, one for a local candidate and the other for a party. The Lower House is divided into equal components of constituency representatives and legislators drawn from party lists in proportion to each party's popular vote. Such an electoral system has often been recommended in Canada in place of the existing one, which tends to exaggerate regional divisions within the country. Of course, the German electoral system usually leads to a coalition government because no party obtains a total majority, but such a coalition is an alternative and quite possibly superior means of reconciling regional and cultural diversities.

Another German innovation that might usefully be adopted in Canada is the greater extent of public funding of political parties. This derives from a strong sense of egalitarianism and the feeling that a social democratic party should not be placed at a considerable disadvantage to a party funded largely by corporate donations. (Since such funding also exists at the Länd level, it is one of the few factors encouraging the autonomy of these regional party organizations.) Whatever one thinks of the ideological aspect of this policy, it would be advantageous to alleviate the endless haggling between federal and provincial wings of the Liberal and New Democratic parties over limited resources, and it would probably allow all three parties to appeal more effectively to all regional and ethnic groupings in the country.

In short, the high degree of integration between federal and state wings of the parties in Germany is a reflection of that country's lack of deep-seated societal cleavages as well as of institutional arrangements such as the Bundesrat. Given these fundamental differences from Canada, it is in the areas of electoral reform and party finance that the German model provides the most useful suggestions for helping Canada overcome some of its problems.

The relevance of the American experience is similarly limited by the fact that American and Canadian social divisions and federal systems are not identical. For example, American regional and sectional conflicts were much sharper 100 years ago than they are today, when the fundamental problems can be termed those of race and class.[10]

The United States is characterized by a totally decentralized party and electoral system. National parties basically do not exist beyond a state-based national convention and a temporary national election committee set up for presidential elections every four years. Instead, parties are organized and operated at the state and local levels. Some presidential candidates come from state politics, such as governors Reagan and Carter, but others establish themselves in the national political arena, such as the Kennedys and George Bush. Party membership, finance, organization and everything except a certain amount of presidential election planning is a function of state parties. Indeed, even they have been increasingly superseded by candidate organizations in recent years.

The basic message of the American system is that a strong national government can co-exist with state-based political parties and flourish in the virtual absence of national parties. By almost all accounts, the American federal system is less decentralized than Canada's federal system, but this seems to have little to do with political party organization. Canada might well wish to retain strong, independent national political parties, but the American example indicates that closely integrated federal-provincial parties are not a prerequisite of a system of government that can cope with regional and ethnic demands.

Observers may disagree about how successfully the American party, electoral, federal and general governmental systems have addressed the fundamental racial-class problem, but the means of doing so at least bear examination. The crucial contrast with Canada has probably been in the looser degree of party discipline at the national level and the constant bargaining among various interests and groups. Individual members of Congress are able to espouse regional, state, ethnic, class or other causes and attempt to arrive at compromises with those representing rival concerns. The American case argues strongly for a diminution of party discipline in Canada so that regional and ethnic compromises can be arranged at the federal level. Many Canadian observers have remarked over the years that if provincial, regional and ethnic interests were better accommodated within the national government (by means of a reformed electoral system and loosened party discipline), these interests would not have to seek satisfaction in the provinces or become the subject of federal-provincial conflict.

In short, the American experience suggests that state-based or candidate-based parties are no detriment to a strong national government and that reforms in the area of the electoral system and party discipline might increase our parties' capacity to accommodate regional and ethnic demands within that national government.

RECOMMENDATIONS

From every perspective examined in this study – historical and contemporary, domestic and comparative – it has been concluded that an increased integration of federal and provincial parties would not necessarily enhance their capacity to represent significant groupings in Canadian society more effectively. In fact, the American example demonstrates that within the U.S. political system, national political parties hardly even exist, and the current Canadian Conservative example indicates that a national party can thrive without counterparts in two of the largest provinces. The Conservative example also shows that a confederal relationship with such provincial wings as do exist is a highly satisfactory arrangement.

Even given the American example, there is no reason to suggest that Canada would be better off without strong political parties at the national level; on the contrary, all evidence points to the need for our national parties to be strengthened. But the same evidence leads to the conclusion that this can be done, and done best, without increasing federal-provincial party integration. The Liberals and New Democrats (and the PCs too, for that matter) should be given every encouragement to strengthen their national parties by building up federally oriented memberships, constituency associations, branch offices and independent finances. This does not necessarily mean reducing their links with provincial branches; such relationships should be maintained where they are advantageous to *both* levels of the party but otherwise should be recast so that the national party receives its fair share of attention, commitment, activity and resources. Whatever structures are in place, a basic common core of party activists will continue to ensure a large amount of cross-level cooperation and commonality of purpose, and close cross-level staff and caucus relationships will remain.

One of the most specific means of strengthening national parties in Canada would be to reform the system of party finance so that national parties would have more resources. Such resources would likely allow them to pursue the twin goals of power and national integration, whether by using the funds to hire party organizers, hold policy conferences, establish party foundations or merely run more effective election campaigns in all parts of the country. The current success of the PC party can probably be attributed, to a large extent, to its ample financial resources. The other two parties waste a great deal of time in financial negotiations with their provincial wings, either to extract badly needed money from them or to give them money that the federal party cannot really afford. Thus, unless other innovative ways are found to encourage a more generous and more equitable distribution of private contributions to Canadian parties, the German and other overseas examples would suggest a greater element of public funding in this respect.

At the present time, Canada has one national and 12 distinctive provincial and territorial election laws with respect to party and election finance, some of them mere fragments. Although one of the main advantages of a federation is that regional variations in public policy are possible, the disadvantages are quite evident in this field. First, especially in such provinces as Newfoundland and Saskatchewan, there is an unintended stretching of the federal legislation to provide tax credits for contributions to provincial parties because no provincial tax credit is available. However helpful this arrangement may be to all parties in such provinces, it is not one that should be encouraged; and the federal legislation should be amended to remove this anomaly, which is both inappropriate and bothersome to the national parties. Given the integrated nature of certain federal-provincial party financial relationships, however, it may be very difficult to prohibit such tax credits under the federal law. In any case, all provinces should be encouraged to provide tax credits under their own legislation.

If new federal legislation is passed to enhance the public funding of national parties, it should also ensure that the federal moneys involved are not similarly siphoned off by integrated provincial parties. Indeed, this is one policy area in which it would probably be advantageous to have uniform federal and provincial legislation. Besides being the only way to close all loopholes, a common regime of party and election finance legislation would also simplify the life of party bureaucrats from coast to coast who spend a great deal of time understanding differences in federal and provincial legislation and then explaining them to potential contributors, candidates, chief financial officers and official agents. In addition, it would help integrated federal parties, which are now forced to make idiosyncratic and time-consuming financial arrangements with each of their provincial wings. Such uniformity could hardly be imposed upon the provinces, but it is to be hoped that the quality of the Royal Commission's legislative recommendations on this subject will lead all provinces to see the advantage of enacting a parallel scheme.

Providing national parties with a stronger and more independent financial base would probably go a long way toward allowing them to represent significant groupings in Canadian society more effectively. Beyond this, however, a reform of the electoral system in the direction of the German model would no doubt be advantageous. If each party received national parliamentary representation consistent with its regional or provincial popular vote in federal elections, it would be better equipped to accommodate all regional and ethnic demands than when, as at present, its parliamentary representation exaggerates its regional strengths and weaknesses. Finally, it would be worth taking another look at how the American system (and British system) manages to accommodate various demands at the national level through less rigid party discipline. Beyond the realm of parties and elections, a more representative bureaucracy and perhaps a reformed Senate would also contribute to this end.

NOTES

The author gratefully acknowledges the assistance of the acting national director of the Progressive Conservative Party of Canada, the acting secretary-general and the chief financial officer of the Liberal Party of Canada and the federal secretary of the New Democratic Party of Canada, together with their field officers and the chief administrative officers of all provincial parties in the country. Herman Bakvis and Leslie Seidle of the Royal Commission staff made valuable suggestions; Erich Keser, Dave Paquette and Jeff Kean were very helpful researchers; and Robert Wittmer and Doris Routhier provided indispensable technical assistance.

1. D.V. Smiley (1980, 1987) was the first to provide a theoretical treatment of this subject, employing the terms integrated and confederal, but using asymmetrical rather than truncated. See also Dyck 1989.

2. In this ranking, I must respectfully disagree with Smiley who claims that the Conservatives were generally more integrated than the Liberals. Wearing (1988) appears to support my view.

3. The party constitution allows the federal party to outlaw a provincial party should its constitution and principles be in conflict with those of the federal party. This happened in 1971 when the New Brunswick wing endorsed the principles of the Waffle movement, and it is more or less what happened in the 1987–90 period with respect to the provincial wing in Quebec.

4. Radwanski (1978) writes that Trudeau gave the Ontario Liberals 15 minutes of his time, and Gwyn (1980) notes that Trudeau discoed in New York after telling British Columbia Liberals that he was too busy to attend their convention. Both also note Trudeau's lack of roots in the party, and Gwyn writes that between 1968 and 1972 he had "scarcely given the party the time of day."

5. Smiley (1980, 1987) hypothesizes that ideological differences within the Liberal party are more likely to be province-based (e.g., in the 1960s Quebec and New Brunswick were left of centre and Saskatchewan was right), although in the Conservative case such differences are evident within the national party.

6. Among the many discussions of this phenomenon, see Stewart 1986, Johnston 1980, Penniman 1988, and Frizzell et al. 1989.

7. Interestingly enough, Crosbie was a former provincial Liberal, Masse came from the Union nationale, and Campbell came from Social Credit.

8. Smiley and Watts 1985. Chandler (1987) calls them "jurisdictional federalism" (Canada) and "functional federalism" (West Germany), and argues that territorial politics and jurisdictional federalism lead to confederal parties in Canada. Other good recent sources on West Germany (now Germany) include a special issue of the periodical *Publius* (Fall 1989) and Roberts 1989.

9. Opposition parties often appeal on this basis in Canadian provincial elections too, but the electorate does not always respond, being distracted by purely provincial stimuli.

10. Gibbins (1982) tries to explain why regionalism is a stronger force in Canada than in the United States, arguing that the American system is able to channel spatially delineated interests within the central government, whereas Canada lacks an adequate regional representation within the institutions of the national government. Smiley and Watts (1985) are not so sure that improved mechanisms of "intrastate federalism" would help in the Canadian case, feeling that other factors must also be considered.

BIBLIOGRAPHY

Bakvis, Herman. 1989. "Regional Politics and Policy in the Mulroney Cabinet, 1984–88: Towards a Theory of the Regional Minister System in Canada." *Canadian Public Policy* 15:121–34.

————. 1991. *Regional Ministers: Power and Influence in the Canadian Cabinet.* Toronto: University of Toronto Press.

Barrie, Doreen, and R. Gibbins. 1989. "Parliamentary Careers in the Canadian Federal State." *Canadian Journal of Political Science* 22:137–45.

Black, E.R. 1979. "Federal Strains Within a Canadian Party." In *Party Politics in Canada.* 4th ed., ed. H.G. Thorburn. Scarborough: Prentice-Hall Canada.

Blake, Donald. 1985. *Two Political Worlds: Parties and Voting in British Columbia.* Vancouver: University of British Columbia Press.

Brown, S., B. Kay, R. Lambert and J. Curtis. 1986. "The 1984 Election: Explaining the Vote." Paper presented at the Canadian Political Science Association annual meeting in Winnipeg.

Chandler, Marsha. 1986. "Constitutional Change and Public Policy: The Impact of the Resource Amendment (Section 92A)." *Canadian Journal of Political Science* 19:103–26.

Chandler, William. 1987. "Federalism and Political Parties." In *Federalism and the Role of the State,* ed. Herman Bakvis and William Chandler. Toronto: University of Toronto Press.

Chandler, William M., and Alan Siaroff. 1991. "Parties and Party Government in Advanced Democracies." In *Canadian Political Parties: Leaders, Candidates and Organization*, ed. Herman Bakvis. Vol. 13 of the research studies of the Royal Commission on Electoral Reform and Party Financing. Ottawa and Toronto: RCERPF/Dundurn.

Clarke, H.D., J. Jenson, L. LeDuc and J. Pammett. 1979. *Political Choice in Canada*. Toronto: McGraw-Hill Ryerson.

———. 1984. *Absent Mandate*. Toronto: Gage.

Covell, Maureen. 1991. "Parties as Institutions of National Governance." In *Representation, Integration and Political Parties in Canada*, ed. Herman Bakvis. Vol. 14 of the research studies of the Royal Commission on Electoral Reform and Party Financing. Ottawa and Toronto: RCERPF/Dundurn.

Davey, Keith. 1986. *The Rainmaker*. Toronto: Stoddart.

Diefenbaker, John. 1976. *One Canada*, Vol. 2. Toronto: Macmillan.

———. 1977. *One Canada*, Vol. 3. Toronto: Macmillan.

Dyck, Rand. 1986. *Provincial Politics in Canada*. Scarborough: Prentice-Hall Canada.

———. 1989. "Relations Between Federal and Provincial Parties." In *Canadian Parties in Transition: Discourse, Organization, and Representation*, ed. A.G. Gagnon and A.B. Tanguay. Scarborough: Nelson Canada.

Elkins, David J. 1991. "Parties as National Institutions: A Comparative Study." In *Representation, Integration and Political Parties in Canada*, ed. Herman Bakvis. Vol. 14 of the research studies of the Royal Commission on Electoral Reform and Party Financing. Ottawa and Toronto: RCERPF/Dundurn.

Engelmann, F.C., and M.A. Schwartz. 1975. *Canadian Political Parties: Origin, Character, Impact*. Scarborough: Prentice-Hall Canada.

English, John. 1986. "The 'French Lieutenant' in Ottawa." In *National Politics and Community in Canada*, ed. R.K. Carty and W.P. Ward. Vancouver: University of British Columbia Press.

Frizzell, A., and A. Westell. 1985. *The Canadian General Election of 1984*. Ottawa: Carleton University Press.

Frizzell, A., Jon Pammett and A. Westell. 1989. *The Canadian General Election of 1988*. Ottawa: Carleton University Press.

Gibbins, Roger. 1982. *Regionalism: Territorial Politics in Canada and the United States*. Toronto: Butterworths.

Graham, Roger. 1990. *Old Man Ontario: Leslie M. Frost*. Toronto: University of Toronto Press.

Gruending, Dennis. 1990. *Promises to Keep: A Political Biography of Allan Blakeney*. Saskatoon: Western Producer Prairie Books.

Gwyn, Richard. 1980. *The Northern Magus*. Toronto: McClelland and Stewart.

Hoy, Claire. 1985. *Bill Davis*. Toronto: Methuen.

Johnston, R. 1980. "Federal and Provincial Voting: Contemporary Patterns and Historical Evolution." In *Small Worlds: Provinces and Parties in Canadian Political Life*, ed. D.J. Elkins and R. Simeon. Toronto: Methuen.

McCall-Newman, C. 1982. *Grits*. Toronto: Macmillan.

McDougall, A.K. 1986. *John P. Robarts: His Life and Government*. Toronto: University of Toronto Press.

Pearson, L.B. 1975. *Mike*, Vol. 3. Toronto: University of Toronto Press.

Penniman, Howard, ed. 1988. *Canada at the Polls, 1984*. Durham, NC: Duke University Press.

Perlin, George. 1980. *The Tory Syndrome*. Montreal: McGill-Queen's University Press.

Publius: The Journal of Federalism. 1989. Special issue on West German federalism (Fall).

Radwanski, George. 1978. *Trudeau*. Toronto: Macmillan.

Roberts, Geoffrey. 1989. "Party System Change in West Germany: Land-Federal Linkages." *West European Politics* 12 (4): 98–113.

Smiley, D.V. 1980. *Canada in Question: Federalism in the Eighties*. 3d ed. Toronto: McGraw-Hill Ryerson.

———. 1987. *The Federal Condition in Canada*. Toronto: McGraw-Hill Ryerson.

Smiley, D.V., and Ronald Watts. 1985. *Intrastate Federalism in Canada*. Vol. 39 of the research studies of the Royal Commission on the Economic Union and Development Prospects for Canada. Toronto: University of Toronto Press.

Smith, David. 1975. *Prairie Liberalism: The Liberal Party in Saskatchewan 1905–71*. Toronto: University of Toronto Press.

Stevenson, Garth. 1989. *Unfulfilled Union*. 3d ed. Toronto: Gage.

Stewart, Ian. 1986. "Friends at Court: Federalism and Provincial Elections on Prince Edward Island." *Canadian Journal of Political Science* 19:127–50.

Thomas, Paul. 1985. "The Role of National Party Caucuses." In *Party Government and Regional Representation in Canada*. Vol. 36 of the research studies of the Royal Commission on the Economic Union and Development Prospects for Canada. Toronto: University of Toronto Press.

Wagenberg, R.H., W.I. Romanow, W.C. Sunderland and E.D. Briggs. 1986. "Media Coverage of the 1984 Canadian Election." Paper presented at the Canadian Political Science Association annual meeting in Winnipeg.

Wearing, Joseph. 1981. *The L-Shaped Party: The Liberal Party of Canada 1958–1980.* Toronto: McGraw-Hill Ryerson.

———. 1988. *Strained Relations: Canadian Parties and Voters.* Toronto: McClelland and Stewart.

Whitaker, Reg. 1977. *The Government Party: Organizing and Financing the Liberal Party of Canada 1930–58.* Toronto: University of Toronto Press.

Williams, R.J. 1985. "Ontario's Party Systems: Federal and Provincial." In *Party Politics in Canada.* 5th ed., ed. H.G. Thorburn. Scarborough: Prentice-Hall Canada.

Winn, C., and J. McMenemy. 1976. *Political Parties in Canada.* Toronto: McGraw-Hill Ryerson.

Young, Walter. 1969. *The Anatomy of a Party: The National CCF 1932–61.* Toronto: University of Toronto Press.

4

PARTIES AND REGIONAL REPRESENTATION

Paul G. Thomas

THIS STUDY EXAMINES the role of party caucuses within the Parliament of Canada as vehicles for the representation of regional concerns and demands in the national policy process. Party caucuses are little known, and even less understood, institutions in the Canadian parliamentary process. The term refers to a private meeting of the parliamentary members of a political party. It is said to have originated in the United States and to have derived from a North American Indian word meaning "to consult." In the United States, the term was originally used to refer to a meeting of party leaders to select candidates for office or to plot policy and strategy to further the party's interests. Under cabinet-parliamentary forms of government, party caucuses have acquired a more specifically parliamentary purpose.

The caucus in Canada is a confidential meeting involving all members of Parliament and senators from a given political party. For many years now, national party caucuses have met on Wednesday mornings during parliamentary sessions. Such meetings usually focus on parliamentary business and the tactics to be followed by the parties in pursuing their parliamentary and wider political goals. In addition, all parties now usually meet several times during parliamentary recesses. At each of these meetings, which last a day or two, the caucus discusses such topics as party strategies for upcoming sessions of Parliament, the organization of the parliamentary group and its relations with the party outside of Parliament, and the party's standing in terms of public opinion.

In addition to the national caucuses, all parties now operate regional caucuses and also usually a system of policy committees. According to a former MP,[1] the party caucus is a crucial institution for creating greater awareness of, and sensitivity to, regional issues: "The great regional debates are within caucus. They are emotional; they are spontaneous; they are without written statements. The heartbeats of the country are felt within caucus; and that is where comprehension comes. That does not get out to the House of Commons, because of the secrecy of the party caucus system." The effectiveness of the party caucuses in bringing regional concerns to the national decision-making process and in enhancing the legitimacy of the actions of the national government in all parts of the country is the main concern of this study.

In addition to the representation of regional views, party caucuses serve a number of other functions. They contribute to party unity and to party solidarity in terms of parliamentary behaviour. Within caucuses, an attempt is made to develop a consensus on party positions to be presented in Parliament and beyond. Strategies and tactics for advancing the party's cause are also devised in the caucuses. Caucus meetings allow for two-way communication between the party leadership and their supporters regarding policy issues and the political situation in general. Such meetings are also used to build party morale and to vent disagreements and frustrations. Over time, the importance of party caucuses has grown, although the progress has been uneven and intermittent. Whereas the principal focus for this study is on the caucus as a regional body, these other related functions are also significant and merit attention.

REGIONALISM AND REGIONAL CONFLICT

In a recent book that reviews a decade of national surveys of the attitudes of Canadians on different topics, the authors conclude that regional tensions are now higher than at any other point during the preceding 10 years (Gregg and Posner 1990, 31). Respondents in all parts of the country believed that the national decision-making processes were unfair to their regions. There was a widespread perception that tolerance and fairness were no longer part of the rules of the political game (ibid., 32).

Regional conflicts are not new to Canada. Over the years there have been recurrent complaints about the inequities of national policies, which are alleged to systematically favour central Canada at the expense of the peripheral regions of the country. What is new, and perhaps contradictory, is the feeling today across the country, including Ontario and Quebec, that the national political system does not serve provincial interests adequately.

Definitions of Regionalism

Regionalism is a broad and controversial concept. It refers to the distinctive character of defined geographic areas and to people's perception of, and identification with, such places. This definition is similar to the one used by Schwartz (1974, 309) who defines the concept as a regional view of reality, by which she means a consciousness of belonging to a region with its distinctive features and interests. Regional consciousness is related to, but is not necessarily created by, regional economic, social and political differences. It is necessary to distinguish between regions as economic and social units with distinctive features and the social-psychological component of regionalism.

Regional diversity is seen by many scholars to be the most salient feature of Canadian society. Differences in physical geography, patterns of settlement, economic structures, ethnic composition, language, religion and local histories are said to have produced variations in political outlooks across the country. Rather than one shared national political culture, Canada is seen as a collection of regional political cultures.

Cultural regionalism is encouraged when significant linguistic, ethnic or religious minorities that have resisted assimilation into the larger society are concentrated in defined geographic areas. When cultural pluralism is expressed territorially in this way, members of minority cultural groups may feel their vital interests are better protected by the regional political system than by the national government.

Economic regionalism exists when the economic diversities vary among regions more than they do within. The most prominent economic differences are those between the "have" and "have not" provinces. Regions and provinces compete in economic terms, each trying to improve its economic position, often in relative terms compared to others. Walter Gainer (1976, 42) has argued that "the underlying basis of regional frictions within the Canadian federation stems more from the pursuit of common economic growth and development goals than it does from any great regional differences in dominant values, attitudes and behaviour patterns." In the hinterland or peripheral regions there is a shared dissatisfaction with the concentration of commercial activity and influence in the large urban centres of central Canada.

Economic differences among Canadian regions are related to the extent of industrialization, the relative reliance upon natural resources, the type of resources being developed, the destination of products to domestic or foreign markets and the level of financial and other types of policy support from the federal and provincial governments. Geography and history have combined to identify certain regions with particular types of economic activity. Economic regionalism can serve to reinforce cultural regionalism and may result in extreme political conflict when differences are perceived as unjust (Bell and Tepperman 1979, 198).

Political regionalism refers to the different orientations to politics and the identifications with place of residence expressed by Canadians in various parts of the country. Over the past two decades a large number of surveys have been conducted to determine the regional contours of Canadian political consciousness. Although somewhat ambiguous results have been produced from the surveys (largely it seems because of variations in the ways in which the questions were asked), some of the main findings should be noted here.

A majority of Canadians in every province felt closer to their provincial governments than to the national government, and everywhere, except in Ontario and Quebec, this preference was by a substantial margin (Elkins and Simeon 1980). During the 1980s over 80 percent of western Canadians felt that the political system favours central Canada and almost one in three felt that western Canada got so few benefits from being part of Canada that they might as well go it on their own (McCormick and Elton 1987). Yet strong provincial identities and attachments do not displace strong national loyalties. Nearly 70 percent of Canadians described themselves as Canadians first, with well over three-quarters of anglophones in Ontario and the West identifying themselves in this way; only 40 percent of francophones in Quebec saw themselves as Canadians first (Ornstein et al. 1980). Over the last decade, an overwhelming majority of respondents endorsed the proposition that Canada was the best country in which to live (Gregg and Posner 1990).

Although regional identities exist, they do not determine all aspects of Canadian political outlooks. Regional effects are held to be less marked than social class differences in determining people's sense of political efficacy, participation and most ideological differences (Ornstein et al. 1980). In economic, social and cultural fields, one study discovered a growing convergence in public attitudes, with even the differences between Quebec and the rest of the country not being all that significant (R. Johnston 1986). Whereas regional feelings fluctuate to some extent in content and intensity over time, certain points recur in regional viewpoints.

Regionalism as Symbol, Myth and Ideology

A perennial theme of Canadian politics is that the national government is insensitive and unresponsive to the needs and demands of the peripheries of the country and has catered to the interests of central Canada.

Evidence of these feelings has been reported above. Whether the charge is justified or not, the alleged bias in national decision making in favour of Ontario and Quebec is widely accepted as a fact in the rest of the country. Over time regionalism acquires a symbolic, mythical and ideological quality. Regions become reified and stereotyped; they are seen as unified political actors with no internal divisions, despite the fact that there are disagreements within as well as between regions. Regionalism provides the lens through which people perceive and interpret events. For example, when western Canadians turn on their television sets on election night to find out that a majority government has been elected without them, the event reinforces a strongly developed sense of alienation. Regional discontent takes on a mythical dimension that suggests that nothing is ever done to benefit the outer regions or that beneficial policies are grudging consolation prizes or designed with an eye to political considerations in which regional interests are a minor component. As an ideology, regionalism provides a definition, admittedly vague, of the ideal place of the region in the political system and serves as a guide to action.

The Institutionalization of Regionalism

Regionalism is rooted at least as much in public perceptions as in actual economic and cultural differences. There is no denying an underlying regional dimension and texture to Canadian society, but the importance of regionalism has been heightened by how we have organized our political life. Canadians have been conditioned by the constitutional and institutional arrangements and the associated political processes to think about their political life in territorial terms. Issues become defined in terms of their regional impacts and in terms of which order of government has primary jurisdiction. Although regionalism is often seen as the preeminent fact of Canadian political life, there are significant other social cleavages that increasingly pose new challenges for the political system. If there are regional political cultures, there are also political cultures surrounding the demands of social classes, Aboriginal peoples, women, the elderly, environmentalists and numerous other groups. However, regional tensions stand out among the many issues facing an increasingly fragmented political culture because they challenge the territorial integrity of the political system.

The main structural feature contributing to regionalism is the federal system. Federalism does more than reflect the underlying diversities found in Canadian society, it also reinforces the cleavages that gave rise to federalism in the first place. During this century, federal and provincial governmental activities have assumed growing practical and symbolic importance in the lives of Canadians, resulting in the increased politicization of society. According to Alan Cairns (1986, 55), "we must learn to think in terms of politicized societies caught in webs of interdependence with the state, and we must think of the latter as an embedded state tied down by its multiple linkages with society, which restrain its maneuverability." As governments impinged more on the lives of individuals and groups, they were able to generate and mould public opinion and to foster or discourage certain forms of political representation.

Another dynamic at work, especially since the 1960s, has been increased competition for political credit and loyalty between the two orders of government. With the increased importance of their constitutional responsibilities, their increased political and bureaucratic competence, and their new aggressiveness and visibility in federal-provincial dealings, provincial governments have been able to draw pressure groups into the ambit of their influence and to structure public opinion along provincial lines. It has been suggested that the feeling of belonging has been transferred from the local community to the province, rather than to broader but amorphous regions, such as Atlantic Canada and the West, which have a less clear political definition (Beck 1981). Regionalism is now most vigorously promoted by provincial politicians who are anxious to protect their jurisdictions and serve their self-interest in re-election. Political parties at the provincial level can gain ground by attacking federal authorities for being indifferent, or even hostile, toward provincial concerns.

If federalism is the main contributing factor to regional outlooks, the importance of regionalism is also exaggerated by the simple-majority, single-member electoral system used in national and provincial elections, an issue that is discussed later in this study.

THE LEGITIMACY OF THE NATIONAL GOVERNMENT

Critics of the existing Canadian political system suggest that the institutions of the central government now operate in an unduly centralized and majoritarian way. The legitimacy of national policies is compromised because current methods of political organization do not provide an adequate outlet for the expression and incorporation of territorially based interests in decision making (Smiley and Watts 1985, xvi). Legitimacy is a difficult concept, both in a theoretical sense and in terms of finding empirical measures of the phenomenon in the real world (Connelly 1984). In general terms, political legitimacy consists of the acknowledgement of and support for the institutions and policies of the political system. Several factors appear to affect the level of legitimacy enjoyed by the institutions and policies of the Canadian political system.

The House of Commons

As the most democratically based and broadly representative institution at the national level, the House of Commons should enjoy a high degree of legitimacy. It is the institution at the centre of a wider political process for creating governments, rendering them legitimate, giving assent to policies that become legally binding, and holding governments accountable on a continuous basis. The legitimizing authority of the House of Commons is strengthened by tradition; over time, Canadians have been conditioned to think in terms of policies needing the approval of Parliament. Philip Norton (1990) has suggested that three other functions may be subsumed under the rubric of legitimization: tension release (e.g., the redress of grievances), integration (the aggregation and reconciling of different demands to create a national outlook) and the mobilization of support (raising support for particular policies between elections). In practice, several processes in Parliament serve these functions, although it is open to debate how well each is performed.

The House of Commons is described as representative; however, in terms of the social backgrounds of its members it is atypical of the population it serves. MPs tend to be older, better educated and of higher socio-economic status than their constituents. Women and minority-group members are underrepresented in the Commons in comparison to their presence in society at large. These patterns are not particularly surprising given the fact that we elect legislators on a territorial basis to represent constituencies; we do not select them to create a mirror image of society. Nevertheless, underrepresentation of certain social and economic groups has symbolic importance and may rob policies of support and legitimacy, especially among groups who consider themselves marginal to the political process. For example, the *Canadian Charter of Rights and Freedoms*, passed in 1982, which stresses individual rights and identifies certain social categories of individuals for specific protection, challenges the territory-based definition of pluralism that dominated Canadian political life up to that point.

Government Decision-Making Procedures

The organization and procedures for decision making in government can affect the legitimacy of policies. For example, i. the Cabinet uses its majority in Parliament to push through unpopular legislation, public opposition to the policy may grow because of the way it was adopted.

There is clearly a relationship among different institutions in terms of generating legitimacy for government actions. For example, the adoption of a more formalistic and collective approach to decision making within the Trudeau cabinet system is said to have weakened the Cabinet as a forum for the articulation and accommodation of regional interests. According to some commentators, ministers were given less autonomy to act as regional defenders. Moreover, the complicated procedures for handling policy issues are said to have confused outside pressure groups about how best to gain access to key decision makers in "official Ottawa" at the appropriate point in the policy cycle. Paul Pross (1985) suggested optimistically that the diffusion and confusion of power within the executive arena made Parliament a more attractive target for the messages of pressure groups who were seeking the political legitimacy that the House of Commons could bestow on their viewpoints. Unfortunately, the Commons' own legitimacy has been challenged when contentious policies were pushed through under strict party discipline by governments with little or no elected representation from the sections of the country most directly affected.

The Federal Bureaucracy

The perception of a centralist bias in the operations of the federal bureaucracy may also rob national policies of legitimacy. No one disputes the fact that the bureaucracy has gained influence during this century as the scope and complexity of government has grown. Negative perceptions and mistrust of the bureaucracy have increased over the past two decades. Twenty-two times between 1980 and 1989 a national survey asked about people's level of confidence in the public service. The results showed an erosion of confidence over nine years and on average 83 percent of respondents had hardly any or only some confidence (Scott 1990, 65). When asked in 1987 which level of government they were thinking about, 42 percent of respondents mentioned the federal public service, 31 percent the provincial and 27 percent said both.

Organized along the lines of policy sectors, the frames of reference for federal departments reflect economic, industrial and social categories. Problems that come up within a regional context may be ignored or not seen clearly. John Meisel has suggested that the centralizing tendencies of a powerful bureaucracy sitting in the nation's capital have not been tempered sufficiently by the political process. According to Meisel, "a system of electoral parties – that is, parties which are not programmatic, which are more interested in winning elections than in developing detailed policy alternatives – impedes the creative interaction between our excellent bureaucracy and regional interests expressed by politicians."[2]

Government Effectiveness

In addition to the institutional and procedural aspects of legitimacy, there is also a substantive aspect. Ralf Dahrendorf (1980, 397) has written that "a government is legitimate if it does what is right both in the sense of complying with certain fundamental principles, and in that of being in line with prevailing cultural values in the society." There is also a relationship, albeit not entirely clear, between the perceived effectiveness of government policies and the level of legitimacy within the political system. Dahrendorf (1980, 396) suggests that the relationship is asymmetrical: it is possible for a government to be effective without being legitimate, but it is difficult to imagine a government that is legitimate over the long run without being effective. There is ample evidence, from Canada and elsewhere, that public confidence in governments has declined and it is fair to assume that some part of the decline can be attributed to disappointment with the performance of governments, especially in the realm of management of the economy. Over time, ineffectiveness will erode legitimacy.

Manipulation of Political Symbols

Most members of the general public experience politics at the symbolic level (Edelman 1988). As spectators most of the time, we derive our knowledge of the political process mainly from images in the mass media. Skilful manipulation of the symbols of government by the political leadership can be used to mobilize consent and support. As Edelman (ibid., 123) writes, "While coercion and intimidation help to check resistance in all political systems, the key tactic must always be the evocation of interpretations that legitimize favoured courses of action and threaten or reassure people so as to encourage them to be supportive or to remain quiescent." Contriving events and the use of advocacy advertising have become popular means by which governments seek to bestow legitimacy on their actions.

The Role of the Media

The increasingly adversarial stance adopted by the media and its reporters toward government in all its forms may gradually erode legitimacy. In the case of Parliament, even though it has been televised since 1977, most Canadians develop their image of the institution from the nightly television newscasts and to a lesser extent from the other media. Since conflict captures media attention more than hard work and inspiration, much of the parliamentary coverage paints a rather negative picture that encourages cynicism toward the institution. The sometimes three-ring circus atmosphere of Question Period makes it a prime source for news stories on Parliament, whereas serious discussions in debates and in the committee system generate little coverage. The few surveys available suggest a declining reputation for Parliament.

Legitimacy and Electoral Reform

Citizens may recognize a government as legitimate for many reasons; however, in a system in which legitimacy is low, and the bases of legitimacy not accepted, resort to violence and political disintegration can occur. Although some delegitimization may be taking place in Canada, fortunately it has not descended to that level. Less drastic signs of deteriorating relations between citizens and their governments would be defiance of laws, direct political action, support for protest parties and declining participation in elections. Serious underlying problems of legitimacy could include the following: failure of all citizens to accept the national community (Quebec), lack of acceptance of the structure and procedures for recruiting leaders and making policies (western Canada), and failure by leaders to convince citizens that they are following the right procedures and adopting the right kinds of policies. All of these concerns may seem far removed from the issue of electoral reform, but the identification of numerous sources of legitimacy reinforces the important point that changes to particular institutions are likely to have only a marginal impact on the overall level of political support for the political system and its policies. Put in more concrete terms, changing the electoral system alone is not a panacea to solve regional discontent.

REPRESENTATION AND RESPONSIVENESS

The process of representation of public opinion to government is a complex, multidimensional phenomenon that takes place on many levels and in many locations throughout the political system. Yet Canadian political scientists have not spent much time addressing the conceptual problems related to the role of political parties, Parliament and the process of representation. Instead, they have sought to describe the more obvious dimensions of representation (such as the regional composition of the House of Commons or the socio-economic backgrounds of MPs) without a full discussion of what representation actually is.

Concepts of Representation

The most widely quoted definition of representation is Hannah Pitkin's (1967, 209): "Representation means acting in the interests of the represented, in a manner responsive to them." Implied in the definition is the idea that constituents must have some influence or control, or at least the potential for such, over their elected representatives. Representatives should not, Pitkin suggested, be consistently at odds with the wishes of the represented, without good reason and without explanation. The prevalent approach based upon this definition was to equate representation as congruence between the policy views of constituents and the policy stands taken by their elected representatives. In this view, if an MP and his constituency are in complete agreement on policy, he is seen as acting responsively when he voices their opinions. Such a straightforward example, however, is probably rare in the real world and hides a great deal of the complexity of the concept of responsiveness.

In Canada the puzzle of representation is complicated by the pervasive influence of cohesive, disciplined political parties. Most actions by individual Canadian legislators are actually forms of party behaviour based upon party loyalty and party discipline. How can MPs be responsive to constituency opinion if they are expected to follow the party line? If there is controversy within a constituency over policy, whose views should the MP represent? Should MPs respond only to those members of the electorate who voted for their party or do they have an obligation to balance competing views? Should responsiveness be to the current demands of the public or to what the MP deems to be in the long-term best interests of the population? It is not clear from available research how MPs answer these questions. Most of the literature on Parliament assumes a dual representation role for MPs: they are seen as members of parties with a national mandate and as members who also represent geographic constituencies. This dualistic conception excludes an intermediate territorial dimension of representation: the promotion of the interests of their home province or even groups of provinces. It also ignores the identification that some MPs assume in their representational roles with particular sectors of the economy or segments of the population.

The emphasis on demonstrating the congruence between constituency opinion and legislative behaviour has diverted attention from other types of representational activity undertaken by MPs. Eulau and Karps (1977) sought to correct this deficiency by identifying four components of responsiveness: policy, service, allocation and symbolic.

Policy responsiveness refers to some meaningful connection between the policy preferences of a constituency and the positions taken by its representative in Parliament. Service responsiveness refers to the tangible benefits that the MP is able to obtain for particular constituents. Over the past two decades MPs have equipped themselves with a variety of devices ("householders" advertising their availability, constituency offices, paid staff, etc.) to serve more effectively as liaisons with government on behalf of their individual constituents. Allocation responsiveness refers to efforts by legislators to obtain more generalized benefits for their constituencies through intervention in the legislative and administrative processes. MPs can campaign for the placement of government buildings or contracts within their ridings, advertise the availability of government programs, seek tax breaks for industries that are prominent in the constituency, lobby ministers for grants to support local projects, and so on.

Symbolic responsiveness operates more on a social and psychological level. It refers to the more intangible forms of recognition and reward for the people being served in the representative relationship. As noted earlier, the fact that certain social groups are underrepresented in Parliament may send a symbolic message. Symbolic rewards seldom exist in isolation from material benefits and groups that feel symbolically excluded may also feel they have been denied the tangible benefits of government.

The different components of responsiveness overlap in practice. Pursuing the policy interests of constituents merges with the MP's search for allocative benefits. Delivering a government contract to a local firm becomes an allocation action and an important symbolic occasion. MPs pursue representation opportunities in hundreds of ways, both formal and informal. Much of the representation process takes place behind the scenes away from public notice. It consists of contacts with ministers and the bureaucracy, meetings with interest groups, asking questions in the House of Commons, dealing with the media, responding to queries from constituents and many more activities.

The Need for Further Study

Our understanding of the representative process in all its aspects is seriously underdeveloped. We simply do not know exactly what the cumulative impact of the different types of representation is on the public's confidence in, and support for, the political system. If the earlier cited survey data are accurate, many Canadians are clearly unhappy with the performance of their political institutions and specifically dissatisfied with Parliament. Yet the available survey data do not tell us which aspects of Parliament's performance have been found wanting. The public unease may be tied up with the issues before Parliament at any given time. Impressionistically, it seems that public criticism of Parliament remains unfocused and people do not know what aspects of the institution they wish to change, apart from those types of reforms that the pollsters ask them to endorse or reject.

REPRESENTATION AND POLITICAL PARTIES

The Role of Political Parties

Political parties have long been considered essential to representative and responsible government. Party is the means by which the public puts governments in place and seeks to hold them accountable for their performance. Parties help to shape and organize the various opinions found in society by structuring them in the form of votes and other types of political activity. They give expression to regional and other diversities and integrate them into a definition of the national interest. They act as giant personnel agencies for the recruitment, election and placement of individuals in public office. The party with the greatest number of MPs elected to the House of Commons forms the government and is expected to provide policy leadership in the form of legislative, financial and other initiatives. The other parties perform the function of an institutionalized opposition, something that is considered valuable as a means for holding the political executive, in the form of the Cabinet, accountable for its actions. In theory, MPs from all parties provide parliamentary scrutiny of the bureaucracy, but in practice this function belongs more to the opposition parties who perform it indirectly by holding responsible ministers directly and continuously answerable in public for the performance of departments and other agencies. Opposition parties are also a valuable means for the expression of minority opinions and permit peaceful alternation in office. Finally, political parties organize most aspects of legislative life and provide the energy that drives the institution of Parliament on a daily basis.

The Effectiveness of Canadian Political Parties

Although the importance of political parties to parliamentary democracies is widely recognized, there is a growing unease about their capacity to perform successfully the various functions ascribed to them. Any discussion of the decline of political parties must necessarily take into account these various functions. Because the functions are interrelated and not always complementary, assessments of the effectiveness of the party system vary depending upon which function is under examination.

Canadian parties have been described as both too weak and too strong. They are held to be less than successful in structuring the vote, mobilizing opinion and integrating the mass public into a shared definition of the national interest. Parties have lost ground to other institutions as sources of policy ideas over the last three to four decades. Within parties the focus has been primarily on winning elections, not on preparing to govern. There has not been the willingness to spend the energy, time and resources necessary for serious policy development. Instead, the parties have used their recently gained affluence (largely the result of the election expense law passed in 1974) to employ the new campaign technologies, not to sponsor policy development.

With respect to the recruitment of personnel, the filling of public offices and the organization of government, parties have suffered little or no loss of function. More people seek nominations than in the past, although there are concerns about the "packing" of nomination meetings and the free-wheeling spending that occurs in some nomination contests. In the eyes of many critics, parties have become almost too successful in structuring the operations of cabinet-parliamentary government. They dominate most aspects of parliamentary life. Disciplined and cohesive parties make leadership and coherence possible in terms of legislation and spending. They also enable the public more easily to assign accountability for actions since it is the prime minister and Cabinet who normally control the parliamentary process when a majority government is in place. At the same time, the pervasive influence of parties and the strict partisanship in the House of Commons limit the contribution of both Parliament and its individual members to the process of governing. Members may speak for their regions, but normally they must vote for their parties.

The Brokerage Model

How party caucuses contribute to the expression and accommodation of regional viewpoints is central to the so-called "brokerage model" of political parties. This model has been the dominant metaphor for interpretation of the party system and has been the ideal that the party leaders have sought, at least at the level of rhetoric, to approximate. The classic statement of the brokerage ideal was made by J.A. Corry (1952, 22): "In the aptest phrase yet applied to them, parties are brokers of ideas. They are middlemen who select from all the ideas pressing for recognition as public policy those they think can be shaped to have the widest appeal and through their party organization, they try to sell a carefully sifted and edited selection of these ideas (their programme) to enough members of the electorate to produce a majority in a legislature." Following a market analogy of democracy, one version of the brokerage model sees political parties as profit-seeking entrepreneurs who try to maximize their vote to gain power, and views voters as self-interested consumers who vote for the party whose policies are most likely to benefit them individually.

A second version of the brokerage interpretation sees pragmatic, moderate, accommodationist parties as crucial in a diverse, pluralistic society where national unity is fragile. In this view, Canadian political parties have avoided imposing political debate along social class lines on a country that is already divided along regional, linguistic, religious and other cleavages. The principal function of political parties is said to be the aggregation and accommodation of diverse interests. To do this, the primary concern of party leaders is to keep the party united, not to articulate policy positions. It is desirable that the parties themselves are pluralistic institutions reflecting internally the main interests within society, and there must be "political room" for the élites within the parties to build coalitions through bargaining, compromise and accommodation without excessive pressures from the outside.

Both variants of the brokerage model have attracted their fair share of critics (Brodie and Jenson 1989). Party competition, according to the market analogy, is said to make the political system more responsive and to facilitate accountability, but the critics challenge it on several fronts. They reject the underlying assumption of "consumer sovereignty" in the electoral market, wherein the public has identifiable and stable policy preferences. Mass political beliefs are not fixed, but highly ambivalent and subject to manipulation by political élites. Competition for votes involves not simply responsiveness to mass preferences, but also the shaping of public opinion and the mobilization of political support (Edelman 1971). A second challenge to the market analogy involves the issue of whether parties offer voters any real choice. There is a disagreement among scholars over whether the two parties that have contended for power at the national level really offer voters clear policy alternatives. The majority opinion appears to be that the main parties have avoided principled stands and have not spelled out their policy plans for the benefit of the electorate. Consequently, most elections have settled little in policy terms. Despite the lack of policy differences, voters still develop loyalties to particular parties and these serve as barriers to the entry of new parties into the electoral marketplace.

The market variant of the brokerage model has been less popular than the pluralist version, which calls more direct attention to the sociological realities of Canadian society. In a society characterized by "complex cleavages," political parties are compelled to stress the function of social integration, according to brokerage proponents. There is disagreement, however, over the best way for parties to perform this function. Advocates of the "creative politics" of left–right political debate insist that the development of class-based politics would result in loyalties that transcend regional, linguistic and other conflicts. It is also argued that political parties have been brokerage institutions in terms of incorporating various interests only at the level of votes. Internally, they have been dominated by élites. It was easy for political élites to adopt a "pragmatic" political style emphasizing compromise and mutual adjustment because their issues dominated the parties. The concerns of excluded or politically marginal groups received limited or no attention.

David Smith (1985) provides another criticism of the brokerage model. Writing prior to the victory of the Mulroney Conservatives in the 1984 general election, Smith argued that recent prime ministers had followed a pan-Canadian, rather than a brokerage, approach to national leadership. Prime Ministers Diefenbaker (1958–63), Pearson (1963–68) and Trudeau (1968–79 and 1980–84) sought to transcend regional loyalties by appealing to Canadians on the basis of certain national values and policies, such as northern development, linguistic justice, patriation of the Constitution, the *Canadian Charter of Rights and Freedoms* and a national energy program. Their relative refusal to cater to regional concerns forced provincial governments to become more aggressive in defending their interests and led to demands for reforms to national institutions to make them less centralist in orientation.

The pluralist version of brokerage politics operated more successfully during earlier decades when the underlying social cleavages and the issues of the day were more amenable to the politics of élite accommodation and consensus building. Since the 1960s, the rise of more numerous pressure groups expressing new values has fragmented the political culture. New avenues for political participation were opened, with the somewhat ironic result of increased dissatisfaction among groups who found that their demands could never be fully met. A slowdown in economic growth beginning in the mid-1970s increased controversy over the role of government and created the impression that all public policy decisions involved clear winners and losers. A decline in public confidence, trust and deference toward governmental élites occurred. In this changed social-political context, political parties have faced grave difficulties in achieving the national consensus that brokerage theory ascribes to them. The containment of conflict has become more difficult because of the nature of the issues faced by governments today. In summary, recent history suggests that Canadian political parties are best understood not as bulwarks against social and political conflicts, but as institutions that function best in the absence of such conflicts.

THE ELECTORAL AND PARTY SYSTEMS

There is a dispute among scholars about what contribution, if any, the electoral system has made to the relative weakness of political parties as unifying agencies. The debate was launched by Alan Cairns in an article calling attention to the problems caused by the simple-plurality electoral system (Cairns 1968). Cairns attributed considerable significance to the electoral system, arguing that the party system would not have developed in the way it had without "the selective impetus" provided by the electoral system. It had fostered a party system that "accentuated sectional cleavages." It had reduced the visibility of other types of social cleavages that cut across sections. It had made sections or provinces appear monolithic in their support for particular parties and it had undervalued the partisan diversity that existed within provinces. It had provided parties with an incentive to make sectional appeals during elections and the highly regionalized character of the Cabinets and caucuses of the governing parties may have led to regional biases in national policies. Cairns observed that whether a party adopted policies favourable to provinces where it had strong parliamentary representation or whether it designed policies with an aim to achieve breakthroughs in provinces where it was weak was a matter for investigation in each case. The basic point, he argued, was that sectionalism had been given increased importance by the electoral system and the result was to call into question the political integrity of the country. If these were the disadvantages of the electoral system, it also had a mediocre record in terms of its supposed virtues. During the period from 1921 to 1965, the electoral system had produced majority governments where none would otherwise have existed on half of the occasions; and in about one-third of the elections during the period, the electoral system reduced the opposition parties to "numerical ineffectiveness."

J.A.A. Lovink (1970) argued that the propositions presented by Cairns could not be verified on the basis of the available evidence. The indictment of the electoral system, he said, was premature and probably too severe. He began by pointing out that Cairns had not clearly identified what constituted a regional policy and that in the "real world" almost all national policies had regional significance. According to Lovink, it was not clear to what extent the federal political parties had pursued regionally discriminatory policies. The regional composition of the various parliamentary parties may have led to greater sensitivity to the interests of certain provinces, but this pattern might be the result of pressures from within caucus or of decisions by autonomous leaders playing to their regional strengths or taking into account considerations outside the realm of electoral strategy. Much more research was needed, Lovink concluded, before the sectional nature of Canadian politics could be blamed on the impact of the electoral system on party policy.

The Cairns–Lovink debate over the impact of the electoral system turned more on differing emphases than on fundamental disagreements. Cairns did not argue that the electoral system conjured up regional discontent where none would otherwise exist and Lovink did not suggest that the electoral system was simply a technical factor that contributed nothing to the weakness of parties as unifying agencies. The influences of the electoral rules on parties and on the representation of regional concerns within Parliament can be both direct and indirect and, therefore, the identification of such influences is difficult. The procedures for assigning seats to provinces and for converting votes into seats for the political parties clearly affect electoral outcomes. Seats are the real currency of the parliamentary game and votes are important as they affect the probability of winning or losing seats. The electoral system makes some votes more valuable than others to particular parties. Electoral calculations are bound to figure prominently in both campaign strategies and the formulation of party policies. Pushed to a logical extreme, the winning strategy for political parties would consist of making campaign and policy appeals to marginal voters in marginal ridings so as to maximize the efficiency of the party's votes. However, such a pure vote-maximization approach presumes better political intelligence than is available to parties. Furthermore, party decision making involves more than simple electoral calculations. Parties do not act solely on the basis of the electoral consequences; they are often motivated by more public-spirited considerations such as national unity and fairness. Evidence of the relevance of such considerations for caucus decision making is provided later in this study.

Regional Balance

The most negative consequence of the electoral system has been to create an image of a highly regionalized party system in which whole sections of the country are excluded from the governing process during the terms in office of different parties. Many observers would argue that for the ideal model to work requires that the governing party have breadth of regional support. A "working" majority in the House of Commons is not necessarily a broadly based majority. In an electoral landslide, the winning party inevitably wins seats in all parts of the country. However, such landslides are relatively rare in Canada, especially recently. In the 34 elections held since Confederation, the winning party has won 60 percent or more of the seats in the House of Commons on

13 occasions. Only seven times over the 33 elections since 1872 has the governing party captured a majority of the seats in all four regions of the country – the Atlantic provinces, Quebec, Ontario and the West. Canada's more recent electoral history has featured six minority governments in the 12 elections held since 1957. Only the Progressive Conservatives in 1958 and in 1984 captured more than 60 percent of the seats and managed to win a majority of the seats in all regions. As table 4.1 reveals, historically, Canadian governments have not enjoyed broad regional support in their parliamentary caucuses.

Regional justice will probably not be seen to be done if a government completely lacks representation from particular regions. Even if a region gives a disproportionately small number of MPs to the governing party, there will still be a concern that the region is at a disadvantage when it comes to government attention and favours. Exactly how many seats from a region are needed to induce confidence that regional fairness will prevail is not clear. Writing about the long period of almost uninterrupted Liberal rule from 1921 to 1957, Alan Cairns (Williams 1988, 107) pointed to the success of the party in straddling the two language groups while still achieving "politically adequate representation from western Canada." It may be that the designation of "politically adequate representation" can be assigned only retrospectively. Perceptions of the adequacy of a region's representation within the national government depend on the type of issues that arise and on how a particular region fares in comparison to other parts of the country. It is plausible to argue that the main issues of partisan disagreement during the thirties, forties and fifties related to the development of the welfare state and that because such issues cut across regional boundaries, the Liberal party was able to avoid the appearance of regional bias.

Underrepresentation for a region on the government side of the House of Commons does not necessarily mean underrepresentation in the Cabinet. Prime ministers can strive, and usually do, to make their ministerial teams more regionally balanced than the parliamentary party as a whole. Provided that some MPs are returned from each province, the prime minister usually seeks to include a member from each province in Cabinet, and certain portfolios are usually assigned to MPs from the regions most directly affected. Regional representation in the Cabinet can be a considerable compensation for a region's underrepresentation in the parliamentary party as a whole. An experienced and politically skilful regional minister can protect regional interests, even without the backing of a large regional caucus. In fact, it is suggested later in this study that a large provincial or regional caucus can

Table 4.1

Percentage of seats in each region won by governing party in Canadian general elections, 1867–1988

| Election | Governing party[a] | % seats won by governing party in region | | | | |
		Canada	West[b]	Ontario	Quebec	Atlantic
1867	**Conservative**	55.8	—	56.1	69.2	29.4
1872	**Conservative**	51.5	90.0	43.2	58.5	48.6
1874	**Liberal**	64.6	20.0	72.7	50.8	79.1
1878	**Conservative**	66.5	90.0	67.0	69.2	55.8
1882	**Conservative**	66.2	72.7	59.3	73.8	67.4
1887	**Conservative**	57.2	93.3	56.5	50.8	55.8
1891	**Conservative**	57.2	93.3	52.2	46.2	72.1
1896	**Liberal**	54.9	47.1	46.7	75.4	43.6
1900	**Liberal**	62.0	70.6	39.1	87.7	69.2
1904	**Liberal**	65.0	75.0	44.2	83.1	74.3
1908	**Liberal**	60.2	51.4	41.9	81.5	74.3
1911	**Conservative**	60.2	51.4	83.7	41.5	45.7
1917	**Unionist (Conservative)**	65.1	96.5	90.2	4.6	67.7
1921	Liberal	49.4	8.8	25.6	100.0	80.6
1925	Liberal	40.4	33.3	13.4	90.8	20.7
1926	Liberal	47.3	34.8	28.0	92.3	31.0
1930	**Conservative**	55.9	44.9	72.0	36.9	79.3
1935	**Liberal**	69.8	48.6	68.3	84.6	96.2
1940	**Liberal**	72.7	59.7	67.1	93.8	73.1
1945	**Liberal**	51.0	26.4	41.5	83.1	69.2
1949	**Liberal**	72.5	59.7	67.5	90.4	73.5
1953	**Liberal**	64.2	37.5	58.8	88.0	81.8
1957	PC	42.3	29.2	71.8	12.0	63.6
1958	**PC**	78.5	91.7	78.8	66.7	75.8
1962	PC	43.8	68.1	41.1	18.7	54.5
1963	Liberal	48.7	13.9	61.2	62.7	60.6
1965	Liberal	49.4	12.5	60.0	74.7	45.5

Table 4.1 (cont'd)
Percentage of seats in each region won by governing party in Canadian general elections, 1867–1988

| Election | Governing party[a] | % seats won by governing party in region | | | | |
		Canada	West[b]	Ontario	Quebec	Atlantic
1968	**Liberal**	58.7	40.0	72.7	75.7	21.9
1972	Liberal	41.3	10.0	40.9	75.7	31.2
1974	**Liberal**	53.4	18.6	62.5	81.1	40.6
1979	PC	48.2	73.8	60.0	2.7	56.3
1980	**Liberal**	52.1	2.5	54.7	98.7	59.4
1984	**PC**	74.8	76.3	70.5	77.3	78.1
1988	**PC**	57.3	53.9	46.5	84.0	37.5

Source: Jackson and Jackson (1990, 444).

[a] **Liberal/PC/Conservative** represents majority government; Liberal/PC represents minority government.

[b] West includes the Northwest and Yukon Territories.

be a liability at times if it lacks political direction, cohesion and discipline. Adequate political representation, to use Cairns's phrase, may not require balanced regional caucuses.

Depending on the dynamics of party competition within a particular province, the simple-plurality electoral system tends to "over-reward" the leading party. In so doing, it sometimes assigns whole provinces to particular parties. The most notable example has been the stranglehold that the Liberal party had on the province of Quebec for most of this century. Being able to count on a large number of seats from Quebec (which once had approximately 30 percent of the total seats in the House of Commons and now has about 25 percent) meant that the Liberals began with a built-in advantage in terms of achieving a majority government. Quebec was described as the Liberals' "solid South," a comparison to the role played by the American southern states in placing Democrats in office almost continuously earlier this century.

QUEBEC BLOCK VOTING

The historical attachment of Quebec to the Liberal party helped to create the notion of "block voting" within that province. There are several related propositions involved with the idea that Quebec acts as a block within national politics in a way that other provinces do not. The first is the perception that Quebec voters have a greater tendency than voters elsewhere to support a single party, usually the governing party. As a political minority within the national political system, franco-phones in Quebec, it is suggested, have consciously adopted a strat-egy of not fragmenting their vote among different parties. Calculating which party will gain office nationally, they have placed their support behind that party to ensure their interests are not ignored. Greater homogeneity in voting when combined with support for the winning party has meant the "overrepresentation" of Quebec MPs in both the Cabinet and the caucus of the governing party.

This perceived pattern of political behaviour by the Quebec elec-torate has caused resentment elsewhere in the country. Voters in other provinces see Quebec as deciding which party will form the national government. Even when governments change, the perception persists, especially in the West, that Quebec is crucial to the formation of the new government. It is also suspected that Quebec MPs act as a cohe-sive group within the governing party to dictate policy and to gain benefits for their province, sometimes at the expense of other regions.

The idea of a Quebec block in national politics is part fact and part fiction, and it is also controversial. Alan Cairns (1968) had argued that the stereotype of Quebec as monolithically Liberal was an artifact of the electoral system. He pointed out that, although voter support for the Liberals in Quebec was strong, it was never as unanimous as the elec-toral system made it appear. Historically, only about half of the vote in Quebec went to the Liberal party, but the party benefited from the frag-mentation of the remainder of the vote. It was only at the level of seats, not at the level of votes, that Quebec represented a one-party monopoly, he concluded.

However, Macpherson (1991) has argued that Cairns is wrong in dismissing block voting as easily as he does. Comparing the historical voting patterns of Quebec with Ontario, she concludes that both at the level of seats and the level of votes there is more uniformity of support for a particular party within Quebec than in Ontario. With block vot-ing defined as a particular party capturing 75 percent or more of the seats, it was found that since 1879 Quebec has voted as a block on 23 occasions compared with only four times for Ontario over 31 national elections; when block voting was defined as 55 percent or more of the popular vote going to a particular party, it was found that voters in Ontario engaged in block voting only four times compared with 22 times by those in Quebec (ibid., 6–7). In other words, greater homo-geneity of voting in Quebec is a social fact, not just a contrivance of the electoral system. Furthermore, the concentration of voting support in Quebec for the party that wins the province means that the "efficiency" of the Quebec vote is higher than Ontario's vote. In Quebec the winning party wins proportionally more seats than the winning party in Ontario, where there has typically been a closer split between the two front-running parties and a relatively stronger third-party presence.

The second proposition about block voting suggests that Quebec has tended to support the winning party nationally as a way to protect its interests. Cairns (1968) argued that this was a dangerous myth that caused resentment elsewhere in the country. The recurring pattern of Quebec's MPs on the government benches was a product of the electoral system, not of any devious cunning by Quebec voters. As the second most populous province, Quebec would automatically make a greater contribution to national election results; hence, it would stand a greater chance of being on the winning side. "To a great extent," Cairns argued, "Quebec determines which party will form the government, rather than exhibiting a preference for being on the government or the opposition side of the House" (ibid., 69). The parties need Quebec to win, more than Quebec voters demonstrate a clear tendency to support the winning side.

Cairns may well be correct, but one can question whether he may have been too ready to dismiss the possibility of distinctive electoral behaviour in Quebec. If the number of seats from a province alone determined the strength of its presence in national government, then Ontario would be a more pivotal province than Quebec. At present, Ontario holds 99 seats or 32 percent of the total seats in the House of Commons; Quebec, 75 seats or 25 percent. Historically, the seat advantage for Ontario has been in the four to five percent range. What happens electorally in Ontario should be more decisive in national elections than what takes place in Quebec. However, despite having more seats, Ontario has not used its electoral strength to the same advantage as Quebec has done in terms of placing a particular party in office nationally. Macpherson demonstrates this difference in the relative influence of the two provinces by excluding each in turn from the national results over the last 30 elections and seeing whether the party holding office changes. Excluding Quebec changed the party in government seven times, whereas excluding Ontario changed the party in government only four times (Macpherson 1991, 13). The explanation is again greater concentration of voter support for a single party, which has enabled Quebec to increase its influence in national elections. This is not to say that Quebec enjoys an unfair advantage: if Ontario's voters had acted as cohesively as their Quebec counterparts, Ontario's contribution to the election of the national government would have increased correspondingly.

The Bandwagon Effect

A closely related element of the block-voting theory holds that Quebec voters are susceptible to a political bandwagon effect; instinctively, they support the party that appears headed for a national victory. The evidence on this point is mixed. First, the argument for a bandwagon ignores the fact, or at least fails to explain it adequately, that approximately half of the Quebec electorate on average have not been cunning enough to predict the winner in national elections or have failed to act on their correct political intelligence.

It is assumed that the bandwagon phenomenon applies mainly to French-speaking Québécois who are conscious of their minority status within the political system and vote strategically either to avoid exclusion from the inner circle of the governing party or to maximize their political leverage by providing the seats needed to form a majority government. It is hard to find conclusive evidence that francophone Québécois act with both the prescience and coordination that the bandwagon theory suggests. A recent analysis of shifts in voting intentions during the 1988 federal election provides some evidence that francophone Québécois were more sensitive than other groups of voters to the anticipated outcome of the election and adjusted their voting intentions accordingly (Johnston et al. 1989). In the study, Quebec respondents were asked at five points during the campaign to rate the prospects of the parties. Respondents were divided into two groups: francophones and all others. Using sophisticated statistical analysis, the researchers were able to discern only limited evidence of a bandwagon effect within the francophone group, and only within this group did expectations regarding the electoral performance of the Liberal party have a statistically significant impact on voting intentions. At one stage during the campaign, momentum was building in favour of the Liberals based on their opposition to the Free Trade Agreement. If this was a bandwagon, it apparently stalled, either because the Liberals could not sustain the fears about free trade or because the counterattack from the pro–free trade forces was effective. In Quebec, where the free trade issue was not so volatile, there was more of a voter reaction to the shifting prospects of the parties than to the issue itself. Firm conclusions about the supposed bandwagon effect among francophone Québécois cannot be made at this time. The psychology of voter choice, especially in the final weeks of what have apparently become more volatile election contests, defies definitive analysis. Clearly, the act of voting involves something more complicated than simply jumping on and off bandwagons, especially when it is unclear where they are going.

Quebec Loyalty

Once Quebec voters are behind a particular party, they tend to support that party for a long period of time. Quebec has been the foundation for long periods of Liberal rule. However, it has also shifted loyalties more drastically than other provinces, as in 1958 and 1984 when it swung massively to the Progressive Conservatives after decades of alignment with the Liberals. Whether Quebec is the province that leads in replacing a long-standing governing party, or simply votes with a trend already underway, is open to debate. However, the historical record reveals that Quebec, more than any other province, has had a very strong presence in the caucus of most governments.

Quebec's Overrepresentation

Table 4.2 reveals how Quebec has often been "overrepresented" in the governing caucus. The term overrepresentation refers to a situation in which a province holds a higher percentage of places in the governing caucus than its percentage of seats in the House of Commons. Over 34 elections, Quebec has been in this situation on 24 occasions compared with 20 occasions for the Atlantic region, 14 for Ontario and 11 for the West. Quebec's success in placing a higher percentage of its representatives on the government benches reflects both the volatility of voter support in that province and the periodic tendency for voters to swing strongly behind the main opposition party when they become dissatisfied with national policies or sense a trend in favour of an alternative. In comparison, greater stability in voter preferences for the two main parties has meant less extreme swings in the Atlantic region. In the West, suspicion of established parties has led voters since 1921 to support protest parties and the result has often been to leave the region outside of the governing coalition that comprises a majority government.

THE WEST AND THE ELECTORAL SYSTEM

The crucial importance of Quebec to the formation of a new government and the prominence of its representatives in both the Cabinet and the caucus have been a source of growing resentment elsewhere in the country, especially in the West. Changes in government and a high turnover among MPs do not seem to make any difference in the coalitional basis on which political power is exercised in national politics. In this view, Quebec's votes must be assiduously courted and the views of Quebec's representatives must figure prominently in the setting of

Table 4.2
Regional composition of government caucus and House of Commons,
Canadian general elections, 1867–1988

Election	Governing party[a]	% regional composition of government caucus				% regional composition of House of Commons			
		West[b]	Ont.	Que.	Atl.	West[b]	Ont.	Que.	Atl.
1867	Conservative	—	45.5	44.6	9.9	—	45.3	35.9	18.8
1872	Conservative	8.7	36.9	36.9	17.5	5.0	44.0	32.5	18.5
1874	Liberal	1.5	48.1	24.8	25.6	4.9	42.7	31.6	20.9
1878	Conservative	6.6	43.1	32.8	17.5	4.9	42.7	31.6	20.9
1882	Conservative	5.8	38.8	34.5	20.9	5.2	43.3	31.0	20.5
1887	Conservative	11.4	42.3	26.8	19.5	7.0	42.8	30.2	20.0
1891	Conservative	11.4	39.0	24.4	25.2	7.0	42.8	30.2	20.0
1896	Liberal	6.8	36.8	41.9	14.5	8.0	43.2	30.5	18.3
1900	Liberal	9.1	27.3	43.2	20.5	8.0	43.2	30.5	18.3
1904	Liberal	15.1	27.3	38.8	18.7	13.1	40.2	30.4	16.4
1908	Liberal	13.5	27.1	39.8	19.5	15.8	38.9	29.4	15.8
1911	Conservative	13.5	54.1	20.3	12.0	15.8	38.9	29.4	15.8
1917	Unionist (Conservative)	35.9	48.4	2.0	13.7	24.3	34.9	27.7	13.2
1921	Liberal	4.3	18.1	56.0	21.6	24.3	34.9	27.7	13.2
1925	Liberal	23.2	11.1	59.6	6.1	28.2	33.5	26.5	11.8
1926	Liberal	20.7	19.8	51.7	7.8	28.2	33.5	26.5	11.8
1930	Conservative	22.6	43.1	17.5	16.8	28.2	33.5	26.5	11.8
1935	Liberal	20.5	32.7	32.2	14.6	29.4	33.5	26.5	10.6
1940	Liberal	24.2	30.9	34.2	10.7	29.4	33.5	26.5	10.6
1945	Liberal	15.2	27.2	43.2	14.4	29.4	33.5	26.5	10.6
1949	Liberal	22.6	29.5	34.7	13.1	27.5	31.7	27.9	13.0
1953	Liberal	15.9	29.4	38.8	15.9	27.2	32.1	28.3	12.5
1957	PC	18.8	54.4	8.0	18.8	27.2	32.1	28.3	12.5
1958	PC	31.7	32.2	24.0	12.0	27.2	32.1	28.3	12.5
1962	PC	42.2	30.2	12.1	15.5	27.2	32.1	28.3	12.5
1963	Liberal	7.8	40.3	36.4	15.5	27.2	32.1	28.3	12.5

Table 4.2 (cont'd)
Regional composition of government caucus and House of Commons, Canadian general elections, 1867–1988

Election	Governing party[a]	% regional composition of government caucus				% regional composition of House of Commons			
		West[b]	Ont.	Que.	Atl.	West[b]	Ont.	Que.	Atl.
1965	Liberal	6.9	38.9	42.7	11.5	27.2	32.1	28.3	12.5
1968	**Liberal**	18.1	41.3	36.1	4.5	26.5	33.3	28.0	12.1
1972	Liberal	6.4	33.0	51.4	9.2	26.5	33.3	28.0	12.1
1974	**Liberal**	9.2	39.0	42.6	9.2	26.5	33.3	28.0	12.1
1979	PC	43.4	41.9	1.5	13.2	28.4	33.7	26.6	11.3
1980	**Liberal**	1.4	35.4	50.3	12.9	28.4	33.7	26.6	11.3
1984	**PC**	28.9	31.8	27.5	11.8	28.9	33.7	26.6	11.3
1988	**PC**	28.4	27.2	37.3	7.1	30.2	33.6	25.4	10.8

Source: Jackson and Jackson (1990, 445).

Note: Rows may not add up to 100% because of rounding.

[a] **Liberal/PC/Conservative** represents majority government; Liberal/PC represents minority government.

[b] West includes the Northwest and Yukon Territories.

government policy. Extreme versions of this outlook suggest that only a bilingual Quebecker will ever be prime minister in the future and that no policies will ever be adopted that are unacceptable to the Quebec caucus. Quebec and Ontario together are seen in the West to represent the centre of power in Canadian politics, with almost 60 percent of the seats in the House of Commons. Despite holding 30 percent of the seats in the Commons, the West feels that it lacks influence in national decision making. Over the years the West has experimented with several different strategies to promote its interests at the national level. In 15 of the 21 federal elections held since 1921, voters in the West chose to support the second major party and third parties rather than stand behind the governing party. On only six occasions were the majority of its elected MPs found in the government caucus. The West's political nonconformity contrasts sharply with Quebec's electoral behaviour, which fairly consistently has led the province to place the majority of its parliamentary support behind the governing party. As a region consisting of four separate provinces, it is not surprising that the West has demonstrated less political cohesion than Quebec.

By supporting opposition parties, the West was expressing its dissatisfaction with national policies. Voters in the West also apparently hoped that their denial of support for the major parties would produce minority governments and enable regional pressures to be exerted by third parties holding the balance of power. In Quebec, the electoral system served to produce less proportionate outcomes by giving the strongest party a larger proportion of seats than votes. In the West, it disproportionately rewarded third parties because their electoral strength tended to be highly concentrated. In general, however, third parties failed as dependable long-term instruments of western regional power, although the Co-operative Commonwealth Federation and the Social Credit during earlier decades did force certain issues onto the national agenda. Strict party discipline in the Commons kept the third-party strategy from working as effectively as was hoped because, even when the major parties borrowed the ideas of third parties, there was no public process for the West to be seen getting its way in national decision making.

After approximately two decades of underrepresentation in successive Liberal governments, the West lined up in 1984 behind the new Progressive Conservative government. In some ways, this was a return to its initial approach after entering Confederation of seeking to work within one of the major parties. Expectations of greater sensitivity to the West's concerns were high after the Conservative victory. Of the 86 MPs from the West, 61 were in the government caucus. The western caucus represented 28 percent of the national caucus membership, compared with 27 percent from Ontario and 37 percent from Quebec. However, before the end of the first term of the Mulroney government, there were complaints that nothing had changed. Critics claimed that so long as the West was outnumbered in the Commons and in the caucus, so long as power was concentrated in the Cabinet, and so long as the system operated according to majority rule and strict party discipline, the West was bound to lose.

The pessimism of this viewpoint is fostered in part by the electoral system, which has helped to create negative, and often false, stereotypes of how the political system operates at the national level. The rules for translating votes into seats do have consequences for the type of regional representation found in the House of Commons, and thus far the analysis has been mainly concerned about the impacts of the electoral system on public perceptions. It has also been charged that the electoral system provides incentives for parties to make decisions and to adopt policies in a regionally biased fashion. Although it is desirable for party caucuses to be as broadly representative of the regions as possible, it does not follow necessarily that regional biases in policy making arise when they are not. The following sections examine the role played by party caucuses in providing for the expression and accommodation of regional viewpoints, beginning with a brief history of caucus organization.

A BRIEF HISTORY OF CANADIAN PARTY CAUCUSES

The Early Years

Whereas political parties are now central to all aspects of the parliamentary process, this was not always the case. During the early decades of Confederation, parties were predominantly local, rather than national, in orientation. Individuals were recruited to run for Parliament by local élites and were more responsive to them than to the national party leadership. Dissent from the party position was a regular feature of the early Parliaments, but because successive prime ministers adopted a rather flexible interpretation of what constituted a serious defeat, they never felt compelled to resign or to seek a new election. The development of national parties and the structuring of parliamentary behaviour along party lines took place over many years.

The adoption of the simultaneous and secret ballot in 1878 gradually eliminated the phenomenon of "ministerialists," that is, candidates for office who, sensing the outcome of a staggered election, would declare their support for the leading party. As the franchise was gradually extended during the late nineteenth and early twentieth centuries, parties transformed themselves into mass organizations designed to reach the wider electorate. Individual candidates soon came to depend heavily upon party endorsement and organizational support for their election. Independent MPs, prominent in earlier Parliaments, became almost an extinct species as parties came to dominate recruitment to the House of Commons. Voting in the Commons increasingly occurred along strict party lines, although this trend was slowed somewhat in the 1920s by the appearance of the Progressives who attacked the emerging conventions of party government. The Progressives were particularly concerned to halt the tyranny of the caucus, which, in their view, forced MPs and senators to subordinate the representation of regional and local concerns to the requirements for party unity.

As the first British colony to obtain independence and to combine a cabinet-parliamentary structure with a federal division of powers, Canada had to develop a model for the parliamentary organization of parties without the benefit of precedents. Accounts of the first caucuses in the Canadian Parliament are nonexistent or very limited. It appears, however, that the earliest caucuses were infrequent and dominated by the party leadership. One reason for this could be that Parliament was in session for much shorter periods of time during the first decades of Confederation. The job of the MP did not become nearly full time until probably the 1960s. The internal dynamics of earlier caucuses involved a great deal of reliance upon log rolling and patronage. Without the buffer of party discipline, individual MPs and senators were more openly exposed to pressures from powerful interest groups in their constituencies and provinces. Contemporary reformers who hark back to the "good old days" when party discipline was less rigid should recognize that earlier Parliaments were scarcely models of parliamentary or party democracy.

Improving Caucus Organization

Beginning in the 1930s and the 1940s, both the governing party (usually the Liberals) and the official Opposition (the Progressive Conservatives) took steps to improve caucus organization. The changes were mainly intended to solidify emerging leadership control over the parties; they had little to do with promoting internal party democracy. In this respect, the smaller third party, the Co-operative Commonwealth Federation, was different because its ideology stressed caucus democracy. On the governing side, caucus became an instrument to ensure Cabinet control over the legislative process. It allowed ministers to test their policies and other measures before making them public and forestalled the possibility of open disagreement on the floor of the Commons. Use of caucus in this way paralleled changes to the procedures of the House of Commons designed to ensure completion of the government's expanded workload without undue delay.

Partly to compensate back-bench MPs who lost opportunities to sidetrack government business and saw their right to raise matters through private members' bills or resolutions gradually restricted, some grudging measure of caucus democracy was granted.

On the opposition side in the late 1930s, the practice of establishing a "shadow cabinet" of designated critics to lead the attack on government ministers began. Gradually, the concept became institutionalized within both parties, but it did not achieve full development until late in the 1960s. The purposes of organizing the opposition caucuses into shadow cabinets were to promote the development of parliamentary talent, to encourage the acquisition of specialized knowledge, to meet the growing demands of the media and interest groups for spokespersons on various topics, and in all these ways to create an image of the party as an alternative government in waiting.

Leadership Domination

Although caucus activity increased, leadership domination apparently remained the prevalent pattern. Reports of the government caucus during the time of prime ministers Mackenzie King (1935–48) and Louis St. Laurent (1948–56) suggest that the governing caucus was a quiet and acquiescent group. Ministers became increasingly preoccupied with the challenge of directing growing departments and spent less time on party affairs, including relations with caucus. Caucus meetings were used mainly to boost morale, not to work out policy positions. For the Progressive Conservatives a series of electoral setbacks created internal bickering, and influence within caucus tended to gravitate to members seen as loyal to the leader. After John Diefenbaker became prime minister in 1957, there was little improvement, despite his claims that he welcomed caucus participation. Diefenbaker prohibited the formation of regional caucuses, although provincial groups continued to meet informally. There was a growing rift between Diefenbaker and the members of the Quebec caucus over both their limited representation in Cabinet and the denial of their right to meet as a group. Back in opposition after the 1963 election, challenges to Diefenbaker's leadership grew. Full caucus meetings became raucous emotional affairs with members challenging the right of the leader to decide party positions unilaterally.

Consultation of Caucus

After 1963, Prime Minister Lester Pearson sought to strengthen caucus input by encouraging his cabinet ministers to consult MPs on legislation and matters affecting their regions. In addition, a pre-session meeting of caucus was instituted to allow MPs to discuss the government's legislative plans and to prepare strategy for the session. Although these changes were sold as representing a desire for closer relations between the government and the caucus, they also reflected the minority position of the Pearson government and the need to ensure full support in the Commons. In practice, most ministers failed to consult caucus in advance and eventually the requirement to do so was dropped, allegedly because some MPs did not respect the need for confidentiality in handling proposed legislation.

In 1969, a year after Pierre Trudeau became prime minister, a two-day special meeting of the Liberal caucus was held to discuss several matters, including how much independence MPs would be granted in the new committee system, whether the provincial advisory groups established by the Liberal Federation and the regional desks created in the Prime Minister's Office would supplant the caucus as the main source of political intelligence on the regions, and how the organization and procedures of caucus might be improved. As a result of the meeting, it was made a requirement that ministers preview bills with the appropriate caucus committee. After 1970, the six functional caucus committees had access to professional staff through the Liberal Caucus Research Bureau. Also, in 1969, the full caucus obtained the right to elect its own chair, a formal executive for the national caucus was created and regional caucuses were given a guaranteed place on the agenda of national caucus to which they would report.

Despite these improvements, discontent persisted. Not all ministers complied with the requirement to preview legislation. Caucus committees varied in their levels of activity and effectiveness. Time was always at a premium in full caucus. During the minority Trudeau government (1972–74), the emphasis shifted almost completely to the short-term tactical issues related to political survival. The previous system of standing committees was replaced by ad hoc legislative committees, to which MPs were invited by the minister sponsoring a particular bill. During the majority Liberal government (1974–78), the Liberal caucus succeeded in delaying and amending proposed legislation and participated in a Cabinet-sponsored process to formulate a national industrial policy. Back in office after the short-lived Conservative government led by Joe Clark (1979–80), the pattern of caucus involvement with government decision making did not change all that much. Throughout the Trudeau years, the role of caucus, though improved, remained limited and mainly reactive. It was consulted more frequently than in the past and it was able to exert direct influence on legislation in progress. Regional caucuses became more active, with the Quebec caucus clearly being the strongest.

The fractious tradition of the Progressive Conservative caucus continued during the leadership periods of both Robert Stanfield (1967–76) and Joe Clark (1976–83). Both faced challenges to their leadership, which detracted from the effectiveness of caucus as a forum for organizing challenges to the government. In the case of both leaders, the response was one of patience; they did not force a showdown with the rebels. Instead, they tried to work with caucus by creating extremely large shadow cabinets to give nearly every MP an assignment as a critic. Frequent rotation of the critics' jobs was another way to combat frustrations and to avoid fights over leadership. To discourage any impression of an inside group calling all the shots, Stanfield convened regular meetings of the shadow cabinet to review government proposals, and the outcomes of these debates were taken to full caucus where all members could participate in formulating the party's position. According to former MP Erik Nielsen (1989, 119), this process was also followed by Joe Clark and for a time by Brian Mulroney when he was Leader of the Opposition. Numerous caucus committees were established as another way to encourage back-bench involvement, but they fluctuated in their levels of activity, and attendance by the assigned members was erratic.

No clear pattern of caucus involvement emerged during the brief term of the Clark government. Back in opposition, the challenges to Clark's leadership were renewed and he was forced to agree to a study of caucus organization. Prepared by Frank Oberle, MP, the report was eventually presented to Mulroney, who had replaced Clark as leader in 1983. Most of the 11 recommendations made in the Oberle report were accepted by Mulroney, including the right of full caucus to elect its chair. Before the 1984 federal election, a series of policy committees and party task forces were put to work preparing policy plans for a new Conservative government. Under guidelines developed earlier, the Trudeau government allowed these caucus teams to consult public servants, provided information on new programs, and granted access to departmental budget plans. Although the reports produced by these caucus committees were uneven in quality, some were very influential. Reports were sent first to the Planning and Priorities Committee of caucus and then on to full caucus. The whole exercise represented the most ambitious effort up to that point to develop a policy role for an opposition caucus.

An Overview

This brief historical account reveals that party caucuses have become more active, more structured and more influential over time. The caucus of the governing party is a consultative device more than a decision-making body. It is used mainly as a sounding board for ministers' policies and to gauge the state of support for the government's actions across the country. As is true of most other aspects of party life, the approach to caucus favoured by the party leader determines to a great extent the nature of caucus involvement, although the wider political situation and party traditions also affect the role assigned to caucus. Regardless of which party was in office and who was leader, there were complaints that the Cabinet did not adequately consult the caucus. As early as the 1930s, opposition parties recognized that organizing their caucuses would focus and strengthen their criticisms of the government's performance. It was not until the 1960s, however, that significant reforms were instituted to both government and opposition caucuses. For most of their history Canadian party caucuses have been informal and reactive. Recent gains in caucus democracy are not necessarily permanent.

THE GOVERNING CAUCUS: THE PROGRESSIVE CONSERVATIVES

How the Governing Caucus Functions

The functioning of party caucuses has far more to do with social psychology, leadership, communication and group dynamics than with structures and procedures for decision making. This is particularly true of the caucus of the governing party whose primary role is consultation and communication – not formal decision making. Although there is a typical order of business for a national caucus meeting, printed agendas are seldom prepared, formal votes are not held and no reports are issued from caucus meetings. A great deal of time in caucus meetings is taken up by ministers informing their colleagues about actions that they propose, gauging reactions and mobilizing support. Opportunities are provided for backbenchers to present their views on legislation, spending plans and administrative decisions. Ideological and regional differences are expressed and there is a search for a consensus on the broad policy directions to be followed by government. Formulation of strategy for the parliamentary process and the wider political competition among parties is also a function of caucus. Developing group feeling, fostering teamwork and boosting morale are a big part of the psychology of successful caucus management. All of these functions can be aided by good structures and processes, but there is no neat organizational fix to the challenge of developing policy and maintaining unity in a caucus that reflects the diversities and tensions within the country at large. It is hoped that in the privacy of caucus frank exchanges will lead members to recognize the need to attenuate their views and search for compromises.

Typically, the structure of a governing caucus is relatively fluid, reflecting its size and regional composition, its traditions, the approach of its leader and the leading issues on the government's agenda. The meetings of the national caucuses for all parties have long been held on Wednesday mornings when Parliament is in session. Under Prime Minister Mulroney, the Progressive Conservatives have also adopted the practice of, about twice a year, holding weekend meetings of full Cabinet followed by a daylong meeting with caucus, with one of these meetings taking place in the fall to discuss issues and strategies for the upcoming session of Parliament. In addition to the national caucus, there are a series of provincial caucuses, which usually meet on the Tuesday evening prior to the full caucus on Wednesday. For the larger provinces such as Ontario and Quebec there are also smaller, less formal groupings representing cities or regions within provinces. Although there is not a formal system of policy committees organized within the Progressive Conservative caucus, there is usually at any one time a number of ad hoc policy committees at work, some of which achieve a relatively permanent existence. From time to time special caucus meetings are convened to deal with specific concerns, and there are informal groups and friendships formed along ideological and regional lines. Clearly, caucus provides a number of forums for MPs and senators to present their views, but because parliamentarians are busy people with many duties, they simply do not have the time to utilize all the opportunities presented within the caucus structure. For example, in 1987 an effort was made to organize the right-of-centre MPs in the Conservative caucus into a special group modelled on the British Conservative Party's ultraconservative Monday Club, but even ideologically compatible MPs felt there was no need for another caucus meeting (Riley 1987).

Mulroney's Skills in Maintaining Caucus Unity

Near the close of the first term of the Mulroney government many commentators were impressed by the success of the prime minister in managing his large, regionally and ideologically diverse caucus, especially given the past troubles faced by Progressive Conservative leaders. What made his accomplishment more remarkable was that it was achieved against the difficult political background of eight or nine cabinet resignations, the taint of several scandals, deepening regional tensions and plummeting popularity. There was grumbling in the ranks, to be sure, and there were some cases of open dissent, but through it all the Progressive Conservative caucus remained basically intact.

Being in power provided Mulroney with a number of practical levers to keep his members in line. There is always the hope – however remote – of appointment to the Cabinet. Barring that, a Progressive Conservative MP could always aspire to become a parliamentary secretary to a minister, to chair a parliamentary committee or to serve on a special caucus task force. There is a relationship between the level of back-bench satisfaction and the availability of opportunities outside the caucus for MPs to be involved and use their knowledge constructively. A series of organizational and procedural reforms to the House of Commons was adopted in February 1986 based on the report of a special Commons committee chaired by the Newfoundland MP James McGrath. Standing committees of the House of Commons became more active, and politically sensitive topics were often referred to them for study. The status of committee chairs was enhanced and these individuals tended to be senior backbenchers whose frustrated ambitions might otherwise have led them to become restless.

Being in government meant there was a chance for MPs to obtain the benefits of federal spending for their regions, provinces and local communities: job creation funds, government contracts, community development projects, farm assistance and so on. There were opportunities to host a prime-ministerial visit to their ridings and to be seen rubbing shoulders with other leading political figures and visiting dignitaries. Also, there was the satisfaction of being on the governing side and being part of the action when major initiatives were being planned (even if, in the case of backbenchers, they were on the outer edge of the governing process). As a current senator and former MP suggested in an interview for this study, running a government was a new experience for most of the Conservatives: "Traditionally, the Liberals were the governing party and we were the minority party. And a minority party wakes up every morning and pinches itself when it's in government."

Finally, Mulroney's success in holding the caucus together owed something to the fact that during his successful bid for the leadership he had attracted the support of many of the MPs who had caused trouble for Joe Clark. This group included the rump of MPs left over from the Diefenbaker period, many of the right-of-centre MPs and a number of the single-issue advocates, all of whom lacked the ideological flexibility to get along well in caucus. To this group, Mulroney added a large number of newcomers from Quebec, who had few previous links with the Conservative party and virtually no federal political experience. Opposing this coalition were the Clark loyalists, who were more moderate in outlook. After Mulroney gained the leadership, they eventually rallied to support the party to gain the victory that seemed inevitable in the 1984 election. In office, many of the former Clark ministers have become key ministers in the Mulroney government and they have remained consummate team players.

Getting the caucus members to line up behind a sure winner did not require much skill in political management, but keeping them united through tough political times required superior leadership skills. Mulroney devoted a great deal of effort and energy to achieve caucus unity. He rarely missed a Wednesday morning meeting of the national caucus, which he would use to reach out effectively to his back-bench supporters. A leading national journalist (Fraser 1989, 19) has described the Mulroney style in caucus as "reassuring, cajoling, correcting, encouraging, flattering. Sometimes shamelessly theatrical, he would use birthdays, anniversaries, personal anecdotes, and the tough, funny locker-room talk of political partisans to keep his sprawling caucus united, optimistic, and enthusiastic." A senator interviewed for this study said that the Conservative caucus reminded him of "a high school pep rally without the pretty girls." Several others interviewed for this study thought that Mulroney gave his best speeches in caucus and said that on several occasions there were standing ovations after he spoke.

In addition to using caucus to boost morale, Mulroney often took time to remind members of how they gained power. Week after week he stressed that victory and power depended upon caucus unity. He pointed out that there were over 100 constituencies with more than 15 percent French-speaking population. The historical failure by the Progressive Conservative party to appeal sufficiently to francophones both inside and outside Quebec gave the Liberal party a large head start on the road to national office and Mulroney believed this meant that the Conservative party could not provide truly national leadership: "For the Progressive Conservative caucus to have evolved over a long period of time without the influence on the day-to-day basis in the caucus, in the formulation of policy, of the sensitivity and attitudes of French-speaking members, was quite harmful" (Fraser 1989, 20). One of the best and politically most courageous speeches that Mulroney gave in caucus was in favour of the national party coming to the defence of the language rights of the francophone minority in Manitoba. More than any other of the caucus divisions that tormented Stanfield and Clark, it was the struggle to drag the party to an understanding of Quebec that eventually undermined their leadership.

Mulroney also worked hard at ensuring that individual MPs and senators did not feel neglected and excluded from the exercise of power. Shortly after taking office, he created the position of Caucus Liaison within the Prime Minister's Office (PMO) to help him keep track of caucus opinion and to deal with the concerns of individual caucus members. The first occupant of the position played a very active role in looking after the needs of members, especially since so many were newcomers to Parliament. To avoid the kind of resentment directed at the PMO when Trudeau was in office, Mulroney regularly told caucus members that they "did not have to take any crap from my staff" (Goar 1987). Mulroney went out of his way to be accessible to backbenchers. He regularly invited groups of MPs to breakfast at his residence. He tried to get back to MPs promptly when they sought a meeting. He phoned them for information and advice on how the government was perceived in their regions and on provincial and local issues. He would push ministers in caucus and chase them down if they were seen to be neglecting local issues that could lead to caucus discontent.

How the Caucus Influences Legislation

No formal system of standing policy committees exists within the Progressive Conservative caucus. One was apparently laid down on paper when Parliament began in 1984, but it did not work well. Instead, the parliamentary secretaries, on behalf of their ministers, bring together the Conservative MPs serving on the relevant standing committees of the House of Commons and any other interested members to discuss proposed legislation. Recently, for example, there have been caucus committees on the Goods and Services Tax and the broadcasting bill. One of the recommendations accepted from the Oberle Report on Caucus Reform (1983) was that Conservative ministers should be required to preview legislation with caucus. Barbara Sparrow, Calgary MP, indicated in 1988 that the requirement was not always honoured and that there was usually little time to study legislation: "I am absolutely amazed at how little input private members have into the formulation of legislation, policies and/or regulations. It appears to me that most of the time we are told what a minister will be announcing in forty-eight hours and we do not have any means to study or contribute to the finished product" (Lee 1989, 46). With a trimmed-down majority in the current Parliament, there has been noticeable improvement in caucus consultation on legislation, according to a Conservative MP interviewed for this study: "It is much better than it was. We are gradually getting around to the practice that before bills are introduced, or even drafted, the discussion on the policies that will be put forth takes place in caucus. It is interesting that over the last six years more and more ministers have communicated with caucus prior to drafting bills." Some Conservative MPs have talked about the procedure for caucus approval of bills used by the former Lougheed government in Alberta. All bills had to be voted on by caucus prior to introduction in the legislature. In the case of a majority government, however, a prior vote in the governing caucus would make parliamentary approval even more of a foregone conclusion and might be inappropriate in strict constitutional terms.

All the government members interviewed for this study could think of examples of how caucus delayed or modified legislation. Sometimes this was done through the collective actions of regional caucuses. On rare occasions, such as tax breaks for northern residents, it involved cross-party alliances among MPs to lobby ministers for a more regionally sensitive application of national legislation. Although no standing committees of caucus existed, some special committees, such as those on agriculture and justice, were virtually permanent, and the stronger ministers made a point of consulting them before legislation was tabled. Ministers would also arrange briefings on legislation for the government

MPs who served on the legislative committees of the House of Commons to which bills were referred after second reading. Normally, discussion of legislation did not take up much time at national caucus meetings, but there were several other forums where individuals with specific interests and specialized knowledge could gain influence. Several of the interviewed MPs indicated they did not hesitate to write to or talk to ministers (especially when ministers had "duty days" in the House of Commons) to share their concerns about legislation.

Party Loyalty

No party can remain in office for six years without caucus disagreements arising and the Mulroney government is no exception. However, Mulroney's skills as a conciliator were important in ensuring that backbench discontent did not get out of hand. Although there are examples of dissent during both terms of the Mulroney government, they should not divert attention from the prevalent pattern of strong party loyalty on votes. The chief party whip, as well as a number of regional whips, are responsible for ensuring the attendance and votes of government members. The reduced Conservative majority from 211 MPs in 1984 to 169 in 1988 required that the whips pay more attention to the scheduling of business, both in the Commons and in its committees. James Hawkes, the chief government whip, insisted that party unity rested more on subtle persuasion than on the use of sanctions, such as expulsion from choice committees, exemption from parliamentary delegations overseas, or a personal rebuke from the prime minister. "The maintenance of discipline will work," Hawkes stressed, "if all members have a sense of value" (Howard 1988). Members of Parliament think of themselves as part of a team. Peer pressure and self-discipline lead them to support their party on most occasions. Also, the efforts by the leadership to stay in touch with their opinions contribute to solidarity.

Cleavages within Caucus

The expulsion of two Alberta MPs from the Conservative caucus and the resignation of a third to sit as an independent, and the breakaway by a group of six Quebec MPs, led by former Cabinet Minister Lucien Bouchard, to form the Bloc québécois, received extensive media attention during the second term of the Mulroney government. Several respondents for this study described the three MPs from English Canada as mavericks from the beginning. One reason for their break from the party was opposition to the Goods and Services Tax (GST), but it was pointed out that they had not bothered to attend the briefings on GST provided by the Finance department. As for the Quebec rebels, it was suggested that Mulroney was paying a price for recruiting candidates from the ranks of the separatists and strong nationalists from the province and that the constitutional issue was laden with symbolism and emotionalism.

Caucus confidentiality makes it difficult to obtain a precise indication of the number and the nature of the issues that proved divisive within the government caucus. However, the public would have a mistaken view of the level of conflict if it went by media reports that highlight the periodic disagreements. Impressionistically, the cleavages within caucus appeared to be along moral, ideological and regional lines. In the category of moral issues, three ethically sensitive matters proved difficult during the last two Parliaments for all parties: capital punishment, abortion and legal protection of homosexual rights. Since these were matters of individual conscience, party discipline was relaxed. In all cases, Mulroney arranged for an ad hoc caucus committee, composed of members with opposing views, to hammer out a compromise agreement.

The ideological disagreements within the Conservative caucus revolved around the broad question of the future role of government within the economy and the need to deal with the accumulated public debt. The right wing element within the caucus complained at various times that insufficient progress was being made in curtailing spending, selling Crown corporations and deregulating industries. As part of the prebudget consultations undertaken during the fall of 1990, Quebec and Ontario MPs presented the minister of finance with detailed plans to tighten the federal purse strings (Lounder 1991). Although there was a widespread consensus within the caucus about the need for restraint, there were disagreements over which departments, programs and regions should bear the brunt of cutbacks. In 1986 there was a mini-revolt among rural Tory backbenchers that forced Canada Post, a Crown corporation, to reconsider plans to close rural post offices and raise postal rates. The MPs obtained the right to review the corporation's plan within the Commons standing committee on Government Operations, and eventually a caucus deal was arranged to curtail the reductions (Winsor 1986). Finally, there was an ideological split over reforms to the unemployment insurance scheme proposed by the labour, employment and immigration committee of the House of Commons. The Conservative MP who chaired the committee, James Hawkes (Calgary West), supported the proposals for the series of reforms, which were seen as progressive by policy experts, but he was opposed by a caucus faction led by Don Blenkarn (Mississauga South), Chair of the

Commons finance committee, who supported business organizations in calling for greater curtailment of UIC benefits.

The number of issues on which the caucus divided along regional lines were relatively few according to most of the government members interviewed for this study. On the other hand, MPs can never lose sight of regional sensitivities as expressed by the public and provincial governments. A cabinet minister offered this perspective on the subject of regionalism:

> I think that this country is over-indulged on a regional axis. Everyone sees reality from a regional camp; everyone sees themselves as a minority ... I think that the parochialism is getting worse. Part of that is because for every dollar raised by Ottawa, it can only spend about 60 cents to help you and me. The rest is just used to cover past spending. Therefore Ottawa is more a source of taxation and frustration than it is of benefits which help everyone to feel better. Scarcity politics gives rise to regional anger.

Another MP talked about the problems caused by "regional chauvinists" and the value of caucus in helping members from all parts of the country to overcome "regional narrow-mindedness." When asked to identify issues that aroused regional conflict, the government members could volunteer only a short list, usually consisting of such matters as the amendments to the *Official Languages Act* (1988), the decision to award the overhaul contract for CF-18 aircraft to a Montreal firm over a Winnipeg firm (1986), and the Meech Lake Accord.

Provincial and Regional Caucuses

The Progressive Conservatives operate a provincial caucus for each province where they were successful in electing MPs in the 1988 election. The distribution of Conservative seats at the start of the 34th Parliament was as follows: Newfoundland (2); Prince Edward Island (0); Nova Scotia (5); New Brunswick (5); Quebec (63); Ontario (46); Manitoba (7); Saskatchewan (4); Alberta (25); and British Columbia (12). There is no provincial caucus for Prince Edward Island and no formal caucus for Newfoundland. A formal Saskatchewan caucus was established that had the right to report to national caucus meetings; however, because it was so small, its four MPs were invited to join the Alberta caucus meetings. A four-province caucus for the Atlantic region had existed for several years, and in the fall of 1990 a similar body for the West was started. Formation of a western caucus was intended to combat the public perception that the West's interests were being neglected by the Mulroney government and to offset the political momentum of the Reform movement in the West.

Conservative senators are eligible to attend the regional caucuses for their provinces. In the past, many did not, but the troubles encountered by the Mulroney government in dealing with the Liberal majority in the Senate and the appointment of new Conservative senators served to increase senators' participation. An Atlantic MP offered the opinion that the recent flood of Senate appointments had strengthened the Atlantic caucus. Conservative senators do not meet separately in caucus, but a significant number attend the national caucus meetings and there is always a place on the agenda for the government leader in the Senate to report on developments in the upper chamber. As appointed members, senators lack some legitimacy as regional representatives, but many have extensive political experience and skills, which they use on behalf of their provinces. Although it is fashionable to describe the Senate as a failure as a regional body, such sweeping judgements are usually based on very little knowledge of what senators, both individually and collectively, do on behalf of their regions. Within the governing caucus there are clear examples of how senators play an effective regional role.

The Quebec Caucus

The regional caucuses vary not only in size, but also in level of activity, cohesion and quality of leadership. With 63 MPs, Quebec represents the largest contingent (37.5 percent) in the elected portion of the national caucus. The Quebec caucus has the following five subprovincial caucuses: L'Estrie, Montérégie, Bas-St-Laurent, Quebec City and Montreal. There is a cabinet minister designated to provide leadership for each subprovincial caucus, and at the time of writing Benoît Bouchard serves as the political minister for Quebec as a whole. An election is held to select the chair of the full Quebec caucus.

The Quebec MPs interviewed for this study provided several examples of the provincial influence of the caucus on both legislation and administrative decisions. One related the following: "Back in 1984 we asked that about $30 million be paid to agricultural producers for the drought. We sounded the alarm and the national caucus heard it. It was the same thing when we got the contract for the maintenance of the CF-18s for Montreal. We pointed out the higher unemployment than in Manitoba. It may have been badly publicized, but that issue was handled by the Quebec caucus." In another case, the subprovincial caucus for L'Estrie was successful in convincing both the Quebec and then the national caucus to recommend a government grant for the modernization of the Domtar plant in Windsor, Quebec. The minister responsible had rejected the Domtar request, primarily because the company had made a profit of almost $90 million in 1984. The rejection led to an outcry from the Quebec caucus, the Quebec government (which offered an $83-million grant) and the Quebec media. The prime minister overruled the minister and a $150-million, interest-free loan was provided (Fraser 1989, 310). The Quebec caucus regularly invites interest groups, such as the Union des producteurs agricoles (union of agricultural producers), chambers of commerce and newspaper associations to meet with them.

Opinions varied among those interviewed about the cohesion and effectiveness of the Quebec caucus. A Quebec MP observed: "I think anglophone MPs know the importance of unity better than us. We are not that united. There are always divisions. This is partly because of different personalities. There are also tensions between the city and the country ridings within the province." The failure of the Meech Lake Accord was the most divisive issue faced by the Quebec caucus in recent years. On less symbolic and politically potent issues, the size of the Quebec caucus and its cohesion ensured that its views figure prominently in government decision making. An Ontario cabinet minister offered this assessment: "Generally, I would say that the Quebec caucus is influential because they are very articulate, very well organized, and very focused. It is not because they are being indulged."

The Ontario Caucus

The next largest caucus is Ontario with 46 MPs. It operates a number of subprovincial caucuses. Beginning in 1986, the 10 southwestern Ontario Conservative MPs began holding monthly breakfast meetings to ensure that the area's concerns were being reflected in caucus, Cabinet and Parliament (Ray 1986). As the cabinet minister from the area, Tom Hockin felt that his views would carry more weight if they had the backing of the group. Regular meetings of the cabinet ministers and MPs from the Metropolitan Toronto area are also held. One interviewed MP suggested there was always some tension between the Toronto and non-Toronto groups within the Ontario caucus. According to the minister interviewed for this study, the Ontario caucus probably had the least influence among the various caucuses because it failed to articulate its needs consistently in a focused manner. He explained the problem as follows: "In the Ontario caucus we have always had a struggle in our own minds – whether we should be speaking for Ontario's parochial interests or Canada's national interests ... Our MPs say that because we don't have a wish list or an agenda we get overlooked. There is always that tension. I don't think that it is an unnatural tension for Ontario." When Ontario has pressing concerns, the minister suggested, it was usually able to make an impact. He cited as examples funds for improvements to small-craft harbours, which are visible projects in about 25 Ontario ridings, and the determination to deal with acid rain, which affected Ontario's lakes.

The Alberta Caucus

Effective political leadership from experienced cabinet ministers can more than compensate for a lack of numbers in a provincial caucus. Several respondents mentioned Alberta as having several strong ministers to defend its interests, such as Don Mazankowski, Joe Clark and Harvie Andre. Mazankowski was deputy prime minister and chaired the key Operations Committee of Cabinet, which served, in effect, as the gatekeeper to the Priorities and Planning Committee of Cabinet chaired by the prime minister. Within the Alberta caucus there were regular meetings for the Calgary and Edmonton MPs and there has always been competition between the two cities on select issues. At times the Alberta caucus has asked individuals, or they have volunteered, to prepare reports on particular topics to be used by the other members. Interest groups, such as city councils, chambers of commerce and representatives from marketing boards, regularly meet with the caucus. An Alberta MP described the influence of the provincial caucus:

> When we got rid of the National Energy Program, it was indeed the members from Alberta who worked very closely with the then energy minister, Pat Carney ... When energy prices fell in 1986 we were able to have a Canadian exploration and development program put in. In the area of agriculture, the Alberta and other western caucuses have been extremely influential with advance and drought payments. Alberta depends very heavily on its exports to the U.S.A., and therefore we took the lead on the free trade issue. We were probably the most supportive on that issue.

Another western MP suggested that the issue of the relative influence of various caucuses was mainly a matter of perception. Every region thought other parts of the caucus had greater influence at different times. The formation of the four-province western caucus was a case of learning from Quebec: "We are learning from Quebec how to play political hardball when it's time to play hardball. Up until now we have relied on sweet reason to prevail, but that doesn't always work and sometimes you have to use some political muscle. I understand why

Quebec feels that it has to do that because they are up against the muscle of Ontario all the time. Ontario truly does dominate the national
agenda, economically and politically."

The National Caucus and Regional Concerns

As issues rise and fall on the agenda of the government and as political events transpire, the attention of the national caucus tends to shift
from one set of regional concerns to another. Also, there is a tendency
for the national caucus to respond to situations where regional political problems exist, even if the province has limited representation. A
cabinet minister described how federal approvals for the Hibernia
energy project were moved ahead by caucus pressures to reassure
Newfoundlanders that they would not pay a price for their opposition
to the Meech Lake Accord:

> After Meech Lake failed, our two Newfoundland MPs, with some sen-
> ators, stood up in national caucus and pointed out that Tom Rideout
> (Progressive Conservative leader in Newfoundland) had fought for
> the Accord. Don't punish Newfoundland, they argued, for bringing
> down Meech Lake. That was Clyde Wells, not the PC Party in
> Newfoundland ... The Quebec caucus was feeling hurt and John
> Crosbie said Hibernia was not about giving aid to Wells, it was about
> helping Newfoundland.

In a similar fashion, a former Conservative MP from Manitoba
explained that there was considerable sensitivity among ministers to provide something to Manitoba after the CF-18 maintenance contract went
to Canadair in Montreal rather than to the Winnipeg firm, which had
the less costly and technically superior bid. His contacts with Quebec
MPs at the time suggested to him that they did not see the issue as
Quebec versus Manitoba, but as airplane jobs in Quebec to balance
government support for auto plants in Ontario.

The CF-18 decision illustrates the potency of such events to create
a sense of regional resentment. It was eventually announced in the April
1989 federal budget that a smaller defence contract would go to the
Winnipeg firm that had lost the original competition. The smaller contract was seen as a cynical consolation prize. Moreover, it was part of a
federal budget that removed over $200 million (according to the provin-
cial government's estimate) in forecasted federal spending from the
province, including the planned closure of two national defence bases.
Manitobans felt they had been singled out for a disproportionate budgetary sacrifice because the Conservative provincial government, led

by Gary Filmon, was opposed to the Meech Lake Accord. It was also suggested that the regional minister and the Manitoba caucus had not done an adequate job. Although issues such as the CF-18 affair, which appear to pit region against region, are relatively rare, they contribute significantly to the public perception that regional fairness in national policy making is not being followed.

Caucuses and Constituency Issues

Government MPs were asked if the regional and national caucuses were the appropriate place to raise constituency matters. Most agreed that this was done occasionally, but usually as a final step when satisfaction could not be found in other ways. If an MP has a particular problem with a department or agency, the usual approach is to contact the appropriate minister by telephone, in person in the House of Commons on his duty day or by correspondence. If the problem is not resolved, only then might the matter be raised in the caucus. Should the minister still refuse to act, the MP might threaten to raise the matter in the House of Commons or with the media.

Caucus and the Leadership

The principal constraints on the government caucus have been time and information. Extended discussions about policy are not possible because ministers, and to a lesser extent MPs, simply do not have the time. Not all MPs and senators are anxious to extend their involvement in government decision making. They see their role as supporting the party leadership and taking care of constituency matters. They are content to attend weekly caucus to hear reports and receive encouragement from the leadership, and to rally behind them in Parliament. Other MPs and senators complain about the lack of caucus involvement, but among these are individuals who do not use the opportunities available or fail to do "the homework" necessary to participate effectively. Parliamentarians have more information available today than in the past, through such arrangements as personal staffs, caucus research bureaus, the Research Branch of the Library of Parliament, the standing committees, periodic briefings by public servants and contacts with interest groups. However, it takes hard work to utilize the available information and not all members are prepared to make the effort. With access to departmental and other resources, ministers will always enjoy an information advantage over their back-bench supporters.

Although policy initiative rests with ministers, they usually try to anticipate the reaction of the caucus. In this way caucus has indirect influence. Policy initiation usually involves the development of a climate of ideas and the mobilization of political support for a particular course of action over an extended period of time. Caucus is one of many participants in this diffuse and protracted process. Once the government has formulated its legislative and financial plans, there are several opportunities within the caucus process for MPs and senators to influence those plans. The caucus of the governing party cannot be taken for granted by the prime minister and his Cabinet and it is not. Ministers recognize that the most important parliamentarians they must persuade are their caucus colleagues since it is presumed that members of the opposition parties will inevitably criticize and oppose.

THE OPPOSITION CAUCUSES: THE LIBERALS AND NEW DEMOCRATS

How Opposition Caucuses Function

The orientation of opposition caucuses is different from that of the government caucus since the prime minister and Cabinet are not present and the debates are not about determining government activity but how the party should react to government action or inaction. The emphasis within the opposition is on the daily and weekly routines of parliamentary business, especially on how to challenge the government most effectively: which topics and ministers will be the focus of a Question Period campaign, how the party will react to bills, what topics will be used for opposition "supply days," and what impact activities of the parliamentary party are having on the wider party and on the electorate. The longer-term problems of governing the country are not ignored, but they are addressed more in the strategic terms of winning the permanent election contest that is a big part of parliamentary life than by formulating substantive responses. Without firsthand contact with the work of government and access to the expertise of the public service, the designated critics for the opposition parties (sometimes called shadow cabinet ministers) enjoy less of an information advantage over their caucus colleagues. The party leader has the right to appoint the opposition spokespersons, the House leader for the party in the Commons and a number of other caucus positions. Still, he has far less leverage in the caucus than does a prime minister.

The two opposition parties differ in terms of the leader's right to declare policy. With the Liberals there is some presumed freedom for the leader to pronounce policy unilaterally, but he is expected to respect party resolutions and to heed caucus opinion. The tradition within the New Democratic Party has been to stress the duty of elected members to promote the policy mandate given them in the election, and there is a requirement that the party leader respect the policy positions adopted at party conventions. Unlike the other two parties, the New Democratic Party caucus votes on contentious issues and the results of the votes are intended to be binding on all members. There is less chance within opposition caucuses of the leader and his or her close advisers completely dominating caucus decision making. More real decision making takes place in an opposition caucus than in a government caucus, because the constraints of governing are not involved and the party leaders usually recognize the need to forge a consensus to keep the party united.

The Liberal Caucus

The Liberal party has spent most of this century in office, and its electoral success has done a great deal to hide the internal divisions found in any national party. It is worthwhile to contrast the caucus process when the party was in power from 1980 to 1984 with the pattern when in opposition.

In Power

When the Liberals were returned to office in 1980 after the brief, minority Clark government, they succeeded in electing only two MPs from western Canada, both of them from Winnipeg. The gap in their regional representation led them to adopt several institutional innovations in Cabinet and caucus to compensate for the lack of a western caucus. Furthermore, during this period there were a number of policy initiatives that provoked regional anger and that were a test of whether the new institutional arrangements provided adequate political representation for a region that otherwise seemed to be excluded from the governing process.

Shortly after taking office, the Trudeau government dispatched its two western MPs into the region to hear the concerns of various groups. Their report to the prime minister contained several proposals, which were accepted for the most part. A Western Affairs Committee of Cabinet was established with Lloyd Axworthy, Minister of Transport, as the chair. The other members included the three western senators who had been appointed to the Cabinet to reassure westerners that their interests would not be neglected. Also on the Committee were the other cabinet ministers whose departments had the greatest impact on the region. The Committee reported weekly through its chair to the Cabinet's Priorities and Planning Committee chaired by the prime minister. It had the power to recommend on expenditures from a Western Development Fund of $4 billion created from the higher energy taxes imposed by Ottawa early in the 1980s. In addition, Liberal MPs from other parts of the country were "twinned" with western ridings and expected to keep in touch through contacts with fellow Liberals and interest groups from those areas. The main sponsor of these reforms, Lloyd Axworthy, has described them as a "surrogate for a western caucus" and suggested that they were helpful in resolving several issues of concern to the West (Axworthy 1990, 243–45). He pointed to the signing of Economic and Regional Development Agreements with the four western provinces, the development of a Core Area Initiative for the revitalization of downtown Winnipeg, the passage of the *Western Grain Transportation Act* and the creation of the National Energy Program as examples of the success of the arrangements for making western concerns a priority of the national government.

What would a more detached observer conclude about the success of these arrangements? First, it is significant that the Liberal government felt compelled to fill the gap in regional representation to promote the appearance of regional fairness, as in other examples cited in this study where parties acted to solve their regional deficiencies. Second, the use of senators in Cabinet to represent western interests was clearly a second-best alternative to having elected MPs because the senators did not have the same political legitimacy in the eyes of their colleagues or the public. Some commentators in western Canada went so far as to suggest that the reliance upon senators was a symbolic reminder of the subordination of the region to the political clout of central Canada. Third, critics pointed out that the Western Development Fund may have been announced as $4 billion initially, but the actual spending fell short of this total and the decisions on expenditures were made not by the Western Affairs Committee, which could only recommend, but by the Priorities and Planning Committee of Cabinet where the West's sole representative was Lloyd Axworthy. However, interviews for this study indicated that there was a genuine concern to demonstrate responsiveness to western concerns, that Axworthy had considerable influence despite the lack of political backing from a western caucus, and that the prime minister was highly supportive of the western initiatives.

Two of the policies that Axworthy refers to as successful products of the improvised arrangements illustrate the danger of reifying the concept of region to suggest that the West is a single political unit with common provincial interests. Both the *Western Grain Transportation Act* and the National Energy Program were contentious in western Canada not only because they placed the region's interest in competition with central Canada, but because the region itself was divided in its reaction to these national initiatives.

The Western Transportation Initiative   The prevailing view among
many westerners about the Western Transportation Initiative adopted
in 1983 was that the Quebec Liberal caucus dictated its final content.
The bill provided for an increase in the so-called Crow Rate freight
charges, which had been kept artificially low since 1897. It also proposed to compensate the farmers for the rate increases, to provide
financial support to the railways if they upgraded the western grain
transportation system, and to spend additional funds to promote agricultural and industrial development throughout the country (Laslovich
1985; Skogstad 1987). The debate was over whether the federal compensation would be a split payment to both the railways and the farmers or to just one party. Quebec producers, especially hog farmers,
feared that alterations to the Crow Rates would upset the economic
equilibrium in the livestock and meat processing industries to their
disadvantage. Removal of the Crow Rates would make it no longer
logical to ship both livestock and feed grains to central Canada for
processing and would result in the emergence of a processing industry in western Canada. To avoid this impact, the Quebec producers
favoured payment to the railways. The Parti québécois government
and the Quebec provincial Liberal party supported their province's
producers. The 74-member Quebec Liberal caucus warned that the
party could lose 20 to 25 seats in the province if the split-payment
plan went ahead. Although the decision was made to pay the entire
subsidy to the railways, this outcome was not solely due to the Quebec
opposition.

Western agricultural interests were divided over the original split-
payment proposal. Those groups with a vested interest in the status
quo (e.g., the large cooperative wheat pools) favoured payment to the
railways, whereas those favouring diversification of the agricultural
economy (e.g., livestock producers and agribusiness) favoured payment to the farmers to allow them to pursue more lucrative alternatives to growing grain. Of the four western provincial governments,
Manitoba and Saskatchewan were opposed and Alberta and British
Columbia were supportive. Both Jean-Luc Pepin, the first federal minister in charge, and later Lloyd Axworthy, saw the Western
Transportation Initiative as a response to western alienation and they
went to great lengths to secure a consensus. They tried to compensate
for their lack of western MPs by providing for public hearings in the
West, first by a royal commission and later by the House of Commons
Transportation Committee. When Axworthy replaced Pepin as transport minister in September 1983, he worked with the Liberal MPs on
the Commons Transportation Committee to find a solution. With help

from his parliamentary secretary, Denis Dawson, a Quebec MP, he sought to deal with the Quebec opposition. The Crow Rate debate involved disagreements within regions as much as between them, and was as much about how to pay for the new transportation infrastructure as it was about regional implications.

The National Energy Program   In a similar fashion, the National Energy Program (NEP) announced in October 1980 was the focal point of both ideological and regional disagreements (Doern and Toner 1985). The oil and gas producing provinces of Alberta and Saskatchewan saw the NEP as a unilateral grab by Ottawa for increased jurisdiction and energy revenues. As well as protesting the loss of provincial power over energy development, they supported the energy industry by protesting what was seen as massive intervention by the federal government at a time when public opinion increasingly favoured less government control. Ottawa, the producing provinces and the industry all spent heavily on advertising to promote their points of view, thereby adding to the appearance of conflict.

Opinion polls at the time, however, suggested there was significant public support for the NEP's goals of "Canadianization" of the industry and the redistribution of resource wealth. The NDP government in Manitoba supported the NEP because it fitted the party's ideology, because the province was a consumer of energy and because as a "have not" province Manitoba stood to lose if Ottawa's financial capacity to meet its equalization obligations was undermined by the accumulation of resource wealth in Alberta's treasury. Alberta's intransigence in its energy revenue negotiations with the Government of Canada and the manner in which it flaunted its new wealth in the form of the Heritage Trust Fund caused resentment elsewhere in Canada, where deficits were the order of the day.

It was often suggested in western Canada that a more representative government and Parliament would never have imposed policies like the NEP and the Crow changes on the West. This viewpoint, however, overlooks the fact that there were national as well as provincial interests at stake, that the West was not unified in its responses and that efforts were made by the national government to recognize regional interests. Nevertheless, these two policies and several others became lightning rods for discontent in the West and symbols of the region's subordinate political status. The Liberals elected only two MPs, Turner and Axworthy, from the West in the 1984 federal election. In bottom-line political terms, the Axworthy initiatives did not appear to help the Liberals' recovery in the West all that much.

In Opposition

The Liberal Senators   After the 1984 election, the Liberal caucus under Turner consisted of just 40 MPs and 66 senators. This was a unique situation. In the past, senators, with some notable exceptions, had rarely been active participants in the caucus process. However, before leaving office, Trudeau had appointed a group of young, politically active senators, together with several experienced parliamentarians from the House of Commons. Led by Allan MacEachen, the Senate Liberals were often a better organized, more coherent opposition to the Mulroney government than the smaller, divided group in the Commons. The senators would caucus separately before attending the meeting of the full national caucus on Wednesday morning. As the Leader of the Opposition in the Senate, MacEachen would report on developments in the Senate and tactics that Liberal senators intended to follow in opposing the Mulroney government's legislation. There was seldom any chance for the national caucus to debate the approach being taken by the Liberal senators. The traditional balance was restored within the caucus when 83 Liberal MPs were elected in the 1988 federal election. However, this did not seriously inhibit the Liberal senators from following their own course, sometimes to the consternation of Liberal MPs who felt that obstruction in the Senate was getting out of hand.

Designated Critics   In opposition under first John Turner and now Jean Chrétien, the Liberals have presented a fractious and tattered party image. Both leaders adopted what has become the standard operating practice for opposition parties of appointing a series of designated critics. There were several bases for the assignment of shadow cabinet ministers, regional representation being one. According to two Liberal MPs interviewed for this study, Turner consulted them about their preferences for critic roles, but Chrétien did not. Press reports, however, suggest that Chrétien consulted at least those individuals who ran for the party leadership against him (Gessell 1990). A number of associate critics for particular assignments were appointed and there were disagreements over which MP was to assume the lead role. Even though the perquisites of being a shadow cabinet minister were virtually nil, apart from the greater publicity attached to certain critic roles, there was public grumbling from a few MPs about their assignments. Ideological splits within the caucus also seemed to play a role in the assignment process. Lloyd Axworthy, who had been the party's trade critic under Turner, was shifted to the external affairs post, while Roy MacLaren was given the trade position. It was MacLaren and Paul Martin, Jr., runner-up to Chrétien for the leadership, who led the forces

in favour of Canada entering into a three-way free trade agreement
with Mexico and the United States, while Axworthy, an economic nationalist, opposed such a move (Stewart and Vienneau 1990). In total
Chrétien appointed 114 critics or associate critics, with two or three MPs
being designated for most topics and as many as five MPs sharing the
critic's role for a broad topic such as agriculture. Spreading the jobs
around was obviously intended to keep everyone involved and avoid
any impression of an inside group.

Policy Development   In addition to the critic roles, the Liberal caucus
under Chrétien also created six standing committees dealing with communications, economic policy, external affairs and defence, social policy, sustainable development and political organization. Although the
purpose of the committee system was the development of a coordi-
nated policy approach, the Liberal MPs interviewed for this study agreed
that the main emphasis was on short-term tactical strategy concerning
how to react to the government. One MP suggested there was a split
within caucus about what efforts should be devoted to policy development. Those who opposed more policy work argued that the
Mulroney government would destroy itself, that policy statements
would provide tempting targets for counterattacks by the government,
and that the agenda of national issues would change many times before
the next election, making current policy efforts a waste of time. In fairness to Turner, it should be noted that a great deal of policy-development
work was done with the extraparliamentary wing of the party. A 1986
amendment to the constitution of the Liberal party provided for more
caucus representation on the party's national executive, a linkage that
was previously underdeveloped. In return, the caucus agreed that the
party president and the policy-development chair should be invited to
attend trimestral special caucuses on longer-term issues, but not the
weekly caucus meetings (Wearing 1988).

Leadership   The national Liberal caucus meets Wednesday mornings.
There is usually no printed agenda, although occasionally the notice
for the meeting will indicate a topic for discussion. Under "normal"
conditions, turnout was usually good, but from the start of the leadership race to determine the successor to Turner, absenteeism grew.
Trudeau used to listen attentively to caucus and sometimes took notes.
He would use his opportunity at the close of caucus to debate points
and explain the government's thinking. According to several sources,
Liberal MPs who privately grumbled about Trudeau's leadership were
reluctant to challenge him in caucus, apparently intimidated by his

relentless logic and superior oratory. In contrast, Turner often came to caucus with prepared notes, which left caucus members wondering whether he had made up his mind in advance.

Many of the issues that tested the unity of the governing caucus from 1984 to 1990 also proved difficult for the Liberal party. There were disagreements over the moral issues of capital punishment and abortion. Turner's plan to pre-empt the right of caucus to discuss the party's abortion stand was a significant factor in the moves made by senior caucus members and key Liberal strategists to get the leader to step down in the midst of the 1988 election campaign (Fraser 1989, chap. 9). Ideological disagreements arose over free trade, changes to unemployment insurance and testing of the cruise missile. Turner's decision to contradict party policy by agreeing to cruise testing was taken, according to two MPs interviewed for this study, without full consultation with caucus. Four Liberal MPs broke with their leader on the issue.

Disagreements over leadership and the ideological direction of the Liberal party have been far more common than regional splits since 1984. Of regional issues, the Meech Lake Accord proved to be an even more divisive issue for the Liberals than for the other two parties. Infighting and agonizing shook the parliamentary caucus, as well as the general membership of the party. In his valuable account, Andrew Cohen (1990) describes how Turner lost control of caucus over this issue. The Liberal leader was indecisive. At first, he was too quick to endorse the Accord. Eventually, he was forced to adopt a more critical stance. When the internal caucus divisions became public, he handled the situation poorly. According to Cohen (ibid., 157), "Turner did not seek a consensus and was unable to accommodate dissenters." He was sympathetic to the position of the Quebec caucus and rejected the strict brand of federalism promoted by the former leader. He ignored the party's resolutions on the constitutional question. Although Turner blamed his opponents for using the Meech issue to attack his leadership, it appears that he missed opportunities to provide leadership and effective opposition to the Mulroney government's drive to pass the Meech Lake Accord unchanged.

Regional Caucuses   From 1984 to 1988, the Liberals operated the following regional caucuses: Atlantic (7 MPs), Quebec (17 MPs), Ontario (14 MPs) and the West (2 MPs). Since 1988, the regional composition of their Commons representation has improved: Atlantic (20 MPs), Quebec (12 MPs), Ontario (43 MPs) and the West (6 MPs). The nine Liberals interviewed for this study were asked to assess the relative strength of the four regional caucuses during the 34th Parliament. There was a consensus that the Atlantic and Quebec caucuses were the strongest. A Liberal MP with more than a decade of parliamentary experience offered this impression: "I think that the Atlantic caucus is a very strong regional caucus. We hold 20 of the 32 seats in the region. Historically, the strongest caucuses in the Liberal party are Quebec and the Atlantic. There is very little dissent in the Atlantic caucus and today we are a larger group than either Quebec or the West." The skills of the caucus chair, Ron MacDonald (MP for Dartmouth), an experienced political organizer, were cited as a partial explanation for the success of the Atlantic caucus. For example, MPs from the region, especially from Newfoundland, made the case for months that a high priority for Question Period should be overfishing on the east coast by France and other countries. They successfully insisted that the leader participate in questioning the government to give prominence to the issue and to make the point that it was a national, rather than purely regional, matter.

The Quebec Liberal caucus has a tradition of being well organized and highly focused in its concerns. During the final Trudeau government (1980–84), strict discipline and direction had come from Marc Lalonde, the lead minister from Quebec. According to Christina McCall-Newman (1982, 292), Lalonde "kept track of every riding and every member of the Quebec caucus, 'animating the limp' as he put it and 'channelling the energies of the strong'." With his disciplined caucus behind him, Lalonde could deal with the remainder of the Liberal caucus firmly, constantly reminding his colleagues of Quebec's priorities. The cohesiveness of the Quebec caucus has largely survived the shift to opposition, although three Quebec Liberals bolted to the Bloc québécois after the downfall of the Meech Lake Accord. Even with only nine MPs, Quebec "continues to dominate national caucus," according to a western MP interviewed for this study. A Quebec MP suggested that the provincial caucus was very instrumental in the decision to support the Accord, having convinced Turner to support their position.

Although the Ontario Liberal caucus was the largest during the 34th Parliament, it was not the most influential. There were four subprovincial caucuses for Metropolitan Toronto, eastern Ontario, southwestern Ontario and northwestern Ontario. A former Liberal cabinet minister from Ontario described the provincial caucus as "the least effective," and another former cabinet minister observed that "Ontario has not had a strong regional minister since the days of Donald Macdonald, with all due respect to Herb Gray who has been an absolute loyalist. Even though Ontario is the largest regional caucus, it does not do as well as the Atlantic caucus because it is often fragmented." Another Liberal MP suggested there was a perception in national caucus that Ontario, particularly Toronto, had the leadership and resources to "run the show" and that it got too many benefits from the federal government. Anything done for Toronto, such as a convention centre, had to be offered to the rest of the country, and as the richest province Ontario ended up paying for it, he suggested.

For the last two decades, the Liberal party has enjoyed little electoral success in western Canada and the public perception has grown that the party is insensitive to the region's concerns. Yet in 1968 at the height of Trudeaumania, the Liberals won more votes and seats than any other party in the West, with a total of 27 Liberals compared with 25 Conservatives elected from the 68 available western seats. Despite their number, western Liberal MPs failed to convince the electorate that they had successfully defended the region's interests on such issues as freight rates, grain stabilization, bilingualism and energy pricing. By 1980 the party had fallen back to just two MPs from the region. The institutional improvisations adopted to solve this representation problem (described above) brought only limited, short-term political payoff. After the 1988 election, the Liberals still only had five MPs from Manitoba, their leader from British Columbia, and the two MPs from the Northwest Territories as the basis for a western caucus, joined by the senators from the region. With such small numbers, the caucus is hardly a force to be reckoned with, although the Meech Lake opposition came strongly from the western group. Turner's decision to run in Vancouver had been heralded at the time as a bid to regain the West's confidence. When a western caucus was formed after the 1988 election, Turner spoke to the founding dinner but never appeared again, according to two Liberal MPs interviewed for the study.

Representatives from all regional caucuses indicated that pressure groups from their provinces often approached the caucus for an opportunity to be heard. Although most caucuses were willing to listen to such groups, the western caucus limited access by outsiders to their meetings to save time for parliamentarians to discuss matters among themselves.

The New Democratic Party Caucus

The New Democratic Party has a different internal organizational culture than the other two parties. Although it has had strong leaders in the past, the culture of the caucus is less leader dominated. The general ethos of the party stresses free debate. Successive party leaders have encouraged collective decision making for policy positions taken by the party in Parliament. New Democratic MPs interviewed for this study stressed that their party was the only one that voted in caucus to determine party positions. It is rare, but not unheard of, for the party leader to lose a vote in caucus. Although leaders have at times violated the norm of caucus control, they usually pay a political price for pre-empting the right of caucus to decide. NDP caucus officers are all elected by the caucus and they form an executive to advise the party leader. The emphasis on internal debate has led on occasion to well-publicized splits, but the requirement for caucus involvement has mainly led to greater party solidarity. More than members of the two main parties, New Democrats subscribe to a "mandate theory" of representation, which holds that MPs are elected to represent a set of policy ideas and party resolutions, not to follow their individual views or even the prevailing opinions within their constituencies.

Although the internal norms stress caucus consultation before the leader states the party's position, it does not always happen. According to a former MP interviewed for this study, the amount of caucus consultation on the 1982 *Constitution Act* was very limited and the issue, as well as the process, proved to be highly divisive. The expectation also exists that the party leader will consult the NDP federal council before stating party positions on major policy issues.

With a smaller caucus, the NDP has conducted most of its decision making in full caucus. Ad hoc policy committees are created periodically and are usually chaired by the designated critic for a particular topic. The party leader chooses the designated critics. Party members are asked to state their preferences and the leader's list is formally approved by caucus. Electoral outcomes have dictated the level of regional caucus activity within the NDP. During the 1960s and 1970s, the caucus was dominated by MPs from Ontario, but more recently the balance has shifted to the West. The NDP is committed to the abolition of the Senate and with no members in the upper house, the NDP cannot fill out its regional lineup with senators.

Regional Caucuses

The NDP caucus in the 34th Parliament is the largest in the party's history with 44 members. In the past, some regional caucuses had been largely "paper" entities, but with the current numbers the system of regional caucuses has become more fully realized. The British Columbia caucus, which has almost half (19 MPs) of the total membership, has been able to achieve greater attention for its concerns. From 1984 to 1988, the Ontario caucus was the next largest to British Columbia. A former MP described Ontario as the "least effective" caucus because the province was itself regionally diverse and because "Ontario has the least sense of itself as a distinct region."

Over the years, the NDP has elected only a handful of MPs from the Atlantic region, and has only secured its second Quebec MP ever in 1990. The party has sought to get around its regional shortcomings in a variety of ways. An informal Atlantic caucus consisting of party members, including defeated candidates, was formed in 1989. Since its inception, the NDP has made various kinds of overtures to Quebec, so far with little success. Under Broadbent's leadership, the NDP caucus went to great lengths to stay in touch with Quebec opinion. Staff were hired in the leader's office who were familiar with Quebec. From 1984 to 1988 there was a "surrogate" caucus for Quebec consisting of bilingual MPs and chaired by Michael Cassidy, a bilingual MP from the Ottawa area. During one six-month period in 1986, caucus members visited Quebec 45 times. When the issue of the CF-18 contract arose in November 1986, the shadow caucus for Quebec, supported by the leader, refused to denounce the decision not to award the contract to Winnipeg. "To build political support in Quebec," a Manitoba MP related, "the shadow caucus with very strong support from the leader prevailed over the Manitoba caucus." There has been resentment over such efforts to gain Quebec support. As one MP stated: "It has been largely an unrequited love affair with Quebec and it has cost us valuable votes elsewhere."

Caucus Unity in Opposition

Moulding an opposition caucus is a difficult and delicate task. The problem in an opposition caucus consists not merely of developing a consistent position, but also of persuading the caucus to be reasonably consistent. The pressures for consistency that come from being in office are missing in opposition. Discipline of caucus members, especially more senior MPs, is a sensitive matter. The personality and political skills of the party leader are even more crucial in forging a consensus. Leaders are more likely to get sustained agreement from caucus if caucus is involved in the formulation of party positions. The history of recent tensions within opposition caucuses has been more along ideological than territorial lines, with the exception of the Meech Lake Accord, a symbolic constitutional issue that divided all parties.

THE INDIVIDUAL MP, REGIONAL REPRESENTATION AND OTHER PARLIAMENTARY FORUMS

For this study MPs and senators were asked to share their perceptions of their roles as regional representatives and to compare caucus and other parliamentary forums as vehicles for regional representation. The number of interviewed MPs and senators was small and the questions were open-ended. Of necessity, therefore, the findings are impressionistic and the interpretation of their significance is speculative.

Representation: A Complex Role

The first impression is that, when parliamentarians are not forced to follow the response categories of structured questionnaires, they provide a more kaleidoscopic definition of their representational roles than is usually assumed. Political scientists have a heavy investment in role conceptions that distinguish between the "delegate" who follows the wishes of his or her constituency and the "trustee" who follows his or her independent judgement. The focal point for representation is assumed to be either the constituency or the country as a whole. This simple, dichotomous interpretation of the representational relationship does not fit with the more complex picture of representation in practice described by the interviewed parliamentarians.

MPs see themselves as serving multiple constituencies, not just the one territorial constituency from which they are elected. There are "functional" constituencies in the form of different "policy communities" within territorial constituencies. There are parts of the territorial constituency from which the MP draws more political support and with which he or she may identify more strongly. Parliamentarians are first and foremost members of political parties and both MPs and senators often see themselves as representatives of ideological and policy constituencies within their parties.

Traditional theories of representation also ignore an intermediate level of representational thinking and activity between the national and constituency levels. Although some of the members interviewed spoke of the traditional representational dilemma of being either a constituency representative or a national policy maker, most respondents portrayed their representational world in more complicated terms. Here is how one Quebec MP described his situation: "I see myself as a regional representative from the Eastern Townships, especially from [a city], which is my riding. But [the city] is not an island, since there is a mutual dependence between the city and the region in terms of activities. I also see myself as a representative from Quebec in the House of Commons. I also see myself as a representative of the francophones, in Quebec and elsewhere. These are the different hats I am wearing." A British Columbia MP offered a similarly layered conception of representation:

> It is very difficult to generalize. The primary role is to represent the interests of the people who elected him to Parliament, but this is done within the context of the principles, ideologies and policies of the

party ... Since I come from British Columbia, you can generalize to say that I also defend western interests. But I found with some of the initiatives I promoted that I had more in common with colleagues in other parties who represented similar constituencies in northern Quebec or northern Manitoba ... When I first came here, I found it necessary to develop policy constituencies outside of Parliament in order to have an impact.

A Newfoundland MP suggested that the constituency strategy followed by MPs may change from an "expansionary" phase to a "protective" phase:

> For new members of Parliament it is extremely important to identify with your constituency, with your region, and to demonstrate that you are a voice for them. The balance between how much of your time is spent on national questions versus purely local or regional questions, I think shifts the longer you are here. Once your constituents have built up a degree of trust that you will speak for them and use your best judgement, you have a greater degree of flexibility ... People who have been here for a while have a "safe" constituency and have more flexibility. This does not, of course, remove the need to stay in touch.

Re-election concerns never leave most MPs, even after several terms in Parliament, and most probably exaggerate the risk of defeat. Therefore, throughout their careers, MPs are constantly seeking visibility back home, even though the academic studies say that in Canada there is not a large personal vote (as opposed to a leadership or party vote) to be won (Ferejohn and Gaines 1991). In numerous ways, MPs engage in communication, explaining, contacting, assisting and allocating – all of these activities being part of a broad representational linkage. Representation is, in this sense, less policy-centred than the usual conceptions imply.

Caucus Secrecy and Public Perceptions of Representation

MPs were asked whether the secrecy of caucus meant that their representational efforts on behalf of their constituencies and provinces were not seen and therefore not appreciated by the electorate. Most MPs felt that caucus secrecy did not pose a serious problem. They pointed out that re-election several times and an increasing share of the total vote were the best indicators that their constituents were satisfied with the quality of representation. All of them stressed the importance of advertising their availability and their parliamentary activities. Mailings to all households, use of the local media, monthly town hall meetings, speaking engagements and regular constituency office hours for appointments were among the techniques being used by MPs to maintain a profile in the community. Nearly all MPs also mentioned regular meetings with interest groups, contacts with provincial government officials and dealings with federal departments and agencies in their regions. Others stressed the allocational side of the representational relationship. A Conservative cabinet minister explained: "My region is south, southwestern Ontario. I think that the only way they really assess my efforts is through outputs. I get them dollars for a new auditorium for Windsor. I get them dollars for a convention centre in London. So, yes, I think they do feel that I am producing something for them." In opposition there are few material benefits for MPs to bestow, but there are also not the same constraints on the freedom to voice regional concerns. Most of the opposition effort in Parliament consists of criticizing unpopular government measures. Although the decision to oppose may arise from a secret caucus process, the public does not really care because the opposition party is often criticizing unpopular measures. Government MPs, on the other hand, may get some political credit if a decision favours their constituencies, but conversely they may be seen as ineffective if the decision goes against their constituencies. Caucus confidentiality definitely creates some false impressions that MPs are not working on the public's behalf. Most MPs saw this as the political price that had to be paid to preserve the integrity of the caucus process, which was seen as central to cabinet-parliamentary government. If there were widespread publicity and credit-claiming by individuals and groups who were successful in caucus deliberations, the willingness to compromise would be undermined.

Parliamentary Committees and Regional Representation

MPs were asked to compare service on parliamentary committees to involvement with caucus as a means of regional representation. Their responses may have been coloured by the recent difficulties experienced by the committee system. In February 1986, the committee system was overhauled as part of a more general reform of the organization and procedures of the House of Commons. The detailed study of legislation after second reading was transferred from the existing standing committees to smaller, ad hoc legislative committees. At the same time, the standing committees were reduced in size, the position of chair was enhanced and the committees were granted greater freedom from government control to study matters of interest arising from the Estimates and Annual Reports of government departments and agencies. Budgets for committee staff were to be made available on request. The new committee system was hailed as an opportunity for greater back-bench involvement in policy making, and some committees did indeed exhibit a real streak of independence from party discipline. However, with 26 standing committees (most with 14 members each) and anywhere from 10 to 15 legislative committees meeting during a given period, the demands of the committee system became onerous (Franks 1987, chap. 8). In April 1989, following negotiations with the opposition parties, the government House Leader announced plans to streamline the committee system. The proposal to halve the size of the standing committees remained stalled on the order paper of the Commons because the opposition parties were not prepared to see a reduction in their representation on committees. On a seven-member standing committee on agriculture, for example, the Liberals and New Democrats would probably have only two members each, which would not allow the various party critics on agriculture and different regional representatives to serve as full-time members. In addition, the bitterness in the House late in 1990 brought the committee system to a virtual standstill (Delacourt 1990).

Most MPs indicated that regional interests were a factor in their choice of committee assignments. Committee memberships for government MPs are decided by the party whip in consultation with the government House Leader, and there is competition for the available spots on some committees. Under the current rules, MPs serving as parliamentary secretaries to ministers are not allowed to be on the standing committee that reviews the department's performance. Efforts are made to balance regional, linguistic and other factors in preparing the lists of committee memberships. In the opposition parties, the process is also in the hands of the whips, but the designated critics on various topics have first claim to positions on the relevant Commons committees. MPs can state their preferences for their second standing committee assignment and can request to serve on ad hoc legislative committees studying bills.

Generally, standing committees have a functional approach; they look at policies, programs and administration. There are, however, still openings for MPs to raise local or provincial matters, such as when the Estimates are before the committees and there is a chance to question spending decisions affecting a locality. For example, rural MPs from all parties serving on the Consumer and Corporate Affairs and Government Operations Committee were influential in resisting cutbacks in rural postal services. Likewise, a strong western contingent of Conservative MPs served on the Energy, Mines and Resources Committee as a way to oversee the dismantling of the National Energy Program after 1984. As part of the steering committee that decides the line-up of witnesses, opposition MPs can sometimes highlight the regional implications of national policies. For example, in 1987, Brian Tobin, the Liberal's transport critic, was relentless through countless committee meetings and parliamentary debates in opposing a user-pay provision in a shipping act amendment proposed by the Mulroney government. Almost single-handedly he was successful in forcing the government to withdraw the measure, which would have brought financial hardship to the people he represented on the west coast of Newfoundland (Winsor 1987). Normally, partisanship and government control inhibit the opportunities for committee influence. More autonomous committees, put to work before the government declares its policy position, may be a way to help reconcile regional differences.

CONCLUSION

The Problem of Public Perceptions

It is now widely believed in Canada that the combination of a federal system that highlights regional differences and a cabinet-parliamentary system that centralizes power produces serious tensions within the political system. Regionalism is seen to be on the rise in Canada, and there is declining public confidence in all parts of the country that national policies reflect regional fairness. This study suggests that regionalism involves both objective social and economic facts, as well as subjective perceptions and attitudes held by Canadians in different parts of the country. Constitutional and institutional arrangements have heightened the importance of regionalism and fostered a perception of widespread and severe interregional conflict. The political legitimacy of the federal government and of certain national policies has been undermined by the feeling that regional interests have been ignored or overridden in national decision making.

Without denying the importance of public perceptions, this study concludes that the actual level of interregional conflict in Canadian political life has been overstated. Whereas the federal system is the primary source of the exaggerated importance attached to regionalism, the single-member, simple-plurality electoral system is also a contributing factor. Although there has been a significant loss of public confidence in the national government, provincial governments have also lost public esteem and confidence. Declining faith in and support for governments at all levels reflect much wider sources of disenchantment than organizational arrangements and decision-making procedures. Much of the national malaise cannot be blamed on the electoral system. The problem exists more at the level of public perception than with the actual workings of national institutions and, although perceptions may not be everything in politics, they are nevertheless important.

The Role of the Electoral System

The impact of the electoral system on public perceptions of how the political system operates has served to increase regional tensions. The electoral system contributes to a sense of regional injustice when individual provinces, or even groups of provinces, have all their MPs on the opposition side of the House of Commons, despite the fact that there is significant voter support for the governing party within the province(s) in question.

Another presumed impact of the electoral system has been to weaken the role of parties as agencies of national unity by providing an incentive for regional biases in their policy making. It is assumed that parties will cater to the demands of their regional strongholds and ignore the needs of regions where their parliamentary representation is weak. Although it is desirable for party caucuses to be broadly representative, this has not been the historical pattern in Canada. Yet it is only in the last few decades that there has been talk of a crisis of representation and proposals to reform the electoral system. It seems that the growing strength of the provincial governments, the changed nature of the issues on the national agenda, and the increased emphasis on a functional, rather than a regional, orientation to national decision making, have produced greater regional dissatisfaction. These changes, more than the electoral system per se, explain why political representation in the Commons and the party caucuses, which was once considered adequate, is no longer seen to guarantee regional fairness.

Parties and Regional Concerns

Contrary to the suggestion that parties have forsaken their function to integrate regional concerns, this study found exactly the opposite. The national Conservative, Liberal and New Democratic parties have all been sensitive to the need to recognize and accommodate regional interests. All have sought in various ways at different times to compensate for the gaps in regional representation within their parliamentary caucuses.

National party caucuses have become better organized, more active and more influential since the 1960s. Each party also operates a number of provincial and regional caucuses. These bodies ensure that the regional dimensions of party policy and other regional concerns are articulated and discussed first within the regional caucus and then in the full caucus. Within the governing party, both the national and regional caucuses provide significant opportunities for MPs and senators to influence legislation, spending and administration. The divisions within the Progressive Conservative caucus during the past six years in power have been mainly over ideological and moral issues rather than regional disputes.

In opposition, the Liberal and NDP caucuses have remained more regional in their composition than the Progressive Conservative caucus. They have sought to compensate for deficiencies in regional representation. In the opposition caucuses, debates are mainly about how to react to government proposals and what parliamentary tactics should be used to challenge the government. Actual regional trade-offs do not have to be made. Disagreements that have surfaced within the two opposition caucuses have been mainly over ideological approaches and leadership; splits along regional lines have been far less common.

In all parties, regional caucuses were found to vary not only in size, but also in level of activity, cohesion and the quality of members. In the government caucus, regional ministers are expected to play a lead role in organizing their regional caucuses. The relative influence of different regional caucuses within the governing party was found to depend far more on the political skills of the regional ministers than on the number of members in the provincial caucus. To be underrepresented in the government caucus is not necessarily to be underrepresented in Cabinet if the regional grouping is led by a strong minister.

The number of issues that divide parties along regional lines are relatively few. The same issues were identified time and time again when parliamentarians were asked for examples of policies that proved to be regionally divisive. The analysis of such issues as the National Energy Program, the Crow Rate debate, the CF-18 decision and the Meech Lake Accord suggests that issues were fought within regions as well as between them. Over time, the issues assumed a symbolic importance in the political thinking of western residents that went well beyond their actual impact. This raises the question of whether reforms to existing institutions should be undertaken in response to regional discontent caused by a small number of perhaps atypical issues that are highly emotional and seem to pit region against region.

There is far more regional representation taking place within the parliamentary parties and Parliament in general than is usually assumed. MPs work with multiple definitions of their "constituencies." The usual dichotomy between a constituency and a national focus for parliamentary representation does not capture the complicated ideas of representation that guide the activities of many MPs. In part to enhance their re-election prospects and in part for more "public-spirited" reasons, MPs reach out to contact and respond to the multiple constituencies they serve. It is generally assumed that the Senate has been a complete failure as a regional body, yet senators have recently played an enlarged role in caucus deliberations in both the Conservative and Liberal parties. There is a younger, more professional and more active element in the contemporary Senate that has provided additional capability within regional caucuses.

Because most regional representation takes place in private in Cabinet and in caucus, governments are not seen by the public to be modifying their positions as a result of the expression of demands or concerns from different parts of the country. The absence of visible examples of regional debate and accommodation adds to the sense of exclusion felt by different parts of the country at different times.

Proposals for Electoral Reform

During the late 1970s and early 1980s there was growing concern about the party system and how it was affected by the electoral system. The country seemed destined to experience long periods of Liberal rule with almost no western representation in government, interrupted by brief periods of Conservative rule with almost no Quebec representation. In this context, proposals to reform the electoral system were presented by various task forces and politicians. The election of the Progressive Conservatives in 1984 with strong parliamentary support in all parts of the country took the momentum out of the talk of electoral reform. However, the achievement of regional balance in the governing caucus has not convinced the peripheries of the country, especially the West, that their voices will be heard at the national level.

Western Alienation

Lack of confidence in the national government has grown in both the Atlantic and western regions, but the disenchantment in the West became particularly serious during the 1980s when a series of issues was seen to involve a denial of the region's interest in long-term economic diversification. The disillusionment came out strongly in a 1987 report prepared by the Canada West Foundation:

> Now there are 61 Western MPs in the government caucus, and still western economic interests suffer while massive assistance flows to the centre. The point is not whether the Mulroney government has treated the West marginally better or marginally worse than the

> Trudeau government, but rather that both governments have treated
> the West badly. It does not seem to have made any difference whether
> western MPs sat noisily but impotently on the opposition benches or
> quietly and impotently on the government benches. It now appears
> that electoral reformers were treating the wrong disease. (McCormick
> and Elton 1987, 4)

This study challenges the conclusion in the quotation that the West
has suffered because its MPs were impotent in both opposition and in
government. Nevertheless, the quotation expresses a widely held view
in the West.

The report is also important because it reflects a shift in the thinking of the West about how best to protect its interests. The late 1970s
emphasis on electoral reform to ensure that the West would achieve
some measure of representation in the governing caucus was dropped
in favour of more fundamental constitutional and institutional reforms.
Working within the major parties and using third parties as sources of
regional pressure had not worked satisfactorily. If changing the players did not change the outcomes, it was now time to change the rules
of the game. This is the origin of the West's, particularly Alberta's,
enthusiasm for ideas like decentralization of constitutional responsibilities, Senate reform and more free votes in the House of Commons.
Most of these proposals, however, are beyond the terms of reference
of the present Commission.

If there is a "numbers problem" for the smaller provinces, it cannot be solved by electoral reforms without some departure from the
principle of representation by population. Canada's electoral laws have
never strictly applied the principle of equal value for all votes, but
departures from the principle in the future will be constrained by the
provision in the *Canadian Charter of Rights and Freedoms* that guarantees Canadians equal benefit of the law. The courts have begun to use
this provision to insist upon equal weighting of votes. The authors of
the Canada West study recognized this limit to electoral reform and
therefore argued for a triple-E Senate – that is, an elected, equal and
effective upper house – to counterbalance the majority principle that
operates in the House of Commons.

Proportional Representation

The two main findings of this study – that the regional problem is mainly a matter of perception and that party caucuses have become important forums for the expression of regional concerns – both point to the
continued relevance of electoral reform to achieve more regionally

representative party groupings in the House of Commons. Less regionalized party caucuses would contribute to increased confidence and legitimacy in national policies. Some form of proportional representation (PR) would likely help to correct regional imbalances in the make-up of party caucuses. There are, however, serious implications of PR that must be considered. Still, it is worth reiterating that although the electoral system has been a significant factor in the development of regional discontent, it has not been the only or even the primary one. Federal–provincial disputes and disenchantment with governments in general have been more important contributing factors.

Proportional representation, like ice cream, comes in many flavours; however, the essence of PR is to ensure that the seats awarded to different parties reflect more accurately the actual votes cast. Any version of PR would produce more partisan diversity in the representation in the House of Commons from particular provinces. This outcome might facilitate intraparty accommodation of regional differences. However, it is difficult to see how the Progressive Conservative and Liberal parties would agree to PR if it meant the breakup of the historically large caucuses from Quebec and Ontario that have provided the foundations for majority governments.

Whereas the tendency of the current simple-plurality electoral system to produce majority governments may have been exaggerated, the consequence of PR would be to enhance the prospects for minority government. Six of the last 12 federal elections have resulted in minority governments. During minority governments greater stress is placed on caucus consultation, but there is also greater insistence on strict party discipline to prevent surprise defeats. If implemented on the basis of party lists controlled by the leadership, PR could further contribute to tighter party discipline. Minority governments might avoid initiatives that are regionally sensitive and they might exhibit greater responsiveness to shifting currents of public opinion. However, a series of precariously balanced minority federal governments, whose regional credentials could be challenged, might be weakened in their dealings with assertive provincial governments. National leadership in policy might suffer and in the past at least the smaller provinces have benefited from federally sponsored economic and social programs.

On the other hand, by providing for more regionally balanced party caucuses, PR might lead to greater political confidence in national institutions. Rather than minority governments, PR could lead to the development of a tradition of coalition governments of two or more parties in which the Cabinet's make-up would reflect more accurately than at present the relative voting support for different parties. Even if minority governments were a more common occurrence, they would not necessarily be a formula for legislative deadlock, as the impressive record of legislative accomplishments of the minority Liberal governments during the 1960s reveals. Two further consequences of minority governments are, first, to strengthen the role of the governing party caucus where the opinions of individual MPs must be considered more seriously to prevent surprise defeats in the House of Commons and, second, to increase the likelihood of negotiations among the parties represented in the House of Commons to secure passage of the government's legislative program. Both of these outcomes might increase the responsiveness of the national political system to regional considerations.

Other Approaches to Reform

Beyond electoral reform, there is a variety of possible changes to improve regional responsiveness. These include more free votes in the House of Commons, more autonomy for parliamentary committees, a greater willingness by governments to present their ideas in a tentative form and to make modifications in light of public reactions, and improvements to the caucus process itself. Such proposals deserve more extended discussion than can be presented here. Just as the electoral system does not cause all the regional tensions in the country, it does not represent the only answer to alleviating them.

NOTES

This study was completed in May 1991.

The author would like to acknowledge the excellent research assistance provided by Michel Sarra-Bournet, who conducted most of the interviews with MPs and senators in Ottawa, and Judy White, who provided bibliographic and research assistance in Winnipeg. He would also like to thank the 30 members of the House of Commons and the Senate who shared their knowledge and opinion on the operation of the party caucuses. (To encourage frank and open discussion of the issues examined in this study, the 30 MPs and senators interviewed were promised anonymity.) David McCormick of CBC Newsworld in Ottawa graciously shared his insights into and contacts with the party caucus process. Constructive advice on an earlier draft was provided by Professor Herman Bakvis and two anonymous assessors.

1. W. Huntington, MP, in Minutes of Proceedings and Evidence of the Special Committee on Standing Orders and Proceedings, Issue No. 6, 15 July 1982, p. 33.

2. John Meisel in Minutes of Proceedings of the Special Joint Committee of the Senate and House of Commons on Senate Reform, 28 June 1983, p. 13.

REFERENCES

Axworthy, Lloyd. 1990. "Regional Development Innovations in the West." In *Towards a Just Society: The Trudeau Years*, ed. Thomas S. Axworthy and Pierre Elliott Trudeau. Toronto: Penguin.

Bakvis, Herman, and William Chandler, eds. 1987. *Federalism and the Role of the State*. Toronto: University of Toronto Press.

Beck, J.M. 1981. "An Atlantic Region Political Culture: A Chimera." In *Eastern and Western Perspectives*, ed. David Jay Bercuson and Phillip A. Buckner. Toronto: University of Toronto Press.

Bell, David, and Lorne Tepperman. 1979. *The Roots of Disunity*. Toronto: McClelland and Stewart.

Blishen, Bernard. 1983. "The Development of a Western Regional Consciousness." Sorokin Lectures No. 14. Saskatoon: University of Saskatchewan.

Brodie, Janine, and Jane Jenson. 1989. "Piercing the Smokescreen: Brokerage Parties and Class Politics." In *Canadian Parties in Transition*, ed. Alain G. Gagnon and A. Brian Tanguay. Scarborough: Nelson Canada.

Cairns, Alan C. 1968. "The Electoral System and the Party System in Canada, 1921–1965." *Canadian Journal of Political Science* 1:55–80.

———. 1977. "The Governments and Societies of Canadian Federalism." *Canadian Journal of Political Science* 10:695–726.

———. 1986. "The Embedded State: State-Society Relations in Canada." In *State and Society: Canada in a Comparative Perspective*, ed. Keith Banting. Vol. 31 of the research studies of the Royal Commission on the Economic Union and Development Prospects for Canada. Toronto: University of Toronto Press.

Camp, Dalton. 1981. *An Eclectic Eel*. Ottawa: Deneau Publishers.

Chrétien, Jean. 1985. *Straight from the Heart*. Toronto: Key Porter Books.

Christian, William, and Colin Campbell. 1983. *Political Parties and Ideologies in Canada*. Toronto: McGraw-Hill Ryerson.

Cohen, Andrew. 1990. *A Deal Undone: The Making and Breaking of the Meech Lake Accord*. Vancouver: Douglas and McIntyre.

Connelly, William, ed. 1984. *Legitimacy and the State*. New York: New York University Press.

Corry, J.A. 1952. *Democratic Government and Politics*. Toronto: University of Toronto Press.

Dahl, Robert. 1980. *After the Revolution: Authority in the Good Society.* New Haven: Yale University Press.

Dahrendorf, Ralf. 1980. "Effectiveness and Legitimacy: On the Governability of Democracies." *Political Quarterly* 51 (4): 393–410.

Delacourt, Susan. 1990. "Commons' Panels Face Paralysis." *Globe and Mail,* 6 November.

Doern, G. Bruce, and Glen Toner. 1985. *The Politics of Energy: The Development and Implementation of the National Energy Program.* Toronto: Methuen.

Edelman, Murray. 1971. *Politics as Symbolic Action: Mass Arousal and Quiescence.* Chicago: Markham.

———. 1988. *Constructing the Political Spectacle.* Chicago: University of Chicago Press.

Elkins, David, and Richard Simeon. 1980. *Small Worlds: Provinces and Parties in Canadian Political Life.* Toronto: Methuen.

Elton, David, and Roger Gibbins. 1980. *Electoral Reform: The Need Is Pressing, the Time Is Now.* Calgary: Canada West Foundation.

Eulau, Heinz, and Paul D. Karps. 1977. "The Puzzle of Representation: Specifying Components of Responsiveness." *Legislative Studies* 2 (3): 233–54.

Franks, C.E.S. 1987. *The Parliament of Canada.* Toronto: University of Toronto Press.

Fraser, Graham. 1989. *Playing for Keeps: The Making of the Prime Minister, 1988.* Toronto: McClelland and Stewart.

Gainer, Walter. 1976. "Western Disenchantment and the Canadian Federation." *Proceedings of the Academy of Political Science* 32 (2): 40–50.

Gessell, Paul. 1990. "Chrétien's Picks for Shadow Cabinet Get Mixed Response." Ottawa *Citizen,* 13 September.

Gibbins, Roger. 1980. *Prairie Politics and Society: Regionalism in Decline.* Toronto: Butterworths.

———. 1982. *Regionalism: Territorial Politics in Canada and the United States.* Toronto: Butterworths.

Gidengil, Elisabeth. 1989. "Class and Region in Canadian Voting: A Dependency Interpretation." *Canadian Journal of Political Science* 22:563–88.

Goar, Carol. 1987. "Mulroney Hasn't Lost Grip on Caucus." *Times Colonist,* 18 February.

Gregg, Allan, and Michael Posner. 1990. *The Big Picture: What Canadians Think about Almost Everything*. Toronto: Macfarlane Walter and Ross.

Hodge, Carl. 1990. "The Provincialization of Regional Politics." In *Canadian Politics: An Introduction to the Discipline*, ed. James P. Bickerton and Alain G. Gagnon. Peterborough: Broadview Press.

Horner, Jack. 1980. *My Own Brand*. Edmonton: Hurtig.

Howard, Ross. 1988. "Members of Smaller Tory Caucus May Play a More Demanding Role." *Globe and Mail*, 12 December.

Jackson, Robert J., and Doreen Jackson. 1990. *Politics in Canada: Culture, Institutions, Behaviour and Public Policy*. 2d ed. Scarborough: Prentice-Hall.

Johnston, Donald. 1986. *Up the Hill*. Montreal: Optimum.

Johnston, Richard. 1986. *Public Opinion and Public Policy in Canada*. Vol. 35 of the research studies of the Royal Commission on the Economic Union and Development Prospects for Canada. Toronto: University of Toronto Press.

Johnston, Richard, André Blais, Henry E. Brady and Jean Crête. 1989. "Free Trade and the Dynamics of the 1988 Canadian Election." Paper delivered at the Canadian Political Science Association Annual Meeting, Quebec City.

Kilgour, David. 1990. *Inside Outer Canada*. Calgary: Lone Pine.

Ladd, Everett. 1990. "Public Opinion and the 'Congress Problem.'" *Public Interest* 100 (Summer): 57–67.

Laslovich, Michael J. 1985. *Changing the Crow Rate: State–Society Interaction*. Ottawa: Carleton University, Department of Political Science.

Lee, Robert Mason. 1989. *One Hundred Monkeys: The Triumph of Popular Wisdom in Canadian Politics*. Toronto: Macfarlane Walter and Ross.

Lounder, Jan. 1991. "Massive Cuts Urged." *Ottawa Sun*, 8 January.

Lovink, J.A.A. 1970. "On Analyzing the Impact of the Electoral System on the Party System." *Canadian Journal of Political Science* 3:497–516.

———. 1973. "Is Canadian Politics Too Competitive?" *Canadian Journal of Political Science* 6:341–79.

McCall-Newman, Christina. 1982. *Grits*. Toronto: McClelland and Stewart.

McCormick, Peter, and David Elton. 1987. *The Western Economy and Canadian Unity*. Calgary: Canada West Foundation.

McCormick, Peter, Ernest C. Manning and Gordon Gibson. 1981. *Regional Representation*. Calgary: Canada West Foundation.

MacLaren, Roy. 1986. *Honourable Mentions: The Uncommon Diary of an MP*. Toronto: Deneau.

McNeil, Neil. 1917. "Canadian National Unity." In *The New Era in Canada*, ed. J.D. Miller. Toronto: J.M. Dent.

Macpherson, Laura G. 1991. "Quebec Block Voting." Honours Political Science essay, Dalhousie University.

Mayer, Lawrence. 1970. "Federalism and Party Behavior in Australia and Canada." *Western Political Quarterly* 23:795–807.

Meisel, John. 1981. "The Larger Context: The Period Preceding the 1979 Election." In *Canada at the Polls, 1979 and 1980*, ed. Howard R. Penniman. Washington, DC: American Enterprise Institute for Public Policy Research.

Nielsen, Erik. 1989. *The House Is Not a Home*. Toronto: Macmillan of Canada.

Norton, Philip. 1990. "Parliament in the United Kingdom: Balancing Effectiveness and Consent." *West European Politics* 13 (3): 10–31.

Oberle, Frank. 1983. "Caucus Reform: Update August 1983." Ottawa: House of Commons.

Ornstein, Michael D., H. Michael Stevenson and A. Paul Williams. 1980. "Region, Class and Political Culture in Canada." *Canadian Journal of Political Science* 13:227–72.

Paltiel, Khayyam Z. 1989. "Political Marketing, Party Finance and the Decline of Canadian Parties." In *Canadian Parties in Transition*, ed. Alain G. Gagnon and A. Brian Tanguay. Scarborough: Nelson Canada.

Pitkin, Hannah F. 1967. *The Concept of Representation*. Berkeley: University of California Press.

Pross, Paul. 1985. "Parliamentary Influence and the Diffusion of Power." *Canadian Journal of Political Science* 18:235–66.

Ray, Randy. 1986. "Tory MPs Plan Monthly Meetings." *London Free Press*, 7 November.

Riley, Susan. 1987. "Tories Cool to the Formation of a Right-Wing Caucus." Ottawa *Citizen*, 10 March.

Saltzstein, Grace. 1985. "Conceptualizing Bureaucratic Responsiveness." *Administration and Society* 17 (3): 283–306.

Schattschneider, E.E. 1960. *The Semisovereign People*. New York: Doubleday.

Schwartz, Mildred. 1974. *Politics and Territory: The Sociology of Regional Persistence*. Montreal: McGill-Queen's University Press.

Scott, Gilbert. 1990. "Changing the Corporate Culture of the Public Service." *Canadian Speeches* (December 1990): 64–73.

Simeon, Richard, and Ian Robinson. 1990. *State, Society, and the Development of Canadian Federalism*. Toronto: University of Toronto Press.

Skogstad, Grace. 1987. *The Politics of Agricultural Policy Making.* Toronto: University of Toronto Press.

Smiley, Donald V., and Ronald Watts. 1985. *The Reform of Federal Institutions: Intrastate Federalism in Canada.* Vol. 39 of the research studies of the Royal Commission on the Economic Union and Development Prospects for Canada. Toronto: University of Toronto Press.

Smith, David. 1985. "Party Government, Representation and National Integration in Canada." In *Party Government and Regional Representation in Canada,* ed. Peter Aucoin. Vol. 36 of the research studies of the Royal Commission on the Economic Union and Development Prospects for Canada. Toronto: University of Toronto Press.

Stewart, Edison, and David Vienneau. 1990. "Top Liberals Urge Joining U.S.–Mexico Trade Talks." *Toronto Star,* 12 September.

Thomas, Paul G. 1985. "The Role of National Party Caucuses." In *Party Government and Regional Representation in Canada,* ed. Peter Aucoin. Vol. 36 of the research studies of the Royal Commission on the Economic Union and Development Prospects for Canada. Toronto: University of Toronto Press.

Ullman, Stephen H. 1990. "Political Disaffection in the Province of New Brunswick: Manifestations and Sources." *American Review of Canadian Studies* 20 (Summer): 151–77.

Vance, Rupert. 1968. "Region." In *International Encyclopedia of the Social Sciences,* ed. David Shils. 13:377. New York: Crowell Collier Macmillan.

Wearing, Joseph. 1988. *Strained Relations, Canadian Parties and Voters.* Toronto: McClelland and Stewart.

Weaver, R. Kent. 1985. "Are Parliamentary Systems Better?" *Brookings Review* 3 (Summer): 16–25.

Whelan, Eugene, and Rick Archbold. 1986. *Whelan: The Man in the Green Stetson.* Toronto: Irwin.

Williams, Douglas E., ed. 1988. *Constitution, Government and Society in Canada: Selected Essays by Alan C. Cairns.* Toronto: McClelland and Stewart.

Winsor, Hugh. 1986. "Mulroney Welcomes Flexing of Muscles by Tory 'Nobodies.'" *Globe and Mail,* 18 December.

———. 1987. "Newfoundland MPs Dogged Determination Holed Bill C-75." *Globe and Mail,* 9 March.

5

PARTY COMPETITION AND ELECTORAL VOLATILITY
Canada in Comparative Perspective

Donald E. Blake

CANADA HAS A single-member plurality electoral system. Thus, in contrast to systems using proportional representation, the strongest parties receive a larger proportion of seats than votes, and the total number of effective parties is constrained (Lijphart 1990). This makes plurality systems less competitive in the sense that there are fewer viable options available to the electorate and the system is biased in favour of certain parties over others. However, plurality systems are generally more responsive to election swings than those using proportional representation. By exaggerating the strength of the leading party, relatively small vote shifts can lead to a change of government.

Unlike other countries with plurality systems, Canada does not have a two-party system (Rae 1971, 94), because smaller parties have been sufficiently strong to prevent dominance of election outcomes by the two largest parties, the Liberals and Progressive Conservatives.[1] Cairns (1968) attributes this to the fact that support for some of the smaller parties is concentrated in particular regions, giving them the seat bonus associated with the plurality system in their strongholds. In other words, the Canadian party system offers more competition in the sense of offering the electorate more choice than is the norm in plurality systems.

This research study looks at party competition in Canada compared with that in Great Britain and the United States which, with New

Zealand, are the only other democracies that have extensive experience with the plurality system. As we shall see, Canadian elections are more competitive than those in the other plurality systems in several ways. Besides having a larger number of effective parties, Canada exhibits greater electoral volatility and a higher turnover of members of the national legislature.

The next section looks at volatility or interelection changes in party vote shares in Canada, the United States and Great Britain; this allows us to compare the magnitude of electoral change across the three countries and to look for trends as well. Following that is an examination in the same three countries of changes over time in the turnover of seats between one election and the next. The section after that deals with electoral volatility and competition at the subnational level. This is followed by a final section of conclusions.

VOLATILITY IN CANADA, THE UNITED STATES AND GREAT BRITAIN

One measure of competitiveness, called a volatility index, is used by Blake (1979) to measure net change in the vote between pairs of Canadian elections. This measure is also used by Pedersen (1983) to compare European party systems, as well as by Flanigan and Zingale (1985) for the United States and by Crewe (1985b) for Great Britain. It provides a way of assessing whether the pattern of party competition in a given country is stable or changing. For example, using this measure, Blake (1979) is able to isolate critical elections in Canada, ones in which the balance of power between parties changed substantially to produce a new set of competitive circumstances that persisted until the next disturbance. This measure also allows comparison of interelection changes in different provinces to see whether they emulate or deviate from the national pattern. Thus, Blake demonstrates that the 1935 realignment, which saw the arrival on the scene of the Co-operative Commonwealth Federation (CCF) and Social Credit parties and the decimation of the Conservatives, produced a lasting alteration in the pattern of competition in all provinces except Quebec. On the other hand, the 1958 Diefenbaker sweep, while affecting competition in all provinces to some extent, had long-term effects only in the West.

Moreover, the volatility index is also strongly correlated with other measures of competition such as "swing" (Pfeiffer 1967; Rapoport 1984; Butler and Van Beek 1990), but it has the advantage that it utilizes information about the support of all parties in an election, something that is particularly important in a system with more than two strong parties.

To calculate the measure, the absolute change in vote between one election and the next is calculated for each party and then summed across parties. Because what one party gains another loses, this sum is then divided by two (to avoid double counting). Thus, in 1988, Conservative support dropped by 7.1 percentage points (from 50.0 to 42.9%), the Liberals gained 4.0 points (from 28 to 32%), the NDP support grew by 1.6 points (18.8 to 20.4%), and support for other parties and independents went from 3.1 to 4.6% for a net change of 7.1%. The measure can be viewed as the average gains made by the winning parties in an election, or, alternatively, as the minimum percentage of the electorate that had to shift its support to produce the 1988 result. Of course, gross change, or the percentage of people who actually changed parties, was probably higher. However, some of these changes will have cancelled each other out, resulting in a smaller net shift. Nevertheless, the index remains useful because studies comparing individual-level change (gross change) and aggregate-level change (net change) have shown that they are correlated (Denver 1985).

Table 5.1 shows how Canada compares with the United Kingdom and the United States in postwar elections. In Canada, the average change between elections has been over 8 percent compared to 5.8 percent in the United Kingdom and 3.3 percent in elections for the U.S. House of Representatives. The range and standard deviation are also important indicators of Canada's relative standing.[2] They confirm the relative lack of volatility in U.S. House elections and show that Canada has had more extreme changes than Britain as well as more variability over time. In fact, the figures for Canada resemble those for U.S. presidential elections.

As mentioned above, trends in volatility can be examined for evidence of significant changes in the pattern of competition between

Table 5.1
Electoral volatility in Canada, Great Britain and the United States
(percentages)

	Canada 1949–88	Great Britain 1950–87	U.S. House 1948–86	U.S. Presidency 1948–84
Minimum	3.6	1.7	0.7	2.4
Maximum	16.7	13.3	8.0	18.4
Mean	8.5	5.8	3.3	8.0
Standard deviation	4.8	3.7	2.0	5.3

Calculations for U.S. and Britain based on figures in Flanigan and Zingale (1985) and Crewe (1985b) respectively, updated using Stanley and Niemi (1988) and Craig (1989). Calculations for Canada based on Blake (1979) and Feigert (1989).

parties. For this purpose it is more useful to examine the complete time series of elections than to rely on summary statistics. Figure 5.1 presents the series for Canada, beginning with the 1935 election, which marked the eclipse of Canada's two-party system. Each point on the graph represents the amount of change between a given election and the previous one. Thus, for example, the figure for 1949 represents a net shift of 10.7 percent in support among the parties. Three elections stand out in the figure: the 1958 Diefenbaker landslide election, the subsequent election when the Conservatives lost their majority, and the 1984 Conservative landslide. The figure also shows that while high levels of volatility are generally associated with a change in government, this is not always the case. Government changed hands in 1963, 1979 and 1980, even though volatility levels were very low.

Until 1984, it appeared that Canadian elections had become very stable affairs with only minor net shifts between elections (see also LeDuc 1985; Denver 1985). However, it now appears that 1984 may have ushered in a new era of competition and that this election was thus critical in the sense noted above. It certainly altered the pattern of competition in Quebec, although it is still not clear whether the change will be a lasting one.

Figure 5.1
Electoral volatility in Canada, 1935–88

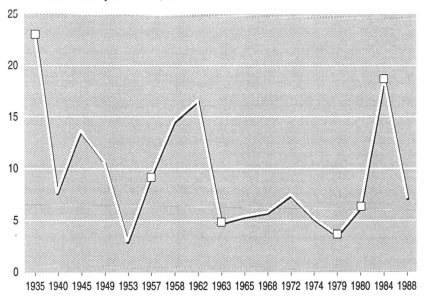

□ Change of government

Source: Based on figures in Canada, Elections Canada (various years).

How do these results compare to those for Great Britain and the United States? Figures 5.2 and 5.3 contain the respective time series for those countries. The pattern of stability in Canada between 1962 and 1979 resembles that for Great Britain prior to the February 1974 election when Labour took power, with volatility hovering around the 5 percent mark. Since then, there have been other substantial shifts as the Conservatives under Margaret Thatcher regained office and the fortunes of the Liberals and the Social Democratic Party (SDP) waxed and waned. Nevertheless, despite lower levels of volatility, government has changed hands in Great Britain five times since 1950 – exactly the same as in Canada.

The pattern for elections to the U.S. House of Representatives stands in sharp contrast to those in both Canada and Britain. Interelection change has rarely exceeded 5 percent, and the mean of 3.3 reported in table 5.1 provides a fairly accurate summary. Moreover, the Democrats retained control of the House throughout the entire period represented in the graph.

In short, it is clear that electoral volatility in Canada has been higher than that in the United States and is higher, on average, than that in

Figure 5.2
Volatility in elections to British House of Commons

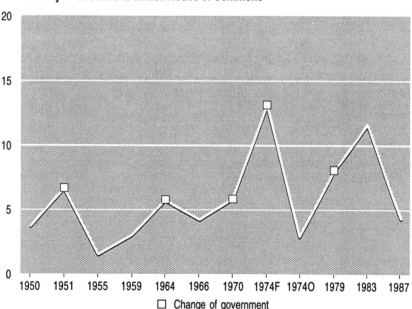

Source: Based on figures in Crewe (1985b) and Craig (1989).
F = February; O = October.

Figure 5.3
Volatility in U.S. House of Representatives elections

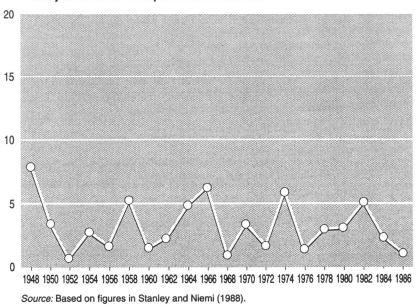

Source: Based on figures in Stanley and Niemi (1988).

Britain. However, on occasion, volatility in Britain has approached the levels exhibited in Canadian elections, and the rate at which elections produce a change in government is roughly the same in the two countries.

TURNOVER IN CANADA, THE UNITED STATES AND GREAT BRITAIN

In an article published in 1973, J.A.A. Lovink suggested that Canadian politics might be too competitive, on the grounds that the turnover in membership of the House of Commons between elections produces such a high percentage of inexperienced members that the operation of Parliament might be negatively affected. He also noted that turnover in Canada was much higher between 1953 and 1965 than in the United States and Britain for comparable periods. The percentage of seats that changed hands was 21.8 percent for the U.S. House of Representatives, 23.0 percent for the British House of Commons, but a huge 76.4 percent for the Canadian House (Lovink 1973, 358).

However, calculating the percentage of seats that changed hands by aggregating results for the entire period gives a misleading picture of the typical turnover rate, because it is greatly affected by the Diefenbaker landslide election and the 1957 election that preceded it. Figure 5.4 provides turnover rates for the entire period from 1935 to 1988.[3] It confirms that turnover during the 1950s was unusually high and that the 1960s and 1970s were marked by relatively low turnover – as would be expected, given the figures on changes in party vote shares reviewed earlier. Again, a comparison with Britain and the United States helps place the Canadian figures in context. It is clear that turnover in Canada is almost always higher than it is in Britain, although sometimes (1970 and 1979) British turnover has approached the lower bounds of the Canadian rate (see figure 5.5). It is also apparent from figure 5.6 that turnover rates in the House of Representatives reflect the low levels of interelection volatility already noted. U.S. turnover has not even approached the minimum Canadian level for almost 20 years. Still, as was the case with electoral volatility, lower turnover rates in the United Kingdom do not mean that its system is less responsive than the Canadian one in the sense of translating election swings into changes of government. Individual MPs are clearly more vulnerable to defeat in Canada than in Britain, but, at least since 1950, governments have fared about as well in both countries.

One explanation frequently advanced for the lack of competitiveness in the United States is the fact that individual members of the House of Representatives enjoy more control over the redistribution process than is the case in Canada or Great Britain.

Figure 5.4
Turnover in Canadian House of Commons
(percentage of seats changing party)

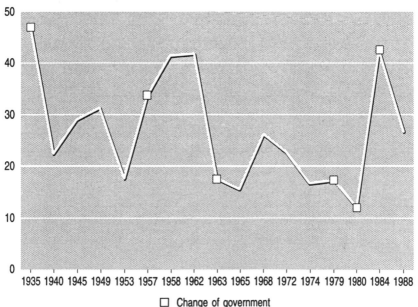

□ Change of government

Source: Based on figures in Feigert (1989).

Figure 5.5
Turnover in British House of Commons
(percentage of seats changing party)

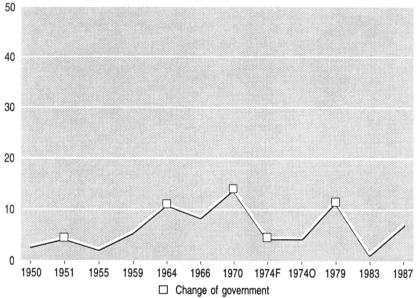

☐ Change of government

Source: Based on figures in Craig (1989).

F = February; O = October.

Figure 5.6
Turnover in U.S. House of Representatives
(percentage of seats changing party)

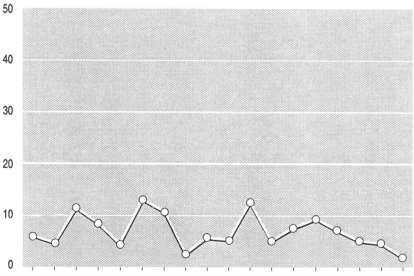

Source: Based on figures in Ornstein (1987).

According to several scholars, one unintended consequence of the judicial push for "one person, one vote" has been an increase in gerrymandering (Baker 1986; Cranor et al. 1989). Tufte has explicitly argued that incumbent members of Congress have been the primary beneficiaries of the reapportionment rules, because they have the ability "to exert significant control over the drawings of district boundaries" (1973, 551). With some exceptions (Jacobson 1987), most scholars agree that the vulnerability of members of Congress to electoral defeat has declined (Cain 1984, 1985; Mayhew 1974; Ferejohn 1977; Fiorina 1977; Bauer and Hibbing 1989). However, Tufte's argument and evidence that partisan redistricting is responsible have been called into question (see especially Ferejohn 1977; King 1989).

Glazer and colleagues come to a similar conclusion after an examination of redistricting for congressional seats during the 1970s. They argue that, at most, the involvement of partisans in redistricting preserved the status quo and that incumbents were not able to benefit at the expense of challengers (Glazer et al. 1987, 680).

Canada has used nonpartisan electoral boundary commissions since 1966 to recommend changes in electoral district boundaries. The effects of this change on party competition in Canada are equivocal. Figure 5.7 presents the percentage of seats won by small margins of victory in each election from 1935 to 1988 and identifies the election immediately following each redistribution. A gap of 10 percent or less is commonly used as an indicator of a marginal seat. By this criterion, the percentage of marginal seats in Canada has averaged 36.7 over the period. The redistributions prior to the 1949 and 1953 elections, which were partisan in the sense that the governing party controlled the outcome, were both associated with reductions in the percentage of marginal seats. The first redistribution produced by an independent boundary commission (in 1968) saw a sharp increase in the next election in the percentage of marginals, as did the redistribution preceding the 1988 election. However, redistribution prior to 1979 produced the lowest percentage of marginal seats for the entire period.

Is Canadian politics too competitive? Posed in this fashion, the question is difficult if not impossible to answer. Much depends on the value one places on stability in the membership of the House of Commons compared with the responsiveness of the electoral system to the wishes of some to change the direction of public policy by altering the membership of the House of Commons. The answer also depends on whether one focuses on periods when, by comparative standards, Canadian elections have produced little change in the balance between parties or in turnover in the House, or on periods when elections have had more dramatic effects.

Figure 5.7
Marginal seats in Canada, 1935–88

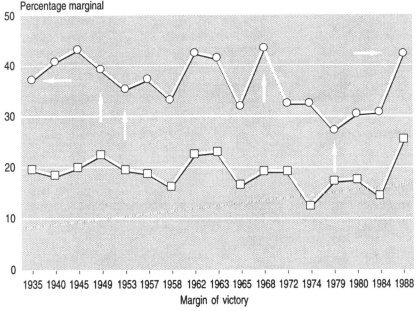

Percentage marginal

Margin of victory

□ Less than 5%　○ Less than 10%

Source: Based on figures in Feigert (1989).
Arrows mark first election after redistribution.

It is more interesting to speculate about why Canadian elections are apparently more competitive than is the case for other plurality systems, especially the United States. LeDuc (1985) argues that it is because Canadian political parties have weak social bases. In other words, parties do not compete as the sole (or even principal) representatives of particular class, religious, regional or ethnic groups. While that is arguably as true of the United States, LeDuc suggests that psychological attachments to parties are stronger south of the border, making voters more resistant to change.

However, it would be unwise to rule out the effects of the electoral system and the party system themselves on party competition. I began by citing the strong evidence for the proposition that plurality electoral systems constrain the number of parties and are associated with two-party systems. However, I also noted that Canada offers somewhat of an exception to this rule because from time to time, and consistently since 1935, there has been at least one party which has been able to challenge Conservative and Liberal dominance. It may be that the availability of more choice is itself a factor in producing greater volatility. This is the conclusion of Pedersen's (1983) examination of differences in electoral volatility between countries in European (including British) elections. Moreover, Spafford (1970) has shown a direct connection between the number of minor-party candidates in the field and the share of seats won by the major parties for a given share of the vote. The existence of more than two viable parties also increases the opportunities for strategic voting, which will also affect the likelihood of switching between elections, and thus will affect measures of electoral volatility.

These possibilities will be explored further in the next section, which examines the patterns of electoral volatility and party competition at the subnational level in Canada.

PARTY COMPETITION AND ELECTORAL VOLATILITY AT THE SUBNATIONAL LEVEL

The preceding analysis has shown that, on the whole, elections for the Canadian House of Commons are more competitive than those for the British House and the U.S. House of Representatives. However, given substantial regional variation in support for political parties, we might expect this to be true of party competition as well. Figure 5.8 reports electoral volatility scores by province for the last three elections. These were calculated in the same fashion as those represented in figure 5.1 and are designed to measure the amount of net change in support for political parties between one election and the next. The measure picks up the dramatic reversal of Liberal and Progressive Conservative fortunes in Quebec during the 1984 election and the gradual disintegration of the Progressive Conservatives' hold on federal support in Alberta. As expected, given the Conservative landslide, volatility was higher in 1984 in most provinces than it was in the previous election. Still, some provinces, Manitoba and Saskatchewan especially, do not seem to have been particularly volatile during this period; and Prince Edward Island and Alberta depart from the recent national pattern which saw volatility peak in 1984.

However, examination of support for the Liberal party, which has dominated politics at the federal level for most of this century, suggests that for a time during the 1970s interelection shifts in party support were becoming more uniform across the country. Figure 5.9 shows the pattern of swing between several pairs of elections, beginning with 1968–72. The 1972 election result, which saw the Trudeau Liberals reduced to a minority government position, was marked by an average 6.5 percentage point shift away from the party. However, just over 60 percent of constituency level results were within 5 points of that magnitude of swing. The 1974 election produced an average pro-Liberal

Figure 5.8
Electoral volatility in the provinces, 1980–88

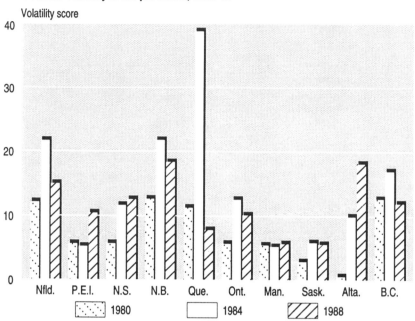

Calculations by author. The higher the bar, the greater the change from the previous election.

swing of 5.0 percentage points. This time, over 80 percent of constituencies were within 5 percentage points of this figure. Swing between 1974 and 1979 cannot be calculated because of redistribution before the 1979 election. However, the 1979–80 election pair was marked by an average pro-Liberal swing of 4.7 points with over 90 percent of ridings within 5 percentage points of the average shift. The latter figure is comparable to those in Britain, where swings have historically been much more uniform across the country (see Butler and Van Beek 1990). However, the 1984 election produced a major disturbance in this pattern. Just one-half of the ridings came within 5 percentage points of the average anti-Liberal swing of 16 percentage points, and a sizable number (largely in Quebec) substantially exceeded this figure.[4]

In the analysis of competition referred to earlier, Lovink (1973) offers a single measure of competitiveness that combines swing, victory margin, and turnover using constituency-level data. Lovink classifies constituencies with an index value of less than 4.9 as marginal, from 5.0 to 14.9 as competitive, and 15.0 or more as safe. The first category in figure 5.10 shows the percentage of marginal seats according to Lovink's definition. The second and third categories combined

Figure 5.9
Uniformity of swing, 1968–84

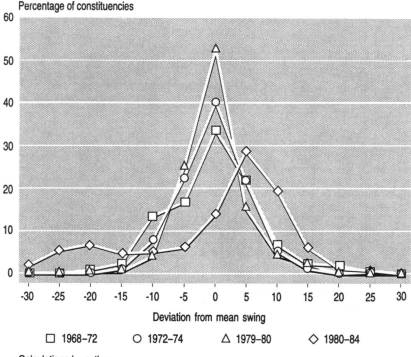

Calculations by author.

correspond to Lovink's competitive category, and the remaining categories are all in his safe seat group. According to these figures, the percentage of seats judged to be marginal dropped from approximately 35 percent of the total in the 1968–74 period to 30 percent in 1979–84. However, this was balanced by an increase in the number of competitive seats, so that the number of seats judged to be safe remained roughly one-third of the total. The average safety score for the latter period was 13.3 compared with 13.0 for 1968–74.

According to this measure, the most competitive areas in federal elections between 1979 and 1984 were the Maritimes, Ontario and Saskatchewan, with average scores of between 6.0 and 8.0. British Columbia came next with 12.0, then Manitoba and Quebec with average scores of 14.3 and 14.6, respectively. Not surprisingly, Alberta had the safest seats in the country, with an average score of 43.6. Figure 5.11 provides a picture of interprovincial differences and changes over time with mean safety scores by province in four sets of elections. The strongest trends in the figure are for Newfoundland and Alberta. Alberta was a very competitive place in the 1950s but distinctly

Figure 5.10
Index of safety, 1968–74 and 1979–84

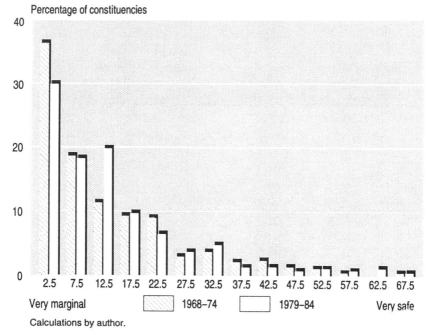

Percentage of constituencies

Very marginal · 1968–74 · 1979–84 · Very safe

Calculations by author.

uncompetitive in the 1980s. The pattern in Newfoundland is exactly the opposite. Other changes are more modest or idiosyncratic. However, the use of average figures obscures some of the more interesting changes in levels of competitiveness. For example, during 1953–58, Ontario contained only 23.4% of the country's marginal seats, whereas 32.3% of all House of Commons seats were allocated to Ontario. By 1968–74, with 33.6% of House seats, Ontario had a much higher proportion (44.2%) of the marginal seats. Finally, in the latest period, 1979–84, Ontario's seat share rose to 34.1%, but its share of the marginal seats jumped to 52.4%.

We can also see from figure 5.11 that whatever the changes in party competition following a redistribution, they were not uniform across the country. Elections from 1953 to 1965 were conducted using the same boundaries, so we should look at the last two bars for each province in the figure. The first nonpartisan redistribution in 1966 is associated with increased competitiveness only in Newfoundland, Ontario, Manitoba, Saskatchewan and British Columbia. In the remainder, competition actually decreased or, as in New Brunswick, did not change appreciably. The redistribution prior to the 1979 election saw increased

Figure 5.11
Competitiveness trends by province, 1953–84

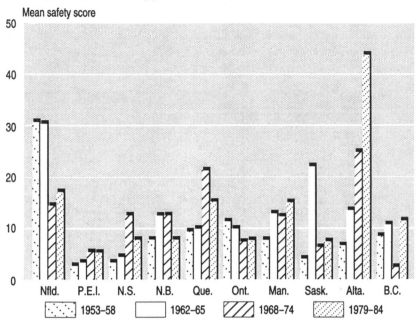

Source: 1953–65 from Lovink (1973); 1968–84 calculations by author.

competition in only three provinces (Nova Scotia, New Brunswick and Quebec), no change in one (Prince Edward Island), and decreased competition in the remainder. With the exception of Alberta, changes in the provinces in 1979, whatever the direction, were rather small.

As noted above, the safety index includes turnover as one component in a weighted combination of competition measures. A look at figure 5.12 suggests that turnover may have been a major factor in the observed decline in the level of safety in New Brunswick and Quebec. Six of ten seats in New Brunswick changed hands as did 57 of 75 in Quebec. However, change of that magnitude would certainly not have been anticipated on the basis of turnover rates in previous elections, especially in Quebec. Another message conveyed by figure 5.12 is that every province has experienced turnover rates of at least 20 percent at one time or another during the past two decades, although Ontario has been most consistent in this regard. Even in Ontario, however, turnover in one election is not a precise guide to what is likely to happen in the next. Alberta is the only apparent exception to this generalization, since its turnover rate was zero for most of the period covered by the figure.

Figure 5.12
Turnover rates by province
(percentage of seats changing party)

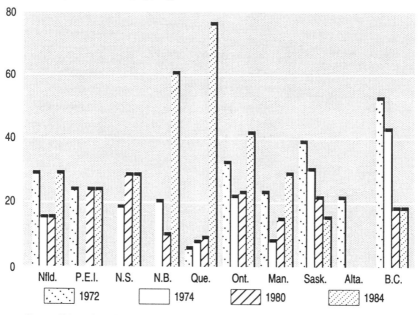

Source: Feigert (1989).

Note: Absence of bar indicates zero turnover in given election year.

There is some evidence that combining the three indicators of competitiveness, as Lovink does, may obscure as much as it reveals. For example, at the aggregate level, marginality is a very poor predictor of turnover. In the 16 elections between 1935 and 1988, the correlation (Pearson r) between the percentage of seats won by margins of less than 10 percentage points and the percentage of seats that changed hands in the next election is only 0.07. The problematic relationship between marginality and turnover is also evident at the constituency level. For example, in the 1980 election the median victory margin in 1979 was 25.8 percentage points for those seats retained by the 1979 winner and 4.9 points for those lost. However, in 1984 the situation was reversed. The median victory margin for the group of seats lost by the 1980 winner was 27.3 points, compared with 15.3 points for the seats won by the 1980 incumbent party. In fact, while the correlation (Pearson r) between victory margin in 1979 and seat retention in 1980 is .42, the figure for victory margin in 1980 and retention in 1984 is –.21.

CONCLUSION

The measures used in this study offer somewhat different ways of looking at the nature of party competition in Canada in order to situate it in an international context and to look for trends. The electoral volatility measure looks at the variability in party vote shares between elections at the level of the province or the nation. Its greatest utility comes from its ability to distinguish shifts in levels of support that are fairly common from those that are large, often indicating major changes in the balance of power between the parties in the system and/or the entry of new parties, or the exit of old ones. National levels of volatility mark Canada as a place where net change between elections is more common than in the other major democracies utilizing the single-member plurality system. The same is true of turnover rates. The probability of defeat for incumbent MPs in Canada is much higher. However, high turnover rates have not made the Canadian system more responsive in the sense of producing more frequent changes of government when compared to Great Britain.

Moreover, examination of the pattern of federal voting by province reveals several with volatility levels below national levels and in two cases, Manitoba and Saskatchewan, levels of stability which approach those found at the national level in the United States. The fact that these two provinces, which have three-party competition in national elections, exhibit substantially lower levels of volatility than provinces such as Newfoundland and Nova Scotia suggests that Pedersen's explanation of international differences may not be applicable at the subnational level in Canada. Interprovincial differences – and the fact that volatility at the national level (figure 5.1) has sometimes increased and sometimes decreased following redistribution – suggest that volatility and this type of electoral reform are independent of each other.

Provincial deviations from Canada's internationally high turnover rate are also apparent and are marked by considerable temporal variation. These differences must be interpreted with caution, because some provinces have so few seats that changes in the party winning only one or two seats can have a substantial effect on percentage figures. The most important messages conveyed by the data are the marked increase in turnover rates in Quebec and turnover rates consistently above 20 percent in Ontario. Given that these provinces elect nearly 60 percent of the House of Commons, they make a significant contribution to the national picture. The safety index data confirm the competitiveness of federal elections in Quebec and Ontario, although this is a recent phenomenon in Quebec. Again, changes in neither measure are correlated with changes in electoral boundaries.

Does this mean that competitiveness is unrelated to questions of electoral reform? I think not. All I have shown is that, in Canada, if boundary changes have an impact on party competition, the direction of the effect (i.e., whether competition is increased or decreased) is not the same across time or space. The same appears to be the case in Great Britain. The issue is still subject to debate in the United States, but the most recent evidence raises serious doubts about whether boundary changes have systematic or lasting effects on competition there as well.

Nevertheless, the competitive circumstances I have described for Canada provide the context within which participants in the political process must function. With large numbers of marginal seats, questions of election finance become very significant. If advertising can affect votes, presumably the greater vulnerability of incumbents in Canada makes the legal framework governing campaign advertising important too. Finally, the existence of large numbers of competitive seats has both positive and negative implications for those who wish to increase the proportion of women in the House of Commons. The evidence presented here suggests that "hopeless causes" are the exception rather than the rule. On the other hand, once they enter the institution, there is no guarantee their stay will be a long one.

NOTES

This study was completed in March 1991.

1. Rae (1971) defines a two-party system as one in which the two strongest parties obtain 90 percent of the seats between them and no single party obtains more than 70 percent. Hence, while elections in Great Britain frequently involve more than two parties, Britain qualifies as two-party using Rae's criteria.

2. Median scores offer even stronger evidence of Canada's distinctiveness. Fifty percent of Canadian elections since 1949 have exhibited net changes of at least 11.8 percentage points. Medians for the other countries are nearly identical to the means.

3. For elections following a redistribution, the turnover rate is based only on those seats whose boundaries remained largely the same.

4. A more detailed analysis of swing can be found in Ferejohn and Gaines (1991).

REFERENCES

Baker, Gordon E. 1986. "Whatever Happened to the Reapportionment Revolution in the United States?" In *Electoral Laws and Their Consequences*, ed. Bernard Grofman and Arend Lijphart. New York: Agathon Press.

Bauer, Monica, and John R. Hibbing. 1989. "Which Incumbents Lose in House Elections: A Response to Jacobson's 'The Marginals Never Vanished.'" *American Journal of Political Science* 33:262–71.

Blake, Donald E. 1979. "1896 and All That: Critical Elections in Canada." *Canadian Journal of Political Science* 12:259–79.

Butler, David, and Stephen D. Van Beek. 1990. "Why Not Swing? Measuring Electoral Change." *PS: Political Science and Politics* 23:178–83.

Cain, Bruce E. 1984. *The Reapportionment Puzzle*. Berkeley: University of California Press.

———. 1985. "Assessing the Partisan Effects of Redistricting." *American Political Science Review* 79:320–33.

Cairns, Alan C. 1968. "The Electoral System and the Party System in Canada, 1921–1965." *Canadian Journal of Political Science* 1:55–80.

Canada. Elections Canada. Various. *Report of the Chief Electoral Officer*. Ottawa: Minister of Supply and Services Canada.

Craig, F.W.S. 1989. *British Electoral Facts, 1832–1987*. Aldershot, UK: Gower.

Cranor, John D., Gary L. Crawley and Raymond H. Scheele. 1989. "The Anatomy of a Gerrymander." *American Journal of Political Science* 33:222–39.

Crewe, Ivor. 1985a. "Introduction: Electoral Change in Western Democracies: A Framework for Analysis." In *Electoral Change in Western Democracies: Patterns and Sources of Electoral Volatility*, ed. Ivor Crewe and David Denver. London: Croom Helm.

———. 1985b. "Great Britain." In *Electoral Change in Western Democracies: Patterns and Sources of Electoral Volatility*, ed. Ivor Crewe and David Denver. London: Croom Helm.

Denver, David. 1985. "Conclusion." In *Electoral Change in Western Democracies: Patterns and Sources of Electoral Volatility*, ed. Ivor Crewe and David Denver. London: Croom Helm.

Feigert, Frank. 1989. *Canada Votes, 1935–1988*. Durham: Duke University Press.

Ferejohn, John A. 1977. "On the Decline of Competition in Congressional Elections." *American Political Science Review* 71:166–76.

Ferejohn, John, and Brian Gaines. 1991. "The Personal Vote in Canada." In *Representation, Integration and Political Parties in Canada*, ed. Herman Bakvis. Vol. 14 of the research studies of the Royal Commission on Electoral Reform and Party Financing. Ottawa and Toronto: RCERPF/Dundurn.

Fiorina, Morris. 1977. *Congress: Keystone of the Washington Establishment*. New Haven: Yale University Press.

Flanigan, William H., and Nancy H. Zingale. 1985. "United States." In *Electoral Change in Western Democracies: Patterns and Sources of Electoral Volatility*, ed. Ivor Crewe and David Denver. London: Croom Helm.

Glazer, Amihai, Bernard Grofman and Marc Robbins. 1987. "Partisan and Incumbency Effects of 1970s Congressional Redistricting." *American Journal of Political Science* 31:680–707.

Grofman, Bernard, and Arend Lijphart, eds. 1986. *Electoral Laws and Their Political Consequences*. New York: Agathon Press.

Gudgin, Graham, and P.J. Taylor. 1979. *Seats, Votes, and the Spatial Organisation of Elections*. London: Pion.

Jacobson, Gary C. 1987. "The Marginals Never Vanished: Incumbency and Competition in Elections to the U.S. House of Representatives." *American Journal of Political Science* 31:126–41.

King, Gary. 1989. "Representation Through Legislative Redistricting: A Stochastic Model." *American Journal of Political Science* 33:787–824.

LeDuc, Lawrence. 1985. "Canada." In *Electoral Change in Western Democracies: Patterns and Sources of Electoral Volatility*, ed. Ivor Crewe and David Denver. London: Croom Helm.

Lijphart, Arend. 1990. "The Political Consequences of Electoral Laws." *American Political Science Review* 84:481–96.

Lovink, J.A.A. 1973. "Is Canadian Politics Too Competitive?" *Canadian Journal of Political Science* 6:342–79.

Mann, Thomas E. 1978. *Unsafe at Any Margin: Interpreting Congressional Elections*. Washington, DC: American Enterprise Institute for Public Policy Research.

Mayhew, David R. 1974. *Congress: The Electoral Connection*. New Haven: Yale University Press.

McCubbins, Mathew D., and Thomas Schwartz. 1988. "Congress, the Courts, and Public Policy: Consequences of the One Man, One Vote Rule." *American Journal of Political Science* 32:388–415.

Ornstein, Norman J. 1987. *Vital Statistics on Congress, 1987–1988*. Washington, DC: American Enterprise Institute for Public Policy Research.

Pedersen, Mogens N. 1983. "Changing Patterns of Electoral Volatility in European Party Systems: 1948–1977." In *Western European Party Systems: Continuity and Change*, ed. Hans Daalder and Peter Mair. Beverly Hills: Sage Publications.

Pfeiffer, David G. 1967. "The Measurement of Party Competition and Systemic Stability." *American Political Science Review* 61:457–67.

Rae, Douglas. 1971. *The Political Consequences of Electoral Laws.* 2d ed. New Haven: Yale University Press.

Rapoport, Ronald B. 1984. "Swing Time: Assessing Causes for Shifts in Congressional Elections." *British Journal of Political Science* 14:222–29.

Rose, Richard. 1984. "Electoral Systems: A Question of Degree or of Principle?" In *Choosing an Electoral System: Issues and Alternatives,* ed. Arend Lijphart and Bernard Grofman. New York: Praeger.

Spafford, Duff. 1970. "The Electoral System of Canada." *American Political Science Review* 64:168–76.

Stanley, Harold W., and Richard G. Niemi. 1988. *Vital Statistics in Congress.* Washington, DC: Congressional Quarterly.

Tufte, Edward R. 1973. "The Relationship Between Seats and Votes in Two-Party Systems." *American Political Science Review* 67:540–54.

6

THE PERSONAL VOTE IN CANADA

John Ferejohn
Brian Gaines

IN THIS STUDY we examine evidence, gathered from recent Canadian elections, of the existence and development of a personal vote – the tendency of citizens to base their voting decisions on characteristics of the incumbent candidate rather than on party or issues.

It was argued in an earlier study that in some electoral systems – among them single-member district, plurality-rule systems – members of Parliament have a systematic incentive to develop bases of personal political support as opposed to party-based support (Cain et al. 1987). This incentive leads members to engage in activities other than those usually associated with the classical or textbook model of representation, such as the passing of laws, or the criticizing or questioning of government policy. Instead they engage in direct activities within their constituencies that are aimed at developing a base of personal support. In single-member district systems, legislators may accordingly establish a reputation for responsiveness to constituent needs and demands by seeking out opportunities to serve constituents directly, by soliciting and responding to constituent requests and by intervening on behalf of their electors in the bureaucratic operation of government. The earlier study yielded evidence that legislators in both the United States and Great Britain engaged extensively in constituency-oriented activities and that their actions had an impact on two areas: policy making (by shaping the policy-making institutions within the governments and by allowing members some independence from party leaders) and elections (by insulating incumbents from national electoral tides).

Although members in both American and British systems try to develop personal political support within their constituencies, it is clear that they have had more success in the United States than in Great Britain. There are many reasons for this, some of them institutional (most prominently, that elections for the British Parliament determine the choice of a prime minister as well as an individual member), and some partisan (British parties are much more cohesive and disciplined than their American counterparts). In this study we focus on the effects of the structurally induced motivations and activities of the members themselves.

American members of Congress command enormous personal staffs and office allocations and are able to employ these publicly financed private bureaucracies to reach regularly and pervasively into their districts. As a result, the typical American member of Congress is able to build a base of broad electoral support and, if he or she is skilful, seldom faces serious or well-financed opposition. Re-election rates for the House of Representatives have remained at around 90 percent for the postwar period and have moved even higher in the last decade (Polsby 1968; Mayhew 1974b; Jacobson 1987a).

Moreover, it is clear that in the United States, the electoral performance of incumbents is not particularly sensitive to their parties' fortunes at any point in time. Most electoral defeats seem to result less from the voters' evaluation of the party's performance on the basis of issues than from a perceived political weakness of the individual incumbent. A scandal is perhaps the most common cause of electoral misery, but other local issues can sometimes become important as well. Viewed from an aggregate perspective, the outcome of congressional elections exhibits little fluctuation from year to year and is relatively insulated from national partisan tides.

In Great Britain, by contrast, members receive virtually nothing in the way of staff or offices – indeed, party leaders regularly oppose increasing these allocations – and must do most of their constituency work alone, without much assistance from either paid staff or party volunteers (Crick 1965; Loewenberg and Patterson 1979). Although there is evidence that incumbents personally engage in high levels of constituency service (more so than American members of Congress) the absence of staff support for such activities limits their electoral impact (Cain et al. 1987). As a result, incumbent performance remains subject to national swings for or against one party or another, although increasingly these swings seem conditioned by regional factors. As was the case in the United States until the 1930s and 1940s, strong electoral tides generally sweep large numbers of incumbents from office.

Nevertheless, there have been important changes in this respect in Great Britain, reflecting higher levels of incumbent insulation now than was common 30 or 40 years ago. Inter-election swings have become more variable, swing ratios have declined sharply and there is evidence of an increase in the level and significance of the personal vote (Crewe 1974; Curtice and Steed 1980, 1982; Cain 1983; Cain et al. 1987).

Again, there are both constitutional and partisan reasons why a lesser personal vote can be expected in Great Britain than in the United States. In Great Britain, the MPs choose a government, so parliamentary elections in that system perform the same function as both congressional and presidential elections in the United States. Some wags have been known to refer to the British House of Commons as a glorified electoral college. In any case, voters cannot separate their choice of member from their choice of government; if they choose to reward their Conservative member for his attention to the constituency, this vote counts as well for the formation of a Conservative government. This linkage between votes for the member of Parliament and votes for the executive works to attenuate the formation of a personal vote.[1]

The British party system is much more tightly organized and disciplined than is the American system. Members of the same party usually vote in much the same way in roll-call votes so that there is no need for the government to garner support in the House of Commons by distributing pork-barrel benefits to constituencies. Thus, because of the relatively high levels of party discipline in parliamentary voting and the absence of distributional components in legislative proposals, there is not much reason for voters to base their votes on the actions of their individual member. In Great Britain, then, the costs of rewarding the individual MP are relatively high, and the benefits of doing so are low.

The Canadian system exhibits both similarities with and differences from those of the United States and Great Britain. Like both of them, it is essentially a single-member district, plurality-rule system. Like the British system, MPs choose a government (although party leadership is determined by the extraparliamentary parties), so that voters cannot reward or punish their member without doing the same to the party. On the other hand, it appears that Canadian parliamentary proposals exhibit more pronounced distributional characteristics than do their British counterparts and that this is tied to the diversity of provincial interests. Although this trait may lead to the expectation of a more developed personal vote, it is also true that parliamentary voting exhibits somewhat more party discipline than in Britain. In this sense, Canadian voters appear to have less motivation to reward or punish members individually for their actions in pursuing provincial or riding interests than do British voters. Then again, Canadian MPs enjoy larger staffs than do their British counterparts and may be able to build a personal vote more efficiently (Fraser 1980; Franks 1987).

On balance, the Canadian system might be expected to demonstrate a personal vote intermediate between that in the United States and Great Britain, although remaining closer in both constitutional and partisan senses to the British system upon which it was based. At the same time, Canada, like its southern neighbour, is marked by regional conflict and federalism, both of which render policy susceptible to particularism.

STUDYING THE PERSONAL VOTE IN CANADA

The authors of *The Personal Vote* (Cain et al. 1987) found it useful to employ several different kinds of data to ascertain the level and significance of constituency-oriented activity. They interviewed members and staff of constituency organizations and surveyed constituents so as to generate a data set that matched constituents with their members. They also employed aggregate statistical data that permitted examination of long-term changes in the personal vote.

In the present study, we are able to employ only aggregate statistical evidence of vote totals for the 20th century, and to examine the 1988 Canadian National Election Study (CNES). Although the CNES contains many of the same items as the 1978 U.S. National Election Study (NES) and the 1979 British Election Study used by Cain, Ferejohn and Fiorina (1987), it has a number of shortcomings that impair its usefulness for a study of personal vote. We cannot, therefore, conduct a fully comparative study of the personal vote since we have no direct evidence on incumbent activities. It is, however, possible to conduct a preliminary evaluation of incumbent visibility, accessibility, constituent evaluation and satisfaction, and the impact of these factors on voting behaviour (although the design of the NES prevents us from making definitive judgements even in these matters). Moreover, using existing aggregate data, we are also able to map long-term changes in the extent to which the composition of Parliament responds to broad national or regional swings.

The first substantive section of this study presents the results of our analyses of the aggregate Canadian election data.[2] We report on a statistical evaluation of the responsiveness of the Canadian electoral system to shifts in votes. To do this, given the limited data available to us, we submit a study that reflects national and regional levels of the swing ratio – the way in which shifts in votes translate into the changing composition of Parliament. We then investigate how inter-election vote swings have evolved over the last half century in relation to both the changing magnitude and variability of these inter-election swings. Finally, we present an extension of the Stokes-Jackman variance components analysis of Canadian elections during this century, which allows us to decompose vote shifts between elections into national, provincial and local components. In effect, we extend Jackman's results (1972) on shifting partisan composition both forward and backward in time to include all comparable election pairs from 1908 to 1988.[3] Moreover, following Stokes's initial paper (1967), we perform a variance components analysis of shifts in turnout over the period.

In the second substantive section, we provide an analysis of the 1988 CNES.[4] Although that study is not fully adequate for a complete investigation of the personal vote, we are able to derive some useful information from it, once appropriate corrections have been made.[5] Moreover, we are able to examine the effects on incumbent recognition rates of the impact of the various ways in which incumbents try to reach their constituents. We are also able to study the manner in which incumbents are evaluated by the Canadian electorate and the role of incumbent constituency activities in determining these evaluations. Using the NES data, therefore, we have tried to conduct our analysis in a way that maximizes the comparability of the present results with those for the United States and Great Britain.

A HISTORICAL OVERVIEW OF CANADIAN ELECTIONS

The development of a large personal vote in the United States has produced a Congress that has been, over time, remarkably stable in its composition. Turnover in the House of Representatives has averaged well under 10 percent for more than a quarter of a century and is, if anything, continuing to decline. We may take this kind of evidence of electoral stability as an indirect indication of the development of a personal vote. Although electoral stability does not, in itself, prove the existence of a personal vote, high levels of volatility would seem to argue against there being an important personal vote phenomenon.

It is interesting, therefore, that the outcome of Canadian parliamentary elections exhibits a great deal of volatility, at least when compared to elections in the United States. It is not unusual for 30–40 percent of the seats to change parties in a single election – numbers that are almost unprecedented in American electoral history. Moreover, turnover of seats exhibits little trend; it is usually around 40 percent, but on occasion it has fallen below 20 percent or risen above 50 percent. There is not even any particular trend when one adjusts to an annual rate based on the number of years that have passed since the previous election. Thus, the apparent volatility is not simply a consequence of government terms being of unequal length.

Of course, not all turnover in Parliament results from seats switching parties. As the data in table 6.1 show, much of the turnover is due to retirements in which members are succeeded by a representative of the same party. When we restrict our attention to partisan turnover, we see somewhat less change, although the legislature still looks volatile by comparison with its British or American counterparts. If we exclude cases that involve changing district boundaries (which are marked with asterisks on the table), partisan turnover is between 20 and 30 percent from 1925 to 1953, increasing to nearly 40 percent until 1962, then shrinking to about 20 percent until 1984. Again, however, more striking than any trend is the magnitude of the turnover throughout this whole period.

It is interesting that our information on retirements belies the perception that Parliament has become more of a vocation in the latter half of this century. The retirement rate per year since the previous election does not appear to decline in recent decades.[6]

Roughly speaking, we can think of changes in the partisan composition of Parliament as the product of two conceptually distinct factors: the rate at which votes are translated into seats (the swing ratio) and the magnitude of inter-election swings in party support. When the swing ratio is large, big inter-election vote swings translate into large seat swings.[7] Thus, if the swing ratio is 2.5 and a party enjoys a vote swing of 10 percent, its parliamentary delegation should increase by 25 percent. This relationship is a rough one for two reasons. First, the national swing in support for a party between two elections is not constant across ridings but exhibits a good deal of variance. Second, there is considerable ambiguity as to what degree of importance ought to be assigned to the swing ratio, since no single number captures all the interesting facets of electoral change. We first examine the variability of inter-election vote swings.

In figure 6.1, we exhibit the standard deviations around the inter-election vote swing for each comparable election pair since 1908 for the major parties. These data reveal a striking general decline since the 1920s in the variability of inter-election swings for the two large national parties. Again, except for the 1984 election, it appears that Canadian constituencies now move much more in unison with national tides than they did 50 years ago. This shift stands in sharp contrast with electoral events south of the border and, to a lesser extent, in Britain. In the

Table 6.1
Turnover in Canadian House of Commons, 1925–88
(percentages)

Election pairs	Defeated	+	Retired	=	Turnover of individuals	Turnover by parties
1925–26	13.5		6.1		19.6	18.4
1926–30	22.4		18.4		40.8	29.8
1930–35	—		—		—	49.6*
1935–40	12.2		27.4		39.6	22.4
1940–45	15.5		29.0		44.5	29.0
1945–49	18.8		17.6		36.4	30.5*
1949–53	9.5		27.5		37.0	17.6*
1953–57	24.9		16.2		41.1	31.3
1957–58	31.3		9.8		41.1	38.1
1958–62	33.2		11.7		44.9	38.5
1962–63	13.6		7.2		20.8	16.2
1963–65	11.7		12.1		23.8	14.3
1965–68	20.1		21.7		41.8	26.3*
1968–72	16.7		23.1		39.8	22.7
1972–74	13.6		8.0		21.6	17.0
1974–79	14.8		25.0		39.8	20.1*
1979–80	14.9		5.0		19.9	16.0
1980–84	31.2		22.0		53.2	42.6
1984–88	21.6		19.9		41.5	27.0*

Note: Table 6.1 is compiled from Lovink (1973), Feigert (1989) and the authors' calculations made using *Chief Electoral Officer Reports* (Canada, Elections Canada). Individual turnover for 1930–35 is omitted because of difficulty in obtaining the data. Column 5 of the table shows the percentage of the total number of seats that changed parties in the second election of the pair. Across elections between which redistricting occurred (marked with asterisks), column 5 is based on the number of ridings comparable to their predecessors before redistricting (not on the total number of seats): $N(1935) = 230$, $N(1949) = 245$, $N(1953) = 244$, $N(1968) = 190$, $N(1979) = 225$ and $N(1988) = 196$. Columns 2, 3 and 4 are the percentage of members elected in the first election in the pair.

United States, roughly the opposite phenomenon has transpired: variability around inter-election swings has increased from the mid-1960s to the present (Jacobson 1987b). In Britain, although trends are weaker, there appears to have been a shift away from what psephologists in that country term the *uniform swing* since the early 1970s (Crewe 1974; Curtice and Steed 1982).

Figure 6.1
Standard deviations of electoral swings in percentages

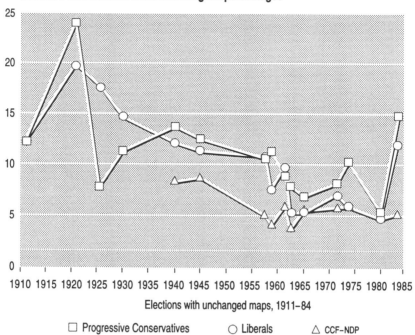

Elections with unchanged maps, 1911–84

☐ Progressive Conservatives   ○ Liberals   △ CCF–NDP

In the United States, and to a lesser extent in Great Britain, increasing variability of inter-election swings is sometimes attributed to the growth of incumbency and of the personal vote. As individual members gain the capacity to insulate themselves from national swings, the outcomes of local races tend increasingly to reflect candidate-centred factors, and the variability of the swing increases. Or, so the story goes. The Canadian data alert us to a difficulty with this explanation. There is, as we shall see, some evidence of an increase in the personal vote in Canada, and even of the appearance of an incumbency effect, but at the same time, it appears that the variance of inter-election swings has actually decreased.

It is worth noting that the decline in the variability of inter-election swings occurs at both provincial and national levels. If these data are examined separately for each of the four regions of Canada, a similar secular decline is evident to some degree in each case. Moreover, the large standard deviations in 1984 are cut nearly in half once region is taken into account. Thus, riding-to-riding variability is genuinely lower in the post-1957 period than previously, after suitable adjustment for regional effects.

In figure 6.2 we investigate the extent to which turnout swings move in concert. Although we do not have data from before the 1950s, there seems to be some evidence of a decline in the variability of turnout in the mid-1950s. Thus, as in the case of partisan divisions, the Canadian aggregate evidence points in the direction of an increase in nationalization (or possibly, as in Britain, of an increase in regionalization) of short-term forces. Leaving aside problems of determining the swing ratio, these data suggest that, if anything, the responsiveness of the partisan composition of Parliament to shifts in votes ought to be increasing, which would suggest that there has been a decline in the magnitude of the personal vote.

The data on inter-election swings in partisan composition and turnout are consistent using either a nationalization or a regionalization hypothesis. While fluctuations around national swings are declining, so too are those around regional shifts. To separate these hypotheses, we employ a statistical technique introduced by Donald Stokes, which is aimed at decomposing the variance in vote swings into national, provincial and local sources.[8]

In his original article, Stokes found evidence of the nationalization

Figure 6.2
Deviations of turnout swings by region

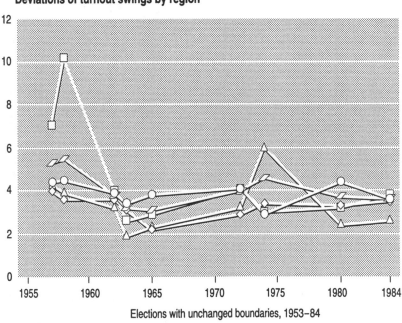

Elections with unchanged boundaries, 1953–84

☐ Maritimes   ○ Quebec   △ Ontario   ◇ West   ⟋ Canada

of short-term forces on partisan division and turnout in both the United States and Great Britain. He speculated there and in later work with David Butler that the cause of this nationalization was traceable mainly to the development of national media markets and to other technological forces associated with the development of large integrated market economies (Stokes 1967; Butler and Stokes 1969). Subsequent work has qualified these results, at least in the United States. It now appears that, because of the growth of the incumbency effect, there has been no substantial nationalization of short-term forces on the partisan composition of the vote in congressional elections (Ferejohn 1977; Fiorina 1977). The results on turnout, however, remain accepted.

Robert Jackman (1972) applied Stokes's technique to Canadian electoral data for the period from 1925 to 1965. His most remarkable comparative finding is that regional effects are a great deal more pronounced in Canada than in either the United States or Great Britain, although national effects are accordingly smaller. In table 6.2, we extend Jackman's Canadian results to the period 1908–84, when data are reported for each set of elections in which riding boundaries remained unchanged, and we focus on the Liberal party vote.

As Jackman found, national effects in Canada are generally small and fluctuate sporadically. The provincial and riding effects also show considerable temporal variability and are of roughly similar magnitudes. It appears that these data do not permit a general conclusion as to the relative magnitudes of provincial and riding effects, though it seems clear that national effects are small in any case. We apply the same method to decompose the Conservative vote in table 6.3.

In contrast to the Liberal vote data, the riding effects on fluctuation of the Progressive Conservative (PC) vote are uniformly larger than are the provincial effects. The Canadian data are still markedly different from those for the United States and Great Britain in that the national forces are so small, but one cannot conclude that regional forces are stronger than local ones in all cases. Indeed, the sporadic appearance of stronger provincial effects in the Liberal vote data may suggest that such effects are due to the interplay of support among the (hegemonic) Liberal party and provincial or ethnic issues and smaller parties.

In the shorter series of elections in which it is possible to replicate this analysis for the Co-operative Commonwealth Federation-New Democratic Party (CCF-NDP), displayed in table 6.4, the most telling result again is the negligible size of national forces.

Finally, we apply Stokes's technique to turnout data over the time series for which those data are available. Here we find some evidence of more substantial nationalization (as Stokes did with U.S. data) and

Table 6.2

Components of variance in Liberal proportion of total vote by electoral period in Canada, 1908–84

	1908–11	1917–21	1925–30	1935–45	1953–58	1962–65	1968–74	1979–84
National	0.01	0.01	0.02	0.09	0.15	0.02	0.04	0.15
Provincial	0.14	0.65	0.30	0.37	0.50	0.52	0.38	0.53
Riding	0.85	0.34	0.68	0.54	0.35	0.46	0.57	0.32

Note: Periods cover one electoral map and contain three elections, except that 1908–11 and 1917–21 contain two elections, and 1953–65 is one electoral map.

Table 6.3

Components of variance in PC proportion of total vote by electoral period in Canada, 1908–84

	1908–11	1917–21	1925–30	1935–45	1953–58	1962–65	1968–74	1979–84
National	0.03	0.18	0.02	0.00	0.30	0.02	0.01	0.17
Provincial	0.09	0.34	0.37	0.38	0.18	0.42	0.47	0.33
Riding	0.87	0.48	0.61	0.61	0.52	0.56	0.52	0.49

Note: Periods cover one electoral map and contain three elections, except that 1908–11 and 1917–21 contain two elections, and 1953–65 is one electoral map.

Table 6.4

Components of variance in CCF-NDP proportion of total vote by electoral period in Canada, 1935–84

	1935–45	1953–58	1962–65	1968–74	1979–84
National	0.05	0.00	0.02	0.00	0.00
Provincial	0.59	0.57	0.40	0.53	0.57
Riding	0.35	0.43	0.58	0.47	0.43

Note: Periods cover one electoral map and contain three elections, except for 1953–65, which is one electoral map.

indications that the provincial effects are substantially smaller. Of course, there are too few data here to ascertain any real long-term change. Indeed, our evaluation of electoral swing variation suggests that most of the real movement in the time series occurred before 1953, so we cannot really say if there is a genuine nationalization occurring in turnout on the basis of table 6.5 alone.

Table 6.5
Components of variance in turnout by electoral period in Canada, 1953–84

	1953–58	1962–65	1968–74	1979–84
National	0.27	0.09	0.07	0.22
Provincial	0.15	0.21	0.28	0.27
Riding	0.58	0.70	0.65	0.51

Note: Periods cover one electoral map and contain three elections, except for 1953–65, which is one electoral map.

We turn now to examine the swing ratio – the rate at which vote shifts are translated into seat shifts in Parliament. The idea of a swing ratio presents a fundamental ambiguity that ought to be described at the outset. If we think of the swing ratio as the rate at which vote shifts translate into seat shifts, the ratio is supposed to describe the dynamic connection between seats and votes. Traditionally, however, swing ratios have been measured by calculating the proportion of seats that a party would gain if it were to enjoy a 1 percent (or uniform) swing across all of its constituencies. Thus measured, the swing ratio describes a feature of the (static) distribution of election margins across constituencies. Roughly speaking, this method of estimation will produce high swing ratios when a large proportion of seats are won by small margins. Indeed, for U.S. data, one of the more popular ways of illustrating the decline in swing ratios is by showing the decline in the proportion of marginal seats (e.g., Jacobson 1987b). In figure 6.3, we plot the historical incidence of electoral victories by less than 10 percent and by less than 5 percent, as two plausible boundaries of genuine marginality.

These data suggest that there has been little systematic change in the distribution of election margins over time, although, if 1988 is ignored, the proportion of seats won by less than 10 percent does decline somewhat over the period for which we have data. This decline, however, is not substantively large. This is in sharp contrast with the results in the United States, where the proportion of marginal victories in congressional elections has plummeted over the past three decades (Mayhew 1974b).

Although the data do not allow us to calculate a swing ratio using the classical method, we can estimate a rough approximation by noting that if 20 percent of the seats are won by margins of 5 percent or less and if the distribution is roughly symmetric with respect to the two major parties, then a 5 percent shift in the vote in favour of one of these parties should yield an increase of 10 percent of the seats in Parliament.

Figure 6.3
Margins of victory in Canadian general elections

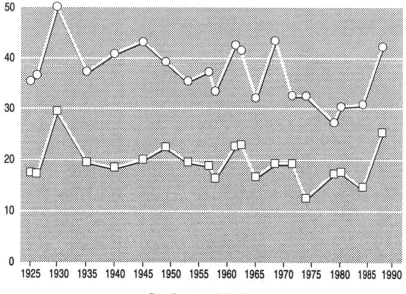

Canadian general elections, 1925–88

○ Percentage of MPs winning by margins smaller than 10%

□ Percentage of MPs winning by margins smaller than 5%

Thus, the swing ratio should be around 2. Note that, except for a few years (of which the most recent is 1984), the estimated swing ratio is less than 2, and tends to be even lower if we do the same calculation for seats won by less than 10 percent of the vote. Of course the validity of this calculation depends on the uniform swing hypothesis, and, to the extent that it fails, these estimates may understate the true votes–seats translation.

From the data we have already seen, it is clear that the hypothesis of uniform swing is not a very good approximation in Canada, although it is a better one after the 1950s than it was before that time. Thus, a measure of this sort might be expected to yield only a very rough estimate of the swing ratio. In addition, the presence of several parties makes the uniform swing hypothesis even less defensible. For this reason, scholars have invented other methods for estimating the votes–seats translation. The most plausible such measure in our view is the regression of historical seat proportion on vote proportion, which is a measure of exactly how actual shifts in votes have translated into shifts in seat distributions. This measure captures the historical reality of votes–seats translation and does not depend on a conjecture as to how vote swings will be distributed. In a multi-party system, it is necessary to perform such estimations for each party separately, and, because of the regionalism of Canadian politics, it is also advisable to carry out estimations within regions. We do so in table 6.6.

These estimates suggest that historical swings in Canada for the two major parties have tended to be above 2 and that there is some variation by region, with the larger ratios found in the Maritimes and the smaller ones in Quebec and the West. These estimates depend on a somewhat questionable hypothesis of homogeneity over time. However, the fact that the time series is so short inhibits any systematic effort to apply this method to briefer historical timeframes.

We may summarize the results of our investigation of aggregate trends in Canadian federal elections as follows. First, since the mid-1920s, there is little evidence of a substantial decline in either the rate at which seats change hands or the rate of shifting among parties. In any case, the rate of partisan turnover in seats in this era, averaging 27 percent, is large by comparative standards. Second, there is little evidence of a growth in local effects of the sort that would be produced by an increase in incumbency voting in parliamentary elections. There may be good reasons to believe that incumbents have an advantage in elections at both the provincial and federal levels, but the fact that the proportion of close races has not changed much, the variability of vote swings has declined and the partisan turnover of seats has remained fairly constant provides little evidence for such an advantage, and no

Table 6.6
Regression estimates of swing ratio in Canada, 1935–84

	PC	Liberal	CCF-NDP
Maritimes	3.3	3.3	0.1
Quebec	1.9	2.3	—
Ontario	2.5	3.2	0.6
Prairies	2.1	2.5	1.7
British Columbia	2.1	2.9	1.8
Canada	2.4	2.7	0.7

Note: Table entries are coefficients from a simple regression of seat percentage on vote for the particular party. Thus, 3.3 indicates that, over the period we examine, the PC party gained 3.3 percent of the federal seats in the Maritimes for each 1 percent increase in popular vote it achieved. Standard errors for these coefficients are about 0.22, so a difference of 0.4 is significant statistically. No ratio is calculated for the NDP in Quebec because there is no variation in the dependent variable (that is, they never won a seat).

reason at all to believe that the magnitude of this advantage has increased much over time.

Of course, our evidence is indirect and awaits clarification by a historical study of the incumbency effect throughout the 20th century. Such a work, by focusing explicitly on legislators' careers, would facilitate comparison between Canada and the United States, where incumbency has been studied in depth, yielding some general results (for a survey see Alford and Hibbing 1981; see also Alford and Brady 1989). Thus, for example, the accumulation of incumbency advantage in Congress is usually front-loaded in the incumbent's second election in what is called the sophomore surge. There is a parallel trend in the way of a decline in party vote share accompanying any incumbent's retirement – a retirement slump – that also seems credibly related to personal vote. Whether Canadian legislators' careers follow similar paths or involve similar personal vote benefits remains, as yet, unclear.

ANALYSIS OF CANADIAN NATIONAL ELECTION STUDY

Our purpose in this section of the study is to investigate the personal vote phenomenon at the level of the individual voter. We begin with a comparison of the visibility of Canadian MPs compared with their British and American counterparts, a natural starting point if the presumption is that a personal vote cannot be built without fairly high visibility of the candidate. Table 6.7 demonstrates the extraordinary levels of incumbent visibility in the Canadian sample. This finding, unfortunately, seems to be largely due to the filtering used in the NES study: the filtered Canadian sample is extremely attentive to politics compared with its American and British counterparts, and all constituency members are very likely to report knowing the identity of their incumbent. Less than a third of the Canadian sample was actually asked whether or not they had been in contact with their MP or their MP's staff and whether they could recall the identity of their MP. Thus, our insight into how Canada compares with similar nations in this regard is minimal.[9]

In table 6.8 we see that, in comparison with respondents in the United States and Great Britain, the Canadian electorate seems to be in constant communication with its representatives. Again, however, our results depend heavily on filtering in the survey. If we assume that those who were not asked the questions would have reported no contact (as we do in the second row in each category), the Canadian marginals can be read as much more comparable with those of the other countries. Since this procedure rests on a conjecture that we cannot test with these data, we think further investigation is warranted. Meanwhile,

Table 6.7
Comparative visibility of U.S. members of Congress, British MPs and Canadian MPs
(percentages)

	Name of member	
Status of member	Recall	Recognition
United States		
Incumbents	32	82
Democrats	31	81
Republicans	32	83
Challengers	12	43
Democrats	12	43
Republicans	12	43
Great Britain		
Incumbents	65	—
Labour	64	—
Conservative	65	—
Liberal	78	—
Nationalist	67	—
Challengers	48	—
Labour	48	—
Conservative	42	—
Canada		
Incumbents	93	—
PC	95	—
Liberal	87	—
NDP	89	—
Challengers	58	—
PC	64	—
Liberal	63	—
NDP	51	—

it would appear that Canadian MPs do communicate with their constituents, perhaps at levels that are comparable with their American and British counterparts.

Although there is some dispute as to whether their reasons for doing so are electorally oriented, there seems little doubt that Canadian legislators, like those elsewhere, devote a considerable amount of attention to their constituencies and that such efforts have the effect of bringing them into contact with citizens in a variety of ways. Thus, in table 6.9, we ask first about the bivariate effects of the various ways incumbent MPs come into contact with their constituents and the influence this may have on their images in the constituency. These contact items are the closest we can come with the NES data to getting at

Table 6.8
Citizen contact with incumbents

Type of contact	United States (%)	Great Britain (%)	Canada N	Canada Denominator	Canada %
Met personally	14	12	545	1 003	54
				3 609	15
Attended meeting where he or she spoke	12	7	434	1 003	43
				3 609	12
Talked to staffer	9	4	121	458	26
(asked of only those who did not meet MP)				3 609	3
Received mail	54	25	944	1 003	94
				3 609	26
Read about in newspaper or magazine	52	32	950	1 003	95
				3 609	26
Heard on radio	25	7	637	1 003	64
				3 609	18
Saw on TV	43	16	757	1 003	75
				3 609	21
Second-hand	29	15		n.a.	
None whatsoever	21	44	2 606	3 609	72

Note: Table entries for Canada are *N*'s, with percentages calculated twice. The denominator of 1 003 corresponds to all actually asked the given contact question. The second denominator, 3 609, represents the assumption that all of those not asked the given contact question would have responded negatively, had they been asked.

n.a. = not applicable.

something like "home style" (Fenno 1978). We turn first to examine the bivariate effects of contacts on visibility.

In table 6.9, note that, compared with the effects of contacts in Great Britain and the United States, the impact of incumbent contact is very small in Canada. Indeed, at first glance, it might seem as though there is little that an incumbent can do to increase visibility in the constituency. Part of the reason for this probably lies in the fact that, since almost all respondents in the sample reported the ability to recall the incumbent, there is very little variability in the recall variable. If, as in table 6.8, we assume that those who were not asked these questions would have been unable to recall either contact with the MP or his or her identity, much larger differences emerge. To take one example, the effect of having met the MP under this (admittedly extreme) assumption would be 96% − 13% = 83%. Of course, it is impossible to tell how respondents who were not asked these questions would actually have responded,

Table 6.9
Association of member visibility with reported contacts
(percentages)

Type of contact	Recall		
	United States	Great Britain	Canada (N = 1 003)
Met MP	62	87	96
Not met MP	30	62	89
Heard MP speak	66	88	96
Not heard	30	63	90
Talked to MP's staff	59	92	93
Not talked	32	64	86
Received mail	49	82	93
No mail	17	60	78
Read about MP	48	81	92
Not read	18	37	92
Heard on radio	52	84	93
Not heard	28	63	92
Saw on TV	47	83	92
Not seen	25	61	93

so we can only speculate that the contact effects are substantially larger than those reported here. Moreover, since, as previously noted, there was no checking on the accuracy of reported recall, these figures may over-estimate the true recall rate in any event.

In table 6.10 we report a similar set of bivariate results for incumbent reputation and constituent satisfaction with the incumbent. Respondents were asked whether they thought their MP could be counted on to look after the interests of their riding. Of the 931 who responded, we investigated the effect that contacts between MPs and their constituents had on those who strongly believed that the incumbent could be counted on in this fashion. In the same table, we report the percentage of constituents who had had some form of contact with the incumbent and were very satisfied with that contact.

The effect of contacts on the incumbent's reputation for attentiveness to the constituency is uniformly large, even without correcting for filtering effects. The same reasoning as outlined above suggests the likelihood that these are under-estimates of true effects, but the degree of the under-estimation must remain obscure until better data become available. We suspect that the reason that relatively substantial effects were found here rather than in table 6.7 is that the question about visibility posed a purely cognitive or informational challenge

Table 6.10
Incumbent reputation, respondent satisfaction and contacts

	Percentage saying incumbent would represent interest of riding	Percentage very satisfied with incumbent
Met MP	64	51
Not met MP	44	9
Heard MP speak	64	40
Not heard	48	14
Contacted MP's staff	61	41
No contact	38	0
Mail contact with MP	57	24
No mail	35	13
Read about MP	56	24
Not read	42	17
Heard MP on radio	58	27
Not heard	49	17
Saw on TV	60	27
Not seen	41	13

to the respondents, all of whom had already passed demanding informational tests even before being questioned on this issue. Here, the respondents were asked an evaluative question and, to some extent, we would expect their answers to such questions not to be strongly forced by the study design.

Likewise, when we turn to the bivariate effects on satisfaction of contacts with the incumbent, we find them to be consistent and substantive. All of the contact variables have a visible impact on satisfaction with the incumbent; and, again, we suspect that, if anything, these estimates probably understate the true effects. Taken together, our previous tables suggest that there is some reason to believe that incumbent activity may very well have effects on constituent perceptions and evaluations of incumbents in Canada and that these effects are similar in direction to those found in the United States and in Great Britain. Because the data are not particularly comparable with the American or British data, we cannot be confident in making magnitude comparisons, but a tentative conclusion would indicate that the effects observed in Canada are not dissimilar to those found in Great Britain.

Turning to multivariate analysis, it is worth stressing once again that the following findings are at best preliminary. Because of various data problems stemming from the CNES design, we must caution that the estimates that follow are somewhat problematic. Our interpretations should be read accordingly.

As might be expected, given the lack of variability in the dependent variable, the results for incumbent visibility shown in table 6.11 are quite weak. Virtually everyone in the sample could recall the incumbent independent of having had contact with him or her, and so there is not much scope for incumbent initiative to make a difference. Indeed, not even sharing partisan identification with the incumbent – quite a reliable variable in the other countries – has an effect in the Canadian sample. Nevertheless, the fact that some of the contact variables are significant and have the expected signs offers some reason to believe that incumbent activities might well affect incumbent visibility in the constituency. Incidentally, we attempted to see if regional differences had any effect on this relationship and could find no evidence that they do.

Table 6.12 shows that we were somewhat more successful in modelling the incumbent's reputation for access. Here, we had an even smaller sample to work with (433 observations), but, as table 6.10 demonstrates, the question we use as a dependent variable, concerning perception of an incumbent's ability to look after the riding, exhibited a considerable amount of variability.

Although these estimates are not fully comparable across countries – the Canadian estimates are regression coefficients whereas those from the other nations are probit coefficients – the pattern of statistical significance is worthy of some attention. Although contact alone does not appear to induce Canadians to regard their incumbents as more accessible, the occurrence of satisfying or somewhat satisfying contacts does produce such judgements just as they do in both Great Britain and the United States. Also, as in the other nations, sharing party identification with the incumbent leads citizens to regard the incumbent as accessible, as does the ability to recall his or her name. In broad terms, then, it appears that Canadian incumbents are able to develop reputations for accessibility in ways that are similar to those in the other nations. We do not have sufficient information at this point to go into any finer detail as to how they might do this; this would seem to require direct information on incumbent activities. There is, in any case, some reason to believe that incumbents who are able to leave constituents satisfied with their contacts enjoy an enhanced reputation. But does this reputation for accessibility translate into electoral rewards?

In table 6.13, we present a simple model of vote determination that permits a preliminary look at how constituency-oriented activity might be related to the vote. In this case we report the Canadian data alone, since lack of comparability between questions forces us to use a

Table 6.11

Probit equations of incumbent contacts and visibility

Independent variables	Name recall		
	Canada[a]	United States[b]	Great Britain[c]
Party affiliation			
Same as incumbent	−0.16	0.23*	0.22**
Independent (none)	0.02	−0.22*	−0.11
Attention to politics: High	0.11	0.90**	0.13*
Medium	—	0.47**	—
Low	—	0.37**	—
Manual occupation	—	—	0.30*
White-collar occupation	—	—	0.48**
Saw MP–R at meeting	0.13	0.33**	0.27*
Mail from MP–R	0.69**	0.52**	0.44**
Read about MP–R	0.10	0.28**	0.40**
Heard MP–R on radio	−0.02	0.19*	0.10
Saw MP–R on TV	−0.13	0.17*	0.45**
Met MP–R	0.67**	0.19*	0.49**
Talked to staff	—	0.01	0.21
Hearsay	—	0.26**	0.10
Incumbent characteristics			
Subcommittee chair	—	0.09	—
Ministerial ladder	—	—	0.01
Opposition spokesperson	—	—	−0.03
Year elected	—	0.00	0.01*
Constant	0.42	−1.58**	−1.44**
N	(890)	(1 483)	(1 267)

Note: Table 6.11 is compiled from tables 1.2 and 1.3 of *The Personal Vote* (Cain et al. 1987) and original calculations using the 1988 CNES. The Canadian dependent variable is based on a question asking respondents if they knew whether any candidate was already their member.

[a]1988.

[b]1979.

[c]1978.

*$p < .05$; **$p < .01$.

specification for Canada quite different from those reported in *The Personal Vote*.

The estimates in this table suggest that, after controlling for party and the reputation of the prime minister, there is some reason to believe that constituency work – at least, successful constituency work – is not

Table 6.12
Reputation for access in three nations

Independent variables	Canada[a]	United States[b]	Great Britain[c]
Contact			
Personal	0.15	0.13*	0.56**
Media	—	0.36**	0.23**
Second-hand	—	0.32**	-0.02
Casework			
Very satisfied	1.32**	0.90**	0.92**
Somewhat satisfied	0.53**	-0.32*	-0.60*
Not satisfied	-0.57**	-1.18**	-1.39**
Second-hand casework	—	—	0.57**
Satisfied	—	0.36**	—
Somewhat satisfied	—	0.40*	—
Not satisfied	—	-1.22	—
District service	—	0.53**	0.55**
Party affiliation			
Same as incumbent	0.65**	0.30**	0.41**
Independent	0.33*	0.04	0.24*
Minor party	—	—	-0.44*
Recall incumbent	0.57**	0.30**	0.05
Recall challenger	-0.14	-0.49**	-0.02
Year elected	—	0.01*	0.01
Constant	-0.07	-0.26	0.14
N	(433)	(1 135)	(821)

Note: Table 6.12 is compiled from table 2.2 of *The Personal Vote* (Cain et al. 1987) and original calculations made using the 1988 CNES. The Canadian dependent variable is based on the question of whether the respondent agreed that a particular candidate would "look after the interests of your riding." This is as close as the Canadian study comes to replicating the questions used in the British and American studies to capture a candidate's reputation for effective constituency service: "If you had a problem that your Representative/MP could do something about, do you think that he/she would be very helpful, somewhat helpful, or not very helpful to you?" Canadian respondents were given a five-point scale, which we condense to strong agreement, agreement and other replies.

[a]1988.
[b]1979.
[c]1978.
*$p < .05$; **$p < .01$.

solely its own reward. There is evidence of an electoral pay-off. Although the ability to recall the incumbent does not make much difference for the vote (since almost everyone in the sample can do that), those very satisfied with incumbent contact are significantly more likely to vote for the incumbent than those who are dissatisfied. Moreover, those incumbents with a reputation for accessibility do significantly better at the

Table 6.13
Probit equation of voting for incumbent in Canadian elections

Independent variables	
Party affiliation	
Same as incumbent	1.48**
Independent	0.48**
Satisfaction with contacts	
Very satisfied	−0.02
Not satisfied	−0.35
Recalls incumbent	0.35
Incumbent accessible	0.21**
Prime minister reputation	0.001*
Region	
Quebec	0.49**
Ontario	0.20
West	0.13
Constant	−2.43**
N	(497)
Log likelihood	−260
Percentage correctly predicted	74

Note: The "prime minister reputation" variable is the thermometer rating of Prime Minister Mulroney if the incumbent is a Conservative, and is the negative of that score if the incumbent is from another party. Thus, higher values are expected to aid PC incumbents and hurt Liberal or NDP incumbents.

$p < .05$; $**p < .01$.

polls. Finally, note that incumbents from Quebec seem to enjoy a measurable advantage at the ballot-box relative to those from most other regions. Ontario incumbents are thought to be even more accessible than their counterparts from Quebec and part of this advantage is transmitted through the incumbent accessibility variable (Krashinsky and Milne 1983, 1985, 1986).

CONCLUSION

We have found some evidence of the development of a personal vote in Canada. Incumbents seem to have an opportunity to develop favourable personal reputations in their constituencies that can have an effect on their electoral fortunes. Given the limitations of the data for the current report, we cannot actually connect incumbent activities to the development of an electoral advantage, but the evidence displayed here is sufficiently similar to that for the United States and Great Britain that we feel entitled to suspect that similar connections to incumbent actions could be discovered. Following the logic of *The Personal Vote*, we would expect the development of a loyal personal following in the constituency to translate into an incumbent advantage. This could, in turn, lead to a situation in which election margins are relatively large, there is substantial variability in vote swings and parliamentary turnover is low. Such symptoms, which reflect a similar situation in the United States, might well be called the American disease.

Having put the matter like this, we can see that the Canadian data are somewhat perplexing. From Krashinsky and Milne, we do find evidence of an actual incumbent advantage, and there seems to be some echo in our survey findings and the aggregate data. On the other hand, Canadian election data do not seem to exhibit the other characteristics: the variability in vote swings is relatively small and declining, electoral margins are small and relatively constant over time and partisan parliamentary turnover seems relatively high and, again, unchanging over time. In short, although there is micro-level evidence that perhaps the American disease has spread northward, there is little aggregate indication of it. Indeed, in the aggregate, the Canadian electoral system seems to exhibit levels of responsiveness comparable with those of Great Britain in the halcyon days of the 1950s.

We must conclude this report, therefore, in a humbler tone than we had anticipated. There are simply too many puzzling linkages that need to be investigated in Canada for us to make final claims about the health of the Canadian electoral system. In the United States, there is concern precisely because personal vote campaigning has progressed to the point that incumbents almost never lose, turnover is slight and policy responsiveness is, at best, marginal. When elections cannot act as sensitive barometers of public sentiment and judgements on the conduct of government, democracy would seem to be on shaky ground. In Canada, analysts still worry about the opposite problem – an insufficiently experienced, or professional, Parliament. Viewed from the south, this trait seems refreshing. However much the personal vote has sunk into Canadian electoral politics, it has not yet transformed Parliament into a re-election machine comparable to the United States Congress, and that is probably all the better for Canada.

NOTES

Mr. Gaines would like to thank the Social Sciences and Humanities Research Council for its financial support (SSHRC 452-90-1217). We wish to thank Richard Johnston and Bruce Cain for advice on and criticism of an early draft.

1. We should remark that "the collective action problem" at the level of Parliament – the fact that an MP is just one among hundreds – gives some leverage for the formation of the personal vote in parliamentary systems. This is, of course, just the appeal that constituency-oriented members make to adherents of other parties.

2. The Canadian election data we use in the historical section of this study were very kindly supplied by Donald Blake and Richard Johnston of the University of British Columbia. Our N's do not always exactly match the actual total number of seats; however, for no election are we missing more than six ridings, including the two or three Northern ridings and the dual ridings in the Maritimes, which are normally omitted. The impact of these omissions is almost certainly negligible, given that we focus on aggregate measures.

3. Throughout this study, the term *comparable* when applied to elections means that boundaries of ridings were not shifted between elections, and when applied to ridings means that their particular boundaries were not shifted in a redistricting.

4. The 1988 CNES was made available by York University. Neither the principal investigator nor York University is responsible for any use we make of the data in this study.

5. Our comparative aspirations are thwarted by three critical design differences between the 1988 CNES and its counterpart studies of the United States and Great Britain, which guided the authors of *The Personal Vote* (Cain et al. 1987). First, several important questions from the previous studies were not repeated in the 1988 CNES. Second, the absence of contextual data in the current version of the 1988 CNES file prevents us from including individual MP traits (such as seniority or cabinet status) in models of MP recognition or responsiveness. It also means that we can never verify respondent accuracy: for example, we must assume that people who claim to recall their MP's name can actually do so. The third and most serious difference concerns the technique by which respondents were filtered out of the sample with certain questions in these different studies. Only the pre-election portion of the 1988 CNES had all the questions necessary for looking at the personal vote, and its sample of 3 609 was unfortunately filtered according to the presence of candidates in a respondent's riding, respondent knowledge, and respondent ability to name the incumbent. Thus, fewer than 1 010 respondents were asked most of the questions that interest us. Our problem, therefore, is that the filter has eliminated so many respondents by the time these questions are asked that those respondents who remain in the sample are unusually politically aware and are unlike those who were asked similar questions in the larger British and American samples.

6. Although there is a small literature concerned with an apparent increase in the rate of voluntary retirement from the U.S. House of Representatives,

retirements there still occur at a level well below that in Canada. Thus, the total number of retirements from Congress through the 1960s was 81, and through the 1970s, a much higher 153. This amounts to an average of 3.5 per cent retirement per year. In Canada, meanwhile, over this same decade, the comparable average was about 5.0 percent (for the Canadian data, see table 6.1; on the United States, see Hibbing 1982).

7. For a more extensive documentation of the volatility of Canadian elections, see Donald Blake's study (1991) submitted to this Royal Commission.

8. For the technical details of variance components, please see the original work by Stokes (1967).

9. For example, 116 of the 131 respondents who said that an NDP member was their incumbent also claim to remember this NDP candidate's name. This represents a mammoth 89 percent recall, and the average incumbent recall for the three national parties was 93 percent. Yet, this level of retention cannot plausibly be imputed to those 2 604 who were never even asked if any candidate was their current MP. It also seems illegitimate to assume that none of these people would have claimed to remember the name of their current MP, had they been asked. Also, to generalize that this cohort would have reported very low recall since it consists of those who report low knowledge of candidates is unfair, given that some portion of these respondents correctly answered that their riding had no candidate from a given party (at the time of the pre-election survey). Others, who were filtered due to their response that there was a candidate but that they knew little or nothing about the candidate, may have assumed incorrectly that the party already had a candidate and attributed ignorance to themselves, when in fact the particular party's tardiness in nomination was to blame for their deficient knowledge.

REFERENCES

Alford, John R., and John R. Hibbing. 1981. "Increased Incumbency Advantage in the House." *Journal of Politics* 43:1042–61.

Alford, John R., and David W. Brady. 1989. "Personal and Partisan Advantage in U.S. Congressional Elections, 1846–1986." In *Congress Reconsidered.* 4th ed., ed. Lawrence C. Dodd and Bruce I. Oppenheimer. Washington, DC: Congressional Quarterly Press.

Blake, Donald. 1978. "Constituency Contexts and Canadian Elections." *Canadian Journal of Political Science* 11:279–305.

———. 1991. "Party Competition and Electoral Volatility: Canada in Comparative Perspective." In *Representation, Integration and Political Parties in Canada*, ed. Herman Bakvis. Vol. 14 of the research studies of the Royal Commission on Electoral Reform and Party Financing. Ottawa and Toronto: RCERPF/Dundurn.

Butler, David, and Donald Stokes. 1969. *Political Change in Britain*. London: Macmillan.

Cain, Bruce E. 1983. "Blessed Be the Tie That Unbinds: Constituency Work and the Vote Swing in Great Britain." *Political Studies* 31:103–11.

Cain, Bruce, John Ferejohn and Morris Fiorina. 1987. *The Personal Vote.* Cambridge: Harvard University Press.

Campbell, Colin, and Harold D. Clarke. 1980. "Conspectus: Some Thoughts on Parliamentary Reform." In *Parliament, Policy and Representation,* ed. Harold D. Clarke et al. Toronto: Methuen.

Canada. Elections Canada. Various. *Report of the Chief Electoral Officer.* Ottawa: Minister of Supply and Services Canada.

Clarke, Harold, Richard Price and Robert Krause. 1975. "Constituency Service among Canadian Provincial Legislators." *Canadian Journal of Political Science* 8:520–42.

Crewe, Ivor. 1974. "Do Butler and Stokes Really Explain Political Change in Britain?" *European Journal of Political Research* 2:47–92.

Crick, Bernard. 1965. *The Reform of Parliament.* Garden City, NJ: Doubleday.

Cunningham, Robert. 1971. "The Impact of the Local Candidate in Canadian Federal Elections." *Canadian Journal of Political Science* 4:287–90.

Curtice, John, and Michael Steed. 1980. "Appendix 2: An Analysis of the Voting." In *The British General Election of 1979,* ed. David Butler and Dennis Kavanaugh. London: Macmillan.

———. 1982. "Electoral Choice and the Production of Government: The Changing Operation of the Electoral System in the United Kingdom since 1955." *British Journal of Political Science* 12:249–98.

Feigert, Frank. 1989. *Canada Votes: 1935–88.* Durham: Duke University Press.

Fenno, Richard F. 1978. *Home Style.* Boston: Little, Brown.

Ferejohn, John A. 1977. "On the Decline of Competition in Congressional Elections." *American Political Science Review* 71:166–76.

Fiorina, Morris P. 1977. "The Case of the Vanishing Marginals: The Bureaucracy Did It." *American Political Science Review* 71:177–81.

Franks, C.E.S. 1987. *The Parliament of Canada.* Toronto: University of Toronto Press.

Fraser, Alistair. 1980. "Legislators and Their Staffs." In *Parliament, Policy and Representation,* ed. H.D. Clarke et al. Toronto: Methuen.

Hibbing, John R. 1982. "Voluntary Retirements from the U.S. House of Representatives: Who Quits?" *American Journal of Political Science* 26:467–83.

Hoffman, David, and Norman Ward. 1970. *Bilingualism and Biculturalism in the Canadian House of Commons.* Ottawa: Queen's Printer.

Irvine, William P. 1982. "Does the Candidate Make a Difference?" *Canadian Journal of Political Science* 15:755–83.

Jackman, Robert. 1972. "Political Parties, Voting, and National Integration: The Canadian Case." *Comparative Politics* 4:511–36.

Jacobson, Gary C. 1987a. *The Politics of Congressional Elections*. Boston: Little, Brown.

———. 1987b. "Running Scared: Elections and Congressional Politics in the 1980s." In *Congress: Structure and Policy*, ed. Mathew D. McCubbins and Terry Sullivan. Cambridge: Cambridge University Press.

Kay, Barry. 1990. "Improving Upon the Cube Law: A Regional Swing Model..." Paper presented at the annual meeting of the Canadian Political Science Association, Victoria.

Krashinsky, Michael, and William Milne. 1983. "Some Evidence on the Effect of Incumbency in Ontario Provincial Elections." *Canadian Journal of Political Science* 16:489–500.

———. 1985. "Additional Evidence on the Effect of Incumbency in Canadian Elections." *Canadian Journal of Political Science* 18:155–65.

———. 1986. "The Effect of Incumbency in the 1984 Federal and 1985 Ontario Elections." *Canadian Journal of Political Science* 19:337–43.

Loewenberg, Gerhard, and Samuel C. Patterson. 1979. *Comparing Legislatures*. Boston: Little, Brown.

Lovink, J.A.A. 1973. "Is Canadian Politics Too Competitive?" *Canadian Journal of Political Science* 6:342–79.

Mayhew, David R. 1974a. *Congress: The Electoral Connection*. New Haven: Yale University Press.

———. 1974b. "Congressional Elections: The Case of the Vanishing Marginals." *Polity* 6:295–317.

Perlin, George, ed. 1988. *Party Democracy in Canada*. Toronto: Prentice-Hall.

Polsby, Nelson. 1968. "The Institutionalization of the U.S. House of Representatives." *American Political Science Review* 62:144–68.

Scarrow, Howard. 1962. *Canada Votes: A Handbook of Federal and Provincial Election Data*. New Orleans: Hauser Press.

Stokes, Donald E. 1967. "Parties and the Nationalization of Electoral Forces." In *The American Party Systems*, ed. William N. Chambers and Walter D. Burnham. New York: Oxford University Press.

Thomas, Norman C. 1980. "An Inquiry into Presidential and Parliamentary Government." In *Parliament, Policy and Representation*, ed. H.D. Clarke et al. Toronto: Methuen.

Thomas, Paul G. 1980. "Parliament and the Purse Strings." In *Parliament, Policy and Representation*, ed. H.D. Clarke et al. Toronto: Methuen.

7

THE CONSEQUENCES OF ELECTORAL VOLATILITY
Inexperienced Ministers 1949–90

S.L. Sutherland

INTRODUCTION

THIS RESEARCH STUDY of Canadian postwar cabinets attempts to determine the extent to which they have been composed of political "amateurs" appointed to Cabinet at the start of their parliamentary careers. The purpose is to see whether ministers having little or no parliamentary experience have been more likely to become a political liability to the government than ministers who, at the time of appointment to cabinet office, were more experienced parliamentarians.

The research question, then, is what is a typical outcome for individuals who are appointed to ministerial office without first having gained an appreciable experience of Parliament through service in the House of Commons? Does a prime minister who includes in the Cabinet novices to parliamentary politics take a considerable risk, or is the factor of parliamentary experience unimportant? A subsidiary question is then whether electoral volatility is an important "cause" or reason for appointments of inexperienced politicians to the Cabinet. In other words, when a prime minister appoints neophyte politicians to the Cabinet, does he seem to do so mainly because he had little or no choice?

The failure of the party to consolidate a broad-based and long-lasting leadership inside Parliament could be important to our politics. The legislature is the most legitimate route to high political office, and the repeated appointment of non-parliamentary politicians or complete amateurs to ministerial jobs could discourage career politicians and work against the development of principled politics in which parties take seriously the task of consolidating long-term interests into coherent alliances.

John Porter asked in the mid-1960s, "How can a political system operate with such unstable patterns of élite recruitment?" and the question is equally valid 25 years later. Where politics is so permeable, a government party is closer to an accidental collection of passengers on an airplane than to a classical political formation. These instant ministers might factually perform less well in House politics than more seasoned parliamentary politicians. For example, they might be less serious about the weight of their responsibility, perhaps less sensitive to appearances, and less alert than more experienced ministers as to how particular actions could be made to look bad by the opposition in the House of Commons.

In research terms, the implicit or null hypothesis is that experience in parliamentary politics makes no difference to the fate of a minister. One can then look for evidence to contradict this hypothesis.

The identification of a minister as a serious political liability is measurable in at least two ways. The most extreme indication that a minister is in trouble, as noted, is his or her resignation from an active Cabinet on the basis of individual ministerial responsibility or because of a policy disagreement with the government. A more qualitative indication of the performance of a minister in cabinet office can be obtained through a review of Commons *Debates* during the inexperienced politician's first period in ministerial office, looking for episodes in which the House had become focused on some matter involving a new minister that puts the government on the defensive. One can control for the temper of the times by pairing each amateur-politician minister with one or more ministers who were appointed to the Cabinet at the same time, but who had more experience in parliamentary politics. The question as to the impact of amateur ministers upon the success of a government becomes researchable when it is posed as a question about the relative frequency of serious difficulty.

Cabinet Composition and Electoral Volatility

The research study also attempts to probe one conventional response to the question of why Canadian prime ministers so frequently entrust positions in the Cabinet to rank newcomers.

The conventional response is that the federal nature of Canadian Cabinet-making conventions entails rigid regional criteria. It is conventionally said that a prime minister must represent in the Cabinet, through the geographical home bases of ministers, all major regions and important sections of large cities. In this view, the appointment to the Cabinet of parliamentary neophytes is made to seem a consequence of unsafe seats.

While it appears true that Canadian electoral politics are much more volatile than American politics and somewhat more volatile than British politics (Blake 1991; Ferejohn and Gaines 1991), aggregate volatility cannot really tell us much about why particular appointments of neophyte ministers are made. Rather, one must ask in the case of each appointment of a neophyte politician to the Cabinet whether the prime minister had a range of experienced parliamentarians, possessing what one might call "the correct geography," from which to choose. One needs to study the detail of election outcomes.

Still another qualitative issue is whether the relative absence of the notion of "career" in Canadian parliamentary parties (certainly in comparison to Britain) lowers the quality of Canadian politics as expressed in the House of Commons. At least two reasons suggest themselves for thinking that this might be so. The back bench is widely viewed as a place of boredom and futility, even while it is admitted that it takes years there before a politician understands how business is organized in the House, and the strategic uses of procedure. Therefore, it may be that even a very small corps of experienced parliamentarians could make parliamentary life very difficult for a less-experienced government. Alternatively, it may be that "avocational politicians," individuals who plan to have only short parliamentary careers, would be less restrained in their behaviour by respect for the institution. Their presence may more directly change the "game" of parliamentary politics.[1] Whatever the mechanism, it appears that there has been a decrease in the quality of political discourse in the House of Commons, and that the response of the Canadian public is seen in the steady decline in popular support for the parties. (See Johnston 1986, chap. 2.)

The third thrust of the paper is to bring such data as are readily available to bear on the propositions dealing with the prime minister's range of choices for forming each Cabinet and the House of Commons' reception of the neophyte minister.

RESEARCH PROCEDURES

Sample of Cabinets

The cabinet membership of each government for the 14 postwar governments from 1949 to the present was recorded, using the list of "members of the government" provided in the Commons *Debates*. It may be noted that "members of the government" are ministers of departments, ministers without portfolio, and, after 1970, ministers of state. Seven of the 14 governments lasted for four or more years: in these cases, a second list of ministers was compiled for a later session of the Parliament. The membership of Cabinet was thus recorded and studied 21 times. The initial observation relates to the first session, while the second date represents a session as near to midterm as possible given the length of the particular Parliament.

The list of ministers presented in the *Debates* is in order of precedence (established by the date of entry of the person to this or previous cabinets) at the last date of the session. Exceptions to the date rule are the first St. Laurent government, when the first date available is for the swearing in of the initial Cabinet; the fourth government of Pierre Elliott Trudeau, where the Parliament largely consisted of one long session; and the second government of Brian Mulroney, where the first and second sessions together lasted only about one month of the first eight months of 1989, and therefore only one observation was taken in 1990.

The *Canadian Parliamentary Guide* of the relevant year was then consulted for each member of each Cabinet to establish the date of entry to the House of Commons as an elected member, the date of first appointment to the Cabinet, and whether there had been provincial or municipal political experience. This process identified the cabinets' ministers as either experienced or inexperienced politicians.

"Experience" Defined

The definition of "minister lacking parliamentary experience" is that, at the time of appointment, the new minister had two or fewer years of experience as a sitting member of the House of Commons or of a provincial legislature.[2] Because John Porter had used a four-year criterion in his study of parliamentary careers conducted as part of his *Vertical Mosaic* (1965), the data were initially investigated in the light of a four-year cut-off. But the two-year criterion was eventually chosen for two reasons. First, the four-year or "whole Parliament" criterion takes in only three or four more individuals than the two-year criterion and thus makes a less clear statement. Second, minority governments were more frequent after than during the period of Porter's research. Their duration (from election to election) is less than one year in three cases, and is always at least a quarter short of three years. In these minority governments, a great deal of a calendar year can be spent in election-related activity, and Parliament does not sit for months at a time. It can take five calendar years for an MP to gain three or four years of experience as a sitting MP after his or her first victory, and the computations become problematic. The two-year criterion demonstrates that an individual will have been identified almost immediately as being "ministrable."

Data Compilation

Basic data were compiled on each government ("members of the government"), comprising seats held by the government over total seats in the House of Commons, the number of inexperienced ministers, and the name, gender, riding and first portfolio of each inexperienced minister.

The total number of ministerial appointments in the sampled cabinets can be calculated by adding the memberships of the 14 governments at the first point in time, plus the new appointments made at midterm where a midterm Cabinet is sampled, and then subtracting the prime ministers (who make the appointments). This makes 412 appointments – not to be confused with individual persons, for which the number is smaller because some persons are appointed two or more times. The number of appointments to Cabinet of persons having fewer than two years of parliamentary experience in this list is 57 (54 individuals).

Next, a list was compiled of novice politician-ministers and, loosely speaking, their "experimental controls" – the ministers immediately above and below on the precedence list of the relevant Cabinet. This control or pairing by the use of the precedence list holds constant the amount of cabinet experience and also the political climate of the time: all other things being equal, only the length of parliamentary experience varies. There are 162 names (54 times 3) on the "subjects plus controls" list. Many are duplicates and/or other inexperienced ministers because new people tend, in the nature of things, to be taken on in batches. In most cases, however, it was possible to establish at least one experienced "control" minister for each politically inexperienced new minister; that is, the desirable control is a person new to the Cabinet but possessing more parliamentary experience than the inexperienced minister.

Hypothesis Testing

As a first step, the list of 412 ministerial appointments was cross-referenced to the Library of Parliament's compilation, "Ministerial Resignations to Date." The identities of both inexperienced and experienced appointees who have resigned from the sampled cabinets were thus established, and an analysis was then conducted that assessed the association between lack of experience and ministerial resignations. Resignation is defined as the discontinuation of a minister's presence in an active Cabinet (that is, before dissolution of a Parliament).

There have been 60 resignations since the start of the 1949 St. Laurent Cabinet, involving 58 individuals. A content analysis of the text of the Library of Parliament collection of official reasons given for the prime minister's acceptance of a tendered resignation resulted in the 11 categories listed in table 7.A1 in the Appendix. (See also Sutherland 1991, where resignations are classified from 1867. The scheme there is slightly different: most notably, "minority government victims" are placed in a miscellaneous category.) The body of data consisting of formal reasons is acceptable because it reflects the prime ministers' judgements of the "best" interpretations for resignations that they have to offer the public in the light of constitutional understandings and precedents, and which also plausibly cover the events leading to the resignations.

The first category of formal reasons for resignation covers the possibility that a minister may have resigned because of a personal administrative error.

The second category concerns acts judged to be unworthy of a minister of the Crown. Accusations of misconduct in office that cause ministers to resign – in most cases, no formal process is undertaken – are subdivided into financial, legal and security. Financial conflict of interest is a clear case of the former, and interference by a minister in the legal system is an example of the second. The subcategory "security" is for any case where it is thought that a minister's action has put the state somehow at risk.

The third category allows for the possibility that a resignation has been brought about by accusations that would, in a majority situation, simply be dismissed. These ministers who are sacrificed to the voting strength of the opposition in difficult political times are designated "minority government victims."

Solidarity covers cases where ministers resign when they cannot accept the Cabinet's policy.

The above set of four reasons constitutes all resignations which can be frankly said to be politically significant: all the ministers whose behaviour has led to significant political embarrassment for the government will be in one of these categories.

The private misconduct category is made up of actions that cast some doubt on the minister's moral standards, but which have no relevance to the portfolio and neither arise from the job nor suggest that the minister did not take office seriously.

Ministers also resign in order to be able to accept an appointment offered by the prime minister under the Order in Council (OIC). Government appointment here means only the job offers that were used to move people out of the Cabinet. Thus, many more cabinet members than are noted here will have received an OIC appointment at some stage in their career, but not in connection with their exit from the Cabinet. Ministers may, of course, also leave to take up a private-sector opportunity. Task finished, health, purely personal reasons and the residual category complete the classification scheme.

A quick review of the main pattern of table 7.A1 in the Appendix shows that the largest single reason that Canadian ministers leave an active Cabinet is to take up a job in the prime minister's gift. It is offered about 35 percent of the time. Resignations related to error or misconduct total 10 cases, or 21 percent. Policy disagreement ("solidarity"), on the other hand, is cited only 8 times, or just over 15 percent of the time. It is with regard to the latter that British practice deviates: there, one finds that about 80 percent of all resignations are for reasons of policy disagreement. (See Sutherland 1991; Butler and Butler 1989.)

Resignation, as noted, is only the first half of the story of the success or lack of success of ministers in Cabinet. A test was also conducted of the qualitative prediction that inexperienced politicians will be more likely to commit errors that affect the stride of the government – without, however, bringing on a resignation – and will therefore incur the disapproval of the House of Commons more often than experienced politicians who know its ways and sensitivities.[3] *Debates* indexes were studied to identify the government in which an inexperienced politician or a control minister was appointed to Cabinet and were also studied for the succeeding government if the same minister continued to serve.[4] The goal was to see whether novice politician-ministers are more likely to commit errors, not grave enough to require a resignation, but which nonetheless create trouble for the government. Thus it can be noted explicitly that the operating assumption is that lack of experience as a backbencher in the House of Commons is never compensated for by cabinet experience; that is, experience in the House is qualitatively different. The impressions gathered in this exercise helped to elaborate the characters or themes of different parliaments. A search was conducted of the following indexes:

- the names of the subject minister and the control(s);
- the headings "Cabinet" and "Cabinet ministers" as a subject and a subheading under "Government" to follow up on calls for resignation and negative references to subject ministers or their controls;
- the entries under the name of the prime minister were searched to establish if he had found it necessary to defend either the subject minister or one of the controls during the session; and

- in later years, entries under the title "prime minister" were searched for references as above to see if the prime minister was under fire for his handling of a particular episode that was alleged to touch upon cabinet solidarity or performance in his role as head of government.

To probe the more qualitative speculation that prime ministers were not always constrained by narrow requirements for regional representation when they appointed particular ministers, the electoral results were consulted to ascertain patterns of regional and provincial representation in the House of Commons of the time. If there happens to be a selection of experienced members of Parliament from the area represented by an amateur minister, one can suppose that pure geography is less important than is often claimed and that interest representation must then be more so. As for the reception by the parliamentary partisan forces of amateur ministers, the "mood" of the House can be loosely characterized by what seems to be the predominant mode of criticism of the government by the opposition.

FINDINGS AND ANALYSIS

The analysis is offered within "ministries" as the politically significant period of time. A ministry is a continuous period presided over by one prime minister, whether in one government or several. Discussion within each ministry is loosely organized within governments, except where a rigid respect for chronology would create too much repetition.

Each section begins with the most objective indicator, resignation, and then proceeds to the more judgemental information about the kind and intensity of other kinds of trouble suffered by the inexperienced minister-politicians or their control ministers. To keep the quantity of information manageable, attention is concentrated on the most interesting episodes, whether brought forward because of an inexperienced minister or because of a control.

The reader is urged to read the text in conjunction with table 7.A1 and the sample data in the Appendix. (It will be noted that the Clark and Turner governments are omitted from the table because there were no resignations.) The Appendix provides background information on each government, including a listing of the politically inexperienced ministers of each Cabinet. It should be noted that the totals for members elected are taken from the *Parliamentary Guide*, while the numbers of seats retained, gained and lost for each party are taken from Feigert (1989). Feigert's counts are based only on the constituencies that remained the same as in the previous election and are, therefore, always less than the *Guide's* counts, where redistributions are included in the figures. (See the Appendix.) Note also that "seats returned" to a party will always be somewhat greater than the number of members returned, because some individuals will have resigned or even died between elections, and therefore a different person is in the "returned" seat.

St. Laurent Governments

Cabinet Appointments and Resignations
None of the three inexperienced or "amateur" ministers of the first St. Laurent Cabinet of 1949 – Pearson, Gregg and Prudham – resigned from an active Cabinet. But the case of George Prudham (Edmonton West) was not an unqualified success as will be explained below.

When Pearson (Algoma East, Ontario) and Gregg (York–Sunbury, NB) were appointed as novice politicians to the first St. Laurent government in the First Session, St. Laurent had just won an election which had returned to him about 30 Ontario Liberal seats and seven New Brunswick seats; hence there would arguably have been contenders for their portfolios if a regional criterion had in fact been predominant. Prudham faced a smaller field as only two Liberal seats were returned from Alberta in the 1949 election, although the party brought in three new members.

When John Pickersgill, another novice minister, was given a portfolio in the second St. Laurent government of 1953, all seven of Newfoundland's seats belonged to the Liberal party, five being seats that were held from the previous election. It seems safe to suggest, therefore, that Pickersgill had more going for him than geography.

Resignations of ministers did abound during the two governments of St. Laurent's ministry, but all eight were offered by experienced ministers. Departures from the active cabinets comprised six appointments under the Order in Council, one resignation to return to the private sector and one resignation on the grounds that the minister's task was finished.

Qualitative Performance Indicators
Gregg, an inexperienced politician who was given the portfolio of Veterans Affairs, seems to have passed through the Parliament unscathed. His precedence list pairs, Robertson and Mayhew, likewise had quiet Parliaments, although Robertson (minister without portfolio) found himself in some trouble in the House much later in the Parliament (December 1952) for contradicting government policy in a speech he made in a United Nations forum. A number of motions of censure and

want of confidence were proposed on the grounds that the Cabinet was divided. Robertson's faux pas was interpreted as a slight to Pearson. Thus, one can conclude that his appointment was less successful in this regard than was that of Gregg.

It will surprise no one to hear that Pearson, in External Affairs, personally survived House politics. One of Pearson's controls, the experienced politician Stuart Garson, survived a major parliamentary campaign to unseat him from the Justice portfolio through November and December of 1949. At issue was his handling of a case under the *Combines Investigation Act*, related to his alleged suppression of a report on the flour-milling industry. He was designated a "law breaking minister" in the House of Commons, and it was repeatedly held that he was in contempt of Parliament. The matter was taken up by the press on grounds of executive dominance of the House of Commons. Garson was, however, to retain office throughout the Parliament. One can score a definite success for Pearson on the side of amateur ministers.

The end of the first St. Laurent government became more rancorous as the Opposition geared up for the forthcoming general election. A scandal over what was called the Currie Report,[5] a document that severely criticized the standard of management and resource control at the Department of Defence, raged through December of 1952, being punctuated by frequent requests for the resignation of the Minister of Defence, Brooke Claxton. There was no real question of Claxton resigning in that Parliament: he resigned on his own schedule in 1954 to take up a private sector position after seeing the Liberals through the election of 1953.

Given the mood of the session's end, the novice politician-minister George Prudham could not have expected much tolerance from the House when some opposition members accused him of being in a conflict of interest in the dog days of the session. The affair was raised on 9 March 1953 by Social Credit MP Ray Thomas of Wetaskiwin. Prudham, a well-known Edmonton businessman, saw his business affairs (not directly related to his portfolio as Minister of Mines and Technical Surveys) put in a bad light in the House of Commons. Prudham's lumber company had purchased some well-located Canadian National Railways property in the city of Edmonton in a transaction in which no tenders were called. Thomas found it "a strange state of affairs when a minister of the crown can negotiate directly with a crown corporation to buy property without benefit of bidding." (Canada, House, 9 March 1953, 2775. The heading, Alexander Construction, is a rich source of references for the Prudham case in this index.) Prudham made a long speech the following day, when he challenged Social Credit to unseat him in the forthcoming election (he was returned). The House's attention to Prudham was limited only by its larger appetite for the Currie Report. Prudham's control minister (as Prudham was the last minister named to this Cabinet, he has only one "pair") was Walter Harris, who had had 10 years in the House when he was appointed to the Citizenship and Immigration portfolio of this government. Harris drew little fire until the next government. Overall, the inexperienced Prudham proved to be a liability, at least for that Parliament.

As a final note, one can remark that as the first government was drawing to a close, the House was preparing its outraged reception for Pickersgill. This was, of course, before he was appointed to Cabinet. St. Laurent was asked questions about his choice of Pickersgill as Clerk of the Privy Council, and MPs seemed generally aware that Pickersgill was about to shift his field of operations from administration to politics.

When the Liberals returned with 171 seats following the general election of 10 August 1953, Pickersgill thus could not have been expecting a smooth ride. He was the sole "amateur minister" of the government. His first appointment was as Secretary of State, and his control ministers, William Ross Macdonald and Jean Lesage, held the portfolios of Solicitor General and Resources and Development respectively. Macdonald attracted a minor amount of negative comment, all because his base was in the Senate rather than in the House. Lesage appears to have been a flawlessly smooth minister.

Pickersgill's reception to the House was characterized by references to him as "prime minister designate," and, as the Parliament moved along, St. Laurent found it necessary to explain Pickersgill's conduct or absences and to generally defend him more often than the rest of the Cabinet combined: the Opposition was, in effect, picking on Pickersgill. He, of course, did not fail to provide opportunity. An example occurred on 27 April 1955 when Mr. Fulton asked for details of a trip made by Mr. Pickersgill, Minister of Citizenship, together with the Minister of Fisheries and a family group in a private railway car belonging to the government. The return trip between Ottawa and Vancouver took the group nearly two weeks in its rolling hotel suite, during which Pickersgill inspected various offices in Victoria, Vancouver and Calgary (Canada, House, 27 April 1955, 3205).

The Conservative leitmotif during this Parliament was that the Liberals were not providing a democratic parliamentary government because they did not know how to do so. C.D. Howe, Trade and Commerce Minister and Minister of Defence Production, was designated as government "czar." Interestingly, although Howe had first entered Cabinet very much earlier, in 1935, he was portrayed as a typical Liberal minister in that he had never served an apprenticeship for office in Parliament, but had first taken a place in Parliament as a member of Cabinet.

No occasion was missed to characterize the Liberal government in terms of the non-parliamentary nature of its ministerial complement. Opposition member W.M. Hamilton, in the debate following the Speech from the Throne, characterized the government as having "the political morality of an alley cat and the lust for power of a Genghis Khan," and named Pickersgill, Pearson and Campney (National Defence) as evidence of the creeping bureaucratic government which preserved only the trappings of democracy. Hamilton suggested that the civil service, through its use of the Liberal party as a vehicle, was essentially taking over Cabinet for the benefit of outside interests. In effect, the accusation boils down to accusing the Liberal government of having constituted a Cabinet on the basis of interest representation separate and apart from the parliamentary party (Canada, House, 2 February 1955, 787–91).

Thus, these themes of the Liberal party's disregard of democratic and parliamentary tradition and its use of "strong-man" government were fully developed by the time the pipeline debate took place in 1956. The government invoked eight closure motions in the course of this sixteen-day debate. The claim was made that closure had been used only six times before in the history of Canadian government. In the eyes of the Conservatives, the Liberals had all but killed democracy. Speaking on 1 June 1956, Thomas Bell (Saint John–Albert) saw no fewer than "eight members of the present cabinet who had no political savvy whatsoever when they were appointed to the cabinet." The Liberal cabinet members, he said, "do not have that appreciation of the traditions of politics that mean so much to us, or the early training that would have prevented such action at this time ... that is one reason in my opinion why we are having trouble today, because in the cabinet there are eight men *who came up the easy way*" (Canada, House, 1 June 1956, 4609, emphasis added).

Donald Fleming, speaking in the final stages of that "momentous but sad debate," characterized the government as "insane and vicious" for resorting to measures that had been denounced by the Liberals' own heros, Laurier and King, as reducing Parliament to a travesty (Canada, House, 5 June 1956, 4691). Speaking on 7 June, CCF MP Colin Cameron (Nanaimo) tied the Liberal style to its recruitment of amateur, administrator ministers:

> I suggest to you that we have to look further for a solution to this
> strange problem ... of a government so inept that it is unable to get

its measures through the House of Commons within the accepted rules of this House ... It is not an accident that many of the members of that administration have stepped right into cabinet positions without any experience in parliamentary life ... When one looks at the front treasury benches he finds that with two exceptions no minister has sat on the floor of this house as a private member, and no minister at all has sat on the floor of this house as a member in opposition. This creates a very grave situation for parliament. (Canada, House, 7 June 1956, 4829–30)

Cameron's speech is a distillation of the considered Conservative view of the Liberal party, one that explains the Conservatives' conviction that they alone had the moral authority to govern because they alone knew how to respect Parliament:

I am not attempting to deny that eminent university presidents, distinguished corporation lawyers and higher civil servants are men of great ability. They are possibly of greater ability than other men who could be found within the membership of the Liberal party: but their abilities were not the abilities of parliamentarians because there is only one place in which a man can qualify for this difficult business of parliamentary life, and that is in the ranks of parliament itself.

I would suggest that this growing habit on the part of this administration of bringing in from outside the ranks of parliament cabinet ministers without parliamentary experience is destroying the very roots of parliament. This institution has several functions to perform. It is not merely an institution for the passing of legislation by the existing government, it is the developing ground for competent parliamentary leadership.

When we have a party – and I address this to the rank and file of the Liberal party – which has acquiesced in this practice, it has been acquiescing in the degradation of parliament because these men, eminent as they are, lack one thing. They are men who have not, like the Minister of Finance and like the Minister of National Health and Welfare, been prepared in their earlier years to take the grave risks involved in embarking upon a political career. On the other hand, they have sought their eminence in other fields and later came to crown it with political eminence. That is a most dangerous precedent and practice for parliament to follow, when parliament should be composed of ordinary men and women representing ordinary men and women throughout the nation ... I can understand that the minister of external affairs may perhaps feel badly about my comments, but I want to say to him that the very qualities which make him a valuable servant of the people in the civil service are not qualities that make him valuable in the House of Commons when it comes to dealing with difficult parliamentary situations ...

It will not be until we get back to the original purposes of parliament, to the original proceedings and traditions of parliament, that we shall avoid the sort of tragic mess into which we got last week. (Canada, House, 7 June 1956, 4830)

In closing, one can say that the Conservatives were able to use Pickersgill's appointment to good effect against the government: although his cabinet performance was smooth, he fit into the theme that the Conservatives wanted to elaborate.

Diefenbaker Governments

Cabinet Appointments and Resignations
One might therefore expect that the following period spanned by the Diefenbaker governments would see a dramatic reduction in entry to Cabinet from outside the parliamentary party. In the first government, which formed after the general election of 1957 with a minority of 112 of 265 seats, only two amateur ministers were appointed. One was Paul Comtois of Nicolet–Yamaska, who was given the Mines portfolio. The other inexperienced minister of this Cabinet, Sidney Earle Smith (Hastings–Frontenac), was appointed to the External portfolio before being elected in a November by-election.

The total number of seats that changed in the 1958 election was 101, for a turnover statistic on the previous electoral map of 38 percent. The Progressive Conservatives retained 108 seats, a very good proportion of their 1957 strength, and took on as well the task of socializing 97 new members from seats gained. The Liberals were reduced to 45 retained seats and 3 new members.

After the election, Mr. Diefenbaker added one more amateur minister, Raymond O'Hurley (Lotbinière), giving him the Defence Production portfolio, and reappointed both Comtois and Smith. (Smith had been president of the University of Manitoba and of the University of Toronto before his cabinet appointment. He died suddenly on 17 March 1959. The news affected Mr. Diefenbaker so severely that he asked the House to adjourn for the day.)

At midterm, Mr. Diefenbaker brought in another small group of new parliamentarians to Cabinet: David Walker (Rosedale), Pierre Sévigny (Longueuil) and Noel Dorion. Diefenbaker had no real choice but to appoint novice ministers because the party had gained 41 new Quebec seats in the House of Commons. When Diefenbaker was returned with a minority government after the general election of 1962, he did not add any inexperienced politicians to Cabinet.

The Diefenbaker governments were not characterized by scandal. During the ministry, there was a total of six resignations from active cabinets. Three of these were to take up OIC appointments, two were for health reasons, and one was a solidarity resignation. Only one of these resignations was that of an inexperienced minister: Paul Comtois (elected for the first time in 1957 and re-elected in 1958) resigned to accept the lieutenant-governorship of Quebec late in 1961 at the age of 60. Douglas Harkness, an experienced appointee, was the solidarity resignation, leaving his job as Minister of Defence in February 1963 because of a disagreement with the government's policy regarding nuclear weapons.

Qualitative Performance Indicators

In the first short 1957–58 government, the qualitative search reveals nothing of major interest about either the amateur ministers or their four control ministers from the precedence list. The Liberal line of attack was essentially to tell Mr. Diefenbaker that he could not hope to govern without more strength in Quebec, and that in forming his Cabinet, he had not even done a good job of using the available francophone talent, leaving out of Cabinet such solid individuals as Marcel Lambert from Edmonton.

In the second Diefenbaker government, the novice minister O'Hurley was castigated for holding "dictatorial powers" as minister of Defence Production. These problems were dwarfed by a scandal concerning O'Hurley's experienced control minister from the precedence list, Henri Courtemanche, Secretary of State. Courtemanche was a director and treasurer of a Montreal hospital during his session as Solicitor General, and it was thought unsuitable that he might have been acting as a solicitor for an organization that was in the process of receiving government funds. Through the fourth session, which ran from 17 November 1960 to 29 September 1961, Courtemanche was accused of financial irregularities at least four times, with several opposition MPs being involved in each onslaught. He resigned citing health reasons on 19 January 1960, but then immediately accepted Mr. Diefenbaker's offer of a Senate position.

Another inexperienced minister, Sévigny, got into difficulty considerably later, in February of 1962, when he was quoted as saying that the "yellow peril" was a threat to civilization, an expression that observers thought unsuitable in the mouth of an Associate Minister of National Defence. Mr. Sévigny eventually rose in the House on 12 February 1962, on a matter of privilege, to say that when he used the phrase in a speech in Montreal on 8 February, he had intended only to flag the threat presented by the military strength of communist China. Sévigny's control ministers, David Walker and Hugh Fleming, do not appear to have blundered through the course of the Parliament. In effect, this Parliament results in a *match nul* – a draw – or close to it, with one inexperienced minister causing embarrassment to the government, matched by problems created by an experienced control minister.

After 1958, the Liberal Opposition was fascinated by the Conservative government's enormous back bench, which it found excessive to the needs of any government, and predicted that its management would be difficult.

As is noted in the Appendix, the second Diefenbaker government operated without parliamentary assistants or any sign of need for them for nearly two sessions after its return in strength in 1958. Between 1943 and 1957, these positions had been conferred through Order in Council and remunerated under a line in the Estimates. Instead of continuing this way, the Diefenbaker government proposed legislation providing for much the same role in Bill C-37.[6] There are probably more questions about assistants than on all other cabinet topics combined. The only other major concern was the government's potential replacement for the late Sidney Smith.

The Liberal parliamentary party (45 seats retained) coped with opposition life with lightness of spirit. When the Liberals advised the Conservatives of their shortcomings as a government, it was frequently with tongue in cheek, as in the following analysis of the geography of the Conservative cabinet by Paul Martin, assisted by a gesturing Pearson:

> The Minister of Transport, the Minister of Finance and the Minister without Portfolio who represents the constituency of Greenwood all come from Toronto. Then the Minister of Citizenship and Immigration comes from a place not far from Toronto ... [Hamilton] Then the Minister of Labour lives in Oshawa, some 40 miles from Toronto ... Then of course while the late Secretary of State for External Affairs represented a riding that was not in Toronto but was close to Oshawa, nevertheless he himself came from Toronto. As the Leader of the Opposition [Pearson] now observes ... in his effective coaching method, they are all in the same television area.

But the great regret is that as a result of the concentration of my right hon. friend's ministers from Ontario in the Toronto-Hamilton-Oshawa district, the fact is that central Ontario, southwestern Ontario, eastern Ontario and northern Ontario are all unrepresented in the cabinet of my right hon. friend ... The Prime Minister now will have the opportunity, not of making changes in the cabinet – I am sure that is not possible – but at least of rectifying the situation somewhat by appointing parliamentary secretaries taking into account the geographical areas of Ontario that are not now represented in his cabinet. (Canada, House, 8 April 1959, 2359)

Pearson Governments

Cabinet Appointments and Resignations
In the two Liberal minority governments of Lester Pearson which followed, inexperienced ministers, appointed in number, took a battering. Comparatively few seats (for Canada) changed hands in the 1963 election, which saw the Liberals regain the power they would be unable to wield. They had 43 retained seats in Ontario and 33 in Quebec, but they had little strength westward with only two seats in Manitoba – one seat retained, one new member – one new member in Alberta and four retained seats and three new members in British Columbia.

Of nine inexperienced politicians appointed as ministers in 1963, none would resign during the two years the government lasted, but four of this group fell shortly after the election returning the second Pearson government of 1965. The inexperienced ministers were Walter Gordon, appointed to Cabinet in preference to several experienced contenders from Toronto; Mitchell Sharp, for whom the same was true; Arthur Laing from Vancouver South; Maurice Lamontagne of Outremont–Saint-Jean, Guy Favreau of Papineau and René Tremblay of Matapédia–Matane, whose jobs could have gone to experienced Quebec colleagues; Charles Mills Drury of Westmount, the traditional Quebec anglophone from the constituency at the heart of anglophone power; John Robert Nicholson of Vancouver Centre; and Harry Hays, a new Liberal MP from Calgary South with no experienced competition.[7]

For convenience, one can flag the novice ministers of this Cabinet who ran into serious trouble after the next election. Walter Gordon resigned on the basis of individual ministerial responsibility on 11 November 1965 – only days after Pearson had been returned with a minority government – on the grounds that he had given bad advice to the Prime Minister. Gordon was soon back in Cabinet and resigned again in 1968 to take up an OIC appointment. Maurice Lamontagne and

René Tremblay resigned together on 17 December 1965 as a scandal raged over their slowness to pay for furniture they had accepted from a Montreal company that was going bankrupt. These ministers did not resign on the basis of individual ministerial responsibility. Prime Minister Pearson accepted their resignations on the grounds that they had been so damaged by opposition tactics that they could no longer serve effectively; in effect, they were victims of minority government. Guy Favreau resigned somewhat later, on 4 April 1967, officially to take up a judgeship, but again, in effect, the victim of the minority situation, his own inexperience and that of his aides in the mishandling of the Rivard affair. One can note that he had been moved out of the Justice portfolio and into the position of President of the Privy Council some time before Pearson offered the position. Thus, one might argue that the lack of sensitivity to appearances, perhaps due to a lack of experience in the House of three of Pearson's ministers – or of their ministerial staffs – was to contribute to the difficulty of the second government in the context of the minority situation and the partisan style of the Opposition.

Of these nine novice ministers, only Mitchell Sharp and Charles Drury (representing the ridings of Eglinton and Saint-Antoine–Westmount) continued to be elected and to hold places at the centre of political life throughout the continuous period of Liberal power ending with Pierre Trudeau's third government. (Gordon's second resignation has already been noted.) Mitchell Sharp resigned some 13 years later in 1976 (from a "holding" position), saying that he wanted to make a place for younger ministers. Charles Drury resigned the same year as Minister of Public Works and Science and Technology, offering the same formula. (See "Task finished" in table 7.A1.)

As for resignations during the first (1963–65) Pearson government, all six were of experienced ministers. Only one was due to a political scandal, bringing about a resignation on individual ministerial responsibility, a conflict of interest. This was the case of Yvon Dupuis, a minister without portfolio who was well experienced, having first been elected in 1952. The minister was said to have exercised undue influence in an attempt to get a racetrack constructed in his riding. It was also alleged that he was a party in some business dealings connected with the project. He resigned in January 1965.

Let us now return to the harrowing life of the second Pearson government. There were nine ministerial resignations in the life of this government between November 1965 and June 1968. Three that were under opposition pressure have already been reviewed: Tremblay, Lamontagne and Favreau, all inexperienced ministers who had first been appointed in the previous short minority government. Gordon is classified under "Other" because he resigned for having offered poor political advice rather than for any failing in his portfolio-related performance. The other resignations included an OIC appointment (Pickersgill), Gordon's second resignation, Winters' contest for the leadership, LaMarsh's exit on grounds of irreconcilable differences with the incoming Prime Minister (Trudeau) and the remaining resignation on grounds of health.

In some contrast with the first batch of novice politicians named ministers by Pearson, both novice ministers appointed by Pearson following the general election of 1965 did very well. Pierre Elliott Trudeau, who entered the House of Commons in that election, was made Minister of Justice in early 1967, after which he rose to the prime ministership in 1968. Jean Marchand held cabinet office until June 1976, when he resigned as Minister of the Environment, not in difficulty, but citing a cabinet policy disagreement over the handling of an air controllers' strike.

In summary, of the total of 11 ministers appointed to office without notable experience in the House of Commons, the success of the ministry was arguably affected by their inexperience in four cases.

Qualitative Performance Indicators
Let us start with the Pearson government of 1963, formed after the defeat of Diefenbaker's Conservatives. Diefenbaker lost the election, according to Peter Newman, because he put too much faith in his own capacity to vanquish "vague bureaucratic villains of his own devising" (Newman 1963, 323). One of these "villains," a particular target of Diefenbaker, was, of course, Maurice Lamontagne, a former economic adviser in the Privy Council who had been forced to resign by the Conservatives when they took power in 1958. The Conservative campaign themes as identified by Peter Newman became the notions that would dominate the following Parliament: "In 1962, he [Diefenbaker] attempted to distract attention from the nation's problems by setting up an enemy for the voters to hate. By personal attacks, which grew in intensity to become the main theme of the campaign, he tried to portray in the public mind an image of the Liberal party as 'the same old bunch' – a group of unrepentant, unsavoury characters dedicated to fooling the population under the guise of socialistic promises that would ruin the country" (ibid., 324).

The proportion of Liberal "civil servant ministers" was on occasion alleged to be as high as a third of all ministers. Clement Vincent (Nicolet–Yamaska), one of eight Quebec Conservatives remaining after the Liberal victory, asked Mr. Drury whether the Liberals might now start appointing politicians to bureaucratic jobs in order to compensate for the raid they had made on the ranks of the civil service (Canada, House, 28 June 1963, 1704). Written questions included several of the following kind: "How many of the present ministers of the crown were employees of the federal public service; who are they, and what position did each one hold?" (ibid., 2 October 1963, 3117).

Behind this was the serious theme that the civil service influence led to an attitude of arrogance, as in the following remark by W.B. Nesbitt (Oxford): "One finds this kind of thinking: we know what is good for you; we are not interested in consulting people at a lower level; we are imposing this on you from on high" (Canada, House, 30 October 1963, 4187).

Of the inexperienced ministers in this first Pearson government, Walter Gordon and Harry Hays likely came in for the most unfavourable attention early in the government. Gordon created a minor scandal in June 1963 in connection with his handling of the budget. While responding to criticism that he had favoured American financial interests by removing a tax on Canadian shares sold to non-residents, he left the impression that there were a couple of business "special advisors" working in his department as consultants, and that these consultants had enjoyed privileged and illegitimate knowledge of the content of the budget before the sensitive tax decision. Gordon eventually apologized on 24 June for having created a "misunderstanding" (Canada, House, 24 June 1963, 1498).

The Albertan, Hays, on the other hand, was a steady problem: his absence from the House in connection with his activities as a cattle auctioneer and as a civic politician was often remarked on (a breach of House rules). The Opposition repeatedly suggested that the portfolio was being run in Hays's name by an eastern minister.[8] In comparison, only one of Hays's control ministers, Postmaster Azellus Denis, attracted much unfavourable attention. In December 1963, there was a dispute about a list of approved consultants to the Post Office for which he was allegedly responsible, and which happened to include a number of Liberals who had been defeated in the recent election (Canada, House, 18 December 1963, 6075–76). In comparison to the steadiness of the supply of problems from Hays, the Denis scandal was less significant.

If Lamontagne was the favoured target of Mr. Diefenbaker, Erik Nielsen would hound Favreau. As early as May 1964, Nielsen was calling for the resignation of Mr. Favreau for a variety of reasons. Then in the fall, a bone with some meat on it fell into the House of Commons. It was alleged, in a confused context of Hal Banks, drug traffic, bail and possible extradition of an offender to the U.S., that a bribe had been offered to someone in Favreau's office (Favreau being the Minister of Justice) by an official (exempt staff) working in the office of the Minister of Citizenship and Immigration (Tremblay).

Nielsen and Diefenbaker orchestrated a campaign of destruction of the Justice Minister throughout the last week of November, using the Justice Estimates as a vehicle. They proposed to reduce the departmental budget in order to censure Favreau's handling of the alleged bribe. Then, Diefenbaker, building upon the idea that funds from unions associated with Banks were exactly the same as a direct personal payment (that is, a bribe) from Banks, urged the Liberals to name the six Quebec ministers who were the creatures of Hal Banks.

Diefenbaker used the House of Commons as though it were a court, arguing as the lawyer for the prosecution, weaving together hints and presumptions. He did this in the absence of standards of evidence, due process or a disinterested judge to weigh the evidence. (See the testimony for 26 November 1964: 10560–72.) The guilt of the ministers' assistants simply had to be assumed as a building block in order to create a case that could reach ministers, so this was done.[9] Then, in a *coup de théâtre*, Nielsen alleged that his office telephone lines had been tapped because of his dedication to the exposure of these scandals (ibid., 10575–76). From a potential image of bully and muckraker, motivated by anti-French antagonism, he transformed himself into an embattled figure, courageously standing against the power of the state apparatus. Bryce Mackasey, whose decency in the event has never been adequately celebrated, was alone in speaking about the dilemma of the officials. He pleaded with MPs to take a little care with the allegations against officials, because they were prevented from defending their actions in the House. As Mackasey deplored, much of the press reported every new presumption as factually true (ibid., 10583–85).

A few months later, in February 1965, the Dupuis case, already mentioned above, came to public attention. There was an RCMP investigation, and Dupuis resigned. In a reply to a rub-it-in question from Diefenbaker on 16 February Pearson, alluding to Diefenbaker's own handling of the Courtemanche case, scored a point: "The honourable gentleman resigned. He was not appointed to the Senate." A couple of days later, in an accusation that apparently came to nothing, the Opposition accused the Minister of Veterans Affairs, an experienced minister, of having taken money for exercising influence. As the months wore on, corruption was increasingly the main theme: the motion for adjournment of debate and almost any other occasion was used to ask for debates on the grounds of the corruption of the government, and occasionally accusations were made outside the House. Walter Dinsdale, for example, made some remarks on television which Pearson challenged him to substantiate in the House (Canada, House, 18 December 1964, 11313–14, 11324).

The general election of November 1965 solved nothing as it returned a Liberal government with most of its personnel intact, and duly returned to cabinet positions. Thus the stories of Lamontagne, Favreau and Tremblay could be pursued to their resignations. They were finished politically, the health of two of them fatally broken. Trudeau attracted some criticism in the Justice portfolio, and there were several calls for his resignation and a condemnation of his personal style. But it cannot be said that either he or Marchand, or their control ministers, were given much attention by the Opposition.

In the second session the mood changed, almost as though the House wanted to draw back from the viciousness of the first session. Pearson stepped down as Prime Minister in favour of Trudeau. Diefenbaker was replaced by Robert Stanfield as Conservative leader. The House received the news of the death of René Tremblay. Gordon made way for Sharp in Finance, and Pickersgill, the epitome of everything the Conservative parliamentary party had hated in the earlier Liberal style, resigned to accept the plum of the chairmanship of the Canadian Transportation Commission. As the still-seatless Stanfield, the new PC leader, watched from the gallery, T.C. Douglas rounded out the themes of the era in his farewell to Pickersgill, the archetypical Liberal administrative politician: "I think it was Senator Chubby Power who said that a member of parliament could only get out of politics in one of two ways, either by dying or by being defeated, and the first was so final and the second so humiliating. However, Mr. Pickersgill has managed to find a third way. It is not every member who can write his own ticket or draft the bill for his own final haven of rest" (Canada, House, 25 September 1967, 2400).

In summary, one can say that the review of the qualitative indicators on general performance pertaining to this ministry shows that the novice politician-minister did open the government to considerable trouble. This occurred because the Opposition had decided to exploit the issue of "integrity" and to capitalize upon the ineptness of the novice ministers, using their own parliamentary experience to exploit every opportunity and gain momentum. This concentration was, in effect, at the expense of a sustained interest in the substance of government policy. In any event, these two Parliaments demonstrated that a parliamentary party is indeed capable of being mobilized to stamp out what it sees as dilettantism in politics to devastating effect.

Trudeau Governments

Cabinet Appointments and Resignations

The general election of 25 June 1968 was another election with, for Canada, relatively low turnover (50 of 264 seats changing parties). In forming his first Cabinet, Mr. Trudeau worked conservatively, largely from the resources of the 75 returned Liberal seats. Central Canadian ministers were chosen exclusively from "returned" ranks. His "amateur" ministers were Donald Jamieson from Newfoundland (who had entered the House in a by-election in 1966), James Richardson from Winnipeg and Otto Lang, Saskatoon–Humboldt. Lang was initiated as a Minister without Portfolio. No one new appeared at mid-government.

Similar care was shown in cabinet making after the general election of fall 1972, which returned a minority to the Liberals. The only inexperienced ministers of this government were Marc Lalonde and Jeanne Sauvé. Both were from Quebec, and both were appointed to ministerial office over a strong contingent of experienced members from the 55 returned Liberal seats. Lalonde was not of the "civil servant" species hated by the Tories, but rather a party activist who had served as a policy adviser to the Prime Minister before becoming his principal secretary (not to be confused with parliamentary secretaries) from 1968 to 1972. His first cabinet post was the department of National Health and Welfare. Jeanne Sauvé, a beginner in the sense Lalonde was not, was initiated more gradually with the position of Minister of State for Science and Technology. Thus, one can say that Mr. Trudeau deviated from caution only to bring in a trusted colleague and to increase the representation of women in Cabinet.

Even with a small majority Mr. Trudeau did not become adventurous. Following the general election of 1974, building a huge Cabinet of 39, he brought in only two neophytes. These were Anthony Abbott of Mississauga and Iona Campagnolo from British Columbia. Geography clearly did not force Trudeau's hand in Abbott's appointment, as he had 36 retained seats in Ontario. It is as likely that gender as geography forced his hand in Campagnolo's appointment, because 8 BC Liberal seats had been retained, of which a couple were held by members who had experience in the House.

Trudeau's caution seems to have paid off. Of all seven inexperienced politicians he appointed to Cabinet in all three of his governments, only one was to resign from an active cabinet: James Armstrong Richardson resigned, not in difficulty, but for policy reasons in November 1976 after having served many years in a Trudeau government.

A review of resignations of experienced politician-ministers from the Trudeau government shows 6 from the first government and 11 from the third.

From the first government, Paul Hellyer and Eric Kierans resigned for policy reasons, two ministers quit to accept offers of OIC appointments and two quit for health reasons. No minister resigned from the second government.

In the third government there was considerably more trouble. Two ministers resigned on individual ministerial responsibility: André Ouellet and John Munro, both for showing too little respect for the independence and the dignity of the judicial system. One minister, Francis Fox, resigned in the middle of a storm of outrage over a moral question: he had falsely signed a husband's name on a formal medical permission for an abortion to be performed on the wife. Jean Marchand left for policy reasons, and two other ministers, John Turner and Bryce Mackasey, not openly admitting policy differences, left respectively to return to the practice of law and to contest a provincial election. Two ministers, Sharp and Drury, as noted above, left saying that their work was finished, and two others, Donald Macdonald and Ron Basford, left for personal reasons. Only one OIC appointment was offered, to Gérard Pelletier.

A summary of the 11 years of the first three Trudeau governments (table 7.A1) shows the balance sheet. Two ministers erred with regard to the system of justice and resigned on individual ministerial responsibility. Four explicitly refused Mr. Trudeau's leadership, as noted, with other reasons being offered in a couple of cases, for a total of 18 resignations during the period.

Qualitative Performance Indicators

All three of Trudeau's novice-politician ministers in the first government seem to have succeeded uneventfully. One of Jamieson's experienced control ministers, however, did not have a calm Parliament. Eric Kierans served as Postmaster General during much of this government, and there were many remarks censuring his performance in handling a postal strike, disputes, rural post office closings and postal rates. There were a number of calls for his resignation (he later resigned as communications minister). Lang attracted some fire as the minister for the Wheat Board. Almost as much attention was given to Marc Lalonde, at that point still in the Prime Minister's Office, on the grounds that he was becoming too powerful in the Liberal party. Other developments included the creation of the "Minister of State" title. Sauvé was the first to occupy one of these positions, effectively a job for a junior minister but nonetheless carrying cabinet status.

The next government was smooth sailing for Jeanne Sauvé as well as for Marc Lalonde. The Parliament is notable perhaps mainly for the emergence of Thomas Cossitt (PC, Leeds) who began his trademark inquiries into the Prime Minister's expenditures. The persistence of his questioning changed the whole look of the *Debates* index, from that time forward, to show massive clusters of page references for the expenditures of the PM, cost of his cars and residences and so on, and for the PMO.

By the third Trudeau government, the Opposition's gloves were off with regard to Sauvé, and several calls for her resignation and remarks about her incompetence were made. Lalonde's absenteeism from the House was brought into the record. It is, of course, to be expected that Lalonde would be a continuing subject of interest to the Opposition, if only because of his power as Quebec minister and his position as Trudeau's close counsellor. Neither Iona Campagnolo nor Anthony Abbott had an easy time, probably as much because the temper of Parliament was souring as because of their own performances. Broadbent, for example, called for Campagnolo's resignation on 5 December 1978 on the basis of the Auditor General's comments on the management of Loto Canada ("Iona in Wonderland"). Abbott was said to be too light to hold down the geography of Toronto. But any shortcomings of Abbott and Campagnolo looked insignificant in the light of the resignation of Abbott's experienced pair, Francis Fox (Canada, House, 30 January 1978, 2350).

Of the inexperienced ministers who began cabinet duty in the earlier Trudeau governments, most continued to perform well. Lang did, however, provide transportation on a Department of National Defence aircraft to his children's nanny, and Jamieson was accused of a possible conflict of interest in reference to his radio stations in Newfoundland. In general, a study of the entries in the indexes and a skimming of the *Debates* lead to two general conclusions about the first Trudeau ministry. It was a considerable success because of the caution and intelligence with which cabinets were made of the available parliamentary party: actually, the best attempt in the Liberal party's history. Second, in seeming contradiction, the ministry witnessed the absolute end of civility as even a minor tradition in Canadian politics. Nothing, certainly not a reading of references to earlier prime ministers and of Commons *Debates* up to this ministry, could prepare the reader for the meanness of the references to Mr. Trudeau that occur through the period, mounting in frequency and vulgarity toward the end.

Thus, one has an apparent paradox. Trudeau's ministry, in fact, was a relatively clean administration, with such scandals as there were taking place largely in the politics-security area rather than emerging from conflicts of interest or ministerial bungling. Frequent probes regarding solidarity led nowhere; the dissident ministers left rather suddenly and neatly: this is the very model of cabinet solidarity. Yet, the impression created by the critical focus of the parliamentary opposition was one of an illegitimate and weak leadership addicted to luxury, a leadership with connections to foreign ideologies and communist states. The few novice politicians that Trudeau allowed himself as ministers were in general successful, at least in comparison to their controls.

Clark Government

The election of 22 May 1979 saw a Conservative minority government with 70 Conservative seats returned. When the 31st Parliament convened in October, it was greeted by a Cabinet which included four novice ministers. All were from Ontario; in fact, three from Toronto were drawn from the 25 gained seats rather than the 16 PC returned seats. Thus it is a moot point as to whether Clark had to bow to political geography. Between the opening of the session and its end in December, there was little controversy to distinguish the new ministers from the more experienced controls, save perhaps the level of controversy caused by de Cotret's elevation to the Senate, now, of course, known to be temporary. By the time the government fell, the Liberals had barely cleared their throats: there was a serious concern about how to handle access to papers of the previous government for the ongoing RCMP inquiry (Macdonald Commission), and they were eager to let their doubts be known regarding Mr. Clark's abilities as a leader, thinking perhaps that the Conservatives might need assistance. There were no resignations from the Clark government while it was active.

Pierre Elliott Trudeau: Fourth Government

Ministerial Appointments and Resignations
In the snap election of 18 February 1980, the Liberals returned with 147 of 282 seats. Mr. Trudeau had 32 retained seats from Ontario and 67 from Quebec, but many of the most valued members of the old team had retired. Although he had some strength in the Maritimes, he had almost none in the West. Five novice-politician cabinet ministers were appointed from the seats gained in the election: two men from Toronto, the mandatory Quebec anglophone from Westmount, an Ontario woman and a Quebec woman. None of the inexperienced ministers appointed by Mr. Trudeau during his fourth government resigned during that government.

Of experienced ministers, none resigned on individual ministerial responsibility because of a portfolio-related error, but Roger Simmons did resign in 1983 for personal financial reasons. (Simmons had experience in the Newfoundland legislature as well as several years in the federal House of Commons.) In effect, this was another near-scandal-free government, in terms of personal disasters brought on by individual ministers.

Qualitative Performance Indicators

Between 1980 and 1983, none of the new ministers attracted concentrated negative comment. Judith Erola, Minister of State for Mines, was requested to resign on 18 November 1982 because of the cost of maps, and Donald Johnston attracted some criticism for cutting back salaries of ministerial staff. Erola's control minister, the experienced politician Lloyd Axworthy, attracted more criticism than the five neophyte politician-ministers together. Hardly one Conservative missed out on calling for Axworthy's resignation. The majority of calls for resignation arose from Axworthy's identity as Minister Responsible for the Status of Women in response to public criticism of him by Doris Anderson when she slammed the door on their past collaboration on the status of women. Mr. Trudeau resolutely left all to defend themselves, speaking only on behalf of Senator Austin, another Erola control minister. Austin was heading the Ministry of State for Social Development and representing the West in Cabinet.

As in his previous government, Mr. Trudeau himself was the target of accusations: he had communist sympathies, hired communists, visited communist countries, avoided war service, was creating a corporate state, was a dictator, stupidly arrogant, a liar, out of touch with the economic situation and a poseur (he also sat for Yousuf Karsh). More than a dozen Conservatives requested, suggested or demanded his resignation. Tom Cossitt, to his last breath, kept track of Trudeau's two Cadillacs. (Cossitt died on 15 March 1982, and his widow, Jennifer, won his seat in a by-election in October 1982.)

The second session of 1983–84 was more of the same. Senator Austin attracted attention in the general disapproval of the creation of the Canadian Development Corporation Company and its later manoeuvres. Among experienced ministers, Mr. Turner drew Mr. Clark's fire for his potential for being in conflict-of-interest situations because of his memberships on certain boards. As the session closed, there was excitement about the alleged existence of a "Mulroney file" in Trudeau's PMO.[10] The file, the Conservatives maintained, had been put together by the Liberals, using taxpayers' resources in order to discredit the incoming prime minister. The Conservatives were thus anticipating a Liberal onslaught on their leader of much the same character as the one they had mounted against Trudeau.

To conclude, the inexperienced ministers caused little pain during this government which, although it lasted for four years, had the character of a pause in Canadian political life. Two impressions emerge. The steadiness and character of personal attacks on Trudeau blunted the House's sensibilities to vicious language and gamesmanship, making it seem quite normal to attribute the most vile characteristics and motives to one's partisan opponents. These attacks against their leader, it seems, also indoctrinated the Liberals with a motive of revenge.

Mulroney Governments

Ministerial Appointments and Resignations

The 1984 election was a great victory for the Progressive Conservatives, who won 211 of 282 seats. One hundred and one of these were returned seats, but only one of these was from Quebec. The Liberals retained only 39 seats, being defeated in 108 of their previous ridings, and the NDP regained 22 seats. The total of changing seats in the House in this election was 120, for more than 40 percent new seats and, of course, a considerably higher percentage of MPs new to the House.

For the first time in Canadian history, Canadians found themselves with a prime minister who himself qualified as a parliamentary neophyte. Mr. Mulroney was first elected to the House in a by-election on 29 August 1983, and began his cabinet experience with the job of Prime Minister on 17 September 1984. He appointed a large Cabinet, which emphasized the need for novice politicians. In the Cabinet of the first session, 33rd Parliament, there were 15 "amateur" ministers of whom 4 were women. It should be noted that the Mulroney cabinets have contained more women than ever before (see the Appendix), and for the first time in difficult portfolios.

Obviously, Mr. Mulroney could not have appointed experienced Quebec politicians to Cabinet: he had only one experienced member among the 58 Quebec seats. While there was a wide choice between the novice Quebec members, the backgrounds and talents of only a few were well known to Mr. Mulroney, most having been recently recruited to stand for the Conservative party. In Ontario, there could not have been any real need to appoint new members to ministerial positions, unless on the elastic geography criterion, because there were 37 seats returned from that province. There were several experienced members available from Toronto alone whom he bypassed. There were also alternatives to both Stewart McInnes and Bernard Valcourt in the Maritimes.

Mr. Mulroney stayed with his basic line-up through the second session, with one major exception. This was the dazzling entry to Cabinet of Lucien Bouchard (Lac-Saint-Jean) as Secretary of State. Mr. Bouchard was named to Cabinet a couple of months before he was elected in June 1988. A sitting member resigned to make way, a rare manoeuvre in modern Canadian politics, except, of course, in the case of party leaders.[11]

Of the total of five resignations that took place during the first session of Mr. Mulroney's first Parliament, only one inexperienced minister resigned. This was Suzanne Blais-Grenier, who resigned in December 1985 from the position of Minister of State for Transport.

Of the four experienced politicians who resigned, three were on the basis of individual ministerial responsibility. John Fraser, who had been in the House from 1972, offered his resignation because of a personal act of maladministration in the portfolio; in fact, he was the only minister in the period 1949–90 to do so. He had overruled a decision of Fisheries inspectors to keep some tuna off the market because they judged it to be too old, although still safe to consume. Sinclair Stevens, a politician-businessman-lawyer who had been elected continuously from 1972, was brought down by the House of Commons for being in conflict of interest in his portfolio, Regional Industrial Expansion. Robert C. Coates's resignation as Minister of National Defence was accepted for conduct showing a lack of security-related judgement given his position: he had passed an evening at a nightclub in West Germany in dubious company. Coates had been in the House continuously since 1957. Neither Coates nor Stevens were candidates in the 1988 election, but Fraser was later fully rehabilitated. He became the first elected Speaker of the House in 1986 when the rules on the speakership were changed, a position to which he was re-elected after the general election of 1988. The final resignation of this session was that of Marcel Masse, for an alleged violation of the electoral law. Masse was eventually found not guilty, and re-entered Cabinet. (Masse qualifies as an experienced member. Although he was first elected to the House of Commons in 1984, he had earlier won two elections to the Quebec assembly.)

Later in the first Mulroney government, two of the novice politician-ministers who had been appointed to Cabinet in the first session ran into grave political difficulties. These were André Bissonnette, who was brought down by the House from the position of Minister of State for Transport for alleged land speculation in his riding, allegedly made possible by insider knowledge gained in Cabinet (although he was eventually found not guilty when his case came to trial), and Michel Côté, who had to offer his resignation in the midst of a storm over allegations of conflict of interest for having accepted a large personal loan while Minister of Supply and Services.

Of experienced politicians, Roch LaSalle, who had been a member of the House since the general election of 1968, was eventually retired because of repeated allegations of influence peddling. David Crombie was the only minister since 1980 to leave Cabinet to take up a patronage job. Crombie, although he was relatively new to the federal House, had been mayor of Toronto.

The election of 1988 returned another Conservative majority; 124 of the Conservatives' seats of 1984 were returned to them. The Liberals did somewhat better overall than in the previous election but still retained only 20 of their 60-odd seats.[12]

Resignations after the re-election (to date, October 1990) were by ministers who had been appointed to Cabinet in the previous government without much experience. Bernard Valcourt's resignation in August 1989 is probably the oddest in Canadian politics. Valcourt had an accident on his motorcycle while he was driving under the influence of alcohol late at night on a deserted road. He apparently was having no difficulty, at least until he was chased by a police car. In practical terms, he needed time out of Cabinet to recover from his injuries. Jean Charest, who had been appointed without House experience in the first Mulroney government, was forced to offer his resignation in January 1990 on the basis of individual ministerial responsibility. He had telephoned a judge regarding a case relevant to his portfolio as Minister of State for Fitness and Amateur Sport. Lucien Bouchard resigned in June 1990 for solidarity reasons. Bouchard, frustrated and disappointed with the failure of English Canada to accommodate the Meech Lake Accord and allow constitutional reform that acknowledged Quebec's distinctiveness in the federation, quit to form a secessionist movement in the House of Commons (and then sustained the Conservatives in power).

Qualitative Performance Indicators
The resignations having been noted, the task here is to attempt to characterize the performance of novice politician-ministers and the mood of the House in more general terms.

In the first session of the first government, Barbara McDougall's resignation was called for on several occasions for reasons to do with her portfolio as Minister of State for Privatization (the failures of the Northland Bank and the Canadian Commercial Bank). One of her control ministers, however, Marcel Masse, actually did have to resign. The

Liberal "rat pack" (Sheila Copps, John Nunziata and Don Boudria, all elected to the House of Commons in 1984, Copps and Boudria having experience in the Ontario Legislature) made up for numbers with energy. With the occasional boost from the NDP, the rat pack turned the tables on the Conservatives. The three subjected Prime Minister Brian Mulroney to a version of the irreverent and highly personal attack to which Mr. Trudeau had been subjected. Mr. Mulroney had fulsomely promised to put a stop to conflict-of-interest situations in government, to refrain from patronage and to govern modestly, promises which provided a focus for the rat pack's investigations.

One need only look at the index under "References" for Mr. Mulroney in 1984–86 to get the idea of the style of accusation to which he was subject: his personal expenses were high, the level of public mistrust was high, he ran money-raising clubs (the 500 Clubs) to bring in funds for the party and dispensed patronage in return, and his travel expenses – subsidized by the public and the Conservative party – were spectacular. Any debate became an opportunity. MP Brian Tobin, for example, worked a nice attack on the Prime Minister's two-airplane Asian trip into a discussion of the *Canada Shipping Act*: "They [ministers] do not ride the buses any more ... While the rest of us are wondering whether Air Canada will land in our riding ... the Prime Minister is taking an L-1011 to Europe. Flying along at a slower pace behind the L-1011 ... is a Hercules aircraft loaded with two trucks and video gear to take pictures of the Prime Minister ... It is a Trojan Horse for the people of Canada to have a peek at the emperor's entourage and the presidential travelling style of the Prime Minister" (Canada, House, 12 June 1986, 14284).

In the second session, Patricia Carney and Roch LaSalle, the experienced control ministers for novice-minister Bissonnette, both came in for a good amount of criticism. Carney was targeted as Minister of International Trade during the free trade negotiations. LaSalle came under fire for fund-raising activities. The overlapping Bissonnette and LaSalle cases were handled together by the opposition parties in an interesting way: a number of MPs, sometimes from both opposition parties, seemed to work together quite closely through a variety of procedural strategies to force the Prime Minister into a stance of almost constant defensiveness. The goal appeared to be to get Mr. Mulroney to say that the reason for his different treatment of the Bissonnette and LaSalle cases was that LaSalle was a long-time Quebec fund-raiser: that is, that he condoned LaSalle because he needed him, but could afford to let Bissonnette go.

Another inexperienced minister, Benoît Bouchard, performed comparatively smoothly. Certainly, he made calmer progress than his control minister, Walter McLean, who was criticized extensively for his performance as Secretary of State, in particular in connection with the citizenship courts.

Over the second half of the first government, references to Mr. Mulroney in the House did not improve. He was called a branch-plant manager, alternately fearful but presidential in temperament. No fewer than five automobiles were devoted to his purely local needs, and his children's nanny was allegedly on the public payroll. His "advance" from the Progressive Conservative party for decorating the Prime Minister's residence was flagged as a possible conflict of interest, and the Deputy Assistant Registrar General was required to make a statement.[13]

As for Lucien Bouchard, he was welcomed to his position as Secretary of State in the second session with allegations that the sitting member who had made his seat vacant for the Bouchard by-election had been bribed to do so, and that the by-election had been bought for Mr. Bouchard by a campaign costing as much as $2 million, part of it public money. Mr. Rodriguez saw an insult to other Quebec members in Bouchard's appointment: "The Prime Minister had to go to Paris to get the ambassador to run in Lac-Saint-Jean to save the Government's skin in Quebec. What message is he giving to the eunuchs in the back-benches who have been elected from that part of the country? ... You fellows will never make it to Cabinet. You were overlooked" (Canada, House, 20 June 1988, 6602).

As the session drew to its end, Suzanne Blais-Grenier made a number of allegations about a "kickback" system in government. Mr. Vincent Della Noce, another Conservative, at first seemed to share her views, but then rose in the House on 22 August 1988 to deny an *Ottawa Citizen* report of 19 August as coming from him. The Deputy Prime Minister explained on 23 August 1988 that the RCMP had interviewed Blais-Grenier, and that her remarks could not be substantiated.

The Blais-Grenier allegations dominated question period on several occasions, with senior Liberals John Turner and Robert Kaplan and senior NDP members joining the more junior Liberals. Sheila Copps, in a debate on the conflict-of-interest legislation, summed up the Liberals' point of view:

> I can understand why the Members of the Conservative Party are so touchy on this issue ... the conflict of interest legislation that is before this House remains an absolute farce so long as the Prime Minister (Mr. Mulroney) refuses to accept his responsibilities concerning the Hon. Member for York–Simcoe [Mr. Stevens]. I did not say that you had an option. I did not set myself up as the patron goddess of purity,

as did the Prime Minister in the debate in 1984. But in fact, it was not the Liberal Party, it was J.M.S. Careless, an eminent Canadian historian, who, when writing about the history of this Government over the last four years, said that it was the first time in the history of Canada that the tone of patronage had changed. In the past, he wrote, Members were trying to do things for their ridings. In this case, you have clear-cut situations of members of the Government, of the Conservative Party, using their parliamentary privilege to fatten their own pocketbooks, to take advantage and to receive personal gain. (Canada, House, 1 September 1988, 19148)

To sum up, of the inexperienced ministers of the second Mulroney government, two (besides Mr. Mulroney himself) had very difficult parliaments. Mr. Charest had to resign: his control minister received no negative comment. Mr. Lucien Bouchard was the other minister under close scrutiny. Everything about his performance was noted, from his office renovations to his absenteeism from the House and, of course, his performance as Environment Minister. Opposition Environment critic Sheila Copps provided a subject-by-subject "report card" for Mr. Bouchard's five months as Minister of the Environment on 8 June 1989. Overall, the inexperienced ministers were more of a general burden upon the government than were the experienced ministers.

Finally, the Mulroney ministry marks the first time that the Liberal party undertook the same partisan focus on a prime minister as had the Conservatives at the end of the Trudeau government. Further, they improved their tactics: an attack is more effective when conducted by several MPs than by one or two, because a multiplicity of speakers creates an impression that condemnation is widespread and a matter of banal public knowledge. The television viewer sees one person after another rise to their feet to condemn some shameful act: it must have happened.

During this period, there appeared to be a markedly decreased opposition attention to the question of cabinet cohesion on policy, and, in fact, a catholic approach to policy by the government: only Blais-Grenier and Lucien Bouchard could not be accommodated.

CONCLUSIONS

Resignations

Are inexperienced ministers more of a risk to a prime minister attempting to form a Cabinet than ministers with experience in the House of Commons? Of a total of 412 appointments studied in the 14 governments,

57 appointees (54 individuals) had two or less years of experience as a backbench Member of Parliament. During the 41-year period 1949–90, there were a total of 60 resignations by 58 individuals. (Lionel Chevrier and Walter Gordon each resigned twice.) Of these 60 resignations, a grand total of 21 were politically significant resignations: 13 ministers resigned on a version of individual ministerial responsibility and 8 ministers resigned on grounds of policy disagreements. Of the resignations dealing with individual ministerial responsibility, one was offered for a personal administrative-type error in the portfolio; nine were due to alleged acts unworthy of a minister and with financial, legal or security ramifications; and three ministers were effectively caught in the trap of the Pearson minority government and were politically destroyed. Of the 13 politically significant error-related resignations, 6 came from among the 57 inexperienced ministers (Favreau, Lamontagne, Tremblay, Bissonnette, Côté and Charest) and 7 from the 355 experienced politicians (Dupuis, Ouellet, Munro, Fraser, Stevens, LaSalle and Coates).

Therefore, a conclusion that one might draw is that, of the resignations that have come about on the basis of individual ministerial responsibility (whether faults were alleged or actual), a disproportionate percentage have been by those ministers almost completely new to parliamentary politics. Almost one-half or 50 percent of all resignations on individual ministerial responsibility have arisen from our base of 57 appointments of novice politicians during the period 1949–90. One would expect, all other things being equal, only about 15 percent of resignations by novice politician-ministers, that is, the same proportion of inexperienced appointees as in all ministerial appointments in the period. Therefore, novice politician-ministers are much more likely to resign on the basis of individual ministerial responsibility than are experienced politicians.

One might look at the data from another perspective, and say that the rate of resignations on individual responsibility among inexperienced appointees is about 11 percent (six disasters from 57 neophyte appointments), while the disaster rate among experienced appointments is much less at seven disasters from a base of 355 appointments (total 412 appointments minus the 57 appointments of inexperienced persons) in the period, or 2 percent. It seems fair, therefore, to say that the parliamentary troops of the opposition find novice ministers easier game.

The risk factor for policy disagreements is not worth calculating: resignations resulting from ministers not agreeing with cabinet policy are rare to vanishing point in Canada. In contrast, about 80 percent of all British cabinet ministers who leave their cabinets do so for reasons of principle (Sutherland 1991). Nothing could form a more telling contrast between Canada and the "Mother of Parliaments" than the difference in importance given to policy as a reason for leaving an active Cabinet.

The other point that must be made is that serious political scandals involving ministers, while they are to be deplored, are rare: if one drops the Fraser resignation and the Pearson minority resignations as largely irrelevant, then only 9 of 412 ministerial appointments ended in a resignation on a serious ground under individual ministerial responsibility (less than 2 percent of all appointments). This is roughly comparable to the British record.

If the reader can forgive a change of perspective on the data, it is interesting to ask whether particular prime ministers have been particularly unlucky or lucky in the way in which *all* their cabinet appointments turned out. The "disaster rates" of prime ministers can be calculated (number of difficult resignations calculated on the base of the number of ministerial appointments they made in the cabinets sampled). St. Laurent suffered no difficult resignations and made 46 of the 412 appointments, or 11 percent; Diefenbaker suffered one problem resignation from 73 appointments, that is, 5 percent of the 21 politically significant problems enumerated from 1949 to 1990 but 17 percent of appointments; Pearson suffered four blows or 20 percent of the difficult resignations and made 55 appointments or 13 percent; Trudeau had six problems or 29 percent of the 21 difficult resignations, but made 138 of the 412 appointments or 33 percent; and Mr. Mulroney made 85 of the 412 appointments sampled (21 percent) and suffered nine of the difficult resignations or 43 percent. In summary, Pearson and Mulroney both experienced more than their share of difficult resignations. Both disproportionately used novice parliamentarians in ministerial office.

Therefore, overall, a risk-aversive prime minister would prefer to appoint experienced politicians to Cabinet if he had the choice, and he almost always does have a choice.

Qualitative Indicators

In fact, pure geography or regionalism seems to do very little to explain the particular composition of Canadian cabinets. That cabinets are regional in terms of their composition is not at issue. The point is that the need to represent the regions in Cabinet cannot often tell us why one particular individual was chosen to be a minister rather than another; the great majority of the time, a prime minister has quite a wide choice between experienced politicians representing a good variety of regions when he chooses his ministers. Of the 54 appointments of inexperienced ministers, fewer than 10 can be strongly justified on the grounds that a prime minister badly needed a neophyte to represent a particular part of the country. One can review and summarize the findings about regional ministers.

In 1957, Diefenbaker did need both Sévigny and Dorion from Quebec. In 1963, Pearson was very light in western representation, thus he probably did need Harry Hays, who made trouble for him. Pearson's government of 1963 was the first in which large numbers of neophyte politicians were made ministers. Up to this time, the Liberals had tended to drop their amateurs into the House one or two at a time: for example, Pearson himself, Sharp and Pickersgill. Nine newly elected MPs were appointed to Cabinet by Pearson, among them being Lamontagne, Favreau and Tremblay. Pearson could have chosen from among very large numbers of returned members from Quebec. (Of course, given his minority situation and the partisan spirit of the Opposition, the Opposition might well have found other weaknesses.)

In 1968, Trudeau did need Lang from Saskatoon and Richardson from Winnipeg to represent the West and also Jamieson in Newfoundland; all three eventually caused trouble in their own ways. And clearly, Mr. Mulroney did need instant ministers from Quebec in 1984, because the sole experienced parliamentarian he had at hand from that province was Roch LaSalle, for a 100 percent disappointment. Still, Mr. Mulroney had a rich choice between freshly elected Quebec members and could have avoided some problems that are obvious with hindsight, such as the matching of members with business interests with business portfolios.

In summary, the need for a regional representative qualifies as an explanation of why a neophyte is appointed less than 20 percent of the time, and almost never accounts for the selection of a particular neophyte. The need for geographical representation in Cabinet seems to be an excuse that can always be made to fit loosely with the facts.

One must now try to summarize the more nuanced qualitative differences between the performances of novice politician-ministers and experienced politician-ministers as controls, short of a resignation on individual ministerial responsibility. In objective terms, novices do not generally appear to seriously worsen in the job, over time.

When one studies the performance of novice ministers and their controls within the various ministries, it is hard to see much difference, except in the case of the Pearson and Mulroney ministries. The sole common element here appears to be that the weaknesses of the inexperienced ministers fell conveniently into a theme on which the Opposition wanted to elaborate. Pickersgill never really slipped, but he caused outrage among Conservatives because he was a civil-service transplant, a mortal sin in Conservative eyes. Prudham, on the other hand, was a novice and erred in appearance by continuing business dealings while a minister of the Crown; but still the Conservatives eventually let him off rather lightly. They were not making a campaign out of business-related integrity, possibly because they were the party of small business, or possibly because their base of power was in Prudham's West.

The Liberals, on the other hand, being the party of expertise, were consciously ready to exploit personal integrity related to business, as Copps noted in the House. Therefore, this study concludes that novice politician-ministers are *made* into liabilities by the Opposition, largely when the apparent weaknesses of novices can be blown into something that looks like a party theme. In the case of a minority government, such a juggernaut can cause great personal tragedy.

During the second half of the period under study, a form of pious outrage appears to have become the main motor of Canadian parliamentary politics. The Conservatives developed their theme of the "easy way" in the Pearson era. The caution that Trudeau exhibited in cabinet making then became a barrier to the Conservative party's attempts to gain power by discrediting the Liberals. Trudeau built cabinets conservatively, avoiding the use of new ministers generally and even inventing the Minister of State position to keep novices on the fringes of power. The response of the Opposition was to target Trudeau personally.

Also, during the Trudeau ministry, the Conservative party began explicitly to promote the idea that it offered a change of governing *team*, as distinct from policies or principles. In the Conservative view, the Liberals were a flawed team, dependent on outside interests and the civil service for personnel, while the Conservatives alone sprang from the people and were imbued with a proper respect for parliamentary government.

Perhaps because they believed their own rhetoric, the Conservative parliamentary party strategists failed to take into account that the old team of the Liberal parliamentary party was also changing quickly from 1979 to 1984: the distant experts and mandarins whom they accused of setting the party's tone were mostly gone. The new recruits were quite capable of carrying out the partisan personal attack. Mr. Mulroney seemed anxious to conciliate the Opposition as it took on one Conservative minister after another. He thus obtained quick resignations from ministers under fire: this appeared to fit with the image the Conservatives had of themselves as honourable parliamentarians. But instead of soothing the Opposition, the resignations confirmed its strategy of dismantling the government *à la pièce* and fuelled the perception by the public that the government was one of inept rascals.

A few cases are enough to create the stereotypes that the public does appear to credit.[14] To become the party of the "easy way," the Liberals only needed six or eight mandarins.[15] To transmute itself from the party of high parliamentary morality to the party of self-enrichment by venal businessmen, the Conservatives needed only two or three clumsy ministers, assisted, of course, by a number of scandals among parliamentary secretaries and backbenchers (Simpson 1989) – and to be in power.

There are signs that the government recognizes the emptiness of these politics without knowing how to stop: in the Throne Speech in May 1991, the government noted that overzealous partisanship and party discipline had led to "empty posturing and feigned outrage" and promised to try to devise measures to alleviate the displays of partisan revulsion.[16] The McGrath reforms of the House of Commons in 1986 were also premised on lessening partisanship, but it appeared that the Liberals were not ready to embrace a regime of "turn the other cheek" until they had taken their revenge.

Although it is a giant inference to move from the qualitative impressions generated in research of this kind to suggestions for reform, it does appear that two suggestions can be made. First, every means should be taken to encourage and assist the political parties to develop policy on a continual basis. This might involve assuring the party organizations of a minimum fund between elections to develop their ideas. Second, we could try to increase the longevity of parliamentary careers in order to develop individuals who are professional parliamentary politicians with a good knowledge of policy issues and with policy preferences. The parties might try to increase the size of a seasoned core of parliamentary politicians by changing "territorial" norms to encourage talented career politicians to move to safe seats in ridings which are not their home territories.[17] Politicians might, therefore, be more prepared for office when it is offered. In the absence of a politics of ideas, Canadians seem almost sure to have a politics of outrage.

APPENDIX

Table 7.A1
Ministerial resignations (1949–90)

Time Period / Duration / Prime Minister / Party	1949–57 6.6 years St. Laurent Liberal		1957–63 5.8 years Diefenbaker Conservative		1963–68 4 years Pearson/Trudeau Liberal		1968–79 11 years Trudeau Liberal		1980–84 4.3 years Trudeau Liberal		1984–90 6.6 years Mulroney Conservative		Total	
Formal reasons	Inexp	Exp	Inexp	Exp	Inexp	Exp	Inexp	Exp	Inexp	Exp	Inexp	Exp	Inexp	Exp
1. Error in portfolio	—	—	—	—	—	—	—	—	—	—	—	Fraser	0	1
2. Misconduct in office														
(a) Financial	—	—	—	—	—	Dupuis	—	—	—	—	Bissonnette Côté	Stevens LaSalle	(a) 2	(a) 3
(b) Legal interference	—	—	—	—	—	—	—	Ouellet Munro	—	—	Charest	—	(b) 1	(b) 2
(c) Security	—	—	—	—	—	—	—	—	—	—	—	Coates	(c) 0	(c) 1
3. Minority government victim	—	—	—	—	Lamontagne Tremblay Favreau	—	—	—	—	—	—	—	3	0
4. Solidarity	—	—	—	Harkness	—	LaMarsh	Richardson	Marchand Hellyer Kierans	—	—	Blais-Grenier L. Bouchard	—	3	5
5. Private misconduct	—	—	—	—	—	—	—	Fox	—	Simmons	Valcourt	—	1	2

Table 7.A1 (cont'd)
Ministerial resignations (1949–90)

Formal reasons	1949–57 6.6 years St. Laurent Liberal		1957–63 5.8 years Diefenbaker Conservative		1963–68 4 years Pearson/Trudeau Liberal		1968–79 11 years Trudeau Liberal		1980–84 4.3 years Trudeau Liberal		1984–90 6.6 years Mulroney Conservative		Total	
	Inexp	Exp	Inexp	Exp	Inexp	Exp	Inexp	Exp	Inexp	Exp	Inexp	Exp	Inexp	Exp
6. Government appointment	–	Mayhew Fournier Rinfret Abbott Bradley Chevrier	Comtois	Pearkes Brooks	–	Chevrier Denis Bendickson Pickersgill	–	Cadieux Benson Pelletier	–	–	–	Crombie	1	16
7. Private sector opportunity	–	Claxton	–	–	–	–	–	Turner	–	–	–	–	0	2
8. Task finished	–	McKinnon	–	–	–	Macdonald Gordon	–	Drury Sharp	–	–	–	–	0	5
9. Health	–	–	–	Courtemanche Macdonnell	–	Cardin	–	McIlraith Greene	–	–	–	–	0	5
10. Private reasons, not explained	–	–	–	–	–	Deschatelets	–	Macdonald Basford	–	–	–	–	0	3
11. Other	–	–	–	–	Gordon Winters	–	–	Mackasey	–	–	–	Masse	1	3
Total	0	8	1	5	4	11	1	17	0	1	6	6	12	48

Source: Canada, Library of Parliament (1990).

DATA ON SAMPLED CABINETS[18]

Louis Stephen St. Laurent, 1949–57

First Government
Following the general election of 27 June 1949: 21st Parliament. Liberal government, with 193 of 262 seats.

Seats Retained, Gained and Lost: Of the Liberals, 113 were returned members. Six sitting members lost their seats. The Progressive Conservatives returned 37 members to their seats, losing 30 and gaining 4 seats that had formerly belonged to other parties. The CCF retained 9 seats, gained 3 and lost 20. Social Credit held on to 10 seats. The total of changed seats for the Parliament was 76, or nearly 30 percent.[19]

First Session, 15 September 1949 to 10 December 1949
Cabinet membership: 21
Women: 0
Inexperienced ministers: 2
  • Milton Fowler Gregg, York–Sunbury, Veterans Affairs
  • Lester Bowles Pearson, Algoma East, External Affairs (previously Under Secretary of State for External, first appointed to Cabinet as Secretary of State for External in 1948, after which he won a by-election)
Parliamentary assistants: 10

Fourth Session, 30 January 1951 to 9 October 1951
Cabinet membership: 20 (2 new appointments)
Women: 0
Inexperienced ministers: 1
  • George Prudham, Edmonton West, Mines
Parliamentary assistants: 13

Second Government
Following the general election of 10 August 1953: 22nd Parliament. Liberal government, with 171 of 265 seats.

Seats Retained, Gained and Lost: Of Liberals, 148 seats were retained and 10 were gained. The Progressive Conservatives returned 31 of their members and elected 18 new members. The CCF retained 11 seats, gained 11 and lost 1. Social Credit held on to 9 of the seats they had in the previous Parliament and gained 5 from other parties. The total of changed seats in the election was 43, or 16 percent.

First Session, 12 November 1953 to 20 November 1954
Cabinet membership: 21
Women: 0

Inexperienced ministers: 1
  • John Pickersgill, Bonavista–Twillingate, Secretary of State (previously
    Clerk of the Privy Council, Secretary to Cabinet, in PMO 1937–52)
Parliamentary assistants: 13

Second Session, 7 January 1955 to 28 July 1955
Cabinet membership: 20 (2 new appointments)
Women: 0
Inexperienced ministers: 0
Parliamentary assistants: 11

John George Diefenbaker, 1957–63

First Government
Following the general election of 10 June 1957: 23rd Parliament. Conservative
minority government, with 112 of 265 seats.

Seats Retained, Gained and Lost: The Conservatives came into power with 47 of
their seats retained and 65 new seats gained. The Liberals held on to 100 seats
and gained 5 from other parties. CCF held on to 19 seats and gained 6. Social
Credit retained 15 seats and gained 4 from other parties. The figure for changed
seats in this election was 83, or about 30 percent.

First Session, 14 October 1957 to 1 February 1958
Cabinet membership: 22
Women. 1
Inexperienced ministers: 2 (no women)
  • Paul Comtois, Nicolet–Yamaska, Mines
  • Sidney Earle Smith, Hastings–Frontenac, External Affairs (first appointed
    in 1957, winning a by-election to enter the House of Commons later that
    year)
Parliamentary assistants: 13

Second Government
Following the general election of 31 March 1958: 24th Parliament. Conservative
government, with 208 of 265 seats. This victory represented nearly 80 percent
of all seats in the House of Commons.

Seats Retained, Gained and Lost: The Progressive Conservative victory resulted
in 108 seats retained and 100 gained. The Liberals retained only 45 seats, losing 60 and picking up 3 new seats. The CCF held on to 8 seats, losing 17. Social
Credit lost 19 seats. The total of changed seats was 101.

First Session, 12 May 1958 to 6 September 1958
Cabinet membership: 23
Women: 1

Inexperienced ministers: 3 (no women)
- Raymond O'Hurley, Lotbinière, Defence Production
- Paul Comtois, Nicolet–Yamaska, Mines and Technical Surveys
- Sidney Earle Smith, Hastings–Frontenac, External Affairs

Parliamentary secretaries: None

Fourth Session, 17 November 1960 to 29 September 1961
Cabinet membership: 24 (6 new appointments)
Women: 1
Inexperienced ministers: 3 (no women)
- David J. Walker, Rosedale, Public Works
- Pierre Sévigny, Longueuil, Associate Minister of National Defence
- Noel Dorion, Bellechase, Secretary of State

Parliamentary secretaries: 16

Third Government
Following the general election of 18 June 1962: 25th Parliament. Conservative minority government, with 116 of 265 seats.

Seats Retained, Gained and Lost: The Progressive Conservatives held on to 111 seats, losing 93 and making no gains. The Liberals retained 40 of the seats they had held in the last election, gaining 60. The NDP retained 8 seats and gained 12 from other parties. Social Credit also made gains, taking 30 from other parties. The total of changed seats in this election was 102, for a turnover figure of close to 40 percent.

First Session, 27 September 1962 to 5 February 1963
Cabinet membership: 22
Women: 1
Inexperienced ministers: 0
Parliamentary secretaries: 16 (1 woman)

Lester Bowles Pearson, 1963–68

First Government
Following the general election of 8 April 1963: 26th Parliament. Liberal minority government, with 129 of 265 seats.

Seats Retained, Gained and Lost: The Liberals retained 95 of the seats they had held in the previous Parliament and gained 34. The Progressive Conservatives held on to 90 seats, gaining 5 from other parties. The NDP (CCF) retained 16 seats, gaining 1. Social Credit held on to 21 seats, gaining 3 from other parties. The total of changed seats was about 16 percent.

First Session, 16 May 1963 to 21 December 1963
Cabinet membership: 26

Women: 1
Inexperienced ministers: 9 (no women)
- Walter Gordon, Davenport, Finance and Receiver General
- Mitchell Sharp, Eglinton, Trade and Commerce (previously Assistant Deputy Minister and then Deputy Minister of Trade and Commerce from 1951 to 1958)
- Arthur Laing, Vancouver South, Northern Affairs and National Resources
- Maurice Lamontagne, Outremont–Saint-Jean, President of the Privy Council
- Charles Mills Drury, Saint-Antoine–Westmount, Defence Production and Industry
- Guy Favreau, Papineau, Citizenship and Immigration
- John Robert Nicholson, Vancouver Centre, Forestry
- Harry Hays, Calgary South, Agriculture
- René Tremblay, Matapédia–Matane, Minister without Portfolio

Parliamentary secretaries: 16

Second Government

Following the general election of 8 November 1965: 27th Parliament. Liberal government, with 132 of 265 seats.

Seats Retained, Gained and Lost: The Liberal government retained 115 seats, gaining 17 and losing 13. The Conservatives retained 83, gaining 13 new seats and losing 12. The NDP held on to 16 seats and gained 1. Social Credit held on to 13 seats, gained 1 and lost 11. The total of changed seats was 38, or 14 percent.

First Session, 18 January 1966 to 8 May 1967
Cabinet membership: 29
Women: 1
Inexperienced ministers: 2 (no women)
- Jean Marchand, Langelier, Citizenship and Immigration/Manpower and Immigration
- Pierre Elliott Trudeau, Mount Royal, Justice

Parliamentary secretaries: 19 (1 woman)

Pierre Elliott Trudeau, 1968–79

First Government

Following the general election of 25 June 1968: 28th Parliament. Liberal government, with 155 of 264 seats.

Seats Retained, Gained and Lost: The Liberals retained 75 seats, gained 26 and lost 17. The Conservatives held on to 50 seats, gained 11, but lost 21. The NDP retained 10, gained 6 and lost 6 others. Social Credit held on to 5 of their old seats, gained 6 new ridings, and lost 4. The total of changed seats was 50, or just under 20 percent.

First Session, 9 September 1968 to 22 October 1969
Cabinet membership: 31
Women: 0
Inexperienced ministers: 3
- Donald Jamieson, Burin–Burgeo, Defence Production, Supply and Services and Receiver General, Transport, within first year
- James Richardson, Winnipeg South, Minister without Portfolio, Supply and Services and Receiver General
- Otto Lang, Saskatoon–Humboldt, Minister without Portfolio
Parliamentary secretaries: 18 (no women)

Second Session, 23 October 1969 to 7 October 1970
Cabinet membership: 30 (no new appointments)
Women: 0
Inexperienced ministers: 0
Parliamentary secretaries: 30 (no women)

Second Government
Following the general election of 30 October 1972: 29th Parliament. Liberal minority government, with 109 of 264 seats.

Seats Retained, Gained and Lost: The Liberals retained 105 seats, gained 4 and lost 50. The Conservatives retained 65, gained 42 and lost 7. The NDP retained 18, gained 13 and lost 4. Social Credit retained 13, gained 2 and lost 1. Total number of changed seats was 60, or 23 percent.

First Session, 4 January 1973 to 26 February 1974
Cabinet membership: 30
Women: 1
Inexperienced ministers: 2 (1 woman)
- Marc Lalonde, Outremont, National Health and Welfare (policy adviser to the PM 1967–68 and principal secretary to the PM 1968–72)
- Jeanne Sauvé, Ahuntsic, Minister of State for Science and Technology[20]
Parliamentary secretaries: 17 (no women)

Third Government
Following the general election of 8 July 1974: 30th Parliament. Liberal government, with 141 of 264 seats.

Seats Retained, Gained and Lost: The Liberals retained 107 seats, gained 34 and lost 3. The Conservatives retained 86 seats, gained 4 and lost 20. The NDP retained 15, gained 1, and lost 16. Social Credit retained 11 and lost 4. The total of changed seats was 45, or 17 percent.

First Session, 30 September 1974 to 12 October 1976
Cabinet membership: 39

Women: 3
Inexperienced ministers: 2 (1 woman)
  • Anthony Abbott, Mississauga, Consumer and Corporate Affairs
  • Iona Campagnolo, Skeena, Minister of State, Fisheries and Amateur Sport
Parliamentary secretaries: 50 (4 women)

Second Session, 12 October 1976 to 17 October 1977
Cabinet membership: 35 (3 new appointments)
Women: 3
Inexperienced ministers: 0
Parliamentary secretaries: 46 (2 women)

Charles Joseph Clark, 1979

First Government
Following the general election of 22 May 1979: 31st Parliament. Conservative
minority government, with 136 of 282 seats.

Seats Retained, Gained and Lost: The Conservatives retained 70 seats, gained
31 from other parties, and lost 7. The Liberals held on to 92 seats, gained 8, but
lost 32. The NDP retained 12, gained 8 and lost 2. Social Credit retained 5, gained
1 and lost 5. Total number of changed seats was 47, or 17 percent.

First Session, 9 October 1979 to 14 December 1979
Cabinet membership: 30
Women: 1
Inexperienced ministers: 4 (no women)
  • Robert Jarvis, Toronto–Willowdale, Minister of State for Federal-Provincial
    Relations
  • Ronald Atkey, Toronto–St. Paul's, Employment and Immigration
  • Robert de Cotret, by-election in 1978, but was defeated in the 1979 gen-
    eral election. Appointed to the Senate in June 1979 to serve as Minister of
    Industry, Trade and Commerce and Minister of State for Economic
    Development, resigning January 1980
  • Michael Wilson, Etobicoke Centre, Finance
Parliamentary secretaries: 22 (1 woman)

Pierre Elliott Trudeau, 1980–84

Fourth Government
Following the general election of 18 February 1980: 32nd Parliament. Liberal
government, with 147 of 282 seats.

Seats Retained, Gained and Lost: The Liberals retained 114 of their seats from
the previous Parliament, gained 33 and lost 2. The Conservatives retained 102,

gained 1 and lost 31. The NDP retained 21, gained 11 and lost 5. Social Credit lost 6. The total of changed seats was 45, or 16 percent.

First Session, 14 April 1980 to 30 November 1983
Cabinet membership: 35
Women: 3
Inexperienced ministers: 5 (2 women)
- Donald Johnston, St-Henri–Westmount, Minister of State for Economic Development and Science and Technology
- Judith Erola, Nickel Belt, Consumer and Corporate Affairs
- Céline Hervieux Payette, Montréal–Mercier, Minister of State Fitness and Amateur Sport
- David Paul Smith, Don Valley East, Minister of State Small Business and Tourism (previously executive assistant to Walter Gordon and John Turner)
- Roy MacLaren, Etobicoke North, Minister of State Finance (previously a foreign service officer)

Parliamentary secretaries: 27 (1 woman)

Martin Brian Mulroney, 1984–90

First Government
Following the general election of 4 September 1984: 33rd Parliament. Conservative government, with 211 of 282 seats. Although this is the largest number of Conservatives ever elected to Parliament, the victory represents 75 percent of available seats, less than the Diefenbaker victory.

Seats Retained, Gained and Lost: The Conservative victory involved retaining 101 of the seats held in the previous Parliament, gaining 110 seats from other parties, and losing only 2. The Liberals held on to 39 seats, losing 108 and gaining 1. The NDP retained 22 seats in the Conservative sweep, gained 8, and lost 10. The total of changed seats was 120, or 43 percent.

First Session, 5 November 1984 to 28 August 1986
Cabinet membership: 40
Women: 5
Inexperienced ministers: 15 (4 women)
- Brian Mulroney, Manicouagan, Prime Minister
- André Bissonnette, Saint-Jean, Minister of State Transport
- Benoît Bouchard, Roberval, Employment and Immigration
- Michel Côté, Langelier, Regional Industrial Expansion
- James Kelleher, Sault Ste. Marie, Solicitor General
- Barbara McDougall, St. Paul's, Minister of State Privatization
- Monique Vézina, Rimouski–Témiscouata, Supply and Services
- Stewart McInnes, Halifax, Public Works
- Pierre Cadieux, Vaudreuil, Labour
- Jean Charest, Sherbrooke, Minister of State Youth

- Thomas Hockin, London West, Minister of State Finance
- Monique Landry, Blainville–Deux-Montagnes, External Relations
- Bernard Valcourt, Madawaska–Victoria, Minister of State Small Business and Tourism
- Gerry Weiner, Dollard, Minister of State Immigration
- Suzanne Blais-Grenier, Montreal–Rosemont, Environment and Minister of State Transport

Parliamentary secretaries: 26 (2 women)

Second Session, 30 September 1986 to 30 September 1988
Cabinet membership: 40 (6 new appointments)
Women: 6
Inexperienced ministers: 1
- Lucien Bouchard, Lac-Saint-Jean, Secretary of State
Parliamentary secretaries: 29 (4 women)

Second Government
Following the general election of 21 November 1988: 34th Parliament. Conservative government, with 169 of 295 seats.

Seats Retained, Gained and Lost: The Conservatives retained 124 seats, gained 5 and lost 38 of the seats they had held in the previous Parliament. The Liberals retained 20 seats, gained 41 and lost 5. The NDP retained 9 seats, gained 7 and lost 4. The total of changed seats in this parliament was 53, or about 18 percent.

Cabinet as of March 1990
Cabinet membership: 39
Women: 6
Inexperienced ministers: 3
- Lucien Bouchard, by-election, 20 June 1988, Lac-Saint-Jean, Environment
- Jean Corbeil, Anjou–Rivière-des-Prairies, Labour and Minister of State Transport
- Gilles Loiselle, Langelier, Minister of State Finance (previously a civil servant in Quebec)

NOTES

1. This explanation was suggested to the author in an informal communication with Richard Johnston of the University of British Columbia.

2. Experience as a mayor of a major city was also taken into account as political experience, although experience as an alderman was not.

3. Although it might be interesting to try to do so, the analysis does not look for "non-fatal" damage, for example, in the form of demotions resulting from particular episodes or scandals. The approach here is cross-sectional

and compares House reactions to the misdeeds of inexperienced ministers and of control ministers in order to address the idea that there may be failure which does not result in resignation on individual ministerial responsibility.

4. The Indexes of the Commons *Debates* are of consistently high quality for the 40-year period reviewed for this study.

5. The Currie Report is at the origin of the much-loved but mythical auditors' finding of "horses on the payroll." The gist of the finding was that a certain job cost more to do using horses than without them, that is, with the help of machines. Waste and inefficiencies in Department of National Defence were big subjects at the time because of the recency of the war effort and the potential for corruption given the scale of the expenditure. The Currie report was allegedly suppressed at the outset, then a copy of it was "purloined" and made its way to the media, after which it was eventually tabled.

6. The term "parliamentary secretary" was at this time substituted for "parliamentary assistant": individuals holding these offices are not members of the government.

7. In making this Cabinet, Pearson achieved almost the textbook Cabinet of the time as described by Douglas Fisher: "Quebec had to have five members of the cabinet, four of whom had to be French Canadian Catholics and one an English speaking Protestant ... and ... the ministers of public works and justice had to come from Quebec" (Canada, House, 24 March 1959, 2193).

8. There are more than 30 references to Hays: see the Index for 1963.

9. The Dorion Report would eventually suggest that Favreau's worst sin was optimism.

10. See the Index for 1983–84, p. 185, for more than a dozen references to the topic.

11. See Canada, Library of Parliament (1989). The St. Laurent Liberals and the Diefenbaker Conservatives were really the last to use the technique, both with a certain frequency of success. Stuart Garson, Frederick Bradley, J.W. Pickersgill, George Marler and Lionel Chevrier were the instant ministers of the St. Laurent ministry, all winning by-elections within a couple of months of their appointments. Mr. Diefenbaker brought in Sidney Smith, Hugh Fleming and Martial Asselin. Pearson brought in only Charles Granger, and Trudeau tried and failed to bring in only Pierre Juneau. Not all of these cases had a constituency vacated for them. Neither were all necessarily completely bereft of parliamentary experience: their shared characteristic is that they had no seat in the Commons or Senate at the time that they were named to Cabinet.

12. Of the 295 members in this House, 127, or 43 percent, were elected for the first time, not greatly different from the 40 percent turnover figure for

seats. For an indication of the variety of rules possible in the subject of political arithmetic, see Robinson (1988), Belacqua (1988) and Wills (1989).

13. See the Indexes for 1986–88. Mr. Rodriguez provides a comprehensive update of Mr. Mulroney's troubles on 31 August 1988.

14. Thus it is this writer's opinion that conflict legislation could not cure the widespread public perception that Canadian politics are relatively corrupt, because it is not founded in reality. For an update on the status of federal conflict legislation, see Canada, Office of the Assistant Deputy Registrar (1990).

15. It is perhaps worth noting that, in promising to cut the numbers of civil servants in 1984, Mr. Mulroney was playing to a long-standing party theme and not merely echoing American neo-Conservatism of the time, as is often alleged.

16. See Hart (1991). Hart appreciates the irony that the speech deploring excessive partisanship should have been read in the Senate: the battle there over the GST, Hart says, "brought us nightly portrayals of such stupefying wrath that there were times I half expected Royce Frith to slap a clip into his Luger and thin those Tories out."

17. John Warren, a long-time parliamentary reporter, discusses the frequency with which leaders run in ridings other than the riding of residence in "Twists and Turns" (1990).

18. A total of 426 cabinet ministers are recorded in this list. Note that appointments are not the same as persons. Some appointees appear more than once: for example, three persons were reappointed to ministerial office after an election, still not possessing two or more full years of experience at the time of the second appointment.

19. These figures are an attempt to demonstrate the stability of the memberships of the parliamentary parties on the assumption that the only factor that matters is electoral volatility. The election statistics are from Feigert (1989). It must be noted that Feigert's figures for changing seats will always be less than other researchers' estimates of total new members to the House of Commons because Feigert's calculations, following a redistribution, are made on the basis of the seats existing in the previous election. Thus the reader should expect discrepancies: the seats retained and gained will not add up to the party's total strength as reported in the *Parliamentary Guide* because of redistributions. There were redistributions in 1948, 1952, 1966, 1976 and 1988. There will also be some divergence because seats and members are not the same thing: parties may hold seats but change candidates.

20. This is the first observed use of the Minister of State title.

REFERENCES

Belacqua, Maurizio. 1988. "Metro's 15 New Faces in Parliament." *Toronto Star*, 27 November.

Blake, Donald. 1991. "Party Competition and Electoral Volatility: Canada in Comparative Perspective." In *Representation, Integration and Political Parties in Canada*, ed. Herman Bakvis. Vol. 14 of the research studies of the Royal Commission on Electoral Reform and Party Financing. Ottawa and Toronto: RCERPF/Dundurn.

Butler, D.E., and G. Butler. 1989. "Ministerial Resignations." In *Ministerial Responsibility*, ed. Geoffrey Marshall. Oxford: Oxford University Press.

Canada. House of Commons. *Debates*. Volumes and dates as indicated.

———. Library of Parliament. Bibliographies and Compilations Branch. 1990. "Ministerial Resignations to Date." Ottawa: LOP.

———. Library of Parliament. Information and Technical Services Branch. 1989. "Ministers Named from Outside Parliament." Compilation no. 11e. Ottawa: LOP.

———. Office of the Assistant Deputy Registrar of Canada. 1990. *Conflict of Interest in Canada: A Federal, Provincial and Territorial Perspective*. Ottawa: Minister of Supply and Services Canada.

Canadian Parliamentary Guide. Published annually from 1867, by the Normandin family from 1926 to 1989, and by Info Globe from 1990.

Corry, J.A. 1946. *Democratic Government and Politics*. Toronto: University of Toronto Press.

Feigert, Frank. 1989. *Canada Votes, 1935–1988*. Durham: Duke University Press.

Ferejohn, John, and Brian Gaines. 1991. "The Personal Vote in Canada." In *Representation, Integration and Political Parties in Canada*, ed. Herman Bakvis. Vol. 14 of the research studies of the Royal Commission on Electoral Reform and Party Financing. Ottawa and Toronto: RCERPF/Dundurn.

Gwyn, Richard. 1965. *The Shape of Scandal*. Toronto: Clarke, Irwin and Company.

Hart, Matthew. 1991. "The Gripes of Wrath: Of Wild Anger, Frenzied Rage." *Globe and Mail*, 18 May.

Johnston, Richard. 1986. *Public Opinion and Public Policy in Canada*. Vol. 35 of the research studies of the Royal Commission on the Economic Union and Development Prospects for Canada. Toronto: University of Toronto Press.

Newman, Peter C. 1963. *Renegade in Power*. Toronto: McClelland and Stewart.

Porter, John. 1965. *The Vertical Mosaic: An Analysis of Social Class and Power in Canada*. Toronto: University of Toronto Press.

Robinson, Jennifer. 1988. "Rookie MPs Learn Ropes of Life on Parliament Hill." *The Gazette* (Montreal), 11 December.

Simpson, Jeffrey. 1989. *Spoils of Power: The Politics of Patronage*. Toronto: Harper and Collins.

Sutherland, S.L. 1991. "Responsible Government and Ministerial Responsibility: Every Reform Is Its Own Problem." *Canadian Journal of Political Science* 24:91–120.

Warren, John. 1990. "Twists and Turns: Leaders Can Take Strange Detours en route to House." *Ottawa Citizen*, 1 October.

Wills, Terrance. 1989. "The Changing Face of Canada's MPs." *The Gazette* (Montreal), 2 April.

8

NEW POLITICS, THE CHARTER AND POLITICAL PARTICIPATION

Neil Nevitte

C AIRNS (1990) IS UNDOUBTEDLY correct in suggesting the *Canadian Charter of Rights and Freedoms* and new patterns of population replacement combine to challenge the effectiveness of representative institutions such as the electoral system and political parties. The Charter expands the constitutional protections for minority rights and, thus, attracts the interest of minority groups seeking to enhance their legal or socio-economic status (Gibson 1985). As Eberts (1985) notes, the Charter makes at least two new avenues of action available to advocates of minority rights. First, they have clear recourse to the courts to seek measurement of *existing* legislative provisions against a revised constitutional standard and, second, they can invoke Charter provisions in an effort to shape the content of legislation *during* the legislative process. As the Charter expanded the protections for designated minorities (e.g., visible minorities), new patterns of population replacement increased the proportion of the population that qualifies as a designated minority. The size of clientele eligible to exercise minority protections is increasing as a consequence of two interrelated dynamics of population replacement. Canadian fertility rates have fallen to the point that current population levels cannot be sustained through natural increase alone. The burden for maintaining these population levels, therefore, has shifted largely to immigration. In the course of the last 25 years or so, the sources from which Canadian immigrants are recruited have changed significantly. New immigrants are increasingly being drawn from nontraditional, non-European sources. Between 1956 and

1960, for example, Canadian immigrants from traditional sources (Europe) outnumbered those drawn from nontraditional sources by a ratio of 12 to 1. By 1980, that trend had reversed; immigrants from nontraditional sources (the Third World) outnumbered those from traditional sources by a ratio of 2 to 1 (Beaujot and Rappak 1988).[1]

As Cairns (1990) points out, the increased cultural heterogeneity of the Canadian population raises important questions about representation. One such question is whether leaders drawn predominantly from one cultural group can adequately represent the interests of publics drawn from different cultural groups. Another question relates to how minorities and minority issues will be politicized. Will minorities be vigorous in their use of Charter provisions to protect and promote their interests? And, more broadly, will minority issues gain widespread public support? Or, will "minority rights" become more politicized and contentious?

The Charter, the particular protections it provides designated groups, and the specific dynamics of population replacement, arguably present challenges that are unique to the Canadian national setting and to Canadian representative institutions.[2] But these challenges and changes may also be cast in a broader light; they may be viewed as aggravated by, and working in tandem with, other transformations that have swept across the political cultures of advanced industrial states. Those transformations, generally characterized as the decline of old politics and the rise of new politics, have far-reaching implications for the kinds of demands citizens place on representative institutions throughout the Western world (Bell 1973, 1976; Dalton 1988; Huntington 1974; Inglehart and Siemienska 1988, 1990; Knutsen 1989; Lasch 1972; White and Sjoberg 1972).

The essential elements of the new-politics thesis can be summarized fairly easily. New-politics theorists argue, inter alia, that there is a massive body of cross-national evidence pointing to the "decline of political parties" and that the increased electoral volatility among mass publics, the weakening of citizen attachments to traditional political parties, and the decomposition of long-standing electoral alignments are not haphazard events. Rather, they point to broad-scale changes that are the consequence of fundamental shifts in the value systems of mass publics in advanced industrial states. The rise of new politics, it is argued, places stress on traditional representative institutions and produces problems of governability for a combination of reasons. First, associated with the rise of new politics is the emergence of a new political agenda. That agenda gives greater prominence to concerns not only about such historically marginalized groups as women,

Aboriginal people and visible minorities (i.e., many of the designated Charter groups), but it is also linked to the emergence of movements promoting environmental protection, animal rights, gay rights, peace, opposition to nuclear power and issues broadly associated with the quality of life. Second, a substantial body of cross-national evidence also shows that support for the new-politics agenda is disproportionately concentrated within particular segments of the citizenry of advanced industrial states – a "new class" that is younger, better educated and better informed than their counterparts of preceding generations. New-politics theorists suggest that the emergence of this new class is linked to the structural changes associated with late industrialism or post-industrialism. The new class is generationally driven, it is increasingly prominent and powerful and it is gradually displacing generations that cleave to old-politics concerns. Representative institutions, consequently, are confronted with a difficult dilemma: how to satisfy a divided public, one segment of which makes political demands geared to a traditional agenda and the other that is driven by a new agenda.

Finally, and perhaps of greatest significance, the rise of new politics is associated with new patterns of political participation (Barnes et al. 1979; Dalton 1988). Cross-national evidence drawn from a large number of advanced industrial states clearly shows that citizens holding new-politics values are not just younger and better educated, they are also more interested in politics; they are more demanding and they are more "issue-driven." In some respects, they exhibit the qualities of the ideal citizen in the democratic polity: they are well informed, articulate, sophisticated and participatory. By the same token, they are also less deferential, more élite-challenging, more critical of the status quo, and more disenchanted with traditional hierarchically organized representative institutions. It is the combination of a new agenda and new political skills that poses challenges to political parties, particularly those geared to traditional assumptions about political leadership and representation. In western European settings at least, the emergence of new politics has not only reoriented and divided old political parties, it has produced new ones. It has stacked the ranks of issue-driven movements, and it has inspired interest groups aiming to advance specific goals of the new-politics agenda (Kitschelt 1989; Baker et al. 1981). New politics, in short, is boisterous politics.

The starting position for the following analysis is that the Cairns analysis (1990) and the new-politics thesis are entirely complementary. The argument is that contemporary difficulties confronting Canadian representative institutions can be understood in terms both of the dynamics of population replacement and the politics of the Charter, and of the broad sea changes induced by new politics, changes that are increasingly prominent in advanced industrial states. The analysis begins by outlining the logic and implications of one well-tested variant of the new-politics perspective, Inglehart's postmaterialism thesis (Inglehart 1971, 1977, 1988, 1990). The bulk of the study will employ available empirical data to examine the following four questions.

1. What is the evidence of the emergence of new politics in the Canadian setting?
2. What impact does new politics have upon citizen attachments to Canadian political parties?
3. What is the relationship between new politics and nontraditional, non-political party forms of political action?
4. How is new politics related to the dynamics of population replacement? And how are new-politics orientations related to attitudinal structures that shape issue positions relating to "Charter groups," women and minorities, as well as to new-politics movements such as environmentalism.

The final section of the study will consider what broader implications the data have for political representation, for the politicization of Charter issues and for political participation in Canada.

NEW POLITICS AND POSTMATERIALISM

Most perspectives on new politics start with the observation that there are fundamental qualitative differences between early and late industrial experiences. Late industrialism is alternatively labelled as "postindustrialism" (Bell 1973, 1976), "technetronic" society (Brzezinski 1970), "postwelfarism" (Lasch 1972), "postbourgeois" or "postmaterialist" society (Inglehart 1971, 1990). Regardless of terminological differences, new-politics analysts generally concur on three important themes. First, advanced industrial states have crossed a series of significant thresholds.[3] Typically, all have experienced unprecedented levels of affluence, economies driven by the tertiary sector, massive expansions in the educational levels, the "information revolution" and a corresponding growth in communications-related technologies, extensive social-welfare networks, and dramatic increases in the social, geographic and economic mobility of populations. From a broad historical standpoint, furthermore, these developments have taken place in a relatively brief time span – in about the last 25 years.

Second, new-politics theorists argue that these structural transformations are linked to fundamental shifts in the value systems of mass publics. Again, the precise contours of these emergent value systems are described in slightly different ways. Some view the shift in terms of a change from group solidarity to self-actualization and regard as central the increased significance that is attached to inner goals (Reisman 1950; Huntington 1974). Others suggest that the value changes have produced a "new morality" (Harding 1986), have given the notion of "success" new meaning (Dalton 1988), have transformed attitudes toward authority, conformity, religiosity and the work ethic (Flanagan 1982) or given rise to the norms of decentralization and autonomy (Toffler 1980; Naisbitt 1982). Yet others focus more explicitly on political values and note the transition from old- to new-politics goals – a decreasing emphasis upon issues such as economic growth, public order, national security and traditional lifestyles – and an increased salience of issues related to individual freedom, social equality and the quality of life (Miller and Levitin 1976; Hildebrandt and Dalton 1978; Dalton 1988). Despite these differences in emphasis and in what is taken to be most significant, there is substantial agreement about the scope and general content of value change.

Third, there is also broad consensus about the political consequences of structural and value change. Whereas the rise of a new agenda and the erosion of traditional patterns of political participation represent two indicators of how new politics is reshaping conventional forms of political behaviour, the advance of new politics is also associated with shifts in the style and content of political discourse and with the emergence of vigorous forms of *unconventional* citizen behaviour – direct-action politics. Political dissent and protest, of course, are not new. Most Western liberal democracies have historical experience of peasant revolts, food riots and, later, of industrial strife and spontaneous protests from the disenfranchised and marginalized. From the standpoint of traditional assumptions about the politics of industrial societies, it would be reasonable to suppose that with an expansion of the franchise, with greater affluence and with redistributive policies aimed at spreading wealth and providing social supports to entire populations, the incidence of protest would wane (Dalton 1988). Available evidence, however, contradicts that expectation. Protest behaviour has increased in advanced industrial states (Barnes et al. 1979), and it is most frequent in those societies that are most affluent (Powell 1982). Protest action associated with new politics differs from traditional forms of protest in two important respects. First, new-politics protest is not just the weapon of last resort for those without voice in the political order. It is, as Dalton (1988, 60–61) notes, the strategy of choice for the politically astute middle class. Second, unlike traditional forms of direct-action politics, the protests of new-politics adherents are not spontaneous. They are deliberate, planned and sustained forms of political action that combine substantial resources and sophisticated techniques – public-awareness campaigns, organized demonstrations and media opportunities – with the goals of mobilizing public opinion and influencing policy makers (Tilly 1975).

Explaining New Politics: The Postmaterialist Thesis

Despite similarities in the prevailing *descriptions* of the origins, character and consequences of new politics, there are significant differences in how new-politics theorists explain *why* value change has occurred. One line of argument is that value change is chiefly the result of the inherent weaknesses of older welfare states, states that have buckled under the impact of the structural stresses induced by late industrialism (Offe 1984). Others focus more squarely on the rise of the new class and reason that the value change is a direct consequence of the rise of the new class (Lipset 1979). Alternatively, it is suggested that the polarities structuring political discourse and behaviour in the earlier phases of industrialism have weakened (Crewe et al. 1977). New politics has emerged, as it were, in the wake of these receding traditional structuring principles. Yet others argue that the ideological climate is just as charged as before, but the polarities organizing politics have shifted to work along different axes.

Within this latter school of thought, Inglehart's postmaterialism thesis (1971, 1977, 1981, 1988, 1990) provides one of the most comprehensive accounts of the origins, nature and consequences of value change. Inglehart identifies the divide between materialist and postmaterialist values as the primary cleavage reorienting the politics of advanced industrial states. He relates the rise of postmaterialism to the structural features of late industrialism, he identifies the specific ways in which postmaterialism has shaped both the content and dynamics of political behaviour, and he forecasts that it will continue to do so with predictable consequences.

The Inglehart variant of the new-politics thesis has been extensively documented elsewhere, and it is sufficiently well known that it no longer requires detailed elaboration. The core elements of the theory hinge on the combination of two hypotheses. The scarcity hypothesis suggests that an individual's priorities reflect the socio-economic environment. According to Inglehart (1981, 881), "one places the greatest subjective value on those things that are in relatively short supply." The socialization hypothesis stipulates that "the relationship between socio-economic environment and value priorities is not one of immediate adjustment: a substantial time lag is involved for, to a large extent, one's basic values reflect the conditions that prevailed during one's pre-adult years" (ibid.). Armed with these hypotheses and informed by Maslow's conceptualization of a needs hierarchy (Maslow 1954), Inglehart identifies a significant intergenerational materialist/post-materialist value divide and then posits the direction of value change. Those age cohorts with direct experience of the collective traumas of the 20th century, the great wars and the Depression, will give relatively high priority to materialist goals – economic security and "safety needs" (Inglehart 1971, 991). Alternatively, those born since 1945, without direct experience of these traumas and "drawn largely from the younger segments of the modern middle class" have, he says, "been socialized during an unprecedentedly long period of unprecedentedly high afflu-ence. For them, economic security may be taken for granted as the supply of water or air we breathe once could" (ibid.). Those cleaving to postmaterialist values, in other words, have moved up the needs hierarchy: they have surpassed concern for material security and instead have placed priority on aesthetic and intellectual needs and on the need for belonging.

The postmaterialist thesis has attracted considerable attention for several good reasons. First, the theory is elegant; it relies on only a few basic assumptions, and those assumptions are well grounded in other research findings. Second, the theory is plausible. Inglehart not only provides an account for why traditional class-based politics has unrav-elled, but he also provides a specific set of predictions regarding the contemporary and future shape of political contests. Third, the post-materialist thesis has been exhaustively tested in more than 20 different countries in the last 19 years. Not surprisingly, Inglehart's version of the new-politics thesis has been the focus of much critical scrutiny.[4] But Inglehart's response to those criticisms has been robust. His central findings have been confirmed by independent researchers employing a variety of methods in a number of different settings (Lafferty and Knutsen 1985; Bakvis and Nevitte 1987) and the basic thesis, though not unscathed, remains intact.

Although Inglehart presents but one perspective on new politics, there are substantive, methodological and practical reasons for exploring new politics in the Canadian setting through the postmaterialist perspec-tive. First, the theory is comprehensive, and it provides a framework from which we can generate specific predictions about attitudes to minorities, the impact of population replacement and evolving patterns of political participation. One prediction is that the rise of postmateri-alist values will produce greater public sympathy for minorities.

Consequently, the expectation is that the advance of postmaterialist politics will encourage the politicization of Charter issues. Another prediction is that postmaterialist values will be concentrated within those segments of the population that are younger and better educated. Furthermore, it predicts that those segments of the population that exhibit postmaterialist values will have weaker attachments to traditional political parties. Thus, postmaterialists are expected to be more likely than their materialist counterparts to engage in unconventional forms of political action and élite-challenging behaviour.

Second, the fact that the postmaterialist thesis has been repeatedly tested by different investigators in a variety of national settings has two important by-products. The stability of the findings from research in a large number of advanced industrial states suggests that the now standard battery of indicators used to tap materialist/postmaterialist orientations are cross-nationally reliable and valid and, because these sustained research efforts have produced a substantial body of secondary evidence, we are well placed to examine Canadian evidence in the context of the broader cross-national findings.

POSTMATERIALISM IN CANADA

By most criteria Canada qualifies as a postindustrial state. It has enjoyed substantial increases in wealth. The GDP has doubled in the last 25 years (International Monetary Fund 1986), and expanded productivity is reflected in substantial increases in individual income. The structure of the Canadian domestic economy has also changed. Technology has been an important driving force behind that shift, and now more than half of the Canadian workforce is employed in the tertiary sector. Because technology places a premium on knowledge-based skills, most post-industrial states have experienced a dramatic growth in educational opportunities, especially for the young. As figure 8.1 illustrates, Canada is no exception to that trend. The proportion of 20–24-year-olds enrolled full-time in educational institutions has tripled since 1960. Expanded educational opportunities, in turn, encourage occupational mobility and, consequently, the middle class has grown.

The influx of women in the workplace in the last 20 years has produced a dramatic shift in the gender composition of the workforce. By 1988, two-thirds of all Canadian women between the ages of 18 and 65 were part of the paid workforce (Organisation for Economic Co-operation and Development 1988). The shifting context of social life can be related to all of these forces. With the decline of rural economies, urban centres have become more powerful population magnets than ever before. Canada is one of the most urbanized societies in the world,

Figure 8.1
Growth of educated publics: Canada in cross-national perspective

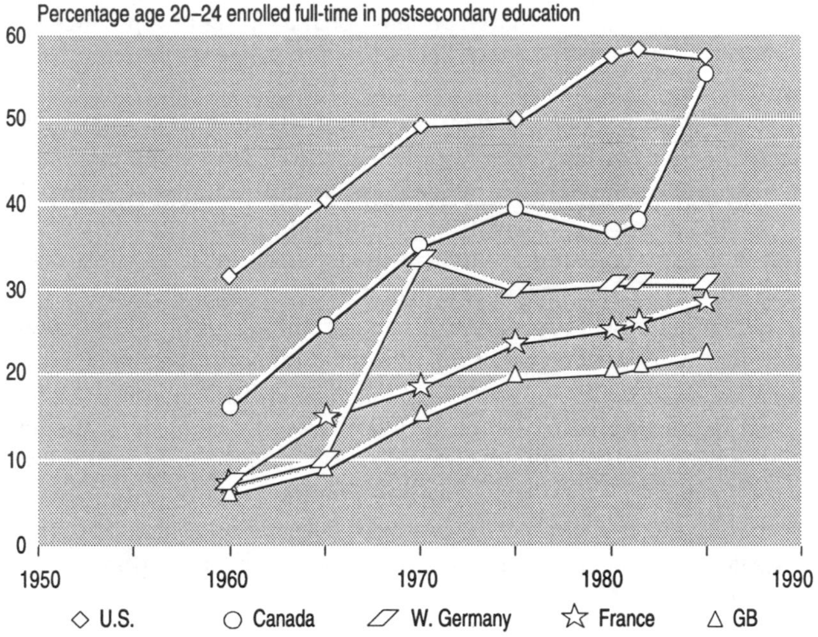

Percentage age 20–24 enrolled full-time in postsecondary education

◇ U.S.   ○ Canada   ▱ W. Germany   ☆ France   △ GB

Source: UNESCO, Statistical Yearbook for the Years 1974, 1984, 1988 (Paris: UNESCO Press, 1975, 1984, 1988).

and social indicators such as higher divorce rates, lower fertility rates and increased levels of delinquency, crime and suicide probably reflect the stresses of mobility and urban life.

In light of the very considerable body of cross-national evidence linking the shift from industrialism to postindustrialism with the rise of new politics, there are good reasons to expect Canadian politics to be shaped by the very same forces that have swept across other postindustrial states. Indeed, it would be remarkable if it were not the case. In this context, it is striking that the postmaterialist thesis has featured so marginally in the analysis of value change in Canadian politics. To be sure, some analysts have provided scattered evidence of Canadian value orientations that are congenial to a postmaterialist interpretation. For instance, Lambert et al. (1986) report findings "that probably represent examples of what Inglehart calls materialist values" in their analysis of the political beliefs among the Canadian electorate. Similarly, Gagnon and Tanguay (1989) suspect that postmaterialism might play a role in the future formations of Canadian political parties. Others note that the groups that are heavy Charter users – the Canadian Civil Liberties

Association, feminist organizations and advocacy groups for the handicapped, the elderly, racial and ethnic minorities, minority-language interest groups and Aboriginal people – bear a strong resemblance to a coalition of interests that promote postmaterialist goals (Morton 1990). Further, it might be argued that the dramatic growth of environmental pressure groups, some 2 500 by one count, along with animal-rights groups, gay-rights activists and citizen-action coalitions at community, provincial and federal levels all indicate that postmaterialist-style politics is on the rise. This conclusion is certainly plausible, but it relies almost exclusively upon inferences drawn from indirect and mostly qualitative evidence. The point is that apart from these speculative post facto commentaries, few attempts have been made to deploy a deliberate postmaterialist construction on Canadian political value change. Significantly, even these efforts have relied on indirect evidence or data collected at a single time-point from limited samples of the Canadian public (Bakvis and Nevitte 1987; Nevitte et al. 1989; Nevitte and Gibbins 1990). In short, our ability to explore the dynamics of value change through the new-politics optic has been hobbled by a major practical obstacle – the absence of direct evidence drawn from national representative samples.

Data and Methods

The following analysis is based on direct evidence; it relies partly on secondary survey evidence drawn from Canadian National Election Studies undertaken since 1965 and partly on two matched national surveys, one conducted in 1981 (N = 1 254) and the other in 1990 (N = 1 730). There are a number of features of the latter two datasets that are particularly noteworthy. First, the sampling procedures employed during the data collection in 1981 and 1990 were precisely the same (see Appendix for a summary of the 1990 survey). Both surveys used stratified random surveys representative of the Canadian population. Second, both surveys, which were the Canadian segments of the first and second rounds of the European Value Systems Study Group (EVSSG)/World Values research projects,[5] contained the same core survey items in both 1981 and 1990. Both also contained the standard Inglehart materialism/postmaterialism value scale. Third, the datasets also match the surveys undertaken in 1981 in 21 other national settings and in 1990 in 41 other national settings. This means that in undertaking cross-time comparisons in the Canadian setting, or in comparisons between the Canadian and other survey evidence, one can be reasonably confident that the findings are directly comparable and that any differences detected in the Canadian national values are not a result of variation in data collection procedures or in instrumentation, but reflect instead genuine value change.

If politics involves conflicts about valued goals, then the central task of analysing value change, new-politics theorists argue, is to track which values take priority in the minds of citizens at different times. An identical battery of value indicators was used in both the 1981 and 1990 Canadian Values Surveys, and responses to these items are employed in the following analysis to generate a single measure of materialist/postmaterialist orientations (Inglehart 1977).

Respondents in both the 1981 and 1990 surveys were asked:

> There is a lot of talk these days about what the aims of the country should be for the next ten years. On this card are listed some of the goals which different people would give as top priority. Would you please say which of these you consider the most important? And which would be the next most important?
>
> Maintaining order in the nation (M)
>
> Giving people more say in important government decisions (PM)
>
> Fighting rising prices (M)
>
> Protecting freedom of speech (PM)

Following standard procedures, respondents are grouped into one of three value clusters according to the rankings given to the four items. Those assigning "maintaining order" and "fighting rising prices" top priority place emphasis on personal and physical security; they are classified as materialists (M). Postmaterialists (PM) assign "giving people more say" and "protecting freedom of speech" top rankings. And those respondents selecting one material and one postmaterial item are classified into a third group; they have "mixed" value priorities.

DIRECT EVIDENCE: CANADA IN CROSS-NATIONAL CONTEXT

The following exploration of postmaterialism in Canada begins with the broad picture and these questions: What is the direct evidence of new-politics values in the Canadian public? How does the Canadian evidence compare with that from other advanced industrial states? And, to what extent has the balance of materialist/postmaterialist values shifted in Canada in the course of the last 10 years? The basic data addressing these questions as presented in table 8.1 and figure 8.2 show first that the proportion of postmaterialists in the Canadian

Table 8.1
Cross-national distribution of materialist/postmaterialist values
(percentages)

Value type	Britain 1981	France 1981	W. Germany 1981	U.S. 1980	Canada 1981	U.S. 1990	Canada 1990
Materialist	23.3	32.2	24.4	34.0	22.1	16.4	11.7
Mixed	62.6	48.2	55.1	56.0	61.9	60.8	62.7
Postmaterialist	14.1	19.6	20.5	10.0	16.0	22.8	25.6
N	(1 199)	(1 145)	(1 243)	(1 614)	(1 183)	(1 940)	(1 645)

Sources: Britain, France, Germany, Canada (1981), World Values Survey (1981); U.S. (1980),
Dalton (1988), extracted from Center for Political Studies (CPS), University of Michigan,
Election Studies; Canada (1990) and U.S. (1990), World Values Survey (1990).

public in 1981 was essentially the same as that of publics in Britain, France, the United States and West Germany at about the same time. Proportionately, there were slightly more postmaterialists in Germany and France than in Canada and slightly fewer in Britain and the United States. Canadians, clearly, occupy the middle ground, but the cross-national differences are small. With respect to the distribution of materialists, the findings indicate greater cross-national variation. The level of materialism in the Canadian public is almost precisely the same as that of the British and German publics in 1981, and all three are somewhat less materialist than the French and American publics. Generally, two findings stand out. First, in all five countries considered, materialists clearly outnumbered postmaterialists in 1981. Second, there is no evidence to suggest that the Canadian public exhibits value priorities that are atypical of other advanced industrial states or that Canadians have escaped the new-politics values that have reshaped political life elsewhere.

When one focuses on the four rightmost columns of table 8.1 and compares the 1981 Canadian data with the 1990 findings, the results are very striking indeed. They indicate that substantial value change has taken place in the last 10 years. The proportion of materialists within the Canadian public has halved while the ranks of the postmaterialists have grown from 16 percent in 1981 to more than 25 percent in 1990. In other words, by 1990 postmaterialists not only outnumbered materialists, they did so by a substantial margin of more than two to one. The data also show a similarly striking value shift within the American public. In both national settings for which contemporary data are available, the proportion of materialists has dropped dramatically, and there has been a similar proportionate increase in postmaterialists; post-materialists now outnumber materialists.

Figure 8.2
Cross-national distribution of materialist/postmaterialist values

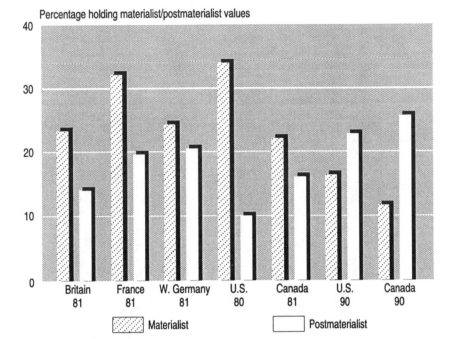

Percentage holding materialist/postmaterialist values

Materialist · Postmaterialist

Britain 81 · France 81 · W. Germany 81 · U.S. 80 · Canada 81 · U.S. 90 · Canada 90

Sources: Britain, France, West Germany, Canada (1981), World Values Survey (1981); U.S. (1980), Dalton (1988), extracted from Center for Political Studies (CPS), University of Michigan, Election Studies; Canada (1990) and U.S. (1990), World Values Survey (1990).

A clearer picture of the scope and location of value change can be provided by disaggregating these findings, and in table 8.2 the data are unpackaged according to a variety of socio-economic, cultural and regional criteria. This table presents a great deal of evidence, but three findings are of particular note. First, when one considers the 1981 data, one can see that the sociostructural distribution of materialist and postmaterialist values essentially conforms to findings that have been generated in other cross-national settings. Postmaterialists outnumber materialists in two categories of respondents: among those reporting a high level of formal education and among professionals. The effects of union membership and age, however, are not strong. Similarly, materialists are disproportionately found, as would be expected, among the unskilled, low income, low education, 54 or older, female and union member categories, and of particular note for the Canadian context, among French speakers.

Second, a comparison of the 1981 data with the 1990 findings in table 8.2 indicates a great deal about the nature of that value change. It shows that there has been a wholesale and secular shift away from

Table 8.2
Materialists and postmaterialists by socio-economic variables
(percentages)

Variable	Category	1981 M	1981 PM	1990 M	1990 PM	M 1990-M 1981	PM 1990-PM 1981
Age	18–33	21.6	15.9	11.0	27.2	-10.6	11.3
	34–53	20.2	15.9	11.1	25.0	-9.1	9.1
	54+	26.0	16.4	13.4	25.2	-12.6	8.8
Education	Low	25.6	14.6	15.4	19.5	-10.2	4.9
	Mid	22.4	12.1	11.3	24.0	-11.1	11.9
	High	14.8	23.8	8.2	34.1	-6.6	10.3
Occupation	Unskilled	31.0	15.0	13.5	21.3	-17.5	6.3
	Skilled-clerical	15.4	17.3	10.6	26.6	-4.8	9.3
	Mgmt.-sales	20.1	14.5	11.2	25.6	-8.9	11.1
	Professional	13.9	27.8	8.3	35.7	-5.6	7.9
Income	Low	26.7	15.1	13.1	23.0	-13.6	7.9
	Mid	20.9	17.2	10.6	28.2	-10.3	11.0
	High	18.5	16.5	8.4	30.9	-10.1	14.4
Language	English	18.0	15.6	9.4	24.2	-8.6	8.6
	French	31.5	16.7	19.2	30.8	-12.3	14.1
Gender	Male	20.0	17.6	9.9	30.4	-10.1	12.8
	Female	24.4	14.3	13.6	21.1	-10.8	6.8
Region	Atlantic			13.6	19.7		
	Quebec			18.3	30.9		
	Ontario		n.a.	9.5	23.5	n.a.	n.a.
	Prairies			8.0	24.2		
	BC			8.7	28.4		
Union	Member	22.9	15.9	12.3	24.9	-10.6	9.0
	Nonmember	16.3	16.3	7.4	32.0	-8.9	15.7

Sources: World Values Surveys (1981, 1990).

n.a. = not available.

materialism and toward postmaterialism across all segments of the Canadian public. Indeed, by 1990, the proportion of respondents reporting postmaterialist orientations outnumbered those in the materialist group in every category. The right-hand columns of table 8.2 provide summary figures indicating the degree and direction of value change, and they show that the largest increases in postmaterialist orientations are to be found among non-union members, those with high incomes, French speakers, males and those within middle or high levels of education. Conversely, the largest decreases in materialist orientations are located in the unskilled occupation group, low-income Canadians, those who are older and French speakers. Notwithstanding the secular pattern of value change between 1981 and 1990, those with high levels of formal education, professionals and non-union members exhibit the highest concentrations of postmaterialists. There are also significant regional variations; the materialist/postmaterialist divide, clearly, is deepest in Quebec, which has significantly more materialists *and* postmaterialists than any other region.

The presence of powerful education effects on the balance of materialist/postmaterialist values comes as no surprise at all. That finding is predicted by Inglehart's theory, and the Canadian evidence conforms to expectations drawn from a large body of evidence from other advanced industrial states. More surprising, perhaps, is the apparent weakness of age-related effects. Both of these findings can be probed further by considering the Canadian evidence, once again, in cross-national context. With respect to age, the data in figure 8.3a not only underscore further the secular nature of postmaterialist value change, but they also point to some intriguing cross-national differences. In the 1981 data, the age effects on postmaterialism in Canada are relatively

Figure 8.3a
Age differences in value priorities

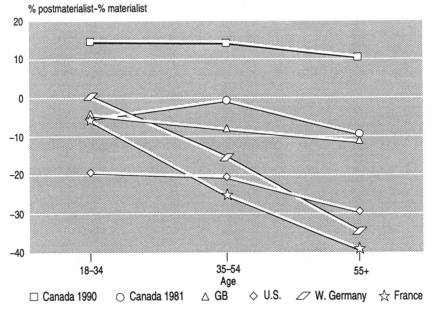

% postmaterialist–% materialist

□ Canada 1990   ○ Canada 1981   △ GB   ◇ U.S.   ◿ W. Germany   ☆ France

Sources: United States, Dalton (1988), extracted from 1980 CPS, American Election Study; Great Britain, West Germany, France, Dalton (1988) extracted from Eurobarometer 18; Canada, World Values Surveys (1981, 1990).

weak, and they are certainly weaker than those evident in the British, West German and French publics. They are, however, similar in shape to those of the American public. The 1990 Canadian results replicate the shape of the 1981 data, but they do so at a different level. One might speculate that the weakness of age-related effects could be a result of a combination of factors. For example, it could be argued that once new-politics values have taken hold within a particular segment of the population, particularly a segment that has moved into the command posts of society (Inglehart 1990), then age-related effects weaken or wash out as new-politics values are projected onto the entire society by increasingly influential groups. Patterns of population replacement may also come into play: as older cohorts, those who are materialist as a result of firsthand experience with the social and economic traumas of the Depression and the wars are replaced by postmaterialists then, in the absence of any massive economic downturn and accompanying social trauma, one would expect cohort effects to weaken. Indeed, in the long run, one would expect age-related effects to disappear entirely.

With respect to the linkages between education and postmaterialism, figure 8.3b illustrates that the 1981 Canadian evidence mirrors

Figure 8.3b
Educational differences in value priorities

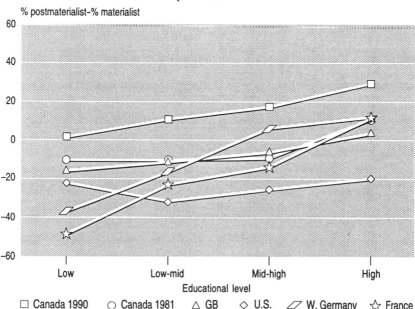

% postmaterialist-% materialist

Educational level

□ Canada 1990   ○ Canada 1981   △ GB   ◇ U.S.   ⬭ W. Germany   ☆ France

Sources: United States, Dalton (1988), extracted from 1980 CPS, American Election Study; Great Britain, West Germany, France, Dalton (1988) extracted from Eurobarometer 18; Canada, World Values Surveys (1981, 1990).

the distributions evident in the four other advanced industrial states under consideration. Although the materialist/postmaterialist value differences between the high and medium-high education groups in 1990 are not quite as sharp as the differences between those same groups in 1981, education clearly appears to be a reasonably strong predictor of postmaterialist leanings. In fact, when one employs a relatively powerful statistical method, stepwise logistic regression, to determine which background variable from table 8.2 provides the best single predictor of postmaterialism in Canada, the results are unequivocal: it is education.[6] This finding carries significant implications because it suggests that, other things being equal, as the Canadian public becomes better educated it will also become more postmaterialist.

NEW POLITICS, POLITICAL PARTICIPATION AND REPRESENTATION

New Politics and the Redistribution of Political Skills
New politics has far-reaching implications for political participation and presents challenges to traditional representative institutions, observers argue, for a combination of reasons. The first relates directly to the content of value change. Postmaterialists, Inglehart contends, emphasize self-expression as a valued goal. More particularly, they give priority to "giving people more say in government decisions" (1977, 40–46). Under conditions of affluence and social tranquillity, Inglehart expects postmaterialists to be more likely to fulfil their potential for participation because " being freed from the need to focus their energies primarily on the struggle for economic and physical security should enable them to devote more attention to postmaterialist concerns – such as politics" (Inglehart 1990, 335).

Second, the rise of new politics is also associated with the redistribution of political skills. With the emergence of extensive political communities that could no longer rely on personal contact and word of mouth, governments required national administrative structures, written records and the performance of complex coordinating functions. This transformation placed a premium on special skills, most notably literacy, and these skills were held by a relatively small élite. It was this small élite, Inglehart argues, that had a vision of, and the skills to address, national politics (1990, 337). The skill gap between élites and publics narrowed somewhat with the process of industrialization. With industrialization, populations became more urbanized, more literate and less parochial (Lerner 1958); they experienced, in Deutsch's words, social mobilization (Deutsch 1963, 1966). The basic thresholds of social mobilization – substantial levels of industrialization, widespread literacy, universal suffrage, the massive shift to urbanization – were crossed, Inglehart suggests, a long time ago. But a core process, the dissemination of the skills necessary to cope with extensive political communities, or "cognitive mobilization," continues (Inglehart 1977; Dalton 1984; Dalton et al. 1984). In postindustrial society, the gap between the political skills of élites and the public, then, has further narrowed, and, consequently, postmaterialists will be more "cognitively mobilized," more likely to discuss and be interested in politics.

Third, new politics produces new types of political participation. A very large body of empirical evidence demonstrates that education increases an individual's level of "subjective political competence" and levels of political participation (Almond and Verba 1963; Milbrath 1965; Verba et al. 1978; Barnes et al. 1979). Participation, in turn, is related to membership in organizations (Verba and Nie 1972; Nie et al. 1969). Paradoxically, however, cross-national evidence drawn from advanced industrial states indicates that such conventional forms of political behaviour as voting have levelled off (Dalton 1988, 39). In fact, in the case of the 1988 American presidential elections, voting turnout dropped to its lowest level since the 1950s. The apparent paradox can be resolved because, according to Inglehart, "while the individual level preconditions for political participation have been improving, external mobilization has been in decline, as a result of the decay of political party machines, labor unions, and religious institutions" (1990, 336).

From the postmaterialist standpoint, the distribution between older and newer forms of political participation is crucial. In the late 19th and early 20th centuries, Inglehart points out, publics were effectively mobilized by élite-dominated hierarchical organizations, such as traditional mass-based political parties. Following Converse (1972), Inglehart argues that publics had relatively low political skills and traditional organizations "usually produced only a relatively low qualitative level of participation, generally the simple act of voting" (1990, 339). The growing segments of contemporary publics with high political skills, however, are less dependent on permanent hierarchical organizations. More than that, hierarchical organizations, in general, are less attractive. In this respect, changes in the workplace are instructive. Technologically driven economies gain a competitive edge and thus reward innovation. Autonomy and the ability to make decisions free from hierarchical constraints are crucial to innovation, and it is impossible to prescribe innovation from above. Experience in this kind of nontraditional, less hierarchical work environment encourages broad participation in decision making in the workplace. Those transferring such work-experience skills to political life are less likely to be satisfied with traditional political institutions that provide little room for meaningful participation (ibid., 338–40). Consequently, postmaterialists are more likely to turn instead to nontraditional, élite-challenging and unconventional forms of political participation.

Briefly summarized, the Inglehart perspective provides a variety of expectations about how postmaterialism affects political participation. To date, none of these expectations has been systematically explored in the Canadian setting. To do so, one can begin by examining the available Canadian evidence in a broad, cross-national context.

Starting first with levels of political discussion, the evidence presented in table 8.3 indicates that in 1981 Canadians were as likely as British, French and West German publics to discuss politics frequently and about as likely to never discuss politics. American respondents are the outliers: they are much more inclined toward political discussion. But a comparison of the two rightmost columns of table 8.3 shows a striking increase in the levels of political discussion in Canada in the last decade. The proportion of Canadians reporting frequent political discussion has more than doubled, and the size of the group responding that they never engage in political discussion has shrunk from about 32 percent in 1981 to just 24 percent in 1990. The political-discussion profile of Canadians in 1990, in other words, approaches the 1981 American profile. Finally, figure 8.4 clearly provides support for the hypothesis that postmaterialists are, in one sense, more politically articulate than materialists. Materialists massively outnumber postmaterialists in the "never" category, and, although the proportion of materialists frequently discussing politics has increased since 1981, they still remain far below the proportions of postmaterialists who do so.

Table 8.3
Cross-national distribution of political discussion
(percentages)

	Britain 1981	France 1981	U.S. 1981	W. Germany 1981	Canada 1981	Canada 1990
Frequently	10.9	11.7	23.2	10.6	9.7	19.5
Occasionally	52.0	51.6	57.1	54.5	58.4	56.7
Never	37.1	36.7	19.6	34.8	31.9	23.8
N	(1 226)	(1 194)	(2 305)	(1 283)	(1 247)	(1 722)

Sources: World Values Surveys (1981,1990).

The question reads: "When you get together with your friends, would you say you discuss political matters frequently, occasionally, or never?"

Figure 8.4
Political discussion by value priorities: Canada, 1981 and 1990

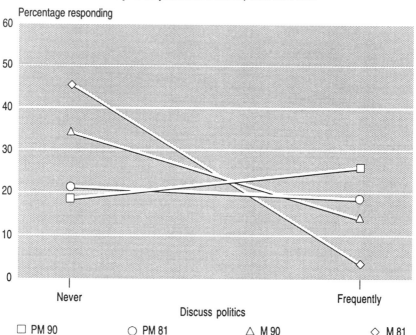

Percentage responding

Discuss politics

Never   Frequently

☐ PM 90   ○ PM 81   △ M 90   ◇ M 81

Sources: World Values Surveys (1981, 1990).

The question reads: "When you get together with your friends, would you say you discuss political matters frequently, occasionally, or never?"

A second clear expectation of the postmaterialist perspective is that those cleaving to new-politics values will be more interested in politics than those of the old-politics tradition. Table 8.5 presents evidence that clearly supports that prediction. There is good reason to expect political interest and political discussion to be related and for the Canadian data the correlation is powerful ($r = .56$). Consequently, it is not surprising that the 1981 cross-national distributions of political interest roughly mirror the 1981 cross-national findings with respect to political discussion. Nor is it surprising that American respondents are both more likely to discuss politics and to express more interest in politics than their western European and Canadian counterparts. If the increase in levels of political discussion in Canada between 1981 and 1990 can be described as striking (table 8.3) then the increased levels of political interest that have taken place over the same period (table 8.4) are even more remarkable. The proportion of Canadians reporting that they are very interested in politics has more than doubled in the last

Table 8.4
Cross-national distribution of political interest
(percentages)

	Britain 1981	France 1981	U.S. 1981	W. Germany 1981	Canada 1981	Canada 1990
Very interested	5.6	6.5	11.5	6.4	7.2	20.7
Somewhat	33.0	56.6	36.8	42.0	45.5	38.4
Not very	33.0	11.2	31.0	37.1	26.9	26.7
Not at all	28.5	25.7	20.7	14.6	20.4	14.2
N	(1 229)	(1 197)	(2 276)	(1 287)	(1 251)	(1 723)

Sources: World Values Surveys (1981, 1990).

For all 1981 data, the question reads: "Which of these statements comes nearest to describing your interest in politics?
  1. I take an active interest in politics.
  2. I am interested in politics but don't take an active part.
  3. My interest in politics is not greater than other interests.
  4. I'm not interested in politics at all."

For the 1990 Canadian data, the question reads: "How interested would you say you are in politics? Very interested, Somewhat interested, Not very interested, or Not at all interested."

decade; indeed, it has nearly tripled. It rose from 7.2 percent in 1981 to 20.7 percent in 1990. The Canadian 1990 levels of political interest far surpass those found in the 1981 United States sample.

Figure 8.6, which disaggregates reported levels of political interest in Canada according to value type, also yields a revealing finding. It shows that in 1981 the main difference between materialists and post-materialists was that materialists were much more likely to report no interest in politics. The differences between the proportion of post-materialists and materialists responding very interested in 1981 were, in fact, quite small. But these patterns have changed dramatically in the space of a decade. By 1990, Canadian postmaterialists were more than twice as likely as materialists to be very interested in politics.

The argument that publics are increasingly sophisticated, that the balance of skills between élites and publics have shifted and that citizens, consequently, are less dependent on traditional élites and reference groups and more self-sufficient in politics is an important one. New-politics theorists, Inglehart and others (Dalton 1984, 1988; Dalton et al. 1984), view cognitive mobilization as driving these changes. Cognitive mobilization implies that, with the expansion of education, publics are better equipped to evaluate political information relatively independently. Evidence of higher levels of political interest means that publics are motivated to do so, and the information revolution, particularly the expanded reach of the mass media, implies that political knowledge is

Figure 8.5
**Political interest by value priorities: Britain, France, U.S., West Germany, 1981;
and Canada, 1981 and 1990**

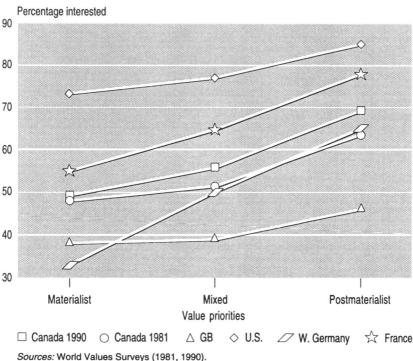

Percentage interested

Value priorities

☐ Canada 1990   ○ Canada 1981   △ GB   ◇ U.S.   ⧄ W. Germany   ☆ France

Sources: World Values Surveys (1981, 1990).

more accessible and a more widely held political resource than before.

Education and political interest provide two indirect indicators of cognitive mobilization.[7] Evidence already presented has shown rising levels of education in the Canadian public (figure 8.1) and greater interest in politics (table 8.4). If the postmaterialist thesis has any application at all to the Canadian setting, then, one would expect to find evidence of increased levels of cognitive mobilization in the public at large and higher levels of cognitive mobilization among postmaterialists than materialists. Drawing from Canadian National Election Studies from 1965 to 1988, figure 8.7 illustrates that the proportion of the Canadian public that rates "high" on the cognitive mobilization scale was relatively small, slightly less than 45 percent of respondents, at the time of the 1965 election. The proportion declined somewhat by the 1974 election, but since then, according to these data, it has increased sharply. By the 1984 election, more than 55 percent of Canadians sampled were highly cognitively mobilized, and by 1988 the proportion increased again to include nearly two out of three Canadians.

Figure 8.6
Political interest and value priorities: Canada, 1981 and 1990

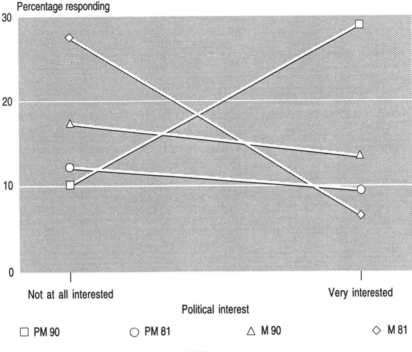

Sources: World Values Surveys (1981, 1990).

The widest time-points for which direct evidence of both materialist/postmaterialist and cognitive mobilization indicators are available are the 1981 and 1990 Canadian World Values Surveys. These data, presented in figure 8.8, provide further confirmation that levels of cognitive mobilization increased between 1981 and 1990 and that postmaterialists exhibit much higher levels of cognitive mobilization than either those falling in the mixed or materialist categories. These findings, in short, provide further evidence not only of postmaterialism in the Canadian setting but also of a changed public. Like citizens of other advanced industrial states, the Canadian public is more politically sophisticated than before and postmaterialists, as predicted, are more politically sophisticated than their materialist counterparts.

New Politics and Political Participation

In the past 25 years, the study of political participation has perhaps become the single most thoroughly analysed aspect of élite and public political

Figure 8.7
The advance of the cognitively mobilized

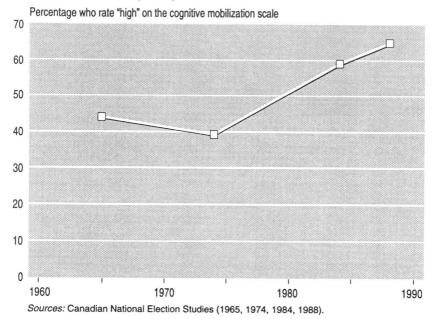

Percentage who rate "high" on the cognitive mobilization scale

Sources: Canadian National Election Studies (1965, 1974, 1984, 1988).

Figure 8.8
Cognitive mobilization and value priorities: Canada, 1981 and 1990

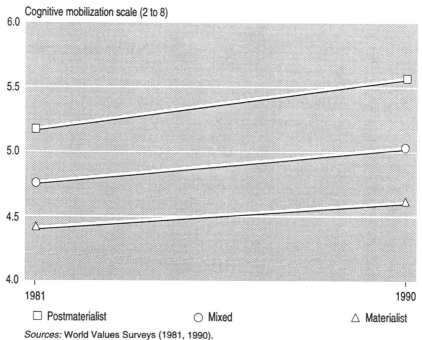

Cognitive mobilization scale (2 to 8)

☐ Postmaterialist   ○ Mixed   △ Materialist

Sources: World Values Surveys (1981, 1990).

behaviour. An enormous body of literature, drawn mostly from multiple studies of advanced industrial states, has focused attention on the extent to which patterns of political participation, particularly conventional forms of political participation such as voting, are shaped by sociostructural factors (Rokkan 1970; Dahl 1966; Rose 1974). This line of analysis typically stresses how such ascriptive variables as religion, language and ethnicity combine with variables relevant to the industrialization experience – class, education, income and occupation – to produce a matrix of "cleavage structures" through which political participation may best be explained (Lipset and Rokkan 1967). Comparative analysts take the same logic one step further and argue that cross-national similarities and differences in patterns of political participation can be understood in terms of how the *same* variables interact in unique or similar ways. Not surprisingly, a large number of Canadian analysts have followed the same approach to explore Canadian patterns of political behaviour. Many reached the hotly contested conclusion that in one significant respect Canadian patterns of participation are unlike those of comparable industrial settings in that the levels of class voting appear to be atypically low (Alford 1963; Mishler 1979; Pammett 1987). And one popular explanation has been that the political significance of class has been overridden by such other variables as region, religion and ethnicity (Wilson 1968).[8]

These traditional approaches usually worked from the assumption that individual attitudes played little independent role in shaping political participation and that assumption appeared justified. Converse's (1964) classic study of the political-belief systems of mass publics, after all, seemed to demonstrate that the political attitudes of most citizens were vague, unstructured and lacked stability over time. An emerging contemporary literature, however, presents a somewhat different picture. This literature (Pomper 1972; Page and Brody 1972; Miller and Levitin 1976; Weisberg and Rusk 1970) suggests that cleavage structures are not "frozen" for all time; rather, they have "thawed." Individual perceptions about policy alternatives, candidate and party evaluation, and issue positions, the literature argues, are becoming increasingly important in shaping both conventional and unconventional forms of political participation. Whereas such institutional constraints as electoral rules, party organization and "opportunity structures" remain significant factors (Kitschelt 1989), individual values, nonetheless, are increasingly coming into play. Furthermore, within this school of thought, cross-national evidence has shown that the materialist/postmaterialist divide is relevant not only to citizen attachments to traditional representative institutions such as political parties, to voting intention, to confidence in governmental and non-governmental institutions, but also to emerging forms of unconventional political behaviour (Inglehart 1977, 1990; Barnes et al. 1979; Dalton et al. 1984).

A full exploration of how individual values bear on political participation in Canada would require a thorough study of how both sociostructural factors and individual values interact in the Canadian setting. It would, in fact, entail another project. The following questions addressed in this study, however, are more focused and modest. Is there any evidence that the materialist/postmaterialist divide shapes conventional forms of political participation in the Canadian setting? Do Canadian materialists and postmaterialists, like their counterparts in other advanced industrial states, differ in how much confidence they have in governmental and non-governmental institutions? And, does the rise of postmaterialism hold any implications for such unconventional forms of political participation as protest behaviour?

The 1988 Canadian National Election Study asked respondents a battery of questions about partisanship, about the strength of individuals' attachments to political parties and about voting intention. One such question was: "Thinking of federal politics, do you usually think of yourself as a Liberal, Conservative, NDP, or none of these?" Figure 8.9 illustrates the distribution of partisans, nonpartisans, and those reporting no party identification, according to value type. It shows that partisans outnumber nonpartisans across all value types. But it also shows that postmaterialists are more likely than those in the mixed and materialist categories to be nonpartisans. The differences, moreover, are statistically significant. Figure 8.10 elaborates these findings by presenting the data in a slightly different way. Here, the precise partisan orientations of respondents are displayed, and they underscore two significant findings. First, postmaterialists are clearly more likely than materialists to report no party identification. Second, those postmaterialists who do identify with a political party are relatively evenly distributed between the two traditional major political parties – the Liberals and the Progressive Conservatives – and the long-standing other large party, the New Democrats. Furthermore, when the data are probed in greater detail a consistent pattern emerges: when strength of party identification is considered, materialists are more strongly attached to traditional political parties than are postmaterialists.[9] Materialists are more likely than postmaterialists to report that they voted. And of those respondents who voted, postmaterialists are more likely than materialists to vote for candidates from nontraditional polit-

Figure 8.9
Value priorities and partisanship

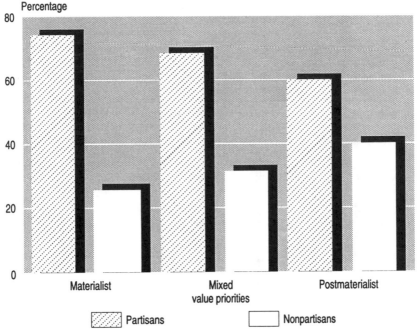

Source: Canadian National Election Survey (1988).

ical parties. These findings are consistent with comparable evidence drawn from other advanced industrial states (Inglehart 1990; Dalton 1988). They suggest that postmaterialists' attachments to traditional political institutions, political parties, are weaker and that their patterns of conventional political participation, voting, are indeed systematically different from those of their materialist counterparts.

New Politics and Confidence in Institutions

It has already been noted that new-politics theorists, in general, and postmaterialists, in particular, view increased electoral volatility and partisan dealignment as just the "tip of the iceberg." Such factors indicate, but do not completely tap, the deeper and wider value changes taking place within the publics of advanced industrial states. For reasons already outlined, Inglehart contends that postmaterialists are less likely to be satisfied with passive, élite-directed forms of political participation; they are more concerned about the quality of participation and the openness of institutions. There is some scattered evidence that suggests that Canadian postmaterialists share these concerns. For example, when the

Figure 8.10
Value priorities and party identification in 1988

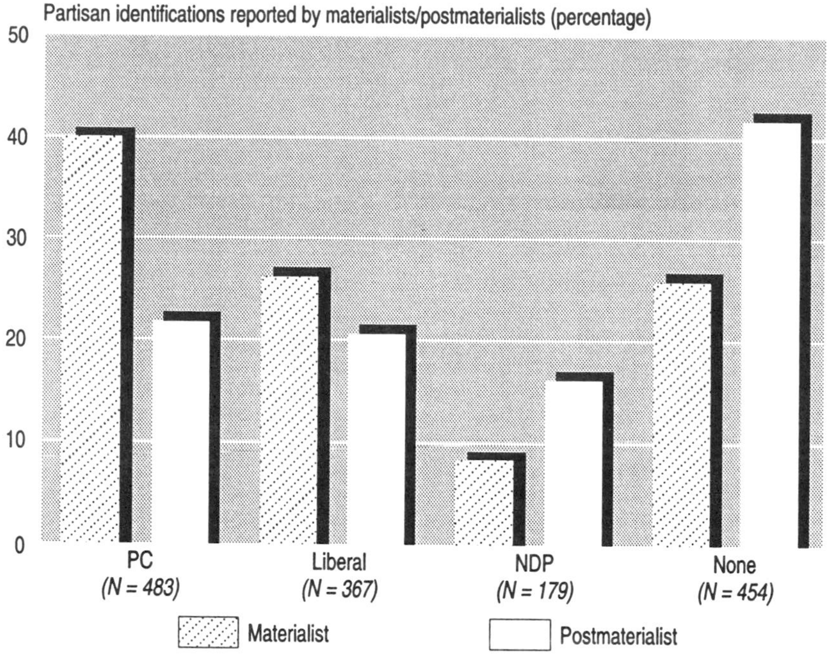

Partisan identifications reported by materialists/postmaterialists (percentage)

| | PC (N = 483) | Liberal (N = 367) | NDP (N = 179) | None (N = 454) |

Materialist   Postmaterialist

Source: Canadian National Election Survey (1988).

1988 Canadian National Election Study presented respondents with the statement "Our government should be made more open to the public," postmaterialists were significantly more likely than materialists to agree.[10]

There is nothing inherent in postmaterialist values, according to Inglehart, that predisposes postmaterialists to be dissatisfied with political institutions: "It depends on the relationship between one's values and the setting in which one lives" (1977, 311). Thus, in those settings in which postmaterialist concerns are given relatively high priority, postmaterialists may be relatively satisfied with, and confident in, the performance of institutions (Inglehart 1977). Furthermore, weak attachments to traditional political parties may provide no generalizable clues about postmaterialists' confidence in a broader array of governmental or non-governmental institutions.

Reporting that "x" percent of respondents are satisfied with institution "y" and "z" percent are not, are findings that carry relatively little meaning when they are viewed in isolation. Comparative evidence provides a more revealing picture. Both the 1981 and the 1990 World Values Surveys asked respondents about their confidence in a variety of institutions, and, as before, the Canadian 1981 evidence can be placed in a larger cross-national perspective. Table 8.5 summarizes these data, and they show, broadly, that Canadians' attitudes toward a variety of governmental and non-governmental institutions were relatively similar to those of publics in Britain, France and West Germany, all of which were somewhat different from those in the United States. Canadians expressed less confidence in Parliament, for example, than did publics in the United States, France and Germany, but they were slightly more confident in Parliament than were their British counterparts in the British Parliament. But a comparison of the two rightmost columns in table 8.5 indicates that noticeable changes took place in Canada between

Table 8.5
Confidence in institutions
(percentages)

Institution	Confidence	Britain 1981	France 1981	W. Germany 1981	U.S. 1981	Canada 1981	Canada 1990
Legal system	Very	18.3	7.9	15.1	18.4	14.1	10.0
	Somewhat	47.4	48.5	51.4	34.8	50.3	44.0
	Not very	29.0	33.7	29.0	41.4	31.5	39.2
	Not at all	5.3	9.8	4.4	5.4	4.1	6.8
Press	Very	4.5	2.2	2.2	12.3	6.3	5.5
	Somewhat	23.8	30.3	28.1	37.5	38.9	40.8
	Not very	58.2	48.2	56.5	43.8	46.4	46.6
	Not at all	13.4	19.2	13.2	6.3	8.4	7.1
Unions	Very	4.7	4.0	4.9	10.7	4.9	5.0
	Somewhat	20.5	36.4	33.9	27.7	28.7	29.9
	Not very	52.0	39.4	47.2	48.4	50.8	49.4
	Not at all	22.8	20.2	13.9	13.2	15.6	15.7
Parliament	Very	8.7	6.5	8.6	14.7	7.1	5.6
	Somewhat	31.0	48.3	42.8	37.5	36.0	31.7
	Not very	48.7	32.0	43.5	40.7	44.3	52.0
	Not at all	11.7	13.2	5.0	7.1	12.6	10.7
Civil service	Very	7.9	4.3	3.8	17.1	7.4	6.1
	Somewhat	39.2	47.7	28.5	41.1	43.9	43.5
	Not very	45.2	36.4	56.2	35.2	40.2	43.0
	Not at all	7.7	11.5	11.2	6.6	8.6	7.5
Companies	Very	9.7	3.6	4.4	12.7	10.6	6.1
	Somewhat	40.4	45.1	29.5	36.9	45.8	45.3
	Not very	41.6	35.4	45.9	41.5	35.0	42.4
	Not at all	8.3	15.9	20.2	8.9	8.6	6.3
Canadian political system	Very						5.7
	Somewhat						32.1
	Not very						50.1
	Not at all						12.1

Sources: World Values Surveys (1981, 1990).

1981 and 1990. For example, public confidence in Parliament clearly dropped. Confidence in the legal system also eroded, but compared to other institutions, confidence in the legal system still ranked considerably higher than unions, the civil service or the press.

It has been shown that postmaterialism/materialism is related to the strength of citizen attachments to political parties. Does that value divide underpin differences in levels of confidence in a broader array of institutions that mediate individual–state relations? Figure 8.11 sheds light on that question and it shows how the levels of confidence of both postmaterialists and materialists have changed over the last 10 years.

Several findings are worth noting. First, with but one exception, the case of unions in 1990, postmaterialists consistently exhibited less confidence than materialists in all institutions under consideration. The gap is wide and consistent in the cases of the civil service, companies and the legal system – all institutions that in other settings are associated with maintaining the established status quo. Second, in only one instance, the case of the press, has the level of confidence on the part of postmaterialists increased. But then the press may be characterized more as a watchdog institution than as a supporter of the status quo. The third and perhaps most striking finding relates to confidence in Parliament. Plainly, postmaterialists had little confidence in Parliament in 1981. In fact, Parliament along with unions ranked lowest of all institutions, and that assessment did not change by 1990. What did change, according to these data, was how materialists viewed Parliament. The cumulative picture presented by these data is fairly clear. They suggest not only that postmaterialists have weaker attachments to traditional political parties but also that they have much less confidence than their materialist counterparts in a wide array of governmental and nongovernmental institutions. The Canadian data, in sum, are consistent with findings from other advanced industrial states. The rise of new politics *is* associated with weaker support for traditional representative institutions, and postmaterialism, as expected, does appear to depress conventional forms of political participation.

New Politics and Unconventional Forms of Political Participation

The erosion of conventional forms of citizen participation presents one challenge to representative institutions, the emergence of unconventional élite-challenging, and the rise of protest behaviours another. Postmaterialism, Inglehart claims, encourages unorthodox political behaviours because traditional representative institutions do not readily respond to, or accommodate, the political demands made by an increasingly well informed and politically sophisticated public (1990, 339–43).

Figure 8.11
Value priorities and confidence in institutions

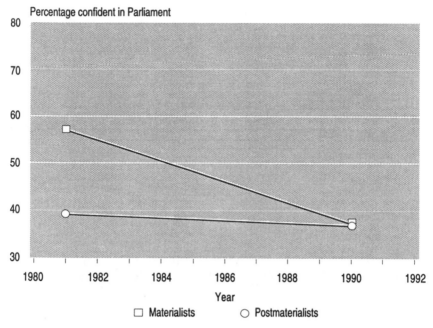

Percentage confident in Parliament

☐ Materialists   ○ Postmaterialists

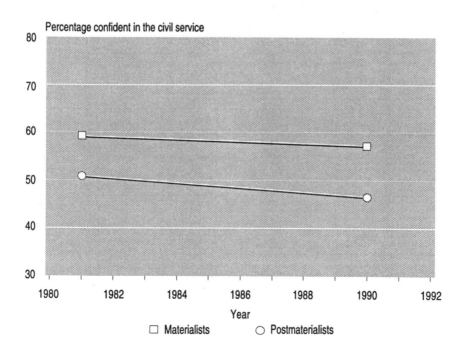

Percentage confident in the civil service

☐ Materialists   ○ Postmaterialists

Figure 8.11 (cont'd)
Value priorities and confidence in institutions

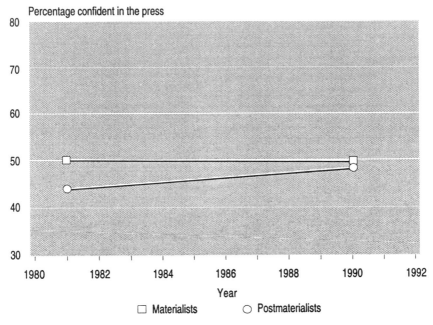

Percentage confident in the press

☐ Materialists   ○ Postmaterialists

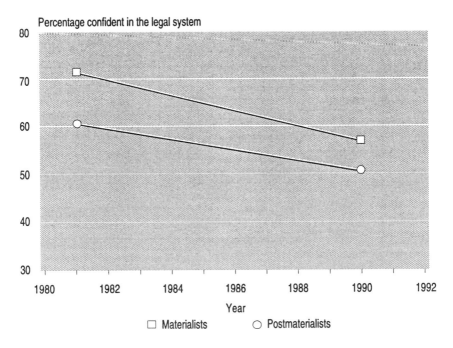

Percentage confident in the legal system

☐ Materialists   ○ Postmaterialists

Figure 8.11 (cont'd)
Value priorities and confidence in institutions

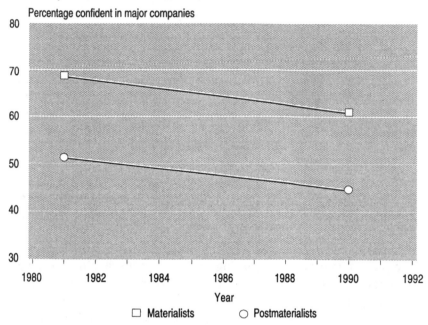

Percentage confident in major companies

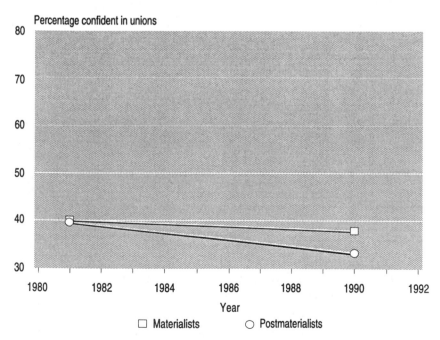

Percentage confident in unions

Sources: World Values Surveys (1981, 1990).

Despite the fact that protest behaviour has a long history in most Western states, the systematic empirical study of protest behaviour is a relatively recent phenomenon. It was stimulated by the proliferation of protest activities of middle-class groups – environmentalists, consumer activists, those advocating the rights of senior citizens, women, minorities – that adopted direct-action techniques during the 1970s (Dalton 1988; Farah et al. 1979). One result of the burgeoning study of protest behaviour in the last 15 years (Marsh 1977; Verba et al. 1978) has been the emergence of some conceptual consensus about how to tap unconventional political behaviours. These studies and others (such as Kaase and Marsh 1979) have suggested that it is useful to consider protest behaviour in terms of a hierarchy or continuum anchored at one end by such relatively benign protest activities as "signing a petition" and topped at the other by much more extreme protest activities, such as damage to property or personal violence. Figure 8.12 is adapted from a now widely used scale of protest behaviour, and it schematically depicts such a hierarchy of protest. The protest continuum, according to Dalton (1988, 65), is marked by several thresholds.[11] The precise locations of the thresholds are open to dispute, but the central point underscored by cross-national empirical evidence is that unconventional political behaviours are cumulative. Individuals engaging in protest at, say, the mid-point in the hierarchy typically also engage in the milder forms of direct action at lower levels in the protest hierarchy (ibid., 63 66).

Several cross-national studies, the World Values Surveys included, now routinely employ the same indicators of protest behaviour. Respondents in the 1981 surveys and the 1990 Canadian segment of the World Values Survey were presented with a card listing the protest activities, and each was asked "whether you have actually *done* any of these things, whether you might do it or would never, under any circumstances, do it." Table 8.6 reports the responses to these questions put to the British, French, West German, American and Canadian publics in 1981 and also to the 1990 Canadian survey. The results are revealing on several counts. First, the 1981 data suggest that the responses of the Canadian public are fairly typical of those of publics in other advanced industrial states. When one scans the responses in the "done" columns, for example, there is nothing to suggest that Canadians are less likely than other publics to have signed a petition or joined a boycott. The French public appears to have been most likely to have attended an unlawful demonstration, occupied a factory or joined an unofficial strike. Moreover, if the "never do" category measures aversion to protest, these data provide no evidence that Canadians are more "deferential"

Figure 8.12
Hierarchy of political protest action

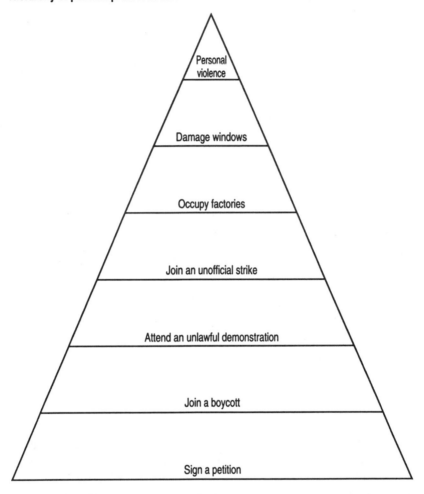

Personal violence

Damage windows

Occupy factories

Join an unofficial strike

Attend an unlawful demonstration

Join a boycott

Sign a petition

Source: Dalton (1988, 65).

or less inclined than publics in most other comparable states to engage in élite-challenging behaviour. In other words, there is no evidence of any historical residues of passive political behaviour to be found in the Canadian public of 1981.

A second striking finding is that the protest potential of the Canadian public appears to have increased significantly across all categories by 1990. The finding that the proportion of Canadians prepared to "sign a petition," an entirely legal activity that lies squarely within the norms of democratic behaviour, increased from just over 62 percent in 1981

Table 8.6
Forms of political protest action

Action	Response	Britain 1981	France 1981	W. Germany 1981	U.S. 1981	Canada 1981	Canada 1990
Sign a petition	Done	63.3	45.3	47.4	63.9	62.1	77.6
	Might do	28.1	33.0	37.3	24.0	27.0	14.4
	Never do	8.6	21.8	15.3	12.1	10.9	8.1
Join a boycott	Done	7.2	11.5	7.5	15.4	14.9	23.5
	Might do	31.4	38.1	34.0	37.1	44.8	42.8
	Never do	61.4	50.4	58.5	47.5	40.3	33.7
Attend an unlawful demonstration	Done	9.9	26.7	14.7	13.0	13.4	22.2
	Might do	35.1	31.5	36.9	14.1	45.3	42.4
	Never do	55.0	41.8	48.4	46.9	41.3	35.4
Join an unofficial strike	Done	6.9	10.1	1.8	3.4	4.7	7.5
	Might do	18.7	26.3	14.1	18.0	17.7	28.0
	Never do	74.5	63.6	84.0	78.7	77.7	64.7
Occupy factories	Done	2.5	7.3	1.5	1.7	2.5	3.2
	Might do	12.6	25.6	12.7	10.1	16.4	20.4
	Never do	84.9	67.2	85.8	88.2	81.1	76.3
Damage windows	Done	2.1	0.6	1.3	1.5	1.4	
	Might do	1.6	4.8	1.3	1.8	3.0	n.a.
	Never do	96.2	94.6	97.5	96.7	95.6	
Personal violence	Done	0.9	1.0	1.3	1.9	1.3	
	Might do	4.1	8.1	2.2	3.8	4.3	n.a.
	Never do	95.0	90.9	96.6	94.4	94.4	

Sources: World Values Surveys (1981, 1990).

n.a. = not available.

to more than 77 percent in 1990, may be little cause for concern. A more problematic challenge to the political status quo, perhaps, is the evidence of increased potential for other sorts of protest action. By 1990, only about a third of respondents reported that they would never join a boycott or attend an unlawful demonstration. Moreover, whereas in 1981 more than three-quarters of Canadians claimed that they would never join an unofficial strike, by 1990 the proportion of the public taking the same position slipped to less than two-thirds.

Evidence has been presented that unequivocally points to the rise of new politics in Canada, and the data presented in table 8.6 clearly show that the protest potential of Canadians has unequivocally increased since 1981. There is circumstantial evidence, then, for drawing the inference that the advance of postmaterialism is linked, as Inglehart predicts, to protest behaviour. But what is the direct evidence? A comparison of the protest behaviours of materialist and postmaterialist value types yields truly striking differences. The differences are statistically significant ($p < .01$) and strong (gamma = .29).[12] Postmaterialists are far more likely to engage in protest behaviour. According to the 1990 data, just over 45 percent of postmaterialists had engaged in at least two protest behaviours, although less than 20 percent of materialists reported that they had done so.

The graphic presented in figure 8.13 presents both a more complete and more complex picture. It shows, first, that there were consistent

Figure 8.13
Hierarchy of political protest action by value priorities: Canada, 1981 and 1990
(percentages)

1981				1990		
Percentage done	Materialist	Post-materialist		Percentage done	Materialist	Post-materialist
1.3	1.2	1.1	Personal violence	NA*	NA*	NA*
1.4	1.9	2.2	Damage windows	NA*	NA*	NA*
2.5	2.8	3.8	Occupy factories	3.5	1.7	5.9
4.7	4.4	7.1	Join an unofficial strike	7.4	4.4	10.4
13.4	9.1	23.0	Attend an unlawful demonstration	22.3	14.7	32.4
14.9	9.7	23.5	Join a boycott	24.1	12.6	32.9
62.1	54.0	66.1	Sign a petition	77.5	65.8	86.2

Sources: World Values Surveys (1981, 1990).

*NA = not asked.

differences in the protest activities of materialists and postmaterialists both in 1981 and in 1990. Postmaterialists were more likely to engage in every form of protest at both times. There were no 1990 data for the most extreme forms of protest, but the available data show that, on average, materialists were more likely to engage in protest in 1990 than they were in 1981. But then so were postmaterialists. In fact the gap in protest behaviours of materialists and postmaterialists widened substantially by 1990. These patterns of protest provide further support for the postmaterialist thesis. The findings are consistent with evidence from other advanced industrial states, and they suggest, once again, that the consequences of emergent new politics in Canada are similar to those found in other national settings.

Postmaterialism, Issue-Driven Politics and the Charter

Thus far, this analysis has shown that the levels of new-politics values in Canada are comparable with those found in other advanced industrial states, that the rise of new politics is associated with the redistribution of political skills and that there are predictable consequences of the rise of new politics for both conventional and unconventional patterns of political participation. What remains to be explored is the question of whether there are any substantive links between the political agenda of new politics and Charter issues. One feature of the political changes associated with postmaterialism is that publics are increasingly "issue-driven" (Inglehart 1990, 340-42). Armed with new political skills and guided by new-politics values, new-politics adherents are not only averse to traditional representative institutions, but they are also promoters of a nontraditional agenda. A variety of studies employing evidence from western European and American publics have made significant advances in mapping out the issue space that separates the traditional and new agendas (Sears and Citrin 1985; Dalton and Baker 1987). One such issue space has to do with attitudes toward government. Traditional political conflicts typically revolved around the "size of government." The old Left sought an expanded, redistributive state, and the old Right resisted "big government." Recent longitudinal evidence suggests, however, that publics, particularly adherents of new politics, are increasingly critical of big government. At the same time, they are also accustomed to the policy scope of the modern state (Lipset and Schneider 1983). Available survey evidence suggests that new-politics adherents are less tolerant of tax increases, but they do not seem prepared to have those programs promoting social equality dismantled (Jowell and Witherspoon 1985). Canadian research has produced similar findings (Nevitte et al. 1989).

"Peace and pollution" represent a second cluster of issues that concern new-politics adherents. New-politics support for antinuclear power and antiwar and environmental movements has been amply documented in both western Europe and the United States (Buerklin 1987; Chafer 1986; Kitschelt 1988; Mueller-Rommel 1985; Reudig 1988). Linkages between opposition to environmental degradation and support for new-politics values have also been found in the Canadian setting (Bakvis and Nevitte 1990). And table 8.7 provides more definitive evidence that amplifies earlier findings. It shows that on seven of the eight survey items tapping environmental attitudes in the 1990 Canadian segment of the World Values Survey, postmaterialists are more concerned than materialists about ecological issues. In responses to the eighth item, a very general question, "Do you approve or disapprove of the ecology movement or nature protection?", the approval ratings of both materialists and postmaterialists were so high that statistical tests of difference would be meaningless.

Table 8.7
Environmental issues and value priorities

Question	Response	Materialist (%)	Postmaterialist (%)	Chi square (dof)	Sig
I would give part of my income if I were certain that the money would be used to prevent environmental pollution.	Agree Disagree	58.7 41.3	81.1 18.9	32.81 (1)	.00
I would agree to an increase in taxes if the extra money is used to prevent environmental pollution.	Agree Disagree	57.4 42.6	73.7 26.3	15.14 (1)	.00
The government has to reduce environmental pollution but it should not cost me any money.	Agree Disagree	62.4 37.6	38.3 61.7	29.14 (1)	.00
All the talk about pollution makes people too anxious.	Agree Disagree	59.5 40.5	39.2 60.8	20.78 (1)	.00
If we want to combat unemployment in this country, we shall just have to accept environmental problems.	Agree Disagree	38.8 61.2	26.2 73.8	8.95 (1)	.00
Protecting the environment and fighting pollution is less urgent than often suggested.	Agree Disagree	24.9 75.1	15.1 84.9	7.51 (1)	.01
Do you approve or disapprove of the ecology movement or nature protection?	Approve Disapprove	96.3 3.7	96.7 3.3	.00 (1)	1.0

Source: World Values Survey (1990).

More central to the *Canadian Charter of Rights and Freedoms* than to the size of government and "peace and pollution," however, are issues that specifically relate to Charter groups – women and minorities. Postmaterialists, Inglehart has argued, are concerned about the quality of life, and for postmaterialists the concept of quality of life is an expansive one. Its reach includes not just environmental issues and issues relating to peace and to qualitatively different forms of political participation; it also encompasses issues relating to social equality for women and for racial and ethnic minorities (Inglehart 1990, 177–211, 371–92). If the rise of new politics has implications for Canada's representative institutions because it increases the chances that issues relating to the status of women and minorities will be politicized, then one would expect to find systematic differences between materialists and postmaterialists in attitudes to Charter groups. The 1990 Canadian segment of the World Values Survey contained a variety of items probing attitudes about the role of women in the family and the workplace, and table 8.8 displays materialist and postmaterialist responses to eight such questions. First, these data show that there are systematic and significant differences between materialists and postmaterialists on four of the eight items. On three of the remaining questions the differences between the two value types are not significant but they operate in the predicted direction. For example, that materialists are more likely than postmaterialists to agree that "the best way for a woman to be an independent person" is "having a job" and that "both the husband and wife should contribute to household income" is not surprising. Both responses are consistent with the economic preoccupations of materialists. The responses to the eighth item, an item that combines elements of both the materialist and postmaterialist agendas, indicate no consistent pattern.

The 1990 survey also included questions that tapped attitudes about a variety of issues relating to minorities, race and immigrants, and more generally issues about tolerance. Table 8.9 compares materialist and postmaterialist responses to minority issues and the results are again consistent with postmaterialist predictions. Postmaterialists are more trusting of immigrants; they are less likely to object to having immigrants, or "people of a different race," as neighbours, they disapprove more strongly of apartheid and they are less likely than materialists to support a Canadians-first policy in the workplace. Somewhat surprisingly, materialists are more likely to rate "tolerance" as an important value for children.[13]

Considered together, the evidence presented in tables 8.8 and 8.9

Table 8.8
Women's issues and value priorities

Question	Response	Materialist (%)	Postmaterialist (%)	Chi square (dof)	Sig
A working mother can establish just as warm and secure a relationship with her children as a mother who does not work.	Agree Disagree	66.0 34.0	72.8 27.2	2.60 (1)	.11
A preschool child is likely to suffer if his or her mother works.	Agree Disagree	62.4 37.6	49.5 50.5	8.20 (1)	.00
A job is all right but what most women really want is a home and children.	Agree Disagree	55.8 44.2	34.4 65.6	21.71 (1)	.00
Being a housewife is just as fulfilling as working for pay.	Agree Disagree	74.2 25.8	69.6 30.4	1.10 (1)	.29
Having a job is the best way for a woman to be an independent person.	Agree Disagree	60.4 39.6	53.2 46.8	2.47 (1)	.12
Both the husband and wife should contribute to household income.	Agree Disagree	72.3 27.7	65.4 34.6	2.46 (1)	.12
When jobs are scarce, men have more right to a job than women.	Agree Disagree	30.8 69.2	12.4 87.6	26.89 (1)	.00
Do you approve or disapprove of the women's movement?	Approve Disapprove	81.0 19.0	88.8 11.2	5.92 (1)	.01

Source: World Values Survey (1990).

clearly suggests that postmaterialists are generally more sympathetic to status-of-women and minority issues. The implication, then, is that the advance of postmaterialism will increase the likelihood that women's issues and minority issues will attract higher levels of support within the Canadian public. It is important to emphasize, however, that these findings relate to *general* attitudes toward women and minorities. Collectively, these data tap orientations that fall well beyond the more particular scope of the Charter.

A more reliable guide to the potential politicization of Charter issues can be provided by limiting our attention to three questions that more closely relate to section 15 Charter issues.[14] Respondents were asked:

1. When jobs are scarce, men have more right to a job than women. (Agree/Disagree)
2. When jobs are scarce, employers should give priority to Canadians over immigrants. (Agree/Disagree)

Table 8.9
Minority issues and value priorities

Question	Response	Materialist (%)	Postmaterialist (%)	Chi square (dof)	Sig
Would you *not* like to have as neighbours: people of a different race?	Mention	8.8	4.5	3.21 (1)	.07
	Not mention	91.2	95.5		
Would you *not* like to have as neighbours: immigrants/foreign workers?	Mention	8.8	5.5	1.54 (1)	.22
	Not mention	91.2	94.5		
When jobs are scarce, employers should give priority to Canadians over immigrants.	Agree	63.3	45.8	14.64 (1)	.00
	Disagree	36.7	54.2		
Which qualities do you consider especially important for a child to learn at home? (Tolerance and respect for other people.)	Mention	21.2	15.6	2.60 (1)	.11
	Not mention	78.8	84.4		
Do you approve or disapprove of the anti-apartheid movement?	Approve	85.0	88.0	0.59 (1)	.44
	Disapprove	15.0	12.0		
Do you trust recent immigrants?	Trust	66.1	79.2	6.93 (1)	.01
	Do not trust	33.9	20.8		

Source: World Values Survey (1990).

3. When jobs are scarce, people should be forced to retire early. (Agree/Disagree)

All three questions probe respondent attitudes in the workplace. The first explores discrimination on the basis of sex, the second addresses discrimination on the basis of nationality and the third, age. All relate to provisions in section 15 of the Charter. A straightforward comparison of materialist and postmaterialist responses to each question shows that postmaterialists tend to disagree and materialists to agree that, under conditions of job scarcity, giving priority to men, Canadians and the young is permissible. The differences, moreover, are significant in each case ($p < .01$). When one considers all questions together, by simply constructing an additive Charter scale,[15] the data show that materialists are about four times as likely as postmaterialists to agree with all questions. Postmaterialists, conversely, are about twice as likely as materialists to disagree with all questions. As would be expected, the differences are statistically significant, and the association among value type, scores on the materialist-postmaterialist scale and location on the Charter scale is reasonably strong (gamma = .25).

The findings presented in this section are revealing in several respects. If, as has been argued, new politics produces a more skilled, more élite-challenging and more issue-driven public, then the likelihood that new politics will encourage challenges to traditional representative institutions and the politicization of Charter issues hinges partly on the extent to which the issue spaces occupied by new-politics adherents and old-politics adherents are congruent or divergent. Cross-national evidence unequivocally shows that old- and new-politics adherents do not share issue space with respect to issues such as the size of government or "peace and pollution," and available Canadian evidence reproduces the same findings. But it has also been shown that new- and old-politics adherents diverge significantly on both general orientations toward minorities and the status of women and to more particular orientations that are more closely tied to section 15 provisions in the Charter – issues relating to discrimination on the basis of sex, nationality and age. Figure 8.14 graphically summarizes these findings. It illustrates the extent to which materialists and post-materialists hold divergent positions on Charter issues, on issues that classically separate adherents of new and old politics, such as environmentalism, and on the kinds of strategies both value types are inclined to adopt in pursuing their agendas.

This study began with the proposition that challenges to the Charter in Canada and the difficulties confronted by Canada's traditional representative institutions may be unique examples of a more general phenomenon – the rise of new politics. It was argued that some insights into problems relating to governability or the future prospects for domestic political tranquillity might be gained by exploring the hypothesis that new politics provides an optic through which problems of representation might be understood. To this point, the task has focused on examining separately and serially the connections between materialist/postmaterialist orientations and political discussion, political interest, cognitive mobilization, citizen attachments to established political parties, confidence in institutions, protest behaviours and issue space; however, more critical to the shape of future politics, to the likelihood that new politics feeds Charter challenges and promotes direct-action strategies outside conventional political avenues, is the question of whether, and how, new-politics orientations encompass or link Charter attitudes and protest behaviour. To explore the connectedness of these issues requires a somewhat different statistical approach: path analysis. Figure 8.15 schematically illustrates the links between new-politics orientations, and Charter and protest orientations for the Canadian public in 1990. Two basic findings emerge from the path analysis. The

Figure 8.14
The Charter, the environment and protest activity by value priorities

Materialist and postmaterialist support for Charter issues

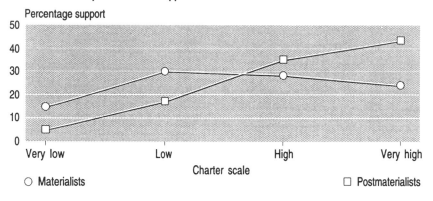

Percentage support

Charter scale

○ Materialists   □ Postmaterialists

Materialist and postmaterialist support for environmental issues

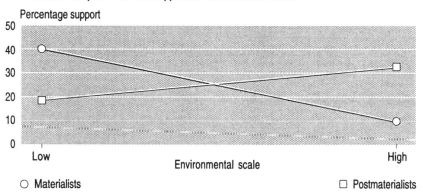

Percentage support

Environmental scale

○ Materialists   □ Postmaterialists

Materialist and postmaterialist protest activity

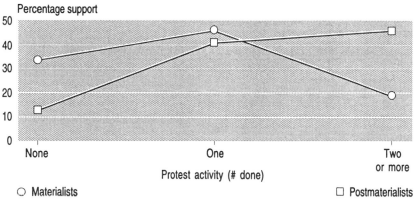

Percentage support

Protest activity (# done)

○ Materialists   □ Postmaterialists

Source: World Values Survey (1990).

first is that new-politics orientations are directly related both to respondents' positions on the Charter and to protest behaviour. Significantly, the strength of the linkage between postmaterialism and Charter position is only very slightly weaker than the linkage between postmaterialism and public positions on environmentalism – the issue that has been most often associated with new-politics orientation. Put more simply, postmaterialism is almost as good a predictor of Charter orientations as it is of environmental orientations. The second basic finding is that protest orientations are at best only very weakly related to orientations to the Charter. Or, conversely, a respondent's position on Charter issues provides no reliable guide for predicting a respondent's attitudes toward conventional or unconventional political behaviours. New-politics orientations provide a reliable guide for a respondent's inclinations toward protest and Charter orientations, but Charter orientations and protest attitudes are not, by themselves, connected.

The analysis presented in figure 8.15 is based on pooled data, on a sample of the entire Canadian population. But, it is reasonable to suppose, on the grounds of self-interest alone, that different segments of the Canadian public, for example men and women, may hold widely divergent attitudes toward Charter issues and exhibit quite different patterns of linkage between new politics, the Charter and protest.

Figure 8.15
New politics, the Charter and protest behaviour: a path analysis

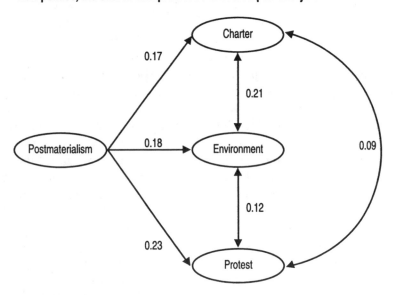

Source: World Values Survey (1990).

Figure 8.16 replicates the path analysis presented in figure 8.15 but it does so first for women respondents only and then for men. The findings in figure 8.16 can be most usefully evaluated by comparing the data with those presented in figure 8.15. The findings show, as predicted, that new-politics orientations and Charter position are more strongly linked for women respondents than for men; however, the path between postmaterialism and protest is somewhat stronger for male respondents than it is for females. More striking, perhaps, is the finding that the link between protest and Charter orientations is stronger for women than for men. For women, position on the Charter is a better predictor of protest activity and vice versa. Parallel findings have been reported elsewhere for public attitudes toward Canada's native people (Wohlfeld and Nevitte 1990).

Apart from women, minorities make up a second group that clearly stands to gain or lose with the politics of the Charter. Canada, as many observers have pointed out, is increasingly a society of minorities, and, consequently, the politics of minority–state relations will become an increasingly important axis in Canadian political life (Nevitte and Kornberg 1985). Cairns (1990) correctly argues that the dynamics of population replacement present new challenges to representative institutions, and one field of play for the battle of minority rights will undoubtedly be the Charter. Cairns's initial position was that the changing structural shape of the Canadian population raises the problem of how Canadians from one cultural group could be represented by Canadians from another group. At the outset, this study expanded the range of issues relevant to the representation of minorities to include other questions – namely, how will minorities themselves seek to promote their goals and explore the practical score of their rights? And, how will the Canadian public respond to the politicization of minority issues? In the light of the preceding analysis one might also ask: What does new politics have to do with these questions?

In general, any analysis of the impact of population replacement on issues such as the politics of value change has to take into account both the natural replacement of domestic populations and immigration-emigration. Postmaterialist theory contains explicit expectations to the effect that age, life-cycle and cohort effects will have a significant impact upon the distribution of new-politics values. The initial cross-national analyses of postmaterialism (Inglehart 1971, 1977) demonstrated quite powerful age-related effects on value change. Those age effects have, however, weakened, and when the recent Canadian evidence of the linkages between generations and postmaterialism was explored (figure 8.3) the data indicated that generational effects in Canada were

Figure 8.16
**New politics, the Charter and protest behaviour: a path analysis
for Canadian females and males**

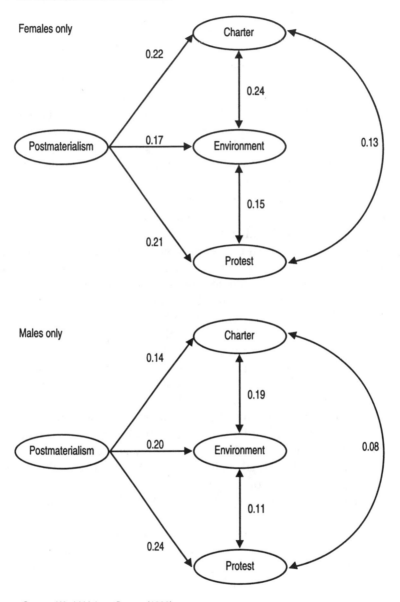

Females only

Males only

Source: World Values Survey (1990).

unusually weak compared with those found in other national settings.
Indeed, stepwise logistical regression analysis demonstrated that the age

effects could be discounted almost entirely in contemporary Canada. In that context the potential impact of immigration becomes crucial.

One speculation was that the shifting patterns of Canadian immigration, i.e., the substantial decline in immigrants from Europe and the increased significance of the Third World as a source of population replacement, might be explained in economic terms. The standard-of-living gap between Canada and Europe has narrowed, but it remains wide between Canada and the Third World. If immigration is driven by these economic considerations alone, it is reasonable to suppose that there would be substantial differences between those born in Canada and those born outside the country when it comes to locations on the materialism/postmaterialism scale. The evidence, somewhat surprisingly, suggests otherwise.[16] The data indicate that respondents born outside of Canada rate as high as the Canadian-born respondents on the postmaterialism scale and that ethnicity and years of residence in Canada have no significant impact on postmaterialist/materialist inclinations.[17]

Even though few differences between the postmaterialism of Canadian-born and non-Canadian-born respondents can be detected in the data, the linkages between new-politics orientations, the Charter and protest can nonetheless be quite different. Indeed, the path-analysis results of these two groups presented in figure 8.17 reveal significant differences. Not surprisingly, the results of the path analysis for Canadian-born respondents are similar to those of the Canadian population as a whole (figure 8.15). The connection between postmaterialism and Charter orientation, moreover, is somewhat stronger than for the pooled sample as is the path between postmaterialism and protest. These findings, however, stand in stark contrast with those for non-Canadian-born respondents. For them, the linkage between postmaterialism and position on the Charter is very weak indeed, and the connection between postmaterialism and protest is also weaker than for their Canadian-born counterparts.

Two important implications flow from these findings. The first is that for native-born Canadians, new politics clearly encourages the politicization of Charter issues. This group scores high on the Charter scale, the data suggest, for principled reasons that have their roots in new politics itself – a preference for social equality. The clear implication is that the advance of new politics produces greater support for Charter-related causes.

The second finding is that the same logic does not apply to minorities themselves. That is, minorities are likely to support and pursue Charter issues not because of new-politics orientations but because they *are* minorities. The data show that for non-Canadian-born respond-

Figure 8.17
New politics, the Charter and protest behaviour: a path analysis
for Canadian- and non-Canadian-born respondents

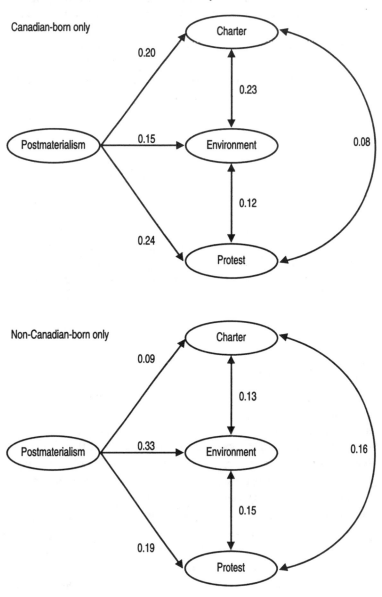

Source: World Values Survey (1990).

ents there is still a significant linkage between new-politics orientations and protest, but the linkage is weaker than for the rest of the Canadian population. But the data also show that the connection between Charter and protest orientations is much stronger than for the rest of the population. For non-Canadian-born respondents, in fact, the path between protest and Charter orientations (.16) is almost as strong as the path between protest and postmaterialism (.19). In summary, the advance of new politics does appear to have significant implications for the politicization of Charter issues. The political environment in which the non-Canadian-born segment of the population lives is increasingly supportive of Charter issues, and it is more supportive, the data suggest, because of the rise of new politics.

CONCLUSION

In bringing this analysis to a close it is useful to synthesize and review some of the central findings and to consider, more generally, what implications the findings have for political representation and for the politics surrounding the Charter. The very first question posed was: Is there evidence of new politics in the Canadian setting? The answer to that question, according to the evidence presented, is unequivocally "yes." Two findings are of particular significance in that respect. First, by most structural criteria, Canada clearly does qualify as an advanced industrial state, and so there are reasons to believe that new-politics values would take hold in this national setting as they have in others. The direct evidence demonstrates not only that Canada has not escaped the advance of new politics, but also that the levels of new-politics values are comparable with those found in other advanced industrial settings at a similar time. Those values, furthermore, are distributed throughout the Canadian public in proportions that are comparable with the distributions found in other states.

Second, the proportion of the Canadian public cleaving to new-politics values has clearly increased in the course of the last decade. The evidence is striking in that the rate of increase is neither marginal nor glacial. The size of the new-politics segment of the Canadian public has increased by about 15 percent in less than 10 years. One in four Canadians, in 1990, exhibited new-politics values. The data are striking in another respect. The value change is not limited to one segment of the Canadian public; it is secular. The evidence points to a sea change, and by 1990 postmaterialists outnumbered materialists.

The next broad question examined was: What impact does new politics have on citizen attachments to political parties? The central answer to that question is that new politics has the same impact on citizen attachments to political parties in Canada as it has had on comparable publics in other advanced industrial states. They weaken. When other factors are taken into account, postmaterialists are less likely than others to identify with traditional political parties, and they are less likely to vote. Inglehart's explanation for why those adhering to new politics are less enchanted with traditional institutions has to do with the narrowing of the political-skills gap between élites and publics. This analysis has provided some support for that explanation; postmaterialists are politically more skilled than others, they are better informed about politics and they are more interested in politics. The evidence also suggests that the relatively weak attachments of postmaterialists to political parties tells only part of a larger story. Postmaterialists also exhibit less confidence in a variety of other governmental and nongovernmental institutions that mediate individual–state relations.

The third part of the analysis explored the implications of advancing new politics for unconventional forms of political behaviour, protest politics. By no stretch of the imagination, the evidence shows, can new-politics adherents be discounted as mere non-participants or apathetic. Quite the contrary. The rise of new politics is unequivocally linked to the rise of protest behaviour in Canada, as it is elsewhere. New-politics adherents are not only more skilled and better informed about political life, they are also more interested and motivated to participate, but they are more likely to do so through direct-action strategies; they have a larger political-action repertoire. Systematic analyses of political protest in Canada are few and far between (Welch 1975; Clarke et al. 1985). Political discontent, of course, is not new, and voicing complaints about policy and politicians is fair game, even popular sport, in most advanced industrial states. The politics of discontent, certainly in the 1970s and 1980s, could be adequately described in terms of the absence of a policy or national mandate (Clarke et al. 1984). The rise of new politics, however, introduces another dimension, *the absence of a "process mandate."* New-politics adherents are concerned not only about policy but also about the *quality of political participation.*

The final substantive section of the analysis addressed the questions: How are new-politics orientations related to attitudinal structures that shape issue positions relating to Charter groups, women and minorities? And, how are these related to the dynamics of population replacement? The findings, once more, are clear. New-politics adherents, the evidence shows, obviously do occupy an issue space that encompasses orientations and issues relevant to Charter politics. New-politics adherents, in Canada and in general, are more responsive to what might be called women's and minority issues. The data suggest then that the advance of new-politics values would likely produce greater support for these groups and others striving for greater social equality. That general support, it appears, also translates into support for more specific, section 15-type Charter challenges. The dynamics of support, however, appear to work in slightly different ways for different segments of the population. For women, holding postmaterialist values has a powerful bearing on their position on Charter issues. For racial and ethnic minorities, materialist orientations are all but irrelevant; orientations toward Charter issues are a function of their objective social locations, not postmaterialism. The implication is clear. Cairns (1990) is correct in supposing that to the extent that the dynamics of population replacement encourage greater cultural heterogeneity, they also increase the likelihood of Charter challenges. To that conclusion, however, there is also another aspect to consider, namely, postmaterialism itself also encourages the broader politicization of Charter issues in the segment of the population that is not a minority. Both dynamics, in turn, are related to the potential for protest behaviour.

It is only possible to speculate about the long-term implications of new politics for the broad issues relating to political representation in Canada. Inglehart, it must be emphasized, makes no claim that the advance of new politics is inevitable or that it is destined to increase at all times. Indeed, the expectation is that the advance of new-politics values is contingent upon a variety of socialization factors and, importantly, structural factors such as continued affluence. Thus, a substantial reversal of economic fortunes, presumably, would result in a decline in postmaterialism and an increase in materialism. Indeed, such a short-term decline, a period effect, was detected in western European publics during the first oil crisis. But, to the extent that advanced industrial states continue to enjoy relatively stable growth, the increase of new politics appears likely. Furthermore, if, as the data suggest, educational levels do drive new politics, then to the extent that advanced industrial states continue to expand postsecondary education opportunities for citizens (and they can hardly afford not to do so), the political-skill gap between élites and publics can be expected to continue to narrow. The evidence presented in this study suggests that the challenge to traditional representative institutions comes from the interaction of both more widely held political skills and the emergence of a new agenda. The increase in protest potential, in turn, both indicates that publics will be more difficult to govern and provides a measure of the extent to which traditional representative institutions have failed to respond to the new challenges. Kitschelt (1990, 1–2) analyses the dilemma in essentially similar but broader terms:

Whereas the economic challenge of international competitiveness has led to a realignment of economic interests in the acquisition of revenue among capital and labour between sectors, regions and occupational groups of labour, the cultural challenge of reproduction involves a transformation of cognitive frames and normative preferences. At stake is no longer how to reach what everyone takes to be valuable in society (income, power), but to value new experiences that are not provided by the market society itself.

Quality of participation, or what has been called the process mandate, appears to be one such nonmarket value that is central to resolving some of the issues related to representation. Clearly, one crucial question that emerges is: How can representative institutions respond? Presumably, political parties are not merely vehicles for satisfying the narrowly defined interests of contributors; the *manner* in which parties and other representative institutions respond to a claim-making public has symbolic significance. As Kitschelt (1989, 41–74) notes, "the way parties conduct their internal life sends a message to voters about what kind of society its activists and leaders aspire to." The specifics of how political parties and other representative institutions can respond to the challenges, what are the available opportunities, possible strategies and constraints, fall beyond the scope of this study. The western European experience, however, suggests that several factors are pertinent (Gallagher and Marsh 1988; Katz 1990; Strom 1990). The extent to which party organizations are flexible or rigid, the extent to which representative institutions respond to or deflect the forces of change, has to be evaluated from a variety of perspectives including the following: membership and leadership recruitment; resistance to, or acceptance of, new ideas from below, middle-level functionaries and leaders; how interests, visions, routines and ideas combine to allow or to resist change; and the role of party conferences. Clearly, political parties share a broad interest to the extent that they aspire to hold or keep office. Yet it is also clear, according to some analysts of western European parties, that the interests of party leaders, functionaries and members can conspire to resist innovation, to avoid change and to reinforce continuity at the cost of innovation. Ironically, under these circumstances representative institutions threaten to become both the accomplices of the process and, in the end, victims.

APPENDIX
A SUMMARY OF THE 1990 WORLD VALUES SURVEY (CANADA)

The quota sampling procedure was designed to produce an approximation of the adult civilian population, 18 years and older, living in Canada, except for those persons in institutions such as prisons or hospitals, or those residing in far northern regions.

The sample design incorporated stratification by six community-size groups, based on the 1986 census data: cities of 500 000 population and more, those between 100 000 and 500 000, 30 000 to 100 000, 10 000 to 30 000, 1 000 to 10 000 and rural farm and rural nonfarm areas.

The population was arrayed in geographic order by community size and, within these classifications, by census enumeration areas. Enumeration areas, on average, contained about 500 to 1 000 people.

A total of 140 enumeration areas were selected randomly from this array. Within urban centres, a random-block sampling procedure was used to select starting points for interviewers. The interviewer was provided with a map of the enumeration area, showing the location of the starting-point, and was required to follow a specified route in the selection of households. Within the household, the youngest male, 18 years and over, at home at the time of the interview, was questioned. If no male was available, or when the male quota was completed, the youngest female, 18 years and over, was interviewed.

The selection of rural farm and rural nonfarm interviewing locations follows the sample design established for urban centres in terms of geographic dispersion and random selection of enumeration areas. Because of the low population density and wide dispersion of households, the random-block sampling procedure was replaced by quota sampling based on sex and age.

The design of this sample was based on population statistics from the Census of Canada (1986). The author of this study can be contacted for further design details.

NOTES

Much of the analysis in this study would not have been possible without the generous assistance of the Donner Canadian Foundation, which provided financial support for the 1990 Canadian segment of the World Values Survey. I would like to express my gratitude to the Donner Canadian Foundation for its support and to thank Lori Davis for her very capable research assistance.

1. If traditional migrants were motivated primarily by economic opportunity, then it is reasonable to suppose that the trend of increased immigration from the Third World will continue as long as the European standard of living remains close to the Canadian standard of living.

2. Strong parallels, though, can be found in the Australian experience. See Nevitte and Gibbins (1990).

3. Huntington (1974, 163–64) summarizes the thresholds used to distinguish postindustrial from industrial and agrarian societies in the following way:

   a. the economic predominance of the service sector in contrast to the industrial and agricultural sectors;

   b. the predominance in the labour force of white-collar rather than blue-collar workers and, particularly, the widespread and critical role in the economy of professional, technical, and managerial workers;

   c. a central role in the economy and society of theoretical knowledge, technology, research and development as opposed to physical capital and, consequently, the predominance not of factories but of institutions, such as universities, think-tanks, and media devoted to the creation and transmission of information;

   d. high and widespread levels of economic well-being and affluence, leading to increased leisure for the bulk of the population, with a few isolated "pockets" of poverty, in contrast to a small prosperous élite and widespread poverty;

   e. higher levels of education for the bulk of the population, with a college education becoming general, in contrast to a norm of primary education;

   f. a new "postbourgeois" value structure concerned with the quality of life and humanistic values, in contrast to a "Protestant" inner-directed work ethic.

4. For example, attacks have been levelled against the Maslowian underpinnings of the theory; it has been claimed, for example, that the notion of a needs hierarchy remains underspecified. It has also been argued that the relative weight attached to the scarcity and socialization hypotheses has shifted, and, on the methodological front, issue has been taken with how postmaterialism is operationalized. In addition, questions have been raised about whether postmaterialism captures more than a single dimension and whether generational effects have been successfully isolated from period and life-cycle effects. A representative selection of the literature surrounding these debates would include the following: Flanagan (1982); Boeltken and Jagodzinski (1985); Marsh (1975); Van Deth (1983); Lafferty and Knutsen (1985); Bakvis and Nevitte (1987); Inglehart (1985).

5. A comparison of longer-term trends evident in Eurobarometer, European Community Studies and Center for Political Studies (CPS), University of Michigan election data covering the period 1970–86 yields very similar results. See Inglehart (1990, 91–103) and Dalton (1988, 83–85).

6. In this case postmaterialism enters the equation as the dependent variable, and all other structural variables listed in table 8.2 (i.e., age, education, occupation, income, language, gender, region and union membership) operate as independent variables. Essentially, stepwise logistic regression (SLR) procedures compute maximum-likelihood estimates of a logistic model in which

independent variables may be either categorical or continuous and in which no assumptions about normality are made (see Engelman (1983, 941–69)). The SLR procedure enters independent predictor variables in an order determined hierarchically in terms of goodness of fit (chi square) through successive data sweeps. Thus, SLR conducts an initial sweep of all independent variables (step 0) to identify which term provides the best single predictor of postmaterialism. Successive sweeps of the data enter the best predictor (i.e., education) as a control and then scan the remaining independent variables in search of those that significantly contribute to the remainder of the model. The results of the SLR procedures can be summarized as follows:

Step 0	p value	Step 1	p value	Step 2	p value
		Control: education		Controls: education, gender	
Education	.0027				
Occupation	.0435				
Language	.0486				
Gender	.0496	Gender	.0579	Language	.0937

7. For the purposes of the following analysis the cognitive mobilization index is built as an additive scale from a standard, trichotomized education variable (1 = less than high school, 2 = completed high school, 3 = more than high school) and a trichotomized political interest variable (1 = little or no interest in politics, 2 = moderately interested in politics, 3 = very interested in politics). Respondents scoring 2 or 3 on the additive scale are simply categorized as "low" on cognitive mobilization. Those scoring 4, 5 or 6 on the scale are rated as "high" on cognitive mobilization.

8. This extensive debate features a number of dissenting views. For example, Porter (1965), Wiseman and Taylor (1974) and Simeon and Elkins (1974) produce evidence that the impact of class and status on political participation varies by region.

9. The differences between materialists and postmaterialists are statistically significant across the "very strong," "strong" and "not very strong" categories.

10. A very large proportion of all respondents (91.7 percent) agreed. The proportions of postmaterialists and materialists doing so were 94.4 percent and 85.2 percent, respectively.

11. Thus, "signing a petition" and "joining a boycott" may be relatively benign protest activities, but they represent a transition from orthodox to unorthodox behaviours. The next threshold, "attending an unlawful demonstration" or "joining an unofficial strike," marks a shift to unconventional direct-action strategies. "Occupying a factory" entails illegal but nonviolent action, whereas "damaging windows" and "personal violence" represent both illegal and violent protest actions.

12. The statistical comparison is based on the number of protest behaviours in which materialists and postmaterialists reported they had participated. The range is from none (materialists, 33.7 percent; postmaterialists, 13.5 percent) to five (materialists, 0.0 percent; postmaterialists, 3.6 percent).

13. One explanation for what appears to be an inconsistent result might relate to the format for the question. Respondents were presented with a fixed battery of values considered important for children. Forced choice rankings, however, are sensitive to the interaction effects between a single item and other items on the scale, and to that extent they are less reliable.

14. The section 15 Charter provision applies to relationships involving governments directly or relationships regulated by government. See *Retail, Wholesale and Department Store Unions, Local 580 et al. v. Dolphin Delivery Ltd.*, (1986), 33 D.L.R. (4th) 174 (S.C.C.).

15. The Charter scale is constructed here simply by assigning respondents a score of one if they agree with a question and two if they disagree. The scale thus ranges from a possible low of 3 to a possible high of 6 (disagree with all the questions).

16. One possible explanation that cannot be ruled out is that the survey was conducted in only English and French. Consequently, respondents not functional in either language, likely recent immigrants, would not be included in the sample. Therefore, the 1990 survey, like most others, almost certainly underrepresents this segment of the population.

17. The only two differences are noteworthy. Respondents indicating Asia as region of birth were higher than Canadian-born respondents with respect to both materialism and postmaterialism (i.e., few fell in the "mixed" category). Second, those who had resided in Canada for between three and five years were slightly less postmaterialist than those of shorter or longer residence. The categories, however, are small; thus the data have to be read cautiously.

REFERENCES

Alford, Robert R. 1963. *Party and Society*. Chicago: Rand McNally.

Almond, Gabriel, and Sidney Verba. 1963. *The Civic Culture: Political Attitudes and Democracy in Five Nations*. Princeton: Princeton University Press.

Baker, Kendall, Russell Dalton and K. Hildebrandt. 1981. *Germany Transformed*. Cambridge: Harvard University Press.

Bakvis, Herman, and Neil Nevitte. 1987. "In Pursuit of Postbourgeois Man: Postmaterialism and Intergenerational Change in Canada." *Comparative Political Studies* 70:357–89.

———. 1990. "The Greening of the Canadian Electorate: Environmentalism, Ideology and Partisanship." Paper presented at the annual meeting of the Canadian Political Science Association, Victoria.

Barnes, Samuel, Max Kaase et al. 1979. *Political Action*. Beverly Hills: Sage Publications.

Beaujot, Roderic, and Peter J. Rappak. 1988. *Immigration from Canada: Its Importance and Interpretation*. Population Working Paper No. 4. Ottawa: Employment and Immigration Canada.

Bell, Daniel. 1973. *The Coming of Postindustrial Society*. New York: Basic Books.

———. 1976. *The Cultural Contradictions of Capitalism*. New York: Basic Books.

Boeltken, M., and W. Jagodzinski. 1985. "In an Environment of Insecurity: Postmaterialism in the European Community, 1970 to 1980." *Comparative Political Studies* 17:353–84.

Brzezinski, Zbigniew. 1970. *Between Two Ages: America's Role in the Technetronic Era*. New York: Viking.

Buerklin, W. 1987. "The Greens: Ecology and the New Left." In *West German Politics in the Mid-Eighties*, ed. H.G. Wallach and G. Romoser. New York: Praeger.

Cairns, Alan C. 1990. "Representation and the Electoral System." Issue paper prepared for the Royal Commission on Electoral Reform and Party Financing. Ottawa.

Chafer, T. 1986. "Politics and the Perception of Risk: A Study of the Anti-Nuclear Movements in Britain and France." *West European Politics* 8:5–23.

Clarke, H., A. Kornberg and M. Stewart. 1985. "Politically Active Minorities: Political Participation in Canadian Democracy." In *Minorities and the Canadian State*, ed. N. Nevitte and A. Kornberg. Oakville: Mosaic Press.

Clarke, H., J. Jenson, L. LeDuc and J. Pammett. 1984. *Absent Mandate: The Politics of Discontent in Canada*. Toronto: Gage.

Converse, Philip. 1964. "The Nature of Belief Systems in Mass Publics." In *Ideology and Discontent*, ed. D. Apter. New York: Free Press.

———. 1972. "Change in the American Electorate." In *The Human Meaning of Social Change*, ed. A. Campbell and P. Converse. New York: Russell Sage.

Crewe, Ivor, Bo Sarlvik and James Alt. 1977. "Partisan Dealignment in Britain, 1964–74." *British Journal of Political Science* 7:129–90.

Dahl, Robert, ed. 1966. *Political Oppositions in Western Democracies*. New Haven: Yale University Press.

Dalton, Russell. 1984. "Cognitive Mobilization and Partisan Dealignment in Advanced Industrial Democracies." *Journal of Politics* 46:264–84.

————. 1988. *Citizen Politics in Western Democracies*. Chatham: Chatham House.

Dalton, Russell, and Kendall Baker. 1987. "The Contours of West German Opinion." In *West German Politics in the Mid-Eighties*, ed. H.G. Wallach and G. Romoser. New York: Praeger.

Dalton, Russell, Scott Flanagan and Paul Beck, eds. 1984. *Electoral Change in Advanced Industrial Democracies*. Princeton: Princeton University Press.

Deutsch, Karl. 1963. *The Nerves of Government*. New York: Free Press.

————. 1966. *Nationalism and Social Communication*. Cambridge: MIT Press.

Eberts, Mary. 1985. "The Use of Litigation under the Canadian Charter of Rights and Freedoms: Can Politicians and Judges Sing in Harmony?" In *Minorities and the Canadian State*, ed. N. Nevitte and A. Kornberg. Oakville: Mosaic Press.

Engelman, Laszlo. 1983. "Stepwise Logistic Regression." In *BMDP Biomedical Computer Programs*, ed. W.J. Dixon et al. Berkeley: University of California Press.

Farah, Barbara, Samuel H. Barnes and Felix Heunks. 1979. "Political Dissatisfaction." In *Political Action*, ed. Samuel Barnes, Max Kaase et al. Beverly Hills: Sage Publications.

Flanagan, Scott C. 1982. "Changing Values in Advanced Industrial Societies." *Comparative Political Studies* 14:403–44.

Gagnon, Alain G., and A. Brian Tanguay. 1989. "Minor Parties of Protest in Canada: Origins, Impact and Prospects." In *Canadian Parties in Transition: Discourse, Organization, and Representation*, ed. Alain G. Gagnon and A. Brian Tanguay. Scarborough: Nelson Canada.

Gallagher, Michael, and Michael Marsh, eds. 1988. *Candidate Selection in Comparative Perspective*. London: Sage Publications.

Gibson, Dale. 1985. "Minority Rights, Human Rights and the Charter." In *Minorities and the Canadian State*, ed. N. Nevitte and A. Kornberg. Oakville: Mosaic Press.

Harding, Steve. 1986. *Contrasting Values in Western Europe*. London: Macmillan.

Hildebrandt, Kai, and Russell J. Dalton. 1978. "The New Politics." In *German Political Studies: Elections and Parties*, vol. 3, ed. M. Kaase and K. von Beyme. Beverly Hills: Sage Publications.

Huntington, Samuel. 1974. "Postindustrial Politics: How Benign Will It Be." *Comparative Politics* 6 (January): 163–91.

Inglehart, Ronald. 1971. "The Silent Revolution in Europe: Intergenerational Change in Post-Industrial Societies." *American Political Science Review* 65:991–1017.

———. 1977. *The Silent Revolution*. Princeton: Princeton University Press.

———. 1981. "Postmaterialism in an Environment of Insecurity." *American Political Science Review* 75:880–900.

———. 1985. "New Perspectives on Value Change: Responses to Lafferty and Knutsen, Savage, Boeltken and Jagodzinski." *Comparative Political Studies* 17:485–532.

———. 1988. "The Renaissance of Political Culture." *American Political Science Review* 82:1203–30.

———. 1990. *Culture Shift in Advanced Industrial Society*. Princeton: Princeton University Press.

Inglehart, Ronald, and Renata Siemienska. 1988. "Political Values and Dissatisfaction in Poland and the West." *Government and Opposition* 23:440–57.

———. 1990. "A Long-Term Trend Toward Democratization? Global and East European Perspectives." Paper presented at the annual meeting of the American Political Science Association, San Francisco.

International Monetary Fund. 1986. *World Economic Outlook*. Washington, DC: IMF.

Jowell, Roger, and Sharon Witherspoon, eds. 1985. *British Social Attitudes*. London: Social and Community Planning Research.

Kaase, Max, and Alan Marsh. 1979. "Political Action Repertory: Changes over Time and a New Typology." In *Political Action*, ed. Samuel Barnes, Max Kaase et al. Beverly Hills: Sage Publications.

Katz, Richard S. 1990. "Party as Linkage: A Vestigial Function?" *European Journal of Political Research* 18:143–61.

Kitschelt, Herbert. 1986. "Political Opportunity Structures and Political Protest." *British Journal of Political Science* 16:57–85.

———. 1988. "Left-Libertarian Parties: Explaining Innovation in Competitive Party Systems." *World Politics* 40:194–234.

———. 1989. *The Logics of Party Formation: Ecological Politics in Belgium and West Germany*. Ithaca: Cornell University Press.

———. 1990. "Social Democracy and Liberal Corporatism: Swedish and Austrian Left Parties in Crisis." Paper presented at the annual meeting of the American Political Science Association, San Francisco.

Knutsen, Oddbjorn. 1989. "The Priorities of Materialist and Post-Materialist Values in the Nordic Countries." *Scandinavian Political Studies* 12:221–43.

Lafferty, William J., and Oddbjørn Knutsen. 1985. "Postmaterialism in a Social Democratic State: An Analysis of the Distinctiveness and Congruity of the Inglehart Value Syndrome in Norway." *Comparative Political Studies* 17:411–30.

Lambert, Ronald D., James E. Curtis, Steven D. Brown and Barry J. Kay. 1986. "In Search of Left/Right Beliefs in the Canadian Electorate." *Canadian Journal of Political Science* 19:541–63.

Lasch, Christopher. 1972. "Toward a Theory of Post-Industrial Society." In *Politics in the Post-Welfare State*, ed. M. Donald Hancock and Gideon Sjoberg. New York: Columbia University Press.

Lerner, Daniel. 1958. *The Passing of Traditional Society*. New York: Free Press.

Lipset, S.M. 1979. "The New Class and the Professoriate." In *The New Class?*, ed. B. Bruce-Biggs. New Brunswick: Transaction Books.

Lipset, S.M., and Stein Rokkan. 1967. *Party Systems and Voter Alignments*. New York: Free Press.

Lipset, S.M., and William Schneider. 1983. *The Confidence Gap*. New York: Free Press.

Marsh, Alan. 1975. "The Silent Revolution, Value Priorities and Quality of Life in Britain." *American Political Science Review* 69:1–30.

———. 1977. *Protest and Political Consciousness*. Beverly Hills: Sage Publications.

Maslow, A.H. 1954. *Motivation and Personality*. New York: Harper.

Milbrath, Lester. 1965. *Political Participation*. Chicago: Rand McNally.

Miller, Warren. 1975. "The Cross-National Use of Party Identification as a Stimulus to Political Inquiry." In *Party Identification and Beyond*, ed. I. Budge, I. Crewe and D. Farlie. New York: Wiley.

Miller, Warren E., and Teresa Levitin. 1976. *Leadership and Change: New Politics and the American Electorate*. Cambridge, Mass.: Winthrop.

Mishler, William. 1979. *Political Participation in Canada*. Toronto: Macmillan of Canada.

Morton, F.L. 1990. "The Supreme Court as the Vanguard of the Intelligentsia." Calgary: University of Calgary, Department of Political Science.

Mueller-Rommel, F. 1985. "New Social Movements and Smaller Parties." *West European Politics* 8:41–54.

Naisbitt, John. 1982. *Megatrends*. New York: Wagner.

Nevitte, Neil, and Roger Gibbins. 1990. *New Elites in Old States*. Toronto: Oxford University Press.

Nevitte, Neil, Herman Bakvis and Roger Gibbins. 1989. "The Ideological Contours of New Politics in Canada: Policy, Mobilization and Partisan Support." *Canadian Journal of Political Science* 23:475–503.

Nevitte, Neil, and Allan Kornberg, eds. 1985. *Minorities and the Canadian State.* Oakville: Mosaic Press.

Nie, Norman, G. Bingham Powell and Kenneth Prewitt. 1969. "Social Structure and Participation: Developmental Relationships, Parts 1 and 2." *American Political Science Review* 63:361–78, 808–32.

Offe, Claus. 1984. *Contradictions of the Welfare State.* Cambridge: MIT Press.

Organisation for Economic Co-operation and Development. 1988. *Historical Statistics, 1960–1986.* Paris: OECD.

Page, Benjamin I., and Richard A. Brody. 1972. "Policy Voting and the Electoral Process." *American Political Science Review* 66:979–95.

Pammett, Jon. 1987. "Class Voting and Class Consciousness in Canada." *Canadian Review of Sociology and Anthropology* 24:269–90.

Pomper, Gerald M. 1972. "From Confusion to Clarity: Issues and American Voters, 1956–1968." *American Political Science Review* 66:415–28.

Porter, John. 1965. *The Vertical Mosaic.* Toronto: University of Toronto Press.

Powell, G. Bingham. 1982. *Contemporary Democracies.* Cambridge: Harvard University Press.

Reisman, David. 1950. *The Lonely Crowd.* New Haven: Yale University Press.

Reudig, W. 1988. "Peace and Ecology Movements in Western Europe." *West European Politics* 11:26–39.

Rokkan, Stein. 1970. *Citizens, Elections and Parties.* Oslo: Universitets forlaget.

Rose, Richard, ed. 1974. *Comparative Electoral Behavior.* New York: Free Press.

Sears, David, and Jack Citrin. 1985. *Tax Revolt.* Cambridge: Harvard University Press.

Simeon, Richard, and David Elkins. 1974. "Regional Political Cultures in Canada." *Canadian Journal of Political Science* 7:397–437.

Strom, Kaare. 1990. "A Behavioral Theory of Competitive Political Parties." *American Journal of Political Science* 34:565–98.

Tilly, Charles. 1975. "Revolutions and Collective Violence." In *Handbook of Political Science*, vol. 3, ed. Fred Greenstein and Nelson Polsby. Cambridge: Harvard University Press.

Toffler, Alvin. 1980. *The Third Wave.* New York: Morrow.

Van Deth, Jan. 1983. "The Persistence of Materialist and Postmaterialist Value Orientations." *European Journal of Political Research* 11:63–79.

Verba, Sidney, and Norman Nie. 1972. *Participation in America: Political Democracy and Social Equality.* New York: Harper and Row.

Verba, Sidney, Norman Nie and T.O. Kim. 1978. *Participation and Political Equality.* New York: Cambridge University Press.

Weisberg, Herbert F., and Jerrold G. Rusk. 1970. "Dimensions of Candidate Evaluation." *American Political Science Review* 64:1167–85.

Welch, Susan. 1975. "Dimensions of Political Participation in a Canadian Sample." *Canadian Journal of Political Science* 8:553–59.

White, Orion, and Gideon Sjoberg. 1972. "The Emerging 'New Politics' in America." In *Politics in the Post-Welfare State,* ed. M. Donald Hancock and Gideon Sjoberg. New York: Columbia University Press.

Wilson, John. 1968. "Politics and Social Class in Canada: The Case of Waterloo South." *Canadian Journal of Political Science* 1:288–309.

Wiseman, Nelson, and K.W. Taylor. 1974. "Ethnic vs Class Voting: The Case of Winnipeg, 1945." *Canadian Journal of Political Science* 7:314–28.

Wohlfeld, Monika, and Neil Nevitte. 1990. "Postindustrial Value Change and Support for Native Issues." *Canadian Ethnic Studies* 23 (3): 56–68.

9

INCENTIVES CREATED BY THE INSTITUTIONS OF REPRESENTATIVE DEMOCRACY
Their Effect on Voters, Political Parties and Public Policy

Réjean Landry

THIS STUDY DEALS with how the institutions of representative democracy translate voter preferences into public policy and whether there are any institutional arrangements that can encourage political parties to adopt public policies that satisfy such criteria of efficiency as the Pareto optimum.

The institutional arrangements through which representative democracy functions create incentives that structure the behaviour of voters and political parties. In a world of perfect knowledge where decisions are unanimous, parties adopt policies that result in the efficient allocation of resources. However, imperfect knowledge combined with either the plurality or the proportionality system makes it difficult to allocate resources efficiently.

We discuss this difficulty first in terms of the economic theory of representative institutions. Rather than pursuing mathematical perfection at the expense of relevance, we develop deductive models that shed light on the fundamental principles forming the basis of representative institutions. We begin by examining the principles underlying the operation of a representative democracy in which everything is agreed on unanimously in a world of complete, free information. These conditions create a political setting for allocating resources efficiently. We go on to broaden these principles gradually so that the scenario more closely resembles the existing institutions of representative democracy. We then examine the effects of the absence of perfect information on the actions and strategies of voters and political parties in matters of public policy. Our look at the consequences of electing politicians by simple plurality and by proportional representation highlights cases where competition between two or more parties revolves around one or more cleavages. This comparative analysis demonstrates that all public policies that are not unanimously adopted in a world of perfect information carry biases that systematically benefit certain categories of voters at the expense of others.

The biases revealed by this theoretical examination are compared with the results of empirical studies on the redistributive effect of public expenditures and the manipulation of macroeconomic policy by parties in office. The results of the comparison lead us to some conclusions about reform of the election system in Canada. The summary of these conclusions is followed by several proposals for change.

THEORY

Elements of an Economic Analysis of Public Policy

What roles do parties and voters play in determining public policy? How can the fundamental relationship between them be strengthened? This relationship can be understood as a series of interactions between the demands of consumers (voters) and the offers of producers (politicians).

Demand

In the private sector, consumers reveal their preferences by purchasing products from various producers. Willingness to pay the asking price is an indication of consumer preference. Consumers could therefore be said to indicate their demand for various products in the private market by voting with their dollars. Voters, on the other hand, express their preferences for policy options offered in the political market-place by means of various institutions: the vote, political parties, lobbying, opinion polls, petitions, public hearings, demonstrations, legal challenges and various other methods, even civil disobedience and violence. None of these institutions perfectly translates citizen preferences into particular public policies. It is therefore difficult, if not impossible, to identify real voter preferences, that is, genuine citizen demand for various public policies. In such a situation, particular attention should be paid to the incentives that various institutional arrangements create.

The vote is one of the main methods of expressing demand for public policies. Like consumers who choose to purchase those articles that return the highest net benefit, citizens vote for candidates whose platforms promise the greatest benefits at the lowest personal cost. However, there are several differences in the choices offered to consumers and to voters. Consumers in the private market-place can purchase products from various producers in quantities that give them the maximum benefit. A consumer can purchase a computer manufactured by IBM or Apple, bread produced by a grocery store or a small bakery, a vehicle made by GM or Nissan. Consumers are able to buy from various competing suppliers, purchasing the products that best suit their needs. But collective choices in the political market-place are a different matter. Voters can choose one producer for its computer, another for its bread and a third for its car. They cannot choose one party for its social security program, another for its economic policy and a third for its defence policy. Voters have to choose between the complete platforms of various candidates, which are often made up of dozens or even hundreds of individual government policies. Furthermore, voters do not have the luxury of selecting particular policies. A single vote serves to express a voter's preferences for a number of policies, without representing the voter's preferences for all policies. Usually, voters do not approve of every aspect of the platform of the candidate for whom they vote. This type of all-or-nothing support greatly reduces the ability of voters to express their preferences on specific policy issues.

Offers

Like suppliers who offer goods on the private market to gain a profit, politicians offer various public policies to gain votes. Politicians can be motivated by such factors as the public interest, a desire for fame or compassion for the poor. Whatever their ultimate motivation, however, politicians can achieve their objectives only if they win elections. The competition for votes is a strong incentive for candidates to attach enormous importance to the implications of their platforms at election time. Politicians or parties who refuse to adopt policies that maximize votes because they believe the policies to be harmful from a moral or economic viewpoint risk being defeated by those who pay more attention to maximizing votes.

The Political Process and the Allocation of Resources
in a World of Perfect Knowledge

The interaction between voters' demands and the policies and programs offered by politicians gives rise to public policies. Analysing supply and demand in the political market would necessitate examining the attributes of three categories of factors: individuals, policies and institutional arrangements. These attributes vary greatly among countries. It would be impossible to deal with all the variations; to simplify our task and to establish a reference point, we begin by examining an ideal world in which public policies are neutral, that is, contain no biases that would benefit certain categories of voters at the expense of others.

To create an ideal world, however, many conditions must be met. For institutional arrangements, an ideally functioning representative democracy presupposes that 27 postulates are met (table 9.1). The most fundamental postulates in this lengthy list involve the information and aggregation rules. Our ideal world assumes that both voters and politicians have perfect knowledge about the costs and benefits of policies. This ideal world also presupposes that perfect information is free; that is, people have access to it without spending money or time. In addition to everyone being equally informed, people would have to make all their decisions according to the unanimity rule, whether in electing representatives to the legislature, adopting public policies or sharing the costs and benefits of policies.

Establishing an ideal world also requires that voter preferences be similar for all policies and in all ridings. Finally, this model presupposes that voters vote for the party whose platform best contributes to increasing their benefits (material and non-material).

Laws adopted by a legislature are the public policies. In an ideal world, they would assume the attributes of pure public good, that is, indivisible and nonexclusionary. In other words, it would be impossible to divide the benefits of policies among voters, and no rule would allow any voter to be prevented from receiving the benefits resulting from the application of a public policy (table 9.2).

Finally, the model presupposes that voters maximize the benefits from party platforms while politicians maximize votes; that is, politicians prefer being elected to being defeated (table 9.3). Together tables 9.1 to 9.3 present 32 conditions that define an ideal representative democracy.

We may deduce two general propositions from these 32 conditions. The first is that candidates and parties formulate platforms to maximize votes. The second is that policies adopted by parties always follow the Pareto optimum (table 9.4). In other words, the allocation of resources among the various public policies is such that no voter could increase his or her goods by a reallocation of resources without decreasing the resources of someone else.

The first proposition implies that candidates are willing to adopt any political program that maximizes votes, while the second restricts their choice to any program that fits with the Pareto optimum. This second proposition flows from the rule of unanimity (postulates I-4.3, I-4.6 and I-7.1), which excludes the adoption of policies that impose costs on third parties. The rule of unanimity is the best institutional arrangement to protect voters against the imposition of costs by third parties (Buchanan and Tullock 1962). Thus, voters and candidates exercise their right to veto in cases where policy imposes external costs on them, that is, costs resulting from the decisions of third parties. Since the unanimity rule accords a veto right to each individual, only policies that do not impose any external costs will be adopted. The curve in figure 9.1 indicates that as the proportion of individuals who must agree to a decision approaches unanimity (100 percent), external costs decrease. The unanimity rule, however, generates some decision-making costs. These costs result from the time required to influence and to

Figure 9.1
External costs

External costs

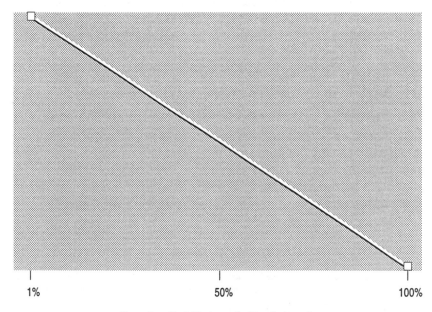

Proportion of individuals required to adopt a policy

Table 9.1
Postulates on institutional arrangements

Taking our cue from the explicit and implicit postulates of Downs (1957), we reinterpret and classify the institutional arrangements of representative democracy according to seven categories of generic rules proposed by Ostrom (1986):

I.1.1	Position rule:	Individuals can choose to be voters or candidates.
I.1.2	Position rule:	Voter preferences are the same from one election district to another.
I.1.3	Position rule:	Voters feel equally strongly about all public policy issues.
I.1.4	Position rule:	A political party is a coalition of candidates.
I.1.5	Position rule:	The candidates of the various parties are equally good at promoting their platforms and their past accomplishments.
I.1.6	Position rule:	Candidates for a given party have the same preferences in all districts.
I.2.1	Boundary rule:	Voters are free and equal.
I.2.2	Boundary rule:	Candidates promote the party platforms.
I.2.3	Boundary rule:	Each party presents its platform to the voters during election campaigns.
I.3.1	Authority rule:	Each voter is entitled to one vote only at time of election.
I.3.2	Authority rule:	Party actions and decisions cannot restrict freedom of electors or other parties.
I.3.3	Authority rule:	Electors vote for the party candidate whose platform or past accomplishments most enhance their interests.
I.3.4	Authority rule:	Electors evaluate the interests they gain from party programs by comparing their personal positions to official party positions.
I.3.5	Authority rule:	Electors vote only if the advantages gained from the policies exceed voting costs.
I.4.1	Aggregation rule:	Elections are held at regular intervals.
I.4.2	Aggregation rule:	Elected candidates constitute the legislative assembly.
I.4.3	Aggregation rule:	Legislative assembly decisions are taken by unanimous consent.
I.4.4	Aggregation rule:	The territory is divided into electoral districts with equal numbers of voters.
I.4.5	Aggregation rule:	The voters in each district elect a candidate to represent the preferences of that district.
I.4.6	Aggregation rule:	Candidates are elected on platforms that receive the unanimous consent of the electorate.
I.5.1	Information rule:	Voters are fully informed about the costs and benefits of party platforms and about parties' past accomplishments.
I.5.2	Information rule:	Party leaders have a perfect knowledge of voter preferences for public policy and of the implications of their platforms for winning votes.
I.5.3	Information rule:	The information needed by the voters and the party candidates is available at no cost.

Table 9.1 (cont'd)
Postulates on institutional arrangements

I.6.1	Scope rule:	The voters and candidates comply with the rules of institutional arrangements in a representative democracy.
I.6.2	Scope rule:	The election dates cannot be changed by the parties of candidates who are elected.
I.7.1	Payoff rule:	The costs of public policies are shared by unanimous consent.
I.7.2	Payoff rule:	Once offered, the benefits of public policies are automatically made available to all voters.

Table 9.2
Postulates on the nature of public policies

The party platforms concern the production of public good with the following characteristics:

II.1	Difficult exclusion: No rule allows any voter to be prevented from taking advantage of the public good once it is offered.
II.2	Indivisible: The benefits of the good that is offered are impossible to divide among the voters. In other words, the good that is offered is a pure public good.

Table 9.3
Postulates on the motivation of voters and candidates

III.1	Voters maximize the utility they receive from public policies.
III.2	Candidates maximize their number of votes, that is, they would rather win elections than lose them.
III.3	Candidates who lead parties maximize the number of party candidates who are elected, that is, they prefer more seats to fewer seats.

Table 9.4
General propositions derived from the postulates describing an ideal world

P.1	Candidates and parties formulate platforms with a view to maximizing their votes.
P.2	Public policies adopted by Parliament always yield the Pareto optimum.

discuss and negotiate with other participants in the decision-making process. There are also costs associated with making concessions. The costs of reaching a decision depend on the proportion of individuals who must agree to the policy before it is adopted. The curve in figure 9.2 shows that the cost of making a decision decreases as this proportion declines.

Figure 9.2
Costs of making a decision

Costs of making a decision

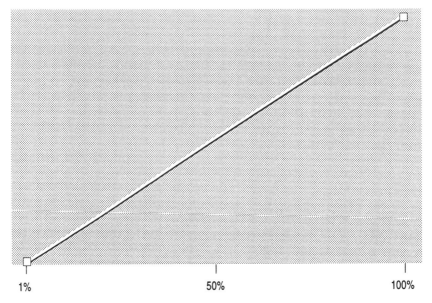

1%   50%   100%

Proportion of individuals required to adopt a policy

The unanimity rule protects voters against external costs, but it generates very high costs for making decisions. For this reason, representative democracies adopt rules that do not require the unanimous consent of voters and elected candidates. Otherwise, the status quo would prevail in all situations in which the voters could not agree unanimously (Rae 1975), effectively paralysing society and preventing any change in public policy. To avoid this, voters adopt rules that do not require unanimous consent to make decisions. It is therefore necessary to relax the three postulates requiring unanimous consent in favour of a formula that lowers the cost of making decisions.

Adding external costs to the cost of making decisions produces the total cost of interdependence (figure 9.3). The majority rule, chosen by the voters and parties, is optimal when the costs of interdependence are as low as possible. In figure 9.3, the optimal majority is denoted by M^*. Optimal majority M^* has three properties (Frey 1983, 39; Buchanan and Tullock 1962):

- The higher the external costs (all else being equal), the higher M^* becomes; the higher the cost of making decisions (all else

Figure 9.3
Total costs of interdependence

Costs

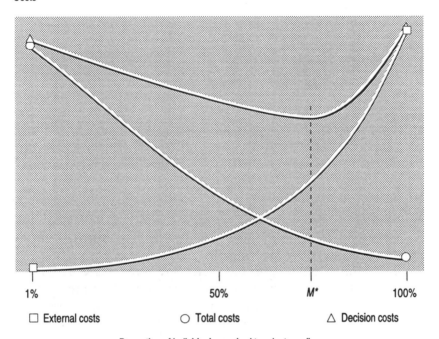

☐ External costs   ○ Total costs   △ Decision costs

Proportion of individuals required to adopt a policy

being equal), the lower M^* becomes.
- The shape of the curves denoting external costs and decision-making costs varies from one public policy to another.
- The optimal majority rule can be 50 percent for some public policies. This result, however, is pure coincidence. It should be emphasized that the simple majority rule has no particular significance as a decision-making principle in the adoption of public policies.

Suppose that, to reduce decision-making costs, decisions concerning the adoption of laws and the sharing of costs generated by policies are made by a majority in a world in which politicians are elected according to the plurality rule (table 9.5). In that world public policies adopted by the legislature can generate external costs (table 9.6).

Voters may not agree with all the policies in the platforms of elected representatives. Electing representatives on the basis of plurality means that some voter preferences will not be promoted

Table 9.5
Introduction of the plurality rule

I.4.3	Aggregation rule:	Decisions of Parliament are made according to majority rule.
I.4.5	Aggregation rule:	The candidate whose platform receives the greatest number of votes is declared elected.
I.7.1	Payoff rule:	Costs of public policies are distributed according to majority rule.

Table 9.6
Proposition ensuing from the introduction of the plurality rule

P.3	Public policies adopted by the legislative assembly can entail external costs.

by the elected representatives. In addition, adopting policies on the basis of the majority rule means that a majority of representatives can vote for policies that award benefits to all while imposing costs on a nonconsenting minority. As Gwartney and Wagner (1988, 18) have pointed out, if your rich uncle says that he is willing to pay for 49 percent of everything you purchase, you are likely to spend more on housing, food and transportation than you would if you had to pay for everything yourself. The same principle applies to public policy decisions adopted under the majority rule. The majority will adopt more expensive policies than if unanimous consent were necessary. The postulate of perfect knowledge means that the minority is fully aware of the costs. It is more realistic, however, to assume that voters and candidates act in a world where knowledge is imperfect and, consequently, the minority is not fully aware of what a policy will cost.

This produces the first bias in the system: unlike the situation in which unanimity was required, the majority rule allows the adoption of public policies that transfer resources from the minority to the majority.

The Political Process and the Allocation of Resources in a World of Expensive, Incomplete Knowledge

In a world of perfect knowledge, candidates cannot influence how individuals vote. All voters are perfectly aware of the costs and benefits of various political policies. If voters act rationally, this knowledge of the costs and benefits renders them immune to any attempt to influence their vote in favour of one party or another. Furthermore, even though they may ardently wish for the victory of the party for which they intend to vote, voters know that there is no use attempting to influence other citizens to vote as they will. In such a situation, the choice of public policies would depend entirely on the rules governing institutional arrangements.

The lack of perfect knowledge is a determining condition that has a decisive effect on the choices made by voters and candidates. It is therefore important to relax the conditions that define the ideal world to move closer to reality. But the conditions involved in the functioning of a real democracy vary greatly among countries, even provinces. Since it is unthinkable to consider all these variations, the model of the ideal world can be modified by gradually increasing the number of conditions that bring it closer to reality, without having to understand this reality in all its detail.

This investigation of representative democracy continues with a study of the implications of a model in which voters and parties must act based on incomplete information. We then consider the consequences of government subsidies to political parties and the effects on party strategies of financial contributions from voters. Next, we compare the implications of electing candidates by plurality and by proportional representation, examining cases in which two or more parties compete around one or more cleavages. Although several implications are surprising, they constitute fundamental biases resulting from the attributes of the institutional arrangements that govern voters' and candidates' actions and strategies in a world where uncertainty reigns supreme.

Introduction of Uncertainty

The model of the ideal world must be modified to include two facts: voters have imperfect knowledge of the costs and benefits of party platforms; and the parties are imperfectly informed about voters' public policy preferences (table 9.7). To come closer to reality, we also assume that a public policy may call into question interests to which voters attach varying degrees of importance. In addition, we presuppose that the functioning of the economy leads the same voter to play the role of consumer on some occasions and the role of producer – as a worker or entrepreneur – on others. To complete this picture, we hypothesize that the information gathering and analysis required by the parties and voters are expensive in time and money.

The model of the ideal world assumed that parties could promise only the production of public goods. Parties may also promise to award private goods to voters (table 9.8). Private goods involve divisible benefits and explicit exclusionary criteria. Examples of this type of policy include one that increases pensions (divisible) to seniors (explicit exclusionary criterion) or one that reduces a subsidy program (divisible) to textile companies (exclusionary criterion).

The introduction of these changes seriously affects how a representative democracy functions. We demonstrate that ignorance and abstention are rational, that voters are more motivated to become informed and to make public policy demands as producers than as consumers, that voters and parties are encouraged to trust ideologies rather than party platforms, and that the supply of public policies is biased in favour of producers and oriented toward the short term rather than the long term. We now examine in greater detail the propositions presented in table 9.9 to understand all their implications.

Voters Have Little Incentive to Become Informed about Government Policies
Information about party platforms influences voters' choices. Thus, voters can be motivated to reconsider their support for a given party as a result of information that reveals costs or benefits they had previously underestimated or overestimated. The information voters demand depends on the relationship between the costs and benefits of that information. In other words, the acquisition and analysis of information generate costs in time and money that voters must weigh. The same is true when one buys a newspaper and takes the time to read it. The main benefit of knowledge is that it helps to avoid voting for the wrong party because of a lack of information about its policies. This benefit is hard to evaluate, however, before policies are put into effect.

The marginal benefits of information tend to decline while the marginal costs of gathering and analysing it tend to rise (Frey 1983, 199). As shown in figure 9.4, up to a certain point, voters have something to gain by becoming informed. Voters do not have an interest in being totally ignorant because their investment in the acquisition and analysis of information at first produces more benefits than costs. Conversely, voters have no interest in being perfectly informed; beyond a certain point, the costs of gathering and analysing information outweigh the benefits. Voters are encouraged to invest in acquiring and analysing information up to the point where the marginal-benefit curve and the marginal-cost curve cross. This point of optimal investment varies from one voter to another and from one public policy to another. Similarly, voters' optimal-investment points can be low for some policies and high for others.

The incentive to invest in acquiring and analysing information is weaker when a voter's vote has little chance of playing a decisive

Table 9.7
Introduction of uncertainty in institutional arrangements

I.1.1	Position rule:	A single voter can sometimes play the role of a consumer or taxpayer, and at other times the role of producer (as a worker or an owner).
I.1.3	Position rule:	The stakes in public policy programs do not imply identical interests for all voters.
I.5.1	Information rule:	Voters do not have perfect knowledge of party policies and resulting costs and benefits, nor of the utility conferred by past achievements of various parties.
I.5.2	Information rule:	Candidates who lead parties do not have perfect knowledge of voter preferences for public policies and voter reactions to policy alternatives.
I.5.3	Information rule:	It is expensive to acquire and analyse the information needed by voters and party leaders.

Table 9.8
Nature of public policies in an uncertain world

Public policies can confer two types of good:

- pure public good; and
- pure private good.

Table 9.9
General propositions derived from the introduction of uncertainty

P.4	Voters have little incentive to become informed about government policies.
P.5	Voters are better informed about public policies that affect them as producers than about policies that affect them as consumers or taxpayers.
P.6	Voters as producers have more incentive to demand government policies that affect them than they do as consumers.
P.7	Voters and parties are inclined to reduce the cost of acquiring and analysing information by associating specific platforms with general political ideologies.
P.8	Parties are inclined to maintain the same ideological position as long as they do not suffer a crushing defeat. If they do, they are inclined to modify their ideological position in the direction of the party that defeated them.
P.9	Most individuals have an incentive not to vote because of the likelihood that no single vote will have a decisive effect on the outcome.
P.10	Political parties are inclined to offer public policies that concentrate benefits in the hands of producers while spreading the costs across all consumers and taxpayers.
P.11	Politicians are inclined to offer public policies that produce benefits in the short term because they will not be able to reap the rewards of policies with long-term benefits.

role in the election. There is an interesting comparison here between the incentive to invest in information in the private market-place and the incentive in the electoral market-place. By comparison shopping – which is an investment in information – consumers of private goods may save money, which will accrue to them personally. Thus those intending to buy a new car may decide to bear the costs of visiting several dealerships to save $500. In a representative democracy, the purchase of a car at the optimal price would require majority approval. Voters, therefore, can enjoy the benefits of their investment in information only if they can also persuade the majority to vote as they do. Since it is extremely expensive to attempt to persuade other voters to change their minds, comparison shopping in the electoral market-place produces much less net benefit than comparison shopping in the private market-place. In the private market-place, investment in information provides benefits that accrue directly to the consumer. In the political market-place, this investment may lead a voter to change his or her vote, but the chances that this vote will prove decisive in the election are extremely low. Since the election results will not, in all likelihood, be influenced by the amount

Figure 9.4
Determination of the amount of demand for information

Marginal costs and marginal benefits

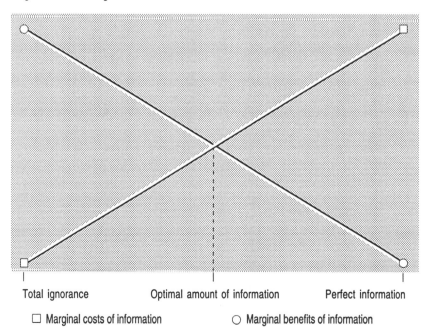

| Total ignorance | Optimal amount of information | Perfect information |

☐ Marginal costs of information   ○ Marginal benefits of information

of knowledge one particular voter accumulates, a rational response is to remain relatively ill-informed about most public policy issues. Indeed, Downs (1957) concluded that voter ignorance is a rational reaction.

Voters Are Better Informed about Policies That Affect Them as Producers Than about Policies That Affect Them as Consumers or Taxpayers Because it is difficult for voters to reap the benefits of their investment in political information, they tend to be content with whatever information is available without charge. The main sources of free information are government publications and brochures on policies; information produced by political parties; information conveyed by interest groups; information relayed through the media; information obtained through discussions with other voters; and information accumulated as producers, consumers or taxpayers. Voters receive far more free information as producers than as consumers or taxpayers (Downs 1957, 255–56). Two factors cause this imbalance. The first is that individuals have an advantage in their role as producers because they specialize in accumulating technical information related to only a few facets of production. As consumers, however, they must accumulate information about many products and services. The second factor is discussed below.

Voters as Producers Have More Incentive to Demand Government Policies That Affect Them Than They Do as Consumers The second factor is the effect of public policies on both producers and consumers, such as the setting of milk prices. Here the benefits to individual producers are much higher than the costs to individual consumers. This imbalance arises because most people earn the bulk of their income from a single factor of production, while their expenses are spread over a vast array of goods and services. Each good or service represents only a small fraction of the total.

The first factor explains why voters are better informed as producers than as consumers, and the second factor explains why voters are more inclined to demand government intervention on matters that affect them as producers than as consumers. Together, these factors also explain why voters' preferences vary according to the public policy issue involved.

Voters and Parties Are Inclined to Reduce the Cost of Acquiring and Analysing Information by Associating Specific Platforms with General Political Ideologies According to Downs (1957), uncertainty encourages the emergence of political ideologies. An ideology provides a general view of society, which then finds concrete expression in the form of various government policies. Ideologies free voters from the need to compare every new public policy issue with their basic principles and their general view of society. Ideologies therefore help to reduce the cost to voters of acquiring information, allowing them to compare the principles on which policies are based rather than the details of every policy proposed. Ideologies can be seen as summaries of the policy differences between parties. Rather than gathering and analysing information on the costs and benefits of every policy proposal in socio-economic terms, voters can simply compare the positions of the parties according to four general principles that underlie socio-economic policy:

- whether the means of production should be publicly or privately owned;
- whether government should play an extended or limited role in planning the economy;
- whether there should be more or less redistribution of wealth from the rich to the poor; and
- whether social programs should be expanded or cut back.

Since basic ideological principles and party policies are strongly related, ideologies are a reliable substitute for information in allowing voters to make rational decisions. Voters are encouraged to minimize the cost of gathering information by referring to basic ideologies rather than to the details of party platforms.

Parties respond by developing ideologies to reduce voters' costs of gathering and analysing information. Even if parties use ideologies to maximize votes, they cannot make radical, sudden changes to their ideologies. The party's ideology and individual policies must be maintained at a high level of correlation. Otherwise, voters could not rely on ideologies to reduce the cost of information.

Parties Are Inclined to Maintain the Same Ideological Position as Long as They Do Not Suffer Any Crushing Defeat. If They Do, They Are Inclined to Modify Their Ideological Position in the Direction of the Party That Defeated Them If this reasoning is sound, we can conclude that the more a party has been identified with certain fundamental principles that provide it with its ideological stamp, the more difficult it is to redefine those principles. As far as voters are concerned, any redefinition of principles produces costs for gathering and analysing information. Conversely, new parties have a greater margin for manoeuvring because they are not yet closely identified with a particular set of principles; as a result, new parties tend to embrace principles that will maximize their votes. It follows that established parties do not change their basic ideologies unless they suffer a crushing defeat at the polls. A defeat prompts them to change their ideologies by adopting certain philosophical principles that helped ensure the winning party's victory.

Most Individuals Have an Incentive Not to Vote Because of the Likelihood That No Single Vote Will Have a Decisive Effect on the Outcome The immediate result of incomplete information is that it prevents voters from distinguishing among parties. They cannot tell how close their personal policy positions are to those of the parties. The only way for them to resolve this problem is to invest in gathering and analysing information. However, a rational voter is prepared to make this investment only if the expected benefits outweigh the costs. Little by little, this cost-benefit analysis causes voters to wonder about the likelihood that their votes will have a decisive effect on the outcome of the election. Even if voters were perfectly informed, their vote could well have no effect on the outcome of the election.

The probability (P) that an individual's vote will make a difference to the election result declines as the size of the electorate increases. The utility (U) of an individual's vote depends on the probability (P) that this vote will create or break a tie in favour of the voter's preferred candidate, multiplied by the value of the benefit (B) resulting from this vote minus the cost (C) of the vote:

$$U = PB - C$$

If $C = \$1$, and if the constituency includes 80 000 voters, $P = 1/80\ 000$. In this case, a rational individual would vote only if B is equal to or greater than \$80 000. This type of argument led Downs (1957) and Tullock (1967) to conclude that abstaining from voting was a rational choice. Several other researchers, especially Riker and Ordeshook (1968), attempted to reinterpret the elements in this equation to make voting rational. They hoped to explain the fairly high rate of voter turnout in various kinds of elections. Several of these explanations tend to justify the propensity to vote in an ad hoc fashion by pointing to motivating factors outside party platforms. It is possible, as with participation in interest groups, that individuals are motivated not only by material incentives but also by axiological (purposive) incentives, as well as by incentives arising from a feeling of solidarity (Clark and Wilson 1961; Cook 1984; Tillock and Morrison 1979; Walker 1983).

Political Parties Are Inclined to Offer Public Policies That Concentrate Benefits in the Hands of Producers While Spreading the Costs Across All Consumers and Taxpayers This proposition deserves attention because it is one of the main tenets of those who support the theory of collective choices.

Party platforms can be considered both from the point of view of benefits – whether they are concentrated in the hands of producers (B_C) or diffused among consumers and taxpayers (B_D) – and from the point of view of costs – whether they are concentrated (C_C) or diffused (C_D). This approach makes it possible to distinguish four types of government policy.

The most hotly debated strategy since the works of Downs (1957) and Olson (1965, 1983, 1986) is one in which party leaders propose policies that would concentrate benefits in the hands of producers while spreading the costs among all consumers and taxpayers (B_C/C_D). This strategy benefits party leaders because it attracts support from the producers while not prompting any loss of votes. In concrete terms, this strategy offers divisible benefits to producers, while counting on consumers and taxpayers to pay little attention to small increases in prices or taxes. This method of redistribution can be considered consensual, because those who lose are not inclined to oppose the policies. They may not even be aware of the costs because they are difficult to measure. The reliability of this analysis rests on the hypothesis that diffused costs are imposed on broad groups of consumers and taxpayers who are unable to deal with the "free-rider" problem.

The reverse strategy – in which party leaders offer policies that provide diffuse benefits while concentrating the costs (B_D/C_C) – produces a situation in which the electoral gains are smaller than the losses. In this case, the diffusion of benefits is not sufficient to encourage consumers and taxpayers to become informed and to organize to pressure party leaders to maximize their benefits. The producers, meanwhile, are highly motivated to organize collective action to inform politicians of the costs of their programs. Proposals related to consumer protection or pollution control are good examples of this strategy. Party leaders may attempt to modify this situation to their advantage by reducing the costs to producers while maintaining some benefits for consumers and taxpayers. Party leaders can do this by proposing policies that have indivisible benefits coupled with costs that are hard to measure. This involves adopting basic positions that associate the party positively with an issue while minimizing the electoral costs incurred because of opposition from producers.

The third strategy used by party leaders consists of offering policies that have both concentrated benefits and concentrated costs (B_C/C_C). In electoral terms, this strategy amounts to a zero-sum game, since the gains and losses in votes tend to even out. There are two variations to this approach: both the costs and the benefits can accrue to a single group of producers; or one group can enjoy the benefits while another group bears the costs. The regulation of working conditions tends to fall into this category. This political strategy encourages those who enjoy the benefits to organize themselves to protect and augment the concentrated benefits, while also stimulating opposition on the part of the producers who are bearing the costs. In addition to creating a zero-sum game, this type of policy is more likely than any other to generate intense conflicts. The polarization it can cause can be reduced by offering divisible benefits coupled with costs that are difficult to measure.

The fourth strategy that party leaders can adopt is to offer policies that spread costs and benefits over all consumers and taxpayers (B_D/C_D). Fighting crime or reducing poverty are examples of this fourth strategy. This type of public policy is not likely to produce substantial gains at the polls. Policies for which costs and benefits are diffuse are the least likely to prompt people to organize to pressure politicians. The diffuse nature of the benefits means that those who potentially will benefit have little incentive to become informed and to organize to influence the party leaders. Similarly, the diffuse nature of the costs means that taxpayers and consumers are not likely to inform themselves and organize to oppose the policies. In other words, the diffusion of benefits and costs makes those who receive the benefits vulnerable to the "free-rider" problem. The same applies to consumers and taxpayers paying the cost. Party leaders are therefore inclined to invest as few tangible resources as possible in this type of policy because of the minimal electoral benefit. Party platforms with diffuse costs and benefits produce most votes for a party if the benefits are small and divisible and the costs are difficult to measure. This associates the party positively with policies that are symbolically important.

This examination of the impact of party platforms on voter behaviour reveals the anti-consumer and anti-taxpayer bias in the political market-place. This bias has the following characteristics:

1. The policies that party leaders should adopt most often are those with concentrated benefits and diffuse costs (B_C/C_D), since the increase in votes is greater than the losses under these circumstances $(I > L)$.
2. The policies that party leaders should adopt least often are those with diffuse benefits and concentrated costs (B_D/C_C), since in this situation the increased vote is smaller than the losses that are caused $(I < L)$.

3. The two other types of policies, those with concentrated benefits and concentrated costs (B_C/C_C) and those with diffuse
benefits and diffuse costs (B_D/C_D), create zero-sum situations
in which increases and losses are equal $(I = L)$. Politicians, therefore, adopt these types of policies less often than $I > L$ policies
but more often than $I < L$ policies. The B_C/C_C strategy is preferable, however, to the B_D/C_D strategy. When the benefits of the
policies are divisible and the costs difficult to discern, the increase
in votes among producers will be higher than the loss of votes
among consumers and taxpayers. The difficulty in overcoming
the problem of incomplete knowledge makes the B_C/C_C strategy
electorally more attractive than the B_D/C_D strategy.

In summary, in a world where knowledge is incomplete and expensive, parties can maximize their votes by offering policies that combine
costs and benefits in the following order:

$$(B_C/C_D) > (B_C/C_C) > (B_D/C_D) > (B_D/C_C)$$

This platform strategy assumes that diffuse costs for taxpayers and
consumers leave them unable to solve the problem of incomplete knowledge. It relies, as we have seen, on consumers and taxpayers paying
little attention to small tax and price increases.

There is a strategy, however, that is more advantageous (Landry
and Duchesneau 1987). This strategy consists of making groups that
receive benefits fully aware of them, while keeping those who pay the
costs unaware. In concrete terms, the best strategy for winning votes is
not the combination B_C/C_D but the combination B_C/C_I – that is, concentrated benefits combined with indefinite costs. It is then impossible
to determine the cost of promises to producers. In the B_C/C_I situation,
producers receive benefits for which costs are totally hidden.
If the B_C/C_D strategy is based on the anti-consumer, anti-taxpayer bias
of the political market-place, the B_C/C_I strategy is based on fiscal illusion, because everyone knows that promises are paid through higher
taxes, with everyone paying for illusory benefits. In theory, fiscal illusion should serve the interests of producers because the benefits they
receive are easier to identify than the benefits to consumers and taxpayers.
The benefits to producers are large enough that they are motivated to
become informed and organize to bring pressure to bear, while the benefits accruing to consumers and taxpayers are such that they cannot solve
the free-rider problem. The previous theoretical prediction, therefore,
should be revised to take these new elements into account:

$$(B_C/C_I) > (B_C/C_D) > (B_D/C_I) > (B_D/C_D) > (B_I/C_I) > (B_I/C_D) >$$
$$(B_C/C_C) > (B_D/C_C) > (B_I/C_C)$$

Politicians Are Inclined to Offer Public Policies That Produce Benefits in the Short Term Because They Will Not Be Able to Reap the Rewards of Policies with Long-Term Benefits   The theory of property rights (Barzel 1990) can help us better understand the way the private market-place and the electoral market-place allocate resources based on time. The private owner with exclusive and transferable rights to a piece of property is inclined to invest in projects that will generate future benefits with current value greater than the costs, even if all or most of the costs are incurred now. This is the case, for example, of a forest products company, which plants and cares for trees that cannot be harvested for 40 or 50 years. The value of the trees obviously increases over time, reflecting the value of the expected profits when they are harvested. According to Gwartney and Wagner (1988, 12–13),

> Private property rights also provide resource owners with an incen-
> tive to conserve for the future. If scarcity and strong demand are
> expected to push up the price of a resource at an annual rate in excess
> of the interest rate, self-interest dictates that private owners conserve
> the resource for the future. When private property rights are present,
> prices and interest rates tie the future with the present and provide
> decision-makers with the information and incentive to see that
> resources are properly cared for and used efficiently.

How does the electoral market-place settle the problem of public policies for which costs and benefits are spread over time? Representatives of the political party that has a majority in the legislature cannot behave like the forest products company. The benefits that politicians can claim as their own and translate into votes are only those that emerge before the next election. Their claim to benefits that emerge after the election depends on their success in being re-elected. This success, or lack of it, depends on their strategy for distributing the costs and benefits of policies over time. Four different strategies can be distinguished (table 9.10).

The best strategy for maximizing votes consists of offering policies that will generate benefits before the next election, while the costs will be delayed until after the election (strategy B,A). In a world of incomplete and expensive information, parties can win most votes by exaggerating the immediate benefits while underplaying the future costs. The worst strategy for winning votes is to propose policies that

Table 9.10
Strategies for distributing the costs and benefits of policies over time

	Costs of the policies emerge	
	Before the next election	After the next election
Benefits of the policies emerge		
Before the next election	B, B	B, A
After the next election	A, B	A, A

will bring costs before the next election while the benefits will show up only after the election (strategy *A,B*). The two other strategies – *B,B* and *A,A* – have little effect on winning or losing votes. When policies generate costs that emerge before the next election, parties are eager to have the benefits become apparent in the short term rather than the long term. In a competitive situation, parties that adopt policies with long-term benefits could easily be defeated by parties that adopt policies with short-term benefits. Thus, a party in office that adopts policies that will reinforce the economy only after the next election could be defeated by an opposition party that emphasizes policies with short-term benefits. Lee and McKenzie (1987, 131) underscore the short-term nature of the incentives inherent in political institutions:

> Politicians ... are in much the same position as the buffalo hunters of the 1870s. Each knew that all would be better off in the long run if everyone reduced his slaughter of the buffalo. But in the absence of private ownership, each also knew that the buffalo he did not shoot today would be shot by someone else tomorrow. Individual buffalo hunters found themselves in a situation in which there was little to gain, but much to lose, from taking a long-term perspective and exercising restraint in the extermination of the buffalo. Political decision-makers find themselves in a situation in which there is little to gain, but much to lose, by refraining from placing short-term demands on the economy that will, in the long run, exterminate much of our productive capacity.

Political parties therefore find themselves in a situation corresponding to "the tragedy of the Commons" (Hardin and Baden 1977; Ostrom 1988). Each party has an interest in basing its policies on the short term, even though such policies, though effective electorally, are less than optimal for the long-term interests of the society.

The tendency of parties to lean toward the short term to the detriment of the long term is aggravated in countries such as Canada and the United Kingdom, where the prime minister can select the date of the election to suit his or her convenience – that is, at a time when the polls indicate that public support is peaking.

Granting Government Subsidies to Political Parties

Granting government subsidies to political parties has become a common practice in most Western countries (Alexander 1989). Most of these subsidies are used to finance national election campaigns. They take two main forms:

- direct financial assistance to parties; and
- free access to television air time and space in the print media.

These subsidies reduce the constraints on party leaders (table 9.11). Their main effect is to change the relative cost of the factors of production of election campaigns. Financial assistance is more easily used in a capital-intensive election campaign than in a campaign that relies heavily on party workers. Subsidies, therefore, encourage party leaders to replace the work of party members with capital-intensive national campaigns based on extensive use of the national media (Strom 1990). All things being equal, the more subsidies are used to finance a large part of election campaign expenses, the less party leaders need to listen to the policy preferences of party members.

Financial Contributions from Voters

Voters contribute money to parties to increase their net benefits from public policies (table 9.12). Their motivation to contribute is greater if the competition between the parties is close and their policy choices are different from the policies that might be adopted if they did not contribute.

Even when the race between parties is close, all voters are not equally motivated to contribute. Those voters who have the most to win or lose as a result of public policy are the producers. The reason is simple: most people derive the bulk of their income from their possession of a single factor of production, whether it is the labour of a worker or the capital and know-how of an entrepreneur. Conversely, consumers spend their income on a multitude of goods and services, the cost of each representing only a small fraction of the total. This imbalance causes voters to contribute more to parties that promote policies that benefit them as producers rather than as consumers. Producers are also

Table 9.11
Granting government subsidies to parties

I.2.4	Boundary rule:	Parties that had successful candidates in the previous election receive subsidies from Parliament.

General proposition derived from awarding government subsidies to parties

P.12	Granting subsidies to parties encourages leaders to run expensive election campaigns.

Table 9.12
Introduction of financial contributions by voters

I.3.6	Authority rule:	Voters can make financial contributions to political parties.

General propositions derived from the introduction of financial contributions by voters

P.13	Voter contributions depend on the costs and benefits of party platforms.
P.14	Voters as producers are more inclined to make financial contributions to political parties than voters as consumers.
P.15	Voter contributions persuade parties to remain sensitive to the policy preferences of their contributors.

organized into interest groups, and contribute to promoting their interests through these groups. The market-place of financial contributions to political parties therefore has a tendency to be dominated by contributions from producers and the groups representing them.

Voters contribute to party finances to persuade parties to advance public policies they would not otherwise have adopted. On the other hand, voters may stop contributing if parties do not respond positively to their expectations. As a result, financing parties through voter contributions forces parties to be sensitive to these policy needs and demands (table 9.12).

The Political Process and the Allocation of Resources in a World of Expensive, Incomplete Information in Which Candidates Are Elected According to the Plurality System or Proportional System

Voter and party strategies of offering or demanding policies are determined not only in a context of incomplete and expensive information, but also in a context of collective rules that translate votes into representatives and seats. These rules determine how the votes will be handled, varying between the two extremes of the plurality system and the proportional system. Since these rules can produce a different number of seats for the same number of votes, they naturally affect the strategic calculations of voters and parties. The rules of plurality and proportional representation may be applied under conditions that vary greatly among countries and even provinces. To understand this diversity, we examine the implications of the plurality rule in five political contexts:

- two parties compete around a single cleavage;
- several parties compete around a single cleavage;
- two parties compete around several cleavages;
- several parties compete around several cleavages; and
- parties compete in a world where voter preferences vary among regions.

The implications of proportional representation will be examined in three political contexts:

- several parties compete around a single cleavage in a world where the distribution of voter preferences is unimodal and symmetrical;
- several parties compete around a single cleavage in a world where the distribution of voter preferences is multimodal and symmetrical; and
- several parties compete around several cleavages.

Plurality

Competition between Two Parties around a Single Cleavage   The simplest political scenario would be to assume that only two parties compete around a single cleavage (table 9.13). Such would be the case if a left-wing party were to propose increasing government intervention to stimulate economic growth and a right-wing party proposed the opposite.

The hypothesis of rationality supposes that voters opt for the party whose platform or ideology most closely resembles their own views. Similarly, parties adopt positions that maximize the number of votes they receive. If voter preferences were to be frozen for a moment, their choices would depend on the positions adopted by the parties. If one party adopts position L and another position C, the first party is certain to attract all voters to the left of L while the second attracts all voters to the right of C (figure 9.5). If the two parties are equidistant from the median, they will split the votes equally, with the votes to the left of the median going to party L, and those to the right going to party C. The competition for votes, therefore, will be extremely close, with each party winning half the votes.

Table 9.13
Competition between two parties around a single cleavage

I.1.7	Position rule:	Voters express their preferences around a single issue.
I.1.8	Position rule:	Voter preferences regarding this issue can be represented by a line running between points *a* and *b*.
I.1.9	Position rule:	Voter preferences can be represented in the form of a continuous distribution between *a* and *b*. This distribution is unimodal and symmetrical.
I.1.10	Position rule:	A voter's preferences can be represented by point *x* to be found at point *a*, point *b* or any other point between the two. The voter accordingly prefers an ideology or political platform that is closer to *x* to an ideology or platform that is further away.
I.1.11	Position rule:	Party policies can be located on the line at a particular point representing the party's ideological position or the average position of the party's policies (the average of the various points representing the various party policies).
I.2.4	Boundary rule:	The competition for votes unfolds between two political parties.

General proposition derived from competition between two parties around a single cleavage

P.16   Competition encourages parties to adopt platforms, and therefore ideologies, that tend to become increasingly similar.

If the first party adopts a position closer to the median while the second maintains its original position, party *L* will win a majority of votes and thus the election. Since party *C* also attempts to maximize its votes, it will be inclined to move closer to the median to attract more votes to its left. Both parties, therefore, have an incentive to move their political and ideological positions slowly toward the median. The median constitutes the optimal position for both because no other position on the line can provide more votes, regardless of the position adopted by the other party. The median also constitutes a position of equilibrium. If both parties adopt it, neither will have any incentive to leave it unilaterally. On the other hand, if both parties adopt the median position, voters will become indifferent to them because they have adopted identical positions. If this were to happen, voters would have to base their decisions on criteria other than the costs and benefits of public policy.

The median is the optimal political position in all two-party races with only one cleavage, even if the distribution of voter preferences does not result in a unimodal symmetrical curve. Therefore, the same logic applies in the case of a bimodal non-symmetrical curve like that in figure 9.6. Even if most voters are to the right of the median, a party that adopts this position would be easily defeated by a more left-wing

Figure 9.5
Competition between two parties with a unimodal, symmetrical distribution of voter preferences

Number of voters

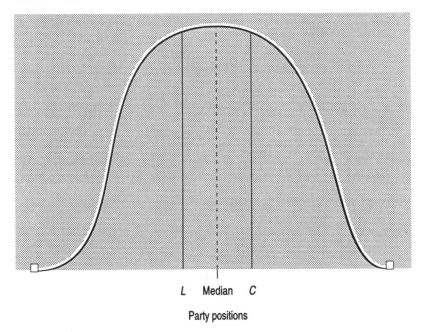

L   Median   C

Party positions

opponent that moved toward this position but remained to the left between the median and the peak of the curve.

Competition among Several Parties with One Cleavage   Suppose that parties L and C have adopted median positions, or at least positions very close to it. Suppose further that a third party enters the race and takes up a position to one side of the median, say to the right. It can be shown that the new party, N, can win a plurality of votes even if the area under the curve to the right of N is less than one-third of the total area (see table 9.14 for rule and proposition governing this scenario). As Brams has shown (1978, 14), if the hatched area is larger than half the non-hatched L–C area, N will get more votes than L and C. In addition, N will also get half the votes to its left between its position and the median. L and C will share the remaining votes. For this reason, N can win a large number of votes with less than a third of the electorate to its right (figure 9.7).

In the same way, it could be shown that a fourth party, P, could take up a position to the left of the median and that it could even succeed

Figure 9.6
Distribution of voter preferences on a bimodal, non-symmetrical curve

Number of voters

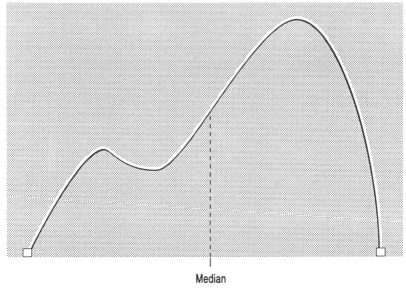

Median

Party positions

in defeating party N if it decided to move closer to the median than did N. In conclusion, in a two-party competition around a single cleavage, the two parties can be defeated by a third or fourth party if the two first parties adopt positions at the median.

Brams (1978, 15–16) has also shown that in a two-party competition around a single cleavage, the two parties can be defeated by a third or fourth party regardless of the position adopted by the first two parties for practically any distribution of voter preferences. In conclusion, a new party can always adopt some position that will defeat one or more competitors. In the case of a single cleavage, three-party competitions

Table 9.14
Competition among several parties around a single cleavage

I.2.4   Boundary rule: Competition for votes is among several parties.

General proposition derived from competition among several parties around a single cleavage

P.17   In a two-party competition, no position is invulnerable to the entry of a third or fourth party regardless of the distribution of voter preferences (Brams 1978, 16–17).

Figure 9.7
Three-party competition with a unimodal, symmetrical distribution of voter preferences

Number of voters

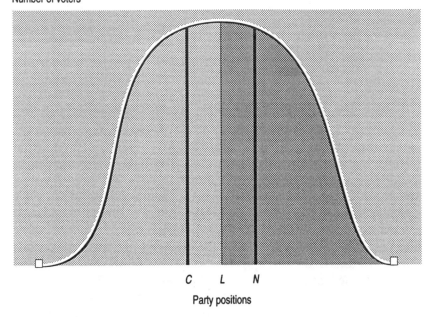

C   L   N

Party positions

tend to become unstable, while two-party competitions tend to remain stable. From this, one can conclude with Taagepera and Grofman (1985, 344) that the plurality rule tends to engender a two-party system when the electoral competition revolves around a single cleavage.

Competition between Two Parties with Several Cleavages   Only during crises does the competition for votes involve just one political cleavage. Lijphart's empirical study (1984b, 128) shows that a single cleavage is unusual; the political competition generally involves more than one cleavage. His study of 21 democratic party systems indicates that parties distinguish themselves from each other by the positions they adopt in one or more of the following dimensions:

- socio-economic: As defined earlier in this study.
- religious: Party positions may be based on secular or religious principles and may contrast on such issues as the death penalty, abortion, pornography, etc.
- ethno-cultural: This type of cleavage exists in countries that are ethnically or linguistically heterogeneous.

- urban–rural: Lijphart (1984b) notes that this cleavage is disappearing. In a country like Canada, the division is not between the city and the country but between the centre and the regions.
- support for the system: This type of cleavage appears when some parties are opposed to the democratic system.
- foreign policy: The parties may distinguish themselves from each other by their positions on international issues.
- materialist–postmaterialist: Some parties may espouse materialist values while others espouse postmaterialist values.

It is much more difficult for voters to gauge the distance between their personal views and party positions if several dimensions are involved in an election (table 9.15). The same holds true for parties, which will experience greater difficulty determining their optimal position. Resolving this problem is all the more complex because voters attach a different value to each dimension. Some voters may consider the parties' positions on the socio-economic dimension to be much more important than their ethno-cultural positions. Other voters may take the opposite view. The relative importance voters attach to various party positions makes it impossible to apply unidimensional spatial analysis to elections involving several issues (table 9.15).

Despite these difficulties, it is still important to investigate the implications of elections revolving around several cleavages. Suppose that two parties, L and C, have different socio-economic and ethno-cultural policies, that they can propose using the power of the state to further stimulate the economy, e, or to oppose doing this, e', and that they can propose to support the demands of a certain ethnic group, r, or to oppose doing this, r'. It follows that each party can adopt one or other of the following four programs: er, $e'r$, er' or $e'r'$. Suppose, finally, that there is a three-person electorate whose preferences are as shown in table 9.16. (The logic of this example was taken from Hillinger 1971 and Brams 1978, 29–31.)

What platform should a party adopt to maximize its votes? This question could be answered by determining the winning position for

Table 9.15
Competition between two parties around several cleavages

I.1.7	Position rule:	Voter preferences revolve around several cleavages.
I.2.4	Boundary rule:	Two parties are competing.

General proposition derived from competition between two parties around several cleavages

P.18	Any political platform adopted by one party may be defeated by a different platform proposed by another party.

Table 9.16
Preferences of three voters on four political platforms

Voter	Preferences			
	1st choice	2nd choice	3rd choice	4th choice
1	er	er'	$e'r$	$e'r'$
2	er'	$e'r'$	er	$e'r$
3	$e'r$	$e'r'$	er	er'

each cleavage, as if voters voted separately on each of the two cleavages. Accordingly, if e is preferred to e' by voters 1 and 2, and r is preferred to r' by voters 1 and 3, one could conclude that the er platform would maximize votes.

This conclusion is incorrect, however, because voters 2 and 3 prefer $e'r'$ to er. Thus a platform supported by a majority of voters when the cleavages are considered independently of one another can be defeated by a platform supported by minorities only. Downs (1957, chap. 4) concluded that parties are prone to develop platforms that attract coalitions of minorities.

The discrepancy between the results of preferences concerning cleavages taken in isolation and preferences concerning platforms that combine positions on two cleavages is caused by a voting paradox (Brams 1978, chap. 2). In the example in table 9.16, the voting paradox means that no political platform is invincible. As shown by the arrows in figure 9.8, which denote majority preferences among various platforms, every platform that receives majority support in an election can be defeated by another majority in a second election. These are called cyclical majorities.

The main conclusion drawn from this example is that in an election involving two cleavages, no platform is invincible. Any platform adopted by a party may be defeated by a different platform adopted by another party. As a result, "In a coalitions of minorities situation, one party may win an election in a given year on a given platform and lose the following election on the same platform without any shift in the preferences of the voters" (Frohlich and Oppenheimer 1978, 135).

Introduction of Regional Variations – Parties Have an Incentive to Invest Their Resources in Districts Where Their Chances of Winning Are Best and to Ignore Other Districts   The plurality rule leads parties to divide

Figure 9.8
Cyclical majorities in regard to voting on political platforms

Marginal costs–Marginal benefits

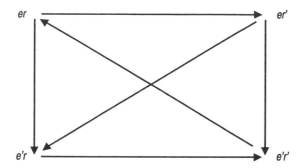

Table 9.17
Introduction of regional variations

I.1.2	Position rule:	Voter preferences vary from one district to another. In other words, preferences vary from one region to another.
I.2.4	Boundary rule:	There are several parties competing for votes.

General propositions derived from the introduction of regional variations

P.19 Parties have an incentive to invest their resources in districts where their chances of winning are best and to ignore other districts.

P.20 Parties have an incentive to become involved in local campaigns.

P.21 Third parties benefiting from support that is regionally concentrated may have more candidates elected than those whose support is evenly distributed across all districts.

P.22 Each party has a single optimal opponent in each district (Katz 1980, 26).

P.23 The optimal opponents are not the same in each district (Katz 1980, 26).

P.24 Voters may vote strategically for a party that does not come closest to meeting their preferences.

districts into two categories: those where they have a high chance of winning and those where their chances are low. Since the resources of parties are limited, they are likely to invest much more in districts where their chances of winning are higher than in others.

Parties Have an Incentive to Become Involved in Local Campaigns The plurality rule leads parties to become involved in local campaigns. Because individuals vote for local candidates of a party, they may attempt to downplay or disregard the costs of some policies in the party platform while exaggerating the local benefits of other party policies. In an election in which one candidate attempts to win votes by emphasizing local benefits, candidates who concentrate on their party's national platform run the risk of losing the election. The emergence of one candidate who emphasizes local concerns, therefore, leads the other candidates to do the same.

Third Parties Benefiting from Support That Is Regionally Concentrated May Have More Candidates Elected Than Those Whose Support Is Evenly Distributed across All Districts   Under the plurality rule, parties are rewarded not for the proportion of votes they win nationally but for the order in which they stand in each district. In a three-party race, therefore, if L receives 34 percent of the votes in all districts, while C and N each receive 33 percent, L wins 100 percent of the seats with only 34 percent of the votes. The plurality rule is disadvantageous to parties whose support is scattered across the nation. The only method of mitigating this disadvantage is to invest some party resources in concentrating votes in certain electoral districts or in the blocks of districts that the regions represent. This system of incentives causes regional parties to emerge. They may succeed in electing enough candidates to engage in an electoral bargaining process that is costly for the whole country.

Each Party Has A Single Optimal Opponent in Each District and This Opponent May Vary from One District to Another   Under the plurality rule, parties are not inclined to accord the same strategic importance to all their adversaries. Since winning seats depends on the order in which parties finish on the electoral district level, the most beneficial transfers of votes occur between the candidate who stands first and the candidate who stands second. Thus, as Katz says (1980, 26), the political race reaches its greatest intensity between the two parties leading the pack:

> The differing values of votes depend on what parties they are coming from or going to. This phenomenon may be illustrated by a simple example. Suppose three parties competing in a single-member district currently share the vote in a ratio of 48:46:6. Then, the party in the middle can afford to lose 1.5 votes to the small party for every vote it gains from the big party until, having gained just over 4 percent from one side while losing just over 6 percent to the other, it moves into first place.

The plurality principle engenders a two-party race at the district level. As a result, each party has an incentive to behave as if it had one optimal opponent in each district. Moreover, if the party standings vary from district to district, each party has a different optimal opponent in the various districts (Katz 1980, 26). This also prompts some parties to run candidates in certain districts only. These third parties could be called regional parties.

Voters Can Be Induced to Vote Strategically   Under the plurality rule, voters whose preferred party has a good chance of winning the election have no difficulty deciding how to vote. However, if the preferred party has no chance of winning the election, the voter may decide to vote for another party that has a better chance of gaining power. Voters in this position vote strategically to avoid wasting their vote. This type of behaviour can transform a race between several parties into a two-party race, falsely suggesting that the two parties that are ahead in the election represent the actual preferences of the voters.

Proportional Representation

The plurality rule results in systematic biases in public policies that divert the choices of voters and parties. Proportional representation, which attributes to each party the number of representatives commensurate with the percentage of votes obtained, is often presented as a far superior alternative. We shall demonstrate that proportional representation also carries a number of biases as far as the attributes of public policies are concerned. We shall compare these biases by highlighting situations in which the distribution of voter preferences is unimodal and symmetrical or multimodal and symmetrical in a world where parties compete around a single cleavage; finally, we shall deal with situations where competition revolves around several cleavages.

Unimodal Distribution of Voter Preferences in a Competition around a Single Cleavage   In addition to assuming that candidates are elected by proportional representation, we also assume that competition occurs among several parties around a single cleavage, with voter preferences being distributed unimodally and symmetrically. To complete this portrait, we assume that according to the rules of the game, voters vote for the list of candidates of one party rather than for a specific candidate and that the candidates' order of appearance on this list is determined by party leaders (table 9.18).

The general proposition deriving from these conditions has already been demonstrated in the examination of the plurality rule: in a single-cleavage world where voter preferences are unimodally and symmetrically distributed, competition among several parties tends to be unstable. Centrist parties tend to be caught in the middle and lose votes to their opponents, who, although they are to the left or right, will move toward the centre.

Table 9.18
The principle of proportional representation

I.1.2	Position rule:	Voter preferences vary from one region to another within a district.
I.1.7	Position rule:	Voter preferences revolve around a single cleavage.
I.1.9	Position rule:	Voter preferences have a unimodal, symmetrical distribution.
I.2.4	Boundary rule:	The competition for votes involves several parties.
I.2.4	Boundary rule:	Candidates exist as members of party lists.
I.3.6	Authority rule:	Party leaders establish the order in which candidates appear on party lists.
I.3.7	Authority rule:	An individual's vote constitutes selection of a party's list of candidates.
I.4.4	Aggregation rule:	The territory consists of a single electoral district.
I.4.6	Aggregation rule:	Each party is assigned a number of representatives commensurate with the percentage of votes it obtained throughout the entire territory.

General proposition derived from implementing proportional representation

P.25   The two parties positioned close to the median, regardless of that position, are vulnerable to the entry of a third or fourth party.

Multimodal Distribution of Voter Preferences   Voter preferences around a single cleavage may also be distributed multimodally, as shown in figure 9.8 (see also table 9.19). Introducing this variable has several implications, which will be examined one by one.

Party Platforms and Associated Ideologies Contrast More Sharply Than in Situations Where Voter Preferences Have a Unimodal, Symmetrical Distribution Consider an electorate in which voter preferences are as reflected in the multimodal, symmetrical distribution curve of figure 9.9. The multiple modes plus proportional representation create conditions that facilitate the emergence of a party at the peak of each mode.

In this example, a state of equilibrium among the five parties is achieved when the distance between each party and its immediate neighbours is the same. Unlike when voter preferences follow a unimodal symmetrical curve, the distribution of preferences in figure 9.9 does not encourage the parties to resemble each other more and more. For instance, party L cannot increase its support by shifting its ground toward N or C. If L moved toward N, it would win additional votes at N's expense, but would lose an equal number to C. The reverse would happen if L moved toward C. As a result, L's interests are best served by not changing its platform and associated ideology. When the competition among several parties revolves around a single cleavage and the

Table 9.19
Multimodal distribution of voter preferences

I.1.9   Position rule: Voter preferences have a multimodal, symmetrical distribution.

General propositions derived from a multimodal distribution of voter preferences

P.26   Party platforms and associated ideologies contrast more sharply than in situations where voter preferences have a unimodal, symmetrical distribution.

P.27   Parties are inclined to invest resources in campaigns conducted throughout the entire territory.

P.28   Parties have two optimal opponents, except parties positioned on the extreme edges of the distribution.

P.29   Proportional representation encourages the concentration of power in the hands of the party leaders.

P.30   Voters have no fear of wasting their vote.

Figure 9.9
Multimodal, symmetrical distribution of voter preferences

Number of voters

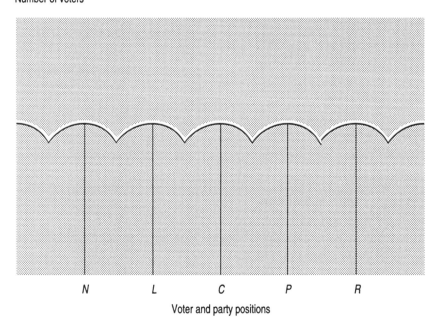

Voter and party positions

voter preferences follow a symmetrical, multimodal curve, the parties are encouraged to distinguish themselves clearly from one another and to maintain the purity of the platforms and ideologies with which they are identified.

Parties Are Inclined to Invest Resources in Campaigns Conducted Throughout the Entire Territory Proportional representation, based on a single voting district, rewards parties for the proportion of votes it obtained throughout the territory rather than for the concentrated support received in certain regions. To this extent, this type of proportional representation is more neutral than the plurality rule because geographically scattered support is valued as much as geographically concentrated support.

Parties Have Two Optimal Opponents In a situation such as the one illustrated in figure 9.8, where parties compete around a single cleavage, each party has at least two optimal opponents; that is, each can attempt to enlarge its voter base among neighbouring voters to its left and right. Thus, party L has two optimal opponents: parties N and C. Katz (1980, 22) offers this explanation:

> Since, by assumption, voters rank their preferences among parties according to the distances between the party platforms and their own most preferred positions in the policy space, the parties against which a candidate should most directly focus his campaign are those most directly competing for the same voters, that is, the voters who are roughly equidistant between the two parties. These are the voters whose opinions would have to be changed the least in order to produce electoral change, and thus it is particularly to these voters that the candidate must appeal.

In a world where competition revolves around a single point, the parties on the extremes have only one optimal opponent. This is the case for party N, whose optimal opponent is L, and for party R, whose optimal opponent is P.

Proportional Representation Encourages the Concentration of Power in the Hands of Party Leaders Under proportional representation in a single electoral district, voters do not vote for a party's local candidate but rather for a list of candidates representing a party. The effect of this rule is to place substantial power in the hands of the party leaders who draw up the lists and determine the order in which candidates appear on them.

Voters Have No Fear of Wasting Their Vote Every vote received by a party contributes to increasing its percentage of the vote and, therefore, the percentage of seats it receives. Voters run no risk of "wasting" their votes as they do under the plurality rule.

Competition around Several Cleavages Parties do not always compete around a single cleavage; they may have to compete around several simultaneously. In this case, and unlike previous situations, parties could have more than two optimal opponents while being encouraged to promote their political platform as a whole (table 9.20).

In a world in which the political competition revolves around several points, parties can be forced to defend themselves against more than two optimal opponents. Take the case of six parties competing around two points (e.g., a socio-economic and an ethno-cultural position). If the party positions on these points are represented by figure 9.10, party *L* competes more directly for votes with *N*, *P* and *C* than with *B* and *R*. Therefore, *L* should concentrate its resources to fight these three parties rather than *B* and *R*. In such a situation, every party has an incentive to concentrate its resources on the struggle against those parties whose platforms most closely resemble its own because these votes are easiest to win or lose. Every party therefore has at least two optimal opponents. A party could find itself forced to compete with more than two optimal opponents, as shown in figure 9.10. An increasing number of cleavages, therefore, helps to increase the number of parties competing directly for votes.

In addition, parties are encouraged to promote their entire political platform rather than emphasizing their positions on one or a few cleavages around which the campaign is revolving. When the race for votes revolves around two cleavages, any platform change to win votes also loses votes. Thus, if party *L* moved from point *L* to point *L'*, it would lose the votes of citizens whose preference hinged on *L*'s position on the ethno-cultural cleavage. According to Katz (1980, 24),

> These results lead to the expectation that rational candidates competing under PR [proportional representation] will stress in their campaigns

Table 9.20
Competition around several cleavages

I.1.7	Position rule:	Voter preferences revolve around several cleavages.

General propositions derived from competition around several cleavages

P.26–30	These are still valid under this modification.
P.31	Parties can be induced to compete with more than two optimal opponents.
P.32	Parties have an incentive to promote their entire platform.

Figure 9.10
Position of five parties on two cleavages

Socio-economic cleavage

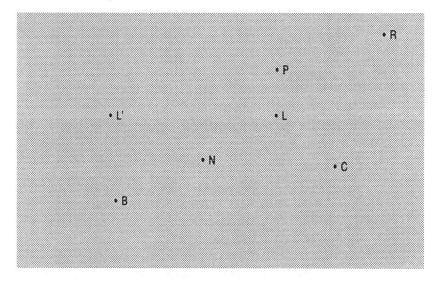

Ethno-cultural cleavage

the virtue of their party's entire platform taken as a whole, and will appeal on the basis of proximity to that point. This is because candidates cannot ignore any relevant dimension for fear of losing voters whose preference for their party is based on that dimension.

RESULTS OF EMPIRICAL STUDIES

Do Parties in Office Adopt Strategies for Redistributing Wealth?
Empirical studies of the redistributive strategies of political parties deal primarily with biases in public expenditures. Until recently, researchers have been much less interested in the redistributive biases in costs and benefits that have been incorporated into law. We look first at redistributive biases in public expenditures.

Biases in Public Expenditures
Empirical studies of public expenditures in Western capitalist economies all address the following question: Does control of the executive by parties with differing ideologies result in changes in public expenditures?

This type of empirical study is based on dependent variables, independent variables, results and limits:

- Dependent variables: Generally measured using national aggregate statistics between 1950 and 1985, these variables include

  - categories of expenditure such as education, health and income; and
  - types of expenditure such as direct expenditures, transfer payments and the taxation system.

- Independent variables: Studies of public expenditures take into account a large number of independent variables. We deal only with the ideological orientations of the public policies of various parties. Parties in office can generally be divided into right-wing and left-wing.

- Results: Statistically, strong left-wing parties are

  - associated with a higher rate of increase in public expenditures (Castles 1982, 85; Van Arnhem and Schotsman 1982, 327);
  - not significantly associated with the increase in public expenditures in the 1973–80 period (Swank 1988, 1139);
  - strongly associated with expenditures on direct government procurement and somewhat associated with expenditures on transfers to individuals (O'Connor 1988, 286);
  - associated with increased expenditure on health care (Castles 1982, 75);
  - associated with income redistribution (Van Arnhem and Schotsman 1982, 323);
  - associated with fiscal redistribution, that is, more progressive taxes (Hicks and Swank 1984, 277);
  - associated with redistributive public expenditures when labour unions are strong and the economy is expanding (Hicks et al. 1989); and
  - strongly associated with redistributive expenditures when right-wing parties are weak (Van Arnhem and Schotsman 1982, 351–52).

The strength of left-wing parties depends on the number of labour unions and the strength of their organizations (O'Connor 1988).

Conversely, strong right-wing parties are statistically

- associated with a slowing in the increase of public expenditures (Castles 1982, 85; Swank 1988, 1133; Van Arnhem and Schotsman 1982, 327); and
- associated with an increase in education expenditures (Castles 1982, 75).

The strength of the political right depends on unity among the parties and the duration of their control of the executive (Borg and Castles 1981, 621).

- Limits:
  - Parties are not easily classified as left or right.
  - The statistical analyses implicitly demand a single cleavage, namely left versus right, expressed as redistribution versus non-redistribution.
  - Being presented in aggregate form, the statistical analyses cannot determine who really benefits from public expenditures.

Statutory Biases

Although there are many studies of the redistributive aspect of public expenditures, there are not many empirical studies of the redistributive aspect of statutes. Landry and his team (Landry 1990, 1991; Landry and Duchesneau 1987) analysed the public statutes adopted by the Quebec National Assembly between 1960 and 1985. The analysis looked at the proposed government intervention and used a questionnaire to determine the nature of the benefits offered as well as the beneficiaries.

The empirical results indicate that

- 13.6 percent of the good provided through statutes constitutes genuine pure public good (Landry 1990, 304);
- 70 percent of the good provided is limited to particular groups by certain restrictions, such as age, sex, the need to pay a fee, etc. (Landry 1990, 304);
- the hypothesis that statutes provide good with benefits going to producers while the costs are assumed by consumers is not borne out by the facts (Landry 1990, 304);
- statutes create benefits for producers more often than for consumers, while the costs of the government action are not mentioned (Landry 1990, 305–306); and
- the hypothesis that social democratic parties create more benefits for workers than for entrepreneurs, while conservative parties do the opposite, is not supported by the facts. Entrepreneurs always receive more benefits than workers, regardless of the ideology of the party in office (Landry 1990, 306).

Are Voters Sensitive to the Economic Manipulations of Parties in Office?

This question has been analysed using the sophisticated statistical techniques of politico-econometric analysis. The basic condition of these empirical studies is that the party that controls the executive improves short-term national economic conditions just before elections. The studies also posit that voters support parties that improve their personal economic situations and punish those that harm them. This relationship between economic policy and elections presupposes that the governing parties are able to manipulate economic policy and that voters are able to respond to the results.

A study of the political economy of U.S. elections by Brown and Stein (1982, 490) summarizes the results of research into the manipulation of economic policy by parties in office:

> Our analysis of the political economy of national elections suggests the existence, at most, of an intermittent four-year economic-electoral cycle. We do find evidence of clear acceleration in real disposable income per capita in the four years when presidents sought re-election (1948, 1964, 1972, 1976). In congressional election years and in presidential election years when the incumbent did not seek re-election, the economy was as likely to decelerate as to accelerate.
>
> The accelerated growth in real disposable income per capita in the four years when presidents (except Eisenhower) sought reelection was caused not by increased transfer payments but by changes in macroeconomic policy, especially tax policy. In each case, a major tax cut stimulated growth ... Accelerated income growth in election years and decelerated income growth in nonelection years are taken as evidence of presidential manipulations of the economy.

The empirical studies undertaken by this school of inquiry indicate that voters are sensitive to fluctuations in the unemployment rate, the inflation rate and personal disposable income (Whiteley 1984; Hibbs 1987; Frey and Schneider 1978a; Minford and Peel 1982).

According to Lewis-Beck (1986, 342), the impact of the economic situation on voting is evident:

> Without doubt, economic circumstances affect British, French, German, and Italian voters. The perception of better (worse) economic performance and policy increases (decreases) their likelihood of voting for an incumbent party. European economic voters appear to arrive at their final choice rather intelligently, on the whole. The view that government has damaged their own financial well-being induces a critical reevaluation of the administration's economic management. If they come to believe that the national economy has suffered or will suffer, due to government economic policies, they withdraw support from the ruling parties.

In general, empirical studies of this type show that people vote for those in office during good economic times, and against parties in office during difficult economic times (Paldam 1981, 194; Minford and Peel 1982, 268; Kramer 1971; Hibbs 1987).

Politico-econometric analyses are based on a number of assumptions that limit their value. They assume that

- voter decisions revolve around a single cleavage: improvement or deterioration of the national economy;
- parties in office are able to manipulate macroeconomic policy in such a way as to produce results that benefit them at elections;
- voters judge their personal economic situation solely with reference to macroeconomic variables such as inflation and unemployment rates;
- voters are sensitive to fluctuations in economic conditions nationally rather than locally or regionally (Alvarez et al. 1990); and
- voters decide how to vote solely on the basis of their opinion of the government, independent of the opportunity cost involved in changing the party in power.

A recent study on the manipulation of macroeconomic policy concluded, "Just how short-term manipulation of the economy fits with the electoral results is unclear" (Williams 1990, 790).

LESSONS FOR THE REFORM OF ELECTORAL INSTITUTIONS IN CANADA

Problems to Be Resolved
Institutional arrangements structure the context in which voters and party leaders make their decisions. This comparative analysis of the institutional arrangements in representative democracies focused on three situations:

1. Representative democracy based on the unanimity rule in a situation of perfect knowledge. The public policies adopted in this situation would reflect the Pareto optimum.
2. Representative democracy based on the plurality rule in a situation of imperfect, expensive knowledge. Although closer to reality than the first situation, the second generates several biases, including the following:

    - The incentive for voters to become informed about party platforms is weak.

- The incentive to become informed is stronger for voters concerned about policies in their role as producers than in their role as consumers.
- Groups representing producers are inclined to demand policies that generate benefits concentrated in the hands of producers and costs diffused among consumers.
- Parties are inclined to offer policies that would concentrate benefits in the hands of producers and that have indefinite costs.
- Parties are inclined to offer policies for which benefits would be realized in the short term.
- Government subsidies for parties persuade them to conduct capital-intensive election campaigns based on extensive use of the national media.
- Financial contributions from voters persuade parties to remain sensitive to the policy expectations of the public.

3. Representative democracy based on the plurality rule. This situation also has several biases, including the following:

- The plurality rule rewards a concentration of votes in certain regions and undervalues diffuse support scattered equally across all regions.
- The plurality rule causes parties to campaign in some regions and ignore others.
- The plurality rule causes individuals to vote strategically when making a choice among more than two candidates.

In addition, empirical studies into biases in public expenditures confirm that they are redistributive, while studies into the effect of statutes show that redistribution largely benefits entrepreneurs and workers. Politico-econometric analyses also show that voters are sensitive to fluctuations in the economy.

In summary, the economic theory of politics predicts that the institutional arrangements of representative democracy generate biases in public policies, and the available empirical studies confirm the existence of such biases in favour of producers.

These biases should be corrected because they cause an inefficient allocation of resources by encouraging parties, as well as voters in their role as producers, to invest resources in creating policies that tend to redistribute existing wealth rather than increase it.

RECOMMENDATIONS

Voters and party leaders are inclined to invest in demanding those changes to the institutions of representative democracy that are in their best interests. When leaders of the major parties are satisfied with the benefits they receive under the existing institutions, significant changes to the status quo are hard to imagine. As a result, attempts must be made to resolve the problems inherent in the current institutions by adopting marginal changes that would produce more benefits than would the status quo.

Marginal Changes to Mitigate the Fiscal Illusion

The party platforms (Landry and Duchesneau 1987) and the statutes adopted by parties in office (Landry 1990) describe the benefits to be provided without mentioning the costs; this is a world of completely unrealistic fiscal illusion. It is currently impossible to force parties to detail the costs of the promises they make in their platforms. This could be attained, however, if relevant statutes were adopted. Therefore, it is recommended that the introduction of bills in the House of Commons be accompanied by informational literature describing how the passage of the statutes would have direct and indirect costs and benefits.

Marginal Changes to Mitigate the Bias in Favour of Producers

The public policy bias in favour of producers probably cannot be turned around in favour of consumers. Furthermore, the fiscal illusion is probably not neutral in its impact and some individuals assume more costs than others. Party leaders would be less inclined to benefit or disadvantage certain categories of individuals if voters were informed about the redistributive effects of policies. Therefore, it is recommended that bills introduced in the House of Commons be accompanied by explanatory material identifying the categories of people who would benefit from the statute and the categories of people who would bear the resulting costs.

Marginal Changes to Reduce the Short-term Thinking of Political Parties

It has been shown that parties are inclined to adopt policies that will quickly bring benefits while the costs are deferred. This inclination partly explains why parties remain silent about the costs of their proposed policies. This vicious circle must be broken, or at least controlled. Therefore, it is recommended that the introduction of bills in the House of Commons be accompanied by documents stating when the benefits of the statute will emerge and when the costs will be paid.

In addition, it is recommended that the introduction of bills in the House of Commons be accompanied by documentation outlining the effect of the proposed statute on the budgetary balance over the next 10 years.

Marginal Changes to Mitigate Party Insensitivity to Voter Demands

When parties receive subsidies from the House of Commons, their leaders become highly independent of party members and are inclined to conduct capital-intensive national campaigns rather than labour-intensive campaigns. Conversely, we have seen that financing parties through voter contributions encourages party leaders to remain sensitive to the public policy demands of their stakeholders. The second outcome appears preferable to the first. Therefore, it is recommended that the subsidies to parties represented in a legislative assembly be reduced gradually and that voters be encouraged to contribute more to financing parties through more generous tax credits.

In addition, it is recommended that voters, but not legal entities, be allowed to make contributions to party finances. This would avoid exacerbating the bias of public policy toward producers as a result of financial contributions from interest groups representing voters in their capacity as producers.

Marginal Changes to Mitigate the Undervaluation of Scattered Support

Because voter preferences vary from one region to another, the election of representatives under the plurality rule creates problems for national parties whose support is scattered. Parties are encouraged to invest their resources in regions where the concentration of votes maximizes the potential number of seats they can win. The advantages gained through a concentrated vote exacerbate regional disparities by punishing parties with popular support spread across the entire territory. Therefore, it is recommended that parties disadvantaged by the distortions arising from the plurality rule be compensated in each of four great regions, namely the Atlantic region, Quebec, Ontario and western Canada. The House of Commons would then have a variable number of members of Parliament, some of whom could be selected from regional lists drawn up by party leaders.

BIBLIOGRAPHY

Abrams, R. 1980. *Foundations of Political Analysis: An Introduction to the Theory of Collective Choice.* New York: Columbia University Press.

Ahmad, K.U. 1983. "An Empirical Study of Politico-Economic Interaction in the United States: A Comment." *Review of Economics and Statistics* 65:173–78.

Aldrich, J.H. 1976. "Some Problems in Testing Two Rational Models of Participation." *American Journal of Political Science* 20:713–33.

Alexander, H.E., ed. 1989. *Comparative Political Finance in the 1980s.* Cambridge: Cambridge University Press.

Alt, J.E. 1979. *The Politics of Economic Decline.* Cambridge: Cambridge University Press.

———. 1980. "Political Business Cycles in Britain." In *Models of Political Economy*, ed. P. Whiteley. London: Sage Publications.

Alt, J.E., and K.A. Shepsle, eds. 1990. *Perspectives on Positive Political Economy.* Cambridge: Cambridge University Press.

Alvarez, R.M., G. Garret and P. Lange. 1990. "What's 'Help' in the Politics of the Business Cycle? Government Partisanship, Policy Uncertainty, and Macroeconomic Performance." Paper presented at the American Political Science Association annual meeting, San Francisco.

Aranson, P.H., M.J. Hinich and P.C. Ordeshook. 1974. "Election Goals and Strategies: Equivalent and Nonequivalent Candidate Objectives." *American Political Science Review* 68:135–52.

Arcelus, F., and A.H. Meltzer. 1975. "The Effect of Aggregate Economic Variables on Congressional Elections." *American Political Science Review* 69:1232–39.

Arrow, J.K. 1963. *Social Choice and Individual Values.* 2d ed. New Haven: Yale University Press.

Ashford, D.E. 1989. "L'État-providence à travers l'étude comparative des institutions." *Revue française de science politique* 39:276–95.

Attali, J. 1972a. *Analyse économique de la politique.* Paris: Presses universitaires de France.

———. 1972b. *Les modèles politiques.* Paris: Presses universitaires de France, Coll. SUP.

Aucoin, P., ed. 1985. *Institutional Reforms for Representative Government.* Vol. 38 of the research studies of the Royal Commission on the Economic Union and Development Prospects for Canada. Toronto: University of Toronto Press.

Auster, R.D., and M. Silver. 1979. *The State as a Firm: Economic Forces in Political Development.* The Hague: Martinus Nijhoff.

Axelrod, R. 1984. *The Evolution of Cooperation.* New York: Basic Books.

Balinski, M.L., and H.P. Young. 1978. "Stability, Coalitions and Schisms in Proportional Representation Systems." *American Political Science Review* 72:848–58.

Barry, B., and R. Hardin, eds. 1982. *Rational Man and Irrational Society.* Beverly Hills: Sage Publications.

Barzel, Y. 1990. *Economic Analysis of Property Rights.* Cambridge: Cambridge University Press.

Blais, A. 1988. "The Classification of Electoral Systems." *European Journal of Political Research* 16:99–110.

———. 1990. "The Debate over Electoral Systems." *Papers in Political Economy* (August): 1–46.

Blais, A., and R.K. Carty. 1987. "The Impact of Electoral Formulae on the Creation of Majority Governments." *Electoral Studies* 6:209–18.

———. 1990. "Does Proportional Representation Foster Voter Turnout?" *European Journal of Political Research* 18:167–81.

Bloom, H.S., and H.D. Price. 1975. "Voter Response to Short-Run Economic Conditions: The Asymmetric Effect of Prosperity and Recession." *American Political Science Review* 69:1240–54.

Bogdanor, V. 1981. *The People and the Party System.* Cambridge: Cambridge University Press.

———. 1987. "Electoral Reform and British Politics." *Electoral Studies* 6:115–21.

Bogdanor, V., and D. Butler. 1983. *Democracy and Elections: Electoral Systems and Their Political Consequences.* Cambridge: Cambridge University Press.

Borg, S.G., and F.G. Castles. 1981. "The Influence of the Political Right on Public Income Maintenance Expenditure and Equality." *Political Studies* 29:604–21.

Brams, S.J. 1976. *Paradoxes in Politics.* New York: Free Press.

———. 1978. *The Presidential Election Game.* New Haven: Yale University Press.

———. 1985. *Rational Politics, Decisions, Games and Strategy.* Washington, DC: Congressional Quarterly Press.

Brams, S.J., and P.C. Fishburn. 1983. *Approval Voting.* Stuttgart: Birkhauser.

Brennan, G., and L.E. Lonasky, eds. 1990. *Politics and Processes: New Essays in Democratic Thought.* Cambridge: Cambridge University Press.

Breton, A. 1974. *The Economic Theory of Representative Government.* Chicago: Aldine.

Brown, T.A., and A.A. Stein. 1982. "The Political Economy of National Elections." *Comparative Politics* 10:479–97.

Browning, R.X. 1985. "Presidents, Congress, and Policy Outcomes: U.S. Social Welfare Expenditures 1949–1977." *American Journal of Political Science* 29:197–216.

Buchanan, J.M. 1975. *The Limits of Liberty: Between Anarchy and Leviathan.* Chicago: University of Chicago Press.

Buchanan, J.M., and R.D. Tollison, eds. 1972. *Theory of Public Choice.* Ann Arbor: University of Michigan Press.

————, eds. 1984. *Theory of Public Choice II.* Ann Arbor: University of Michigan Press.

Buchanan, J.M., and G. Tullock. 1962. *The Calculus of Consent.* Ann Arbor: University of Michigan Press.

Budge, I. 1982. "Electoral Volatility: Issue Effects and Basic Change in 23 Post-War Democracies." *Electoral Studies* 1:147–68.

Budge, I., and D.J. Farlie. 1977. *Voting and Party Competition.* New York: Wiley.

————. 1983a. *Explaining and Predicting Elections: Issue Effects and Party Strategies in Twenty-Three Democracies.* London: George Allen and Unwin.

————. 1983b. "Party Competition – Selective Emphasis or Direct Confrontation? An Alternative View with Data." In *Western European Party Systems,* ed. H. Daalder and P. Mair. Beverly Hills: Sage Publications.

Budge, I., and R.I. Hofferbert. 1990. "Mandates and Policy Outputs: U.S. Party Platform and Federal Expenditures." *American Political Science Review* 84:111–31.

Budge, I., and M. Laver. 1986. "Office Seeking and Policy Pursuit in Coalition Theory." *Legislative Studies Quarterly* 11:485–506.

Budge, I., E. Farlie and M. Laver. 1983. "What Is a Rational Choice?" *Electoral Studies* 2:23–38.

Butler, D., H.R. Penniman and A. Ranney, eds. 1981. *Democracy at the Polls: A Comparative Study of Competitive National Elections.* Washington, DC: American Enterprise Institute for Public Policy Research.

Cadart, J. 1983. *Les modes de scrutin des 18 pays libres de l'Europe occidentale, leurs résultats et leurs effets comparés.* Paris: Presses universitaires de France.

Cairns, A.C. 1968. "The Electoral System and the Party System in Canada, 1921–1965." *Canadian Journal of Political Science* 1:55–80.

Cameron, D.R. 1978. "The Expansion of the Public Economy: A Comparative Analysis." *American Political Science Review* 72:1243–61.

————. 1984. "Social Democracy, Corporatism, Labour Quiescence and the Representation of Economic Interest in Advanced Capitalist Societies." In *Order and Conflict in Contemporary Capitalism,* ed. J.H. Goldthorpe. Oxford: Clarendon Press.

Capron, H. 1987. "Cohérence et estimation des fonctions de popularité: une application au cas français." *Revue économique* 38:1029–41.

Carstairs, A.M. 1980. *A Short History of Electoral Systems in Western Europe.* London: George Allen and Unwin.

Castles, F.G. 1981. "How Does Politics Matter? Structure or Agency in the Determination of Public Policy Outcomes." *European Journal of Political Research* 9:119–32.

———. 1982. "The Impact of Parties on Public Expenditures." In *The Impact of Parties: Politics and Policies in Democratic Capitalist States,* ed. F.G. Castles. London: Sage Publications.

Castles, F.G., and R.D. McKinlay. 1979. "Does Politics Matter? An Analysis of the Public Welfare Commitment in Advanced Democratic States." *European Journal of Political Research* 7:169–86.

Chappel, H.W., and W.R. Keech. 1986. "Policy Motivation and Party Differences in a Dynamic Spatial Model of Party Competition." *American Political Science Review* 90:881–99.

Clark, P.B., and J.Q. Wilson. 1961. "Incentive Systems: A Theory of Organizations." *Administrative Science Quarterly* 6:130–66.

Clarke, H., and P. Whiteley. 1990. "Perceptions of Macroeconomic Performance, Government Support and Conservative Party Strategy in Britain 1983–1987." *European Journal of Political Research* 18:97–120.

Conover, P.J., and S. Feldman. 1989. "Candidate Perception in an Ambiguous World: Campaign Cues and Inferences Processes." *American Journal of Political Science* 4:912–40.

Conradt, D.P. 1970. "Electoral Law Politics in West Germany." *Political Studies* 3:341–56.

Cook, C.E. 1984. "Participation in Public Interest Groups: Membership Motivation." *American Politics Quarterly* 12:409–30.

Courtney, J.C. 1980. "Reflections on Reforming the Canadian Electoral System." *Canadian Journal of Political Science* 23:427–57.

Crain, W.M. 1977. "On the Structure and Stability of Political Markets." *Journal of Political Economy* 85:829–42.

Curtice, J., and M. Steed. 1982. "Electoral Choice and the Production of Government: The Changing Operation of the Electoral System in the United Kingdom Since 1955." *British Journal of Political Science* 12:249–98.

Daalder, H., and P. Mair, eds. 1983. *Western European Party Systems: Continuity and Change.* London: Sage Publications.

Davis, O.A., M.J. Hinich and P.C. Ordeshook. 1970. "An Expository Development of a Mathematical Model of the Electoral Process." *American Political Science Review* 64:426–48.

Dilorenzo, T.J. 1983. "Economic Competition and Political Competition: An Empirical Note." *Public Choice* 40:203–209.

Dinkel, R. 1980. "Political Business Cycles in Germany and the United States: Some Theoretical and Empirical Considerations." In *Contemporary Political Economy,* ed. D.A. Hibbs and H. Fassbender. Amsterdam: North Holland.

Dion, Leon. 1971. *Société et politique: la vie des groupes.* Quebec: Presses de l'Université Laval.

Downs, A. 1957. *An Economic Theory of Democracy.* New York: Harper and Row.

Dummett, M. 1984. *Voting Procedures.* Oxford: Clarendon Press.

Dunleavy, P., and H. Ward. 1981. "Exogenous Voter Preferences and Parties with State Power: Some Internal Problems of Economic Theories of Party Competition." *British Journal of Political Science* 11:351–80.

Eggertsson, T. 1989. *Economic Behaviour and Institutions.* Cambridge: Cambridge University Press.

Elkin, Stephen L. 1985. "Economic and Political Rationality." *Polity* 18:253–72.

Enelow, J.M., and M.J. Hinich. 1984. *The Spatial Theory of Elections: An Introduction.* Cambridge: Cambridge University Press.

———, eds. 1990. *Advances in the Spatial Theory of Voting.* Cambridge: Cambridge University Press.

Erikson, R.S. 1990. "Economic Conditions and the Congressional Vote: A Review of the Macrolevel Evidence." *American Journal of Political Science* 34:373–99.

Eulau, H., and M.S. Lewis-Beck, eds. 1985. *Economic Conditions and Electoral Outcomes: The United States and Western Europe.* New York: Agathon Press.

Fabre, P. 1976. *La décision de majorité.* Paris: Presses de la fondation nationale des sciences politiques.

Fair, R.C. 1978. "The Effect of Economic Events on Votes for President." *Review of Economics and Statistics* 60:159–73.

Farquharson, R. 1969. *Theory of Voting.* New Haven: Yale University Press.

Fiorina, M.P. 1977. "Outline for a Model of Party Choice." *American Journal of Political Science* 21:601–25.

———. 1990. "Coalition Governments, Divided Governments, and Electoral Theory." Paper presented at the American Political Science Association annual meeting, San Francisco.

Franklin, C.H., and J.E. Jackson. 1983. "The Dynamics of Party Identification." *American Political Science Review* 77:957–73.

Freeman, J.R. 1989. *Democracy and Markets: The Politics of Mixed Economies.* Ithaca: Cornell University Press.

Frey, B.S. 1983. *Democratic Economic Policy: A Theoretical Introduction.* Oxford: Martin Robertson.

———. 1984. "Politico-Economic Models and Cycles." In *Theory of Public Choice II*, ed. J.M. Buchanan and R.D. Tollison. Ann Arbor: University of Michigan Press.

Frey, B.S., and F. Schneider. 1975. "On the Modelling of Politico-Economic Interdependence." *European Journal of Political Research* 3:339–60.

———. 1978a. "An Empirical Study of Politico-Economic Interaction in the United States." *Review of Economics and Statistics* 60:174–83.

———. 1978b. "A Politico-Economic Model of the United Kingdom." *Economic Journal* 88:243–53.

———. 1979. "An Econometric Model with an Endogenous Government Sector." *Public Choice* 15:29–43.

———. 1980. "Recent Research on Empirical Politico-Economic Models." In *Contemporary Political Economy*, ed. D.A. Hibbs and H. Fassbender. Amsterdam: North Holland.

———. 1981. "A Politico-Economic Model of the U.K.: New Estimates and Predictions." *Economic Journal* 91:737–40.

———. 1983. "An Empirical Study of Politico-Economic Interaction in the United States: A Reply." *Review of Economics and Statistics* 65:178–82.

Frohlich, N., and J.A. Oppenheimer. 1978. *Modern Political Economy.* Englewood Cliffs: Prentice-Hall.

Gallagher, M. 1975. "Disproportionality in a Proportional Representation System: The Irish Experience." *Political Studies* 23:501–13.

———. 1986. "The Political Consequences of the Electoral System in the Republic of Ireland." *Electoral Studies* 3:253–75.

Golden, D.G., and J.M. Poterba. 1980. "The Price of Popularity: The Political Business Cycle Reexamined." *American Journal of Political Science* 24:696–714.

Grofman, B., and A. Lijphart, eds. 1986. *Electoral Laws and Their Political Consequences.* New York: Agathon Press.

Grofman, B., A. Lijphart, R.B. McKay and H.A. Scarrow, eds. 1982. *Representation and Redistricting Issues.* Lexington: Lexington Books.

Grunberg, G. 1985. "L'instabilité du comportement électoral."
In *Explication du vote: un bilan des études électorales en France*, ed. D. Gaxie.
Paris: Presses de la fondation nationale des sciences politiques.

Gudgin, G., and P.J. Taylor. 1979. *Seats, Votes and the Spatial Organization
of Elections*. London: Pion.

Gwartney, J.D., and R.E. Wagner, eds. 1988. *Public Choice and Constitutional
Economics*. Greenwich: JAI Press.

Hanush, H., ed. 1983. *Anatomy of Government Deficiencies*. New York:
Springer Verlag.

Hardin, G., and J. Baden, eds. 1977. *Managing the Commons*. New York:
W.H. Freeman.

Hardin, R. 1982. *Collective Action*. Baltimore: Johns Hopkins University Press.

————. 1988. *Morality within the Limits of Reason*. Chicago: University of
Chicago Press.

Hayes, M.T. 1981. *Lobbyists and Legislators: A Theory of Political Markets*.
New Brunswick: Rutgers University Press.

Hewitt, C. 1977. "The Effect of Political Democracy and Social Democracy
on Equality in Industrial Societies: A Cross National Comparison."
American Sociological Review 42:450–64.

Hibbs, D.A. 1977. "Political Parties and Macroeconomic Policy."
American Political Science Review 71:1467–87.

————. 1982. "On the Demand for Economic Outcomes: Macroeconomic
Performance and Mass Political Support in the United States, Great
Britain and Germany." *Journal of Politics* 44:426–62.

————. 1987. *The American Political Economy: Macroeconomics and Electoral
Politics*. Cambridge: Harvard University Press.

Hibbs, D.A., and D. Christopher. 1988. "Income Distribution in the United
States." *American Political Science Review* 82:467–90.

Hibbs, D.A., and N. Vasilatos. 1982. "Economic Outcomes and Political
Support for British Governments among Occupational Classes:
A Dynamic Analysis." *American Political Science Review* 76:259–79.

Hicks, A., and D.H. Swank. 1984. "Governmental Redistribution in Rich
Capitalist Democracies." *Policy Studies Journal* 13:265–86.

Hicks, A., D.H. Swank and M. Ambuhl. 1989. "Welfare Expansion Revisited:
Policy Routines and Their Mediation by Party, Class and Crisis,
1957–1982." *European Journal of Political Research* 17:401–30.

Hillinger, C. 1971. "Voting on Issues and Platforms." *Behavioral Science*
16:564–66.

Hofferbert, R.I., and H.D. Klingemann. 1990. "The Policy Impact of Party Programs and Government Declarations in the Federal Republic of Germany." *European Journal of Political Research* 18:277–304.

Holden, K., and D.A. Peel. 1985. "An Alternative Approach to Explaining Political Popularity." *Electoral Studies* 4:231–39.

Holm, J.D. 1986. "Party and Policy in Voter Choice: A Study of Reinforcement." *Electoral Studies* 5:47–60.

Irvine, W.P. 1979. *Does Canada Need a New Electoral System?* Kingston: Queen's University, Institute of Intergovernmental Relations.

———. 1982. "Does the Candidate Make a Difference? The Macro-Politics and Micro-Politics of Getting Elected." *Canadian Journal of Political Science* 15:755–82.

———. 1988. "Measuring the Effects of Electoral Systems on Regionalism." *Electoral Studies* 7:15–26.

———. 1991. "Reforming the Electorate System." In *Party Politics in Canada.* 5th ed., ed. H.G. Thorburn. Scarborough: Prentice-Hall.

Jackman, R.W. 1980. "Socialist Parties and Income Inequality in Western Industrial Societies." *Journal of Politics* 42:135–49.

———. 1987. "Political Institutions and Voter Turnout in the Industrial Democracies." *American Political Science Review* 81:405–23.

Jacobson, G.C. 1990. "Does the Economy Matter in Midterm Elections?" *American Journal of Political Science* 34:400–407.

Jonung, L., and E. Wadensjo. 1979. "The Effect of Unemployment, Inflation and Real Income on Government Popularity in Sweden." *Scandinavian Journal of Economics* no. 85:343–52.

Kalecki, M. 1943. "Political Aspects of Full Employment." *Political Quarterly* 14:322–31.

Katz, R.S. 1980. *A Theory of Parties and Electoral Systems.* Baltimore: Johns Hopkins University Press.

Kavanagh, D. 1981. "The Politics of Manifestos." *Parliamentary Affairs* 34:7–27.

Keman, H. 1984. "Politics, Policies and Consequences: A Cross-National Analysis of Public Policy Formation in Advanced Capitalist Democracies (1967–1981)." *European Journal of Political Research* 12:147–69.

Keman, H., and D. Braun. 1984. "The Limits of Political Control: A Cross-National Comparison of Economic Policy Responses in Eighteen Capitalist Democracies." *European Journal of Political Research* 12:101–108.

Kiewiet, D.R. 1981. "Policy-Oriented Voting in Response to Economic Issues." *American Political Science Review* 75:448–59.

———. 1983. *Macroeconomics and Micropolitics: The Electoral Effects of Economic Issues.* Chicago: University of Chicago Press.

Koole, R., and P. Van Praag. 1990. "Electoral Competition in a Segmented Society: Campaign Strategies and the Importance of Elite Perceptions." *European Journal of Political Research* 18:51–69.

Kramer, G.H. 1971. "Short-Term Fluctuations in U.S. Voting Behavior 1896–1964." *American Political Science Review* 65:131–43.

Lafay, J.D. 1982. "Chômage et comportements politiques: bilan des analyses économétriques." *Revue française de science politique* 32:692–702.

Lakeman, E., and J.D. Lambert. 1974. *Voting in Democracies: A Study of Majority and Proportional Electoral Systems.* London: Faber and Faber.

Landry, R. 1984a. "La nouvelle analyse institutionnelle." *Politique* no. 6:5–32.

———. 1984b. "La simulation de la rationalité économique du comportement électoral des Québécois: 1970–1981." In *Le comportement électoral du Québec,* ed. J. Crête. Chicoutimi: Gaëtan Morin.

———. 1990. "Biases in the Supply of Public Policies to Organized Interests: Some Empirical Evidence." In *Policy Communities and Public Policy in Canada: A Structural Approach,* ed. W.D. Coleman and G. Skogstad. Toronto: Copp Clark Pitman.

———. 1991. "Party Competition in Quebec: Direct Confrontation or Selective Emphasis?" In *Party Politics in Canada.* 5th ed., ed. H. Thorburn. Scarborough: Prentice-Hall.

Landry, R., and P. Duchesneau. 1987. "L'offre d'interventions gouvernementales aux groupes: une théorie et une application." *Canadian Journal of Political Science* 20:525–52.

Laver, M. 1981. *The Politics of Private Desire: The Guide to the Politics of Rational Choice.* New York: Penguin.

———. 1983. *Invitation to Politics.* New York: Basil Blackwell.

———. 1986. *Social Choice and Public Policy.* New York: Basil Blackwell.

Laver, M., and K.A. Shepsle. 1990. "Divided Government: America Is Not 'Exceptional.'" Paper presented at the American Political Science Association annual meeting, San Francisco.

Lee, D.R., and R.B. McKenzie. 1987. *Regulating Government: A Preface to Constitutional Economics.* Lexington: Lexington Books.

Lemieux, V. 1984. "La réforme du système électoral." *Politique* no. 6:33–49.

Lewis-Beck, M.S. 1983. "Economics and the French Voter: A Microanalysis." *Public Opinion Quarterly* 47:347–60.

———. 1986. "Comparative Economic Voting: Britain, France, Germany, Italy." *American Journal of Political Science* 30:315–46.

———. 1988. "Economics and the American Voter: Past, Present, Future." *Political Behavior* 10:5–21.

Lijphart, A. 1984a. "Advances in the Comparative Study of Electoral Systems." *World Politics* 36:424–36.

———. 1984b. *Democracies: Patterns of Majoritarian and Consensus Government in Twenty-One Countries.* New Haven: Yale University Press.

———. 1985. "The Field of Electoral System Research: A Critical Survey." *Electoral Studies* 4:3–14.

———. 1990. "The Political Consequences of Electoral Laws, 1945–1985." *American Political Science Review* 84:481–96.

Lijphart, A., and R.W. Gibbert. 1977. "Thresholds and Payoffs in Lists Systems of Proportional Representation." *European Journal of Political Research* 8:219–44.

Lijphart, A., and B. Grofman, eds. 1984. *Choosing an Electoral System: Issues and Alternatives.* New York: Praeger.

Loosemore, J., and V.J. Hanby. 1971. "The Theoretical Limits of Maximum Distortion: Some Analytic Expressions for Electoral Systems." *British Journal of Political Science* 1:467–77.

Lovink, J.A.A. 1970. "On Analyzing the Impact of the Electoral System on the Party System in Canada." *Canadian Journal of Political Science* 3:497–521.

MacRae, C.D. 1977. "A Political Model of the Business Cycle." *Journal of Political Economy* 85:239–63.

March, J.G., and J.P. Olsen. 1989. *Rediscovering Institutions: The Organizational Basis of Politics.* New York: Free Press.

Meiselman, D. 1984. "Masse monétaire et élections aux États-Unis: existe-t-il un cycle politico-monétaire?" *Problèmes économiques* 1864:28–30.

Merril, S. 1990. *Making Multicandidate Elections More Democratic.* Princeton: Princeton University Press.

Messu, M. 1990. "L'État providence et ses victimes." *Revue française de science politique* 40:81–97.

Mevorach, B. 1989. "The Political Monetary Business Cycle: Political Reality and Economic Theory." *Political Behavior* 11 (2): 175–88.

Minford, P., and D. Peel. 1982. "The Political Theory of the Business Cycle." *European Economic Review* 17:253–70.

Mitchell, G.E., and M.S. Lewis-Beck. 1990. "Does Liverpool Matter? Local Economic Conditions and How Voters Perceive the State of the

Economy." Paper presented at the American Political Science Association annual meeting, San Francisco.

Moe, T.M. 1980a. "A Calculus of Group Membership." *American Journal of Political Science* 24:543–632.

———. 1980b. *The Organization of Interests: Incentives and the Internal Dynamics of Political Interest Groups.* Chicago: University of Chicago Press.

———. 1981. "Toward a Broader View of Interest Groups." *Journal of Politics* 43:531–43.

Mosley, P. 1978. "Images of the Floating Voter: Or, the Political Business Cycle Revisited." *Political Studies* 26:375–94.

Mueller, D.C. 1982. *Analyse des décisions publiques.* Paris: Économica.

———. 1989. *Public Choice II.* Cambridge: Cambridge University Press.

Nordhaus, W.D. 1975. "The Political Business Cycle." *Review of Economic Studies* 42:169–90.

Norpoth, H., and T. Yantek. 1983. "Macroeconomic Conditions and Fluctuations of Presidential Popularity: The Question of Lagged Effects." *American Journal of Political Science* 27:785–807.

Nurmi, H. 1986. "Mathematical Models of Elections and Their Relevance for Institutional Design." *Electoral Studies* 5:167–81.

O'Connor, J.S. 1988. "Convergence or Divergence? Change in Welfare Effort in OECD Countries 1960–1980." *European Journal of Political Research* 16:277–99.

Olson, M., Jr. 1965. *The Logic of Collective Action.* Cambridge: Harvard University Press.

———. 1983. *The Rise and Decline of Nations, Economic Growth, Stagflation and Social Rigidities.* New Haven: Yale University Press.

———. 1986. "A Theory of the Incentives Facing Political Organizations: Neo-Corporatism and the Hegemonic State." *International Political Science Review* 7:165–89.

Ordeshook, P.C., ed. 1989. *Models of Strategic Choice in Politics.* Ann Arbor: University of Michigan Press.

Ordeshook, P.C., and K.A. Shepsle. 1982. *Political Equilibrium.* Boston: Kluver-Nijhoff.

Ostrom, E., ed. 1982. *Strategies of Political Inquiry.* Beverly Hills: Sage Publications.

———. 1986. "An Agenda for the Study of Institution." *Public Choice* 48:3–26.

———. 1988. "Institutional Arrangements and the Commons Dilemma." In *Rethinking Institutional Analysis and Development*, ed. E. Ostrom, D. Feeny and H. Picht. San Francisco: ICS Press.

———. 1990. *Governing the Commons.* Cambridge: Cambridge University Press.

Page, B.I. 1976. "Theory of Political Ambiguity." *American Political Science Review* 70:742–52.

Paldam, M. 1981. "A Preliminary Survey of the Theories and Findings on Vote and Popularity Functions." *European Journal of Political Research* 9:181–99.

Paltiel, K.Z. 1982. "The Changing Environment and Role of Special Interest Groups." *Canadian Public Administration* 25:198–210.

Pampel, F.C., and J.B. Williamson. 1988. "Welfare Spending in Advanced Industrial Democracies." *American Journal of Sociology* 93:1424–56.

Pedersen, M. 1980. "On Measuring Party System Change." *Comparative Political Studies* 12:383–403.

Peretz, P. 1980. "The Effect of Economic Change on Political Parties in West Germany." In *Contemporary Political Economy*, ed. D.A. Hibbs and H. Fassbender. Amsterdam: North Holland.

Petry, F. 1988. "The Policy Impact of Canadian Party Programs: Public Expenditure Growth and Contagion from the Left." *Canadian Public Policy* 14:376–89.

Plott, C.R. 1976. "Axiomatic Social Choice Theory: An Overview and Interpretation." *American Journal of Political Science* 20:511–96.

Pommerehne, W., F. Schneider and J.D. Lafay. 1981. "Les interactions entre économie et politique: synthèse des analyses théoriques et empiriques." *Revue économique* 1:110–62.

Powell, G.B. 1982. *Participation, Stability and Violence.* Cambridge: Harvard University Press.

Przeworski, A. 1985. *Capitalism and Social Democracy.* Cambridge: Cambridge University Press.

Rae, D.W. 1971. *The Political Consequences of Electoral Laws.* New Haven: Yale University Press.

———. 1975. "The Limits of Consensual Decision." *American Political Science Review* 69:1270–99.

Reed, W.R. 1989. "Information in Political Markets: A Little Knowledge Can Be a Dangerous Thing." *Journal of Law, Economics and Organization* 5:355–74.

Riker, W.H. 1962. *The Theory of Political Coalitions.* New Haven: Yale University Press.

———. 1982. *Liberalism Against Populism: A Confrontation Between the Theory of Democracy and the Theory of Public Choice.* San Francisco: W.H. Freeman.

Riker, W.H., and P.C. Ordeshook. 1968. "A Theory of the Calculus of Voting." *American Political Science Review* 63:25–43.

———. 1973. *An Introduction to Positive Political Theory.* Englewood Cliffs: Prentice-Hall.

Robertson, D. 1976. *A Theory of Party Competition.* London: Wiley.

Rosa, J.J. 1980. "Economic Conditions and Elections in France." In *Models of Political Economy,* ed. P. Whiteley. London: Sage Publications.

Rosa, J.J., and D. Amson. 1976. "Conditions économiques et élections: une analyse politico-économétrique." *Revue française de science politique* 226:1101–24.

Rose, Richard. 1984. *Do Parties Make a Difference?* 2d ed. London: Macmillan.

Sainsbury, D. 1990. "Party Strategies and Party-Voter Linkage." *European Journal of Political Research* 18:1–7.

Schlesinger, J. 1975. "The Primary Goal of Political Parties: A Clarification of Positive Theory." *American Political Science Review* 69:840–49.

Schmidt, M.G. 1982. "The Role of Parties in Shaping Macroeconomic Policy." In *The Impact of Parties: Politics and Policies in Democratic Capitalist States,* ed. F.G. Castles. London: Sage Publications.

———. 1983. "The Welfare State and the Economy in Periods of Economic Crisis: A Comparative Study of Twenty-Three OECD Nations." *European Journal of Political Research* 11:1–26.

Schneider, F., and W.W. Pommerehne. 1980. "Politico-Economic Interactions in Australia: Some Empirical Evidence." *Economic Record* 56:113–31.

Shepsle, K.A., and B.R. Weingast. 1984. "Political Solutions to Market Problems." *American Political Science Review* 78:417–34.

Shotter, A. 1981. *The Economic Theory of Social Institutions.* Cambridge: Cambridge University Press.

Sims, C.A. 1983. "Is There a Monetary Business Cycle?" *American Economic Review* 73:228–33.

Sinnott, R. 1989. "Locating Parties, Factions and Ministers in a Policy Space: A Contribution to Understanding the Party-Policy Link." *European Journal of Political Research* 17:689–706.

Spitz, E. 1984. *Majority Rule.* Chatham: Chatham House.

Stephens, J.D. 1979. *The Transition from Capitalism to Socialism.* London: Sage Publications.

Stigler, G.J. 1973. "General Economic Conditions and National Elections." *American Economic Review* 63:160–67.

Strom, K. 1990. "A Behavioral Theory of Competitive Political Parties." *American Journal of Political Science* 34:565–98.

Swank, D.H. 1988. "The Political Economy of Government Domestic Expenditure in the Affluent Democracies, 1960–1980." *American Journal of Political Science* 32:1120–50.

Taagepera, R., and B. Grofman. 1985. "Rethinking Duverger's Law: Predicting the Effective Number of Parties in Plurality or PR Systems." *European Journal of Political Research* 13:341–53.

Taagepera, R., and M.S. Shugart. 1989. "Designing Electoral Systems." *Electoral Studies* 8:49–58.

Taylor, M., and V.M. Herman. 1971. "Party Systems and Government Stability." *American Political Science Review* 65:28–37.

Taylor, P.J., and R.J. Johnston. 1979. *Geography of Elections.* New York: Penguin Books.

Tillock, H., and D.E. Morrison. 1979. "Group Size and Contributions to Collective Action: An Examination of Olson's Theory Using Data from Zero Population Growth, Inc." *Research in Social Movement, Conflicts and Change* 2:131–58.

Tufte, E.R. 1973. "The Relationship between Seats and Votes in Two-Party Systems." *American Political Science Review* 67:540–54.

———. 1975. "Determinants of the Outcome of Midterm Congressional Elections." *American Political Science Review* 69:812–26.

———. 1978. *The Political Control of the Economy.* Princeton: Princeton University Press.

Tullock, G. 1967. *Toward a Mathematics of Politics.* Ann Arbor: University of Michigan Press.

———. 1978. *Le marché politique. Analyse économique des processus politiques.* Paris: Économica.

Van Arnhem, J.C.M., and G.J. Schotsman. 1982. "Do Parties Affect the Distribution of Incomes? The Case of Advanced Capitalist Democracies." In *The Impact of Parties: Politics and Policies in Democratic Capitalist States,* ed. F.G. Castles. London: Sage Publications.

Van Den Doel, H. 1979. *Democracy and Welfare Economics.* Cambridge: Cambridge University Press.

Visser, W., and R. Wijnhoven. 1990. "Politics Do Matter, But Does Unemployment?" *European Journal of Political Research* 18:71–96.

Wagner, R.E. 1977. "Economic Manipulation for Political Profit: Macroeconomic Consequences and Constitutional Implications." *Kyklos* 30:395 410.

Walker, J.L. 1983. "The Origins and Maintenance of Interest Groups in America." *American Political Science Review* 77:390–406.

Weisberg, H.F. 1986. *Political Science: The Science of Politics.* New York: Agathon Press.

Wellhofer, E.S. 1990. "Contradictions in Market Models of Politics: The Case of Party Strategies and Voter Linkages." *European Journal of Political Research* 18:9–28.

Whiteley, P. 1984. "Inflation, Unemployment and Government Popularity: Dynamic Models for the United States, Great Britain and West Germany." *Electoral Studies* 3:3–24.

———. 1986. "Macroeconomic Performance and Government Popularity in Britain: The Short-Run Dynamics." *European Journal of Political Research* 14:45–61.

———. 1988. "Party Incumbency and Economic Growth in the United States: 1929 to 1984." *Political Behavior* 10:293–315.

Whynes, D.K., and R.A. Bowles. 1981. *The Economic Theory of the State.* Oxford: Martin Robertson.

Wilenski, H.L. 1976. *The New Corporatism, Centralization and the Welfare State.* London: Sage Publications.

Williams, J.T. 1990. "The Political Manipulation of Macroeconomic Policy." *American Political Science Review* 84:767–96.

Wittman, D. 1983. "Candidate Motivation: A Synthesis of Alternative Theories." *American Political Science Review* 77:142–57.

Zorn, T.S., and D.T. Martin. 1986. "Optimism and Pessimism in Political and Market Institutions." *Public Choice* 49:165–78.

CONTRIBUTORS TO VOLUME 14

Donald E. Blake	University of British Columbia
Maureen Covell	Simon Fraser University
Rand Dyck	Laurentian University
David J. Elkins	University of British Columbia/University of Ottawa
John Ferejohn	Stanford University
Brian Gaines	Stanford University
Réjean Landry	Université Laval
Neil Nevitte	University of Calgary
S.L. Sutherland	Carleton University
Paul G. Thomas	University of Manitoba

ACKNOWLEDGEMENTS

The Royal Commission on Electoral Reform and Party Financing and the publishers wish to acknowledge with gratitude the permission of the following to reprint and translate material:

Comparative Politics; Éditions Hurtubise HMH Ltée; Lexington Books; Prentice-Hall Canada; Routledge; The Right Honourable Pierre Elliott Trudeau.

Care has been taken to trace the ownership of copyright material used in the text, including the tables and figures. The authors and publishers welcome any information enabling them to rectify any reference or credit in subsequent editions.

~

Consistent with the Commission's objective of promoting full participation in the electoral system by all segments of Canadian society, gender neutrality has been used wherever possible in the editing of the research studies.

THE COLLECTED RESEARCH STUDIES*

---

* The titles of studies may not be final in all cases.

COMMISSION ORGANIZATION

CHAIRMAN
Pierre Lortie

COMMISSIONERS
Pierre Fortier
Robert Gabor
William Knight
Lucie Pépin

SENIOR OFFICERS

Executive Director	*Director of Research*
Guy Goulard	Peter Aucoin

Special Adviser to the Chairman
Jean-Marc Hamel

Research
F. Leslie Seidle,
   Senior Research Coordinator

Legislation
Jules Brière, Senior Adviser
Gérard Bertrand
Patrick Orr

Coordinators
Herman Bakvis
Michael Cassidy
Frederick J. Fletcher
Janet Hiebert
Kathy Megyery
Robert A. Milen
David Small

Communications and Publishing
Richard Rochefort, Director
Hélène Papineau, Assistant
  Director
Paul Morisset, Editor
Kathryn Randle, Editor

Assistant Coordinators
David Mac Donald
Cheryl D. Mitchell

Finance and Administration
Maurice R. Lacasse, Director

Contracts and Personnel
Thérèse Lacasse, Chief

Editorial, Design and Production Services